survey of Operating Systems

survey of

Operating Systems

Third Edition

Jane Holcombe
Charles Holcombe

SURVEY OF OPERATING SYSTEMS

Published by McGraw-Hill, a business unit of The McGraw-Hill Companies, Inc., 1221 Avenue of the Americas, New York, NY, 10020. Copyright © 2012 by The McGraw-Hill Companies, Inc. All rights reserved. Previous editions © 2003 and 2006. No part of this publication may be reproduced or distributed in any form or by any means, or stored in a database or retrieval system, without the prior written consent of The McGraw-Hill Companies, Inc., including, but not limited to, in any network or other electronic storage or transmission, or broadcast for distance learning.

Some ancillaries, including electronic and print components, may not be available to customers outside the United States.

This book is printed on acid-free paper.

1 2 3 4 5 6 7 8 9 0 QDB/QDB 1 0 9 8 7 6 5 4 3 2 1

ISBN   978-0-07-351817-6
MHID   0-07-351817-4

Vice president/Editor in chief: *Elizabeth Haefele*
Vice president/Director of marketing: *Alice Harra*
Publisher: *Scott Davidson*
Sponsoring editor: *Paul Altier*
Director, digital publishing: *Crystal Szewczyk*
Development editor: *Alan Palmer*
Editorial coordinator: *Allison McCabe*
Marketing manager: *Tiffany Russell*
Digital development editor: *Kevin White*
Director, Editing/Design/Production: *Jess Ann Kosic*
Lead project manager: *Susan Trentacosti*

Buyer: *Nicole Baumgartner*
Senior designer: *Anna Kinigakis*
Senior photo research coordinator: *Keri Johnson*
Manager, digital production: *Janean A. Utley*
Media project manager: *Cathy L. Tepper*
Cover and interior design: *Laurie J. Entringer*
Typeface: *10/13 Palatino*
Compositor: *Laserwords Private Limited*
Printer: *Quad/Graphics*
Cover credit: © *Dave Cutler Studio, LLC*

Chapter opening credits: page 1: Fuse/Getty Images; page 39: Chad Baker/Ryan McVay/Getty Images; page 79: Screenshot courtesy of Charles and Jane Holcombe; page 105: Deborah Feingold/CORBIS; page 145: Reuters/CORBIS; page 193: ELOY ALONSO/Reuters/Corbis; page 241: Jan Stromme/The Image Bank/Getty Images; page 275: Image Source/Corbis; page 319: Brian Kersey/Getty Images; page 361: Yuriy Panyukov/Alamy. Timeline photos in Chapter 1: Page 12: Courtesy of the Computer History Museum. Courtesy Xerox Corporation. Page 13: CPU Collection Konstantin Lanzet/Wikipedia. National Museum of American History, Behring Center. ©2004 Smithsonian Institution. Courtesy Apple Computer. Courtesy Microsoft® Corp. Page 14: Ralph Morse/Time Life Pictures/Getty Images. Courtesy of the Computer History Museum. Page 15: Courtesy Apple Computer. Courtesy of IBM Corporation. Page 19: Courtesy of palmOne, Inc. Courtesy Apple Computer. Page 20: Courtesy Apple Computer. Page 22: Software box photograph courtesy of Apple.

The example companies, organizations, products, domain names, e-mail addresses, logos, people, places, and events depicted herein are fictitious. No association with any real company, organization, product, domain name, e-mail address, logo, person, place, or event is intended or should be inferred.

Information has been obtained by McGraw-Hill from sources believed to be reliable. However, because of the possibility of human or mechanical error by our sources, McGraw-Hill, or others, McGraw-Hill does not guarantee the accuracy, adequacy, or completeness of any information and is not responsible for any errors or omissions or the results obtained from the use of such information.

Library of Congress Cataloging-in-Publication Data

Holcombe, Jane.
    Survey of operating systems / Jane Holcombe, Charles Holcombe.—3rd ed.
      p. cm.
    Includes index.
    ISBN-13: 978-0-07-351817-6 (alk. paper)
    ISBN-10: 0-07-351817-4 (alk. paper)
    1. Operating systems (Computers) I. Holcombe, Charles. II. Title.
  QA76.76.O63H6465   2012
  005.4'3—dc22

                                      2011001471

The Internet addresses listed in the text were accurate at the time of publication. The inclusion of a Web site does not indicate an endorsement by the authors or McGraw-Hill, and McGraw-Hill does not guarantee the accuracy of the information presented at these sites.

JANE HOLCOMBE (A+, Network+, MCSE, CTT+, and former MCT) was a pioneer in the field of PC support training. In 1983, while working for a financial planning company, she had the task of moving the accounting and client-management operations to IBM PCs. This project included the use of three different operating systems to run the selected software and the installation of a local area network for sharing of the accounting system and client files. This project revealed the potential of networked PCs in business, and Jane found appropriate training for herself and the staff. Between 1984 and the mid-1990s she was an independent trainer, consultant, and course content author, creating and presenting courses on PC operating systems. Through the late 1980s and early 1990s she taught these courses nationwide. She also coauthored a set of networking courses for the consulting staff of a large network vendor. In the early 1990s she worked with both Novell and Microsoft server operating systems, finally focusing on Microsoft operating systems. She achieved her Microsoft Certified Training (MCT) and Microsoft Certified Systems Engineer (MCSE) certifications in 1996 and later updated the MCSE twice for new versions of Windows. Since 2000 she has worked primarily as a technical writer and technical editor.

CHARLES HOLCOMBE has a high-tech background in the use of computers in the nuclear and aerospace fields. In his 15 years at Control Data Corporation he was successively a programmer, technical sales analyst, salesman, and sales manager in the field marketing force. He ran the Executive Seminar program, was Control Data's liaison to the worldwide university community, and was a market development manager for Plato, Control Data's computer-based education system. For the past 28 years he has been an independent trainer and consultant. He has authored and delivered many training courses and is a skilled writer and editor. For a while he claimed he was semi-retired, but helping to write books like this one, and editing for *The eLearning Guild* for the past several years is too much work for him to be able to say that anymore.

Together the Holcombes have authored the *MCSE Guide to Designing a Microsoft Windows 2000 Network Infrastructure* (Course Technology), both the *A+ Certification Press Lab Manual*, and the *MCSE Certification Press Windows 2000 Professional Lab Manual* (McGraw-Hill/Osborne). They have authored both the first and second editions of *Survey of Operating Systems*, contributed chapters to *Mike Meyers' Guide to Managing and Troubleshooting PCs, Michael Meyers' All-in-One A+ Certification Exam Guide*, 5th edition, and *Windows 2000 Administration* (McGraw-Hill/Osborne). They also wrote several chapters for the *Peter Norton Introduction to Operating Systems*, 6th edition (McGraw-Hill). They wrote both the sixth and seventh editions of the *CompTIA A+ Certification Study Guide*. The book you are holding is their third edition of *Survey of Operating Systems*.

About the Contributors

This book was greatly influenced by the comments, suggestions, and feedback from the following group of dedicated instructors. To them we give our heartfelt thanks.

Technical Editors

Gerlinde Brady	*Cabrillo College*
Mark Renslow	*Globe University*
Tom Trevethan	*ECPI College of Technology*
Nancy Woodard	*Moraine Valley Community College*

Reviewers

Ray Adams	*YTI Career Institute*
Shannon Beasley	*Central Georgia Technical College*
Gerlinde Brady	*Cabrillo College*
John Brand	*Rowan-Cabarrus Community College*
Anton Bruckner	*Sinclair Community College*
Art Dearing	*Tarleton State University*
Jacqueline Dennis	*Prairie State College*
Michael Discello	*Pittsburgh Technical Institute*
Eric Ecklund	*Cambria-Rowe Business College*
Connie Fletcher	*National College Youngstown*
Dennis Hunchuck	*Valencia East*
Ruth Parker	*Rowan-Cabarrus Community College*
Mark Renslow	*Globe University*
Nathan Ullger	*Catawba Valley Community College*

Acknowledgments

We were thrilled when our agent called and asked if we wanted to write the third edition of *Survey of Operating Systems*. Much has happened with desktop operating systems since we wrote the first two editions, and we knew it would require a nearly complete rethinking of the content. Along with sponsoring editor Paul Altier and developmental editor Alan Palmer, we wrote a survey that they sent to instructors—some of whom were still using the second edition. From the results of this survey we created the outline for the third edition.

As with the previous editions, knowledgeable peer reviewers scrutinized each chapter and gave us invaluable feedback on the relevancy and accuracy of the content. We can't imagine writing a book like this without these technical reviews.

We thank every member of the talented team of people at McGraw-Hill who ensured the book's integrity. They include Paul Altier, Alan Palmer, Susan Trentacosti, Anna Kinigakis, and Allison Grimes. We particularly want to thank Paul and Alan for their unstinting support, unwavering positive attitude, and professionalism.

We are thrilled with the fresh, creative design for this edition, and we greatly appreciate the expertise of Susan Trentacosti, Anna Kinigakis, and the production group. They all worked hard to make the book look wonderful. Creating and laying out the many elements of this complex book design was a huge task, and they handled it with aplomb.

We truly appreciate all who worked hard to make this book what it is. Thank you!

About This Book

Important Technology Skills

Information technology (IT) offers many career paths, leading to occupations in such fields as PC repair, network administration, telecommunications, Web development, graphic design, and desktop support. To become competent in any IT field, however, you need certain basic computer skills. This book will help you build a foundation for success in the IT field by introducing you to fundamental information about desktop operating systems, a needed basis for working with computers at any level.

Try This!
exercises reinforce the concepts.

Notes and Warnings
create a road map for success.

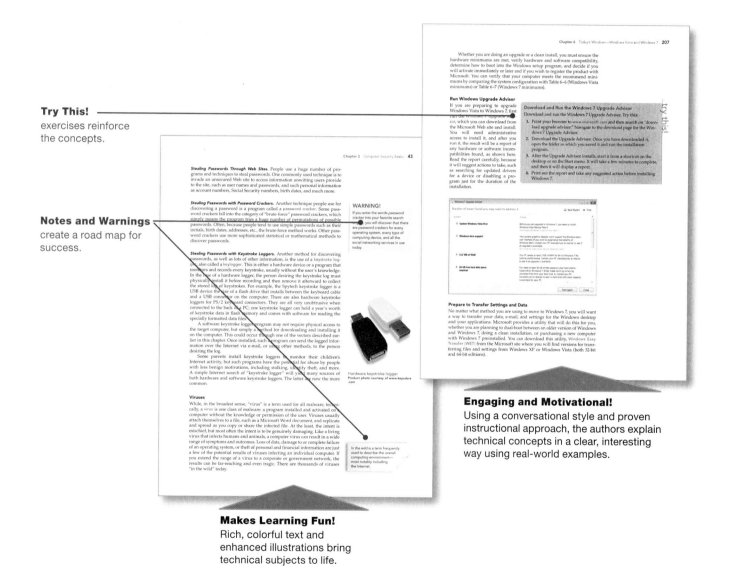

Hardware keystroke logger
Product photo courtesy of www.keycobra.com

Engaging and Motivational!
Using a conversational style and proven instructional approach, the authors explain technical concepts in a clear, interesting way using real-world examples.

Makes Learning Fun!
Rich, colorful text and enhanced illustrations bring technical subjects to life.

Effective Learning Tools

The design of this colorful, pedagogically rich book will make learning easy and enjoyable and help you develop the skills and critical thinking abilities that will enable you to adapt to different job situations and troubleshoot problems. Jane

and Charles Holcombe's proven ability to explain concepts in a clear, direct, even humorous way makes this book interesting and motivational, and fun.

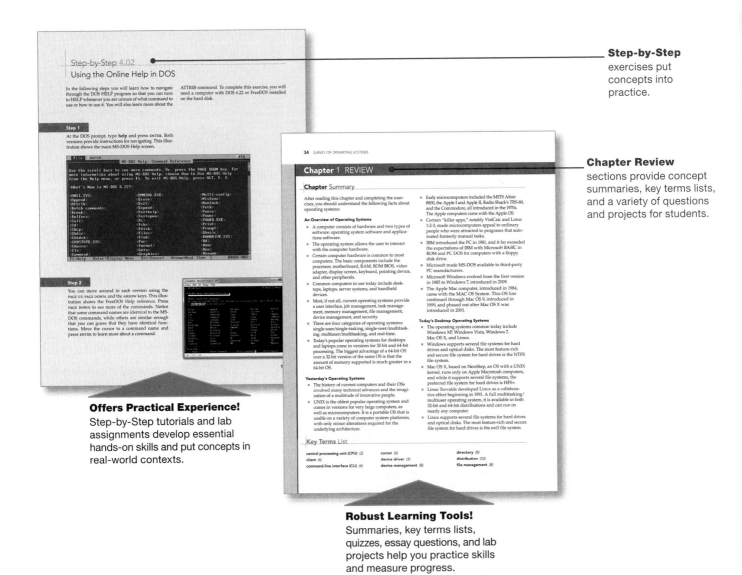

Step-by-Step exercises put concepts into practice.

Chapter Review sections provide concept summaries, key terms lists, and a variety of questions and projects for students.

Offers Practical Experience!
Step-by-Step tutorials and lab assignments develop essential hands-on skills and put concepts in real-world contexts.

Robust Learning Tools!
Summaries, key terms lists, quizzes, essay questions, and lab projects help you practice skills and measure progress.

Each chapter includes:

- **Learning Outcomes** that set measurable goals for chapter-by-chapter progress.
- **Four-Color Illustrations** that give you a clear picture of the technologies.
- **Step-by-Step Tutorials** that teach you to perform essential tasks and procedures hands-on.
- **Try This!** sidebars that encourage you to practice and apply the concepts in real-world settings.

- **Notes** and **Warnings** that guide you through difficult areas.
- **Chapter Summaries** and **Key Terms Lists** that provide you with an easy way to review important concepts and vocabulary.
- **Challenging End-of-Chapter Tests** that include vocabulary-building exercises, multiple-choice questions, essay questions, and on-the-job lab projects.

New to *Survey of Operating Systems*, Third Edition

General changes:

- New design.
- Heavily revised table of contents and updated content.
- New chapters.

Chapter 1 Introduction to Operating Systems

- Removed Overview of Microcomputers section, and some of the content now summarized under first topic, An Overview of Microcomputer OSs.
- Yesterday's Desktop OSs has been updated with appropriate OSs that were previously under Desktop OSs Available Today.
- Section titled Today's Desktop OSs has been updated to include Windows Vista, Windows 7, Windows 8 (briefly), Mac OS X, and Linux.

Chapter 2 Computer Security Basics (New Chapter!)

- This new chapter is based on some content from Chapter 7 in the previous edition and includes, Managing Local Security in Windows, with updates and security information for Mac OS X and Linux.

Chapter 3 Desktop Virtualization (New Chapter!)

- This new chapter on desktop virtualization provides an overview of virtualization followed by sections on virtualization on Windows desktops and on Mac OS X desktops. It includes Step-by-Step exercises on installing virtualization software on both Windows and Mac OS X desktops.

Chapter 4 Disk Operating System (DOS)

- Discussion covers both Microsoft DOS and FreeDOS, and includes instructions on creating a virtual machine for DOS.
- A revised section on Working with the DOS Command Prompt includes examples and Step-by-Step exercises using FreeDOS.

Chapter 5 Windows XP Professional

- Updated to put Windows XP into perspective as an existing but no longer sold OS, the chapter addresses the issues involved with the pending loss of support.
- A new section Securing Windows XP Professional includes information based on the former Chapter 7 including NTFS; Code Signing/Driver Signing, local account management; applying security to files, folders, and printers; and NTFS encryption.

Chapter 6 Today's Windows—Windows Vista and Windows 7 (New Chapter!)

- This new chapter provides an overview of Windows Vista and Windows 7, and discusses installing Windows, managing Windows, and managing local security in Windows.

Chapter 7 Under the Windows Desktop

- Updated information now includes Windows Vista and Windows 7.
- Removed Managing Performance in Windows.
- Moved content of Windows File Systems to Chapter 1.

Chapter 8 Linux on the Desktop

- This discussion of Linux now uses Ubuntu Linux for examples and Step-by-Step exercises. It also includes a new Step-by-Step exercise on downloading Linux and creating a Live CD from an ISO image.
- Added a new section, Securing a Linux Desktop.

Chapter 9 Mac OS X on the Desktop

- A new section on Managing Mac OS X on the Desktop includes updated portions of former sections on Features of Mac OS X Desktop, Getting to Know the Mac OS X Workspace, and Managing Files in OS X. The chapter also includes a new section titled Managing Local Security in Mac OS X and revised Troubleshooting Mac OS Problems.

Chapter 10 The Client Side of Networking

- Includes IPv6 and file sharing features of Windows 7.

Contents

5 | Windows XP Professional 145

6 | Today's Windows—Windows Vista and Windows 7 193

7 | Under the Windows Desktop 241

8 | Linux on the Desktop 275

Introduction

What Will You Learn?

The first two editions of this book were well received by instructors and students. This third edition updates the material and presents new information that is relevant to the topic of desktop operating systems, including Windows, Mac OS X, and Linux. We carefully revised every chapter as needed, with more illustrations and plenty of hands-on opportunities. We have added content throughout, while working to streamline the book in response to feedback we received from instructors. For instance, Chapter 3, "Desktop Virtualization," is new to this edition. We were thrilled when the survey of instructors revealed the need for this chapter because it gave us a chance to call on our decade of experience with desktop virtualization.

We also changed the order of the chapters in response to the surveys. The world has become more dangerous in the years since the second edition, so we moved security from Chapter 7 in the second edition to Chapter 2, "Computer Security Basics," which now includes discussions of security on Windows, Mac OS X, and Linux desktop computers.

Once again, we included a chapter on the venerable Windows XP operating system because so many people still use it. Perhaps we won't need to write about it in the fourth edition. Here is a summary of each chapter:

- Chapter 1, "Introduction to Operating Systems," provides an overview of microcomputer hardware, introduces you to the basic functions common to all operating systems, and introduces the desktop operating systems you will study in this book.

- Chapter 2, "Computer Security Basics," will help you to recognize security threats and vulnerabilities to desktop PCs and users while presenting methods and technologies you can use to protect against threats to computers running Windows, Mac OS X, or Linux.

- Chapter 3, "Desktop Virtualization," will teach you how to install and configure available free desktop virtualization software so that with a single computer you can run a separate desktop operating system in addition to the installed OS. This will let you experience working with a new OS without the expense of dedicating an entire computer to it.

- Chapter 4, "Disk Operating System (DOS)," may convince you that DOS is not yet dead! We included this chapter at the request of survey respondents. We updated it to include both MS-DOS and a free downloadable DOS, FreeDOS. We give you instructions on downloading and creating a FreeDOS Live CD, as well as installing DOS on a hard drive (or into a virtual machine). You will learn to work at the command prompt to run common DOS utilities, manage directories and files, describe the boot-up process, and troubleshoot common DOS problems.

- Chapter 5, "Windows XP Professional," is included because even after nearly a decade, Windows XP is still on many PCs. You will learn to install, configure, manage, and troubleshoot this popular desktop operating system.

- Chapter 6, "Today's Windows—Windows Vista and Windows 7," combines coverage of these two OSs. While Windows Vista was not adopted as widely as Windows XP, we cannot ignore it. Because it is a very close sibling to its successor, Windows 7, we combined coverage of the two. You will learn about the most important new features, how to install these OSs, how to manage the desktop and files, and how to manage local security.

- Chapter 7, "Under the Windows Desktop," explores Windows topics in greater depth. You will learn about the registry, Windows start-up process, installation and management of device drivers, and how to troubleshoot Windows problems.

- Chapter 8, "Linux on the Desktop," will give you the history of Linux and how it evolved to be an important operating system for a variety of platforms and purposes. You will learn how to select and download a free version of Linux and how to install it as a desktop OS using Ubuntu Linux.

- Chapter 9, "Mac OS X on the Desktop," will guide you through installing and configuring Mac OS X and then provide practice using features of the desktop. Finally, you will learn to troubleshoot common Mac OS X problems.

- Chapter 10, "The Client Side of Networking," will give you practice with the skills required to configure a computer to connect to a LAN and to the Internet. You will begin with an overview of the TCP/IP protocol suite, and then you will work with common clients: e-mail, FTP, Internet browsers, and file and print servers. Last, you will learn to troubleshoot common client connection problems.

How Will You Learn?

We don't want to simply give you an encyclopedia of information because it can feel like you're standing in front of an information fire hose, and we've been there ourselves many times in the past decades. Rather, keeping in mind that "less is more," we present just the key points about operating systems, and guide you in your own exploration of the specifics of the technology. One book simply can't give you everything you need to know about operating systems, but we do hope to empower you and to increase your ability to use widely available tools and resources to figure out the answers to your questions. Such tools as the Internet and the help program in your OS are aids you should turn to when you need to learn more about a topic, and when you want to enhance your skills in working with each of these operating systems—and with computers in general.

Each chapter uses many techniques to help you learn. We start by listing learning outcomes, follow that up with a lucid explanation of each topic, and support it with real-world experience and a liberal use of graphics and tables. To give you hands-on experience and to help you "walk the walk," each chapter contains detailed Step-by-Step tutorials and short Try This! exercises to reinforce the concepts. To build vocabulary to help you "talk the talk," each chapter contains computer term definitions, highlighted in a Key Terms List and compiled into a Glossary at the end of the book.

We've also included notes, which provide handy pieces of knowledge to use with your desktop OS. Warnings will help you prevent mishaps.

You can measure what you've learned with end-of-chapter Key Term, Multiple-Choice, and Essay quizzes. In addition, Lab Projects challenge you to independently complete tasks related to what you've just learned.

Let's Get Down to Work

OK, enough of this introductory stuff. This is the last time in this book that you'll see so many words without illustrations. From now on it's downright exciting. Learn a lot and *have fun*!

Supplements

For teachers using this book in the classroom, a powerful collection of teaching tools written by the authors is available online at www.mhhe.com/holcombe3:

- An Instructor's Manual that maps to the organization of the textbook and provides additional instructor tips and activities to use with the book.
- A test bank for each chapter available online in either Word or EZ Test format.
- Engaging PowerPoint slides on the lecture topics, including key points and illustrations from the chapters.

Jane Holcombe

Charles Holcombe

1

Introduction to Operating Systems

"Physics is the universe's operating system."

—**Steven R. Garman**

"I do not fear computers. I fear lack of them."

—**Isaac Asimov**

"The computer was born to solve problems that did not exist before."

—**Bill Gates**

Understanding operating systems (OSs) is critical to your future success in life. It is. Just believe us. You don't? You say you drive a car just fine, but you don't understand its engine, transmission, or other systems? So why can't you just use your computer? Why do you have to even know it has an OS? If you can successfully operate a car, you actually know more about its internal workings than you admit. You turn on the ignition, shift to the correct gear, press the accelerator, and drive down the street without hitting anything. You stop it (in time, usually). You use your car to go somewhere, making the car your transportation tool. Having only superficial knowledge of the workings of your car is adequate if you never intend to repair your car or to explain to a mechanic the symptoms of a problem. And just as you can use a car without much in-depth knowledge of how it works, you can use your computer to write a letter, send e-mail, create a report, or surf the Internet. You only have to know how to turn it on, call up the application program you wish to use, make the application program do what you want it to do, and turn it off.

Learning Outcomes

In this chapter, you will learn how to:

LO **1.1** Describe the purpose and functions of operating systems.

LO **1.2** Describe major events in the evolution of operating systems.

LO **1.3** List and compare the common operating systems in use today.

But if you ever want to understand how your car actually works, you need to spend time studying it. And if you want to be involved in any aspect of the computer industry, you need to understand how the most critical software component, the computer's operating system, works.

This chapter provides an overview of operating systems—specifically, those commonly found on desktop and laptop computers. We'll begin with a brief look at microcomputers—their components and their general types. Then we'll explore the functions that operating systems perform, as well as describe the classic categories of operating systems, while we introduce you to the OSs you will find in home and office computers today. ✺

LO 1.1 | An Overview of Operating Systems

An **operating system (OS)** is actually a collection of programs that gives a computer the critical functionality that lets you use it for work and entertainment. This book will explore the common operating systems used on microcomputers, but before we do, let's answer a few general questions you may have: What is a microcomputer? What's inside a microcomputer? What types of microcomputers are in use today? This section answers these questions.

A typical PC with components
Product photo courtesy of Hewlett-Packard

What Is a Microcomputer?

A **microcomputer** is a computer built around a **microprocessor**, a special integrated circuit (IC) that performs the calculations, or processing, of the computer. An IC, commonly called a chip, is a small electronic component made up of transistors (tiny switches) and other miniaturized parts. The first patents for integrated circuits were issued in 1959 to Jack Kilby of Texas Instruments and Robert Noyce of Fairchild Semiconductor Corporation. Today there are many ICs in a computer in addition to the microprocessor or **central processing unit (CPU)**, also simply called a processor. A microcomputer is small enough and cheap enough to be dedicated to the use of a single person. This was a revolutionary idea in the 1970s, when microcomputers first became available; in the previous decades, computers were physically very large because bulky vacuum tubes served the purpose that microscopic transistors now serve.

What's Inside a Microcomputer?

Our friend Brianna uses a PC at work and a Macintosh at home, and she will soon take night classes in which she will use a laptop PC that she carries to and from school. She wants to learn more about the computers that she uses each day, beginning with the hardware.

Sixty years ago, most people would have laughed at the thought of dedicating an entire computer to the use of an individual because computers were far from "micro." They filled rooms and weighed tons. The expensive, high-maintenance machines were dedicated to the use of a government agency, university, or company. In 1949, *Popular Mechanics* published the following prediction: "Computers in the future may have only 1,000 vacuum tubes and perhaps only weigh 1½ tons." Over the years, computers not only have become physically ever smaller, but they also have become vastly more powerful than their predecessors.

The Basic PC

Each computer that Brianna and the rest of us use is a metal and plastic hardware contraption composed of many components, some of which allow us to interact with the computer. In computerese, we call interaction with a computer **input/output (I/O)**. When you send something into the computer—for instance, when you enter information via the keyboard or have your word processing program read a file from a disk—it is being input. When something comes out of the computer, such as the text and graphics you see on the display screen or the printed results on paper, it is being output from the computer.

Regardless of the brand of microcomputer you use, the common hardware components are basically the same. In general, they include at least one CPU per computer, a central circuit board called a motherboard, and random-access memory (RAM) that acts as the main memory for holding active programs and their data. There are one or more chips called ROM BIOS, a keyboard, a pointing device (mouse or some sort of touch pad), disk drives, and other peripheral devices such as printers, scanners, and cameras.

More About ROM BIOS

Central to any motherboard, and as critical to the operation of a PC as the CPU, is the system ROM BIOS (read only memory basic input output system). System ROM BIOS contains the program code that informs the processor of the devices present and how to communicate with them. Additionally, most components and peripherals have their own ROM BIOS with program code for operating that component. The ROM BIOS for most components is limited to small programs for basic communication between the operating system and the component. Supplementing or replacing the ROM BIOS—even parts of the central system ROM BIOS—are device drivers, special programs installed into an operating system. Each device driver contains code for controlling a component. These are an extension of BIOS, usually allowing much more control of a device than the small programs stored in that device's ROM BIOS.

You can see evidence of the system ROM BIOS and other BIOSs in a PC if you carefully watch the screen as you power up the computer, as shown in Figure 1–1. Each ROM BIOS that powers up with the computer will perform a test. The system ROM BIOS test is known as the power on self-test (POST) and much of the information you see on the screen is the result of the POST and the tests of additional ROM BIOSs on the computer's components.

What Types of Microcomputers Are in Use Today?

In the 1970s, very few computers were small enough to sit on a desk. One computer, the Control Data 160A, actually *was* the desk! But people wanted computers *on* their desks, so what they used was a dumb terminal consisting of a CRT (cathode-ray tube) and a keyboard connected to a large mainframe computer. (Large stand-alone computers are called mainframes.) In the late 1970s, when computers became small enough to sit on a desk, someone coined the word *microcomputer* and it became widely used to describe the early forms of these computers. We're now more likely to use the term personal computer (PC), which applies to computers that comply with hardware standards set and supported by Microsoft, Intel (the largest computer chip manufacturer), and to a lesser extent, other companies. We call these the Microsoft/Intel standards (also called Wintel). However, many important microcomputers don't

```
Phoenix — Award BIOS v6.00PC

Copyright (C) 1984-2003, Phoenix Technologies, LTD


Main Processor : AMD Athlon (tm) 64 X2 Dual Core Processor 3000+

Memory Testing : 1720000K OK
```

FIGURE 1–1 An example of a BIOS start-up message

comply with these standards—most notably, those from Apple and the small handheld computers such as smartphones that are so popular today.

Desktops and Laptops

A desktop computer is a computer designed to spend its useful life in one location—on a desk. A portable computer is designed to be easily carried from one location to another. There are many sizes and types of portable computers. Our discussion of operating systems in this book is limited to the most common operating systems that run on modern desktop and laptop computers. They include Windows and Linux, both of which run on PCs, and Mac OS X, which runs on Apple computers.

Early Macintosh computers came with sophisticated graphics abilities that made them attractive to users requiring high-quality graphical and multimedia support. Part of Apple's early marketing plans simply gave computers to schools, so today the Macintosh has ardent supporters in education and in the graphics businesses. Eventually Microsoft/Intel compatible computers closed the gap in graphics and multimedia capabilities.

In the decades since the introduction of the IBM PC, the majority of desktop and laptop computers used in private and public organizations complied with the Microsoft/Intel standard, with Macintosh computers a distant second. In recent years Apple desktop and portable computers have made great gains in market share. In fact, according to IDC, a market research firm, Apple is third in portable computer sales if you count the company's iPad models along with the MacBook laptop models. If you exclude iPads, Apple is fourth in sales.

Servers

You can also use a PC or Mac as a **server**, a computer that plays several important roles in a network. In all of these roles, it provides services to other computers, which is why it is called a server. We call a computer on the receiving end of these services a **client**. We may base server functions on the same hardware components found in desktop computers, but they are beefed up considerably for a server to which hundreds or thousands of users must connect—resulting in the computer equivalent of a heavyweight versus a lightweight boxer. The cost, which can run in the thousands of dollars for a server versus only a few hundred dollars for an average PC, reflects this difference.

What kind of services does a server provide? When we use a server to store all of the data files of the users in a department or company, we call it a file server. If a server has one or more printers connected to it that it shares with users on the network, we call it a print server. We call a server doing both tasks a file and print server, and even though it sounds like two services, they combine into one service called a file and print service. Note that one server can offer multiple services at the same time. Other servers may offer messaging services (e-mail and fax), Web services, and many, many others. It takes specialized software to provide each type of server service, and complementary client software to request each type of service.

Handheld Devices

Computers today include a long list of various devices that don't have *computer* in their name, such as handheld devices, games, stoves, refrigerators, TVs, and DVD and Blu-ray players. Many handheld devices, often proprietary,

A PC laptop
Product photo courtesy of Hewlett-Packard

Two MacBook laptops
Product photo courtesy of Apple

In this chapter we will use the term *microcomputer* in the historical context when referring to the computers that evolved into today's desktop and laptop computers. Going forward in the book, we will use the terms *desktop computers* and *laptop computers*.

This book is not about the OSs for servers. We focus instead on common desktop and laptop operating systems.

comply with no, or very few, standards in their design, but they are still computers because they contain processors. They include a wide variety of products ranging from simple handheld computers to multifunction mobile devices, such as the devices used in grocery stores to track inventory. Many handheld devices run proprietary OSs, while others run scaled-down versions of desktop OSs.

The most popular handheld devices are wireless phones, called smartphones, that not only allow voice communications, but also let you connect to the Internet, view your e-mail, and do many other things on their small color screens. Examples of smartphones are Apple Computer's iPhone, RIM's BlackBerry, Microsoft's Windows Phone, and various models by Palm, Nokia, HTC, Samsung, LG, and others. Operating systems designed specifically for use on smartphones include Google's Android, Palm's webOS, Apple's iOS, and Windows Mobile.

Functions of Operating Systems

Justin works part-time in a legal office and is a full-time student at a community college, where he is in the computer information systems (CIS) track. Recently, he took a Saturday community education class in computer graphics. At work, he has Windows 7 on his desktop computer; at home he uses Windows XP; and in his graphics class, he used a Macintosh. His next class at the community college will involve working with Linux. Although Justin's experience might seem extreme, it illustrates that you are likely to encounter different desktop operating systems at work, school, and home. In addition, as computers proliferate, it becomes more important to learn the common characteristics that they share.

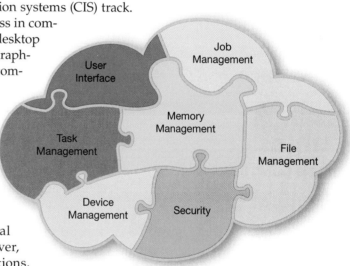

The functions of an operating system

Justin spends most of his time on each computer he uses working in one or another specific application, such as a word processor, a graphical drawing program, or an Internet browser. However, he must also perform tasks outside of these applications, such as logging onto the computer, launching each application, managing files, and even troubleshooting the occasional problem that may arise with the computer. But each of these different computers requires different ways of doing things so he wants to gain a better understanding of the OSs so that he can both perform better on the job and feel more comfortable while working on the various computers. He wants to learn what an OS is and what functions it performs, as the following sections describe.

An operating system is the software (or group of programs) that acts as the central control program for the computer. As such, it is loaded (or "booted up," a derivation of the adage "lifting yourself by your own bootstraps") when the computer is turned on. Its main component, the kernel, always remains in memory while the computer is running, managing low-level (close-to-the-hardware) OS tasks. The operating system acts as an intermediary between the applications and the hardware. Until we made the transition from single-purpose machines to multipurpose machines, there was no need for an operating system between an application and the hardware, since the single-purpose software interacted with all of the hardware of the system.

When programmers (also known as "developers") write an application, they design the application to interact with the operating system and make all requests for hardware services through the operating system. To do this, they must write the program to use the correct commands to request operating system services. The operating system, in turn, interacts with the hardware on behalf of the application and fulfills the requests the application made. Today, because our computers are no longer such dedicated systems, the operating system performs several functions. We'll study them next.

User Interface

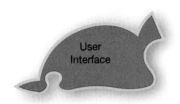

The user interface is the software layer, sometimes called the shell, through which the user communicates with the OS. The OS, in turn, communicates with the computer. Thus, the user interface includes the command processor, which loads programs into memory, as well as the many visual components of the operating system (what you see when you look at the display). On a computer running DOS or Linux (without a graphical shell), this visual component consists of a character-based command line that provides only sparse amounts of information. This is the command-line interface (CLI). Figure 1–2 shows the classic DOS prompt: white characters against a black screen, with a blinking cursor waiting for you to type a command at the keyboard. A cursor in a CLI is merely a marker for the current position where what you type on the keyboard will go. Further, only a limited set of characters can appear on the screen, each in its own little equal-sized grid of space.

To become proficient at working in a CLI, you must memorize the somewhat cryptic commands and their modifiers and subcommands. On the other hand, Apple's Mac and Microsoft's Windows operating systems provide an information-rich graphical user interface (GUI), fully integrated into the operating system. It is through this GUI that you communicate with the OS and the computer. The GUI offers menus and graphical icons (small graphics) that allow you to use a pointing device to select programs to run and to perform many other tasks, such as opening a word processor file.

FIGURE 1–2 MS-DOS prompt

Although you do not have to memorize arcane commands, working within a GUI does require you to learn the meaning of the various graphical pieces that make up the GUI and how to navigate among these pieces to find your programs and data. In addition, you must learn how to make a program become active (to start it running) so that you can get your work or play done. Figure 1–3 shows a GUI screen. Notice the icons and other graphical components, such as the bar at the bottom containing the button showing the Microsoft logo and the cursor. In a GUI the cursor is sometimes replaced by a graphical pointer that can have a variety of shapes that you can move around by manipulating a pointing device—usually a mouse, trackball, or touch pad (on a laptop). The pointer allows you to select or manipulate objects in the GUI, which serves as a metaphor for commands. For example, to delete an item, you pick it up and put it into the recycle bin. By contrast, in a CLI, you would type a command such as "delete myfile.txt."

Although Linux traditionally had a command-line interface, most current versions of Linux also allow you to use GUIs.

Job Management

Job management is an operating system function that controls the order and time in which programs are run. Two examples of programs that may perform this function are a scheduling program that schedules other programs or batch files to run on a certain day and time, and a print program that manages and prioritizes multiple print jobs.

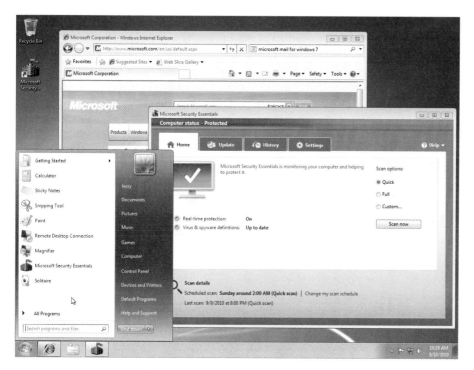

FIGURE 1–3 A typical GUI screen

Task Management

Task management is an operating system function found in multitasking operating systems. Multitasking implies that a computer is simultaneously running two or more programs (tasks) at the same time. In reality, a computer cannot run more tasks simultaneously than the number of processors that exist within the computer. Until recently, most desktop and laptop computers had only a single processor, switching between tasks so fast that it seems to be executing a number of tasks at the same time. New processors can have multiple CPUs within a single chip, so they have true multitasking.

Task management controls the focus (where the system's attention is at any given moment). It also allows the user to switch between tasks by giving the focus to the application the user brings to the foreground. In Windows, this application runs in the current window—the window that is on top of other windows on the screen and the window that receives input from the keyboard when the user types.

Memory Management

Memory management is an operating system function that manages the placement of programs and data in memory, while keeping track of where it put them. In the case of advanced operating systems, such as Windows XP and later Windows versions, this involves a scheme for making optimal use of memory. Virtual memory allows more code and data to be in memory than what the actual physical system memory can hold. Using a memory management OS component called the virtual memory manager, these operating systems move code and data, as necessary, to a portion of the disk defined as virtual memory, meaning that this disk space is used as if it were memory, not just disk storage space. The OS performs this transfer for code and data that are part of any program that currently does not have the user's attention because this unneeded-now information does not have to be kept in RAM for immediate use, so other programs that do need to use the memory now can do so.

The memory management function may not be included in every definition of an operating system, but it is a very important function, especially in the Windows, Macintosh, and Linux operating systems surveyed in this book.

File
Management

File Management

File management, also referred to as data management, is an operating system function that allows the operating system to read, write, and modify data, while managing the logical storage of the data. Each operating system has at least one scheme of logical organization, called a file system. A file system is the logical structure used on a storage device for the purpose of storing files, as well as the code within an operating system that allows the OS to store and manage files on a storage device. The logical structure is written to a storage device when an operating system uses a technique called formatting. The operating system maps the logical organization of the file system to physical locations on the storage device, (most often a conventional hard disk drive or solid state drive so that it can store and retrieve the data. The logical structure of a file system stores metadata, which is data about the stored files.

Normally, a single storage device will have only a single file system, residing in a single area defined as a partition, but most operating systems allow a storage device to have more than one partition. A partition may be an entire drive volume or just a portion of a drive, and it is assigned some identifier, for example, a drive letter like C. In DOS and Windows, the drive letter is followed by a colon, so that a complete drive name may be C:. We often call this a logical drive.

Within the logical structure of a file system, data is organized into entities called files that are saved to storage devices (usually disks). File management also allows users to organize their files, using other special files that act as containers. These special files, called folders or directories, can contain files as well as other folders.

There are file systems for magnetic media (hard drives), file systems for optical media, and special file systems for working over the network. Each of the operating systems discussed in this book supports several types of file systems.

Examples of file systems for magnetic media include the FAT file system that originated with both PC DOS and MS-DOS; the ext2, ext3, JFS, VFS, and ReiserFs file systems for Linux; the FAT32 and NTFS file systems for Windows; and the Mac OS files systems, HFS and HFS+. Learn more about the file systems for Windows, Linux, and Mac OS in the chapters devoted to each operating system.

Examples of file systems for optical media include ISO9660, Universal Disk Format (UDF). File systems for sharing files over a network are independent of the file system used on storage media. Example of such network files systems include NFS, used by Mac OS X and UNIX, and SMB/CIFS used by several OSs.

Device
Management

Device Management

The device management function controls hardware devices by using special software called device drivers, which are installed in the operating system. Device drivers are unique to the device and the manufacturer of the device creates them to work with a specific operating system. For instance, a printer or video adapter will come with drivers for several different operating systems. The device driver contains the commands understood by the device and uses these commands to control the device in response to requests it receives from the operating system. You need a component-specific device driver for each unique hardware component with which the operating system interacts.

Security

Security

The security function of an operating system provides password-protected authentication of the user before allowing access to the local computer and may restrict what someone can do on a computer. For example, Rachel is the accounting clerk in a small company. She has confidential information on her computer, and she doesn't want just anyone to be able to walk up to her computer and access the information stored there. Rachel can set up her computer so that anyone getting into it must log on with a user name and password from a user account. A user account is nothing more than a name and an associated password stored inside the PC. Security is a large topic—one that would take many books and weeks of your time to really master—but to go much farther in this book without addressing computer security would be foolish, so Chapter 2 is devoted to computer security basics. There you will learn about threats to computers, what security is built-in to the operating systems discussed in this book, and the steps you can take to protect yourself from threats.

Categories of Operating Systems

Operating systems are organized into four categories, three of which are based on the number of simultaneous tasks and the number of simultaneous users that can be served, while one category, real-time, is based on an entirely different set of characteristics. The categories are:

- Single-user/single-tasking
- Single-user/multitasking
- Multiuser/multitasking
- Real-time

We'll discuss each in turn.

Single-User/Single-Tasking

A single-user/single-tasking operating system is one that allows only a single user to perform a single task at a time. A task is a function such as reading a file from disk, performing a math calculation, printing a document, or sending a request over the Internet to a Web server. Small and simple OSs can only manage a single task at a time. (See Figure 1–4.)

FIGURE 1–4 Single-user/single-tasking

Examples of single-tasking OSs are MS-DOS and the Palm OS, used on the palmOne handheld computers. Because they take up very little space on disk or in memory when they are running, a single-tasking OS does not require a powerful and expensive computer. The current OSs on the iPhone and the iPad fall into this category because they only allow a user to run one user application at a time.

Single-User/Multitasking

An operating system that allows a single user to perform two or more functions at once is a single-user/multitasking operating system. Early versions of both Microsoft Windows and the Macintosh operating systems were examples of this category. Thanks to these OSs and the applications that run on them, people could accomplish more in less time, increasing their productivity. For instance, a single user can have two or more programs open, share data between programs, and can instantly switch between them. (See Figure 1–5.)

Multiuser/Multitasking Operating Systems

A multiuser/multitasking operating system allows multiple users to run programs simultaneously. We have had such operating systems for decades on mainframes and on today's network servers, sometimes called terminal servers. This is not at all the same as connecting to a network server for the sake of accessing files and

FIGURE 1–5 Single-user/multitasking

printers. When a computer connects to a file and print server to access document files to edit, the client computer performs the processing work locally. Not so with a multiuser server OS that gives each user a complete operating environment on the server that is separate from all other users. A terminal client is software on the user's computer that establishes a connection to the terminal server. In a multiuser/multitasking operating system server environment, all or most of the computing occurs at the server. (See Figure 1–6.)

When connected to a multiuser/multitasking server, each user may have either a full-fledged PC or a thin client (a minimally configured PC). The terminal client runs software under Windows, Mac OS, or Linux, but with far lower hardware requirements than it would need if it ran all the processes locally. The terminal server providing a multiuser/multitasking OS to client computers may be a Unix, Linux, NetWare, or a special version of Microsoft Windows server.

The multiuser capabilities of today's OSs carry over to the user environment. Multiple users can have accounts on a single computer—desktop or server—and when each user logs on he sees his desktop with all his favorite gadgets and other settings, and he has access to his files and installed programs. The desktop operating systems we survey in this book—Windows XP, Windows Vista, Windows 7, Linux, and Mac OS X—all are multiuser/multitasking operating systems with one caveat: only one user at a time can interactively log into the computer. However, a logged on user can simply log out, and leave their entire session of open applications and windows intact, and another user can log in and run a separate session, thus switching the current user. Therefore, Windows OSs support multiple but not simultaneous interactive users. All of the desktop OSs surveyed in this course support multiple simultaneous user connections over a network.

In this context, an *interactive user* is one who is physically sitting at the local computer, controlling the keyboard and mouse.

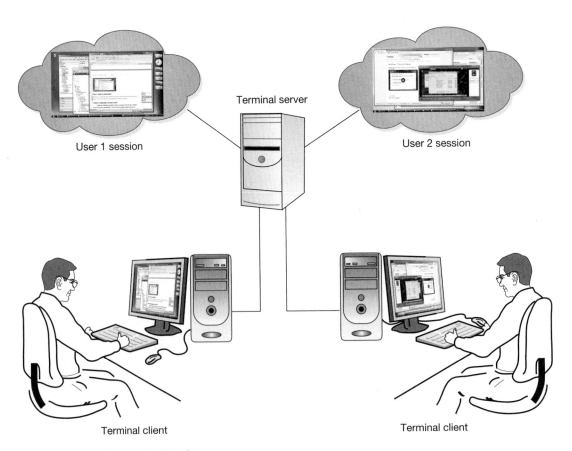

FIGURE 1–6 Multiuser/multitasking

We can take the "multiuser" part of this a step further with the concept of virtualization, discussed in detail in Chapter 3. In brief, virtualization is the creation of an environment that seems real, but isn't. When we talk about virtualization of an OS we usually mean running an OS within a virtual machine within another OS. For instance, you can run Windows XP in a virtual machine on a computer running Windows 7, or you can run Windows 7 within a virtual machine on an iMac computer running Mac OS X.

Real-Time Operating Systems

A real-time operating system (RTOS) is a very fast and relatively small OS. A real-time operating system's speed and ability to work with special real-time application programs defines it. Often embedded, meaning it is built into the circuitry of a device and not normally loaded from a disk drive, a real-time operating system runs real-time applications. It may support multiple simultaneous tasks or it may only support single tasking. A real-time application responds to certain inputs extremely quickly—thousandths or millionths of a second (milliseconds or microseconds, respectively). They run medical diagnostics equipment, life-support systems, machinery, scientific instruments, and industrial systems. Real-time OSs are used in aviation and aerospace where the code must run within the allotted time. Output must be provided in time to make a course correction (in the case of aviation software), make a flow correction (in the case of a ventilator), or provide a warning to an operator. Examples of real-time operating systems include BlueCat Linux by LynuxWorks, QNX Neutrino by QNX Software Systems, Operating System Embedded (OSE), pSOS, and Windows CE.

Real-time embedded systems are everywhere. Devices with real-time embedded systems control the movement of surveillance cameras suspended by cables over a sports arena. Other devices gather data from racecars and transmit the data and live video images of the race from each car. Real-time embedded systems are also used in unmanned military ground vehicles, and you'll find real-time embedded systems in very large-scale machines, such as the huge sack, parcel, and large parcel sorting machines found in U.S. Postal Service bulk mail centers. (See Figure 1–7.)

16-, 32-, and 64-Bit OSs

We call an operating system that can take advantage of the addressing and processing features of a processor an *x*-bit OS. The original MS-DOS was a 16-bit OS, as was Windows 3.0 and its sub-versions. Windows 95, Windows 98, and Windows Millennium Edition were really hybrids, with mostly 32-bit pieces but some 16-bit pieces for downward compatibility. Windows XP had a 64-bit version, but it was not widely used, and you are unlikely to encounter it in the wild. The Windows versions, Mac OS X, and Linux OSs we discuss in this book are available in both 32-bit and 64-bit versions.

All things being equal, the 64-bit version of an operating system will be faster than its 32-bit counterpart, but the biggest difference between the 32-bit and 64-bit versions of Windows is in the address space used by both system RAM and other RAM and ROM in your computer (see Table 1–1). Windows 64-bit does

FIGURE 1–7 Example of a device containing a real-time embedded system
© Michael Pimentel/www.isiphotos.com/Corbis

TABLE 1–1 Windows Memory Limits

Edition	RAM Limit in 32-Bit Version	RAM Limit in 64-Bit Version
Windows XP Professional	4 GB	128 GB
Windows Vista Ultimate/Enterprise/Business	4 GB	128 GB
Windows Vista Home Premium	4 GB	16 GB
Windows Vista Home Basic	4 GB	8 GB
Windows 7 Ultimate/Enterprise/Professional	4 GB	192 GB
Windows 7 Home Premium	4 GB	16 GB
Windows 7 Home Basic	4 GB	8 GB

not use the maximum theoretical address space of a 64-bit CPU, which is 2^{64}, or 9.2 quintillion (nine followed by 18 digits).

A 64-bit operating system requires 64-bit applications, although Microsoft has offered ways to support older applications in each upgrade of Windows, as described in each of the Windows operating system chapters in this book. To determine if a Windows Vista or Windows 7 computer is running a 32-bit or 64-bit version, type "system" in the Start menu's Start Search box (simply Search in Windows 7) and select "System" from the resulting list of Programs. The System Type field will say "32-bit Operating System" or "64-bit Operating System." If you purchase a new computer today with either Windows or the Mac OS preinstalled, it is most likely to be a 64-bit OS.

LO 1.2 | Yesterday's Operating Systems

Sometimes people think that they can simply take the newest and best computer or other gadget and make it work without understanding anything about how it came to be. Well, they can. But they probably can't fix it, modify

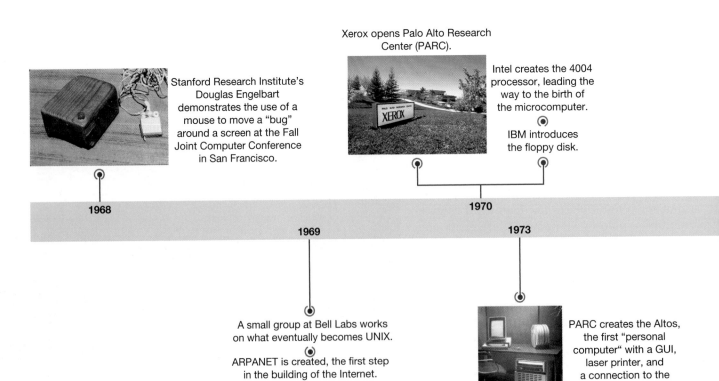

Xerox opens Palo Alto Research Center (PARC).

Stanford Research Institute's Douglas Engelbart demonstrates the use of a mouse to move a "bug" around a screen at the Fall Joint Computer Conference in San Francisco.

Intel creates the 4004 processor, leading the way to the birth of the microcomputer.

IBM introduces the floppy disk.

1968

1969

1970

1973

A small group at Bell Labs works on what eventually becomes UNIX.

ARPANET is created, the first step in the building of the Internet.

PARC creates the Altos, the first "personal computer" with a GUI, laser printer, and a connection to the first Ethernet network.

it, or use it effectively without understanding how and why it came to be in the form it's in now. One really can't understand current PC technology without having a grasp of older PC technology. In other words, studying history is important to understand how we arrived at today. We'll begin with arguably the oldest OS still in use today, with beginnings that predate microcomputers. Then we'll explore the history of computers leading to today's PCs and Mac desktop computers and the operating systems that evolved for each of these hardware platforms.

UNIX—The OS for All Platforms

In the context of this book, we have put UNIX under Yesterday's Desktop OSs because UNIX has a longer history than any other popular operating system. It grew out of an operating system developed for an early Digital Equipment Corporation (DEC) computer and went through several generations of changes before it emerged from the Bell Labs Computing Science Research Center (Bell Labs) as UNIX version 6 in 1975. This was a portable operating system for minicomputers and mainframe computers distributed via government and commercial licenses and inexpensive academic licenses. A portable operating system is one that you can use on a variety of computer system platforms, with only minor alterations required for the underlying architecture.

The University of California at Berkeley licensed UNIX, modified it, and distributed it to other schools as Berkeley Software Distribution (BSD) version 4.2. Later versions have followed. The schools paid licensing fees to

> **Research the History of UNIX**
>
> Read a history of the UNIX operating system. Try this:
>
> 1. Point your Web browser to www.bell-labs.com/history/unix.
> 2. Read the article "The Creation of the UNIX Operating System."
> 3. Read about the contributions of Dennis Ritchie and Ken Thompson.
> 4. Research more recent history of UNIX by entering "UNIX history 2010" into a search engine.

try this!

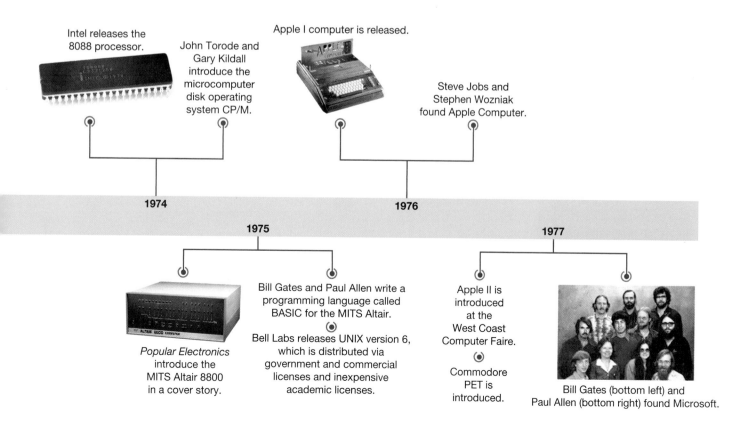

Intel releases the 8088 processor.

John Torode and Gary Kildall introduce the microcomputer disk operating system CP/M.

Apple I computer is released.

Steve Jobs and Stephen Wozniak found Apple Computer.

1974

1976

1975

1977

Popular Electronics introduce the MITS Altair 8800 in a cover story.

Bill Gates and Paul Allen write a programming language called BASIC for the MITS Altair.

Bell Labs releases UNIX version 6, which is distributed via government and commercial licenses and inexpensive academic licenses.

Apple II is introduced at the West Coast Computer Faire.

Commodore PET is introduced.

Bill Gates (bottom left) and Paul Allen (bottom right) found Microsoft.

Bell Labs. Students and others improved on and added to UNIX, freely sharing their code with each other. This tradition still prevails today with such versions of UNIX as Free BSD, Net BSD, Open BDS, and Open Solaris. Commercial versions of UNIX today include AIX, OpenServer (derived from SCO UNIX), and HP/UX.

In certain environments UNIX is still very much alive. The current commercial versions of UNIX include Sun Microsystems' Solaris, Hewlett-Packard's HP-UX, IBM's AIX, and Compaq's Tru64 UNIX. These versions are high-end server applications and quite expensive, as are the computers they run on. There are also many open source versions of UNIX, including FreeBSD and NetBSD. Open source is a certification standard of the Open Source Initiative (OSI) through which a program's source code (the original language in which a program is written) is made available free of charge to the general public. Learn more about open source at www.opensource.org. Even with these free versions available, however, it is worthwhile to buy one of the modestly priced packages from companies that charge small fees just for the value they have added to the OS in the form of additional software, installation and configuration instructions, and documentation.

In addition to portability to many computer platforms, UNIX supports time-sharing and multiuser systems, and some versions run on personal computers. UNIX can be found today on very large computer systems (still referred to as mainframes) and on Intel desktop systems, as well as on a variety of midsize computers. Most versions of UNIX also offer several different user interfaces. Some use character mode, like the traditional shells, such as the Bourne shell and the C shell. Others use a graphical interface such as GNOME or KDE.

Even fierce UNIX advocates do not see UNIX taking over the desktop any time soon. However, it is an excellent server operating system, because it uses resources carefully, allowing you to load only the services currently needed. It is also very secure, and versions of UNIX are present on many of the world's Internet servers.

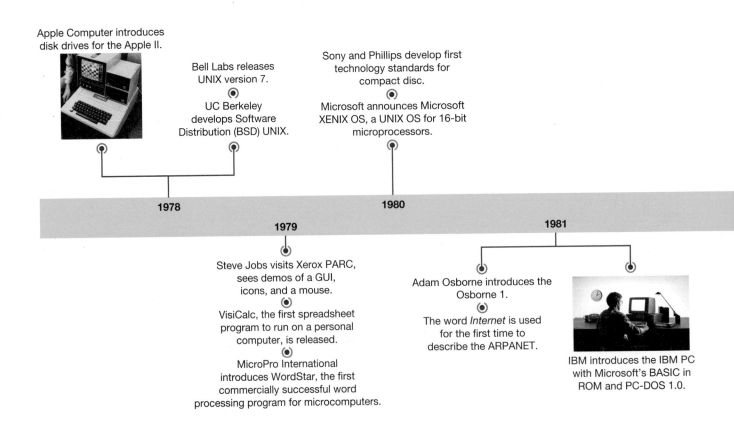

Apple Computer introduces disk drives for the Apple II.

Bell Labs releases UNIX version 7.

UC Berkeley develops Software Distribution (BSD) UNIX.

Sony and Phillips develop first technology standards for compact disc.

Microsoft announces Microsoft XENIX OS, a UNIX OS for 16-bit microprocessors.

1978

1980

1979

1981

Steve Jobs visits Xerox PARC, sees demos of a GUI, icons, and a mouse.

VisiCalc, the first spreadsheet program to run on a personal computer, is released.

MicroPro International introduces WordStar, the first commercially successful word processing program for microcomputers.

Adam Osborne introduces the Osborne 1.

The word *Internet* is used for the first time to describe the ARPANET.

IBM introduces the IBM PC with Microsoft's BASIC in ROM and PC-DOS 1.0.

The Evolution of Operating Systems

Computers didn't arrive yesterday. You could argue that they started with the computers designed (but never built) by Charles Babbage in the 1820s. Or perhaps you would start with the U.S. military's World War II computers. In general, consumers encountered their first microcomputers in 1977 with the introduction of Apple's Apple II, Radio Shack's TRS-80, and Commodore's PET.

Although computers and microcomputers existed before the Apple II, this computer was the first to combine the critical elements that make what today we consider a desktop or laptop; these include a keyboard, a monitor, an operating system, a pointing device, desirable and useful applications, and a reasonable price tag.

The idea for a complex and powerful operating system like what you see on your desktop or laptop today didn't just magically pop into someone's head. An operating system as a separate entity didn't exist in the early years of digital computing (defined roughly as from World War II into the 1950s). Each computer was dedicated to a single purpose, such as performing trajectory calculations for weapons or mathematical analysis for a science lab, in addition to the system I/O functions. Loading a new program into a computer was a time-consuming process.

Operating systems evolved through many small steps, some in the form of technical advances and others in evolutionary changes in how people used computers. The reason they evolved is because people saw the need to use computers as multipurpose devices. The "user," at first a government agency, research institute, or large business, would define the computer's purpose at any given time by the program chosen to run. In the 1950s, some early "operating systems" managed data storage on tape for mainframe computers, but it was much more common for application programmers to write system I/O routines (the stuff of today's OSs) right into their programs. By the mid-1960s, as disk systems became more common on large computers, we needed operating systems to manage these disks and to perform other common system-level routines.

Apple II

The MITS Altair 8800 was an important predecessor to the Apple II, TRS-80, and PET computers. Although featured in a cover article of the January 1975 issue of *Popular Mechanics*, it was not for ordinary people. Whether you bought the $395 kit or the fully assembled $495 version, the input method was switches that you flipped to program it, and the result of these efforts (the output) was a pattern of blinking lights. As a portent of the future, the Altair 8800 gave Bill Gates and Paul Allen their very first sale of the computer language of BASIC.

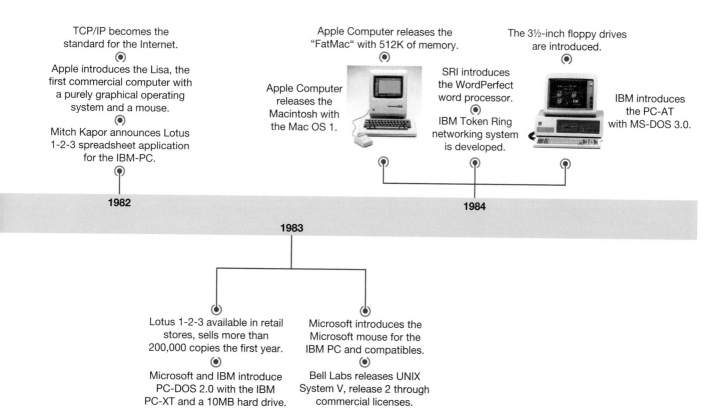

TCP/IP becomes the standard for the Internet.

Apple introduces the Lisa, the first commercial computer with a purely graphical operating system and a mouse.

Mitch Kapor announces Lotus 1-2-3 spreadsheet application for the IBM-PC.

Apple Computer releases the "FatMac" with 512K of memory.

Apple Computer releases the Macintosh with the Mac OS 1.

SRI introduces the WordPerfect word processor.

IBM Token Ring networking system is developed.

The 3½-inch floppy drives are introduced.

IBM introduces the PC-AT with MS-DOS 3.0.

1982

1984

1983

Lotus 1-2-3 available in retail stores, sells more than 200,000 copies the first year.

Microsoft and IBM introduce PC-DOS 2.0 with the IBM PC-XT and a 10MB hard drive.

Microsoft introduces the Microsoft mouse for the IBM PC and compatibles.

Bell Labs releases UNIX System V, release 2 through commercial licenses.

The computer enthusiasts who bought the earliest microcomputers of the 1970s, such as the MITS Altair, were infatuated with the technology. Slow CPU speeds, very limited memory, clumsy I/O devices, and lack of software did not deter them. They would network with like-minded people, have informal meetings and discussions, and then gather in self-help groups and form clubs such as the Home Brew Computer Club in California's Silicon Valley. They shared their techniques for creating hardware and programming language software for these computers. Almost every one of these early microcomputers exceeded the expectations of their makers and users, but before long, for a variety of reasons, most of the early entrepreneurial companies and their products disappeared.

When a software publisher creates an entirely new OS, they give it a version number, usually 1.0. Software publishers constantly receive feedback from customers about problems and the need for particular additional features in each OS. In response, a publisher often introduces a modified version of the original product, in which case the number to the right of the decimal point will probably change (say, from version 1.0 to version 1.1—people often abbreviate *version* as simply "v"). An entirely new version number generally reflects an important change to an OS.

> A OS version by any other name, such as Snow Leopard or Windows 7, is still a version and still has a number. Sometimes you just need to look for the number.

The Killer App

For a microcomputer to truly become a successful, widely accepted product—used in businesses as well as by hobbyists—it had to be a tool that performed an important task; it had to have an application that many people needed. We call such an application a killer app.

One of these important tasks was spreadsheet calculations. Before microcomputers, people created spreadsheets manually, on large sheets of paper. They would enter a column of numbers—say, sales for one product in a drugstore—day-by-day for a month. Then they would add up the daily columns to get the total sales for that product for that month. The next column was for the next product, and so on. The process was tedious and error prone, but very valuable to the manager of the drugstore.

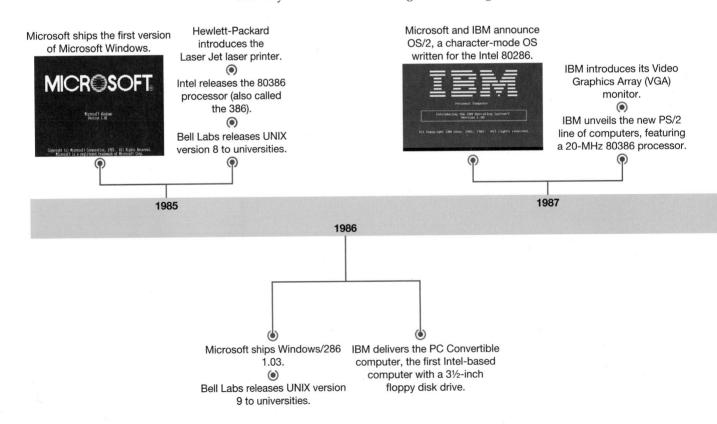

Microsoft ships the first version of Microsoft Windows.

Hewlett-Packard introduces the Laser Jet laser printer.

Intel releases the 80386 processor (also called the 386).

Bell Labs releases UNIX version 8 to universities.

Microsoft and IBM announce OS/2, a character-mode OS written for the Intel 80286.

IBM introduces its Video Graphics Array (VGA) monitor.

IBM unveils the new PS/2 line of computers, featuring a 20-MHz 80386 processor.

1985

1987

1986

Microsoft ships Windows/286 1.03.

Bell Labs releases UNIX version 9 to universities.

IBM delivers the PC Convertible computer, the first Intel-based computer with a 3½-inch floppy disk drive.

Thus, when VisiCalc, an electronic spreadsheet program that ran on early microcomputers, appeared, it became a very successful application. It automated this thankless job, remembered the formulas for the calculations, and allowed people to recalculate a whole column of numbers after a single change was made. VisiCalc did more than this, though; it gave people a reason to want a personal computer. Many people were introduced to VisiCalc on the Apple II computer (running the Apple OS), and this contributed to the success of the Apple II in the late 1970s. However, as the 1980s arrived, Apple failed to come out with a successor to the Apple II in a timely fashion. So, when IBM introduced the IBM PC in 1981, the market was ready for a new microcomputer.

Another fateful series of events revolved around the choice of an OS for the IBM PC. IBM representatives came to Microsoft, then a fledgling software company, for the Microsoft BASIC interpreter, which other machines were using at that time. The result of that visit was that IBM licensed Microsoft's BASIC interpreter and installed it in the ROM of the IBM PC. The IBM folk also talked to Bill Gates about providing an OS; but he did not have one, and so he sent them to another company, Digital Research, the creators of the then-popular CP/M OS. Digital Research, however, refused to sign a contract with IBM, so the IBM guys went back to Bill Gates for the OS. Consequently, Microsoft bought an OS from another company, and this was the basis of the first versions of IBM PC DOS.

Want to learn more about the history of PCs? Our favorite book on the subject is *Fire in the Valley: The Making of the Personal Computer* by Paul Freiberger and Michael Swaine (ISBN 0-07-135892-7).

The IBM PC came with Microsoft's BASIC interpreter installed in ROM, which allowed programs written in the BASIC programming language to run on the PC. For those computers that had the optional floppy drive rather than just the tape drive, the IBM PC came with either PC DOS or a version of Digital Research's CP/M as the operating system. IBM, however, priced CP/M far higher than it did PC DOS, which contributed to the demise of CP/M. The IBM PC far exceeded IBM's sales forecast, which was for about a quarter of a million units during the predicted five-year lifetime of the product. According to one account, IBM took orders for half a million computers in the first few days after introducing the IBM PC. Many enthusiasts bought it, despite its roughly $5,000 price tag for a typical configuration, just to see what it

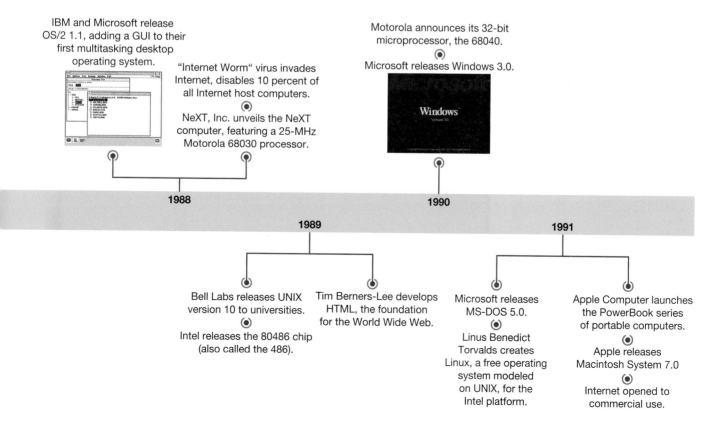

IBM and Microsoft release OS/2 1.1, adding a GUI to their first multitasking desktop operating system.

"Internet Worm" virus invades Internet, disables 10 percent of all Internet host computers.

NeXT, Inc. unveils the NeXT computer, featuring a 25-MHz Motorola 68030 processor.

Motorola announces its 32-bit microprocessor, the 68040.

Microsoft releases Windows 3.0.

1988

1989

1990

1991

Bell Labs releases UNIX version 10 to universities.

Intel releases the 80486 chip (also called the 486).

Tim Berners-Lee develops HTML, the foundation for the World Wide Web.

Microsoft releases MS-DOS 5.0.

Linus Benedict Torvalds creates Linux, a free operating system modeled on UNIX, for the Intel platform.

Apple Computer launches the PowerBook series of portable computers.

Apple releases Macintosh System 7.0

Internet opened to commercial use.

could do. However, the IBM name behind the product also inspired many business users to buy it because this name implied that it was a serious business computer.

The Second Killer App

Although many say that just having the letters *IBM* on the box was what sold that computer, the groundwork laid by VisiCalc left people ready for what was arguably the second killer app, Lotus 1-2-3 by Lotus Corporation. Introduced in 1983, this spreadsheet application ran on the DOS operating system and used all of the 640KB of memory available to software (OS plus application) on the IBM PC. Both the 1-2-3 program and the spreadsheet were in memory while the user worked. It was very fast compared to VisiCalc, which was written to run under the CP/M OS and designed to use much less memory. And 1-2-3 had additional functionality, such as database functions and a program that could create and print graphs from the spreadsheet data. Lotus 1-2-3 was the real killer app, the software that made the IBM PC and PC DOS a must-have combination for people who worked all day crunching numbers and doing what-if calculations. Figure 1–8 shows the Lotus 1-2-3 program with a sample spreadsheet.

Apple OS

In 1976 Steve Jobs and Stephen Wozniak—two guys literally working out of a garage—founded Apple Computer, based on their first computer, the Apple I. Their real notoriety began in 1977 when they introduced the Apple II at the West Coast Computer Faire in San Francisco. This created interest in the brand, and the addition of disk drives in 1978 made it a sought-after product for the technically adventurous consumer. But the OS for the Apple computers at this point did not have a GUI interface—that showed up on the short-lived Apple Lisa computer.

In 1982 Apple introduced the Lisa, the first commercially available computer with a purely graphical operating system—and a mouse. However, this

Through the 1980s, PCs with DOS and a variety of DOS applications made great inroads into organizations of all sizes. In the decade after its introduction, thousands of applications were written for DOS, but Lotus 1-2-3, dBase (database management), and WordPerfect (word processing) were the de facto business standards at the end of that decade. All contributed to the mass adoption of PCs at work, at school, and at home.

There were several notable West Coast Computer Faires. Chuck Peddle also introduced his Commodore PET computer at that first West Coast Computer Faire in 1977. Reports state that more than 12,000 people attended, and among the 180 exhibitors were Intel, MITS, and Digital Research. At the fourth West Coast Computer Faire, in 1979, Dan Bricklin demonstrated VisiCalc (the first "killer app" discussed earlier). At the sixth, Adam Osborne introduced the Osborne 1 computer.

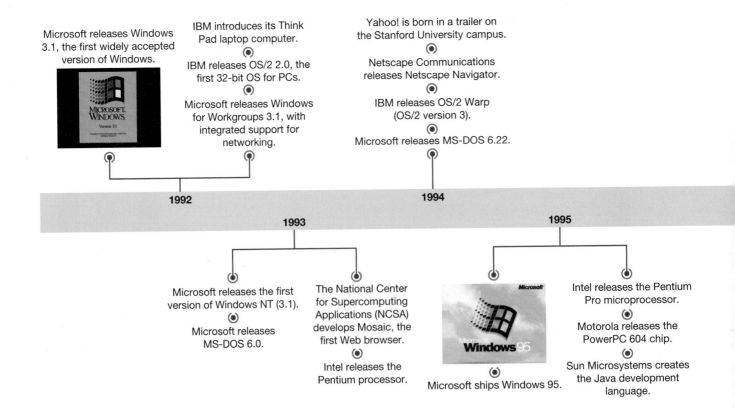

```
A1:                                                              MENU
Worksheet  Range  Copy  Move  File  Print  Graph  Data  System  Quit
Global, Insert, Delete, Column, Erase, Titles, Window, Status, Page
         A          B          C          D          E          F          G          H
1
2   Acme Drugs              Monthly Product Sales Report            May
3   Store #84
4              SKU 13    SKU 25    SKU 53    SKU 57    SKU 61    SKU 73
5          1        6         6        54        32        21        31
6          2        3        31        21        12        54        34
7          3        2         0        78         5        14        15
8          4        8         5        31        87        15        24
9          5        9        53        11        14        21        32
10         6       13        12        14        21        24        14
11         7        3        52        87        65        19        18
12         8        7        13        54        54        23        19
13         9        2        25        21        21        26        17
14        10        8        46        11        14        28        24
15
16  Total          61       243       374       325       245       228
17
18
19
20
27-May-2002  09:42 PM                                      NUM
```

FIGURE 1–8 Lotus 1-2-3 spreadsheet

computer lacked something very important for consumers—applications. It was not successful, and Apple's own Macintosh computer, released in 1984, overshadowed the Lisa and marked the beginning of consumer excitement and the near-cult following of the Apple computer products. The Macintosh came with Mac OS System 1, a GUI operating system that used a mouse. Apple improved the Mac OS over the years to include many easy-to-use features. The final release of the classic Mac OS family was Mac OS 9, introduced in 1999. With its roots in the original 1984 OS, Apple revised and improved the operating system to support multiple users, but it was weak in memory management and full multitasking. In 2001 it was replaced by a completely new operating system—Mac OS X, based on UNIX. Learn more about OS X later in this chapter.

Early in Apple's history, the company strategically targeted schools and universities as places to sell its products, which, over the years, has resulted in large numbers of people who learned computing on a Mac and has contributed to Apple's loyal following. Recently, Apple computers—both desktop and laptops—are gaining market share against PC models and could eventually overtake the mostly Microsoft Windows PCs.

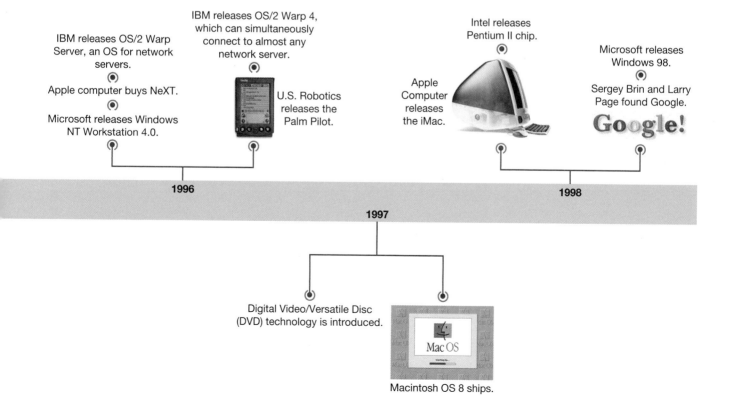

MS-DOS

DOS, which stands for "disk operating system," provides support for interaction, or input and output (I/O), between the memory and disk drives. It is a single-tasking OS with very limited memory support, no support for virtual memory, no native GUI, and no built-in security function. *MS-DOS* refers to the several versions of DOS developed by Microsoft—each major version of DOS being released to support new disk capacities. PC DOS 1.0 supported single-sided 5¼-inch floppies; PC DOS 1.1 added support for double-sided 5¼-inch floppies; and PC DOS 2.0, released with the IBM PC-XT, included support for the XT's 10MB hard drives. DOS 3.0 was released with the IBM PC-AT and included support for the larger AT hard drives. Support for 3½-inch floppies and the larger hard drives of the IBM PS-2 computers were added in DOS 4.0. MS-DOS 6.22 was the last widely used version of MS-DOS.

DOS has a text-mode, command-line interface that requires users to remember cryptic commands and their subcommands to perform file management functions and to launch DOS applications. Figure 1–9 shows a good example of how cryptic DOS can be. Using this OS requires knowledge of many, many concepts. Learn more about DOS in Chapter 4.

Although you will not find DOS as the preferred OS on desktop computers, you might find it as the OS on some handheld devices that do not require a GUI interface. In the past, computer professionals often found DOS handy as a very small OS that fit on a floppy disk, to which they added various utilities for troubleshooting computers. This practice has all but disappeared today, and those same techs are now more likely to carry either optical disks or flash drives loaded with specialized software for their work.

OS/2

In 1987, Microsoft and IBM introduced their jointly developed OS/2 (Operating System/2), intended to replace DOS. However, version 1.0 was underpowered in that they wrote it for the Intel 80286 processor, which had serious

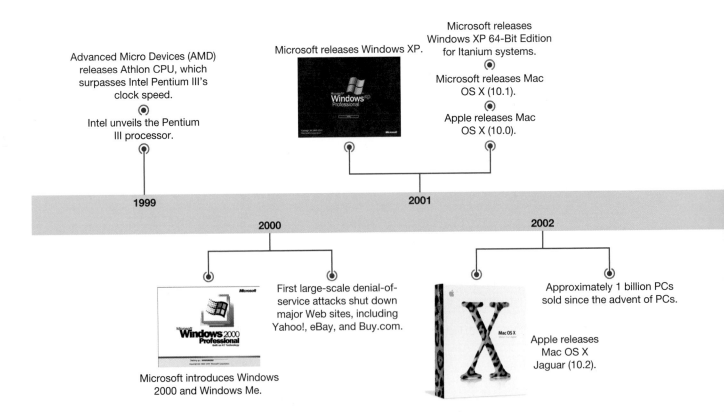

Advanced Micro Devices (AMD) releases Athlon CPU, which surpasses Intel Pentium III's clock speed.

Intel unveils the Pentium III processor.

Microsoft releases Windows XP.

Microsoft releases Windows XP 64-Bit Edition for Itanium systems.

Microsoft releases Mac OS X (10.1).

Apple releases Mac OS X (10.0).

1999

2001

2000

2002

First large-scale denial-of-service attacks shut down major Web sites, including Yahoo!, eBay, and Buy.com.

Microsoft introduces Windows 2000 and Windows Me.

Approximately 1 billion PCs sold since the advent of PCs.

Apple releases Mac OS X Jaguar (10.2).

```
A:\>format c: /s /u

WARNING: ALL DATA ON NON-REMOVABLE DISK
DRIVE C: WILL BE LOST!
Proceed with Format (Y/N)?y


Formatting   502M
Format complete.
System transferred

Volume label (11 characters, ENTER for none)?

  526,106,624 bytes total disk space
      212,992 bytes used by system
  525,893,632 bytes available on disk

        8,192 bytes in each allocation unit.
       64,196 allocation units available on disk.

Volume Serial Number is 3A4E-17DA

A:\>_
```

FIGURE 1–9 MS-DOS prompt with the Format command

memory and mode limits. Despite the memory limits, it still required much more memory and disk space (2MB of memory and 8MB of disk space) than either PC DOS or MS-DOS. This was at a time when 2MB of memory and a 40MB hard drive (considered large in the late 1980s) cost several thousand dollars. Although the first version of OS/2 could multitask applications in memory, only one application could be visible on the screen at a time. Also, people had to write applications specifically for OS/2, because it had very limited support for DOS applications.

In the 1990s, IBM introduced OS/2 Warp, a greatly improved version of OS/2 with a very nice GUI. After about 18 months, however, IBM retreated from the battle for the desktop and targeted the high-end server market. It never rivaled Windows or UNIX in terms of sales. In 2003, IBM announced it

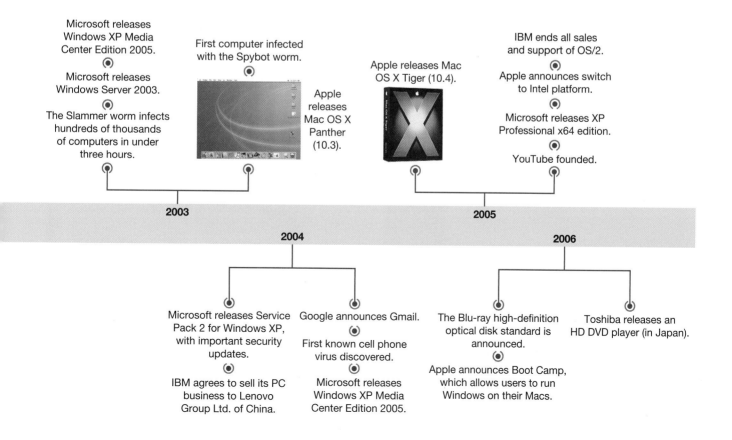

would not develop any future versions of OS/2, and in December 2004 IBM sold its PC division to China-based Lenovo Group.

Microsoft Windows

We'll begin our discussion of Windows by explaining Windows versions and editions, and then briefly go through the versions in chronological order.

Windows Versions and Editions. Before we get too far into a discussion of Windows, we would like to clarify what the terms *versions* and *editions* mean in the context of Windows. Each Microsoft Windows version is a new level of the Windows operating system, with major changes to the core components of the operating system as well as a distinctive and unifying look to the GUI. A version sometimes has a simple ordinal number, as in Windows 1 or Windows 2. Then some sub-versions appeared, such as Windows 3.1. In the mid-1990s, Microsoft moved away from the old convention and modified the names of several OSs to coincide with the calendar year, as in Windows 95, Windows 98, and Windows 2000. Then, it created names such as Windows XP and Windows Vista, but underneath it all Microsoft still maintained a numeric version number, which resurfaced in the naming of Windows 7. The next Windows OS may be Windows 8. The versions we will cover in this book are the strictly desktop versions in use today: Windows XP, Windows Vista, and Windows 7.

Then there is the issue of editions. In recent years, Microsoft released separate products of each Windows version, such as Windows XP Professional, Windows Vista Business, and Windows 7 Professional. We'll start our discussion of yesterday's Windows versions with the first version and make our way to Windows XP, which presently spans the gap between the old and the new.

Windows 1 through 3. In 1985, when the first version of Windows appeared, it was more smoke than OS. It consisted of a not-very-good GUI balanced precariously on top of MS-DOS. The GUI code was separate from the OS code. It

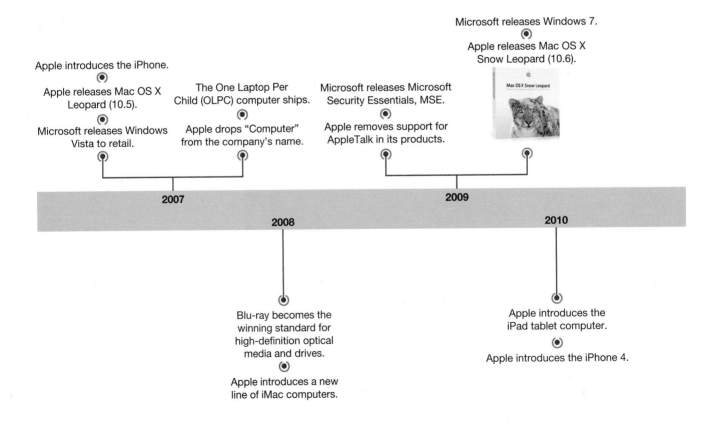

was slow and had a flat look—you couldn't lay one graphic on top of another. The ability to overlap graphical elements, such as windows and icons, did not show up until a later version. However, the GUI gradually improved with each version.

From 1985 to 1990, Microsoft continued to work on both Windows and DOS, but Windows was not much more than a pretty face until 1990 and Windows 3.0, which supported the three Intel processor modes of operation available at that time. Microsoft called these modes, as supported in Windows, Real mode, Standard mode, and 386 Enhanced mode. In Real mode, Windows 3.0 was just a GUI that ran on top of DOS. In the other two modes, it added functionality to DOS to take advantage of the 286 (Standard mode) and 386 (386 Enhanced mode) processor modes.

The most important feature of Windows 3.0 was better support for legacy DOS applications within Windows. This was possible in the 386 Enhanced mode. This meant that both DOS apps and Windows apps could run simultaneously. This version still had its quirks, but for the first time, IT managers saw a potential GUI replacement for DOS as the desktop OS of choice.

In the spring of 1992, Microsoft brought out a minor upgrade, Windows 3.1, which many organizations adopted as the standard desktop OS. The fact that Microsoft's entire suite of productivity applications was also available in versions for Windows 3.*x* helped encourage adoption.

Figure 1–10 shows the Windows 3.1 desktop. Notice that there is no graphical task bar at the bottom of the screen, just the Program Manager window (the main window) with other windows nested in it.

Windows for Workgroups. DOS and Windows OSs through Windows 3.*x* included only the operating system functions. If you wanted to connect to a network, you added a network operating system (NOS) on top of your installed OS. This separate network operating system might be from 3COM or Novell, or it might be Microsoft's LAN Manager NOS, developed in the late 1980s.

Novell and LAN Manager were both server network operating systems that combined the operating system functions with the networking functions and provided file and print sharing services to other computers. Additionally,

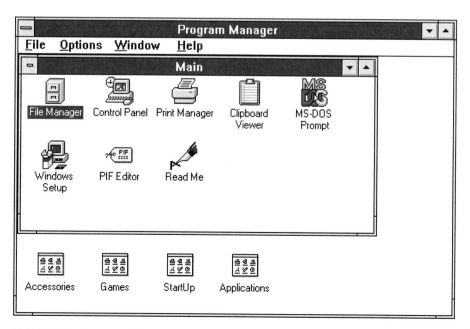

FIGURE 1–10 MS Windows 3.1 desktop

to connect to a server, a client computer needed special client software so it could connect and request services from it.

Early client network software included underlying networking components called drivers and protocols. A protocol is a standard, or a set of standards, that everybody agrees to abide by when they build a piece of software or hardware. Products that adhere to a specific protocol will be able to work together, regardless of who made them. In practice, we use the word *protocol* to describe a software implementation of a protocol, such as the IP protocol, part of the TCP/IP protocol suite. You will learn more about protocols in Chapter 10. Among the protocols are those required to actually "see" and communicate with a certain type of server on a network. Client software includes these protocols. The network software Microsoft provided for DOS and for Windows 3.1 on top of DOS included only the client component. However, beginning in October 1992 with Windows for Workgroups 3.1, Microsoft included both the client and server software in all of its Windows OS products. This enabled peer-to-peer networking, meaning desktop computers could act as servers to their peers. This worked well in a small work group environment of 10 or fewer computers.

Windows NT. Because it had the same user interface as Windows 3.1, Windows NT was introduced in 1993 as Windows NT 3.1. That was where the similarity ended. To begin with, it was a server operating system, which included server protocols in its integrated network support. Furthermore, unlike Windows 3.*x* and Windows for Workgroups, the GUI did not sit on top of DOS, but was an entirely new operating system with a new file system, NTFS.

The NTFS file system includes a new disk file management technology with an entirely new logical structure. It has unique security features that continue to be substantially unchanged today in Windows systems. Learn more about this file system later in this chapter in the section titled, "Windows NTFS File Systems."

Windows NT was the first Microsoft OS to take full advantage of the capabilities of the special protected mode that Intel introduced in its processors manufactured after 1986. A major benefit of this was more stability and security in the OS. In fact, NT was so powerful that Microsoft decided to make two versions of NT: one designed mainly for servers, and another geared more toward individual user systems—what some folks call workstations. Thus, the next version of NT (NT 3.5) was also the first Windows OS to have separate products: Windows NT Workstation and Windows NT Server. Both of these used the same kernel (a kernel is the main OS component) and interface, but the Server version had enhancements and components that were needed only on a network server. Microsoft configured the Workstation version as a desktop operating system.

In 1996, Microsoft introduced Windows NT 4.0, which had a GUI similar to that of Windows 95 as well as other improvements and enhancements to the OS. Figure 1–11 shows the Windows NT desktop. Microsoft no longer sells or supports Windows NT 4.0 Workstation.

Windows 95. Windows 95, released in 1995, predated Windows NT 4 Workstation. It was still a continuation of the Windows 3.X model with the graphical environment simply "sitting" on top of the DOS operating system. It did have some improvements in the operating system, including both 16-bit and 32-bit code. The greatest improvements were in the GUI, which made it the most popular operating system up to that time.

Windows 98. Windows 98 was an evolutionary development in the Windows desktop operating system, including improvements in both visible and

Windows for Workgroups 3.1 was followed a year later by Windows for Workgroups 3.11, with the usual obligatory fixes and improvements including faster network and disk I/O operations. However, users were still working with a Windows OS that was running on top of DOS; that is, first DOS was started and then Windows. Windows depended on DOS, which had to be installed on the computer.

FIGURE 1–11 MS Windows NT 4.0 desktop with open windows

under-the-hood components. It offered more stability than its immediate predecessor, Windows 95, meaning that it was less likely to stop in its tracks just when you were about to complete that book order on Amazon. Although improved, Windows 98 was not as stable as the newer Windows OSs. Figure 1–12 shows the Windows 98 desktop. Its biggest drawback was lack of security. It did not have a local security accounts database for local authentication, and it lacked support for the NTFS file system for file and folder security.

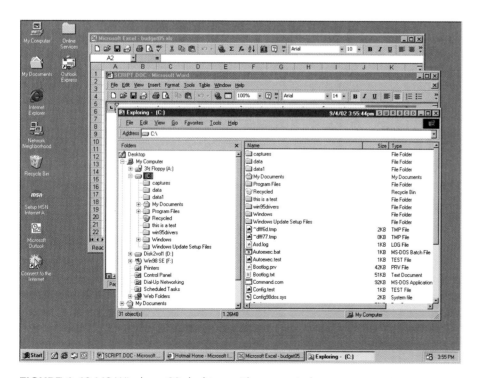

FIGURE 1–12 MS Windows 98 desktop with open windows

Windows 98 offered new options for customizing the GUI, including tighter integration with Microsoft's Web browser, Internet Explorer (IE). This feature allows users to configure Windows so that they can, if they wish, always appear to be in an Internet browser, even when they are not browsing the Internet. Windows 98 came with drivers and support for devices, such as DVD drives, that were not included in Windows 95. As usual with an upgrade to an OS, Microsoft cleaned up existing problems and made the OS run faster.

Windows Me (Millennium Edition). Windows Me (Millennium Edition) targeted the home market, especially the home gaming user, when introduced in 2000. It was essentially Windows 98 with improved music, video, and home networking support. It included the new System Restore utility, which allowed users to roll back the PC software configuration to a date or time before they made a bad change to the computer. The Windows Movie Maker allowed users to digitally edit, save, and share their home videos, and the Windows Media Player gave users a tool for organizing digital music and video. This was the last Microsoft OS based on the Windows 95 internals (mainly the kernel). Windows Me was installed on many computers that were sold to individuals, but it is not an OS that organizations adopted. You are not likely to encounter it in a work environment.

Windows 2000. In 2000, Microsoft introduced the Windows 2000 family of OS products, which brought together the best of Windows 98 and Windows NT. Microsoft had now united its operating systems in a group of products that all shared the same kernel and covered OS needs from the desktop to the enterprise server. The several editions of Windows 2000 include Windows 2000 Professional (the desktop OS), Windows 2000 Server (for a network server on a small network), Windows 2000 Advanced Server (for a network server in larger networks), and Windows 2000 Enterprise Edition (with lots of features for *really* big servers in *really* big networks). Figure 1–13 shows the Windows 2000 desktop.

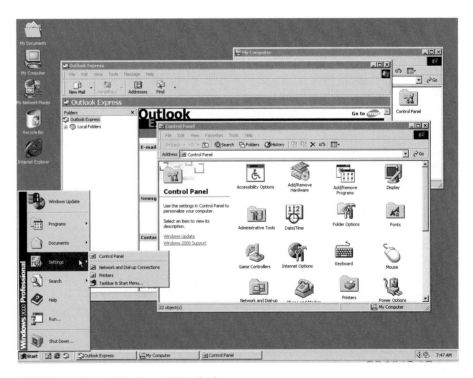

FIGURE 1–13 MS Windows 2000 desktop

Windows XP. With its Windows 2000 products, Microsoft brought all of its OSs together, building them on top of the same core internal piece (the kernel). Some of us, especially those whose jobs include support of both desktop and server computers, thought it would simplify our lives. We really liked that idea because we could learn just one OS for both the desktop and server. However, with Windows XP, Microsoft departed from that model. Windows XP was intended only for the desktop or other consumer-type computer, not for the server environment. The new server products, introduced after Windows XP, began with Windows Server 2003.

There were several Windows XP editions, but the three most common were Windows XP Home Edition, Windows XP Professional, and Windows XP Media Center. All were 32-bit OSs and had the same improved GUI and shared many of the same features, but only Windows XP Professional included several network- and security-related features. Additionally, Microsoft offered Windows XP 64-bit Edition, which supported only 64-bit software and was limited to computers with the Intel Itanium processors.

The Windows XP default desktop was very different from that of its main predecessor, Windows 98, in that by default the recycle bin (where deleted files go) was the only icon on the desktop. In addition, Microsoft redesigned and reorganized the Start menu, as shown in Figure 1–14.

The last service pack for the 32-bit version of Windows XP was SP 3, and as of June 30, 2009, Microsoft no longer permits its retail partners or its original equipment manufacturers to sell

Learn About the Microsoft Support Lifecycle

The Microsoft Support Lifecycle Policy defines the types of support Microsoft provides for its products and how long each support type will be available. Learn more about it; try this:

1. Point your browser to **support.microsoft.com/lifecycle**.
2. Select your country or region and click the arrow button.
3. On the Microsoft Support Lifecycle page there are links to general information on the Support Lifecycle Policy and to the lifecycle of specific products.
4. Explore the Lifecycle information for Microsoft products you use.

try this!

FIGURE 1–14 MS Windows XP desktop with open windows

Windows XP. The company ended support for Windows XP Service Pack 2 (all 32-bit editions) in July 2010. The 64-bit edition did not include a third service pack, and support for the 64-bit edition of XP SP 2 is scheduled to end in April 2014, when support also will end for SP 3 of the 32-bit edition. This is Microsoft's published policy, called the Microsoft Support Lifecycle. Learn more about Windows XP in Chapter 5.

LO 1.3 | Today's Desktop OSs

Today's desktop operating systems include Windows Vista, Windows 7, Mac OS X, and Linux. The latest versions of all of these OSs are multiuser/multitasking operating systems, with support for virtual memory and security, and each comes in editions that support either 32-bit or 64-bit processors.

Table 1–2 summarizes the current desktop OSs covered in later chapters of this book, listing the publisher, platform, and types of applications that you can run natively on each OS. All of these OSs can run virtualization software that will run other OSs, and therefore, other types of applications, but we will defer discussion of virtualization to Chapter 3.

What follows is a brief description of each of these OSs, including a little history to provide perspective. We also reveal where you'll most likely encounter each operating system.

> We do not include Windows Server 2003 or Windows Server 2008 in Table 1–2, because they are not available in desktop versions.

Today's Windows for the Desktop

We discussed Windows XP in the previous section on yesterday's operating systems because we consider it a transitional desktop operating system. We include a chapter on Windows XP only because it is still in use on many desktops today, but Microsoft will soon stop supporting Windows XP with security updates, especially since the release of Windows 7. Therefore, the versions of Windows described in this section on today's operating systems are Windows Vista, Windows 7, and the little we know of the next version of Windows, which we refer to as Windows 8.

Windows Vista

Microsoft released the first retail version of Windows Vista early in 2007. Seen more as an upgrade of Windows XP, it included improvements in how Windows handles graphics, files, and communications. The GUI has a new look compared to previous versions of Windows (see Figure 1–15), and, on computers that can support it, a feature called Aero, which provides translucent windows, live thumbnails, live icons, and other enhancements, further enhances the GUI. Windows Vista was not widely adopted due to problems with speed, high hardware requirements, and the annoyance of a new security feature, called User Account Control (UAC), explained in Chapter 2. Support for Windows Vista without any service packs ended in April 2010. Learn more about Windows Vista in Chapter 6.

TABLE 1–2 Summary of Current Desktop OSs

OS Version	Company	Platform	Applications Supported
Windows XP through Windows 7	Microsoft	Intel/Microsoft	DOS, 16-bit Windows, 32-bit Windows, 64-bit Windows applications
Mac OS X	Apple	Apple Mac	Macintosh applications
Linux	Various	Intel/Microsoft	UNIX/Linux applications

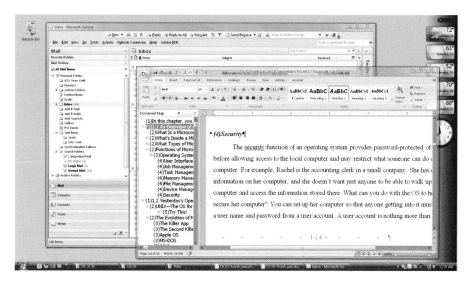

FIGURE 1–15 The Windows Vista desktop

Windows 7

Released in October 2009 Windows 7 is the best version of Windows to date. It includes several improvements to Windows Vista—correcting the short-comings that kept Windows Vista from being widely accepted. Windows 7 is faster than Windows Vista in several ways, from starting up, to going into and out of sleep mode, to recognizing new devices when you connect them. Windows 7 has many new features. The short list includes a redesigned desktop (see Figure 1–16) with a new taskbar that has many new features of its own, such as jump lists. Learn more about Windows 7 in Chapter 6.

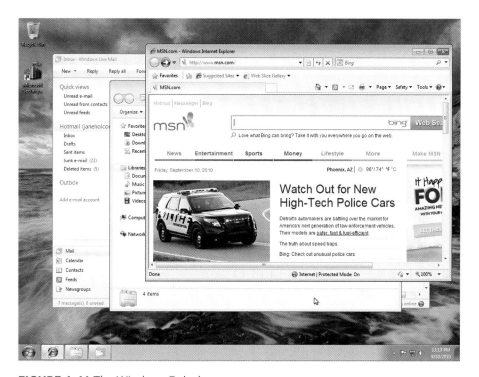

FIGURE 1–16 The Windows 7 desktop

What Is the Latest on Windows 8?

Use a search engine to find out what is happening with the next version of Windows, rumored to be named Windows 8. Try this:

1. Use your favorite search engine to search on "Windows 8" and find out what happened to this version of Windows since the writing of this book.
2. Find the list of features.
3. What improvements does this OS offer over Windows 7?

Windows 8

At this writing, the next version of Windows, rumored to be named Windows 8, is projected to come out in late 2011 or early 2012. While all is speculation, the expected new features include improved support for wireless connectivity and other new features such as stereoscopic 3-D, facial detection, USB 3, and hardware acceleration. Experts expect Windows 8 to support virtualization—perhaps with a built-in hypervisor, which is software that provides the simulated hardware of a virtual machine. It may use virtualization of applications to separate running applications from the core of the OS. Applications virtualized remotely on a server could leave the OS with a much smaller footprint on the desktop. While 32- and 64-bit support is a given, some speculate that Windows 8 may go further with 128-bit support.

Windows File Systems

Depending on the version of Windows you use, you can select from two or three supported file systems when you format a disk. The main file systems supported for hard drives today are FAT32 and NTFS. Windows recognizes several formats for optical drives. Following is a discussion of the FAT file systems (several versions), the NTFS file system, and file systems for optical drives.

FAT File Systems in Windows. The FAT file systems include FAT12, FAT16, FAT32, and exFAT. Each has a logical structure that includes a file allocation table (FAT—hence the name of the file system) and a directory structure. The FAT enables the OS to allocate space on disk to files, while a directory gives the OS a place for identifying information about each file. The FAT file system used by DOS on hard disks is now called the FAT16 file system. The FAT32 file system was introduced in Windows 95 OEM Service Release version 2. The FAT32 file system can use larger hard disk partitions and allocates disk space more efficiently. DOS and Windows OSs only use the FAT12 file system when formatting a floppy disk, and floppy disk drives have all but disappeared from modern computers.

The numbers 12, 16, 32 refer to the size of each entry in the FAT table. On a FAT12-formatted diskette, each entry is 12-bits long; on a FAT16-formatted drive, each entry is 16-bits long, and on a FAT32-formatted drive, each entry is 32-bits long. These entries hold binary values used to number the allocation units on the volume. Therefore, the length of the entry limits the number of entries the FAT table can hold, and thus the maximum number of clusters that you can use on a disk. The data space on each disk volume is divided into the number of clusters the FAT table can handle. There may be 1 sector per cluster (on a diskette), but on hard disk volumes the cluster size may be as large as 64 sectors. The FAT32 file system, with its ability to manage more clusters, has smaller cluster sizes, and wastes the least amount of space, but it has serious limits, especially a complete lack of support for security.

The way in which they allocate space limits the FAT file systems discussed so far to a maximum volume size that is much smaller than the current hard drives. Therefore, to use FAT file systems you need to create several volumes per disk, which is fraught with many potential roadblocks and problems we won't detail here. Additionally, these versions of the FAT file system do not support file-level security.

The exFAT file system first appeared in Microsoft's Windows Embedded CE 6.0, a version of Windows for embedded applications. This proprietary file system is for use with solid-state storage devices, such as flash drives. While exFAT theoretically supports volume sizes up to 64 zettabytes (ZBs), the recommended maximum is 512 terabytes (TBs).

A zettabyte is 2^{70}, while a terabyte is 2^{40}.

Windows NTFS File Systems. The NTFS file systems are available in all versions of Windows beginning with Windows NT, but excluding Windows 9x and Windows Me. The main NTFS logical structure is a Master File Table. Windows uses a transaction processing system to track changes, adding a measure of transaction-level recoverability to the file system, similar to what your bank uses to track transactions and it will roll back incomplete transactions. NTFS allocates disk space more efficiently than FAT, and the latest version theoretically supports a volume size of 256TB (terabytes), but the actual limit within Windows is much less and depends on the version.

NTFS first appeared in Windows NT, and Microsoft upgraded it with improvements over the years. From the beginning, the NTFS file system provided file and folder security not available on FAT volumes. Today, in addition to file and folder security and transaction processing capability, NTFS supports many features. The short list includes file compression, file encryption, and an indexing service. NTFS is the preferred file system for hard drives in Windows and the default created when you install Windows today.

File Systems for CDs and DVDs. Optical discs require special Windows file system drivers. The CD-ROM File System (CDFS) allows Windows OSs to read CD-ROMs and to read and write to writable CDs (CD-R) and rewritable CDs (CD-RW). The Universal Disc Format (UDF) is a file system driver required for Windows to read DVD ROMs and to read and write DVD-R and DVD-RW. Windows XP has a DVD-RAM driver that supports the 5.2GB DVD-RAM disc standard.

Microsoft introduced a new file system for optical drives in Windows Vista, the Live File System, which allows you to write to an optical disc, notably the DVD-RW and CD-R optical discs, adding files at any time, as long as the disc has room.

Mac OS X

The Apple Inc. strategy has been to produce proprietary hardware and software for better integration of the OS and the hardware. This has historically resulted in a higher price for a Mac than for a comparable PC. For several years, beginning in the mid-1990s, Macintosh computers used the Motorola PowerPC chip with an architecture enhanced for graphics and multimedia. Since 2005 the Apple Mac line of computers are Intel-based, but the Mac OS is only licensed to run on an Apple Mac.

The Mac OSs in common use today are versions of Mac OS X (X is the Roman numeral for 10). OS X is a revolutionary change from the previous Mac OS 9. Apple based OS X on NextStep, an OS with a UNIX kernel. Until Mac OS X, the Macintosh OSs were strictly GUI environments, with no command-line option. Mac OS X, with its UNIX origins, gives you the option of a character-based interface, but most users will happily work solely

FIGURE 1–17 Mac OS X GUI

in the GUI (see Figure 1–17). The preferred file system for Mac OS X is HFS+, a robust file system that includes support for file permissions, but it also supports other file systems.

Linux

Linux, an operating system modeled on UNIX and named in honor of its original developer, began as a project in 1991 by Linus Benedict Torvalds while a student at the University of Helsinki in his native Finland. He invited other programmers to work together to create an open-source operating system for modern computers. They created Linux using a powerful programming language called C, along with a free C compiler developed through the GNU project called GNU C Compiler (GCC). Linux has continued to evolve over the years, with programmers all over the globe testing and upgrading its code. Linus Torvalds could not have predicted in 1991 how accepted the new operating system would be.

Linux is a full multitasking operating system that supports multiple users and multiple processors. Available in both 32-bit and 64-bit distributions, it can run on nearly any computer. A **distribution** or "distro," is a bundling of the Linux kernel and software—both enhancements to the OS and applications, such as word processors, spreadsheets, media players, and more. Although Linux natively uses an awkward command-line interface, Windows-like GUI environments, called shells, are available that make it accessible to almost anyone. A GUI is also an important part of many Linux distributions.

Like Windows, Linux supports several file systems for various media types. It has had several file systems for hard drives beginning with the very limited Minux file system and its successor, the extended file system (ext). The ext2 file system, created in 1992, was the preferred file system for many years. It was faster than the previous file system, but had problems with corrupted files after a system crash, which is not an uncommon problem with any file system under an OS. The successor to ext2 is ext3, a file system that employs journaling to avoid file corruption after a system crash and does journaling and all other file system tasks very fast compared to ext2. Other current journaling file systems are ReiserFS, Journaled File System (JFS), and XFS.

The biggest nontechnical difference between Linux and other operating systems is its price and installation. Anyone can get a free copy of Linux on the Internet. Commercial versions of Linux, which are very inexpensive when compared to the cost of other powerful operating systems, are also available from a variety of vendors that provide the Linux code free and charge only for the extras, such as utilities, GUI shells, and documentation. At this writing, Linux vendors Ubuntu, Red Hat, and SUSE are among the top 10 sources of Linux desktop distributions. We'll discuss selection of a Linux distribution in Chapter 8.

Students and teachers have flocked to Linux, not only for its technical advances, but also to participate in the global community that has built up around the operating system. This community invites Linux users and developers to contribute modifications and enhancements, and it freely shares information about Linux and Linux-related issues. Although Linux is a popular server platform, an increasing number of software companies are writing new desktop applications or modifying existing ones for Linux. Figure 1–18 shows an example of a Linux directory.

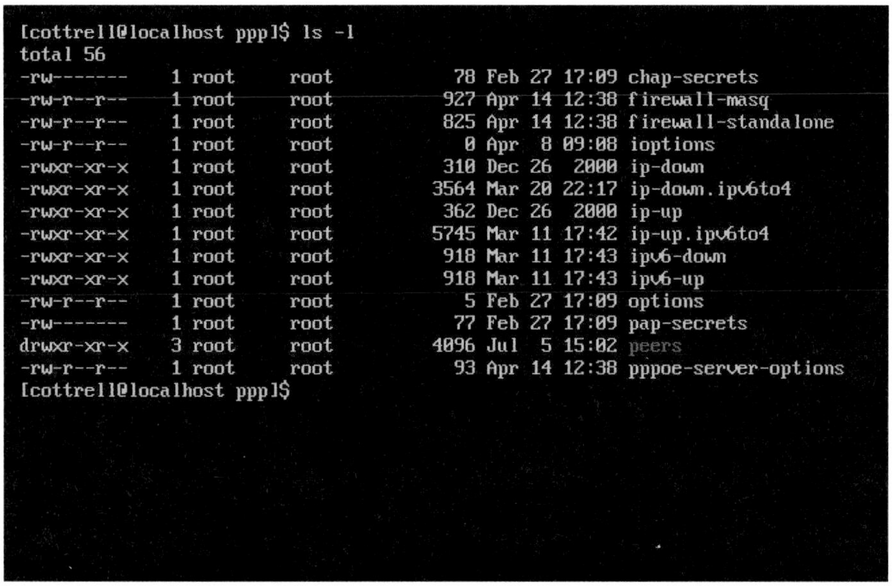

```
[cottrell@localhost ppp]$ ls -l
total 56
-rw-------   1 root     root          78 Feb 27 17:09 chap-secrets
-rw-r--r--   1 root     root         927 Apr 14 12:38 firewall-masq
-rw-r--r--   1 root     root         825 Apr 14 12:38 firewall-standalone
-rw-r--r--   1 root     root           0 Apr  8 09:08 ioptions
-rwxr-xr-x   1 root     root         310 Dec 26  2000 ip-down
-rwxr-xr-x   1 root     root        3564 Mar 20 22:17 ip-down.ipv6to4
-rwxr-xr-x   1 root     root         362 Dec 26  2000 ip-up
-rwxr-xr-x   1 root     root        5745 Mar 11 17:42 ip-up.ipv6to4
-rwxr-xr-x   1 root     root         918 Mar 11 17:43 ipv6-down
-rwxr-xr-x   1 root     root         918 Mar 11 17:43 ipv6-up
-rw-r--r--   1 root     root           5 Feb 27 17:09 options
-rw-------   1 root     root          77 Feb 27 17:09 pap-secrets
drwxr-xr-x   3 root     root        4096 Jul  5 15:02 peers
-rw-r--r--   1 root     root          93 Apr 14 12:38 pppoe-server-options
[cottrell@localhost ppp]$
```

FIGURE 1–18 Red Hat Linux directory listing (ls command)

Chapter 1 REVIEW

Chapter Summary

After reading this chapter and completing the exercises, you should understand the following facts about operating systems.

An Overview of Operating Systems

- A computer consists of hardware and two types of software: operating system software and applications software.
- The operating system allows the user to interact with the computer hardware.
- Certain computer hardware is common to most computers. The basic components include the processor, motherboard, RAM, ROM BIOS, video adapter, display screen, keyboard, pointing device, and other peripherals.
- Common computers in use today include desktops, laptops, server systems, and handheld devices.
- Most, if not all, current operating systems provide a user interface, job management, task management, memory management, file management, device management, and security.
- There are four categories of operating systems: single-user/single-tasking, single-user/multitasking, multiuser/multitasking, and real-time.
- Today's popular operating systems for desktops and laptops come in versions for 32-bit and 64-bit processing. The biggest advantage of a 64-bit OS over a 32-bit version of the same OS is that the amount of memory supported is much greater in a 64-bit OS.

Yesterday's Operating Systems

- The history of current computers and their OSs involved many technical advances and the imagination of a multitude of innovative people.
- UNIX is the oldest popular operating system and comes in versions for very large computers, as well as microcomputers. It is a portable OS that is usable on a variety of computer system platforms, with only minor alterations required for the underlying architecture.

- Early microcomputers included the MITS Altair 8800, the Apple I and Apple II, Radio Shack's TRS-80, and the Commodore, all introduced in the 1970s. The Apple computers came with the Apple OS.
- Certain "killer apps," notably VisiCalc and Lotus 1-2-3, made microcomputers appeal to ordinary people who were attracted to programs that automated formerly manual tasks.
- IBM introduced the PC in 1981, and it far exceeded the expectations of IBM with Microsoft BASIC in ROM and PC DOS for computers with a floppy disk drive.
- Microsoft made MS-DOS available to third-party PC manufacturers.
- Microsoft Windows evolved from the first version in 1985 to Windows 7, introduced in 2009.
- The Apple Mac computer, introduced in 1984, came with the MAC OS System. This OS line continued through Mac OS 9, introduced in 1999, and phased out after Mac OS X was introduced in 2001.

Today's Desktop Operating Systems

- The operating systems common today include Windows XP, Windows Vista, Windows 7, Mac OS X, and Linux.
- Windows supports several file systems for hard drives and optical disks. The most feature-rich and secure file system for hard drives is the NTFS file system.
- Mac OS X, based on NextStep, an OS with a UNIX kernel, runs only on Apple Macintosh computers, and while it supports several file systems, the preferred file system for hard drives is HFS+.
- Linus Torvalds developed Linux as a collaborative effort beginning in 1991. A full multitasking/multiuser operating system, it is available in both 32-bit and 64-bit distributions and can run on nearly any computer.
- Linux supports several file systems for hard drives and optical disks. The most feature-rich and secure file system for hard drives is the ext3 file system.

Key Terms List

central processing unit (CPU) *(2)*

client *(4)*

command-line interface (CLI) *(6)*

cursor *(6)*

device driver *(3)*

device management *(8)*

directory *(8)*

distribution *(32)*

file management *(8)*

file system *(8)*

folder *(8)*

formatting *(8)*

graphical user interface (GUI) *(6)*

input/output (I/O) *(2)*

job management *(6)*

kernel *(5)*

memory *(3)*

memory management *(7)*

microcomputer *(2)*

microprocessor or processor *(2)*

motherboard *(3)*

multitasking *(7)*

operating system (OS) *(2)*

partition *(8)*

personal computer (PC) *(3)*

real-time operating system (RTOS) *(11)*

ROM BIOS (read only memory basic input output system) *(3)*

security *(8)*

server *(4)*

task management *(7)*

user interface *(6)*

version *(22)*

virtual memory *(7)*

Key Terms Quiz

Use the Key Terms List to complete the sentences that follow. Not all terms will be used.

1. The _____ is the main component of an OS that always remains in memory while the computer is running, managing low-level OS tasks.

2. If you save confidential data on your local hard drive, you should be using an operating system that includes a/an _____ function, which protects local files and folders from unauthorized access.

3. A/an _____ takes care of the interaction between a program and a computer's hardware, freeing application programmers from the task of including such functions in their programs.

4. An operating system that uses _____ will allow you to simultaneously run more programs than the physical memory of the computer will hold.

5. When you run several applications at once and switch between them, you are experiencing the _____ feature of an operating system.

6. Interaction with a computer involving getting data and commands into it and results out of it is called_____.

7. The role of a _____ is to provide services to other computers on a network.

8. Software that allows the operating system to control a hardware component is a/an

   _____.

9. Modern OSs are _____ operating systems.

10. The _____ function of an OS includes the visual components as well as the command processor that loads a program into memory.

Multiple-Choice Quiz

1. Which of the following operating systems cannot be licensed for a PC?
   a. Mac OS X
   b. Windows Vista
   c. Windows 7
   d. Red Hat Linux
   e. Windows XP

2. Which of the following is a small electronic component made up of transistors (tiny switches) and other miniaturized parts?
   a. Peripheral
   b. Integrated circuit (IC)
   c. Handheld
   d. Mouse
   e. Vacuum tube

3. Introduced in 1983, this application program became the "killer app" that made the IBM PC a must-have business tool.
   a. Microsoft Word
   b. VisiCalc
   c. BASIC
   d. PC DOS
   e. Lotus 1-2-3

4. Which of the following is not available as a desktop operating system?
   a. MS-DOS
   b. Macintosh OS X
   c. Windows 7
   d. Linux
   e. Windows Server 2008

5. Which of the following is a computer input device?
   a. Display
   b. Printer
   c. Keyboard
   d. RAM
   e. ROM

6. On a network, the purpose of this computer is to allow end users to save and access files stored on this computer, as well as to print to printers connected to this computer.
   a. Desktop computer
   b. File and print server
   c. Handheld computer
   d. Laptop
   e. PC

7. Which of the following characterizes a real-time operating system?
   a. A GUI and the ability to run great games.
   b. Single-tasking.
   c. Large and fast.
   d. Speed and the ability to support real-time application programs.
   e. Runs on a terminal server.

8. Max OS X is built on NextStep, an OS based on what kernel?
   a. Linux
   b. UNIX
   c. DOS
   d. Windows
   e. BASIC

9. In the early 1950s, a typical computer end user would have been a:
   a. Computer gamer
   b. Medical doctor
   c. Politician
   d. Government agency
   e. Secretary

10. An operating system is to a computer as a _____ is to a department.
   a. Salesman
   b. Spreadsheet
   c. Steering wheel

   d. Ignition
   e. Manager

11. Which of the following accurately describes the overall trend in computing during the past 60-plus years?
   a. Toward physically larger, more powerful computers.
   b. Toward physically larger, less powerful computers.
   c. Toward physically smaller, less powerful computers.
   d. Toward physically smaller, more powerful computers.
   e. Toward physically smaller, single-use computers.

12. A client computer accesses a file and print server, opens a file and edits it. In this scenario where is the processing done?
   a. In the keyboard.
   b. On the client computer.
   c. On the file and print server.
   d. Over the network.
   e. In the file and print client software.

13. A specialized form of this type of computer would be used by an individual you might see in a grocery store aisle, taking inventory.
   a. Laptop
   b. Handheld
   c. Desktop
   d. Server
   e. Mainframe

14. This chip contains the basic input/output system for a computer.
   a. Microprocessor
   b. CMOS
   c. RAM
   d. ROM BIOS
   e. Floppy disk

15. What is the very first thing a user must do to gain access to a secure computer?
   a. Back up all data.
   b. Connect to the Internet.
   c. Log on with a user name and password.
   d. Double-click the Start menu.
   e. Reboot.

Essay Quiz

1. Write a few sentences describing every interaction you have had with computers in the past 24 hours.

2. If you use more than one operating system on a regular basis, describe some of the similarities and differences you have noticed between two of those operating systems. You are not limited to the operating systems described in this chapter. (If you use a smartphone and a desktop computer, these will have two different operating systems.) If you do not work with more than one operating system, find someone who has (classmate or other) and interview that person to answer this question.

3. Explain why Windows 98 was not a good choice of operating system for a laptop computer used by a person who works from different locations and holding confidential information.

4. Describe virtual memory and list an OS described in this chapter that does not use it.

5. In studying the common operating systems, you have considered the availability of software that runs on each OS and the general reasons you may choose one over the others. Put yourself in the position of an information technology professional in a new company that will open its doors on day one with 50 employees who will need computers on their desks connected to a corporate network and will need to work with standard business applications. What are some other practical considerations that you can think of that must come into play when making this decision? Your answer does not need to specify a particular OS.

Lab Projects

LAB PROJECT 1.1

To understand the relative cost of each of the operating systems you are studying and the availability of each system, use a paper catalog from a software retailer or a Web site such as www.us.buy.com or www.amazon .com to research the price of each of the operating systems listed in Table 1–3. You are not bargain hunting, so you don't need to look for the lowest price; just find the relative cost of the operating systems, packaged with an optical disk. You will also find that some are not available as new retail products, although you may find them at other sources. We have listed the full retail versions separately from the upgrade versions. You can install the full versions on a computer that does not have a previous version of Windows installed. The upgrade versions are cheaper than the full versions, but will not install without a previous version of Windows. Also, do not include any version sold as being for "system builders" because these versions are not sold as separate products, but are sold to system builders who install the OS on computers before sale. In Table 1–3, enter the cost of each product.

TABLE 1–3 Price and Availability Comparison

Operating System	Cost	Operating System	Cost
Windows Vista Upgrade		Windows 7 Ultimate Upgrade	
Windows Vista full		Red Hat Linux	
Windows 7 Professional full (32-bit and 64-bit)		Mac OS X Tiger	
Windows 7 Professional Upgrade (32-bit and 64-bit)		Mac OS X Snow Leopard	
Windows 7 Ultimate full			

LAB PROJECT 1.2

Examine the operating system on your class lab computer, and answer questions related to the operating system functions described in this section. If you're not familiar with the operating system on your lab computer, you may need to do some research to answer some of these questions. If so, you can search several places. First, look for a Help program in the OS, or read any documentation that is available to you for this OS. If you cannot find the answers in one of these sources, use a search engine on the Internet to find another source of information for your OS.

For this Lab Project, you will need the following:
- A computer with a desktop operating system
- Internet access

1 Start your computer and record the name and version number of your operating system here.

_____

2 In your own words, describe the user interface.

_____

③ Can you see an indication that this operating system provides a job management function? If so, provide a description next.

_____

_____

④ If your operating system supports task management, explain how you can demonstrate the task management functions to someone else.

_____

_____

⑤ Look for tools used to manage files. Then describe how you can copy a file from a location on your hard drive to a flash drive.

_____

_____

⑥ Did you see any evidence that this OS provides security? If so, describe why you believe this is so.

_____

_____

2 Computer Security Basics

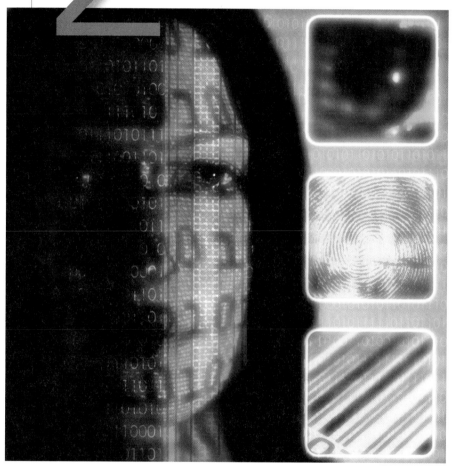

Why do our latest operating systems have a long list of security features? Why do we need to apply security patches to operating systems? Why has computer security become a multibillion-dollar business worldwide? Why? Because it's dangerous out there. And, as you will learn in this chapter, "out there" seems to be everywhere, because no place or technology seems safe from some sort of threat. That includes the Internet, corporate extranets, desktop and laptop computers, and even your cell phone or other portable digital devices. Here you'll learn about the threats, and the methods, practices, and technologies for protecting your computer systems.

In this chapter we first attempt to instill a healthy dose of paranoia in your mind, and then we identify methods for securing a computer, such as authentication and authorization, encryption, firewalls, anti-spam, antivirus, anti-popup, privacy protection, and other types of protections. Then, in later chapters, as you learn about each of these Windows operating systems, as well as Linux and Mac OS 10, you will implement OS-specific security.

Learning Outcomes

In this chapter, you will learn how to:

LO **2.1** Describe security threats and vulnerabilities to desktop PCs and users.

LO **2.2** Identify methods for protecting against security threats.

LO **2.3** Troubleshoot common security problems.

LO 2.1 | Threats to Computers and Users

What are you risking if your computer is not secure? The short answer is that you risk your identity, the work you have created, your company's integrity, and your own job if you are responsible for loss of the company's equipment or data. Today, government regulations, such as the Sarbanes-Oxley Act or the Health Insurance Portability and Accountability Act (HIPAA) require that organizations protect certain personal information, such as health and personal financial data. The consequences to an organization that does not comply with these regulations, or experiences a breach of security involving such data, can be very severe. In the extreme, malware can cause death when it infects critical national defense software or software in computers onboard an airplane or in a train switching system. We'll begin the long answer with an overview of the most common threats and how they gain access to computers.

Malware

Malware, a shortened form of "malicious software," is a term that covers a large and growing list of threats, including many that you no doubt know about, such as viruses, worms, Trojan horses, or spam. But have you heard of pop-up downloads, drive-by downloads, war driving, bluesnarfing, adware, spyware, back doors, spim, phishing, or hoaxes? Read on and learn about all of these and their methods of infecting computers and networks.

Vectors

A vector is a mode of malware infection. While some malware may use just a single vector, multivector malware uses an array of methods to infect computers and networks. Let's look at a few well-known vectors.

E-Mail Vectors. Some malware infects computers via e-mail. You may have believed it was always safe to open e-mail as long as you didn't open attachments, but the simple act of opening an e-mail containing the Nimda virus can infect a computer, depending on the software you are using to read the message. This was true with Microsoft's Outlook Express e-mail client. Microsoft released a patch to close this vulnerability, and it has replaced Outlook Express with Windows Mail in Windows Vista and Windows 7, but you will find Outlook Express running on Windows XP computers. This is an argument for keeping your software updated with security patches. Clicking on a link in an e-mail message can launch malware from a Web site. Read on.

Code on Web Sites. Some malware infects computers by lurking in hidden code on Web sites. An unsuspecting user browses to a site and clicks on a link that launches and installs malware on her computer. Clicking on the link gives the program permission to run.

Trojan Horses. A Trojan horse, often simply called a Trojan, is both a type of malware and a vector. The modern day Trojan horse program gains access to computers much like the ancient Greek warriors who, in Homer's famous tale, gained access to the city of Troy by hiding in a large wooden horse, presented as a gift to the city (a Trojan horse). A Trojan horse program installs and activates on a computer by appearing to be something harmless, which the user innocently installs. It may appear as just a useful free program that a user downloads and installs, but it is a common way for malware to infect your system.

Searching for Unprotected Computers. Still other malware searches for computers with security flaws and takes advantage of the flaws to install itself on the computer and even throughout a private network.

Trojan horse image
Carol and Mike Werner/Alamy

Trojans are on the rise! Bit-Defender conducted a six-month survey from January through June 2009 and reported, "Trojan-type malware is on the rise, accounting for 83 percent of the global malware detected in the world."

Sneakernet—the Oldest Vector. Yet another vector is as old as PCs. In the days when it was uncommon for computers to connect to any network, the mode of sharing data between computers was to carry a floppy disk containing data or programs from one computer to another. The slang for this practice is sneakernet. Sometimes, the floppy disk contained malware, making sneakernet the oldest vector. Sneakernet still exists today, but the storage device of choice is the flash drive, and the computers are usually also on a real network, which extends the risk when malware infects a single computer. In August 2010 the U.S. Deputy Defense Secretary declassified the information that a flash drive, inserted into a U.S. military laptop in 2008 on a military post in the Middle East, was the vector for malicious code that caused a significant breach of military computers. News outlets in 2008 reported the breach and cited anonymous Defense Department officials as stating that this attack originated from outside the United States.

Back Doors. In computing, a back door is a way in which someone can gain access to a computer, bypassing authentication security. Sometimes a program's author installs a back door into a single program so she can easily access it later for administering and/or for troubleshooting the program code. Or an attacker may create a back door by taking advantage of a discovered weakness in a program. Then any program using the back door can run in the security context of the invaded program and infect a computer with malware. In one well-known situation, the Code Red worm took advantage of a specific vulnerability in Microsoft's Internet Information Server (IIS) Web server software, to install a back door. The result was that the worm displayed a message on every Web page on the IIS server. The message included the phrase, "Hacked by Chinese." Then, the Nimda worm took advantage of the back door left by the Code Red worm to infect computers.

Rootkits. A rootkit is malware that hides itself from detection by anti-malware programs by concealing itself within the OS code or any other program running on the computer. Someone who has administrator (root) access to the computer installs a rootkit, giving an attacker administrator privileges to the computer. Once installed, he can then run any type of malware to quietly carry out its mission. "Rootkit" also refers to the software components of a rootkit.

Pop-Up Downloads. A pop-up is a separate window that displays (pops up) uninvited from a Web page. The purpose of a pop-up may be as simple as an advertisement, but a pop-up can be a vector for malware. A pop-up download is a program that is downloaded to a user's computer through a pop-up page. It requires an action on the part of a user, such as clicking on a button that implies acceptance of something such as free information, although what that something may actually be is not made clear. The program that downloads may be a virus or a worm.

Drive-By Downloads. A drive-by download is a program downloaded to a user's computer without consent. Often the simple act of browsing to a Web site, or opening an HTML e-mail message, may result in such a surreptitious download. A drive-by download may also occur when installing another application. This is particularly true of certain file-sharing programs that users install to allow sharing of music, data, or photo files over the Internet. Some drive-by downloads may alter your Internet Explorer home page and/or redirect all your browser searches to one site. Any drive-by download may also install a virus, a worm, or even more likely, adware or spyware (which we describe later in this chapter).

War Driving. War driving is the name given to the act of moving through a neighborhood in a vehicle or on foot, using either a laptop equipped with

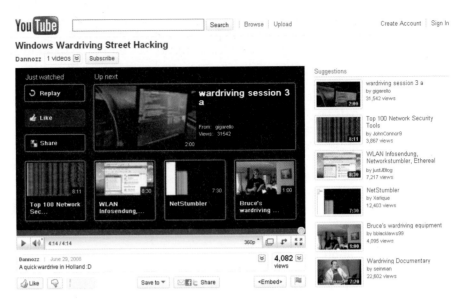

Online videos show examples of war driving.

Wi-Fi wireless network capability or a simple Wi-Fi sensor available for a few dollars from many sources. The users are searching for open hotspots, areas where a Wi-Fi network connects to the Internet without using security to keep out intruders. In a practice called war chalking, the war drivers will often mark a building where a hotspot exists so people "in the know" can later use that hotspot to access the Internet. Not only are they using Internet access illegally, riding on the subscription of the hotspot owner, but they also can capture keystrokes, e-mail, passwords, and user names from the wireless traffic. And if the individual computers on the wireless network, or other networks connected to it, are unprotected, unauthorized people may access those computers, making this a vector for malware. Some people create hotspots intentionally, and more and more hotspots are being made available for free or for a small charge by various businesses, such as coffee shops, bookstores, restaurants, hotels, truck stops, and even campgrounds. Using an unsecured hotspot can expose you to threats unless your computer is secure. If you need to be inspired to secure your Wi-Fi network, check out the Internet where tons of Web sites describe how to war drive, as well as how to protect your data from theft. There are even many war driving videos on YouTube, as shown above.

Bluesnarfing. Similar to war driving, bluesnarfing is the act of covertly obtaining information broadcast from wireless devices using the Bluetooth standard, a short-range wireless standard used for data exchange between desktop computers and mobile devices such as personal digital assistants (PDAs) or cellular phones. Bluetooth devices have a range of from 10 centimeters to 100 meters, depending on the power class of the device. Using a cell phone, a bluesnarfer can eavesdrop to acquire information, or even use the synchronizing feature of the device to pick up the user's information—all without being detected by the victim.

Stealing Passwords

We first considered calling this section "Discovering Passwords," but that phrase is far too innocent sounding—as if the perpetrator was innocently walking along and "discovered" your password lying on the sidewalk. What really happens is theft with intent to break into computers and networks. It is stealing, so let's call it that! Many methods are used to steal passwords.

Stealing Passwords Through Web Sites. People use a huge number of programs and techniques to steal passwords. One commonly used technique is to invade an unsecured Web site to access information unwitting users provide to the site, such as user names and passwords, and such personal information as account numbers, Social Security numbers, birth dates, and much more.

Stealing Passwords with Password Crackers. Another technique people use for discovering a password is a program called a password cracker. Some password crackers fall into the category of "brute-force" password crackers, which simply means the program tries a huge number of permutations of possible passwords. Often, because people tend to use simple passwords such as their initials, birth dates, addresses, etc., the brute-force method works. Other password crackers use more sophisticated statistical or mathematical methods to discover passwords.

Stealing Passwords with Keystroke Loggers. Another method for discovering passwords, as well as lots of other information, is the use of a keystroke logger, also called a keylogger. This is either a hardware device or a program that monitors and records every keystroke, usually without the user's knowledge. In the case of a hardware logger, the person desiring the keystroke log must physically install it before recording and then remove it afterward to collect the stored log of keystrokes. For example, the Spytech keystroke logger is a USB device the size of a flash drive that installs between the keyboard cable and a USB connector on the computer. There are also hardware keystroke loggers for PS/2 keyboard connectors. They are all very unobtrusive when connected to the back of a PC; one keystroke logger can hold a year's worth of keystroke data in flash memory and comes with software for reading the specially formatted data files.

A software keystroke logger program may not require physical access to the target computer, but simply a method for downloading and installing it on the computer. This could occur through one of the vectors described earlier in this chapter. Once installed, such a program can send the logged information over the Internet via e-mail, or using other methods, to the person desiring the log.

Some parents install keystroke loggers to monitor their children's Internet activity, but such programs have the potential for abuse by people with less benign motivations, including stalking, identify theft, and more. A simple Internet search of "keystroke logger" will yield many sources of both hardware and software keystroke loggers. The latter are now the more common.

Hardware keystroke logger
Product photo courtesy of www.keycobra
.com

Viruses

While, in the broadest sense, "virus" is a term used for all malware, technically, a virus is one class of malware: a program installed and activated on a computer without the knowledge or permission of the user. Viruses usually attach themselves to a file, such as a Microsoft Word document, and replicate and spread as you copy or share the infected file. At the least, the intent is mischief, but most often the intent is to be genuinely damaging. Like a living virus that infects humans and animals, a computer virus can result in a wide range of symptoms and outcomes. Loss of data, damage to or complete failure of an operating system, or theft of personal and financial information are just a few of the potential results of viruses infecting an individual computer. If you extend the range of a virus to a corporate or government network, the results can be far-reaching and even tragic. There are thousands of viruses "in the wild" today.

In the wild is a term frequently used to describe the overall computing environment—most notably including the Internet.

Worms

Like a virus, a **worm** is a program installed and activated on a computer without the knowledge or permission of the user. But a worm replicates itself on the computer, or throughout a network. In other words, a worm is a network-aware virus that does not require action from the unwitting user to replicate, and it can have a similar range of outcomes. In recent years the Netsky and MyDoom worms caused chaos and loss of productivity just in the amount of network traffic they generated. The typical worm resides in a single file that it replicates onto multiple machines. However, the Nimda worm changed all that by inserting its code into other executable files on the local drive of each machine to which it replicates itself, making it hard to locate and remove the worm.

Botnets and Zombies

A **botnet** is a group of networked computers that, usually unbeknown to their owners, have been infected with programs that forward information to other computers over the network (usually the Internet). A bot, short for robot, is a program that acts as an agent for a user or master program, performing a variety of functions—both for good and evil. An individual computer in a botnet is a **zombie** because it mindlessly serves the person who originated the botnet code. Most often affecting home computers, botnets have grown to be one of the biggest threats on the Internet.

Spyware

Spyware is a category of software that runs surreptitiously on a user's computer, gathers information without the user's permission, and then sends that information to the people or organizations that requested it. A virus may install Internet-based spyware, sometimes called tracking software or a spybot, on a computer, as can many other means of secretly installing software. Spyware can be used by companies to trace users' surfing patterns to improve the company's marketing efforts; it can be used for industrial espionage; it can be used by law enforcement to find sexual predators or criminals (with appropriate legal permissions); and it can be used by governments to investigate terrorism.

Adware

Adware is a form of spyware software downloaded to a computer without permission. It collects information about the user in order to display targeted advertisements to the user, either in the form of inline banners or pop-ups. Inline banners are advertisements that run within the context of the current page, just taking up screen real estate. Pop-ups are a greater annoyance, because they are ads that run in separate browser windows that you must close before you can continue with your present task. Clicking to accept an offer presented on an inline banner or a pop-up may trigger a pop-up download that can install a virus or worm.

Browser Hijacking

We received a call the other day from Dave, a finance officer at a large farm implement company. Every time he opened Internet Explorer, the home page pointed to a site advertising adware removal software. This is an example of **browser hijacking**, a practice that has been growing. Some unscrupulous people do this so that their Web site will register more visitors and then they can raise their rates to advertisers.

Dave was able to reverse this by changing the default page in Internet Options, but it was very annoying. He was lucky; sometimes hijackers make it very difficult to defeat the hijack by modifying the registry so that every time you restart Windows or Internet Explorer the hijack reinstates. Or you may even find that a registry change makes Internet Options unavailable.

Spam and Spim

Spam is unsolicited e-mail. This includes e-mail from a legitimate source selling a real service or product, but if you did not give the source permission to send such information to you, it is spam. Too often spam involves some form of scam—a bogus offer to sell a service or product that does not exist or tries to include you in a complicated moneymaking deal. If it sound too good to be true it is! Spam perpetrators are called spammers, and spam is illegal. Some corporate network administrators report that as much as 60 percent of the incoming e-mail traffic is spam. Spam accounts for a huge amount of traffic on the Internet and private networks, and a great loss in productivity as administrators work to protect their users from spam and individuals sort through and eliminate spam.

> **try this!**
>
> **Research Spam Statistics**
>
> Find out the latest bad news on the amount of Internet e-mail identified as spam. Try this:
>
> 1. Open your browser and connect to your favorite search engine, such as Google, Bing, or AltaVista.
> 2. Search on the words "spam statistics." For a more targeted search include the current year in your search string.
> 3. In the results list, many of the links will be for anti-spam programs that provide individual statistics. Review the results and select a link that appears to give actual statistics on spam occurrences for Internet e-mail users. Discuss the results with your classmates.

Spim is an acronym for *sp*am over *i*nstant *m*essaging, and the perpetrators are spimmers. A spimmer sends bots out over the Internet to collect instant messaging screen names, and then a spimbot sends spim to the screen names. A typical spim message may contain a link to a Web site, where, like spam, the recipient will find products or services for sale, legitimate or otherwise.

Social Engineering

Social engineering is the use of persuasion techniques to gain the confidence of individuals—for both good and bad purposes. People with malicious intent use social engineering to persuade targeted people to reveal confidential information or to obtain something else of value. Social engineering is as old as human interaction, so there are countless techniques. Following are just a few categories of computer security threats that employ social engineering.

Phishing

Phishing is a fraudulent method of obtaining personal financial information through Web page pop-ups, e-mail, and even paper letters mailed via the postal service. Think of the metaphor of a fisherman preparing and casting his bait in an ocean full of fish. Even if only one in a hundred fish take the bait, he is statistically likely to have many successes. We'll concentrate our discussion on Web page pop-ups and e-mail. A phishing message ("bait") often purports to be from a legitimate organization, such as a bank, credit card company, retailer, and so on. In a typical phishing scenario, the e-mail or pop-up may contain authentic-looking logos, and even links to the actual site, but the link specified for supplying personal financial information will take recipients (the "phish") to a "spoofed" Web page in which they are asked to

Take a Phishing Test!

It is often difficult to discern which e-mails are legitimate and which are "phish." Try this:

1. Use your Web browser to connect to the phishing test at **www.sonicwall .com/phishing/.** If this url no longer works, use a search engine to find a phishing test.
2. After reading the instructions and helpful hints, start the test.
3. You will be presented with 10 e-mails and you must decide whether each is legitimate or phish.
4. When you finish you will be presented with the correct answers. Each e-mail also has a detailed explanation as to why it is either legitimate or phish. Read these explanations carefully.

enter their personal data. The Web page may look exactly like the company's legitimate Web page, but it's not at its site. A common practice is for a phisher to use the credit information to make purchases over the Internet, choosing items that are easy to resell and having them delivered to a destination address to which the phisher has access, such as a vacant house.

Be very suspicious of e-mail requesting personal financial information. Legitimate businesses will never contact you by e-mail and ask you for your access code, Social Security number, or password. Phishing is just an old-fashioned scam in high-tech dress.

Hoaxes

A hoax is a deception intended either for amusement or for some gain with malicious intent. Hoaxes take many forms. One example is an e-mail message from someone you know claiming she took an unplanned trip to London where she was mugged in the subway. The e-mail address looks legitimate, but when you respond, you receive a message from someone else stating that your friend is now in jail and needs bail money. Sounds outlandish? We received such a message, but we were suspicious and called our friend who reported that she was safe at home, and that several of her friends had responded to the message and received the plea for money.

Hoaxes take many forms.
Henrik Kettunen/Alamy

Enticements to Open Attachments

Social engineering is also involved in the enticements to open attachments to e-mails. Called "gimmes," these are found either in the subject line or in the body of the e-mail message. Opening the attachment then executes and infects the local computer with some form of malware. A huge number of methods are used. Sadly, enticements often appeal to the less noble human characteristics such as greed (via an offer too good to be true), vanity (physical enhancement products), or simple curiosity (with a subject line that appears to be a response to an e-mail from you). More tragic, these enticements may appeal to people's sympathy and compassion by way of a nonexistent charity or by fraudulently representing a legitimate charity.

Fraud

Fraud is the use of deceit and trickery to persuade someone to hand over money or other valuables. Fraud is often associated with identify theft, because the perpetrator will falsely claim to be the victim when using the victim's credit cards and other personal and financial information. Obviously, many hoaxes are also frauds.

Identity Theft

Identify theft occurs when someone collects personal information belonging to another person and uses that information to fraudulently make purchases, open new credit accounts, and even obtain new driver's licenses and other forms of identification in the victim's name. They may not even be interested in actual financial information; simply obtaining your Social Security number and other key personal information may be enough to steal your identity. There are many ways not directly involved with computers for thieves to steal your identity. Identity theft is a huge business involved in the theft of large numbers of persons' data from large databases. These criminals sell such identity information for pennies per record. Several Web sites maintained by the U.S. government offer valuable information for consumers who wish to protect themselves from identify theft.

Learn More About Identity Theft

Learn more about identity theft in general, how to protect yourself, and how to report suspected identity theft. Try this:

1. Open your browser and use a search engine to search on "FTC id theft." (Omit the quotation marks.)

2. In the search results select the site identified as the U.S. government's central Web site for information about identity theft.

3. At the Federal Trade Commission's ID theft Web site, explore the various links from this page to learn more about identity theft and related topics.

4. If it is available, watch the video on identity theft. You may be surprised at how easy it is to be a victim of identity theft.

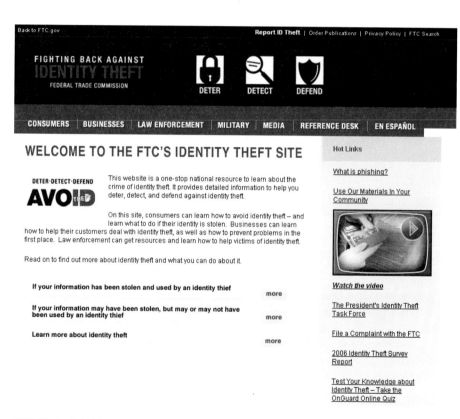

FTC ID theft Web page

Exposure to Inappropriate or Distasteful Content

The Internet, and especially the World Wide Web, is a treasure trove of information. It is hard to imagine a subject that cannot be found somewhere on the Internet. However, some of this content may be inappropriate or distasteful. To some extent, only an individual can judge what is inappropriate and distasteful, however, circumstances in which certain content is harmful to some individuals—such as young children—is considered a threat and thus is inappropriate.

Invasion of Privacy

One can also view many of the threats discussed so far as invasions of privacy. Protecting against privacy invasion includes protecting your personal information at your bank, credit union, both online and at bricks-and-mortar retail stores, athletic clubs, or almost any organization in which you are a customer, member, or employee. All steps you take to make your computer more secure also contribute to the protection of your privacy.

Invasion of privacy
Troy Aossey/Digital Vision/Getty Images

Misuse of Cookies

A more subtle form of privacy invasion involves the misuse of something called cookies. Cookies are very small files an Internet browser saves on the local hard drive at the request of a Web site. The next time you connect to that same Web site, it will request the cookies saved on previous visits—often giving you the convenience of automated log-ins to each site. Cookies are text files, so they cannot contain viruses, which are executable code, but what they may contain includes the following:

- User preferences when visiting a specific site.
- Information you may have entered into a form at the Web site, including personal information.
- Browsing activity.
- Shopping selections on a Web site.

The use of cookies is a convenience to a user who does not have to reenter preferences and pertinent information on every visit to a favorite Web site. In fact, users are not overtly aware of the saving and retrieving of cookies from their local hard disk, although most good Web sites clearly detail whether or not they use cookies and what they are used for. You can find this information in the privacy statement or policy of the site. Cookies are only accessible by the Web site that created them, or through some subterfuge of the Web site creator. A first-party cookie is one that originates with the domain name of the

URL to which you directly connect. A third-party cookie refers to a cookie that originates with a domain name beyond the one shown in your URL. An ad embedded in a Web page—often called banner ads—can use cookies to track your Web surfing habits, and third-party cookies play a part in this type of tracking.

Computer Hardware Theft

Of course security includes something as simple as locking doors, keeping hardware locked away from prying eyes and sticky fingers. That's obvious. What may not be obvious to you, especially if you use a laptop as your principal computer, is what happens if someone steals your computer. You would be astonished at how many computers, especially laptops, are stolen each year, and unless your computer has been properly secured, and all the data backed up, there goes your business information, your data files, your financial information, your address book, everything! Although a large percentage of computer theft occurs just so the thief can sell the hardware quickly and get some quick cash, an increasing number of thieves are technically sophisticated and will go through your hard drive looking for bank account, credit card, and other financial data so they can steal your identity.

Guard against computer theft.
Image Source/Getty Images

Accidents, Mistakes, and Natural and Unnatural Disasters

Accidents and mistakes happen. We don't know of anyone who hasn't accidentally erased an important file, pressed the wrong button at the wrong instant, or created a file name he can't remember. Disasters also happen in many forms. Just a few are fires, earthquakes, and weather-induced disasters such as tornadoes, lightning strikes, and floods. Predicting such events is imperfect at best. The principal way to protect against accidents, mistakes, and disasters is to make frequent, comprehensive backups. You can make backups of an entire hard drive using programs that make an image of the drive, or you can use programs that back up your critical data files on a periodic basis. Organizations that have a lot of valuable data even make multiple

Computer accidents
**R and R Images/Photographer's Choice/
Getty Images**

backups and keep copies off-site. Then, in case of fire, flood, earthquake, or other natural disaster that destroys not only the on-site backups but also the computer, they can still recover.

Keeping Track of New Threats

We cannot begin to cover all the methods currently used to victimize computer users. However, various organizations work to keep track of these threats, counter them, and inform the public. The Federal Trade Commission (FTC) Bureau of Consumer Protection is one such organization. It maintains a Web site (www.ftc.gov/bcp/) with a list of documents about various consumer issues and threats. If you locate the tab labeled "Consumer Protection" and select the sub-tab "Consumer Information" (as shown in Figure 2–1), the resulting page has a list on the left labeled "Consumer Categories." If you select the "Computers & the Internet" or "ID Theft, Privacy, & Security," you will find lists of documents related to the security issues discussed in this chapter. These documents are worth reviewing from time-to-time to learn about new threats.

The People Behind the Threats

The people behind computer security threats are as varied as are their motivations. They come from all walks of life and are scattered all over the globe.

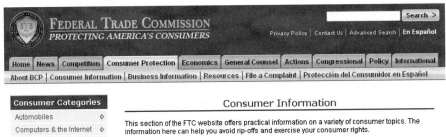

FIGURE 2–1 The FTC Bureau of Consumer Protection Web site

Organized crime is a growing source of these threats. Organized crime cartels exist in every major country in the world, with certain areas notorious for their homegrown crime organizations. Online banking and online shopping are just two areas where billions of dollars are exchanged every day, and these cartels step in to exploit weaknesses. Organized crime specialists work at stealing bank account log-in information and also are the source of many fraud attempts and money laundering via online shopping.

As any group of people engaged in similar endeavors grows and matures, it develops a set of terms and participant competency rankings. For years, the term *hacker* has been used, particularly by the press, to mean someone who uses sophisticated computer programming skills to invade private computers and networks to cause havoc, steal passwords, steal identities and money, and so on. But the people who work to invade others' systems actually fall into several classifications describing their action—classifications defined by the people within that community themselves or those who work to bring them to justice.

Although these levels of competency are worth understanding, from the standpoint of someone trying to protect systems against invasion, it doesn't much matter what level of attacker you are facing. The point is to protect systems against attack. So, for the purposes of this book, and because the term is widely understood, we'll use *hacker* to mean any attacker.

Organized crime
Digital Vision/Getty Images

Hackers

A hacker is an expert programmer with sophisticated skills who is also a networking wizard. Hackers are highly trained, fluent in a number of programming languages, and motivated by the challenge of solving complex problems. They belong to a community, a shared culture, which traces its history back decades. The members of this culture originated the term *hacker*, and they were involved in building the Internet, making the UNIX operating system what it is today, running Usenet, and making the World Wide Web work. Although in the past some hackers were involved in damaging attacks, in general, genuine hackers are involved in solving complex problems and contributing to the computing community.

Hacker
Comstock/Getty Images

Crackers

A cracker is a member of a group of people who proudly call themselves hackers, but aren't. These are mainly adolescent males who get a kick out of causing damage after breaking into computers and making phone systems do things they aren't supposed to do (the latter is called phone phreaking). Real hackers call these people "crackers" and want nothing to do with them. Real hackers mostly believe that being able to break security doesn't make you a hacker any more than being able to hot-wire a car makes you an automotive engineer. The basic difference is this: Hackers build things, crackers break them. They are both harmful!

Script Kiddies

A script kiddie is someone who usually lacks the knowledge to personally develop a security threat, but uses scripted tools or programs created by others to break into computer systems to cause damage or mischief. The name implies enough knowledge to run computer scripts or programs, even from a command line.

Click Kiddies

A click kiddie is similar to a script kiddie, but with even less knowledge than a script kiddie, requiring a GUI to select and run a hacking tool. A click kiddie browses the Web, searching for sites that make it even easier by providing forms the click kiddie can fill out, enter a target IP address, and click to initiate an attack. Such sites provide the additional benefit of anonymity to the perpetrator.

Packet Monkeys

Packet monkeys are similar to script kiddies and click kiddies in that they need to use programs created by others to perform their attacks. They typically have little understanding of the harm they may cause, and their exploits are often random and without a purpose other than the thrill of trying to get away with something. Hackers call packet monkeys "bottom feeders."

Packet monkeys create denial-of-service attacks by inundating a site or a network with so much traffic (data packets) that the network is overwhelmed and denies service to additional traffic. Their attacks may be on a broad scale which makes it more difficult to trace the identity of the packet monkey.

LO 2.2 | Defense Against Threats

No simple solutions exist to the damaging and mischievous threats that lurk on the Internet and on private networks, but doing nothing is not an option. We need to make our best efforts to thwart these threats, even if a determined and skilled invader cannot be deterred. Most people do not have the necessary skills, motivation, or access to sophisticated tools, so implementing basic security will keep the majority out. Here are some basic defensive practices that you can apply in operating systems to avoid being a victim. Often you will need to install a third-party program (free or commercial) to add protection your operating system does not provide.

Education

This chapter may be just the beginning of your education about how threats, such as viruses, get access to computers and networks and how our own behavior can make us vulnerable to such threats as identity theft. Beyond understanding how these things can happen, also be actively alert to signs of a virus or that someone is using your credit.

artpartner-images.com/Alamy

Any unusual computer event may indicate that your computer has been infected by a virus, some sort of browser hijack, or other form of spyware, adware, and so on. Signs to look for include:

- Strange screen messages.
- Sudden computer slowdown.
- Missing data.
- Inability to access the hard drive.

Similarly, unusual activity in any of your credit or savings accounts can indicate that you are a victim of identity theft, including:

- Charges on credit accounts that you are sure you or your family did not make.
- Calls from creditors about overdue payments on accounts you never opened.
- A rejection when applying for new credit for reasons you know are not true.
- A credit bureau reports existing credit accounts you never opened.

Along with education about threats comes paranoia. However, if you use a computer at home, work, or school, and are on a network and/or the Internet, a touch of paranoia is healthy. Just don't let it distract you from your day-to-day tasks. Take proactive, responsible steps, as we outline here.

Security Policies

Follow established security policies describing how an organization protects and manages sensitive information. Security policies define data sensitivity and data security practices, including security classifications of data, and who (usually based on job function) may have access to the various classes of data. For instance, a security policy may state, "Only server administrators and advanced technicians may access the server room, and must not give access to any other individuals." Security policies should also describe the consequences of breaking policy rules.

Security policies should exist in both document form and software form. For instance, at work or school, if you are logging into a Microsoft domain or a Netware network, administrators may configure the servers to enforce a password policy that accepts only strong passwords. How they define a strong password depends on the settings selected, such as minimum password length or complexity. Complexity requirements may say the characters must include a combination of lowercase alphabetical characters, uppercase alphabetical characters, numerals, punctuation characters, and math symbols. In addition, they may require that you create a new password every month, and that you cannot repeat any of the previous 10 passwords.

Install Comprehensive Security Software

A logical progression through the appropriate defense against computer security threats would have us look at authentication and authorization at this point. However, because we include activities that require that you access the Internet, we will first talk about the comprehensive security software that should be in place before you connect to the Internet. This does not mean that security software is more important than authentication and authorization. They are all important pieces of every security defense strategy.

Comprehensive security software may come in one bundle of software from one source, or it can be separate software from many sources. The pieces should include (at minimum) a personal firewall, antivirus software, anti-spam software, and an e-mail scanner. Figure 2–2 shows the console for AVG Internet Security with both the security components and various tools for

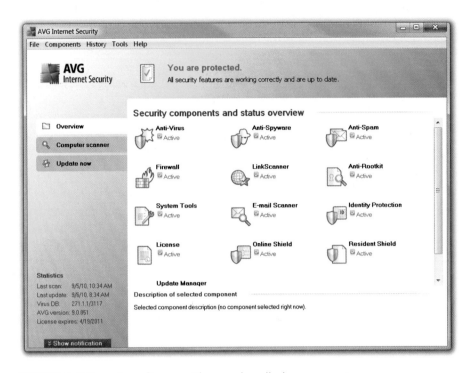

FIGURE 2–2 Security software with many bundled components

managing the security package, such as the Update Manager that automatically checks the AVG site for updates and downloads and installs them. The following sections will describe some of these security components.

Firewalls

A firewall is either software or a physical device that examines network traffic. Based on predefined rules, a firewall rejects certain traffic coming into a computer or network. The two general types of firewalls are network-based hardware firewalls and personal firewalls that reside on individual computers. We recommend that you always have a reliable personal firewall installed, even if your computer is behind a super-secure hardware firewall. An attack can be from another computer behind the firewall, and that is when your personal firewall becomes your last line of defense between your computer and the world. Let's look at these two general types of firewalls.

Network-Based Firewalls. A network-based firewall is a hardware device designed to protect you against the dangers of having an unprotected connection to the Internet. It sits between a private network and the Internet (or other network) and examines all traffic in and out of the network it is protecting. It will block any traffic it recognizes as a potential threat, using a variety of techniques. Table 2–1 lists some of the most common technologies normally included in a firewall, although some of these are not strictly firewall technologies. Your ISP and most corporations employ hardware firewalls, expensive and specialized computers manufactured by companies such as Cisco, 3COM (now owned by Cisco), Netgear, and others, and these sophisticated firewalls require highly trained people to manage them. At work or at school, the network is probably protected by such a firewall.

At home or in a small office, most people have a consumer-grade hardware firewall that comes in a small device that performs many of the same functions performed by a more professional-grade firewall. The most common name for these devices is broadband router or cable/DSL router. They combine the function of a firewall, a router (a device that "routes" traffic from

TABLE 2–1 Firewall Technologies

Technology	Description
IP packet filter	An IP packet filter inspects (or filters) each packet that enters or leaves the network, applying a set of security rules defined by a network administrator. Packets that fail inspection may not pass between the connected networks.
Proxy service	Sometimes referred to as an application-layer gateway, a proxy service watches for application-specific traffic. For example, a Web proxy only examines Web browser traffic. Acting as a stand-in (a proxy) for internal computers, it intercepts outbound connection requests to external servers and directs incoming traffic to the correct internal computer. You can configure a proxy service to block traffic from specific domains or addresses.
Encrypted authentication	Some firewalls require external users to provide a user name and password before they can open a connection through a firewall. Since the authentication information (user name and password) must pass over the Internet, it is important to encrypt it. This authentication involves the use of one of several encryption protocols. Encrypted authentication is a security service that is not limited to firewalls and is not always implemented on a firewall.
Virtual private network (VPN)	Also not a true firewall technology, a virtual private network (VPN) is a virtual tunnel created between two endpoints over a real network or internetwork, done by encapsulating the packets. Other security methods usually applied include encryption of the data and encrypted authentication. When set up in combination with properly configured firewalls, a VPN is the safest way to connect two private networks over the Internet.

one network to another), an Ethernet switch, and even a wireless access point all in one tiny box. These inexpensive devices can handle the traffic of just a few computers, while the more serious devices employed by ISPs and large organizations can handle thousands of simultaneous high-speed transmissions. These consumer-grade devices now come with the "one button" configuration that automatically configures a simple connection to the Internet, with the latest security turned on. You can also access the built-in Web page to make manual changes to the settings. Figure 2–3 shows the security page of a Cisco Wireless-N Router, which includes support for all the technologies listed in Table 2–1 and many more features, including support for the 802.11N standard for Wi-Fi communications and security. The setting labeled "Firewall" is just one option for securing your home network. Even with this device, you would need to research the impact of the various settings before changing from the default settings.

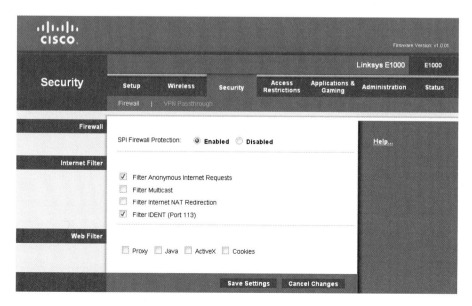

FIGURE 2–3 Security page from a Cisco Wireless-N Router

A firewall makes decisions about allowing traffic into the private network based on how an administrator configured it, the types of computers residing within the private network, and how they will interact with the Internet. If all the computers on a private network are simple desktop computers that connect to the Internet to browse Web pages and access FTP sites, the firewall protecting the network has a simple job. It simply blocks all in-bound traffic that is not the result of a request from a computer on the internal network. In other words, it matches incoming traffic with previous outgoing traffic that made requests that would result in incoming traffic. For example, when you connect to a Web site, outgoing traffic from your computer to the Web site requests to see a page. That page comes to you as incoming traffic. A firewall will allow it through based on your initial request.

But if the private network includes servers that offer services on the Internet, then the firewall must allow initiating traffic to come through, but it does not allow all incoming traffic through. In this case, you configure a firewall to allow incoming traffic of the type that can only communicate with the internally based servers. The various types of traffic include e-mail, Web, FTP, and others. Each type of traffic has a certain characteristic the firewall can recognize. Figure 2–4 shows a firewall protecting a network containing both servers and desktop computers (shown as clients).

A network professional would look at the simplified example of a firewall shown in Figure 2–4 and immediately talk about setting up a DMZ, named for a wartime demilitarized zone. In networking, a DMZ is a network between the internal network and the Internet with a firewall on both sides. It is where an organization puts any servers that it wishes to have offer services to the Internet.

Personal Firewalls. You may also choose to install a personal software firewall utility on any desktop computer, whether it directly connects to the Internet or is behind a hardware firewall. Because many attacks come from within a private network, personal firewalls have become standard. Ever since the introduction of Service Pack 2 for Windows XP, the Windows Firewall has been

Zone Labs (www.zonelabs.com) offers many excellent security products, including Zone Alarm, a personal firewall.

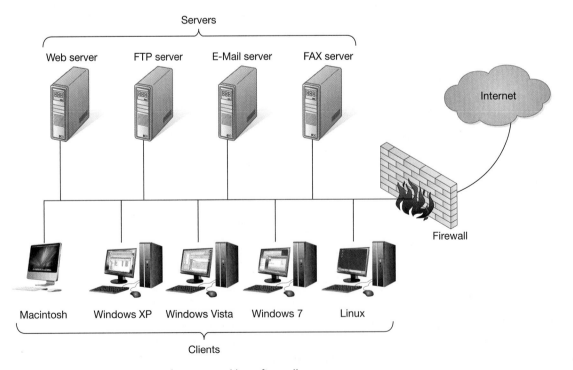

FIGURE 2–4 A private network protected by a firewall.

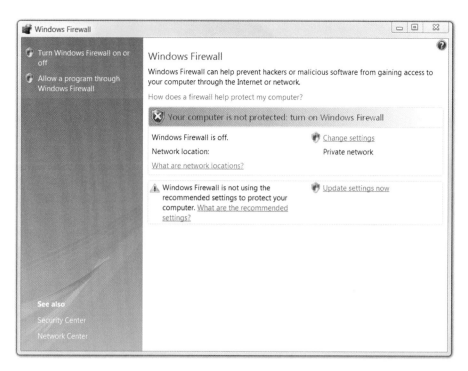

FIGURE 2–5 This message can simply mean that you are using a third-party firewall, and Windows Firewall is disabled.

included in Windows. Mac OS X comes with a firewall that is enhanced in OS X Snow Leopard, and there are many third-party firewalls for Windows, Mac OS X, and Linux.

If you have installed a third-party firewall—either separately or as part of a security suite—the Windows Firewall will be turned off, and opening the Windows Firewall applet in Control Panel will show you a disturbing message, such as the one shown in Figure 2–5.

Anti-Spam Software

There are many software products—called spam filters—designed to combat spam by examining incoming e-mail messages and filtering out those that have characteristics of spam, including certain identified keywords. In a larger organization with centralized network and computer management, special filter software installed on central mail servers can remove spam before it gets to a user's desktop. Other network administrators use Internet-based spam filtering services that block spam before it reaches the corporate network. However, individuals connected to the Internet from home or in small businesses are often on their own when it comes to eliminating spam. Luckily, many e-mail clients now offer spam filtering. Without some sort of spam filter you must sort through your own e-mail to find and delete the spam. Spam filters are not perfect—they often filter out legitimate messages, while allowing some spam messages through. For this reason, most spam filters require some configuration on the part of the user using rules or filters that will automate the process of removing spam from known sources. And the user will still often need to review a list of suspected spam messages. Figure 2–6 shows the Advanced AVG Settings from AVG Internet Security displaying the anti-spam settings with a long list of additional settings shown on the left. You can select the option to Train Anti-Spam to allow it to learn from the decisions you make on your e-mail. It will then remember those actions, such as deleting messages, and take the same action for other messages from the same source.

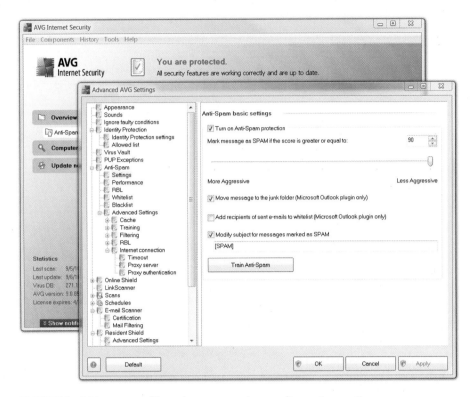

FIGURE 2–6 Most spam filters have extensive configuration options.

Antivirus Software

An antivirus program can examine the contents of a storage device or RAM looking for hidden viruses and files that may act as hosts for virus code. Effective antivirus products not only detect and remove viruses, but they also help you recover data that has been lost because of a virus. To remain current, they require frequent updating as to the virus threats to watch for. An antivirus program includes an antivirus engine (the main program) and a set of patterns of recognized viruses, usually contained in files called definition files. Retailers of antivirus software commonly charge an annual fee for updates to the antivirus engine and the definition files. There are excellent free services for home users. One example is AVG antivirus from GRIsoft. Software companies that offer free security software usually also offer a feature-rich commercial version to which you can upgrade for a fee. The free version gives you a chance to see if you like the interface before you put out any money. Once installed, you can configure most antivirus programs to automatically connect to the manufacturer's Web site and check for these updates.

Pop-Up Blockers

Many free and commercial programs are available that effectively block various forms of adware, especially pop-ups, which are the easiest to block and the most annoying because a pop-up advertisement appears in its own window and must be closed or moved before you can see the content you were seeking. A program that works against pop-ups is a **pop-up blocker**, and all major Internet browsers now have built-in pop-up blockers and so do most software security bundles. You can configure a pop-up blocker so that it will block pop-ups quietly, but you can

FIGURE 2–7 The Internet Explorer Pop-Up Blocker Settings page

also configure one to make a sound and/or display a message allowing you to choose to make a decision on each pop-up or to automatically and quietly block all pop-ups. We have found a few Web sites where blocking all pop-ups has blocked much of the content we were seeking. In that case, we may disable our pop-up blocker for that session or configure it to display a message allowing a decision to be made for each pop-up. You can enable the pop-up blocker feature on the Privacy page of the Internet Options dialog box for Internet Explorer. Once enabled, click the Settings button to open the Pop-up Blocker Settings page, as Figure 2–7 shows.

Privacy Protection and Cookies

Web browsers and security programs offer privacy protection options. In Microsoft Internet Explorer, you can configure privacy settings, including the pop-up blocker, through the Internet Options dialog box, accessible from either the Control Panel or the Tools menu in Internet Explorer. This is also where you determine how Internet Explorer handles cookies. The settings range from "Block all cookies" to "Allow all cookies," with a variety of settings in between. Experiment with the settings by choosing one and then spending some time browsing the Internet. The balance here is between the convenience of cookies for automated log-in to frequently accessed sites and the risk of an invasion of privacy. The Sites button in Internet Explorer will block specific sites; you will see a list of known bad sites listed here. The Advanced button allows you to customize the handling of cookies, as shown in Figure 2–8. We recommend that you allow first-party cookies and block third-party cookies.

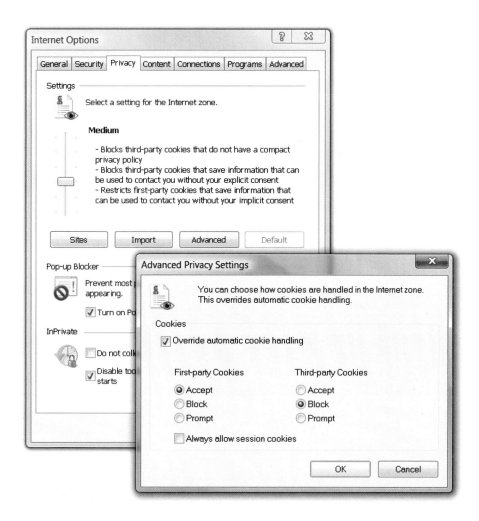

FIGURE 2–8 Use the top part of the privacy page in Internet Options to control the use of cookies.

FIGURE 2–9 The Content tab in Internet Options

Using your favorite Web search engine search on "Web content filter" to learn more about this topic and to find third-party Web content filters.

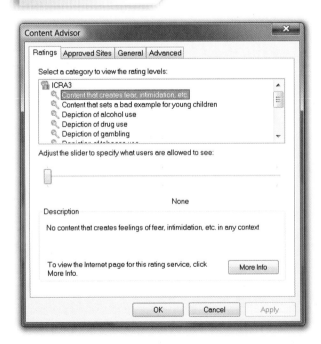

FIGURE 2–10 Content Advisor page displays when you click the Enable button in Internet Options

Parental Controls

Parental Controls, accessed from the Content tab in Internet Options, is a feature in Internet Explorer (see Figure 2–9). It allows parents to protect their children from harm by setting specific Parental Controls for a child's user account. Only someone using a password-protected administrator account can enable and configure Parental Controls, and there must also be an existing standard account for the child. The parent can then set time limits, game limits, and software restrictions. Windows Vista allows a parent to block Web sites with inappropriate content through Parental Controls. If you need this feature in Windows 7, you must add it by downloading the free Windows Live Essentials Suite from the Microsoft site and installing the Family Safety program. This will then show in the Parental Controls dialog box under More Settings.

Content Filtering

You can use software that blocks content, called a content filter, to enable protection from inappropriate or distasteful content. The most common type of content filter used on the Internet is a Web content filter, a software program designed to work with a Web browser to either block certain sites or to allow only certain sites. As with most types of software, you can find both free and commercial versions of Web content filters on the Internet. In fact, you may already have a Web content filter in your Web browser that you only need to enable and configure.

Many services are available on the Internet to evaluate Web site content and give each site ratings based on such parameters as language, nudity, sex, and violence. A content filter may use one or more of these rating services, and allow the administrator to choose the rating level to permit or exclude. Not all Web sites are rated, so if you enable a Web content filter, you will also have to decide what it should do in the event the user connects to an unrated site.

Microsoft Internet Explorer comes with a content filter called Content Advisor that you can enable and configure through the Content tab of the Internet Options dialog box. Clicking the Enable button will turn on this service as well as open a new dialog box for configuring the Content Advisor (see Figure 2–10). From here you have a variety of choices to make. The Ratings page will allow you to configure the level of ratings for language, nudity, sex, and violence. At this writing, the current version of Internet Explorer uses the Recreational Software Advisory Council (RSAC*i*) ratings service, an organization replaced by the Internet Content Rating Association (ICRA). You may also choose a different rating bureau. Before you can use such a bureau, you will need to contact one separately and arrange for this service, which will usually involve a fee.

Check Out the Content Advisor in Internet Explorer

The Internet Explorer Content Advisor is easy to enable, but not so easy to configure once enabled. In this exercise you will enable the Content Advisor and view the configuration options. To complete this exercise, you will need the following:

- A computer running Windows Vista or Windows 7 and Internet Explorer version 8 (or greater).
- A username and password for an account that is a member of the Administrators group.

Step 1

From the desktop click the Windows icon on the far left of the taskbar. In the Start Search (Windows Vista) or Start (Windows 7) box enter "Internet Options" and press the ENTER key.

Step 2

In the Internet Properties dialog box select the Content page. Click the Enable button located in the Content Advisor area of the page.

Step 3

In the Content Advisor dialog (see Figure 2–10), notice the lock and key icon next to the name of the rating service that it will use to rate sites. Below that are the categories this service has rated. When you select one of the categories a slider will display in the middle of the box. Use this slider to select what rating level the user may view in each category.

Step 4

Click on the Approved Sites tab where you can create a list of Web sites that are either always viewable or never viewable. This is configurable per Web site. Enter a Web site and click the Always button. Enter another Web site and click the Never button. You will need this "disapproved" Web site to complete the last step.

Step 5

Select the General tab and notice that the first setting under User Options is deselected. This means that, by default, when Content Advisor is turned on, users may not view pages that haven't been rated by the rating service. Another default allows a Supervisor to use a password to let users view restricted content. Clear this check box.

Step 6

You cannot change the Content Advisor settings or turn it on or off without a supervisor password. On the General tab page of the Content Advisor click the Create password button and the Create Supervisor password dialog box will display. Create a password, as well as a hint to help you remember this password. (You will need this password for Step 10.) A message box will confirm creation of the password. Click OK to close the message box and return to the Content Advisor dialog.

Step 7

The Ratings systems portion of the General page allows you to configure the ratings system(s) available to this computer. A rating system that is available to the Content Advisor provides a file with a .rat extension. To see the current list of ratings systems, click the button labeled Rating systems. Do not select another ratings system, but return to the Content Advisor dialog box by clicking Cancel twice.

WARNING!

Microsoft warns that using a different ratings bureau than the default will add a delay to Web browsing, as the browser contacts the new ratings bureau for each new Web page visited.

Step 8

Before the Content Advisor settings will take effect, you need to close and restart Internet Explorer. Do that now. Click OK to close Content Advisor. Close all open Internet Explorer windows.

Step 9

Open Internet Explorer. If you have a home page, it will display only if you approved it in Content Advisor. It you did not approve it, you will see a navigation cancelled message similar to the one shown here.

Step 10

Disable Content Advisor by opening Internet Options and navigating to the Content page as you did in Steps 1 and 2. Locate and click the Disable button. When prompted, enter the Supervisor password and click OK. You should see a message stating that Content Advisor was turned off. Click OK, and then restart Internet Explore and attempt to browse to any Web site you were not able to access previously.

Keep Up-to-Date

You should be sure to keep your operating system and applications up-to-date with security patches, especially if you are running Windows. Microsoft continues to update each version of Windows for several years (see the Microsoft Support Lifecycle at www.microsoft.com), and the versions discussed in this book automatically check for the updates that plug security holes that malware perpetrators exploit.

Authentication and Authorization

One of the first defenses against threats is authentication and authorization by a security system built into the operating systems on your local computer and on network servers. With the exception of DOS, the desktop OSs surveyed in this book support authentication and authorization. In fact, Linux, Windows, and Mac OS X require it.

After you, as the administrator, set up an account for Rachel, who is in accounting, she must enter her username and password when she logs on to her computer. Before giving her access to the computer, security components of her operating system will verify that she used a valid user name and password. This validation of the user account and password is *authentication*.

A recently hired part-time clerk, Kirsten, works at night entering accounts payable information into Rachel's computer. To allow Kirsten to also log on to Rachel's computer, you can create a new user account for Kirsten. Although only Rachel and Kirsten can log on to this computer, Rachel does not want Kirsten to be able to access the payroll information, also stored there, because this is private information. What might you do to help Rachel with this problem? One thing you could do (if her operating system supports it) is to set up Rachel's computer so that she can assign special permissions to the files and folders on her hard disk, giving each user account the level of permission it needs. For instance, one of Kirsten's tasks is to add accounting information to the accounts payable files, so you could give Kirsten's account the *authorization* that will allow her to write to the files in the accounts payable folder. You will not give Kirsten's account access to any of the other folders, and you will give Rachel's account full control of only the folders that she needs to use.

Right about now you're thinking that we're wrong about Windows and Mac OS X requiring authentication. Your computer is running the latest version of Windows or Mac OS X, but you don't have to enter a username or password to access your desktop and all your personal settings and data. So, obviously, you are not authenticated. Right? Wrong! Windows, Mac OS X, and Linux always require authentication, but each has a feature called automatic login that the OS installation program system turns on under certain circumstances, such as when you bring home a PC or Mac that you just bought in a retail store. Automatic login authenticates anyone who powers up your computer using the same credentials and they have access to everything that you normally do. You should never enable automatic login on a computer at school or work.

Authentication

Authentication is the verification of who you are. Authentication may be one-factor, two-factor, or even three-factor. One-factor authentication is your use of a user name and password as you log on to your computer. In this case, you are authenticated based on something you know—your user name and password. Two-factor authentication involves the use of something you know plus something you have, referred to as a token. If you use a cash card at an ATM, you are familiar with two-factor authentication, because the something you know is your PIN (personal identification number) code, while the token is your cash card. For even more security, consider three-factor authentication, adding biometric data, such as a retinal scan, voice print, or fingerprint scan to the token and password.

Authorization

Authorization determines the level of access to a computer or a resource (files, folders, printers, and so on) to an authenticated user. Authorization includes authentication, plus verification of your level of access to a computer or resource, including permissions and/or user rights. When you connect to a shared folder on your LAN, the security system of the computer hosting the folder will perform authorization, authenticating you, and verifying that your account has some level of access to the folder. This level of access is called permission. Permission describes an action that may be performed on an object. An example of a permission found on a file system is the read permission that allows reading of the contents of a file or folder, but by itself does not allow any other action on that file, such as deleting or changing it. Another component that affects level of access is a user right. A user right defines a systemwide action a user or group may perform, such as logging on to a computer or installing device drivers.

Passwords

A password is a string of characters that you enter, along with an identifier such as a user name, to authenticate you. A password is an important piece of the security puzzle. Don't take your password for granted. In fact, that should be plural, because you should not use the same password everywhere, and you should put a great deal of thought into creating passwords that truly help you protect yourself. This is important because, unless you deal strictly in cash, and do all your transactions in person at the bank, secure authentication is your basic defense against an invasion of your privacy, and your password is central to having secure authentication. Passwords are a very important part of any security system. Most experts recommend using passwords that are at least eight characters long and that contain a mixture of numbers, letters (both uppercase and lowercase), and nonalphanumeric characters. It's easy to guess passwords that use common words—such as the name of a pet—and therefore they offer little in the way of real security.

Establish a method for creating strong passwords—whether it is some scheme that you think up or software that helps you create these passwords. Begin by thinking of a phrase that is easy to remember such as: "I love the Boston Red Sox." Then take the first letter of each word in that phrase and string the letters together. In our example, the result is: iltbrs. Now turn it into a more complex password by capitalizing some of the alpha characters and inserting numbers and other symbols between the letters: i-l,T.b+r-s. If this meets the minimum password requirements you have a password. Now, the trick is to remember this password without the use of sticky notes!

Security Account Basics

A security account is an account that can be assigned permission to take action on an object (such as a file, folder, or printer) or the right to take some action on an entire system, such as install device drivers into an operating system on a computer. A security account may identify a single entity (individual or computer) or a group of entities. Security accounts exist in security databases, such as those maintained by Novell servers, UNIX or Linux systems, Mac OS X desktop and server OSs, and Windows server and desktop operating systems (excluding the Windows 9x family).

WARNING!

Blank passwords or those written on a sticky note and kept handy near a computer provide no security. Always insist on nonblank passwords, and do not write down your passwords and leave them where others can find them.

User Accounts

All operating systems discussed in this book have robust security that begins with using user and group accounts and the requirement to log in to the computer with a user account. The most common type of security account is an individual account, called a user account, and assigned to a single person. In the security database, a user account contains, at minimum, a user name and password used to authenticate a user. Depending on the structure of the security accounts database, a user account may contain additional identifying information. Typically, a user account will include the user's full name, a description, and a variety of other fields including e-mail address, department, phone numbers, and so on. User accounts exist in all Windows security accounts databases.

Built-In User Accounts. Each OS has a very special, very privileged built-in account—a super user—that can perform virtually all tasks on a computer, from installing a device driver to creating other security accounts. In Windows this privileged built-in user is Administrator. In those operating systems with their ancestry in UNIX—Mac OS X and Linux—Root is the most powerful user account, as it is in UNIX. We'll discuss these accounts in the appropriate chapters.

At the other end of the privilege spectrum, we have a guest account, found in Windows, Mac OS X, and Linux. This account is the least privileged and is disabled by default in Windows. If this account is enabled, a stranger can log in with the account (usually with no password), but cannot see anyone else's files and cannot make changes to the system.

Account Types: Standard versus Administrator Accounts. Linux and the versions of Windows and the Mac OS featured in this book all have the notion of types of user accounts. In Windows Vista and Windows 7 a standard user account (previously called a limited account in Windows XP) is for an "ordinary" user without administrator status. A user logged on with a standard account can change her password and other personal settings, but cannot change computer settings, install or remove software and hardware, or perform other systemwide tasks. In contrast, a user logged on with an administrator account, called a computer administrator in Windows Vista, can perform systemwide tasks. The first account created in any of these systems must be an administrator account type, and then you may use this account to create additional accounts. Figure 2–11 shows the Windows dialog box for creating a Standard User account.

In Mac OS X, the difference between an administrator account and a standard account is a single checkbox in the Accounts dialog for a single user: the "Allow user to administer this computer" checkbox. If this is checked, the user account is an administrator; if it is unchecked the account is a standard account. As with the Windows administrator accounts, a Mac OS X administrator account can install programs and do a range of systemwide tasks. A Mac OS X standard user is limited much as a Windows standard user is.

The administrator type of account in Linux includes the all-powerful root, and some other accounts, whereas in Linux the standard account type is not as clear. For instance, *standard user* is the term used to describe the long list of accounts some distributions will create automatically if you choose a special installation. Red Hat Linux, according to the Red Hat Linux Reference Guide for version 9, uses the term *standard account* when referring to the 48 accounts created during an Everything installation. Since this includes the root account and others with a wide range of permissions, it is not the same as the standard type of account used in Windows and Mac OS X.

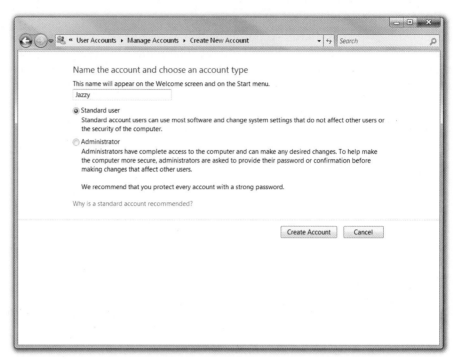

FIGURE 2–11 An administrator account may create accounts of either type.

Group Accounts

A group account is a security account that contains one or more individual accounts, and, in some security accounts databases, may contain other groups. Group accounts exist in the security accounts databases of all the OSs discussed here—some are built in and privileged users can create others. We will concern ourselves only with those groups that exist in the security accounts database on a desktop computer and not with what security accounts exist on a network server, such as a Windows 2008 Domain Controller. We call the accounts on a desktop computer local user and group accounts. The built-in local groups in Windows include Administrators, Users, and Guests (see Figure 2–12).

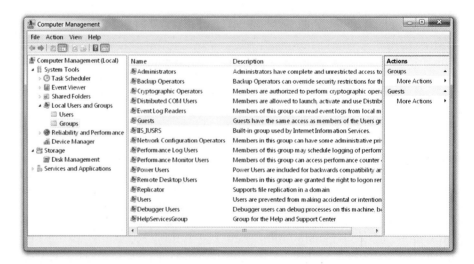

FIGURE 2–12 The Local Users and Groups node in Computer Management shows all groups, including Built-in Groups, administrator-created groups, and those created by some programs as they install.

Computer Accounts

Computers (and sometimes devices) may also have security accounts within a security accounts database maintained by a network server, such as in a Microsoft Windows Active Directory domain. This means your computer actually joins a domain before you, as a user, can log on to the network. When this occurs, new group accounts appear in the accounts database on your desktop Windows computer as it integrates into the domain. The details of this relationship are beyond the scope of this book, but be aware that this is the case if your computer is part of a Windows Active Directory Domain. How could this affect you? If you bring your personal laptop to the office, you will not be able to log on to the corporate network in the same way that you do from your desktop until an administrator makes your computer a member of the domain. If joining your personal laptop to the network is not desired, then there are other methods to give you access to the corporate network.

User Account Control

Before Windows Vista, if you wanted to make changes to your system such as installing a new device or program, you had to log on as an administrator. This meant, if you were already logged on with an account that did not have administrative access, you would have to log off and log on with an administrator account before you could perform a major system task. To avoid this annoyance, many people stayed logged on all day every day using an account with administrator access. This meant that if malware infected your computer, it would have full control over your computer because it has the same level of access as the logged-on user. To prevent this, Microsoft introduced User Account Control (UAC) in Windows Vista. This effective but annoying security feature prevents unauthorized changes to Windows.

With UAC enabled, there are two scenarios. In the first, a user logged on with a privileged account with administrative rights only has the privileges of a standard account, until the user (or a malicious program) attempts to do something that requires higher privileges. At that point, UAC makes itself known, graying out (dimming) the desktop, and displaying the Consent Prompt with a message, "Windows needs your permission to continue." Further, it asks for your response, "If you started this action, continue," and displays the name of the program that is attempting to run. You must click Continue or Cancel. If you click Continue, the task runs with your administrative privileges, and you return to working with standard privileges in other programs.

In the second scenario, a user logs on with the privileges of a standard user and attempts to do something that requires administrative privileges. In this case, UAC displays the Credentials Prompt requiring the user name and password of an account with administrative privileges. If you provide these, the program or task will run with these elevated privileges, but you will return to the standard user privileges for all other activities. In either case, if you do not respond in a short time, UAC will time out, cancel the operation, and return the desktop to you. By default UAC is on in both Windows Vista and Windows 7, although Microsoft made changes to Windows 7 that reduced the number of prompts you will see because it changed the number of Windows programs that require approval to run.

Even with UAC turned off, you still may not be allowed to perform all tasks and will see a message such as "The requested operation requires elevation" when you attempt to perform certain functions.

Mac OS X also has a function similar to Windows UAC, but it is more subtle. Certain dialog boxes have a lock symbol on the lower left. It will appear locked in some instances and unlocked in others. If you are in a dialog box, such as Accounts, you will find that when the lock symbol is locked you can

FIGURE 2–13 Unlock a dialog box in Mac OS X to access advanced settings.

still make certain changes, such as changing your own picture, without a problem, but unlocking the lock reveals more settings that only an administrator may change. If you wish to access the advanced settings, you simply double-click on the lock and enter the user name (it will default to the currently logged-on user) and password of an administrator account, as shown in Figure 2–13. So, even if you have logged on with an account with administrator privileges, it acts like Windows UAC by requiring you to take an extra step before making systemwide changes.

Best Practices When Assigning Permissions

The most important practice in assigning permissions to accounts in any operating system is to use the principle of least privilege. Give permissions to each user or group that allows each user the amount of access required to complete assigned tasks, but do not give users more than required. Thus, the user has the least privileges necessary to function.

Best Practices with User Names and Passwords

You may actually have habits that make you vulnerable to identity theft or another type of attack on your computer, data, or personal information. Consider the following questions:

- Do you have too many passwords to remember?
- When you have an opportunity to create a new password, do you use your favorite password—the one that you use everywhere?
- At school or work, do you have your password written on sticky notes or your desk calendar?
- Have you used the same password for more than a few months?

If you can answer "yes" to any of these questions, you are at risk! And the risk is not only with your password. Because many Web sites allow you to provide a user name to use when you log in, you may also be reusing the same user name and password combination. Now a hacker doesn't even have to guess your account name.

Don't Give Away Your User Name and Password

If you use the same user name and password at your bank as you do at a Web site where you took what seemed like a harmless personality test, you may have put your bank account and your other financial assets at risk. Perhaps the Web site was created to surreptitiously gather just such personal information, or it may have an innocent mission, but simply employ weak security practices. Either way, the outcome may be the same—someone now has information that could allow access to your bank account. "But," you say, "I didn't provide them with my bank account information." Are you sure? If you provided any personal information to the Web site, they may be able to use it to search online databases (some containing information illegally gathered), and to discover, or guess, which bank you use. Then, even though the bank has much better security practices than the Web site you went to, you have just given someone the key (so to speak) to your assets.

Create Strong Passwords

A strong password is one that meets certain criteria, and these criteria change over time as hackers create more techniques and tools for discovering passwords. Microsoft defines a strong password as one that contains at least eight characters, includes a combination of letters, numbers, and other symbols (+, −, $, etc.) and is easy for you to remember, but difficult for others to guess.

Always use strong passwords for the following types of accounts:

- Banks, investments, credit cards, and online payment providers.
- E-mail.
- Work-related accounts.
- Online auction sites and retailers.
- Sites where you have provided personal information.

> Learn more about protecting your computer with passwords. Use an Internet search engine to search on "strong passwords." You will find great tips on how to create complex passwords that are easy to recall, but hard for others to crack.

Never Reuse Passwords

Every account should have a unique name (if possible) and a unique password (always). Many Web sites require your e-mail address as the user name, so these will not be unique.

Avoid Creating Unnecessary Online Accounts

Many Web sites ask that you create an account and join, but what are the benefits of joining? Why do they need information about you?

Don't Provide More Information Than Necessary

Avoid creating accounts with Web sites that request your Social

Get Help Creating Passwords

There are programs that will help you create passwords. While we strongly recommend that you come up with your own method to create and remember strong passwords, it is helpful to see some strong passwords. Try this:

1. Open your browser and connect to your favorite search engine. Search on "random password generator" (without the quotation marks).
2. Select a password generator from the results list and experiment.
3. For instance, the Secure Password Generator on the PC Tools Web site (www.pctools.com) allows you to define the password rules and then after you click the Generate Password button it will generate a password that complies with the rules.
4. Try creating a password, but do not use one you generated in this fashion. Rather, devise your own scheme for creating secure passwords. Then you are more likely to remember your password.

try this!

Security number and other personal and financial information. Avoid having your credit card numbers and bank account information stored on a Web site. Although it's not easy to do online, you can do this with a merchant in person: If asked for your Social Security number, ask these four questions:

1. Why do you need it?
2. How will you protect it?
3. How will you use it?
4. What happens if I don't give it to you?

You may have to make a decision as to whether to do business with that merchant if you don't receive satisfactory answers.

Encryption

Encryption is transformation of data into a code that you can decrypt only by using a secret key or password. A **secret key** is a special code used to decrypt encrypted data. You can encrypt data you are sending over a network. In addition, you can encrypt data files that are stored on a local computer or network server. Encryption protects sensitive or valuable data and only someone who knows the password or holds the secret key can decrypt the data back to its original state. The secret key may be held in a **digital certificate** (also called a security certificate, or simply a certificate), which is a file stored on a computer.

Without being aware, you participate in encrypting network traffic when you do online banking or shopping. Look at the address line and you will see the protocol prefix "http" replaced by "https." This means that you are now using **Secure HTTP (HTTPS)**, which encrypts the communications between you and the bank or e-commerce server. HTTPS uses the **Secure Sockets Layer (SSL)** security protocol. For this encryption method, the user certificates contain identifying information used for verifying the holder of the certificate (your bank or the online retailer) including the holder's public key for use in encrypting a message for the user. Only the user holds the private key to decrypt the message. Your Web browser and its security protocols manage it all for you. If the browser detects a problem with a certificate as a page is loading, you will receive a warning that a Web site's security certificate is invalid. You should not continue loading the page and should add this Web site to your browser's security settings.

Encryption is very useful for data stored on a laptop or in professional settings, where data theft is a real concern. Beginning with Windows 2000, Microsoft NTFS file system allows you to encrypt files and folders through a feature called **Encrypting File System (EFS)**. You turn on encryption through the Advanced button of the Properties dialog box of a folder residing on an NTFS volume, and then all files created in that folder become encrypted. Figure 2–14 shows the Advanced Attributes dialog that opens from the Advanced button on the Properties of a folder named *Ch_02_Security*. Clicking the check box labeled Encrypt Contents To Secure Data will turn on encryption for this folder.

BitLocker Drive Encryption, a feature of the Ultimate Editions of Windows Vista and Windows 7, allows you to encrypt an entire drive.

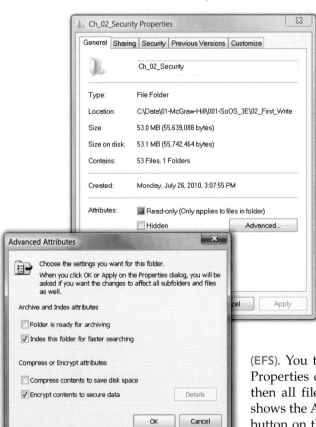

FIGURE 2–14 Turn NTFS encryption on or off using the Properties of a folder.

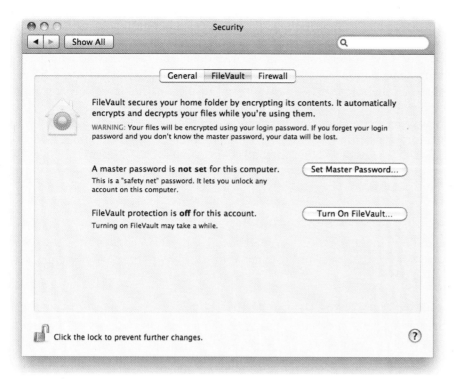

FIGURE 2–15 Configuring FileVault in Mac OS X

Mac OS X has a feature called FileVault that will encrypt all the files in your Home folder. Figure 2–15 shows the Security dialog box in which you can enable Mac OS X FileVault, which presently only encrypts the files in your Home folder. In both OSs, only someone logged on with your credentials can access the encrypted files.

Data Wiping

When you move computers from user to user or remove a computer from service within an organization and sell or give it away, you should remove the data on the computer. This goes beyond a simple delete operation, because there are many methods for "undeleting" such files. To be sure that a determined person will not access your old files, you must remove them completely. The permanent removal of data from a storage device is data wiping. A reformat of the hard drive is one method, but it's not truly very secure, and it's a problem if you wanted to keep the operating system and programs on the disk. Another method is to use data wiping software that uses an algorithm for writing over an entire drive volume, or just those portions of a drive that contain data—whether it has been deleted or not. You can perform data wiping on any storage media that is rewritable, including hard drives, optical drives, and solid-state storage. Both free and commercial data wiping programs will do the trick for most purposes. Such programs are available for all storage types. Those written for hard drives can take advantage of a government-approved ability built in to newer hard drives—Secure Erase. You cannot recover data once you have used such a data wiping program.

The free data wiping programs are not easy to use and, therefore, not for beginners. To learn more about data wiping, and why it is required in some instances, check out the ReadMe file that comes with the Freeware Secure Erase Utility available from the University of California at San Diego's Center for Magnetic Recording Research, written by Dr. Gordon Hughes and Tom Coughlin. At this time, the utility and ReadMe link are available at http://cmrr.ucsd.edu/people/Hughes/SecureErase.shtml.

Physical Security

Physical security of computers and networks is yet another huge topic that we can only touch on here. Physical security for desktop computers and networks includes limiting who has access to the building or room in which the desktop computers or network servers reside. Physical security is part of a school or other organization's security policy, and that policy must define its implementation. Small organizations often simply rely on the trustworthiness of their employees—with mixed results—while larger organizations implement formal physical security protection. This can include a mode of identifying someone trying to get entry to a building or room. This mode can be a guarded entrance with confirmation of a person's credentials, key card access, or a variety of other methods depending on the security needs of the organization. Securing laptops and other mobile devices has its own challenges, addressed next.

Security for Mobile Computing

In addition to the practices outlined above as defenses against threats, special considerations are required when traveling with laptops or other mobile computing devices.

Be Extra Wary of the Danger of Theft

The very portability of laptops and other mobile computing devices obviously makes them more susceptible to physical theft, so you should be alert to that threat and never leave them unattended while traveling.

Encrypt Sensitive and Confidential Data

In addition to applying permissions, you should further protect any sensitive data on the laptop with encryption, using NTFS encryption on a Windows laptop with an NTFS-format drive, or use FileVault for files in the Home folder on Apple laptops.

LO 2.3 | Troubleshooting Common Security Problems

Security is a huge topic, as is troubleshooting security problems. Therefore, this chapter has tried to limit our security discussion to the desktop operating system, and here we have selected some common security problems we have encountered on desktop computers.

Troubleshooting Log-On Problems

There are certain nearly universal log-on problems. They include the following.

Caps Lock Key Turned On

Everyone does it! You're in a hurry, and when you type in your user name and password, you don't notice the placement of your hands and one or both of them are incorrect. You receive an error message indicating that the user name or password is incorrect, as in Figure 2–16. No problem; you type it in

FIGURE 2–16 Log-on error message

again, but don't notice that you have the caps lock on. Some operating systems, including Windows Vista and Windows 7, will warn you of this, but other operating systems will not. Therefore, be careful about the placement of your hands and ensure that Caps Lock is off before entering your user name and password.

Too Many Log-On Attempts

On a bad day, like your first day back at work after a vacation, you may try several times before you enter the password correctly. If you're logging onto a corporate network, it is counting all these tries and you may exceed a limit on the number of log-on attempts. This limit is part of account policies, which you learned about earlier in this chapter.

FIGURE 2–17 Log-on lockout message

Exceeding the number of log-on attempts (account lockout threshold) may result in your user account being locked out of the computer and the network for a period of time (account lockout duration), and you will see a message similar to that in Figure 2–17. There is usually a third parameter used for account policy: the period of time after which the counter for the number of log-on attempts is reset to zero.

If a message like this appears when you are trying to log on to a network at school or work, you will have to call an administrator for help. An administrator may be able to override the lockout so that you can try again. Type carefully this time!

If no administrator is available, you will have to wait for the account lockout time to expire. An administrator configures these settings, usually to comply with a company's security standard (see Figure 2–18). So, it could be a matter of minutes, or it could even be days! Although at the time it can be a huge inconvenience, this is your protection against password crackers, which may need to make many tries before they guess the correct password.

In the unlikely event that you receive a lockout message when attempting to log on to a stand-alone or work group Windows computer, someone will have to log on with an account that is a member of the administrators group and modify the account lockout policy, or you will have to wait out the lockout duration period.

Troubleshooting a Suspected Malware Attack

If you suspect a computer is infected by a virus and have an antivirus program installed, run a scan of all drives and memory to see if you can discover

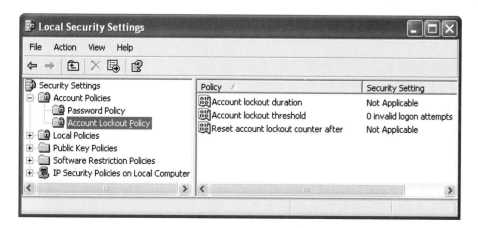

FIGURE 2–18 The Account Lockout Policy with values set for lockout duration, threshold, and a period of time after which the counter resets

try this!

Perform an Online Virus Scan

Try one of the online virus scanners. All you need is a Windows computer with a Web browser and a connection to the Internet. Use the online scanner at Trend Micro, or search the Internet for another one to use. Try this:

1. Open your browser and connect to http://housecall.trendmicro.com.

2. On the Trend Micro Housecall page, select the Download HouseCall 7.1 button. You will need to answer a question or two, including responding to a security warning before the engine and pattern files download, install, and you can finally choose the drive or drives to scan. Follow the on-screen instructions to run the scan.

3. When finished, close all open windows.

and remove the virus. If this does not discover a virus, but you are still suspicious, or if you do not have an up-to-date antivirus program installed, you can connect to one of many Web sites that offer free online scans. Just one example of such a scanner is House-call, found at http://housecall.trendmicro.com. This scanner is by Trend Micro, which also offers a commercial security suite at www.trendmicro.com.

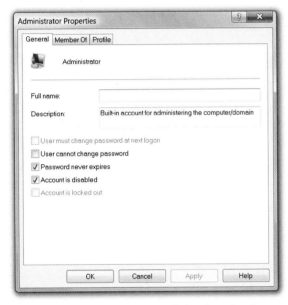

FIGURE 2–19 The Properties dialog box for the Administrator account shows it disabled by default in Windows Vista and Windows 7.

Using the Administrator Account in Troubleshooting

Windows has an administrator account, cleverly named Administrator. Disabled by default, this account has no password in Windows Vista and Windows 7, as shown in Figure 2–19. The administrator account is enabled if your computer is *not* a member of a Windows Active Directory domain and it starts in Safe Mode. In this case, you can log on with this account and attempt to troubleshoot the reason for the computer going into Safe Mode.

Chapter 2 REVIEW

Chapter Summary

After reading this chapter and completing the exercises, you should understand the following facts about computer security.

Threats to Computers and Users

- Threats include malware, phishing, social engineering, identity theft and fraud, exposure to inappropriate or distasteful content, invasion of privacy, misuse of cookies, hoaxes, and computer hardware theft. Other threats include accidents, mistakes, and natural and unnatural disasters.

- A vector is a mode of malware infection, such as e-mail, code on Web sites, Trojan horses, searching out unprotected computers, sneakernet, back doors, rootkits, pop-up downloads, drive-by downloads, war driving, and bluesnarfing.

- The people behind computer security threats come from all over the world, and increasingly they are part of organized crime. Certain terms, describing their techniques, define the individuals. These terms include hackers, crackers, script kiddies, click kiddies, and packet monkeys.

- Many methods are used to steal passwords, including capturing them from unsecured Web sites, using password crackers, and keystroke loggers.

Defense Against Threats

- Education is an important defense against threats. It includes knowing what the threats are and learning to recognize the signs of a threat or an infection.

- Security policies describe how an organization protects and manages sensitive information. You should follow and enforce security policies.

- You should install comprehensive security software, including (at minimum) personal firewalls, anti-spam software, antivirus software, and pop-up and privacy protection.

- You will improve your security if you understand authentication and authorization and its implementation on your computer and in your organization.

- You can combat threats by following the rule of least privilege when assigning permissions and using best practices with user names and passwords.

- Encryption technologies protect your data.

- Data wiping practices can remove even deleted data from computers.

- Physical security of computers and networks is also important, especially for mobile computing.

Troubleshooting Common Security Problems

- Log-on failure may be the result of something as simple as having the Caps Lock key turned on. The OS can lock you out from logging on to your computer if you exceed the number of failed log-on attempts configured in the Account Lockout Policy for a network or an individual computer. An administrator may need to modify the policy.

- If you suspect a computer is infected by a virus and have an antivirus program installed, run a scan of all drives and memory. If this does not discover a virus, and you are still suspicious, connect to one of many Web sites that offer free online scans, such as http://housecall.trendmicro.com.

- Windows has an administrator account, "Administrator." Disabled by default, this account has no password in Windows Vista and Windows 7. The Administrator account is enabled if your computer is *not* a member of a Windows Active Directory domain (the norm for a home computer) and it starts in Safe Mode. In that case, you can log on with this account and attempt to troubleshoot the reason for the computer going into Safe Mode.

Key Terms List

administrator account type *(65)*

adware *(44)*

authentication *(63)*

authorization *(64)*

back door *(41)*

bluesnarfing *(42)*

botnet *(44)*

browser hijacking *(44)*

content filter *(60)*

cookies *(48)*

data wiping *(71)*

digital certificate *(70)*

DMZ *(56)*

drive-by download *(41)*

Encrypting File System (EFS) *(70)*

encryption *(70)*

FileVault *(71)*

firewall *(54)*

first-party cookie *(48)*	pop-up *(41)*	third-party cookie *(49)*
group account *(66)*	pop-up blocker *(58)*	token *(63)*
guest account *(65)*	pop-up download *(41)*	Trojan horse *(40)*
identity theft *(46)*	rootkit *(41)*	user account *(65)*
keystroke logger *(43)*	secret key *(70)*	User Account Control (UAC) *(67)*
keylogger *(43)*	Secure HTTP (HTTPS) *(70)*	user right *(64)*
limited account *(65)*	Secure Sockets Layer (SSL) *(70)*	vector *(40)*
malware *(40)*	security account *(64)*	virus *(43)*
Parental Controls *(60)*	social engineering *(45)*	war driving *(41)*
password *(64)*	spam *(45)*	worm *(44)*
password cracker *(43)*	spim *(45)*	zombie *(44)*
permission *(64)*	spyware *(44)*	
phishing *(45)*	standard user account *(65)*	

Key Terms Quiz

Use the Key Terms List to complete the sentences that follow. Not all terms will be used.

1. A/an _____ defines what a user or group can do to an object such as a file or folder.

2. Programs on a Web site may send very small text files called _____ to a Web browser, along with a request that the Web browser save the file to disk.

3. Unsolicited e-mail, usually sent to market a service or product (legitimate or otherwise), is called _____.

4. _____ occurs when someone collects personal information belonging to another person and uses that information fraudulently to make purchases, open new credit accounts, or even obtain new driver's licenses and other forms of identification in the victim's name.

5. In Windows, a/an _____ defines a systemwide action a user or group may perform, such as logging on to a computer or installing device drivers.

6. _____ includes authentication, plus determination of a person's level of access to a computer or a resource.

7. The EFS feature in Windows NTFS and the Mac OS X FileVault feature are both examples of _____ at the file system level.

8. _____ is verification of who you are.

9. A parent wanting to protect a child from inappropriate Web content may use _____.

10. A person or program with administrative access can install malicious code or a/an _____, which hides itself from detection within the operating system or other program code on a computer.

Multiple-Choice Quiz

1. An organization should have a written set of these defining rules and practices for protecting and managing sensitive information.
   a. Firewalls
   b. Security policies
   c. Comprehensive security software
   d. Content filtering
   e. Antivirus

2. This type of annoyance appears uninvited in a separate window when you are browsing the Web and can provide a vector for malware infections.
   a. Inline banner
   b. Pop-up
   c. Spam
   d. Adware
   e. Back door

3. With this Windows Vista/7 feature turned on (as it is by default) a logged-on user only has the privileges of a standard account, even if that user is an administrator, and must provide credentials to perform most administrative tasks.
   a. Account lockout threshold
   b. EFS
   c. Lockout policy
   d. UAC
   e. Account lockout duration

4. This term describes unsolicited messages received via instant messaging.
   a. Spam
   b. Spyware
   c. Zombie
   d. Spim
   e. Bot

5. You open your browser and, rather than pointing to your home page, it opens to a Web page advertising adware removal or antivirus software. You reconfigure the browser to point to your home page, but when you restart the browser, it again points to the wrong Web page. This behavior is a symptom of what type of malware?
   a. Spyware
   b. Worm
   c. Browser hijacking
   d. Keystroke logger
   e. Trojan horse

6. What type of malware installs on a computer without the knowledge or permission of the user, and replicates itself on the computer or throughout a network?
   a. Virus
   b. Utility
   c. Worm
   d. Scam
   e. Spim

7. What term is used for a seemingly harmless program that has malicious code hidden inside?
   a. Worm
   b. Trojan horse
   c. Antivirus
   d. Optimizer
   e. Cookie

8. What utility or feature of a browser is used to inhibit the annoying windows that open when you are browsing the Web?
   a. Content filter
   b. Firewall
   c. Antivirus
   d. Spam filter
   e. Pop-up blocker

9. Strange screen messages, sudden computer slowdown, missing data, and inability to access the hard drive may be symptoms of what?
   a. War riding
   b. Spam
   c. Encryption
   d. Virus infection
   e. Fraud

10. This device sits between a private network and the Internet (or other network) and examines all traffic in and out of the network it is protecting, blocking any traffic it recognizes as a potential threat.
    a. Router
    b. Firewall
    c. Bridge
    d. Worm
    e. Keystroke logger

11. After several failed log-on attempts, a message appears stating that your account was locked out. This is the result of exceeding this setting in Account Lockout Policy on a Windows computer.
    a. Password length
    b. Account lockout threshold
    c. Account lockout duration
    d. Maximum password age
    e. Password complexity requirements

12. This type of malware is also a vector, concealing itself within the OS code and giving someone administrative access to a computer.
    a. Rootkit
    b. Pop-up download
    c. Drive-by download
    d. Worm
    e. Hoax

13. What is the term used to describe the use of persuasion to gain the confidence of individuals?
    a. Hoax
    b. Fraud
    c. Phishing
    d. Social engineering
    e. Enticement

14. What term describes the action of a password cracker that simply tries a huge number of permutations of possible passwords?
    a. Keystroke logging
    b. Brute force
    c. Statistical analysis
    d. Mathematical analysis
    e. Phishing

15. This firewall technology inspects each packet that enters or leaves the protected network, applying a set of security rules defined by a network administrator; packets that fail are not allowed to cross into the destination network.
    a. Proxy service
    b. VPN
    c. IP packet filter
    d. Encrypted authentication
    e. DMZ

Essay Quiz

1. Explain automatic log-in and why you should not allow it in a situation in which you require security.

2. Consider the following statement: User Account Control limits the damage that someone can do who accesses your computer when automatic log-in is enabled. Elaborate on this statement, describing why it is true, and why there is still a great risk.

3. Why should you disable the Guest account?

4. In your own words, describe why the use of Internet cookies can be an invasion of privacy.

5. Differentiate between permission and user right.

Lab Projects

LAB PROJECT 2.1

Research identity theft to answer the following questions:

1. What is the estimated annual cost of identity theft in the United States in a recent year? What is the trend compared to previous years?

2. Identity theft can involve computers, but in many cases, computers play only a small part in identity theft. Find a recent article on an identity theft ring and describe how the thieves operated.

3. Share your findings with others in your class and compare the information you found.

LAB PROJECT 2.2

Research the latest malware threats. Many organizations, including antivirus vendors and security services, post information on the Internet about the latest malware threats. Use your favorite Internet search engine to research the latest threats, which you may find at one of the top security software manufacturers, such as McAfee or Symantec. Using the information from one of these sites, make a list of five current threats and research each to learn more about it. Briefly describe each threat and how you will use security software or behavior to defend your computer from each one.

LAB PROJECT 2.3

Security is a huge topic today, and organizations require trained specialists to keep their computers and networks secure. One way prospective employers can determine how much someone knows about security is by requiring job applicants to hold certain appropriate security certifications that require study, experience, and passing exams. Find and research a security certification and give a brief description of this certification, including the organization that is behind this certification, who should seek it, what domains (topics) are included in the exam, and the job titles this certification would apply to.

3 Desktop Virtualization

"We're three years old and we're competing against companies that have been around for decades. It is happening because desktop virtualization is going mainstream."

—Stephen Dukker

CEO of NComputing, manufacturer of a thin client device, as quoted in a September 24, 2010, article by Dean Takahashi on GamesBeat at VentureBeat.com

In the 1990s if you wanted to test a new version of Windows or try a Linux distribution (distro), you had to dedicate an entire computer to this task. Similarly, in the mid-1990s when preparing to teach classes on the latest Windows server OSs, a Microsoft certified trainer needed several computers to create the same mix of desktop computers and servers he would encounter in the classroom. Likewise, the Novell administrator and engineer classes of the mid-1990s required that you pair a server and client computer at each desk, so students could experience setting up a server and configuring a client to connect to that server.

As the 1990s ended and the new millennium began, virtualization of operating systems evolved, allowing us to run multiple operating systems on a single computer. The student experience changed, as instructors configured classes in which each participant worked with one or more servers and clients—all on a single PC. Today, all you need in addition to specialized virtualization software to emulate hardware is a computer with the processing power and enough RAM and hard drive space to support the number, and types, of OSs you wish to run. You also need appropriate licenses for all the software you run, including the OSs running in the virtual machines. In this chapter, we will explore the exploding phenomenon of OS virtualization, while preparing you to install the desktop OSs described in this book into

Learning Outcomes

In this chapter, you will learn how to:

LO **3.1** Explain the evolution of desktop virtualization and list the common features of today's desktop virtualization products.

LO **3.2** Select and implement a desktop virtualization option on a Windows Vista or Windows 7 desktop.

LO **3.3** Describe desktop virtualization options for a Mac OS X desktop.

virtual machines (VM), which will save you the cost (and physical desktop space) of working with multiple physical computers. In this chapter we will examine the options available for hosting desktop VMs on Windows and Mac OS X hosts. ✹

LO 3.1 | Virtualization Overview

In this section, we will define virtualization and many of the terms associated with it, describe its background, and tell how it has led to the virtualization of desktop operating systems.

Ubiquity of Virtualization

Virtualization is the creation of an environment that seems real, but isn't, and today it seems like virtualization is everywhere in the computing world, and there are many types. You can explore a virtual world, such as Second Life or VMware's vmworld (see Figure 3–1). In a virtual world a user often selects an animated computer-generated human, or avatar, to represent him or her within the virtual world. Virtual worlds are used in online training, in marketing of products, and in games. Many organizations use storage virtualization in which client computers can utilize many networked hard drives as though they are one. Network engineers work with network virtualization involving a network addressing space that exists within one or more physical networks, but which is logically independent of the physical network structure. Then there is server virtualization, in which a single machine hosts multiple servers, each of which performs tasks as independently from the others as separate physical machines would. Companies that provide low-cost Web hosting services can create a separate virtual Web server for each customer.

With only a small leap we come to desktop virtualization, the virtualization of a desktop computer into which you can install an operating system, its unique configuration, and all the applications and data used by (normally) a

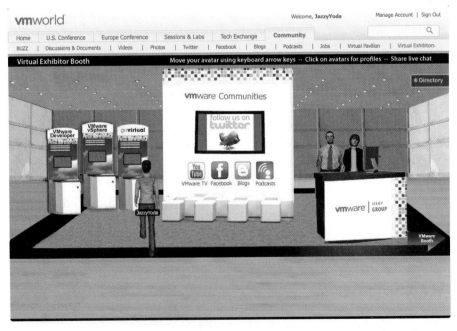

FIGURE 3–1 VMware's Virtual Pavilion showing Jane's avatar (JazzyYoda) walking into an exhibitor's virtual booth

single person. This virtual desktop may reside on a server, allowing a user to access it from a computer with specialized client software, or it may exist on the local computer. Each individual virtual environment in both server virtualization and desktop virtualization is a virtual machine—the software emulation of all hardware with which an operating system must interact. But wait, there's more! There is application virtualization, in which a user connects to a server and accesses one or more applications rather than an entire desktop environment. This chapter is devoted to today's desktop virtualization, but first we will look at the past.

Your (Great?) Grandfather's Virtual Machine

Today's virtual machines have a very long pedigree—they can trace their roots back to the 1960s when mainframe computer manufacturers, such as IBM, routinely created multiple discrete environments on a single computer. A user connected using a dumb terminal that was little more than a keyboard and display with a connection to a host computer (mainframe or minicomputer), but it had no native processing power (hence the term *dumb*). A dumb terminal would connect to the host computer, sending keystrokes, and displaying the keystrokes and responses on the display. Each user connected to a discrete area on the host called a partition. A single terminal session could access each partition on a server. Partitioning is the process or act of creating a partition. The partition to which each user connected was not a true virtual machine, as today's virtual machines are, but an area in which the user had access to programs and data. This type of a partitioning of a mainframe computer's resources is different from the partitioning of disk drives described in Chapter 1 and referred to later in this chapter. After the advent of the IBM PC in the 1980s, a PC configured to emulate a dumb terminal often replaced the dumb terminal.

For years, this model prevailed for those organizations that wished to have a centralized system where all the programs and data resided, with the individual users connecting from whatever served as a terminal. The 1990s implementation of this model included servers or minicomputers running terminal services to which users connected nearly seamlessly to partitions from their desktop PCs using terminal client software. These were not, however, virtual machines because the entire hardware and operating system environment was not part of the partition to which users connected. They did not have a fully configurable desktop operating system, such as Windows, to work with beyond their application and data.

A 1970s-era computer terminal
Chilton Computing/Atlas Computing Division/Rutherford Library

Today's Virtual Desktops

In the past decade, many large organizations have adopted the thin client for their desktop users. A thin client is a low-cost PC, usually without such common peripherals as diskette drives (now gone from most PCs), expansion slots, and optical drives. The purpose of a thin client is to connect to a server, allowing the user to work in a server-hosted environment. When that environment provides the entire OS experience and working applications it becomes a virtual desktop, or a full virtual machine. This virtual machine may reside on a server and be accessed by a client computer (thin or not), or it may reside on a desktop computer. This allows the interactive user (the one sitting in front of that computer) to switch between the host OS, the operating system installed directly on the computer, and one or more guest OSs, the operating systems running within a virtual machine.

The term used today for hosting and managing multiple virtual desktops on network servers is virtual desktop infrastructure (VDI). The term is attributed to VMware in distinguishing its virtual desktop server products from the products offered by competitors, specifically Citrix and Microsoft products that did not provide a full desktop environment. Today VDI applies to any server product that provides the full virtual desktop support.

Type I and Type II Hypervisors

A hypervisor, also called a virtual machine monitor (VMM), is the software layer that emulates the necessary hardware on which an operating system runs. The hardware virtualization allows multiple operating systems to run simultaneously on a single computer, such as a network server. Each hypervisor normally emulates a computer separate from the underlying computer, but it must use a virtual processor compatible with that of the underlying machine—mainly either an Intel processor or an AMD processor. There are two types of hypervisors, Type I and Type II. A Type I hypervisor—sometimes called a bare-metal hypervisor—can run directly on a computer without an underlying host operating system. A Type II hypervisor requires a host operating system.

> In place of a full-featured operating system as its host OS, a Type I hypervisor has software that has as its sole purpose the interaction with the physical computer for support of virtual machines.

Bare-metal hypervisors first appeared on high-powered servers. While it may have been possible to run one of these on desktop computers, until recently these computers lacked the hardware support required for virtualization of some hardware. Of course, that was not a big hurdle, and now bare-metal hypervisors have been introduced, or at least announced, by the major hypervisor manufacturers—notably Citrix and VMware. Citrix's XenClient is a Type 1 hypervisor targeted at laptops. Announced in July 2010, Citrix offers a free evaluation version, XenClient Express, at its Web site, www.citrix.com.

Most hypervisor products for the desktop today are still Type II, and the hypervisors we discuss in this chapter are all Type II hypervisors requiring an underlying operating system. Whatever hypervisor you use for hosting, you will find more and more organizations deploying server-based virtual machines that are the users' everyday work environment. The reason for this is easier central management of the operating systems and user environment. While most of these virtual machines will continue to be hosted on servers, there may be a trend by late 2011 of corporations moving to desktop- or laptop-hosted Type 1 hypervisors.

> The term *x86* applies to a PC (processor, motherboard, and other components) that conform to the Intel 32-bit x86 specification and can run 32-bit software.

You have several choices for Type II hypervisors for desktops, but today some of the newer ones run only on computers with hardware-assisted virtualization features, which means they require a computer with either the Intel Virtualization Technology for x86 (Intel VT-x) or AMD Virtualization (AMD-V) architecture extensions, which improve the performance of virtual machines on the host. You can install a Type II hypervisor on your desktop and test another operating system without the expense of a separate computer. Figure 3–2 shows Windows 7 running in a virtual machine on a Mac OS X OS.

There are several choices of desktop Type II hypervisors, depending on both the hosting OS and the desired guest OSs. The ones we will discuss in this chapter all have several things in common. These are the tasks required

FIGURE 3–2 A Windows 7 virtual machine running in OS X on an Apple computer

to create a virtual machine, the order in which you do them, and how the host and guest OS share the mouse and keyboard.

1. Prepare the computer by taking a few cautionary actions: Confirm that the computer's hardware and operating system meet the minimum requirements for the hypervisor you intend to install. Back up your hard drive in case something goes wrong. Remove any conflicting software. In particular, be wary of installing a second hypervisor on a single host operating system. Do this on a nonproduction computer, if possible.

2. Install the hypervisor, such as Oracle's VM VirtualBox hypervisor (see Figure 3–3).

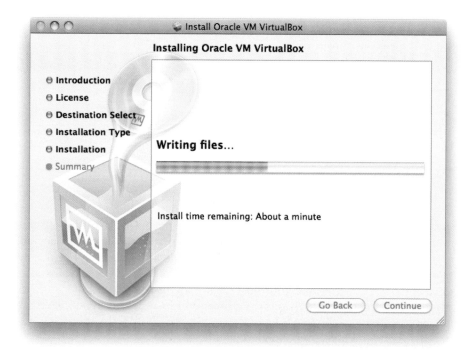

FIGURE 3–3 Installing a hypervisor

3. Install a virtual machine, selecting from a list of guest OSs that the hypervisor supports. Each hypervisor has default settings for each OS, the based on the minimum requirements of the guest OS. This normally creates two files on the host: a virtual machine file and a virtual hard drive file. The first contains the settings for the virtual machine, while the second contains all the operating system, program, and data files of the VM appearing as a hard drive when the VM is running. Other files may be created at this time, such as log files, but the virtual disk file and virtual machine file are the most important.

4. Install the guest OS. This normally requires the full retail version of the OS on disc, although there are exceptions. One exception is that you can bring in compatible pre-created virtual machines. You must have a legal license for each guest OS. Be sure to password protect each guest OS.

5. Install appropriate utilities for the guest OS. The hypervisor provides these utilities, and they include special software for making a virtual machine work better for the guest. Depending on the hypervisor in use, you may be prompted to install the guest utilities the first time you run each guest OS, and you may be notified of updates to the installed guest utilities. Next, secure the OS with security software.

6. Finally, once you have an OS installed into a virtual machine, you need to realize that the guest OS and host OS are sharing the same physical hardware, and certain things aren't easily shared. The keyboard and mouse are good examples of hardware that can serve only one master at a time. Normally, you give a VM control of a mouse by mousing into the VM and clicking inside the guest window. The virtual machine captures the mouse and keyboard, giving the VM the focus. To release the mouse and keyboard, there is a host key, which varies in each hypervisor. In VirtualBox on a Mac, it is the left Command key, while in Virtual PC it is the right Alt key. You will normally see a message about the host key during the installation or the first time you run the guest OS. Make sure you write down what key or key combination is the host key and keep the information handy. Practice using it right away.

WARNING!

If you already have a hypervisor installed on your computer, do not install a second until you uninstall the first. We knew better, but we were in a hurry and also sure we had uninstalled the previous one. Installing the second hypervisor caused the computer to crash. It was Jane's production computer. We had to repair the OS and jump through a few more hoops before the computer was up and running again. The moral of this story? Don't be in a hurry, uninstall conflicting software, and don't use a production computer for testing software.

Major Hypervisor Sources

The major sources of hypervisors are Citrix, VMware, Parallels, Microsoft, and Oracle. There are many other players in the field, with virtualization topics appearing in the technical press every day.

LO 3.2 | Desktop VMs on Windows Desktops

You have several options—both commercial and free—for running Linux, DOS, or Windows on a Windows desktop computer. At this writing you cannot run any version of Mac OS X in a VM on a PC, due more to licensing issues than technical issues. The hypervisors we describe here are free. Two are from Microsoft, one is from VMWare, and one is from Oracle. Unlike other software publishers that offer free desktop virtualization software, Microsoft does not require that you register with it to acquire a Microsoft hypervisor, nor does it require that you use any type of key to make it work. However, the installation program will verify that your host OS is a legitimate version of Windows before the Microsoft virtualization products will install. The hypervisors we will explore here are Microsoft Virtual PC, Windows XP Mode, Windows Virtual PC, VMware Player, and Oracle VirtualBox.

Microsoft Virtual PC 2007

Microsoft Virtual PC 2007, as its name implies, is an older version of Microsoft's hypervisor. It will install and run on certain editions of Windows XP, Windows Server 2003, and Windows Vista. You can create VMs and install other versions of Windows, Linux, and DOS. An important distinction between Microsoft Virtual PC 2007 and its successor, Windows Virtual PC (discussed next), is that Virtual PC 2007 does not require a CPU that supports hardware virtualization, but Windows Virtual PC does require this support.

The requirements for Virtual PC 2007 are:

1. Host OS: Windows Vista Business; Windows Vista Enterprise; Windows Vista Ultimate (Windows Vista must have at minimum Service Pack 1); Windows Server 2003, Standard Edition; Windows Server 2003, Standard x64 Edition; Windows XP Professional; Windows XP Professional x64 Edition; or Windows XP Tablet PC Edition. Windows XP must have Service Pack 3 (SP3).

2. An x64-based or an x86-based computer with a 400 MHz or faster (1 GHz recommended) processor with L2 cache.

3. Processor: AMD Athlon or Duron, Intel Celeron, Intel Pentium II, Intel Pentium III, Intel Pentium 4, Intel Core Duo, and Intel Core2 Duo.

4. RAM: Add the RAM requirement for the host operating system that you will be using to the requirement for the guest operating system that you will be using. If you will be using multiple guest operating systems simultaneously, total the requirements for all the guest operating systems that you need to run simultaneously.

5. Disk space: To determine the hard disk space required, add the requirement for each guest operating system that you will install.

6. Guest OS: Windows 98, Windows NT Workstation, Windows 2000, Windows XP, OS/2, Windows Vista, Windows 2000 Server, and Windows Server 2003.

> The term *x64* (or *x86-64*) refers to a PC (processor, motherboard, and other components) that conform to the 64-bit architecture required to run 64-bit operating systems and applications.

If you are unsure of the edition of Windows or the system type of your computer (32-bit or 64-bit), open the Start menu, right-click on Computer, and select Properties.

If you are thinking that you would like to run Virtual PC 2007 on your Windows 7 computer that does not have hardware support for virtualization, you are in luck as long as you don't mind doing some research on exactly how to achieve this. Be warned that while it is possible to do this, Microsoft does not officially support it. One good article on how to achieve this is on the Virtual PC Guy's Blog at http://blogs.msdn.com/b/virtual_pc_guy/archive/2009/08/19/running-virtual-pc-2007-on-windows-7.aspx. Rather than type in this URL, open a search engine and search on "Virtual PC 2007 on Windows 7." Omit the quotation marks. You may find a more recent article with updates.

Download Microsoft Virtual PC 2007

You can download Virtual PC 2007 from the Microsoft site. This requires a high-speed broadband connection, but the 30 MB file should take only a minute or two to download. Try this:

1. Use a search engine to locate the Microsoft download site for Windows Virtual PC 2007. At this time the site offers Microsoft Virtual PC 2007 SP1 (Service Pack 1) for Windows Server 2008, Vista SP1 and Windows XP SP3, but you may find an even newer update available.

2. Select the appropriate architecture version for your operating system (32-bit or 64-bit), and begin the download.

3. Verify that the file, presently named "setup.exe," was saved to the Download folder or to the location you selected.

4. You are ready to install Virtual PC 2007 on your Windows computer.

try this!

Step-by-Step 3.01

Installing Microsoft Virtual PC 2007

Using the file you downloaded in the Try This! on the previous page or a file provided to you by your instructor, install Microsoft Virtual PC 2007 on your Windows XP or Windows Vista computer. For our example, we will use Windows Vista. To complete this exercise you will need the following:

- A computer running Windows Vista with a minimum of 2 GB of RAM installed.
- The user name and password of an administrator account for this computer.
- A broadband Internet connection.

Step 1

Locate and double-click the installation program. This will start the Microsoft Virtual PC 2007 Wizard.

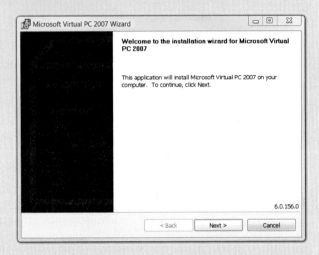

Step 2

Click Next on the Welcome page and follow the instructions. You will need to accept the License Agreement.

Step 3

Enter the Username (this does not need to match your user account name) and Organization information in the Customer Information page. Notice that Microsoft automatically entered the Product Key on this page, and grayed it out, so you cannot change it.

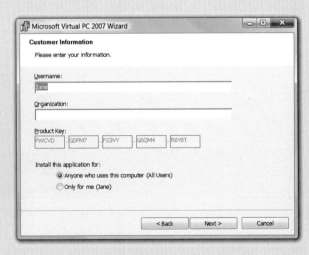

Step 4

Click Next on the Customer Information page and on the Ready to Install the Program page. Notice the location in which the program will be installed. You will normally allow it to install in the default location, but if you need to change this, click the Change button and browse to another location. When you are ready to have the installation begin, click the Install button.

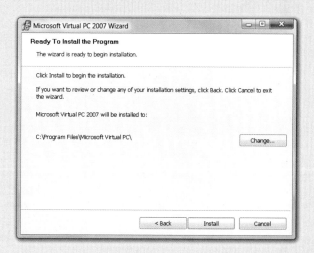

Step 5

The Installing Microsoft Virtual PC 2007 page shows the status of the installation with a progress bar. When the installation is complete, the Next button will become active; click it to proceed to the Installation Complete page.

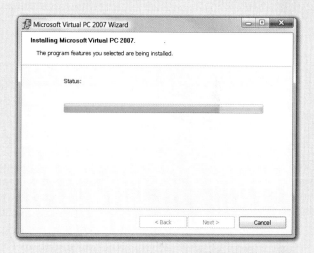

Step 6

Click the Next button when the progress bar shows that the installation is complete. On the Installation Complete page click Finish.

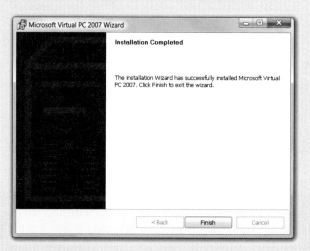

Step 7

Verify that Virtual PC was installed by clicking Start | All Programs. Virtual PC will be highlighted as a new program.

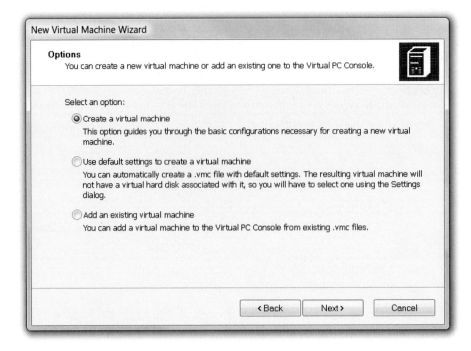

FIGURE 3–4 Select the correct option

As with any hypervisor, once you have installed Virtual PC 2007, the next step is creating a virtual machine appropriate for the first operating system you wish to install. Begin by launching Virtual PC 2007 from Start | All Programs. This launches the New Virtual Machine Wizard. On the Welcome page click the Next button. On the Options page, there are three choices, as shown in Figure 3–4. The first choice lets you create a virtual machine, allowing you to customize the configuration beyond the bare minimum for the operating system you will install. This includes both the virtual machine (saved in a .vmc file) and the virtual hard disk (saved in a .vhd file). We prefer to use this when creating a virtual machine. The second option is quicker, but creates a virtual machine with the default settings, but no virtual hard disk. You would choose this if you wanted only a minimally configured virtual machine and will use a previously created virtual hard disk. The third option lets you add a preexisting virtual machine, which means you need an existing .vmc file.

If you select the first option to create a virtual machine and click Next, the Virtual Machine name and Location page appears. Enter a meaningful name—such as the name of the OS you plan to install, as shown in Figure 3–5. Use the Browse button only if you want to specify a location other than the default location. Click Next, and in the Operating System page select the operating system you plan to install. Figure 3–6 shows this page with the dropdown box open and displaying the list of supported Guest OSs. Select Other if you wish to install DOS or Linux.

Select an OS and click Next to proceed to the Memory page. On this page, you may either keep the default setting for the selected OS or choose to adjust the amount of RAM used by the virtual machine and click Next to move to the Virtual Hard Disk Options page. Select the option to create a new virtual hard disk and click Next. On the Virtual Hard Disk Location page, keep the disk location, unless you wish to move it to a drive with more space. Then click Next to continue. The Completing the New Virtual Machine Wizard page displays a summary of the choices you made. Double-check the choices, and if it is OK, click Finish. You can configure several virtual machines—even

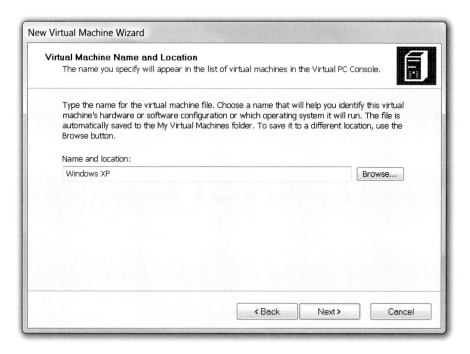

FIGURE 3–5 Enter a name for the virtual machine.

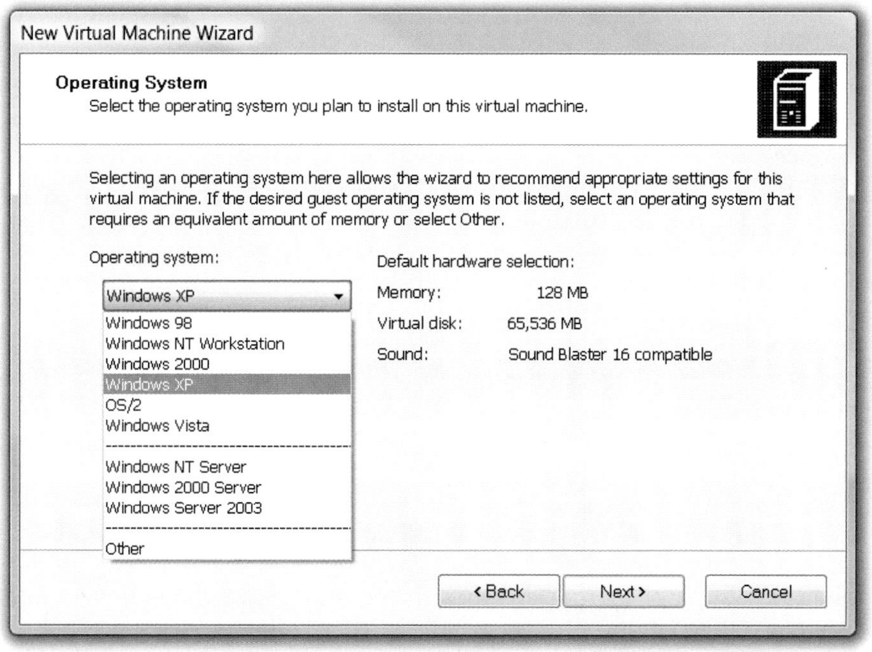

FIGURE 3–6 Select from the list of supported OSs.

before you begin installing the guest operating systems. If you do, the Virtual PC Console will list all the virtual machines, as shown in Figure 3–7.

Once you have configured a virtual machine, you are ready to install an OS into it. You will need the distribution disc for the OS you wish to install. You can also provide the file in ISO form. Let's assume you have the disc. Before beginning, place this disc in the host computer's optical drive. To start

FIGURE 3–7 The Virtual PC Console with four virtual machines

an OS installation, open Virtual PC from the Start Menu, which now opens the Virtual PC Console. Select the virtual machine for your OS and then click the Start button. This is the equivalent of turning on your PC. A window will open, and at first the background will be black while it loads the virtual system BIOS. This generally happens so fast that you cannot even read what displays there. It will then boot from your disc, starting the OS installation. From there, you install the OS just as you would on a physical machine, following the instructions in the setup program. We will provide instructions for installing Windows XP, Windows Vista, Windows 7, and Linux in the following chapters. You can install each of these into a virtual machine. You will also receive instructions for installing Mac OS X, but we will not be installing that on a virtual machine.

Windows XP Mode and Windows Virtual PC

Microsoft provides both Windows XP Mode and Windows Virtual PC as free, optional components of Windows 7. Windows XP Mode uses a runtime version of Windows Virtual PC; therefore Windows XP Mode is Windows Virtual PC with Windows XP preinstalled. After you download and successfully install Windows XP Mode and Windows Virtual PC from the Microsoft Web site they appear as two separate menu choices from the Start menu in Windows 7. The main purpose of Windows XP Mode for Windows 7 is to run legacy Windows XP applications that will not run well in Windows 7. Microsoft recommends Windows XP Mode and Windows Virtual PC for small and midsize businesses. For larger organizations Microsoft recommends the Microsoft Enterprise Desktop Virtualization (MED-V), which is server-based desktop virtualization.

With Windows Virtual PC you can also create VMs to run other guest systems, including Windows Vista, Windows 2000, and some versions of Linux. Once installed, it is so well-integrated into Windows 7 that you can start programs installed in the Windows Virtual PC VM from Start menu shortcuts of the host OS. Beyond that, if you have a certain data file type that you prefer to run in a program that is in the VM, you can assign that file type to the program in the host. Then, double-clicking on such a data file will launch the VM and the program within it.

All editions of Windows 7 support Windows Virtual PC, but the Home edition is somewhat limited in that you need to create your own virtual machine for Windows XP using a valid setup disc for the version of Windows you wish to install in the VM.

Windows XP Mode does not require hardware-assisted virtualization technology, but Windows Virtual PC does. You can download Windows XP Mode for Windows 7 at the Windows Virtual PC Web site, shown here.

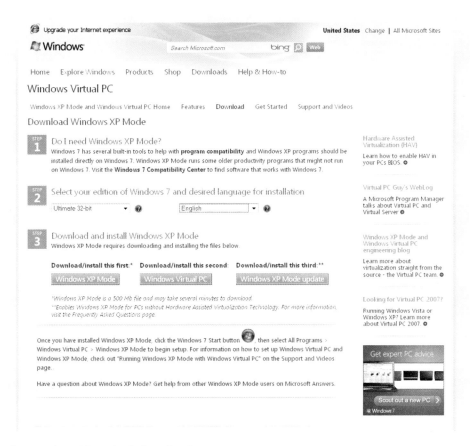

The Windows Virtual PC download page

Run the Hardware-Assisted Virtualization Detection Tool, available separately from the Microsoft Web site, or you can wait and let it run automatically when you initiate a download of Windows Virtual PC from there. If your computer will not support hardware-assisted virtualization, you will receive the message shown in Figure 3–8. If your computer passes, proceed with downloading both Windows XP Mode and Windows Virtual PC and install each in turn.

If your computer does not support hardware virtualization, carefully follow the instructions on the download page. First download Windows XP Mode and install it, then download Windows Virtual PC and install it, and finally, download the Windows XP Mode update, which includes support for running Windows XP Mode on a system without hardware support for virtualization.

If your computer's documentation indicates that the processor supports virtualization, but the computer fails the test, look in the documentation for instructions on enabling this feature.

FIGURE 3–8 This computer cannot run Windows Virtual PC.

VMware Player

VMware, Inc., has been producing virtualization software for more than a decade. The company has both server and desktop hypervisor products. VMware Player 3.0 is the current version of its desktop hypervisor, available as a free trial, and comes in three versions: a 32-bit/64-bit version for Windows hosts, a 32-bit version for Linux hosts, and a 64-bit version for Linux hosts.

The Windows-hosted version requires Windows XP or newer as the host and this hypervisor supports 64-bit guest operating systems. Like Windows Virtual PC, VMware Player allows you to launch VM-hosted programs from the hosting OS—even from the Start Menu. Within a VMware virtual machine you can install one of 200 guest operating systems, including Windows XP, Windows 7, Ubuntu 9.10, and Red Hat Linux. You can also create VMs for Linux, DOS, and BSD UNIX (see Figure 3–9).

If you are running VMware Player 3.0 on a Windows 7 Professional or Ultimate computer on which you have installed the Windows Virtual PC for Windows 7, you can import the virtual copy of Windows XP from a Virtual PC VM (Windows XP mode) into a VMware VM. Additionally, VMware offers the VMware vCenter Converter, which takes an existing Windows installation and converts it to a virtual machine.

Oracle VirtualBox

Oracle VirtualBox may be the most versatile of the free virtual machine products available at this writing because it comes in versions for a variety of host operating systems including Windows, Linux, and Mac OS X. Like the other free VM hosting software discussed here, it will run guest versions of Windows, Linux, and DOS. And like Microsoft's Virtual PC 2007, Oracle VirtualBox will run on hardware that does not support virtualization, so it is yet

FIGURE 3–9 Download the trial version of VMware to test it before deciding to buy it.

another choice for older computers without hardware virtualization support. Because this is available for the Mac, we'll leave our discussion of VirtualBox for the next section.

LO 3.3 | Desktop VMs on Mac OS X

The most compelling reason for using virtualization software on a Mac is to run Windows to access certain Windows apps that aren't available for the Mac OS. There are several options for doing this, including Apple Boot Camp, VirtualBox, and Parallels. Apple Boot Camp is more of a multi-boot solution, but VirtualBox and Parallels offer virtualization on the Apple desktop. Parallels is a commercial product, and you can learn about it at www.parallels .com/products/desktop/. VirtualBox is a free product from Oracle, so we'll describe Boot Camp and VirtualBox.

Apple Boot Camp

Apple Boot Camp is available with Mac OS X. It is a multi-boot option, meaning it allows you to install Windows onto a separate disk partition, and then you can choose to boot into either OS. This is an either-or situation; you need to restart to change from one OS to the other, but you can run both OSs. The advantage is performance—each OS is running directly on the Mac with no performance loss from being in a virtual machine. To create a Boot Camp partition and Windows on your Apple Mac computer you need the following:

- An Intel-based Mac computer with Mac OS X 10.6 or later (strongly recommended).

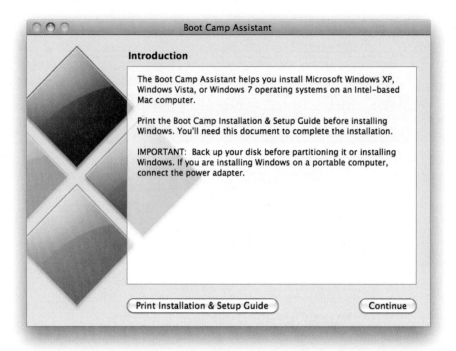

FIGURE 3–10 Print the Installation and Setup Guide before proceeding.

- The keyboard and mouse or trackpad that came with your computer. (Alternatively, use a USB keyboard and mouse.)
- A built-in optical disk drive or a compatible external optical drive.
- A Mac OS X version 10.6 installation disc.
- One of the following as the client OS: Windows XP Home Edition or Professional with Service Pack 2 or later (32-bit version only); Windows Vista Home Basic, Home Premium, Business, or Ultimate; Windows 7 Home Premium, Professional, or Ultimate.

Boot Camp comes with Mac OS X. Before running the Boot Camp Assistant, back up your Mac because the first step requires that you create a new partition for the Windows OS. To begin the installation, run the Boot Camp Assistant program from the Applications | Utilities folder. Notice that the first page, seen in Figure 3–10, gives you the option to print the Installation and Setup Guide for Boot Camp. This is an excellent idea. After you have printed the Guide, click Continue.

Boot Camp Assistant first has you create a partition on which to install Windows. This is especially important because you are not likely to have a second physical hard drive in a standard iMac or MacBook. That also means you should decide how big a partition you wish to have for your Windows OS. Remember that you will be installing applications into Windows, so you will need a bigger partition than the minimum recommended for the version of Windows you plan to install. For instance, when installing Windows 7 on an iMac with a 500 GB hard drive, we considered the minimum requirements for the OS itself (16 GB for 32-bit or 20 GB for 64-bit) and then we considered the requirements of the various applications we wish to install and the data we will generate (unless it is being saved to a server). Considering these needs, and the overall hard drive space, we decided to create a partition of 100 GB, as Figure 3–11 shows. You can click the Divide Equally button to have the disk space split evenly between OS X and Windows, click the 32 GB button to allot 32 GB to Windows, or click

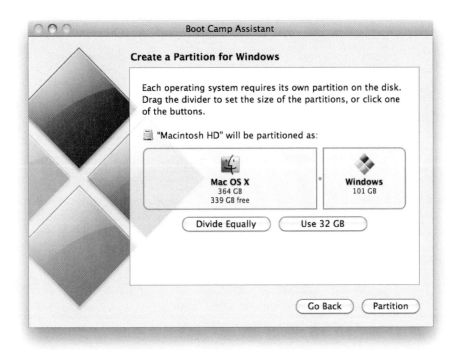

FIGURE 3–11 Partitioning the hard drive

and drag the dot between the two spaces. The iMac described here already contained a single partition using up its entire usable space, but Mac OS X can repartition such a drive, creating two partitions out of one without losing data. Those of us with decades of experience partitioning hard drives in DOS and Windows cringe at partitioning an already fully partitioned drive, but it works.

The next screen prompts you to provide the Windows disc. Once created, the partition appears as another drive device in Finder, as shown here.

The Boot Camp partition appears with other drives under Devices in Finder.

Oracle VirtualBox

Oracle VirtualBox will run on a variety of host operating systems including Windows, Linux, and Mac OS X. Like the other free VM hosting software discussed here, it will run as guest versions of Windows, Linux, and DOS. It will also run on hardware that does not support virtualization.

Once you have downloaded the disk image file, when you are ready to install VirtualBox, simply double-click on the VirtualBox disk icon on the desktop, shown here.

VirtualBox

Download VirtualBox for Mac OS X

You can download VirtualBox for Mac OS X from the VirtualBox Web site. This requires a high-speed broadband connection, but the 30 MB file should take only a minute or two to download. Try this:

1. Point your Web browser to www.virtualbox.org.
2. On the home page locate the Downloads link and click it to navigate to the Downloads page.
3. On the Downloads page locate the link next to the latest version of VirtualBox for OS X Hosts and click on it. This action selects the disk image file (a file with a "dmg" extension) for Mac OS X. (See Figure 3–12 on the next page.)
4. This will first open a dialog box asking if you want to open the file or save it. Select Save File, which will automatically download, showing the progress.
5. You now have a disk image from which to install VirtualBox.

try this!

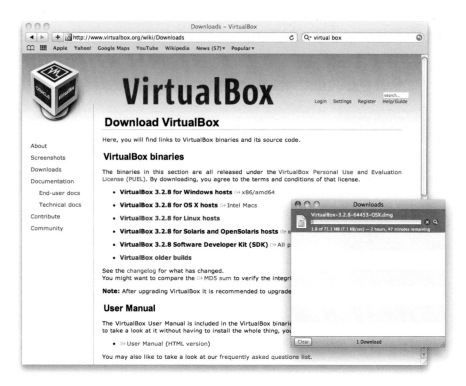

FIGURE 3–12 Downloading VirtualBox

Step-by-Step 3.02

Installing Oracle VirtualBox

Using the file you downloaded in the Try This! or a file provided to you by your instructor, install Oracle VirtualBox. The instructions provided are for installing it into Mac OS X, but the instructions are nearly identical when installing on a Windows PC, although you will work from a downloaded executable or ISO file on a PC, and here we begin with a disk image file (.img). To complete this exercise you will need the following:

- A computer running Mac OS X 10.6 with a minimum of 2 GB of RAM installed.
- The user name and password of an administrator account for this computer (even if you are logged on as an administrator, you will need these credentials to install new software).
- A broadband Internet connection.

Step 1

Locate and double-click the VirtualBox disk image on the desktop. This will open the VirtualBox drive. If you wish to read the documentation, open the UserManual. pdf file. Also, note that the VirtualBox Uninstall tool is located here, for when you decide you do not need this program.

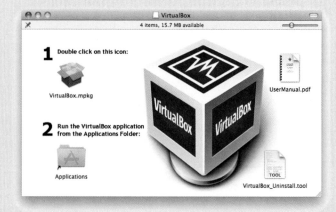

Step 2

To start the VirtualBox installation, double-click on the VirtualBox.mpkg icon. The VirtualBox installation wizard runs. At first it runs a test to verify that the computer can support VirtualBox. Follow the instructions and proceed through the pages, including reading and accepting the software license agreement, after which you can either accept the defaults for a standard install or select a different destination and installation type.

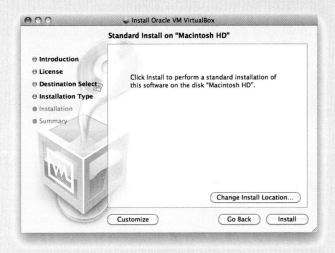

Step 3

In a very short time the installation is complete, and you will find VirtualBox listed in Applications. Launch the program from there to create your first virtual machine from the management console.

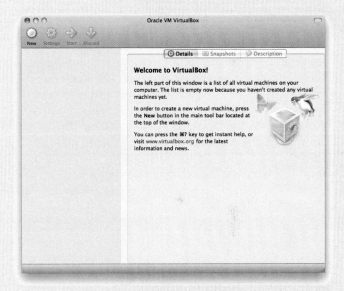

Step 4

Click the blue icon labeled New and the New Virtual Machine Wizard will guide you through the creation of a virtual machine. This process does not require the guest OS, but you do need to know which OS you will install into the virtual machine you are creating. You are simply configuring the machine to accept the guest OS. When prompted to name the virtual machine, use a meaningful name, such as the name and version of the OS you plan to install. Then select the OS you will install and continue.

97

Step 5

On the Memory page select the amount of base memory, initially accepting the default and continuing. On the virtual Hard Disk page ensure that you selected Boot Hard Disk and Create a new hard disk. This will launch the Create New Virtual Disk Wizard. Continue through this wizard, selecting the Dynamically expanding storage type. Continue.

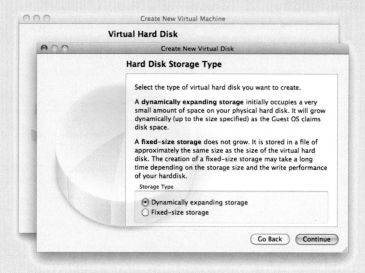

Step 6

On the Virtual Disk Location and Size page accept the defaults because you can come back and modify these settings later—even after you have installed an OS. On the next page you will see a summary of the virtual disk settings. Confirm that these are correct and click the Done button to complete the creation of the virtual disk. Then, you will see another summary page for all the settings for this virtual machine. Confirm the settings and click Done.

Step 7

The console will appear with your new virtual machine, ready for the installation of the OS.

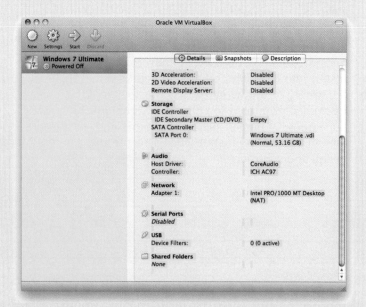

Click Start to begin installing the OS into this virtual machine (providing you have the installation files on disk or in an ISO image). This will launch the First Run Wizard, which will guide you through the process of beginning the installation of your OS.

Secure the virtual machine. Assign a strong password to any user account you create within the guest OS, then update the OS with all security updates, and install antivirus and other security software.

After you install an OS you will probably be disappointed in how the desktop appears within the virtual machine and you may notice that certain features, such as the network adapter, do not function. This is because all hypervisors require that you install additional programs and drivers for the OS to appear and to work well in the VM. Called VirtualBox Guest Additions, you will receive many reminders to install them. VirtualBox allows you to run them from within the VM, launching the setup program from the Start Menu. Figure 3–13 shows the Welcome box for the VirtualBox Guest Additions Setup

FIGURE 3–13 Install the VirtualBox Guest Additions after installing the guest OS.

FIGURE 3–14 VirtualBox with several virtual machines

Wizard. Follow the instruction to install these necessary tools for the virtual machine.

You can create multiple virtual machines in VirtualBox, and launch and manage them from the console, as Figure 3–14 shows.

Chapter 3 REVIEW

Chapter Summary

After reading this chapter and completing the exercises, you should understand the following facts about desktop virtualization.

Virtualization Overview

- There are many types of virtualization today, such as virtual worlds, storage virtualization, network virtualization, server virtualization, and desktop virtualization—the subject of this chapter.
- Virtualization had its roots in the dumb terminal-mainframe systems of the 1960s and the terminal service-terminal client systems of the 1990s.
- Today's virtual desktops can be hosted on network servers or on PCs.
- A hypervisor, or virtual machine monitor (VMM), is the software that emulates the necessary hardware on which an operating system runs.
- A Type I hypervisor (a "bare-metal hypervisor") runs directly on a computer without an underlying host operating system.
- A Type II hypervisor requires a host operating system.
- The major sources of hypervisors are Citrix, VMware, Parallels, Microsoft, and Oracle.

Desktop VMs on Windows Desktops

- There are both commercial and free Type II hypervisors for running Linux, DOS, or Windows on a Windows desktop computer.
- Microsoft Virtual PC 2007 is free and will run on any computer running Windows XP or newer versions of Windows, and it supports Windows, Linux, and DOS guests without requiring hardware-assisted virtualization.

- Windows XP Mode is a free hypervisor that installs on a Windows 7 host with a Windows XP guest preinstalled. It does not require hardware-assisted virtualization.
- The free Windows Virtual PC requires both Windows 7 and hardware-assisted virtualization. Use the Hardware-Assisted Virtualization Detection Tool to test your computer before you download one of these solutions.
- VMware has several commercial hypervisor products. Download and install the trial version of VMware player to temporarily test this product before buying it.
- Oracle VirtualBox is free and runs on several hosts including versions of Windows, Linux, and Mac OS X. It will run on hardware that does not support virtualization.

Desktop VMs on Mac OS X

- You have several choices for hypervisors for Mac OS X that will run versions of Windows and Linux.
- Apple Boot Camp is not actually a hypervisor so much as a dual boot option that allows you to dual boot between Mac OS X and Windows. This gives each OS full use of the hardware, but only one can be loaded at a time.
- Oracle VirtualBox is a free hypervisor and will run versions of Windows, Linux, and DOS on hardware that does not support virtualization.
- Parallels is a commercial hypervisor product for Apple and other hosts, mentioned, but not detailed in this chapter.

Key Terms List

application virtualization *(81)*

desktop virtualization *(80)*

dumb terminal *(81)*

guest OS *(82)*

host key *(84)*

host OS *(82)*

hypervisor *(82)*

network virtualization *(80)*

server virtualization *(80)*

storage virtualization *(80)*

terminal client *(81)*

terminal services *(81)*

thin client *(81)*

Type I hypervisor *(82)*

Type II hypervisor *(82)*

virtual desktop infrastructure (VDI) *(82)*

virtual machine *(81)*

virtual machine monitor (VMM) *(82)*

virtual world *(80)*

virtualization *(80)*

Key Terms Quiz

Use the Key Terms List to complete the sentences that follow. Not all terms will be used.

1. The software layer that emulates the necessary hardware on which an operating system runs is a/an _____.

2. When a network address space exists within two or more physical networks, it is called _____.

3. Many organizations use _____ in which many networked hard drives are seen as one to the client computers.

4. _____ is the creation of an environment that seems real.

5. When you run one desktop OS within another operating system, this type of virtualization is called _____.

6. In the 1960s, a/an _____ was the very simple interface device to a mainframe computer.

7. In the 1990s, you would expect to use _____ software on a PC to connect to a specialized server or minicomputer.

8. A/an _____ is a low-cost PC, usually without such common peripherals as diskette drives (now gone from most PCs), expansion slots, and optical drives, and is used to connect to a special environment on a server that could be simply a partition or a virtual machine.

9. In desktop or server virtualization, the software emulation of all hardware with which an operating system must interface is a/an _____.

10. Second Life is an example of a/an _____.

Multiple-Choice Quiz

1. In which type of virtualization does a user connect to a server and work within a program, without an entire virtualized desktop environment?
   a. Storage virtualization
   b. Application virtualization
   c. Terminal service
   d. Thin client
   e. Virtual world

2. What term describes the hosting and management of multiple virtual desktops on network servers?
   a. Thin client
   b. Terminal services
   c. Minicomputers
   d. Virtual desktop infrastructure (VDI)
   e. Partitioning

3. Which of the following does not require a host OS?
   a. Type II hypervisor
   b. Type I hypervisor
   c. Virtual PC 2007
   d. Windows Virtual PC
   e. Windows XP Mode

4. What term has two definitions that have been described in this book—first, as the space reserved for a terminal session on a mainframe or minicomputer, and, second, as a portion of a physical disk allocated for use by a file system?
   a. Thin client
   b. Virtual machine
   c. Client
   d. Host
   e. Partition

5. What type of hypervisor would you install on a Windows host OS?
   a. Type II
   b. Type I
   c. Boot Camp
   d. A bare-metal hypervisor
   e. A dual-boot hypervisor

6. If you wanted to run Windows XP on an iMac with OS X 10.6, which option would give you the best performance?
   a. Windows XP Mode
   b. Virtual PC 2007
   c. VirtualBox
   d. Parallels
   e. Apple Boot Camp

7. Which free hypervisor, studied in this chapter, runs on Windows, Mac OS X, and Linux OSs?
   a. Virtual PC 2007
   b. Windows Virtual PC
   c. VirtualBox
   d. Apple Boot Camp
   e. Windows XP Mode

8. You upgraded your four-year-old PC to Windows 7 and you would like to install a hypervisor so that you can run and test Linux applications. A test shows that your computer does not support hardware-assisted virtualization. Which of the following can you install on the PC that will work for your purposes?
   a. Windows XP Mode
   b. Windows Virtual PC
   c. Virtual PC 2007
   d. Boot Camp
   e. VDI

9. Which of the following solutions should you select if you wish to run a Windows guest on Mac OS X 10.6, but you need frequent access to both the host and guest OSs?
   a. Windows XP Mode
   b. Windows Virtual PC
   c. VirtualBox
   d. Boot Camp
   e. Virtual PC 2007

10. Which of the following will release the mouse from the control of a virtual machine?
   a. Guest key
   b. Host key
   c. Host OS
   d. VDI
   e. Terminal service

11. Which of the following is synonymous with hypervisor?
   a. Terminal service
   b. Bare metal
   c. Virtual hard drive
   d. Virtual machine
   e. Virtual machine monitor (VMM)

12. Your PC has an AMD processor installed that includes AMD-V technology and the motherboard fully supports this processor. Which is the most capable version of a Microsoft hypervisor you can install on this machine, provided the computer has all the requirements?
   a. VirtualBox
   b. Windows Virtual PC
   c. Windows XP Mode
   d. Microsoft Virtual PC 2007
   e. Parallels

13. What legal issue must you consider when installing a guest OS in a hypervisor?
   a. Copyright of guest OS
   b. Antivirus
   c. Licensing of guest OS
   d. Guest key
   e. Supplying security credentials

14. After downloading VirtualBox to an iMac with Mac OS X 10.6, which of the following is the name of the object you should double-click to install VirtualBox on your computer?
   a. VirtualBox.mpkg
   b. VirtualBox.iso
   c. VirtualBox.exe
   d. VirtualBox.pdf
   e. VM.bat

15. Which of the following is a multi-boot option for running Windows as a second OS on a Mac OS X 10.6 computer?
   a. VirtualBox
   b. Windows Virtual PC
   c. Windows XP Mode
   d. Boot Camp
   e. Parallels

Essay Quiz

1. What is the purpose of each the two most important files created by a Type II hypervisor when preparing a new virtual machine?
2. Explain the significance of the Intel VT-x and AMD Virtualization architecture extensions.
3. Explain why an IT person would want to use a Type II hypervisor on a desktop computer.
4. Why is there (at this writing) no hypervisor for running Mac OS X on a Windows PC?
5. You have Windows XP Mode installed on your Windows 7 computer, and you would like to do a side-by-side comparison of Windows XP Mode and Windows XP in a VirtualBox VM. What precautions should you take and how many computers are required for this comparison?

Lab Projects

LAB PROJECT 3.1

Find out how virtualization is being used in an organization in your area. Arrange an interview with an IT manager, network engineer, or other knowledgeable IT staff person from an organization in your area. Consider approaching someone at a regional hospital or medical clinic because privacy laws require that they meet certain minimum standards in IT, and they often have the best IT staff in a community. Ask if they are using virtualization, and if so, what type? What are their future plans for virtualization? Report your findings to your classmates.

LAB PROJECT 3.2

If you installed a hypervisor on your computer, find another one that will run on your OS. Uninstall the first one without removing the virtual machines created for that hypervisor; install the second one. Compare the similarities and differences. Will the new hypervisor work with the virtual machines you created with the first one? Decide which one you prefer working with. If it is the second, then keep it; if you preferred the first one, uninstall the second and reinstall the first.

LAB PROJECT 3.3

Find out the latest about Type I and Type II hypervisors. Browse the Internet using the keyword *virtualization* and watching for recent articles and news releases. Consider turning on Google alerts with the key term *virtualization*. Watch the number of alerts you receive over just a period of a few days.

4

Disk Operating System (DOS) and the Command-Line Interface

"I've noticed lately that the paranoid fear of computers becoming intelligent and taking over the world has almost entirely disappeared from the common culture. Near as I can tell, this coincides with the release of MS-DOS."

—Larry DeLuca

Quoted by Ian Godman at www.ecademy.com

W ho cares about DOS? Why should you need to learn about an operating system created 30 years ago and used with the very first PCs? Because some organizations still have DOS applications lurking somewhere that they can't or won't replace with newer applications. Because some devices (specialized computers) actually still use DOS. Because Windows, Mac OS X, and Linux OSs still have a DOS-like command-line interface (CLI) for running text-based utilities. And because all of these operating systems have certain administrative utility programs that are available only from a CLI. Developing command-line skills with DOS—any version—will increase your comfort level with a non-GUI interface anywhere you encounter one. Therefore, familiarity with the DOS CLI will prepare you for working with a variety of OSs.

In this chapter your exploration of DOS begins with an overview and brief history of DOS. Then you'll consider reasons DOS is still in use today

Learning Outcomes

In this chapter you will learn how to:

LO **4.1** Identify the versions of DOS, its strengths, weaknesses, and why it is still in use.

LO **4.2** Install DOS on a physical or virtual machine, and create a live CD.

LO **4.3** Work with the DOS command prompt for file management and other tasks.

LO **4.4** Understand the DOS boot-up process.

LO **4.5** Troubleshoot common DOS problems.

and look at the features and limits of DOS OSs. You'll install DOS on your lab computer—either directly or in a virtual machine. If neither of these is practical, you will learn how to create a FreeDOS live CD. You'll practice file management tasks in DOS as you create, copy, move, and delete files and directories. Finally, you'll study the DOS boot-up process.

LO 4.1 | DOS Basics

In this section, you will learn what DOS is, the versions of DOS for PCs, its strengths, and its weaknesses.

What Is DOS?

DOS, short for Disk Operating System, is a single-user/single-tasking operating system. Its name comes from its support of disks—something that is assumed with today's desktop OSs, but a fairly new idea during the emergence of the personal computer in the late 1970s and early 1980s. Many operating systems were called disk operating systems, but from about 1981 into the new millennium, the term "DOS" was most often applied to DOS from Microsoft. In this chapter we will use the term to apply to DOS for PCs, regardless of the version or source of the OS.

DOS has a simple command-line interface, called the **DOS prompt**, that accepts only text (non-graphical) input and produces only text output. This includes alphabet characters, numeric characters, a few math symbols, and special characters. Some would argue that you can create primitive graphics in DOS with special *extended* characters—lines, double-lines, and corners. With these characters you can draw boxes around text, but they are still individual characters that each take up a fixed space, just as the alphanumeric text characters do. For our purposes, we will refer to all the characters available at a command line as "text."

DOS and Linux do not have integrated GUIs, but you can add a GUI shell to either DOS or Linux, in which case, the shell runs "on top" of the OS and is not integrated into the OS. The limits of DOS as a real-mode OS also limit its ability to support a sophisticated GUI shell.

The following is a brief history of DOS, as seen through a discussion of various versions of DOS.

Versions of DOS

Let's look at a few of the various versions of DOS—past and present.

MS-DOS

Many versions of DOS have been used in the three decades since the introduction of the IBM PC. The most commonly used versions of DOS in the 1980s and 1990s came from Microsoft. First there was PC DOS, which Microsoft licensed to IBM for personal computer (PC) products, beginning with the IBM PC in 1981. Later Microsoft licensed DOS as MS-DOS to many other PC manufacturers, often customized and then sold under that company's name as an original equipment manufacturer (OEM) product. IBM sold an OEM version of DOS as PC DOS, Compaq sold an OEM version as Compaq MS-DOS, and many other manufacturers sold versions as well.

The first version of DOS that Microsoft sold as a non-OEM retail product was MS-DOS 5.0. Microsoft no longer offers a DOS product; its last retail version was MS-DOS version 6.22, released in 1994.

> Although Microsoft no longer sells MS-DOS 6.22, many organizations still have licenses for it, and you may encounter it. For this reason, we use MS-DOS 6.22 in many examples in this chapter, and we also use FreeDOS, a free version you can download and use for many of the exercises.

Use the DOS VER command, shown here, to determine the version of DOS. You can also use this command from the Windows command prompt to display the version of Windows. In Windows XP select Start | Run, and type "cmd" (without quotes) to open the command line DOS-like interface. In Windows 7, click on the Windows icon in the lower left corner and in the "Search programs or files" dialog box type "cmd" (without quotes) and press the ENTER key. When the command line window opens, type "ver" at the prompt and press the ENTER key. The system will return the version of your operating system on the following line and the command prompt will display for more input.

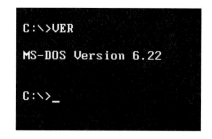

The VER command

PC DOS

IBM continued to offer new versions of PC DOS through PC DOS 2000, released in 1998. They ended defect support for this product January 31, 2001, meaning that it would no longer provide patches or improvements. This and older versions of PC DOS are not available through IBM but may be found at other retail sources. The last versions of PC DOS could install on any Microsoft/Intel compatible computer.

> **Finding the Version Number of DOS**
>
> If you have DOS installed on either a physical or virtual machine, you can discover the version number by using a command that is common in most DOS versions. Try this:
>
> 1. At the DOS prompt, type **ver** and press ENTER. The version information should appear on the screen.
> 2. What version are you running? _____

try this!

DR-DOS

In 1987, Digital Research introduced DR-DOS, a DOS product especially for the IBM PC and compatible market. Novell acquired Digital Research in 1991 and briefly offered DR-DOS (then referred to as Novell DOS). DR-DOS has since changed hands several more times—first to Caldera, then to Lineo, and finally to DeviceLogics in 2002. Lineo updated it to DR-DOS 7.03, adding support for use in ROM or flash memory. DeviceLogics, founded with the goal of offering DOS as a solution for embedded products, brought out a trial release of DR-DOS 8, but they never did a full-scale release. They continue to offer the 7.03 version.

> If you do not have access to a running version of DOS, and you do have a Windows computer, you will find that most of the commands in this chapter are available from the Windows command prompt. Simply open a command prompt and try these commands. Just don't call the Windows command prompt DOS, because it is not DOS any more than Linux is DOS! In Windows the command prompt is simply a command-line interface to a 32-bit or 64-bit OS.

DOS for Free

You can get some versions of DOS without charge. One of these is FreeDOS, distributed under the GNU GPL. GNU (pronounced "guh new") is a project that began many years ago at MIT with the goal of distributing free, open software. People may modify the software, as long as they freely share their modifications with others. This is the GNU General Public License, or GNU GPL. FreeDOS is 100 percent compatible with MS-DOS, but it supports the FAT32 file system. Learn more about FreeDOS at **www.freedos.org**. Later we'll describe how to download FreeDOS and install or run it from an optical disc.

> While IBM no longer offers PC DOS as a retail product, there have been sightings of it in the wild, including a recent Amazon.com listing, with a packaged CD labeled "PC DOS." Only two were available.

DOS Strengths

DOS has lasted for so many years for two reasons: It works with applications written specifically for DOS, and it requires a very small amount of memory. We'll discuss both of these reasons.

DOS for Backward Compatibility

Some people use DOS because they still have special legacy applications that require it. Legacy applications are those written for an older operating system. Take Sophie, for instance. She recently bought a small picture-framing business that included an old PC that uses DOS and an application program that computes frame prices. The program takes the dimensions of a picture and calculates the amount of mat and frame needed. When prices for her supplies change, she can go into the program and enter the new prices. She likes the program and she feels that it works well. However, when her current computer finally wears out, Sophie should consider an alternative to her DOS-based program, since she is dealing with visual arts products. She will find that computer prices have come down, power has gone up, and there are more application choices, even in her field of picture framing.

"Working well" should not be the sole reason for using DOS as the operating system for this application because all versions of Windows can run DOS applications. How well a DOS application runs in Windows depends on how the programmer wrote it—and therein lies the problem. If the application program requests operating system services in a standard way, then it should run in Windows much as it does under DOS, although you may need to make some accommodations in the compatibility settings for newer versions of Windows. If the application requests services in a nonstandard way (bypassing the operating system), then two outcomes are possible: It may either run under Windows much more slowly, or it may not run at all! The best practice is to test your DOS application in Windows before giving up your DOS computer.

> Because DOS was slow at accessing hardware and programmers wanted to make their applications run faster, they wrote many, if not most, DOS applications to request services from the hardware in nonstandard ways.

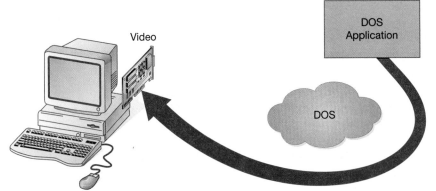

Video

An application "reaching around" DOS to access hardware directly

DOS When You Need a Small OS

Another reason DOS is still around is that it is much more compact than Windows OSs and therefore is useful when you need a very small operating system for embedded systems. Embedded systems are ROM-based operating systems running on a computer embedded in a device such as a handheld computer or a smart kitchen appliance. Although Microsoft offers scaled-down versions of Windows for embedded systems that require a sophisticated GUI interface, DOS is a candidate for embedded systems that do not require such an interface.

Lou, who works at a large sporting goods retailer, showed us an interesting use of embedded DOS. This company uses handheld scanning devices to take inventory. Each scanner is a small computer running embedded DOS and, as you can see in Figure 4–1, each scanner has a tiny screen and a keypad to allow users to work in the inventory application and to enter DOS commands. Both DOS and the application are stored on ROM and loaded into only 640KB of RAM when the device power is on. The device scans the Universal Product Codes (UPCs) on in-store inventory and communicates wirelessly with the store's computerized inventory systems.

The small size of DOS is also attractive because the files required to load DOS into memory (the boot files) easily fit on a 3.5-inch floppy disk or a thumb drive called a boot drive, leaving plenty of room for additional files, such as device drivers and utilities. This ability makes DOS popular as an OS for the software tools used by computer technicians and other computer professionals.

> Any storage device from which an operating system can start up is a boot drive.

A device driver, as described in Chapter 1, is a special program that works with an OS to allow use of a particular piece of hardware, such as a mouse or optical drive. A utility is a program that allows you to perform handy tasks, usually computer management functions or diagnostics such as upgrading the program in your computer's ROM-BIOS or looking for errors on your disk. A utility differs from an application, which is software that allows you to perform useful functions and create results you can use in your personal or business life, such as writing a report or calculating a budget.

Assuming you have a computer with a floppy disk drive, you can also use a DOS boot drive to help install a new operating system if the installation files for the new operating system are located on a file server computer on the company network. In that case, you need to use a start-up disk with special network drivers to boot up the computer and connect it to the file server. Once it is connected, you can run the installation program for the new operating system over the network and install it on the local hard drive.

DOS Weaknesses

DOS has significant user interface, processor mode, memory, multitasking, and hard disk usage limitations. We'll discuss each in turn.

User Interface Limits

The DOS user interface is a challenge to work with, especially for a generation accustomed to a more intuitive GUI interface. To launch programs and perform file management tasks at the CLI, the user must learn and memorize cryptic commands.

DOS processor mode limitations are actually the cause of the memory and multitasking limitations. This is because they wrote DOS for the Intel 8088 processor and the computer architecture (design) of the original IBM PC. The 8088 processor had a limited bag of tricks because it had only one mode of operation—real mode, in which only 1 MB of addresses is available for both RAM and ROM, and it can complete only one task at a time. DOS only understands how to work in real mode. Other than DOS, the OSs discussed

in this book are capable of using the more advanced protected mode of modern processors that allow the processor and the OSs to access vast amounts of memory addresses. This mode also supports multitasking, a basic feature of today's Windows, OS X, and Linux OSs.

FIGURE 4–1 A handheld inventory scanner
Photo courtesy of Intermec

To work with any version of DOS beyond the introduction provided in this chapter requires a commitment of time and effort. You will need to research command usages and memorize cryptic commands.

DOS Memory Limitations

MS-DOS can access only 1 MB of address space. The processor uses each address in the address space to access a location in RAM or ROM.

```
A:\>dir /w
 Volume in drive A has no label.
 Volume Serial Number is 0000-0000

 Directory of A:\

COMMAND.COM    NOSTACK.COM   ZCOM.EXE      KEYBUS.COM    KEYBUK.COM
KEYBSP.COM     KEYBIT.COM    KEYBFR.COM    KEYBSW.COM    KEYBGR.COM
KEYBDA.COM     KEYBNO.COM    KEYBCHF.COM   KEYBCHG.COM   KEYBGK.COM
CONFIG.SYS     AUTOEXEC.BAT  SETUP.EXE     ASSIGN.COM    CHKDSK.COM
DEBUG.COM      SELECT.COM    EXE2BIN.EXE   FIND.EXE      PRINT.COM
RECOVER.COM    SHARE.EXE     SYS.COM       FORMAT.COM    SORT.EXE
GRAFTABL.COM   LABEL.COM     JOIN.EXE      SUBST.EXE     MORE.COM
REPLACE.EXE    APPEND.COM    XCOPY.EXE     DISKCOPY.COM  DISKCOMP.COM
CONFIGUR.COM   DSKSETUP.COM  MODE.COM      SEARCH.COM    APPLY.COM
TREE.COM       COMP.COM      SHIP.COM      ANSI.SYS      DRIVER.SYS
ATTRIB.EXE     EDLIN.COM     FC.EXE        GRAPHICS.COM  UDISK.SYS
ZCACHE.SYS     EMM.SYS       PART.EXE      PREP.EXE      DETECT.COM
ASGNPART.COM   BOOTF.COM     ZSPOOL.COM    RTCLOCK.COM   BACKUP.COM
RESTORE.COM    LINK.EXE      LIB.EXE
        68 File(s)        623,312 bytes
         0 Dir(s)         766,976 bytes free
```

A directory listing of a DOS boot drive with 68 files—many being handy utilities and programs—that take up less than half the available space!

Further, the architecture of the PC allows only the first 640 KB of this for the RAM used as the workspace for the operating system and the application programs and data. We call this 640 KB of memory conventional memory. The remaining 384 KB of addresses is reserved for the system BIOS and the RAM and ROM used on adapters, such as the video adapter and network cards.

Figure 4–2 shows the result of using the DOS MEM command to look at memory usage on a computer with 16 MB of physical memory. It shows that

```
C:\>MEM

Memory Type         Total  =   Used  +   Free
----------------    -------    -------    -------
Conventional         638K       65K       573K
Upper                  0K        0K         0K
Reserved               0K        0K         0K
Extended (XMS)     15,360K    15,360K       0K
                  --------    -------    -------
Total memory       15,998K    15,425K     573K

Total under 1 MB     638K       65K       573K

Largest executable program size     573K  (587,088 bytes)
Largest free upper memory block       0K       (0 bytes)

C:\>_
```

FIGURE 4–2 The MEM command shows DOS memory usage

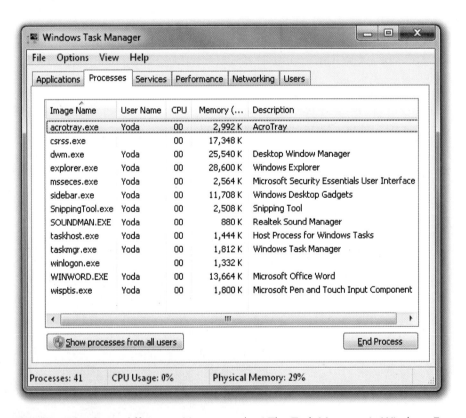

FIGURE 4–3 What a difference 20 years makes! The Task Manager in Windows 7 shows the memory in use by processes (active portions of running programs).

DOS, while still limited to real mode, can use memory more efficiently through special memory management device drivers and through programs that load device drivers and parts of the operating system into the memory areas that DOS by itself cannot use for programs. This leaves more space in the 640 KB of main memory for an application program to use.

the OS is using 65 KB of conventional memory, leaving 573 KB of conventional memory for an application to use. The 15,360 KB of memory shown as extended memory is the physical memory above 1 MB that is not available to DOS. With special drivers added to DOS, certain DOS programs can access this additional memory, but DOS itself is still limited to the first 1 MB of addresses. This is true whether they are for program use or for accessing locations in adapter RAM or ROM. Compare Figure 4–2 with Figure 4–3, which shows the Windows Task Manager on a Windows 7 computer with very few programs running in its 4 GB of RAM memory, but enough to take up nearly a gigabyte of memory!

DOS Multitasking Limits

DOS can't take advantage of the advanced multitasking capabilities of protected mode in the advanced Intel processors. Although DOS can have several drivers and small programs called terminate and stay resident (TSR) programs in memory at one time, it can run only one application program at a time, called single-tasking. The Windows, Linux, and Mac operating systems you will study in this book allow several programs to run in memory at one time, and users can switch among them. This is multitasking, which we introduced as an operating system function in Chapter 1.

DOS Hard Drive Limitations

While not an issue in newer versions of DOS, if you are using MS-DOS on a modern PC you will quickly run into its hard drive limit. MS-DOS 6.22 does not support physical hard drives larger than 7.8 GB. Further, like most OSs, DOS uses logical drives. A logical drive is a portion of a physical hard drive that appears to be a drive with a letter assigned to it. A logical drive resides within a partition, a term we described in Chapter 1 as an area of disk allocated for file storage. You can have one or more logical drives on a physical drive, but MS-DOS can only use logical drives that are each 2 GB or less and within the 7.8 GB total space limit.

LO 4.2 | Installing DOS

Now that you are familiar with the strengths and weaknesses of DOS, you are ready to install DOS on a PC. In this section you will learn the hardware requirements for DOS and the preparation needed before installing it. Then you'll have an opportunity to install DOS onto a hard drive.

DOS Hardware Requirements

One of the strong points of DOS is that it can run on the most minimal of PCs—anything from an original 8088-based PC to one of today's lightning-fast PCs. Therefore, the hardware requirements for DOS are very small. All you need is a personal computer that complies with the old IBM PC standards or one of its Microsoft/Intel descendants.

Following are general DOS hardware requirements for MS-DOS 6.22 and IBM PC DOS 2000, and you can consider these minimum requirements for other versions of DOS:

- An Intel/Microsoft standard PC.
- 6 MB of free hard disk space for the DOS utilities, if installing onto a hard disk.
- 512 KB of memory.

Preparing for DOS Installation

To do a clean install of DOS on a computer hard disk, you must commit to losing any other operating system on the disk. You do not have to prepare the computer hard disk before the installation because the DOS setup program can prepare it. Preparation of a hard disk is a two-step process: the first step is to create a partition, and the second step is to format that partition (we defined partition in Chapter 1). The space within a partition contains one or more logical drives. A logical drive is an area within a partition that an operating system views as a disk drive with a letter assigned to it. (Because this drive is not a physical entity, we use the term *logical* to describe the drive.) The OS must format these logical drives with a file system, such as FAT16, before data can be stored on them. The storage space on a physical hard disk is either a single logical drive, given the letter *C:* when it is the first logical drive on the first hard disk system in a computer, or it can be subdivided into multiple logical drives (for example, C:, D:, E:, and so on).

Partitioning a Hard Disk in DOS

A hard disk comes, fresh from the factory, with its disk space divided into concentric tracks, each of which is divided into equal-sized sectors, often referred to as the physical format of the disk. Each sector has a capacity of 512 bytes. The first physical sector on a hard disk is the master boot record (MBR). Within this sector lies the 64-byte partition table, which a disk-partitioning program uses to define the partition boundaries for that hard disk.

Most operating systems include the partitioning step in a menu-driven process of their installation programs, so that anyone who can answer a few simple questions can at least succeed in creating a partition on which to install the OS. Most people do not fully understand the basics of partitioning, but for some IT jobs this is core knowledge.

Partitioning Programs

While most operating systems include disk partitioning in their setup process, disk-partitioning programs come with most operating systems and you can use them after installing the OS to create additional partitions when you add a new physical drive. FDISK is the one that comes with DOS. FreeDOS has both a basic FDISK program and an extended FDISK program named XFDISK. Regardless of the version of DOS, the documentation may refer to its partitioning program as "FDISK" no matter the actual name of the executable file. Let's look at the basics of hard disk partitioning with FDISK in MS-DOS.

Partitioning with FDISK

Beginning with MS-DOS version 4.0, FDISK can partition hard disks up to 4 GB in size, but DOS's native FAT16 file system does not support this partition size because it is limited to a maximum size of 2 GB per partition. Because of this fact, if you are using MS-DOS, a hard disk between 2 GB and 4 GB in size must be broken down into multiple partitions, each of which does not exceed 2 GB. FDISK can create two types of partitions: primary and extended. A primary partition can contain only one logical drive (C:, D:, and so on), which uses the entire space of the primary partition, while an extended partition can contain one or more logical drives, each of which can use a portion of the partition. FDISK can create only two partitions on a physical drive; only one can be primary, and one can be extended. MS-DOS will boot from a primary partition, but not from an extended partition. Further, a primary partition must be marked as "active" by the FDISK program to be bootable. The first hard disk system in a PC being prepared for the installation of MS-DOS must have a primary partition.

> While MS-DOS 6.22 is limited to the FAT12 and FAT16 file systems, FreeDOS supports these file systems, as well as the FAT32 file system, which is the default file system it will create if you run the installation program that comes with FreeDOS 1.0 Final.

> This discussion applies only to standard MS-DOS. Some OEM versions of MS-DOS, as well as third-party DOS operating systems, have partitioning programs that can create more than one primary DOS partition, and they may create larger partitions as well as partition types beyond those discussed here.

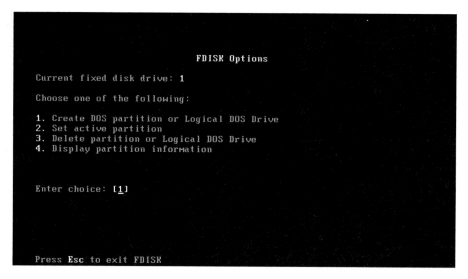

```
                         FDISK Options

Current fixed disk drive: 1

Choose one of the following:

  1. Create DOS partition or Logical DOS Drive
  2. Set active partition
  3. Delete partition or Logical DOS Drive
  4. Display partition information


Enter choice: [1]




Press Esc to exit FDISK
```

FIGURE 4–4 The FDISK Options menu displays the main operations you can perform.

The FDISK program is menu-driven. Figure 4–4 shows the MS-DOS FDISK menu for selecting options. If you were preparing a new unpartitioned hard disk for use, you would first boot from a DOS startup disk that contains the FDISK and FORMAT programs. You would run FDISK, selecting option 1, which would display a menu from which you could choose to create a primary or extended partition, or to create a logical drive on an extended partition (required only for extended partitions). You would select to create a primary partition; then you would follow the instructions, return to this main FDISK options menu, and select option 2, Set Active Partition (or it will not be bootable). Then, after a reboot, you run the DOS FORMAT command like so: FORMAT C: /S. This will format C: and install the DOS system files (discussed later). You cannot use a partitioned hard drive until you have formatted it.

Once the system has formatted a hard disk, reboot and run the FDISK command. Now you can select option 4, Display Partition Information, and see the partition information, as Figure 4–5 shows.

WARNING!

You should use a partitioning program only after learning how it works. For the first hard drive in a computer, the safest way to partition a hard disk is from the setup program during the installation of an operating system because it will include a menu-driven section that will guide you through the disk partitioning process.

```
                 Display Partition Information

Current fixed disk drive: 1

Partition  Status   Type   Volume Label   Mbytes   System   Usage
  C: 1       A    PRI DOS   MS-DOS_6        2047    FAT16     50%



Total disk space is 4087 Mbytes (1 Mbyte = 1048576 bytes)





Press Esc to continue_
```

FIGURE 4–5 The FDISK Display Partition Information displays the partitioning information for a hard disk.

FreeDOS

It's difficult to find a legal copy of MS-DOS, but there are other options for working with non-Microsoft DOS OSs. One is FreeDOS. We will provide instructions for downloading, installing, and working with FreeDOS with the warning that it is free software that changes, and that installing it can be a challenge. We will use both MS-DOS and FreeDOS in the discussions that follow.

Downloading FreeDOS

If you would like to download FreeDOS, point your browser to www.freedos .org, and, to access the download page, click on the link labeled Download FreeDOS. At this writing, you can download either a scaled down 8 MB distribution (fdbasedcd.iso), or a 153 MB distribution (fdfullcd.iso) that includes more utilities and the ability to create a live CD. (A live CD is a CD or DVD from which you can boot an OS without requiring any part of the OS to be resident on a hard disk.)

If you have a broadband connection, we strongly recommend downloading the larger distribution and using the resulting ISO file to create a FreeDOS optical disc. Then you can use this disc to install FreeDOS on a hard disk (or into a VM) or to boot to a live CD version of FreeDOS. Additionally, the larger distribution includes more DOS utilities, and it is the version we use in this chapter. The downside of this larger distribution is that it takes a very long time to load all the utilities during the installation. We decided to install them all; you can choose to be more selective.

FIGURE 4–6 The Virtual PC Console with FreeDOS

Creating a Virtual Machine for FreeDOS

If you would like to install FreeDOS into a virtual machine, or simply run it from a live CD in a virtual machine, prepare a virtual machine following the instructions in Chapter 3. Using Virtual PC, we created a minimally configured virtual machine, selecting first the OS/2 option and then reducing the memory for this VM to 16 MB. We strongly recommend configuring the memory to be smaller than 256 MB because you will receive an error message if you have that much RAM. This will occur if you are installing on either a physical machine or a VM with over 256 MB of RAM. We recommend the minimum your hypervisor will allow, which is why we used 16 MB. Figure 4–6 shows the Virtual PC Console with the FreeDOS virtual machine listed. At this point we had not yet installed FreeDOS, but the listing looks the same as the other virtual machines, which do have OSs installed. Now you are ready to install FreeDOS (or any other version of DOS) into the virtual machine.

Running FreeDOS from a Live CD

Installing FreeDOS is a nontrivial task, so if you would like to avoid some frustration or if you cannot devote a computer to DOS, then simply boot from the FreeDOS disc. We recommend you first create a DOS virtual machine in your hypervisor of choice, then place the FreeDOS disc in the drive and start the virtual machine, which will boot up from the disc. Whether you are doing this on a physical or virtual machine, on the first menu (see Figure 4–7—shown in a VirtualBox VM in Mac OS X) simply press ENTER to select the first option: Continue to boot FreeDOS from the disc. On the second menu (Figure 4–8) select one of the live CD options. This will bring you to a DOS

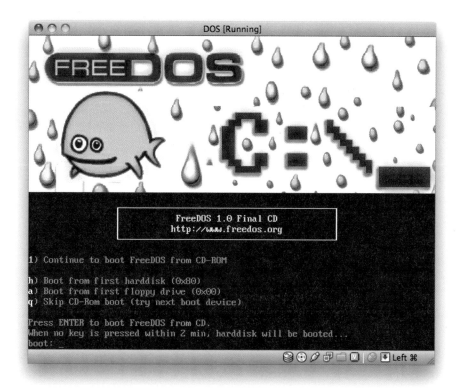

FIGURE 4–7 The initial FreeDOS menu from the Installation/Live CD disc, shown in a VirtualBox VM running in Mac OS X

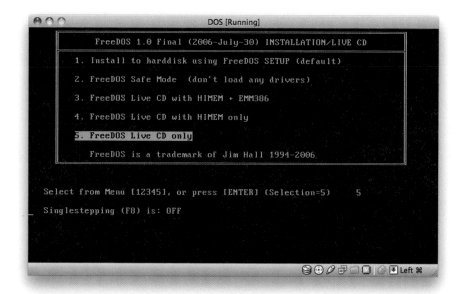

FIGURE 4–8 The second menu from the Installation/Live CD disc. Select one of the live CD options.

prompt (Figure 4–9) that indicates the current drive is A: and is a RAM disk created by FreeDOS.

Once you are at the FreeDOS Live CD DOS prompt, most DOS commands are available to you, and you can do many of the activities in this chapter, including partitioning and formatting a hard drive or virtual hard drive.

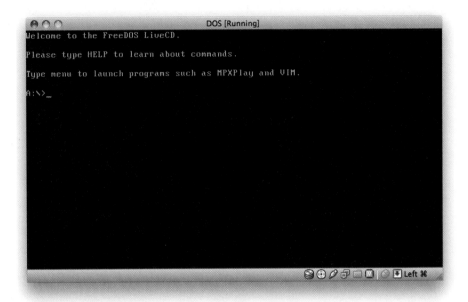

FIGURE 4–9 The FreeDOS Live CD DOS prompt

Installing FreeDOS

Once you have created a virtual machine, or have a physical machine prepared, proceed to Step-by-Step 4.01.

Step-by-Step 4.01
Installing FreeDOS

In the following steps, you will install FreeDOS on a hard disk or into a virtual machine. It will take as long as an hour to do this and you will need to pay close attention to the messages to successfully install FreeDOS. To complete this exercise, you will need the following:

- A Microsoft/Intel standard personal computer (desktop or laptop).
- An unpartitioned hard drive or a virtual machine you have prepared.
- TheFreeDOS disc (created with fdfullcd.iso).

Step 1

Insert the FreeDOS disc into the optical drive. Then, if you are installing this on a physical computer, restart the computer. If you are installing into a virtual machine, open the virtual machine console, select the FreeDOS virtual machine you created, and start the virtual machine from the console. After the computer or VM restarts, the FreeDOS menu screen appears.

Step 2

Press ENTER to boot FreeDOS from disc and proceed with the installation. This will bring up the Installation/Live CD menu. Here you see it inside the Virtual PC 2007 window. Ensure that the selection highlight is on the first choice, *Install to harddisk using FreeDOS Setup (default)*, and press ENTER to begin the installation.

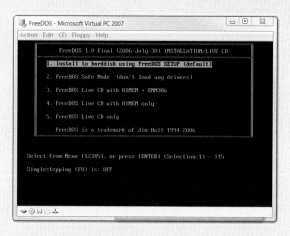

Step 3

Select your language and keyboard layout and press ENTER.

Step 4

Select *Prepare the harddisk for FreeDOS 1.0 Final by running XFdisk* and press ENTER. This starts the eXtended FDisk partitioning program, the FreeDOS equivalent of the MS-DOS FDISK program, although FreeDOS also has an FDISK utility that is a near twin to that of MS-DOS.

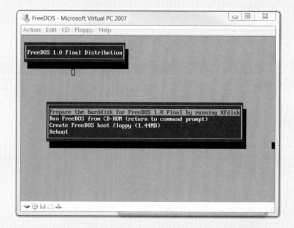

Step 5

Press ENTER to close the XFdisk Options window and accept the defaults in the next two windows by pressing ENTER to accept Primary Partition and, after ensuring that the highlight is on YES, press ENTER again to initialize the partition area.

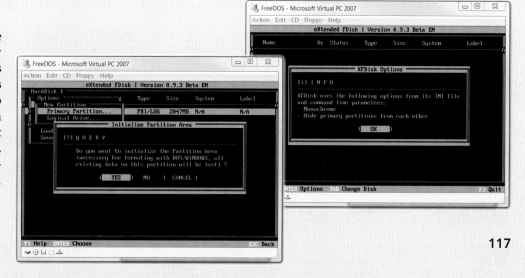

Step 6

Setup will now initialize the partition, after which you will see a message prompting you to format the newly partitioned drive. Move the highlight to *Yes* and press ENTER.

Step 7

Now you see a warning that all data on the nonremovable disk will be lost. If you want the format to proceed, you must *type* YES and press ENTER. Typing a "Y" will result in an error message.

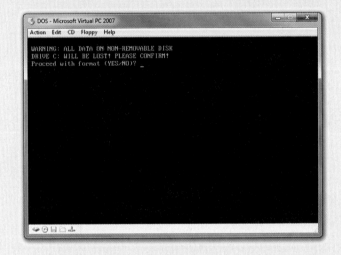

Step 8

After the format is complete, the Setup program will display a menu. Select option 1, *Continue with FreeDOS installation*. On the next page, select yet another option 1, *Start installation of FreeDOS 1.0 Final*.

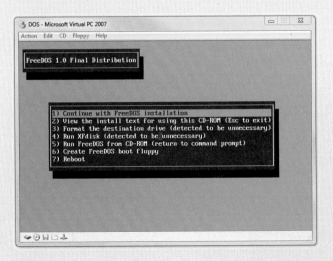

The next screen contains a copyright notice as well as information about the distribution and the license. Press any key to proceed to another screen that asks if you are ready to install and continues: "You should have already created your install floppies, or dumped all the install files into a single directory on your hard disk." If you are using a disc you created with fdfullcd.iso (or the equivalent), all the necessary files are on the disc. Press a key to continue from this screen and press a key to continue on the next screen. The Install program will use the files in the Packages directory. Don't try to change these locations on your first installation.

Press any key to proceed, and a list will display from the first group (the list shown is not the first one). Each list will be different, and you will have the option of moving through the items and clearing the check boxes of the items you do not wish to install. We recommend installing all files the first time you install FreeDOS. Simply move the cursor to Done and press ENTER for each group.

After installing each group of files a message will display, "Done installing this disk series. If you are installing other disk series, please insert disk #1 of the next series in the drive now." If you are installing from disc, ignore the messages to change floppy disks and simply press any key to proceed. You will do this many times during the installation as the setup program continues to find the next group of files and install them. It's confusing, and takes a long time, but hang in there.

119

Step 12

When the FreeDOS Install finishes copying all the files, you will see a black screen with a menu. Select option 8, *Do Not load a packet driver* and press ENTER. You need this only if you plan to connect to a network with this DOS installation.

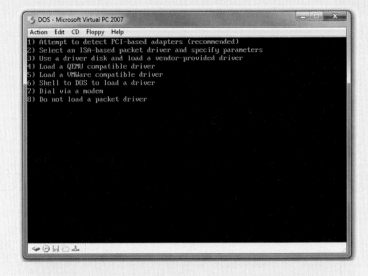

If you see an error message saying that a package conflicts with something, and prompts you to remove it, select *Y* to remove that package. You should eventually see a screen with a menu concerning installing the OpenGEM GUI interface for Free-DOS, as shown here. Select *1* if you wish to install it, after which another message displays about the OpenGEM installation. Press any key to continue, which brings you to the License page. Read the message and press *1* to accept and install OpenGEM. After OpenGEM installs you will see the screen announcing that OpenGEM has installed. Press any key to continue on this screen and again on the following screen.

Step 13

You may have returned to the DOS prompt at this point or, if you installed a packet driver earlier, you will need to respond to prompts concerning installing an e-mail client. We suggest you decline and work your way through these screens until you arrive at a DOS prompt, which signals the end of a successful installation.

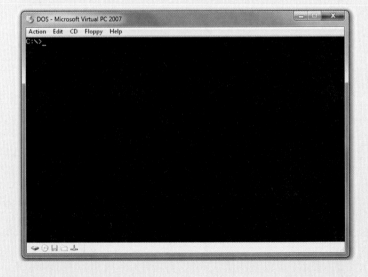

Once FreeDOS is installed, any time the computer (or VM) restarts, and after the BIOS information displays, you will see various messages on the screen, which are the output of special DOS commands that run during start-up, such as drivers and programs loaded from commands in the FDCONFIG.SYS and AUTOEXEC.BAT files. The last line displayed will be a DOS prompt (also called the command prompt), which consists of, at minimum, the drive letter followed by a blinking cursor, indicating that the command interpreter is open for business. If you type at your keyboard, the characters will display at the cursor. Our FreeDOS installation is configured to show the current drive, the current directory, and the greater than (>) sign.

LO 4.3 | Working with the DOS Command Prompt

To work with DOS you need to know how to successfully run commands at the DOS prompt. You also need to become proficient with the handful of DOS commands that are the most useful for managing directories and files. We'll discuss each in turn.

Success at the DOS Prompt

Up to this point, you may have done a few things at the command prompt without much instruction. Were you successful, or did you receive confusing error messages? Success at the DOS prompt means correctly entering commands and getting the results you desired. Before you can achieve either of these goals you need to understand how DOS interprets a command and how DOS locates a program called up from the command prompt. You must also discover which command will accomplish the task you have in mind, determine the correct syntax for that command, and understand how to correctly enter a command at the command prompt. Finally, you must learn how to use DOS operators with certain DOS commands.

How Does DOS Interpret a Command?

You might type a command such as **dir** at the command prompt, which is only the name of a command (which DOS will use to find the command). Or, you might type a command that includes both the command name and instructions to the command, as in **dir a: /a**. In any case, what you enter at the command prompt is interpreted by a special component of your OS called the command interpreter, which, in both MS-DOS and FreeDOS, is COMMAND .COM. This component receives commands, finds the actual program code for the command, loads the program code into memory, and passes any additional instructions (such as the **a: /a**) to the command.

Some commands have no additional instructions, such as the VER command, which only displays the DOS version and does nothing else, but most DOS commands have many instructions you can use. The list of such commands is quite long, but they include DEL, COPY, REN, and XCOPY. Many commands will not work without additional instructions. Figure 4–10 shows the screen output in MS-DOS after running all the commands listed in the preceding sentence without any command parameters. Notice that only the VER command works successfully without any further instructions.

Let's look at this process more closely. When you type something into the command line and press ENTER, the DOS command interpreter kicks into action behind the scenes. It takes what you entered at the command line and

FIGURE 4–10 Parameter error messages

parses it. In this context, parse means to divide the command into its components and determine the meaning of the command. The DOS command interpreter parses your entry based on special delimiter characters. The most important delimiter character to remember is the space character (the result of pressing the space bar). When parsing a command line we call the components parameters. For instance, **dir a: /a** has three parameters: **dir**, **a:**, and **/a**. The first parameter must be the command; the other parameters must be valid parameters that the command understands. A parameter that begins with a forward slash (/) is called a switch.

How Is a Program Found and Loaded?

The next job for the DOS command interpreter is to load the command named at the beginning of the command line. DOS looks for the command by searching in some special places. Let's say you entered the command CHKDSK. You have not provided a file name extension with the command (which is quite normal), so DOS will first check its own list of internal commands. These commands reside within COMMAND.COM and are not stored as separate files on disk. If it finds the command name in that list, DOS doesn't search any further and loads the code into memory, passing on any other parameters that were on the command line. Internal commands are fast because they are small and are already in memory as part of COMMAND.COM.

Our example command, CHKDSK, is not an internal command, which DOS will discover after checking the list of internal commands. Now DOS will look for an external command that matches. An external command is a file stored on disk that contains instructions and has one of the following extensions: COM, EXE, or BAT. (Typing **chkdsk.exe** on the command line would have told DOS earlier that this was an external command.) Because we didn't include the file name extension, DOS is still not sure about the exact file. Now DOS will look for a match, using those extensions. But wait! Where does DOS look for external commands? It first looks in the current directory, and then it consults a list called the search path. The search path, controlled by the PATH command, should be included in the AUTOEXEC.BAT file. If the PATH command looks like path=c:\dos;c:\word, then to find the CHKDSK command after it has searched the internal list and the current directory, DOS searches in the C:\DOS directory and then in the C:\WORD directory. In each location, DOS first looks for CHKDSK.COM, CHKDSK.EXE, and then CHKDSK.BAT, in that order. If it finds a match, it loads the program into memory and doesn't look any further. In the case of CHKDSK, it would stop after finding CHKDSK.EXE in C:\DOS. Since DOS can use external commands only when it can find them on disk, they may not be available to use if they weren't installed.

Which Command Will Accomplish the Task?

To discover which command will accomplish the task you have in mind, you must do some detective work. One way to do this is to ask an experienced DOS expert. Since you probably won't have someone like that handy, a good substitute is the DOS HELP program. Learn to use it. DOS has a fairly simple help program that does not allow you to conduct the more sophisticated searches you will find in other OS help programs. However, many of the command names actually relate to the task the command performs, unlike some of the Linux commands you will study later in this book. At the command prompt, simply type **help**, and you will get a listing of MS-DOS commands with descriptions. Browse through the list to find the command you need.

Strictly speaking, DOS does not require a space before switches (parameters that begin with a forward slash such as /a). But you should get into the habit of always placing a space between parameters when you type a command because it's easier to stick with one practice that always works, and spaces between the parameters always work (as long as you use the correct parameter).

There are about 30 internal commands, but you will use only about half of them frequently, including CD, CLS, COPY, DATE, DIR, MD, PATH, PROMPT, ECHO, REM, RD, SET, TIME, TYPE, VER, and VOL. Use the DOS HELP program to learn more about these commands.

In both versions, the installed DOS directory holds dozens of external DOS commands, but you will normally use only a handful, including ATTRIB.EXE, CHKDSK.EXE, DELTREE.EXE, DISKCOPY.COM, EDIT.COM, FORMAT.COM, MEM.EXE, PRINT.EXE, SYS.COM, TREE.COM, XCOPY, and UNDELETE.EXE.

Both MS-DOS HELP and FreeDOS HELP have onscreen instructions that neglect to tell you that you can use the arrow keys to move the selection highlight and use the ENTER key to select a highlighted item.

Step-by-Step 4.02

Using the Online Help in DOS

In the following steps you will learn how to navigate through the DOS HELP program so that you can turn to HELP whenever you are unsure of what command to use or how to use it. You will also learn more about the ATTRIB command. To complete this exercise, you will need a computer with DOS 6.22 or FreeDOS installed on the hard disk.

Step 1

At the DOS prompt, type **help** and press ENTER. Both versions provide instructions for navigating. This illustration shows the main MS-DOS Help screen.

Step 2

You can move around in each version using the PAGE UP, PAGE DOWN, and the ARROW keys. This illustration shows the FreeDOS Help reference. Press PAGE DOWN to see more of the commands. Notice that some command names are identical to the MS-DOS commands, while others are similar enough that you can guess that they have identical functions. Move the cursor to a command name and press ENTER to learn more about a command.

Step 3

Navigate the Help reference, looking at the information on various commands. If you have trouble moving around in Help, both versions of DOS offer Help on Help (FreeDOS Help on Help is shown here), available from the first page. If you accidentally exit from Help, simply enter the command Help from the command prompt to open the Help program again.

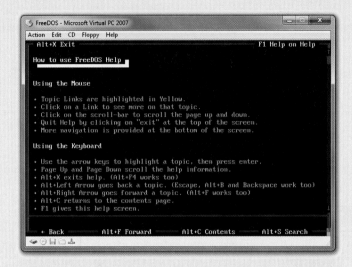

Step 4

Return to the main page of the Help reference, select the ATTRIB command, and press ENTER to view the help information on ATTRIB and to learn how you can see the file attributes of all the files in the current directory, shown here for FreeDOS.

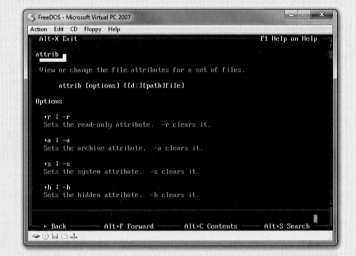

Step 5

When you are finished, press ALT, then F, and then x to exit MS-DOS HELP and return to the DOS prompt. If you are using FreeDOS, press ALT, then x, to exit.

For an online, searchable DOS command reference check out www.computerhope.com/msdos.htm#02.

What Is the Correct Syntax?

The Help reference will help you find the command that will accomplish a task, but you also need to know how to tell the command exactly what to do. This requires that you know the syntax of the command. Syntax for a DOS command is a set of rules for correctly entering a specific command at the command line. This includes the command name and the parameters that act as instructions to the command. You can use the DOS HELP program to find the syntax for a command, or you can type the command name followed by the "/?" parameter. Figure 4–11 shows the result of typing COPY/? at the command prompt. This is identical in both MS-DOS and FreeDOS.

```
C:\>copy /?
Copies one or more files to another location.

COPY [/A ¦ /B] source [/A ¦ /B] [+ source [/A ¦ /B] [+ ...]] [destination
  [/A ¦ /B]] [/V] [/Y ¦ /-Y]

  source        Specifies the file or files to be copied.
  /A            Indicates an ASCII text file.
  /B            Indicates a binary file.
  destination   Specifies the directory and/or filename for the new file(s).
  /V            Verifies that new files are written correctly.
  /Y            Suppresses prompting to confirm you want to overwrite an
                existing destination file.
  /-Y           Causes prompting to confirm you want to overwrite an
                existing destination file.

The switch /Y may be preset in the COPYCMD environment variable.
To append files, specify a single file for destination, but multiple files
for source (using wildcards or file1+file2+file3 format).

C:\>_
```

FIGURE 4–11 The COPY command syntax

It should not come as a surprise to you that DOS syntax is cryptic. Let's look at the syntax of the COPY command. To correctly enter the COPY command, you must first type **copy** followed by the optional and required parameters in the order shown. All optional parameters are in square brackets with required parameters shown without brackets. Of course, you don't use the brackets in the actual command line. The source is the only required parameter, and it is the file or files to copy (you can include the path to a file, as in C:\DOS\). The destination is not required, but if you don't provide it, it will assume the directory you're currently in.

An example of the COPY command in action: **copy myfile.txt c:\data\myfile.bak**. Learn more about commands for file management later in this chapter, and use them in Step-by-Step 4.03.

Operators

A command line operator is a symbol, such as the vertical bar (|) or the greater-than sign (>), that affects the behavior of commands. For instance, if you place a vertical bar between two commands, DOS will use the output from the first command as the input to the second command. We won't talk about all the possible permutations of this, but when you use a command and the output runs off the screen, repeat the command, but add the vertical bar plus the MORE command. For instance, if I want to quickly see the contents of a text file, such as the AUTOEXEC.BAT file, I like to use the TYPE command, but if the file is very long, it will scroll off the screen. Therefore, add the vertical bar and the MORE command: **type autoexec.bat | more**. Figure 4–12 shows the result of running this command. The line containing the command has scrolled off the screen, but the MORE command filters the input it is given and displays it one screenful at a time. The message "More" displays at

Check Out the Syntax for DOS Commands

Once you know the name of a DOS command, you can easily discover the correct syntax. Try this:

1. At the DOS command prompt, type **chkdsk /?** and press ENTER. If you are using MS-DOS 6.22, you may be surprised at the suggestion in the last paragraph of the screen output. It recommends that you use SCANDISK rather than CHKDSK.

2. Check out another command: at the DOS command prompt, type **xcopy /?** and press ENTER.

try this!

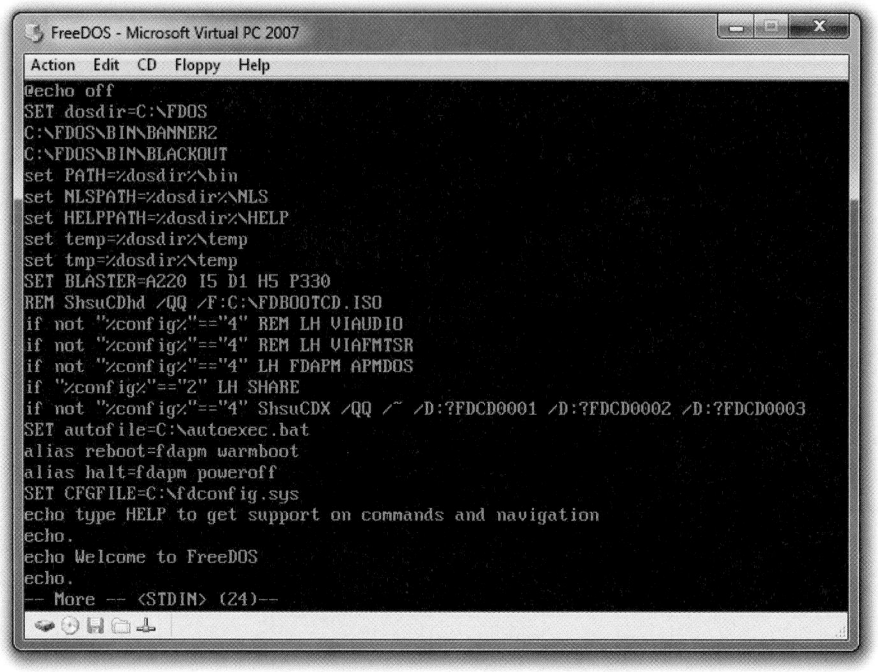

FIGURE 4–12 The result of sending the output of the TYPE command, operating on the AUTOEXEC.BAT file, to the MORE filter

the bottom of the screen, much as it would in MS-DOS, with the exception of the "<STDIN> (24)" which are FreeDOS artifacts. You get no clue that you only need to press any key to see the next screen full.

Another operator, the greater than symbol (>), takes command output and creates a file with the name you provide to the right of the operator if a file with that name does not exist. If a file with that name exists, its contents will be overwritten and lost. Let's say we want to create a backup of the auto-exec.bat file and name it autoexec.bkk. There are other ways to do this, but one way is to enter the following at the command prompt: **type autoexec.bat > autoexec.bkk**.

There are many tricks to using DOS, but these few should get you started. Now it's time to use DOS to manage files and directories.

Learning to Manage Files and Directories

DOS has a no-frills file management system centered on the abilities and limits of the FAT file system. To manage files in DOS, you need to understand DOS file basics, directories, how to design a directory structure for file management, how to create directories, and file management commands. This is worth learning because every Microsoft OS and UNIX/Linux OSs have a similar directory structure that requires the same kind of basic skills and understanding.

DOS File Basics

DOS file basics include file-naming rules, DOS file types, DOS executable files, and DOS file attributes.

DOS File-Naming Rules. When working with files in DOS, you must understand the rules for naming files in DOS, and then you must understand the

> ## WARNING!
>
> You may see the vertical bar and greater-than symbols elsewhere in DOS, but they only work as described when they are within a command line and used with programs that can interact with them. For instance, in the DOS Help program, you will see the vertical bar (|) used to separate information about parameters; and you will see the greater than sign (>) used within the DOS prompt itself, as described earlier. In these instances these symbols are not working as operators. (Are you confused yet?)

concept of file type. DOS can work only with files with a file name of up to eight characters, followed by a period, followed by an extension of up to three characters. This basic rule of file naming is called the 8.3 (eight-dot-three) naming convention. But there is more to it than that. Aside from the dot, which separates the file name from the extension, within the file name and extension you can use only alphanumeric (A to Z and 1 to 0) characters. A DOS file must begin with an alpha character (A-Z) and contain no spaces. DOS only recognizes a few special characters in file names. These special characters are

$ & # @ ! % ' ^ ( ) - _

Other characters, including math symbols and punctuation characters, are illegal or invalid characters in file names. They are

/ \ [ ] | < > + = ; , * ?

Further, DOS does not differentiate between uppercase and lowercase characters. Other OSs do recognize the difference, and these OSs are called case-sensitive. So to DOS, readme.txt is the same as README.TXT, but to another OS, such as Linux, it isn't. Examples of valid DOS 8.3 file names are README.TXT, FORMAT.COM, FDISK.EXE, AUTOEXEC.BAT, MONOUMB.386, and CONFIG.SYS.

Examples of illegal DOS 8.3 file names are READTHOSE.TXT, FORMAT. COM, and README.FILE. The first file name is invalid because the file name portion is too long; the second is invalid because it contains an illegal character; and the third is invalid because the extension portion is too long.

In addition to the file name and extension, you may need to tell DOS exactly where a file is, in which case you need to provide the path to the file. The path to a file includes the drive letter (C:) plus a backslash (\). If you stop at that point (C:\), you are pointing to the root directory. If you follow that with a file name (C:\AUTOEXEC.BAT, for instance), DOS looks in the root directory for the file. If the file is in a subdirectory, you need to include that. C:\DOS points to the DOS subdirectory of the root directory, for example. If you want to point to a file in that directory, you add the name: for instance, C:\DOS\EDIT.COM. The backslash symbol (\) separates directories within directories.

> Make life easier for yourself. Don't try to memorize the valid characters—just avoid using anything but alphanumeric characters, or you will make file naming more complicated than it needs to be, and wonder why DOS will not accept your clever file names!

Use the asterisk (*) and question mark (?) as wildcard characters. The asterisk is the more useful of these two. You can use the asterisk to replace all characters from that point to the end of the file name or all characters to the end of the extension. For example, *.DOC refers to all files with the DOC extension. Similarly, README.* refers to all files with the README file name and any extension. This wildcard is very powerful and useful. For instance, if you wanted to copy all files from the current directory to a target directory on drive C: named BACKUP, you could simply type the command **copy *.* c:\ backup**.

> Learn more about working with directories and subdirectories later in this chapter.

The question mark replaces a single character for each instance of the question mark. For instance, DISKCO??.COM refers to all files that match the provided characters and have any characters in the seventh or eighth place of the file name.

> In three decades of working with DOS, we have used the asterisk wildcard character about a thousand times more than the question-mark wildcard character. Don't waste too much time trying to use the question-mark character.

DOS File Types. DOS recognizes several different file types. Some of these file types contain text data, and others contain program code and are referred to as binary files. We usually don't make DOS guess which is which; we identify the file type of a file with a special extension. An extension is separated from a filename by a period. Following is a list of common file extensions and the file types each identifies to DOS:

BAK	A file containing backup data
BAS	A BASIC program file
BAT	A batch file (a special text file in which each line is treated like a command at the DOS prompt)
COM	An executable binary file (a program)
DOC	A word processor data file, usually containing text plus the special codes for formatting the text when printed
EXE	An executable binary file using a more complicated structure than a COM file (a program)
SYS	A device driver or operating system file
TXT	A file containing text without special codes for formatting the text

DOS Executable Files. DOS considers three types of files to be executable: .COM, .EXE, and .BAT. The .COM and .EXE files both contain programming code; the difference between these two types of files is not important to us in this chapter; .BAT files are batch files, which are not programs but text files that contain commands that you could type at the command prompt, but which you choose to put in a batch file. When DOS executes a batch file, it uses the command interpreter to interpret each line of the batch file. The batch file acts like a script for the command interpreter. This is called batch processing and is a great way to automate tasks you perform frequently. Perhaps you back up the files you are working on every day by copying them to a thumb drive, for instance; you could create a batch file to automate this process. This listing is an example of such a batch file; it assumes the drive letter that is assigned to your thumb drive is drive F:

```
@ECHO OFF
ECHO Data files will be copied to F:
ECHO Please insert a thumb drive into the USB port
PAUSE
XCOPY C:*.TXT F:
XCOPY C:*.INI F:
ECHO Remove the thumb drive and store in a safe place
```

DOS File Attributes. In addition to file types, DOS uses file attributes that are saved in each file or directory entry. These attributes determine how DOS handles the file. For instance, if the file attribute for directory is turned on, or *set*, then the file entry is for a directory, and, rather than pointing to the location of a file, it points to another directory listing. The DOS file attributes are as follows:

- **Read-only**—an attribute that indicates that a file may not be modified or deleted. DOS automatically puts this attribute on certain files as a small measure of protection. Anyone using a program that ignores this attribute, or using a program that lets him turn off this attribute, can delete the read-only file.
- **Archive**—an attribute that, when turned on, indicates a file has been created or modified since the last backup. DOS places this attribute on all new or changed files. Most backup programs can turn off this attribute for each file backed up, allowing the program to keep track of the backed up files.
- **System**—a special attribute that MS-DOS gives to the system files, IO.SYS and MSDOS.SYS.
- **Hidden**—an attribute that will cause a file or directory to be hidden from programs that pay attention to this attribute, such as the DOS DIR command.

- **Volume label**—an attribute used for a special root directory entry, which can be used to give a disk a label or name.
- **Directory**—an attribute that indicates that the entry is a directory, not a file.

These attributes are used in the FAT file system in all OSs, plus other file systems, such as NTFS, have attributes—and some are identical to the DOS FAT file attributes. You should never change the directory attribute manually because the OS creates it when it creates a directory. Likewise you shouldn't mess with the system attribute, because the OS uses it to identify its own special files, such as IO.SYS and MSDOS.SYS (in the case of MS-DOS). It's important for a computer professional to understand the read-only and hidden attributes because the first one may keep you from editing a file someday and the second one may keep you from seeing a file on disk.

try this!

Make a File Read-Only

Use the ATTRIB command to make a file read-only. Try this:

1. Use the DIR command to view the list of files in the current directory, and from the files displayed, choose one to use in the next few steps, using its file name and extension when you see *filename.ext*.
2. At the command prompt, type **attrib +r** *filename.ext* and press ENTER.
3. Confirm that the file is now read-only with the Attrib command: Type **attrib** and press ENTER.
4. If an *R* is displayed by the file name, it is read-only. Try deleting this file: type **del** *filename.ext*.
5. Remove the read-only attribute: type **attrib −r** *filename.ext*.

Root Directory and Other Directories

A directory is a special file that can contain listings of files and other directories. The root directory is the top-level directory, and the only one that the FORMAT command creates. Other programs (such as the DOS setup program) and users can create additional directories, which will be stored below the root, in a hierarchical structure. Sometimes we call a directory that contains other directories a parent directory and a directory contained within another directory a child directory or subdirectory. The information DOS stores in a directory entry for a file includes the file name, extension, date and time of creation or modification, size, attributes, and beginning cluster number. Some of this information appears in the directory listing you see when you use the DOS DIR command, as shown in Figure 4–13 for MS-DOS and Figure 4–14 for FreeDOS. Both of these DOS installations use a setting that ensures that the DOS prompt will display both the current drive and the current directory. In both cases, the DOS prompt ends with a greater than (>) symbol. The backslash (\) is a separator between the directories. The first backslash after the drive letter indicates the root. Also notice that in addition to the directory for the DOS files (DOS in MS-DOS and FDOS in FreeDOS) there are also directories for additional installed programs. The MS-DOS listing shows the Word and Xtree directories created when the user installed applications that needed a place to put program files.

Designing a Directory Structure for File Management

Now you will take a different view of the root directory as you decide what directories to create within it to hold your data files. You can even create directories within directories, so your directory design can get pretty fancy.

When it comes to organizing data in your computer, think "office supplies," and imagine that your computer is a filing cabinet and that each logical

```
C:\>dir

 Volume in drive C is MS-DOS_6
 Volume Serial Number is 2C98-8B17
 Directory of C:\

DOS          <DIR>           04-24-02   5:24p
COMMAND  COM         54,645  05-31-94   6:22a
CONFIG   SYS             50  07-25-02  10:18a
AUTOEXEC BAT             68  07-25-02  10:21a
XTREE        <DIR>           07-25-02  12:47p
WORD         <DIR>           07-25-02  12:48p
        6 file(s)         54,763 bytes
                   2,136,473,600 bytes free

C:\>_
```

FIGURE 4–13 MS-DOS directory listing using the DIR command. Notice the Word and Xtree directories.

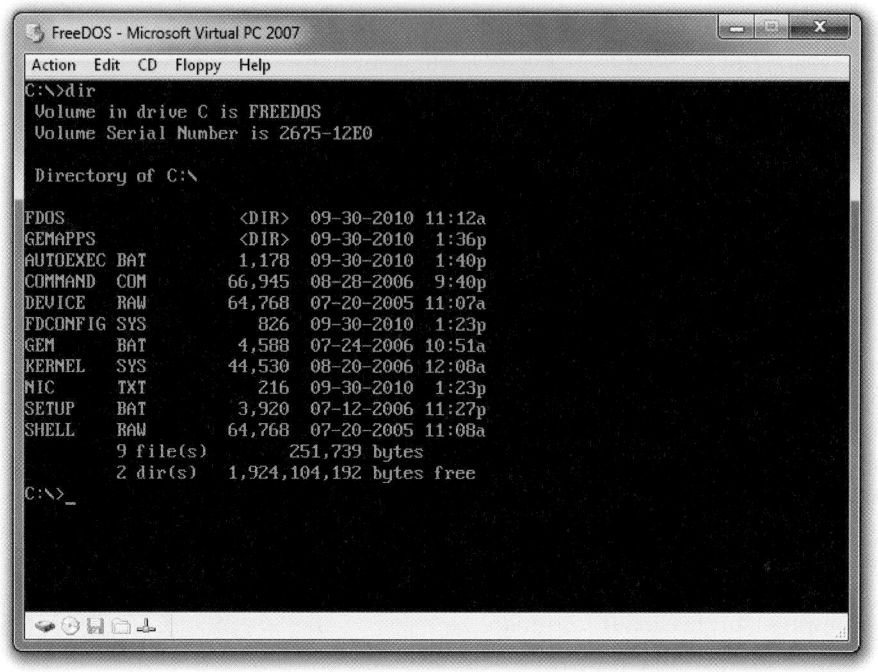

FIGURE 4–14 A directory listing of the root directory in FreeDOS

WARNING!

You should never save data files in the root directory because doing so is like dumping things into a filing cabinet drawer without using folders and dividers to organize them. A technical reason for not saving files in the root directory is that, unlike subdirectories, the root directory can't grow. If you save everything into the root directory it will eventually reach its limit, and you will get a "Disk Full" error message, even though the disk isn't full!

drive (with its root directory) is a drawer in that cabinet. The directories you create at the root would be the large hanging folders, and the directories created at the next level are the smaller folders placed within the hanging folders.

Of course, you can place individual files in any of these directories, but you should design a directory structure that works for your own need to save and organize your files. Always reserve the root directory for the files needed by the OS during start-up and for your top-level subdirectories.

Figure 4–15 shows the result of using the DOS TREE command to view directories. The DOS setup program created the DOS directory, but a user created the other directories. The DATA directory is where he stores all his data files, while the APPS directory is where he installs all his applications. The directory C:\APPS\EXCEL contains the Microsoft Excel program files, while the directory C:\APPS\WORD contains the Microsoft Word program files. He saves the word processing and spreadsheet files that he creates with these two programs in the DATA directory. The logic behind this design, in which he stores the applications in one directory hierarchy and the data in another directory structure, has to do with backups.

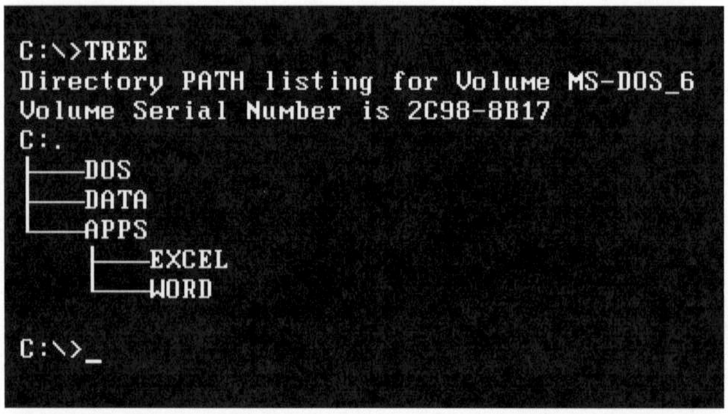

FIGURE 4–15 Directories viewed with the TREE command

Whether he does his backups with an actual backup program or simply uses the XCOPY command, he can start his backup at the top level (DATA or APPS) and back up the contents of all child directories. His data files change more frequently than the application files, so he will want to back up the DATA directory more often than the APPS directory.

Creating and Navigating Directories

Let's say you want to create several new directories to organize your data files. Remember that the directory structure is hierarchical; that is, a directory can contain other directories as well as files. The basic hierarchy is <Drive>:\<Directory Name>\<File Name>. As you add directories to the hierarchy, the path to a single file can look like this <Drive>:\<Directory Name>\<Directory Name>\<Directory Name>\<Directory Name>\|<Directory Name>\<File Name>. Remember that a directory that contains other directories is a *parent* directory, and a directory inside a parent directory is a *child* directory, or subdirectory.

The DOS command to create a directory is MD (Make Directory). The syntax is MD [*drive:*]*path*. For instance, to create a directory named data in the current directory, simply type **md data**; to create the same directory on drive C: type **md c:\data**. The DOS command to move between directories (change the current directory) has two possible common names: CD and CHDIR. Both stand for Change Directory and are identical in function. After executing either command, you will be in the new directory, and, as always, any subsequent commands that you issue that operate on a directory will operate on the directory you are currently in unless you specify a different path as a parameter for the command.

Use File Management Commands

DOS has several commands you can use for file management tasks. These commands let you copy, move, and delete files, as well as create, move, and delete directories. Remember that some of these commands are internal commands, which are loaded into memory along with DOS, ready to run whenever you need them. These small and fast commands include DIR (Directory), CD (Change Directory), CLS (CLear Screen), COPY, REN (REName), MD (Make Directory), CD (Change Directory), TYPE, and RD (Remove Directory).

Three often-used external commands, XCOPY, DISKCOPY, and DELTREE, are enhancements to internal commands. For instance, XCOPY and DISKCOPY can copy in ways that the internal COPY command can't. XCOPY can copy files and entire directories, while COPY can only copy files—it has no understanding of directories. DISKCOPY can make a floppy-disk-to-floppy-disk copy between floppy disks of the same size, creating an exact duplicate of the original floppy disk. The DELTREE command can delete an entire directory and its contents, while the internal RD (Remove Directory) command can delete only an empty directory.

> DOS and Windows use the back-slash (\) as a separator for disk paths, and Linux and the Mac OS X command line use the forward slash. URLs also use the forward slash as a separator on the Internet.

> One convenient shortcut when moving between directories is to use the double dot (..). When you type **cd ..** (or **chdir ..**), you move to the parent directory of the directory you are in. Thus, you can easily move up a hierarchy without having to enter the name of each parent directory. Similarly, **cd ** moves you directly to the root of the current drive.

> As you have already seen with such commands as CD/CHDIR, a number of DOS commands have alternate forms. Use whichever form you can remember most easily.

Step-by-Step 4.03
Managing Files and Directories

Let's practice working with files and directories from a command line. Say you want to create a new directory named *testdata* in the root of C:, copy several files into it, examine the files to make sure they are there, and then delete those copied files and the *testdata* directory. To complete this exercise, you will need

- A computer with DOS installed on a disk or into a virtual machine. You cannot do this exercise on an optical disc unless you have another writable disk. If you do not have a DOS computer, you can perform most of these steps at the Windows command prompt, but the directory structure will be very different.

Step 1

At the command prompt, type **cd** and press ENTER. Then type **dir** and press ENTER. A listing of files and directories in the root (C:\) will be displayed.

Step 2

In MS-DOS, to move down one level into the DOS directory, type **cd dos**. In FreeDOS to move to the FDOS directory, type **cd fdos**. Press ENTER. Your screen display will resemble the FreeDOS screen shown here. MS-DOS will show only the DOS directory, and a few files. FreeDOS will show the FDOS and GEMAPPS (if you installed OpenGEM) directories and a few files.

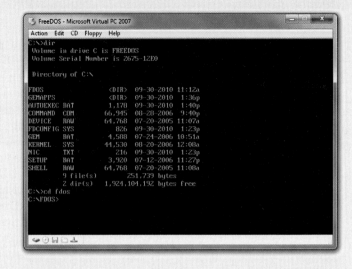

Step 3

With the DOS or FreeDOS directory current, type **dir** and press ENTER. Many of the files rolled up and out of view. Clearly you need to do something else to examine the files contained in C:\DOS or C:\FDOS.

Step 4

Type **dir /?** and press ENTER to get a listing of the available syntax for the DIR command. Notice that if you use the /p (for Pause) switch, the listing will pause after each screenful of data. Try it now. Type **dir /p** and press ENTER. You can now examine the contents of C:\DOS screenful by screenful until you are back at the command prompt.

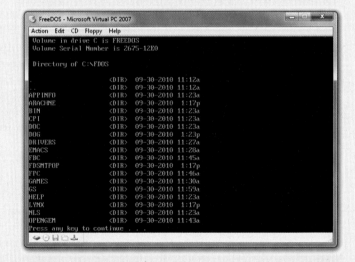

Step 5

Try a few more switches. Type **dir /w** to see a wide listing of directory contents. Then try variations of the sort order switch (/o). Try **dir /on** to sort on name.

Step 6

To return to the root of C:, type **cd ..** (that's two periods or dots) and press ENTER—you are now back at the root of C:. You can also return to the root from any number of levels down by simply typing **cd **. Test that you have indeed returned to the root by typing **dir**.

Now that you are back at the root create your *testdata* directory: type **md testdata** and press ENTER.

Step 7

Confirm that DOS created your directory by typing **dir** again and reading the listing to see if your new directory shows.

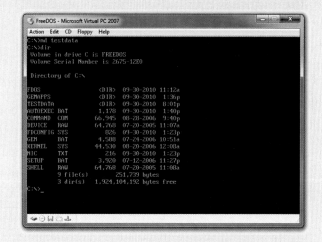

Step 8

Type **cls** (for **CL**ear **S**creen) and press ENTER any time you wish to clear the screen.

It's time to copy some information into your testdata directory

In MS-DOS type **copy c:\dos*.txt c:\testdata** and press ENTER.

In FreeDOS type **copy c:\fdos*.txt c:\testdata** and press ENTER.

Notice that we used the wildcard character (*) to copy all files with the txt extension—and only those files.

Step 9

Check to see if the command worked. Type **cd testdata** and press ENTER to change focus to the testdata directory. Then type **dir** and press ENTER to display the contents of that directory.

You should see a list of files with txt extensions in the testdata directory as shown here in MS-DOS.

Step 10

Let's say you have changed your mind, and now you want to get rid of all the files in testdata. You also want to be very sure to delete only the files in testdata.

Type: **del c:\testdata*.*** and press ENTER to delete all file names with all extensions.

Type **y** and press ENTER when you see the warning:

```
All files in directory will be deleted!
Are you sure (Y/N)?
```

```
C:\>copy c:\dos\*.txt c:\testdata
C:\DOS\COUNTRY.TXT
C:\DOS\README.TXT
C:\DOS\NETWORKS.TXT
C:\DOS\DRVSPACE.TXT
        4 file(s) copied

C:\>cd testdata

C:\TESTDATA>dir

  Volume in drive C is MS-DOS_6
  Volume Serial Number is 2C98-8B17
  Directory of C:\TESTDATA

 .            <DIR>         05-01-02    9:52p
 ..           <DIR>         05-01-02    9:52p
 COUNTRY  TXT       15,920  05-31-94    6:22a
 README   TXT       60,646  05-31-94    6:22a
 NETWORKS TXT       17,465  05-31-94    6:22a
 DRVSPACE TXT       41,512  05-31-94    6:22a
        6 file(s)       135,543 bytes
                  2,137,784,320 bytes free

C:\TESTDATA>_
```

Step 11

From within the testdata directory type **dir** and press ENTER.

The testdata directory should be empty again, with only the dot (.) and dot-dot (..) files that are part of any subdirectory.

We need to remove the testdata directory now.

Type **cd ..** and press ENTER to move up to the root of C:.

Now use the RD command to remove a directory. Type **rd testdata** and press ENTER. Confirm that the testdata directory is gone by typing **dir** and pressing ENTER again. There should be no sign of testdata.

LO 4.4 | The DOS Boot-Up Process

In this section, you will discover why you should learn the boot process for any OS with which you work. Then you will learn about DOS system files, how the DOS boot process works, and how to create a DOS start-up disk.

Why You Should Learn the DOS Boot-Up Process

Personal computers are multipurpose devices. They become the tools you need them to be only through both the installation of hardware components—both internal and external to the computer—and through the OS. The OS usually has modifications in the form of commands that tell it how to behave and device drivers that add the ability to work with the available hardware. The computer finally becomes the tool you need for the jobs in your personal and business life when you install application programs. These application programs rely on the OS for services they need.

Lee, a young computer technician, has now worked with several different OSs and has found that a significant number of problems occur, or make themselves known, during the boot-up (or start-up) process. Therefore, understanding the normal start-up process for personal computers in general, and then for each individual OS, helps him to troubleshoot problems that show up during boot-up. Careful observation will tell him at what point in the process the failure is occurring. Then he can troubleshoot, using his knowledge of what components must be missing or damaged to cause the problem.

DOS System Files

We call certain critical DOS files, collectively, the system files. In MS-DOS they are IO.SYS, MSDOS.SYS, and COMMAND.COM. In FreeDOS they are KERNEL.SYS and COMMAND.COM. These files must be present in the root of drive C: to start DOS from your hard disk, and they must be in the root of a floppy disk to start DOS from that floppy. These files make up the bare-bones OS. In MS-DOS they are all read-only, and the first two have both the hidden and system attributes set. In FreeDOS, only the archive attribute is on for these files. In MS-DOS, IO.SYS handles interaction with hardware and the loading of device drivers during boot up and is the main (or kernel) component of the OS. In FreeDOS the functions of IO.SYS and MSDOS.SYS combine in the single KERNEL .SYS file. In both versions COMMAND.COM is the command interpreter that provides you with the famous command prompt and interprets the commands you enter.

DOS Configuration Files

DOS uses the special MS-DOS configuration files CONFIG.SYS and AUTOEXEC.BAT during boot up. These two files are text files (containing only text), and they have no special formatting codes. What they have in common is that you can read them using any text editor or word processor. In FreeDOS these files are FDCONFIG.SYS and AUTOEXEC.BAT. Let's see when and how DOS uses these files.

The CONFIG.SYS or FDCONFIG.SYS File. You use the CONFIG.SYS file to add device drivers to DOS and to modify DOS settings. To work with a CONFIG .SYS file, you use a text editor to create or modify the file, entering special commands. Then you place the file in the root of the boot disk, which is drive C: if DOS is installed on your hard drive, or it can be on a bootable floppy. DOS automatically looks for CONFIG.SYS immediately after loading the first two system files and before loading COMMAND.COM. If CONFIG.SYS is present, DOS uses its commands. The most common CONFIG.SYS commands are as follows:

BUFFERS	DOS
DEVICE	FILES
DEVICEHIGH	STACKS

All of these commands are used with an equal sign, as in BUFFERS=30. BUFFERS, DOS, FILES, and STACKS should appear only once in a CONFIG .SYS file because each modifies a single setting for the OS. The BUFFERS command controls the number of disk read buffers, the area of memory used during file access. The DOS command controls the location in memory of a portion of the operating system. The FILES command controls the number of file handles available to DOS. (File handles are pointers used to keep track of files that are open in memory.) STACKS controls the number of special areas, called stacks, that are used by programs.

The DEVICE and DEVICEHIGH commands are used to load device drivers and will be used in a CONFIG.SYS file as many times as there are device drivers to install. The difference between DEVICE and DEVICEHIGH is that DEVICE loads drivers into the first 640 KB of memory, whereas DEVICEHIGH loads drivers into special memory above 640 KB, which exists only when special memory management drivers and settings have been loaded.

A CONFIG.SYS file may be as simple as the following:

```
files=10
buffers=10
dos=high,umb
stacks=9,256
```

Below is an example of a slightly more sophisticated CONFIG.SYS that loads the device driver that supports use of the high memory area, the address space between 384 KB and 1024 KB, with the line "device=himem .sys /testmem:off." This CONFIG.SYS also loads a device driver for the CD drive, "device-oakcdrom.sys /D:mscd001." This CONFIG.SYS file also creates a ram disk, a logical drive that uses RAM memory rather than physical disk space.

```
device=himem.sys /testmem:off
device=oakcdrom.sys /D:mscd001
files=10
buffers=10
dos=high,umb
stacks=9,256
devicehigh=ramdrive.sys /E 2048
lastdrive=z
```

AUTOEXEC.BAT. AUTOEXEC.BAT is a special batch file because DOS looks for it immediately after it loads COMMAND.COM. While we use CONFIG .SYS or FDCONFIG.SYS to tell DOS what to *be* (making it an OS that uses the high memory area and works with various devices), we can use AUTO-EXEC.BAT to tell DOS what to *do* every time it starts up. For example, you might tell DOS to run a TSR. However, the most common commands found in AUTOEXEC.BAT are commands that place settings in a special area of memory used to store messages to DOS and other programs. We call this area of memory the **environment**, and commands that add messages, called variables to the environment, include:

PATH

PROMPT

SET

The PATH command allows you to control the search path DOS uses when searching for an entered command. The PROMPT command controls the appearance of the DOS prompt. The SET command adds other values to the environment, as when a DOS application's setup program adds a SET command to the AUTOEXEC.BAT with an entry that contains the directory path to that application's data files. For example, when Norton Utilities for DOS was installed, its setup program put a line in AUTOEXEC.BAT that looked something like this: SET NU=C:\NORTON. Other programs would ignore this entry, but whenever Norton Utilities runs, it would look in the environment for this setting. You can also use the set command to set the path rather than using the PATH command. You can see the current environment settings by simply typing the SET command without additional parameters at the prompt.

As with the CONFIG.SYS file, you may have a very simple AUTOEXEC .BAT file like the following:

```
path=C:\DOS;
prompt=$p$g
```

You may also have a very complicated AUTOEXEC.BAT file, like the one created by the FreeDOS installation program. We won't explain all the commands in this sophisticated batch file, just the commands we selected from it, shown here. Most of the lines create environment variables, but the third and fourth commands execute programs. The first is a program named BANNER2, which is the banner2.com file stored in the BIN directory. BANNER2 .COM displays a FreeDOS banner screen, which displays very briefly before the BLACKOUT command turns it off and then the remainder of the AUTOEXEC.BAT file executes and the command prompt appears. The first and last line use the ECHO command to first turn off the echoing of each command line, which otherwise occurs when a batch file runs. This does not inhibit the result of running a program in AUTOEXEC.BAT. At the end ECHO ON turns echoing back on.

```
@ECHO OFF
set dosdir=C:\FDOS
C:\FDOS\BIN\BANNER2
C:\FDOS\BIN\BLACKOUT
set PATH=%dosdir%\bin
set NLSPATH=%dosdir%\NLS
set HELPPATH=%dosdir%\HELP
set temp=%dosdir%\temp
set tmp=%dosdir%\temp
@ECHO ON
```

If you are at the command prompt in either version of DOS, you can view and edit the configuration files by loading them in the Edit program. To view the FreeDOS FDCONFIG.SYS file simply enter the **edit FDCONFIG.SYS** command at the command prompt. If your version of DOS loaded a mouse

Windows stores environment variables in the registry. You can view the environment variables in Windows by opening a command prompt and entering the set command.

driver, you can move the mouse cursor (a small rectangle) around in the Edit program and use it on the scroll bar on the right. Otherwise, use the Arrow keys to move the blinking cursor.

Using environment settings is such a handy practice that it continues today in Windows. One quick way to see the environment settings in Windows is to open a command prompt and simply type the SET command without parameters. You might be surprised at the long list of settings. For instance, the WINDIR value points to the location of the folder in which Windows is installed, and the USERNAME value shows the user name of the currently logged on user.

Every time you turn your computer on, your computer "learns" what hardware it has attached to it and looks for an operating system to start. It learns about the essential hardware components by reading information stored in special nonvolatile RAM. It has a standard way of looking for an operating system and loading it into memory. The OS, in turn, learns how it will behave and how it will interact with the hardware. This section offers a somewhat simplified description of the boot process, from turning the computer on through loading the operating system with all its configuration settings and device drivers.

The phrase *boot up a computer* comes from the old concept of lifting yourself by your own bootstraps—something that is impossible for humans, but necessary for a computer. The computer starts with nothing and then executes little programs, each of which performs a necessary task or adds more capability until the entire computer is up and running.

The Intel and similar processors used in our PCs have a unique characteristic tied to the PC architecture: When you power up your PC, the processor loads a special ROM-based program called the Power-On Self-Test (POST) into memory. POST runs a series of small diagnostic tests on the hardware. When POST finishes, it passes control to a small program in the ROM BIOS called the bootstrap loader.

You can boot up (or start) DOS several ways. One way is to turn on the power switch of your PC, called performing a cold boot. You can use the other two methods after a computer is powered up. One is to use a key combination that reboots DOS without a power-down and power-up cycle. This key combination is Ctrl-Alt-Delete (pressed simultaneously), and this method is called a warm boot. A third method, also a warm boot, is available on many PCs: Press the Reset button, which (depending on the manufacturer) skips the power-down and power-up cycle and runs POST.

To understand how the bootstrap loader works, you need to understand a little about how a drive is prepared for use. A disk, whether it is a hard disk or a floppy disk, is divided into individual chunks, called sectors, which are each 512 bytes in size. Further, remember that a hard disk can have several areas (partitions) that appear as discrete logical drives (C:, D:, E:, and so on), with many, many sectors in each.

The first sector on each logical drive on a hard disk is the boot sector for that logical drive. When you format a disk (A:, C:, D:, and so on), the OS you are using writes information into the boot sector (not the MBR). This information includes version information about the OS and a small program that calls up the system files for the OS.

The ROM BIOS bootstrap loader looks for a floppy disk in drive A:. If it finds one, it loads the boot sector from that floppy disk into memory, which in turn runs the OS loading program. If the bootstrap loader does not find a floppy disk in drive A:, it looks for an OS on the hard drive. It first looks in the MBR of the first hard drive and reads the partition table, looking for a special type of partition, called a primary partition, that is also "active." This means

When you boot to MS-DOS, it will ask you to confirm the date and time unless you have an AUTOEXEC.BAT file in the root of the start-up disk. That is all you need. The file does not have to have anything in it.

When DOS reigned on PCs, people fondly referred to Ctrl-Alt-Delete as the three-fingered salute.

A floppy disk does not have an MBR, only a boot sector.

This discussion of the boot-up process assumes that the boot order in the BIOS is set to first look at the floppy drive, then to the hard drive.

that it is the specific partition from which to load the OS. The bootstrap loader reads the first sector of the active partition into memory. Remember that this sector is also special. It is the boot sector and contains a special OS loading program.

On a disk formatted by DOS, the OS loading program looks for IO.SYS and MSDOS.SYS (or KERNEL.SYS in FreeDOS). If it finds them, it loads them into memory. MSDOS.SYS or KERNEL.SYS looks for CONFIG.SYS in the root directory of the disk from which it is loaded. If it finds this file, it configures the OS based on the commands in CONFIG.SYS. Then COMMAND.COM is loaded into memory. It looks for AUTOEXEC.BAT. If it finds this file, it executes each command in the file. After this, unless AUTOEXEC.BAT loaded an application, the DOS prompt displays with its little blinking cursor waiting for you to enter a command.

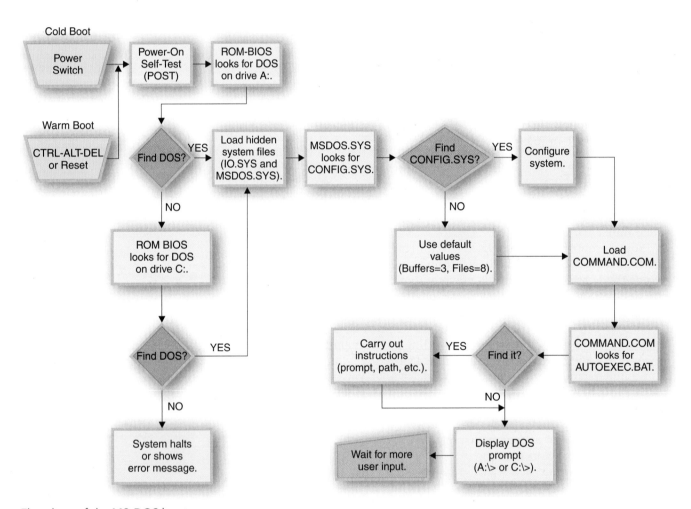

Flowchart of the MS-DOS boot-up process

LO 4.5 | Troubleshooting Common DOS Problems

You may encounter some common problems if you work with DOS. Let's examine some of these problems, looking at the symptoms, the possible causes, and solutions.

"Non-System Disk" Error Message

In this scenario, DOS is installed on your hard disk, but fails to boot up, and an error message appears that includes the words "Non-system disk." This indicates that the OS loader program cannot find the system files (IO.SYS or MSDOS.SYS for MS-DOS or KERNEL.SYS for FreeDOS). The most likely cause is that a data floppy disk has been left in drive A:. The OS loader program from the first sector on the disk is loaded into memory and looking for the system files on drive A:. However, a data floppy disk is one formatted to hold data, but is not a bootable disk, so it lacks the system files. To solve this problem, check to see if there is a floppy disk in drive A: and, if so, remove it and press any key. The boot process should continue successfully.

> The complete message may vary between DOS versions, but includes the words "Non-system disk." This error may not appear on a computer that is set to check other drives if the system succeeds in finding an OS on another drive.

If there is no floppy drive, or if there is and drive A: does not contain a floppy disk, then you have a bigger problem because this means the OS loader was loaded from the first sector on C: and could not find the system files during boot up. In this case, you should boot with a bootable floppy disk or bootable optical disc that also has the SYS.COM program. Then type the following command to have the system files placed back on your drive C:

    SYS C:

Next, remove the floppy disk or optical disc from the drive and reboot your computer. It should now boot to DOS.

> **Cause a Failure**
>
> You can learn what happens when the bootstrap loader fails to find an operating system. If your computer has a floppy drive and is configured to boot from the floppy disk drive first and then from the hard disk, use a blank, formatted floppy disk to "break" your computer and fix it again! Try this:
>
> 1. With your computer turned off, insert a blank, formatted floppy disk in drive A:.
>
> 2. Turn the computer on. After it fails to find an OS, it should display this message:
>
>    ```
>    Non-system disk or disk error
>    Replace and strike any key when ready
>    ```
>
> 3. Simply remove the blank disk from drive A: and press a key. The system should restart and load the operating system from your hard disk.

try this!

"Bad or Missing Command Interpreter" Error Message

In this scenario, DOS is installed on your hard disk, but fails to boot up, and the "Bad or Missing Command Interpreter" error message is displayed. This indicates that the file COMMAND.COM is missing or is a different version than IO.SYS and MSDOS.SYS or KERNEL.SYS. To confirm that this is the problem, locate a DOS start-up disk or FreeDOS disk of the same version as that which is installed on your hard disk, place it in the appropriate drive, and boot up again. After the computer boots up, display a directory of the root of C: using the DIR /A command. The /A will display all files, including hidden files. First, verify that COMMAND.COM is missing. If it is missing, then you have confirmed the problem and can solve it. If COMMAND.COM is present, check the file date and time information in IO.SYS, MSDOS.SYS (or KERNEL .SYS in FreeDOS), and COMMAND.COM. If COMMAND.COM has a different date and time, you need to replace it with one with the correct date and time.

To solve this problem, verify that the COMMAND.COM file on the floppy disk or optical disc is the correct date and time (matching that of the other system files on C:); then copy COMMAND.COM from the floppy disk or optical disc to C:.

> Another fix for this problem is to use the SYS.COM program, if it is present on the DOS start-up floppy disk or optical disc *and* if it is from the same version of DOS as the hard disk. This will transfer the entire matching set of three system files from the floppy disk to the hard drive. Boot from the floppy disk or the optical disc, and enter the following command: **sys c:**.

"Bad Command or File Name" or "File Not Found" Error Message

You have just entered a command at the command prompt and receive the "Bad Command or File Name" message. This means that either the command name or a file name (or directory name) in one of the parameters is incorrect. For instance, on a computer with DOS 6.22 installed, we wanted to delete a directory called DATA1, and we entered the following with a slight typo: **deltree data.** In this case, there was no DATA directory, only a DATA1 directory, so the result was the "Bad command or File Name" message.

If you are running FreeDOS, you will see the "Bad Command or File Name" only if the command parameter is wrong. If a parameter that should be a file name is incorrect, you will see the "File not found" message.

Whenever you see these error messages, whether you are working in DOS or at a command prompt in Windows, look for a typo in the command line you entered, and then reenter the entire line correctly. Typos are the most common cause of these errors.

Request to Enter the Current Date and Time

You boot up a computer with DOS, and you are required to enter the current date and time. This means that DOS did not find an AUTOEXEC.BAT file. If you previously had an AUTOEXEC.BAT file, you may want to investigate how and why DOS cannot find it now. Perhaps, rather than booting from drive C:, your computer booted from drive A:, because a bootable start-up disk was in the drive. If so, the prompt on the screen should show drive A:. If this is the case, remove the floppy disk and restart the computer.

Chapter 4 REVIEW

Chapter Summary

After reading this chapter and completing the exercises, you should understand the following facts about DOS.

DOS Basics

- First there was PC DOS, which Microsoft licensed to IBM for personal computer (PC) products, beginning with the IBM PC in 1981. Later Microsoft licensed DOS as MS-DOS to many other PC manufacturers, often customized and then sold under that company's name as an original equipment manufacturer (OEM) product.
- The major commercial versions of DOS are no longer available, but there are free versions of DOS; we used FreeDOS for the examples and exercises in this chapter.
- One reason DOS is still in limited use today is its small size, which makes it a good choice for embedded systems.
- The DOS user interface is not easy to work with. DOS can access only the real-mode capabilities of the Intel processors. DOS is a single-tasking OS. DOS provides limited services for DOS

applications. DOS applications can only use conventional memory.

Installing DOS

- The DOS Setup program will partition and format a hard drive, if needed.
- The hardware requirements for any version of DOS are minimal: an IBM or compatible personal computer, 6 MB of free hard disk space for the DOS utilities if you are installing onto a hard disk, and 512 KB of memory.

Working with the DOS Command Prompt

- COMMAND.COM interprets commands by parsing what you enter at the command line. The first parameter is assumed to be the command itself, and COMMAND.COM looks for this command in memory and on disk, loading it into memory and passing the parameters to it.
- Internal commands are commands that are part of COMMAND.COM and are always available to use

when you are at a DOS command prompt. They are very fast to access.

- Use the DOS Help program to determine the command to use and the correct syntax for that command.

- DOS and the FAT file system use a naming convention for files and directories called 8.3 (eight-dot-three). It is best to use only alphanumeric characters for 8.3 file names, even though some nonalphanumeric characters work.

- A file's extension can indicate the type of file.

- File attributes determine how DOS handles a file or directory. The file attributes are read-only, archive, system, hidden, volume label, and directory.

- DOS considers three types of files to be executable: COM, EXE, and BAT. COM and EXE files both contain programming code, while BAT files are batch files, which are not programs but text files that contain commands that are interpreted line by line.

- A directory is a special file that can contain listings of files and other directories. The root directory is the top-level directory and the only one that the FORMAT command creates.

Describe the DOS Boot-Up Process and Create Start-Up Disks

- It is important to understand the boot-up process of an OS in order to troubleshoot failures that occur during the process.

- A cold boot of a personal computer occurs when you turn on the power switch. A warm boot of a personal computer occurs when you press CTRL-ALT-DELETE. A computer Reset button resets a running computer without a power-down and power-up cycle.

- The order of events during boot up of DOS is cold or warm boot, then POST, and then the bootstrap loader looks on the A: or C: drive (or any other drive listed in the BIOS setup) and loads the boot record. Then IO.SYS and MSDOS.SYS (or just KERNEL.SYS in FreeDOS) are loaded, CONFIG.SYS (if it exists) is read and used by MSDOS.SYS or (KERNEL.SYS), COMMAND.COM is loaded, AUTOEXEC.BAT (if it exists) is read and used by COMMAND.COM, and finally, the DOS prompt displays.

Troubleshoot Common DOS Problems

- A failed start-up to DOS that results in the "Non-System Disk" error message means the OS loader program cannot find IO.SYS and/or MSDOS.SYS (or KERNEL.SYS in FreeDOS). The most likely cause of the problem is that a data floppy disk was left in drive A:. Check for, and remove, any floppy disks in the drive and reboot the computer.

- A failed start-up to DOS that results in a "Bad or Missing Command Interpreter" error message means the file COMMAND.COM is missing or is a different version than IO.SYS and MSDOS.SYS. Boot from a bootable floppy disk or bootable disc of the correct version, and copy the COMMAND.COM file to the root of C:.

- When you enter a command and see the "Bad Command or File Name" or "File Not Found" error message, check and recheck your spelling and reenter the command.

- If you are required to enter the date and time when you boot up a computer, this most likely means that there is no AUTOEXEC.BAT on the root of the boot disk. Create an AUTOEXEC.BAT file, even if it is empty, and just about any computer built since 1984 will simply use the internal clock to get this information.

Key Terms List

Key Terms Quiz

Use the Key Terms List to complete the sentences that follow. Not all terms will be used.

1. If you have a/an _____ you can boot an OS, without having it installed on the local hard disk.

2. The _____ for a DOS command is a set of rules for correctly entering a specific command at the command line.

3. A restart of DOS that does not require a power-down/power-up computer cycle is a _____.

4. The only directory created when DOS formats a disk is the _____.

5. After the Power-On-Self-Test (POST) the _____, a small program in the ROM BIOS, loads the boot sector from a disk.

6. The type of memory in which DOS, its drivers, and applications can run is called _____.

7. A/an _____ is one of a special set of file directory entries that indicate certain properties, such as read-only, archive, system, or hidden.

8. A DOS command that is part of the COMMAND.COM program and is always available when DOS is running is called a/an _____.

9. A/an _____ is the only hard disk partition type from which you can start MS-DOS.

10. A word processor is an example of a/an _____ program.

Multiple-Choice Quiz

1. In the 1980s, IBM sold OEM MS-DOS under this product name.
   a. System X
   b. PC DOS
   c. IBM MS-DOS
   d. Linux
   e. Compaq MS-DOS

2. Why use DOS today?
   a. It uses the NTFS file system.
   b. It is the OS of choice of gamers.
   c. DOS can take advantage of Intel protected mode.
   d. It does not need much memory or storage space.
   e. It has a great GUI.

3. What DOS product did Novell own at one time?
   a. FreeDOS
   b. PC DOS
   c. Compaq MS-DOS
   d. Mac OS X
   e. DR-DOS

4. Which Intel processor mode can MS-DOS use?
   a. Advanced
   b. Protected
   c. Real
   d. Standard
   e. Read-only

5. How much minimum free disk space is required when you install MS-DOS 6.22 or IBM PC DOS 2000 onto the hard drive of a computer?
   a. 512 KB
   b. 2 GB
   c. 49 MB
   d. 6 MB
   e. None

6. Which one of the following MS-DOS commands would you use to delete a directory and its contents, including subdirectories, in one pass?
   a. DEL
   b. XCOPY
   c. DELTREE
   d. CHKDSK
   e. ATTRIB

7. What is the default file system used by the installation program for FreeDOS 1.0 Final when it formats a hard drive?
   a. FAT32
   b. NTFS
   c. FAT16
   d. FAT12
   e. CDFS

8. Which of the following is true when installing MS-DOS?
   a. You can use the DOS install setup program.
   b. You must have administrator rights to the computer.
   c. You can create a logical drive up to 4 GB.
   d. You must install from CD.
   e. You can't use MS-DOS until you have activated it with Microsoft.

9. The 8.3 file naming convention is a feature and a limitation of DOS and the _____.
   a. NTFS file system
   b. FAT file system
   c. POST
   d. ROM BIOS
   e. IBM PC

10. Which of the following is an illegal character for a DOS file name?
    a. $
    b. (
    c. \
    d. -
    e. _

11. What do you learn from the syntax of a command?
    a. The command's attributes
    b. The rules for entering that command at the command line
    c. The list of possible errors created by the command
    d. The version of the command
    e. How much memory a command uses

12. What BIOS-based program performs diagnostics as a computer powers up?
    a. IO.SYS
    b. COMMAND.COM
    c. MSDOS.SYS
    d. KERNEL.EXE
    e. POST

13. Which of the following is a FreeDOS configuration file?
    a. FDAUTOEXEC.BAT
    b. FDCONFIG.SYS
    c. CONFIG.SYS
    d. IO.SYS
    e. KERNEL.SYS

14. When using FDISK to prepare a primary partition for MS-DOS 6.22, what is the maximum size you can create?
    a. 4 GB
    b. 2 TB
    c. 512 MB
    d. 2 GB
    e. 650 KB

15. What is the most likely cause of the error message: "Bad Command or File name"?
    a. Incorrect switch
    b. Incorrect versions of DOS
    c. Insufficient permissions
    d. You do not have administrator rights
    e. Typos on the command line

Essay Quiz

1. Recalling what you learned in Chapter 1 about operating system functions, answer the following questions:
   a. What operating system functions does DOS support?
   b. What functions are completely unsupported in DOS?
   c. Of the functions supported in DOS, which, in your opinion, are only minimally supported?

2. You're a new employee doing computer support in a small manufacturing company that uses DOS on two computers running an application written in the late 1980s specifically for this company. The company owns two legal sets of the software. The company that created the software went out of business 10 years ago, and your company has never found an off-the-shelf program to replace this program. For many years the enterprise has maintained the two computers running the program, but now one of them has failed. You are to install DOS on a newly purchased computer that has no OS. Your boss left you with the new computer and a copy of the application software. You have found two original sets of MS-DOS 6.22 on 5.25-inch floppy disks, but the new computer has only a 3.5-inch floppy disk drive. The old computer that failed had a 5.25-inch floppy disk drive. The remaining old computer has only a 3.5-inch drive. One of your co-workers believes you must now buy a new copy of DOS. Describe what you believe your options for installing DOS on the new computer are, including the issue of whether you must buy a new copy of DOS.

3. If you had room on a disk or thumb drive for only a few external DOS commands, which ones would you choose? If you do not have much experience with DOS, open the DOS Help program and browse through the commands. Then suggest several that you would want and explain why you selected each command.

4. In a few sentences, describe the DOS boot-up process.

5. Describe the difference between a primary partition and an extended partition.

Lab Projects

LAB PROJECT 4.1

You are to assist a senior desktop support specialist on a service call. The computer is in the distribution warehouse of a large retailer. He installed DOS on a hard drive as well as a DOS application that the warehouse uses for tracking received orders within the warehouse. He created a CONFIG.SYS file with commands that configure DOS with the settings and drivers needed. Then he created an AUTOEXEC.BAT file that calls the application so that it starts every time the computer starts. Running this one application is to be the only thing that this computer does. However, he has had problems with other users deleting the COMMAND.COM, CONFIG.SYS, and AUTOEXEC .BAT files, causing the system to fail to start properly and requiring that someone replace these files on the hard drive. You are to come up with a solution to this problem and to test the solution on the lab computer on which you installed DOS.

You will need a lab computer with MS-DOS installed.

Then do the following:

1 Describe your solution to the problem of users deleting the COMMAND.COM, CONFIG.SYS, and AUTOEXEC.BAT files.

2 Determine the location of the COMMAND.COM, CONFIG.SYS, and AUTOEXEC.BAT files on the hard drive.

3 Implement your solution on your lab computer.

4 Test your solution and explain the results.

LAB PROJECT 4.2

What is the current state of DOS? Use your Web browser to research any new activity concerning DOS. Look for indications that DOS is a viable product today. Write up your findings, including where you believe the future lies for DOS.

LAB PROJECT 4.3

To test your proficiency with DOS, your boss has assigned you the task of creating several directories on 10 computers that all have floppy disk drives. You will create the same directory structure on each computer. In the root of C:, you will create a directory called DATA. Below that you will create two directories: CUSTOMER and SALES. Below CUSTOMER you will create two directories: WHLSALE and RETAIL. Below SALES, you will create three directories: ADS, PROMOS, and PLANS. You realize that manually entering the DOS commands to create those directories at each computer is going to be boring, and when you do a boring job, you tend to make mistakes. Therefore, you have decided to automate this task.

1 To automate the process of creating several directories on 10 computers, create a batch file similar to the listing that follows, and name the batch file with a name, such as NEWDIRS.BAT.

```
@ECHO OFF
ECHO Subdirectories will be created on drive C:.
PAUSE
C:
CD \
MD \DATA\CUSTOMER\WHLSALE
MD \DATA\CUSTOMER\RETAIL
MD \DATA\SALES\ADS
MD \DATA\SALES\PROMOS
MD \DATA\SALES\PLANS
ECHO The directories have been created.
```

2 Copy the batch file onto a floppy disk or flash drive, and take the floppy disk to a computer to test it. Insert the disk or flash drive, make it current by typing the drive letter, followed by a colon and pressing ENTER. Then run the batch file by entering the name of the batch file at the command prompt.

3 Report the outcome, including the amount of time you estimate it will take to run the batch file on 10 computers. Record how much time you estimate it would have taken to do this task manually at each computer.

5 Windows XP Professional

"Any operating system that has been sustainable for 10 years and still has such a huge following must have a lot going for it."

—Ray Wilson
The Bulletin, *Philadelphia*

M icrosoft introduced two editions of Windows XP, Professional and Home Edition, in October 2001. Windows XP did not have a viable replacement (in the minds of computing professionals) until the advent of Windows 7 in 2009. In this chapter, you will work with Windows XP Professional because it still exists on many desktops and you should be prepared to work with it. You will learn its benefits and features, and you will install it, configure it, customize it, and secure it. Finally, you will learn to troubleshoot common Windows XP Professional problems. ✷

Learning Outcomes

In this chapter, you will learn how to:

LO **5.1** Describe Windows XP Professional benefits and features.

LO **5.2** Install and configure Windows XP Professional.

LO **5.3** Manage Windows XP Professional.

LO **5.4** Secure Windows XP Professional.

LO **5.5** Troubleshoot common Windows XP Professional problems.

145

LO 5.1 | Windows XP Overview

This overview includes a description of the various Windows XP versions and Windows XP's enhanced features and benefits.

Windows XP Editions

There are several versions of Windows XP, including some introduced many months after the initial release. Microsoft designed all of them for consumers at home or in business. The Windows XP lineup and target customers include:

- Windows XP Professional, for the business and power users.
- Windows XP Home Edition, for the home or very small business.
- Windows XP Media Center Edition, which allowed users to use a TV remote control to view TV listings and to catalog songs, videos, and pictures.
- Windows XP Tablet PC Edition, for tablet devices and notebooks.
- Windows XP Embedded, for other devices (usually small, handheld devices).
- Windows XP 64-bit Edition, for more advanced PCs with one 64-bit or two symmetric 64-bit Intel Itanium processors, and up to 16 GB of RAM.

What you won't find in this list is a server version of Windows XP. Beginning with the Windows XP products, Microsoft officially separated its small system OSs from the server system OSs.

> Here is a short list of features available in Windows XP Professional, but not in Windows XP Home: the ability to join a Windows Active Directory domain (a grouping of users and computers for central administration of security); support for two processors and for multiple (human) languages; a built-in backup capability; and file encryption on an NTFS volume.

Although Windows XP Home Edition can work well in a small office that has simple security needs, it is not appropriate for most business environments because it doesn't include many of the security and remote management features of Windows XP Professional. The most significant shortfall of Windows XP Home Edition is its inability to join a Microsoft domain. This becomes a real problem for a small business wanting to bring in a Small Business Server edition of Windows, which includes a Microsoft Active Directory domain. The business would have to upgrade every Windows XP Home Edition computer to Windows XP Professional (or newer version of Windows) before users could enjoy the benefits of logging onto a domain.

try this!

Check Out Your Windows XP Version

It is simple to determine what version of Windows XP you have, as well as the Service Pack level. Try this:

1. Open the Start menu, right-click My Computer, and select Properties.
2. The General tab of System Properties displays the version and Service Pack level, as well as information about the registered user, the Product ID code entered at Windows installation, and some information about the processor and RAM.
3. When you are finished, close the System Properties dialog.

The Windows XP desktop (with the default Bliss wallpaper)

The End of the Road for Windows XP

October 22, 2010, marked the last day you could buy a new PC with Windows XP installed. This date was one year after the introduction of Windows 7. Support for Windows XP Service Pack 2 (SP2) ended July 13, 2010. If you are still using Windows XP, ensure that you have Service Pack 3 installed. Microsoft will support Windows XP with Service Pack 3 (SP3) until April 2014. Service Pack 3 is for 32-bit Windows XP; there was no Service Pack 3 for 64-bit Windows XP.

Windows XP's Features and Benefits

At this writing, Windows XP is a decade-old OS that remained on so many corporate desktops only because its successor, Windows Vista, came with its own set of problems. As a result, many organizations—both large and small—stayed with XP rather than make a costly migration to Vista. That changed with the introduction of Windows 7 in the fall of 2009. Now that there is an able replacement for Windows XP, we will not speak of its benefits versus previous OSs, but just look at a few of its features and benefits because you will still encounter it on the desktop for the next few years.

AVG 2011

A shortcut for the AVG program

The Windows XP Desktop

Most students will be familiar with the Windows XP desktop, so we will give only a brief overview of it. The Windows XP desktop has only one default shortcut, the Recycle Bin, but many applications install a desktop shortcut during their installation. A shortcut is an icon that represents a link to one of many types of objects. Double-clicking on a shortcut has the same results as taking the same action directly on the linked object. An object can be a folder, a data file, a program, or any other type of object an icon can represent in Windows. Shortcuts are often, but not always, distinguished by a small bent arrow, as seen here on the shortcut for AVG Internet Security 2011. A shortcut on the Start menu, shown in Figure 5–1, typically does not have the bent arrow.

The Start menu is the central tool for finding your data files and starting a variety of programs in Windows. The Start menu divides into areas containing shortcuts and submenus. On the top left of the Start menu is an area called the pinned-items list, containing your choice of programs you wish to quickly start. To begin with, your default Internet browser and e-mail software will have shortcuts here, but you can add shortcuts by locating a program file or short-cut and dragging it to the start button. The shortcuts in the pinned-items list remain there unless you choose to remove or change them. Remove a program from the pinned items list by right-clicking it and selecting Unpin From Start Menu. A barely visible separator line marks the end of this list and the beginning of the recently used programs list.

If you click All Programs, you will see a list of icons and folders for installed programs. An arrow to the right of a folder icon indicates that you can expand the folder item to display the contents or submenu. Figure 5–2 shows the All Programs menu.

One handy Start menu item is My Recent Documents, which contains shortcuts to recently opened data files. However, this is only on the menu if you select the "List my most recently opened documents" check box in the Advanced options accessed through the Customize button on the Start Menu Properties dialog box (see Figure 5–3).

FIGURE 5–1 The Windows XP Start menu

Additionally, Windows XP Professional can join a Microsoft Active Directory domain, and participate in the security benefits of domain membership. An Active Directory domain is Microsoft's implementation of directory services, a security accounts database shared across multiple servers, known as domain controllers.

Security

Windows XP Professional contains security components, the most important of which are required logon authentication and the ability to set file and folder permissions on an NTFS volume. We'll look at these two security components later.

Stability and Compatibility

The features in Windows XP that make it stable and that support compatibility with older applications include driver signing (introduced in Windows

FIGURE 5–2 The Windows XP All Programs menu

Both the Windows Update and Automatic Update programs require Internet Explorer. Windows Update requires that IE be the default browser. Updates to these programs (and their successors) may also require updates to Internet Explorer.

2000), Program Compatibility options for older-program support, and, for the first time, automated Windows Updates.

Hardware issues are just part of the stability issue. At the time Windows XP was introduced, older programs, often called legacy applications, existed in computers around the globe. Many took advantage of the way that Windows 98 interacted with the video card, which is very different from how Windows XP does. Therefore, Windows XP has special Compatibility settings in the properties dialog box of each executable program file. You can use this to tell Windows XP to emulate, or pretend, that it is Windows 98 by picking Windows 98/Windows Me from the Compatibility Mode list, as shown in Figure 5–4, and Windows XP will run the program in a modified environment that will not affect other running programs. A compatibility mode may or may not resolve a display problem. You could also force Windows XP to use a different screen resolution and/or color depth when running the old application, using settings in the Display Settings on the Compatibility page. Alternatively, you can run the Program Compatibility wizard, as described later in this chapter under "Troubleshooting Common Windows XP Problems."

Updates

Windows XP provides a Windows Update program that allows you to interactively connect to the Microsoft Windows Update Web page. You can configure a second program, Automatic Update, to automatically connect to the Microsoft site and download updates.

File System Support

As stated earlier, Windows XP supports NTFS, which is the preferred file system. For downward capability it also supports FAT12 for floppy disks, and FAT16 and FAT32 for hard disks. Of these choices, only NTFS offers file and folder security. While FAT32 does use disk space more efficiently than FAT16, and, like NTFS, you can use it on very large hard disk partitions, there is only one reason to choose FAT32 on the volume on which you install Windows XP. You should choose FAT32 if your computer is going to dual-boot

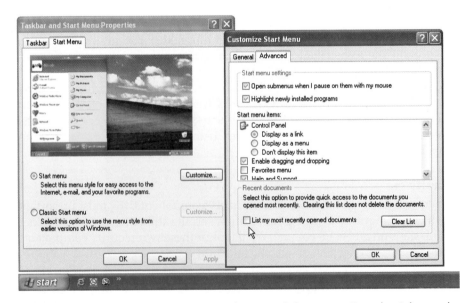

FIGURE 5–3 Select "List my most recently opened documents" on the Advanced page of the Customize Start menu dialog box.

between Windows XP and an OS that does not support NTFS, such as Windows 98 or FreeDOS, and you want to access the volume on which Windows XP is installed from the other OS installation. We have also used FAT32 to format an external hard drive that we move between Windows PCs and an iMac, as FAT32 is a file system that both OSs have in common. However, it does not offer file and folder security.

Similarly, FAT16 would be your choice if you are dual-booting between Windows XP and either Windows 95 (before Service Release 2) or MS-DOS. FAT16 should be your file system of last resort, as it offers neither security nor efficient disk usage.

Recovery Tools

In the area of disaster recovery tools, Windows XP has several tools. These include:

- **Last Known Good (LKG) Configuration** start-up option for start-up failures due to a configuration change. Last Known Good (LKG) only lets you restore the system to a single restore point (not called that), and you only have a narrow window of opportunity in which you can use LKG—on the first reboot after making a configuration change and *before* logging on. Once you log on, XP deletes the former LKG settings, and the new settings with the changes included become the LKG.

- **Task Manager** for stopping errant programs. This Windows utility allows you to see the state of the individual processes and programs running on the computer and to stop one of them, if necessary.

- **Recovery Console**, a character-mode boot-up environment with a command-line interface, accessed either from the installation disc or from the hard drive if you installed it from the disc. You can enter advanced command-line commands to attempt to recover from a major OS failure.

- **Safe Mode** start-up options, a troubleshooting and recovery tool that allows you to select from several options for starting Windows XP with certain components disabled.

- **Device Manager**, to aid in troubleshooting device problems. This Windows Control Panel applet displays the list of hardware and the status and properties of each device. Use this to disable a device or to update or rollback a device driver.

- **System Restore**, a utility that creates restore points, which are snapshots of Windows, its configuration, and all installed programs. If your computer has nonfatal problems after you make a change, you can roll it back to the last restore point.

- **Automated System Recovery (ASR)**, a tool available from the Windows XP Backup program (NTBACKUP.EXE) that you use to recover from damage that prevents the operating system from starting up in any way.

FIGURE 5–4 The Compatibility page allows you to select settings that enable an older program to run.

Check Out Your File System

It is simple to determine the file system on each drive in your computer. Try this:

1. Open the Start menu, double-click Computer/My Computer. Alternatively use the Windows Key + E combination to quickly open Windows Explorer.
2. In Windows Explorer right-click on the Drive C icon and select Properties.
3. On the General page look for the File System field and note the file system.

Automated System Recovery and the Backup Utility are not included in Windows XP Home Edition. Because manufacturers often pre-install Home Edition on computers, many of them attempt to make up for this with a custom system recovery tool, but they may not include a backup utility.

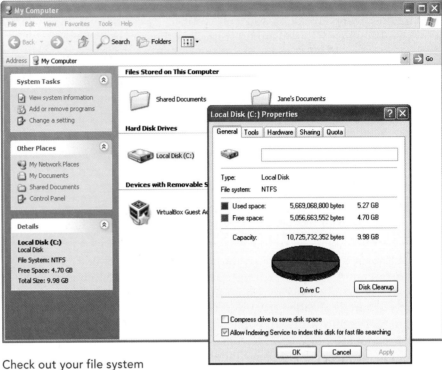

Check out your file system

LO 5.2 | Installing Windows XP

Windows XP is fast approaching the end of its product life cycle, and you are more likely to encounter it on existing computers rather than having to install it, but it is not out of the question that you may need to do so. Today it is much less likely that you will ever need to upgrade an older version of Windows to Windows XP. Therefore, we will only examine how to do a clean install of Windows XP onto an empty hard disk.

Preparing to Install Windows XP

Prepare to install Windows XP Professional by ensuring hardware requirements are met, verifying hardware and software compatibility, determining how to boot into Windows XP setup, and finally, taking time to understand the difference between activation and registration and how to handle both tasks when it comes time to do them during installation.

- Verify that your computer meets necessary hardware minimums by comparing the system configuration with Table 5–1.
- Verify hardware compatibility by running the Windows XP compatibility checker, called the **Upgrade Advisor**, from the installation disc by selecting the Check System Compatibility option. It produces a report with suggestions for resolving incompatibilities, such as locating appropriate drivers for detected hardware. Before installing, be sure that you resolve any compatibility problems, as recommended by the Upgrade Advisor.
- If you do not wish to devote an entire computer to Windows XP, nor wish to dual-boot between Windows XP and another OS, consider creating a virtual machine in which to install Windows XP. Chapter 3 described several options for doing this, including free, downloadable hypervisors. If you choose to do this, create a virtual machine with at least the minimum memory and disk space required by Windows XP, as described next.

As the name implies, the Upgrade Advisor, when run on a computer with an earlier installation of Windows, will test for both hardware and software compatibility.

TABLE 5–1 Windows XP Minimums versus Our Recommended Minimums

Published Minimums for Windows XP Professional	Our Recommended Minimums for Windows XP Professional
Any Intel or AMD 300 MHz or higher processor	Any Intel or AMD 600 MHz or higher processor
128 MB of RAM	512 MB of RAM
1.5 GB of hard drive space	4 GB of hard drive space
Super VGA video card that supports 800 × 600 resolution or greater	Super VGA video card that supports 1024 × 768 resolution or greater
CD-ROM or DVD drive	CD-R, CD-RW or DVD-R drive

When introduced in 2001, Windows XP was not a small operating system in terms of both disk space needed for storage and the CPU and RAM needed to run it and supported programs. But considering that even consumer-grade PCs now commonly come with gigabytes of RAM, terabytes of hard disk space, and video adapters with astounding color and resolution, the Windows XP requirements seem quaint. Table 5–1 shows the minimum hardware requirements to simply install the OS, plus our recommended minimum hardware for a Windows XP installation that would also include common office productivity tools, such as the Microsoft Office suite.

Clean Installation

The goal of a clean installation is to avoid inheriting problems from a previous installation, a downside of an OS upgrade that is installed into the same directory structure of a previous version of the same OS. For this reason, when performing a clean installation, if the hard disk was used previously, you would have the Windows Setup program repartition and format the disk. Recall that a partition defines the boundaries of a logical drive, and repartitioning rewrites the partition information in the master boot record (MBR), making all programs and files on the previous logical drive unavailable. Once you repartition, you must format each logical drive within the partition (one for each primary partition, and one or more for each extended partition).

There are subtle differences in how different OSs partition disks, and some installed utilities (or viruses) may have altered the MBR and boot record on the disk. A repartition and format will truly give you a clean disk.

Now for the bad news: A clean installation is a lot of work when done manually. For this reason, many organizations now use other, more advanced, methods, such as a hands-free, scripted install, or use of an image, which is an exact duplicate of the entire hard drive contents, including the OS and all installed software. But, for the most part, only large organizations employ these methods. Even then, it's important to know how to build a desktop, meaning how to install an operating system and all appropriate software, as well as how to configure it for daily use.

The use of images is very popular in medium-to-large organizations that have dozens, hundreds, or thousands of desktop computers. You create a custom image for a large number of users by installing the OS on a reference computer identical to those on which you will eventually place the images. Then you install all the necessary applications, and finally, you customize the desktop, complete with shortcuts, and add the corporate wallpaper. Next, you use imaging software, such as Symantec's Norton Ghost (www.symantec.com/) or Paragon's Hard Disk Manager (www.paragon-software.com/) to copy the image of the hard drive. You can copy the image onto a CD, but people usually copy it to a network server and distribute it from there. Popular imaging software comes in products for an individual's single images and enterprise products for centrally distributing images out to many desktops.

> The above recommended minimums for hardware are for running Windows XP Professional with application programs that do not require a great deal of disk and RAM space. Be sure to check the hardware requirements of any applications you plan to install into Windows XP Professional.

> IT professionals use scripted installations or some type of imaged installations. These methods often take a great deal of preparation and knowledge and are best used when you must install an OS onto many computers, using identical configurations.

Preparing to Boot into Windows XP Setup

For a clean installation, you need to boot into Windows Setup. The Windows XP CD is bootable, and Microsoft did not include a program to create a set of setup boot disks, as it did with previous versions. Therefore, the simplest approach is to boot from the optical drive. While we don't recommend that you modify the system settings on your lab computer, if you find that you cannot boot from the Windows XP CD, ask your instructor to help you reconfigure the PC to boot from a CD.

In the unlikely event that your computer can't be made to boot from a CD, and if the computer has a floppy disk drive, you can create a set of six (yes, six!) floppy disks as Windows XP setup boot disks using a program downloaded from Microsoft's Web site.

An over-the-network installation requires considerable preparation but we recommend doing it if you need to install Windows on several computers. You must copy the contents of the I386 folder to a network share, and then you must boot up each computer, connect to the network share, and run the Windows XP setup program (WINNT.EXE). If your instructor has prepared an over-the-network installation for you, you will follow the instructions to boot up your computer and connect to the appropriate network share to start the installation.

Registration versus Activation

In one of the final setup steps, setup will prompt you to register your product and to activate it. Many people confuse activation with registration. These are two separate operations for Microsoft software, although we have seen other software that combined these two functions.

Registration is informing Microsoft who the official owner or user of the product is and providing contact information such as name, address, company, phone number, e-mail address, and so on. Registration is still entirely optional. Activation, more formally called Microsoft Product Activation (MPA), is a mandatory new method Microsoft uses to combat software piracy, meaning that Microsoft wishes to ensure that only a single computer uses each Windows XP license.

Mandatory Activation within 30 Days of Installation. Activation is mandatory, but you may temporarily skip this step during installation. You will have 30 days in which to activate the product, during which time it will work normally. If you don't activate it within that time frame, it will automatically disable itself at the end of the 30 days. Don't worry about forgetting because, once installed, Windows XP frequently reminds you to activate it with a balloon message over the tray area of the taskbar. The messages even tell you how many days you have left.

How to Activate. Here is how product activation of Windows XP works. When you choose to activate, either during setup or later when Windows XP reminds you to do it, it generates a product ID from the product key code that you entered during installation and combines it with a 50-digit value that identifies your key hardware components to create an installation ID code. You must send this code to Microsoft, either automatically if you have an Internet connection, or verbally via a phone call to Microsoft. Microsoft then returns a 42-digit product activation code. If you are doing this online, you do not have to enter any codes; it is automatic and very fast. If you are activating over the phone, you must read the installation ID to a representative and

---

If you need to create the setup boot disks, connect to www.support.microsoft.com and search on "KB310994." This is the number of an article that explains how to create the disks and provides links for several versions of the program to create them.

It is important to understand activation because Windows XP Professional is not the only Microsoft product requiring activation, and Microsoft is not the only software vendor using an activation process. Some vendors even stop allowing their older products to automatically activate, which we had happen with our favorite screen capture software after five years. So far, we have not heard of any such problems with Microsoft products.

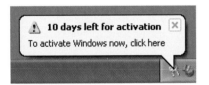

The activate Windows XP reminder balloon message

WARNING!

If you must activate Windows XP by phone, be sure you are sitting at your computer. Our experience is that you have to do all this in real time, entering the code while the representative dictates it; you cannot write the number down and use it later. Your experience may be different from ours.

enter the resulting 42-digit activation code into the Activate Windows By Phone dialog box.

Microsoft Product Activation does not scan the contents of the hard disk, search for personal information, or gather information on the make, model, or manufacturer of the computer or its components, and it sends no personal information about you as part of the activation process. Figure 5–5 shows the dialog box that will open when you start activation by clicking on the reminder message balloon.

Reactivation. The hardware identifier used during activation is called the *hardware hash* because it is generated by applying a special mathematical algorithm to values assigned to the following hardware:

- Display adapter.
- SCSI adapter.
- IDE adapter.
- Network adapter media access control address.
- RAM amount range (for example, 0–64 MB or 64–128 MB).
- Processor type.
- Processor serial number.
- Hard disk device.
- Hard disk volume serial number.
- CD/DVD drive.

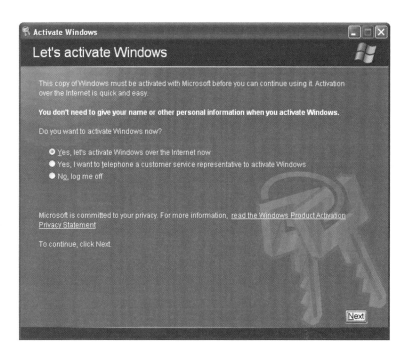

FIGURE 5–5 Activation will take just seconds with an Internet connection.

MPA will occasionally recalculate the hardware hash and compare it to the one created during activation. When it detects a significant difference in the hardware hash, you will be required to reactivate and may have to call and confirm the reason for the reactivation. Adding new hardware, such as disk drives, will not require reactivation, but *replacing* components in the preceding list, or repartitioning and reformatting a drive, will affect the hardware hash. We have had to reactivate after making a great many changes to a computer and again when we decommissioned a computer and used the Windows XP disc from the decommissioned computer to install Windows XP on a different computer.

Learn more about Microsoft Product Activation (MPA) by connecting to **www.support. microsoft.com** and searching on "activation." You will find articles on activation for Windows XP and other Microsoft products. Notice that software purchased with a volume license agreement does not require product activation. Volume licensing is available to organizations needing five or more licenses.

Getting Down to Business: The Installation

Installing Windows XP is simple. The Windows Setup wizard will guide you through every step. The on-screen directions are clear and correct, and you will need to make very few decisions. If you are in doubt about a setting, pressing ENTER will likely perform the correct action by selecting a default setting.

Overall, the installation process takes about an hour. You will spend most of that time watching the screen. Feel free to walk away as the installation is taking place. If it needs input, the installation program will stop and wait until you click the correct buttons.

If you are not available to respond to a prompt on the screen during installation, it will only delay completion. The installation process for Windows XP requires input from you only at the very beginning and at the very end.

Installing Windows XP Professional

This step-by-step describes a clean installation of Windows XP Professional. If you do an upgrade installation or if you install Windows XP Home, the screens will vary from those described here. To complete this exercise, you will need the following:

- A Microsoft/Intel standard personal computer (desktop or laptop) compatible with Windows XP Professional, with at least the minimum hardware and configured to boot from CD, and an unpartitioned hard disk (disk 0, the first hard disk) or a virtual machine you have prepared before beginning the Windows XP installation (see Chapter 3).
- The Windows XP Professional CD.

- The Product ID code from the envelope or jewel case of your Windows XP Professional CD. (The Product ID code was once called the CD key.)
- A 15-character (or less) name, unique on your network, for your computer.
- The name of the work group to use in the class lab.
- A password for the Administrator account on your computer.
- The IP address, subnet mask, and other necessary TCP/IP configuration information, or confirmation from your instructor that you should configure Windows XP Professional to get an IP address automatically.

Step 1

Insert the Windows XP CD and boot the computer. After inspecting your hardware configuration, Windows XP Professional Setup will show the blue screen of character mode setup and copy files to your computer. After copying the files, it will prompt you to remove the CD and reboot the system. Windows Setup will start, load system device drivers, and display the Welcome To Setup screen. Press ENTER to start the installation.

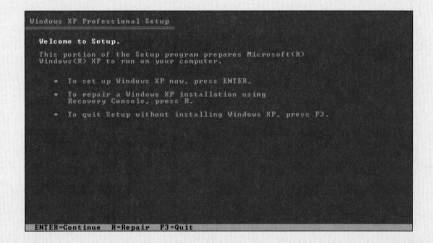

Step 2

The End User License Agreement (EULA) appears. This is your agreement to comply with your license to use Windows XP Professional. Read the EULA; press F8 to acknowledge acceptance of the agreement and to continue.

Step 3

If your hard disk is unpartitioned, create a new partition by ensuring that the highlight is on "Unpartitioned space," and then pressing c to create a partition in the unpartitioned space. On the following screen, you can either accept the default size for the partition or enter a smaller value in the highlighted box. In our example, we decided to use half the disk space. We had to first use the BACKSPACE key to overwrite the default value and enter 2048.

On the next screen select the new partition and press ENTER to install Windows XP on that partition. Then, you need to decide on the file system format for the new partition. Select *Format the partition using the NTFS file system* and then press ENTER. The screen will show a progress bar while formatting the partition.

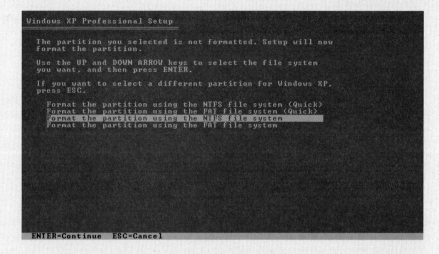

Step 5

Next, setup copies files to the newly formatted partition, displaying another progress bar. On a clean installation, setup creates a folder named Windows in C:\ into which it installs the OS, creating appropriate subfolders below this folder. After it completes copying the base set of files to this location, your computer reboots, and the graphical mode of Windows XP setup begins. On the left of the screen, incomplete tasks have a white button, completed tasks have a green button, and the current task has a red button. Continue with the installation, following the instructions that appear for each new task.

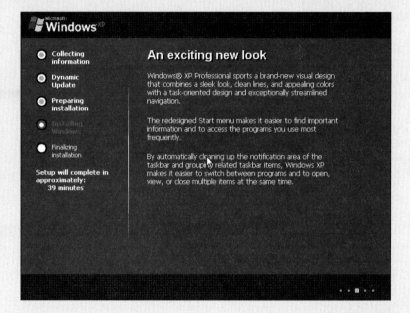

Step 6

On the Regional And Language Options screen, leave the defaults and click Next, unless told otherwise by your instructor. On the Personalize Your Software page, enter your name and the name of your school or employer. Next, you must enter a valid product key for Windows XP. You can find this on the CD case containing your copy of Windows XP. Be sure to enter it exactly, or you will be unable to continue.

Step 7

Next, name your computer; this identifies your computer on a network. Check with your network administrator for an appropriate name. In addition to a valid name for your computer, you need to create a password for the Administrator user account. This password will allow you to modify and fix the computer. Next, set the date, time, and time zone.

Step 8

If it detected a network card, it will install the network components and you'll have an opportunity to configure the network settings. On the Network Settings page, select Typical Settings, unless told otherwise by your instructor. Once you have installed the networking elements, you need to configure the network. Relax. Windows Setup will do most of the work for you. Unless you have specific instructions from your network administrator, the default settings are the preferred choices.

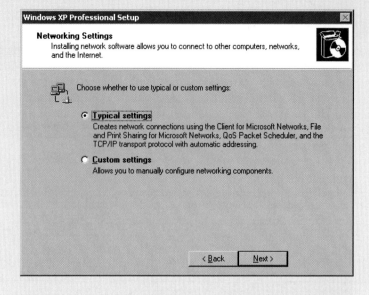

Step 9

If your computer participates in a domain-based network, you need to set the domain options. The computer shown here is on a network without a domain, and we have supplied a work group name. Enter the setting provided by your instructor, and click Next. Be prepared to wait for several minutes while Windows Setup copies files.

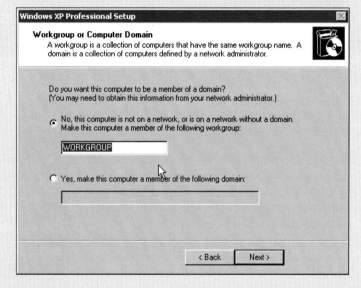

Step 10

After it copies the files required for the final configuration, Windows XP will reboot. During this reboot, Windows XP determines your screen size and applies the appropriate resolution. This reboot can take several minutes to complete, and once the reboot is complete, you must log on as the Administrator. There may be balloon messages over the tray area of the taskbar. A common message concerns the display resolution. If this message appears, click the balloon and allow Windows XP to automatically adjust the display settings.

Step 11

Another message reminds you that you have 30 days left for activation. We suggest that when you do a single install, you test it for a few days before activating it, in case you need to make any significant changes in the hardware. It might appear to the activation program that you have installed it on a different computer or made sufficient changes to a computer after product activation to require reactivation. Delaying activation also allows time to work out any problems with network connectivity. If you are not choosing to activate at this time, click on the close button of the message balloon. Congratulations! You have completed the Windows XP installation and should have a desktop with the default Bliss background.

Post-Installation Tasks

After you install Windows XP, you have a few necessary post-installation tasks. They include verifying network access (assuming you connected to a network) and installing at least the critical updates, including Service Packs. You should complete these tasks before moving on to customizing the desktop for yourself or another user and performing other desktop management tasks.

Verifying Network Access

Once you complete the installation, open the Start Menu | My Computer | My Network Places and see if you can see any computers on the network besides your own. In My Network Places, click on *View workgroup computers*, which is a link in the task pane on the left. This will show all the computers in the work group or domain in which your computer resides (recall the work group or domain setting from the installation). In Figure 5–6 you can see just one computer, Webster01, in the Osborne work group. If you also used a work group name that was different from that chosen by your fellow students, your computer might also be alone like Webster01 is.

To see other work groups and domains, find and click the link labeled *Microsoft Windows Network* in the task pane under Other Places. Figure 5–7 shows three work groups or computers: Htc, Osborne, and Workgroup. Just seeing other work groups and domains on the network is confirmation that a network connection is working because you must connect and communicate on a network to be aware of the other work groups, domains, and computers. However, if you are eager to see other computers, open one of these work groups or domains.

FIGURE 5–6 Osborne work group with one computer showing

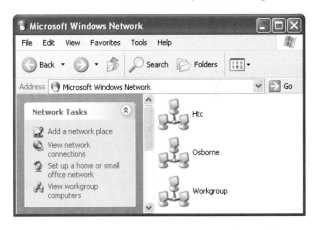

FIGURE 5–7 Microsoft Windows Network with three work groups or domains showing

> My Network Places refers to all groupings of computers as work groups, even though in Figure 5–7, Htc is a domain, and the others are work groups.

Virtual Machine Additions

If you installed Windows XP into a virtual machine, be sure to install the virtual machine additions for Windows. Whatever hypervisor you are using will remind you to do this, usually when you start up the newly installed OS in the virtual machine. How you start the installation of the additions varies by product. You may simply need to respond to a pop-up window or look in one of the menus on the window surrounding your virtual machine. For instance, the Action menu for a VM in Microsoft Virtual PC 2007 contains the option Install Or Update Virtual Machine Additions. Once launched, the Virtual Machine Additions installation program will run within the virtual machine, as shown in Figure 5–8.

Installing Updates

Now that you have verified network access, your next task is to

---

Check Out Your Neighborhood

If your Windows XP computer connects to a network, verify that you can see other computers on the network. Only computers with the Server service turned on are visible. Windows XP turns this on by default during installation, so you should see your computer and maybe other computers on the network. Try this:

1. Select Start | My Computer. In My Computer, under Other Places, select My Network Places. If you share any folders on your network, you may see them in this view. If you see folders, you have verified network connectivity.

2. Under Network Tasks (in the task pane), select View Workgroup Computers. You should, at minimum, see your computer in the work group you specified during installation (see title bar).

3. Under Other Places, select Microsoft Network to see other work groups on your network. When you have finished, close all open windows.

try this!

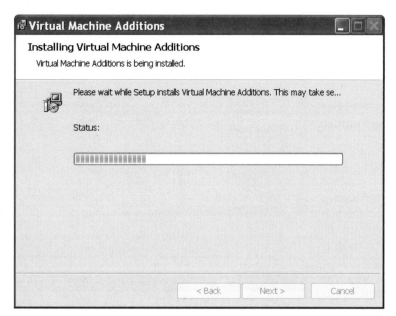

FIGURE 5–8 Microsoft Virtual PC 2007 installing Virtual Machine Additions

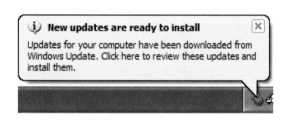

FIGURE 5–9 Windows Update balloon message

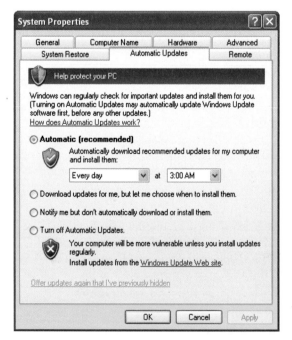

FIGURE 5–10 Choosing to enable automatic updates

install updates. This is important, especially if you are on a network and/or the Internet, because many of the updates close security holes that someone can exploit over a network. How you actually obtain updates will depend on the organization (school or business) where you install Windows XP. In some organizations, the IT department may distribute updates for new installations on CD even before connecting a computer to a network. Other organizations may make them available on a shared folder on the private network. If you have an Internet connection, you can connect to the Microsoft Web site and download them free.

Windows XP actually reminds you to enable Automatic Update. Soon after installing Windows XP (a day or two in our experience), a message balloon (see Figure 5–9) will pop up from the taskbar suggesting that you automate updates. If you click on this message, the Automatic Updates Setup wizard will run, allowing you to configure the update program. You say you've never seen this message balloon, and would certainly like to automate the update process? No problem—simply right-click on My Computer (on the Start menu), select Properties, and then click the Automatic Updates tab and select the settings you desire (see Figure 5–10). Then, whenever your computer connects to the Web, it checks the Windows Update page. What happens next depends on the setting you chose.

If you have a slow Internet connection (dial-up), you may want to disable Automatic Updates and opt to use Windows Update to manually connect and download the updates at times that will not interfere with your work. If you have a faster connection, you may elect to have the updates downloaded automatically, and review and select the updates you wish to install. Whichever option you choose, keeping Windows XP up-to-date should reduce the risk of a virus exploiting a system flaw.

Over its lifetime, Windows XP has had countless updates and three Service Packs. If you install Windows today, the distribution CD may include a Service Pack, depending on the vintage of the CD, but it will be a long way behind the curve as far as the latest updates are concerned. Further, if you wait and allow Automatic Update to bring the Windows XP installation up-to-date, several days will pass before this is accomplished. Therefore, we recommend you use the Windows Update program to manually access the updates. This will still take several iterations, but you will bring it up-to-date sooner this way.

Start Windows Update from a shortcut on the Start menu or from the Control Panel task list. Internet Explorer will open and connect to the Windows Update Web page, and you will see a message asking if you want to install the latest version of Windows Update Control. Click Yes, and follow instructions to install any further updates to the Windows Update program.

After installing the latest updates to Windows Update, the Welcome To Windows Update page will display. Click Express Install to start a quick scan of your computer to determine what

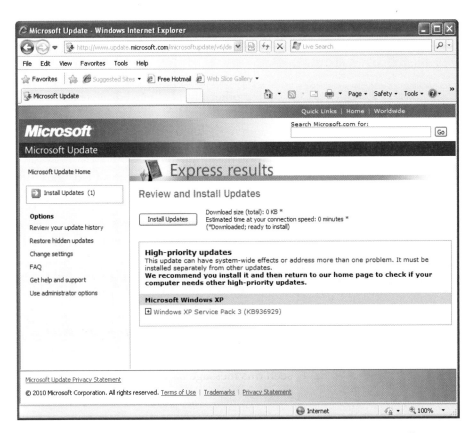

FIGURE 5–11 Continue updating until there are no more updates to install.

high priority updates should install. There will be a delay while it scans and looks for available updates. Then the Express Updates page will display the list of high-priority updates Microsoft recommends for your computer. Click Install Updates to proceed.

Read and accept any End User License Agreements (EULAs). The updates will download and install. After the critical updates install, restart the computer. Now run Windows Update again; click the Custom Install button to initiate another scan. At the conclusion of this scan, review the updates listed, remove any updates you don't wish to install at this time, and click Download and Install now.

Figure 5–11 shows Windows XP Service Pack 3 as the only result. This appeared only after running Windows Update several times, and downloading and installing all the updates that preceded SP3. This effort included several reboots. When you have installed all the Critical updates and all the optional updates you wish, close all open windows.

LO 5.3 | Managing Windows XP Professional

Once you have installed Windows XP Professional, configured the OS to work with your network, and installed updates and service packs, it's time to customize Windows for the user. In the case of a new OS, the first few times you do this, you will need to find familiar tools and perhaps learn how to use new ones.

In this section, you will practice some common procedures for customizing and managing Windows XP, creating a new partition, installing and removing applications and Windows components, and preparing the desktop for users, including modifications to display settings and adding a printer.

Creating New Partitions

If you performed a clean install of Windows XP on a hard disk and created a partition that did not use the entire physical disk space, then you will need

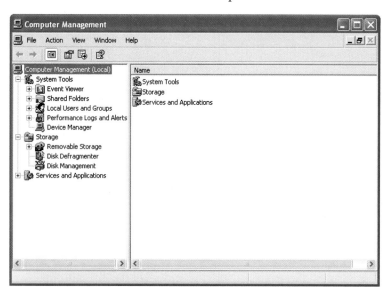

to partition that remaining space. Also, if you add another physical hard drive to your computer you will want to create one or more partitions on the new drive.

Partitioning a very large hard disk into two or more partitions allows the operating system and applications installed into the operating system to "own" the system partition, the partition on which the OS is installed. This also provides a distinct drive or drives that can be devoted purely to data and therefore can be easier to back up.

To create a partition you must log on as an Administrator, open the Start menu, right-click My Computer, and select Manage from the context menu. This will open the Computer Management console. You can also open this console from Start | Control Panel | Administrative Tools.

In Computer Management, click the *Disk Management* folder under the Storage node. After a brief delay, the Disk Management snap-in will appear in the right pane of the console. If you installed Windows XP according to the instructions in Step-by-Step 5.01, drive C: is a primary partition using the NTFS file system. Drive letters are assigned to hard disk drives first and then to optical drives. If there is unallocated space remaining on a hard disk, you will see an area labeled "Unallocated" with the amount of space available.

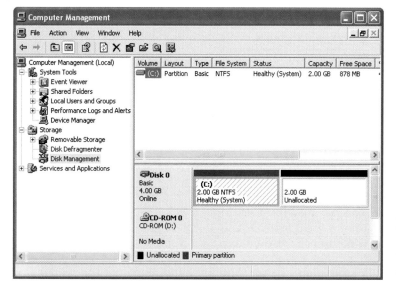

Before creating the new partition on the hard disk, we recommend changing the drive letter of the CD-ROM drive so that drive D will be available for the new partition: Right-click on the area labeled "CD-ROM 0," and select Change Drive Letter And Paths from the menu. In the Change Drive Letter And Paths dialog box, select the Change button and then choose a new drive letter for the CD-ROM drive. Click *OK*, then click *Yes* in the Confirm box, and keep the Computer Management console open to Disk Management.

Right-click in the box labeled "Unallocated," and click New Partition to launch the New Partition wizard. In the Welcome page of the New Partition wizard, select the Next button. In the Select Partition Type page, select *Primary Partition* and click *Next*. In the Specify Partition Size page, select a partition size that is at least 1 MB smaller than the maximum space. Then click *Next*.

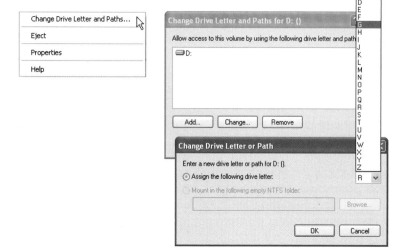

In the Assign Drive Letter page, keep the default drive letter setting (which should now be D:) and click *Next*. In the Format Partition page, keep the default selection, which will format the drive with NTFS, using the Default allocation size (Don't mess with this!), and will name (label) the volume New Volume. Click *Next*.

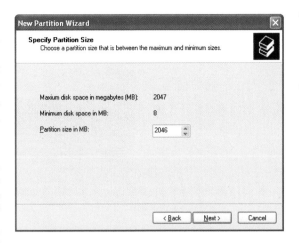

The Completing The New Partition Wizard page displays a summary of the settings you have selected. Review these settings. If you wish to change any of the settings, use the Back button to find the page for the setting. Otherwise, click *Finish* to complete the partitioning. If you watch Disk Management carefully, you will see the Unallocated space change to a partition, then the formatting progress will display, and finally it will be shown as a Healthy volume. Close the Computer Management console.

Installing and Removing Applications

For most people, a computer in itself is not important; it's the work (or play) that we can accomplish using the computer that is important. Therefore, Windows XP is no more than a pretty face until you install the applications that will enable someone to do the desired tasks.

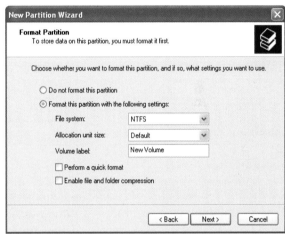

Windows XP allows you to add programs through a Control Panel applet named Add Or Remove Programs. You will rarely need to use this option, as most applications come with setup programs that start as soon as you insert the CD or DVD (if Autorun is enabled, which it is by default). But if this is not the case, and you cannot find the setup program on the CD or DVD, use the Add New Program button in Add Or Remove Programs, and it will search for the setup program.

Installing an Application in Windows XP

All programs today come with mostly automated installation programs—even free programs. Never try to install a program by simply copying its files onto a hard drive. This will not work because when a program installs it normally copies its files to a folder hierarchy and makes changes in the Windows registry that allow the program to

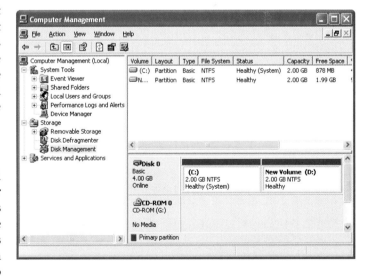

be integrated with Windows components. Learn more about the registry in Chapter 7.

Removing Programs

The longer you have an OS installed on a user's computer, the more housekeeping it requires. One cleanup task is to remove no-longer-needed (or never-really-were-needed) programs.

Computers purchased with Windows XP preinstalled often have many additional programs installed that you'll never use. These programs are

WARNING!

Never remove a program by simply deleting it from disk. Even if you succeed in removing all its files, Windows and other programs may still try to start the program, and you get error messages and no easy way to stop this from occurring.

Creating a New User

Creating a new user account enables that user to log in with a user name and password. This allows an administrator to set the rights and permissions for the user.

Creating users in User Accounts is a straightforward process. You need to provide a user name and an initial password. The user can change the password later. You also need to know the type of account to create: computer administrator or limited.

Unless otherwise specified by an administrator, you should create one limited account (member of the Users group) per user of the computer and one account that is a member of the local Administrators group (in addition to the Administrator account created during installation). The reason for creating two administrator accounts is so that if one administrator is not available, or is not able to log on to the computer, another one can. It's simple redundancy. Windows XP actually reminds you to do this; the first time you try to create a local account after installing Windows XP it will only allow you to create a computer administrator account. After that, it will allow you to create limited accounts.

Password Reset Disk

Windows XP Professional allows the currently logged-on user to create a Password Reset disk to use in case of a forgotten password. This is very important to have because if you forget your password, and an administrator resets the password using User Accounts or Local Users and Groups, then when you log on using the new password, you will find that you will lose access to some items, including files that you encrypted when logged on with the forgotten password. When you reset a password with a Password Reset disk, you can log on using the new password and still have access to previously encrypted files.

Best of all, with the Password Reset disk, users have the power to reset their own passwords. You only have this power if you think to create a Password Reset disk before you forget the password! If you need to create a Password Reset disk for a computer on a network (domain), search the help system for "Password Reset Disk" and follow the instructions for a computer on a domain.

The Password Reset disk is both a convenience and a threat. You only have to create the disk once, regardless of how many times you may later change the password. It is a convenience in that you only have to make it one time and it will always work. It is a threat in that it will always work on your machine, no matter who has it and uses it!

try this!

Add Administrative Tools to the Windows XP Professional Start Menu

Administrative Tools is a special folder containing helpful tools for administration. Make it handy by adding it to your All Programs folder now. You will need the computer on which you successfully installed Windows XP Professional in Step-by-Step 5.01. Try this:

1. Right-click Start Menu, select Properties, select the Start Menu tab, and then click the Customize button next to the words "Start Menu."

2. In the Customize Start Menu dialog box, select the Advanced tab, and scroll the list under Start Menu Items to the bottom to System Administration Tools. Then select the radio button next to Display on the All Programs Menu.

3. Click *OK* twice to close the Customize Start Menu dialog box as well as the Taskbar and Start Menu Properties dialog box.

4. Confirm that Administrative Tools now displays on the All Programs list. You will use Administrative Tools in upcoming step-by-step exercises in this chapter and later in this book.

To create and manage users, you log on as the Administrator or a member of the local Administrators group. Be sure to assign a password to the Administrator account so that only authorized users can access this all-powerful account.

When you create new user accounts on your own computer, create both a computer administrator account and a limited account for yourself. Use the administrator account whenever you need to install new software or make changes to the computer. Use the limited account for your day-to-day work. This protects your computer from viruses that might use the elevated privileges of your administrator account to cause damage.

Encryption is a very advanced feature that you should use only after studying it carefully. It would take more than a chapter just to talk about encryption in depth!

Step-by-Step 5.03

Creating User Accounts and a Password Reset Disk in Windows XP

This exercise describes how to create new user accounts in Windows XP Professional. First, you will create a new account that is a member of the administrators group, and then you will create a limited account. If you are working with Windows XP Home Edition, you will already have an account, in addition to the built-in Administrator, that is an administrator type. After creating the new accounts, you will log on with one of the new accounts and create a password reset disk.

To complete this step-by-step exercise you will need the following:

- A computer with Windows XP Professional installed.
- A USB flash drive or a floppy disk if the computer has a floppy disk drive.
- The password for the Administrator.
- A blank formatted floppy disk.

In this exercise the assumption is that no new accounts were created since creating the Administrator account during installation.

Step 1

Log on as Administrator and open Control Panel. Select the User Accounts applet. Click CREATE A NEW ACCOUNT. On the Name the New Account page enter the first letter of your first name, followed by your last name and click NEXT.

Step 2

On the Pick the Account Type page, the option for limited is grayed out (unavailable) if this is the first account you have created since installation. The first new account (in addition to the Administrator account) can only be a computer administrator. Notice the tasks a computer administrator can do, then click CREATE ACCOUNT.

Step 3

After creating the account, you automatically return to the main page of User Accounts where you should see your new account.

Step 4

Now you can create one or more limited accounts. In this case, you'll create one. Follow the steps you used to create the previous account, creating a user name consisting of your entire first name and the first letter of your last name. *Be sure to read the description of the limited account type on the Pick an Account Type page.* The illustration shows several accounts.

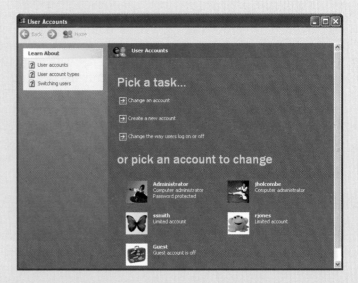

172

Step 5

Back on the main page, the newest account will appear as a limited account, and each of these new accounts has a blank password. Create a password for each account beginning with the computer administrator account. In User Accounts select Change an account. On the Pick An Account To Change page, select the new computer administrator you created above.

Step 6

On the following page, select Create a Password. Before creating a password, click on each of the items in the Learn About list to learn how to create a secure password as well as a good password hint, and a message about what to do when you forget your password. Then, use what you learn to fill in the text boxes for the new password and a password hint, and then click CREATE PASSWORD.

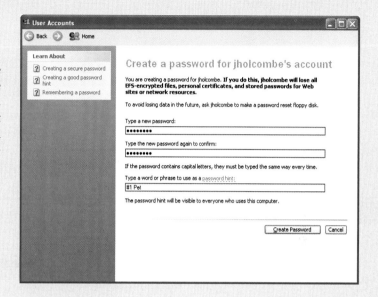

Step 7

Use the BACK button to go back to the Pick an Account to Change page, select each of the accounts you created, and create a password and password hint. When you have created passwords for your accounts, close the User Accounts Pick an Account to Change page.

Step 8

While you were able to create accounts and to create passwords, you were not able to place users in any group accounts other than Administrators or Users or add any additional information. If you want to go beyond the capabilities of the User Accounts tool, you need to open the Computer Management Console. Do that now. Right-click on My Computer and select Manage.

Step 9

In the Computer Management console, select Local Users and Groups and click on Users. The users you created in the previous steps will display, as well as users not shown in User Accounts.

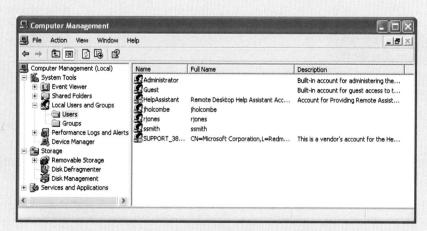

Double-click the limited account you created to open the Properties for this user account. The User Accounts tool used the user name you entered as both the user name and full name. Change the full name to your full name and add a description (such as "student" or "manager").

Select the Member Of tab and click the Add button. In the Select Groups box, click the Advanced button to bring up another Select Groups box that will allow you to view all the local groups in a list from which you can make a selection.

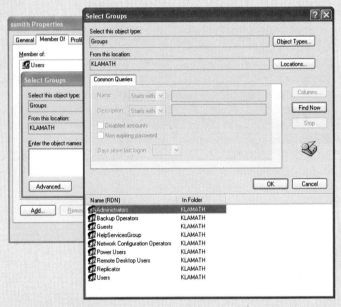

Select Power Users from the list. Then click OK three times to close the three open dialog boxes. When you return to the Computer Management console you may have to refresh the Users node by selecting the Users folder and pressing the F5 key. The full name and description for the limited account should now show. Close Computer Management.

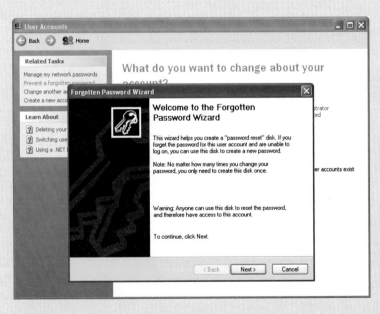

Now create the Password Reset disk. First insert a blank, formatted flash drive into a USB port or insert a blank formatted floppy disk into drive A:. Then open User Accounts and on the Pick A Task page select the account that you are currently logged in on as (Administrator). On the next page select *Prevent a forgotten password* from the list of *Related Tasks* (on the left). Read the Welcome page of the Forgotten Password Wizard, and then click NEXT.

On the Create a Password Reset Disk, select the drive and click next. On the Current User Account Password page enter the current user account password and click NEXT. The Creating Password Reset Disk page will show a progress bar while creating the disk. When it completes, click NEXT, then click FINISH to close the wizard. Remove the flash drive or disk. Make sure you properly label the flash drive or disk, including the account name and computer, then store it in a safe and secure place.

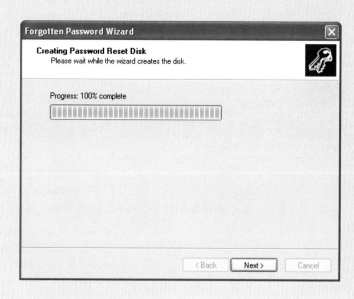

Applying Security to Files, Folders, and Printers

Windows XP Professional fully supports the use of permissions to protect files, folders, and printers. Permissions for files and folders depend on the use of the NTFS file system, as does file encryption. Printer permissions are supported regardless of the file system in use. In this section you will explore NTFS permissions for files and folders and encryption on NTFS volumes.

Securing Files and Folders on an NTFS Drive

Windows XP supports the NTFS file system that allows you to control who has access to specified files and folders by assigning permissions. These permissions restrict access to local users and groups as well as to those who connect to these resources over the network. Although, in the case of those connecting over a network, the share permissions (not related to NTFS permissions) take effect first and may block access to the underlying files and folders. Only NTFS volumes allow you to assign permissions to files and folders. In this section, we will focus on the security features of NTFS in Windows XP, including file and folder permissions and encryption.

File and Folder Permissions. On a volume formatted with the NTFS file system, each folder and file has a set of security permissions associated with it. Each file and folder on an NTFS volume has an associated access control list (ACL), which is a table of users and/or groups and their permissions to the file or folder. Each ACL has at least one access control entry (ACE), which is like a record in this tiny ACL database that contains just one user or group account name and the permissions assigned to this account. An administrator, or someone with the permissions to create ACEs for the file or folder, creates the ACEs. To view the ACEs in an ACL for a file or folder, open the properties dialog box and select the Security tab. Figure 5–20 shows the Security page for a folder named *spreadsheets*. Notice the list of permissions for the user jholcombe. This is an ACE.

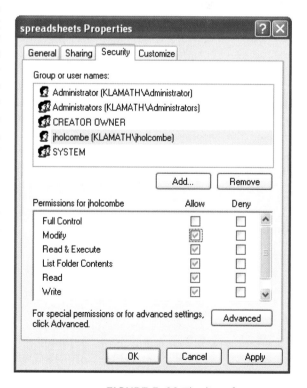

FIGURE 5–20 The list of permissions for a folder

The permissions you can set on folders differ slightly from those that you can set on files. In both cases, there are standard permissions, each of which is composed of several special permissions. For example, the standard file permission called Read permission consists of the following special permissions: Read Data, Read Attributes, Read Extended Attributes, Read Permissions (the permissions on the file), and Synchronize.

The standard file permissions are follows:

- Full Control
- Read
- Modify
- Write
- Read and Execute

The standard folder permissions are the same as the standard file permissions with the added permission of List Folder Contents.

Folders that contain sensitive information, such as payroll files, should be protected from unauthorized access. To do this you can assign permissions to certain users and groups, and you can keep others out, implicitly or explicitly. This is possible because each of the standard permissions and each of the special permissions has three states: Allow, Deny, or implicit denial. You can check only one box at a time for any permission. If both the Allow and Deny boxes are clear, that permission does not apply at all—it's implicitly denied. Checking the Allow box allows that permission, and checking the Deny box denies that permission—it's explicitly denied. Why have these three-state permissions? If you leave a user account off the permissions list, thus implicitly denied access to a file or folder, you can give that user access to the file and folder through membership in a group that has access. On the other hand, an administrator can explicitly grant access to a group or explicitly restrict access to a member of the group using the Deny state of a permission. This will override the permission to the file or folder that was granted to the group.

Most of the time, standard permissions are all you need.

try this!

Research Special Permissions

It is important to understand permissions so that you can protect resources from unauthorized access or damage. Don't try to memorize them—remember that help is just a few mouse clicks away. Use the Windows XP Help and Support Center now to see the list of special permissions that make up each of the standard permissions listed here. Try this:

1. Start Help and Support from the Start menu. In the Windows XP Help and Support Center, use the search box to find articles on special permissions.
2. In the Search Results list, open article *How to set, view, change, or remove special permissions for files and folders in Windows XP* and read the descriptions of each of the special folder permissions.
3. When you have completed your research, close Help.

During installation, the Windows setup program sets default permissions on the folders it creates that allow the OS to function but that keep ordinary users from harming the OS. You can cause harm to the OS if you change these default settings. You should change NTFS permissions only for data files and folders that you create for data files.

Permissions Assigned to Personal Folders. When a new user logs on to Windows the operating system will create personal folders just for that user. In addition, if the local drive is an NTFS partition, it will assign a default set of permissions to those folders designed to keep other users out of those folders. Now you will explore the default permissions set on these folders.

NTFS Permission Inheritance. The folders and files on a disk volume are in a hierarchy, with the drive itself at the top, followed by the root folder and subfolders. A newly created folder or file inherits the permission settings of the parent folder, unless you choose to block this inheritance, which is an option in the Security dialog of the file or folder. When you view permissions on a file or folder, the permissions inherited from the parent will be grayed out, and you will not be able to modify those permissions at that level. You can assign new permissions, but you cannot alter inherited permissions. You can modify them in the folder in which they originated. You can choose to block inheritance on a folder or file to which you wish to assign different (usually more restrictive) permissions. If you block inheritance, Windows XP will prompt you with the option to copy the previous inherited permissions.

Step-by-Step 5.04

Viewing Permissions on Personal Folders

In this step-by-step exercise, you will explore the NTFS permissions automatically assigned to personal folders. To complete this step-by-step exercise, you will need the following:

- The computer on which you successfully installed Windows XP Professional in Step-by-Step 5.01.

- The user accounts created in Step-by-Step 5.03.
- Drive C: set up as an NTFS partition (per the instructions in the installation step-by-step exercise).

Step 1

Log on as the limited account you created in Step-by-Step 5.03. Open My Computer, browse to C:\Documents and Settings, and notice the folders. There will be one for each logged-on user, plus one titled All Users.

Step 2

Open the folder for the account with which you logged on and view the contents that make up the user profile for the user. Created the first time that user logged on, they contain the files that hold that user's desktop files, favorites, the Start menu, and several other important folders and files. Windows creates these folders on any file system that Windows supports, even FAT16 or FAT32.

When a user first logs on to a computer that has NTFS on the boot drive (the drive in which the system files are installed), Windows sets permissions on the personal folders it creates for the user. To view these permissions, right-click the folder named for your user account, select Properties, and then click the Security tab. Click the Permissions button, and you will see the list of users and groups that have permissions to the folder. Notice that the Everyone group is not on the list.

By default, the Security page shows only the standard permissions and lets you assign only the standard permissions. Notice the Allow and Deny check boxes for each standard permission. To see the special permissions, click the Advanced button and then click the View/Edit button to see the special permissions assigned to the selected user. You will rarely need these special permissions. Click Cancel three times to close the Properties dialog box.

Try to open a folder named for another account. You will not be able to do this, because the user account you are using does not have permissions to access the personal folder of another user. Log off.

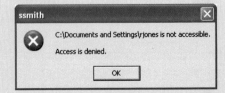

Combining NTFS and Share Permissions

Anyone sitting at your computer who logs on can access files and folders on an NTFS volume if the permissions allow. You might say that person has to go through two security "doors": the authentication door (during logon) and the authorization door in which the security system checks the ACL on each file or folder for NTFS permissions for that user.

If you share a folder on that same NTFS volume, it is visible to network users, and anyone coming over the network comes through three doors. Only this time the authentication door is between the computer and the network (yes, even though it is not apparent, an incoming user authenticates). Then there are two authorization doors: one at the share point (the shared folder) at which Windows checks permissions to see if the incoming user is authorized to have access and another at the NTFS file and folder level where it checks the NTFS permissions.

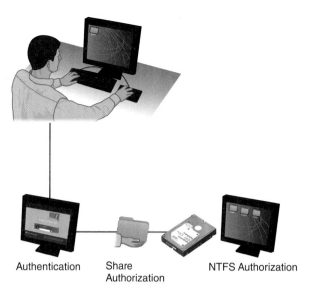

Authentication   Share   NTFS Authorization
                   Authorization

Accessing an NTFS file or folder through a network share

NTFS File and Folder Encryption

Windows XP Professional allows you to make individual files or folders even more secure using the Encrypting File System (EFS), a component of the operating system, to encrypt files and folders saved on an NTFS volume. See how this works in the following scenario.

Jaime is a financial planner who carries his laptop to meetings with his clients. On his hard drive he has files containing confidential data on each of his clients. He needs to be sure to keep this information secure from prying eyes, and he worries that if someone steals his laptop this information would fall into the wrong hands. To guard against this, Jaime has four good practices:

1. He encrypts all confidential data files on his laptop, which is running Windows XP Professional.

2. He makes sure that he always uses a complex password that would be difficult to guess.

3. He changes his password frequently and never reuses old passwords.

4. He always uses the Lock Computer option in the Windows Security dialog box whenever he leaves his computer unattended—even briefly.

Encrypting a File or Folder. Jaime has encrypted a folder on his laptop that he calls Data. While the folder itself is not actually encrypted, all files in this folder are now encrypted and any new files he saves into that folder are automatically encrypted. This may sound rather high tech and inconvenient, but it was quite simple to do, and once Jamie turned on encryption for this folder, he never had to think about it again. As long as he logs on with the same account that he used when he turned on encryption, he simply opens the encrypted files using his normal applications. The security components of the OS verify his authorization to access these files *and* that he is the person who encrypted them. Someone logged on to his computer with a different account will not be able to open these files, even if the person uses an account with Full Control permission to the files.

To encrypt a file or folder, simply open the Properties dialog box, click the Advanced button, and place a check mark in the box labeled *Encrypt contents to secure data*. When you click OK to close the Properties dialog box you must make a decision. In the case of a folder, you must decide whether to encrypt

> Don't use file encryption unless you are an advanced user who has researched it first or unless you have the support of skilled professionals who can take steps to ensure that you can successfully recover your encrypted data.

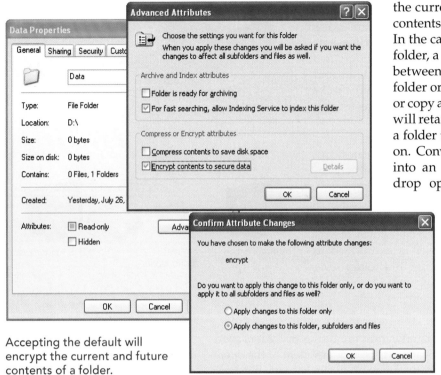

Accepting the default will encrypt the current and future contents of a folder.

The warning message when encrypting a file

If you use a Windows XP Professional computer at school or work, you may discover that encryption isn't available when you look at the Advanced Properties of a file or folder on an NTFS volume. This is because it is possible for a knowledgeable administrator to turn off encryption.

the current contents of the folder and all new contents or to encrypt only the new contents. In the case of a file located in an unencrypted folder, a Warning message asks you to choose between encrypting the file and the parent folder or encrypting only the file. If you move or copy an encrypted file to an NTFS volume, it will retain its encryption, even if it is moved to a folder that does not have encryption turned on. Conversely, moving an unencrypted file into an encrypted folder using a drag-and-drop operation will not result in the file being encrypted. Be sure to only use cutting and pasting (or saving from within an application) to move files into encrypted folders. Further, if you move or copy an encrypted file to a non-NTFS volume it will be decrypted.

Decrypting Files and Folders. The only person who can decrypt a file or folder is the person who encrypted it or a member of a special group called recovery agents. By default, only the local Administrator is a member of this group. Recovery is not the same as being able to directly access the data; it is a very advanced task, described in Windows XP Professional Help and Support.

Securing a Local Printer

In addition to setting permissions on files and folders, you may set permissions on your local printer. A printer has a single set of permissions that affect both the locally logged-on user and users accessing the printer as a share on the network. Printer permissions are simple compared to NTFS permissions. Printer permissions consist of

- Print—permission to send documents to the printer.
- Manage Printer—permission to print plus permission to pause and restart the printer, change spooler settings, share the printer, assign printer permissions, and change printer properties.
- Manage Documents—permission to pause, resume, restart, cancel, and rearrange the order of documents submitted by all users. This permission does not include the print or manage printer permission.

When you add a printer driver, the default permissions allow any user to print; a special group called Creator Owner has Manage Documents permission, but only members of the Power Users and Administrators groups get all of the permissions. Creator Owner refers to anyone printing a document, giving each user the right to manage just their own documents. Figure 5–21 shows the default permissions for a printer named Accounting.

While all users are assigned the print permissions through the Everyone group, an administrator can assign more restrictive permissions, if needed. One way to do that is to remove the Everyone group and explicitly assign permissions to users and groups. Another method is to leave the Everyone group as is, but to explicitly deny Print permission to a single user or group.

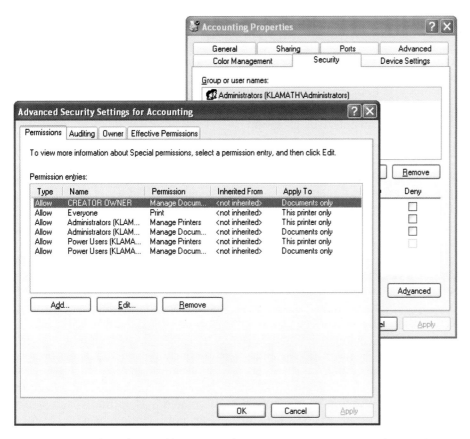

FIGURE 5–21 The Advanced button on the printer properties page shows printer permission details.

LO 5.5 | Troubleshooting Common Windows XP Problems

If life were perfect, then your computer would work all the time, with no problems. However, no matter how hard you work, your computer will find new ways to annoy you. In this section, we will review some features for being prepared for problems and troubleshooting. We will introduce you to the Windows XP Help and Support Center and to proactive tasks that you can perform with the Backup Utility and System Restore.

Where to Find Help

Launch Windows XP Help and Support Center from Start | Help And Support, and you'll see a large menu of options for troubleshooting. From here you can invite someone to connect to your computer and remotely access your desktop to help you correct a problem. You can connect to Microsoft's support site or to a newsgroup to research a problem or to seek help and advice. We won't detail all the choices, but don't overlook this program when you need to troubleshoot or when you simply wish to learn more about Windows.

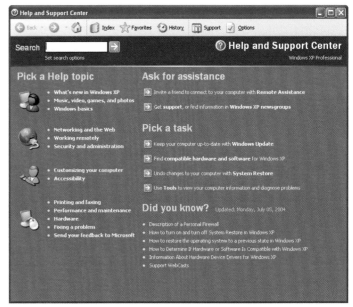

The Help and Support Center should be the first place you look for answers.

Perform Proactive Maintenance Tasks

Someone once said that the best offense is a good defense. Don't wait for problems to occur before you take action. Have a defense strategy in which you take steps to avoid problems. Include backing up data, disk defragmenting, and periodic housekeeping of the files and folders. Be prepared to use the System Restore and Automatic System Recovery features. You should install and configure an antivirus program.

Creating Backups and Automated System Recovery Disks

Yes, we know you've heard it repeatedly. You need to actually back up your data files on removable media, on an external hard drive, or to a network server. This is extremely important! Do it often and do it right. Windows XP Professional, like previous versions, has the Backup Utility, available through Start | All Programs | Accessories | System Tools.

Windows XP Professional has a recovery feature, Automated System Recovery (ASR), which creates a backup of the entire system partition (where the OS is installed) and therefore provides a more holistic repair, restoring your operating system to a certain point in time. ASR requires some planning. You must use the Advanced Mode of the **Backup Utility** (NTBACKUP.EXE) to create an ASR backup set, which includes an ASR diskette to initiate a boot-up into the ASR state, and a system partition backup to media, such as tape, another local hard disk, or a network location that is accessed via a drive letter (a "mapped" drive). Figure 5–22 shows the Advanced Mode of the Backup Utility with the option for running the Automated System Recovery wizard to create an ASR set. An ASR backup set does not include a backup of other partitions, nor does it allow you to select data folders. Therefore, your Windows XP Professional backup strategy should include the occasional creation of an ASR set and frequent backups to save data and changes to the OS since the last ASR set.

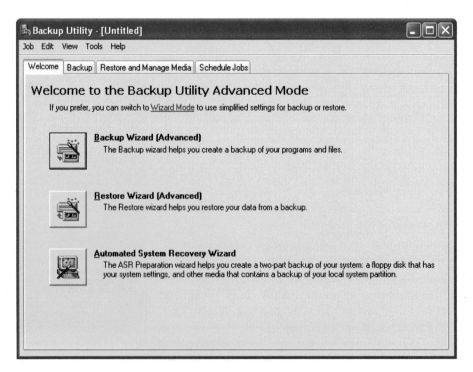

FIGURE 5–22 The Automated System Recovery wizard will walk you through the creation of an ASR disk set.

Explore the Backup Program (NTBACKUP)

The backup program NTBACKUP is the tool provided with Windows XP Professional for creating backups, ASR backups, and ASR diskettes. You should familiarize yourself with this program. To complete this step-by-step exercise, you will need the following:

- The computer on which you successfully installed Windows XP Professional in Step-by-Step 5.01.
- A user name and password for an account that is a member of the Administrators group.

Step 1

Log on as an Administrator. First, run the Backup Utility and examine the Automated System Recovery Preparation wizard. Open the Backup program quickly by entering the command NTBACKUP in the Run box (from Start | Run). In the Welcome page of the Backup Or Restore wizard, click Advanced Mode.

Step 2

In the Welcome page of Advanced Mode, click on the Automated System Recovery Wizard button. This will open the Automated System Recovery Preparation wizard. Click *Next*.

Step 3

On the Backup Destination page, notice the Backup Media Type box. In the very unlikely chance that your system includes a tape backup system it will give you a choice between tape and file. If the Backup Media Type box is grayed out (like the illustration), you can only back up to a file (rather than to tape), and you must provide a destination for this file on any local hard drive or network location available to you.

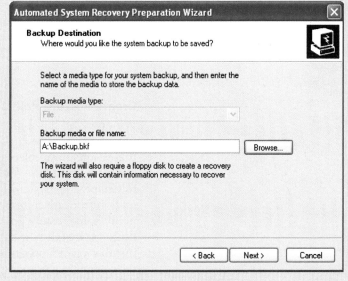

Cancel the Automated System Recovery wizard, and explore the Backup page of Backup Utility. In the left pane, notice the check boxes that allow you to select drives and folders to back up. Click on the words "System State," and the contents of System State will display in the right pane. Placing a check in the box to the left of System State will back up all these items. The grayed-out boxes show you that you can back up all the components of System State, or none of them, but you cannot select individual System State components.

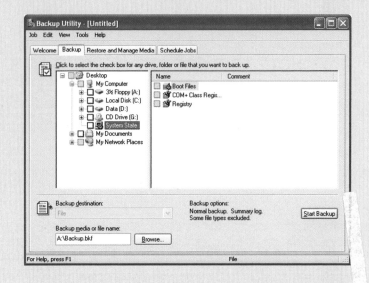

Click on the words "Local Disk (C:)" in the left pane, and the right pane will reveal the contents. Now click on the check box to the left of "Local Disk (C:)," and notice that all the check boxes in the right pane are selected *except* pagefile.sys. This is a special file used by the system for virtual memory and should *not* be backed up; it cannot be selected for backup in the Backup Utility.

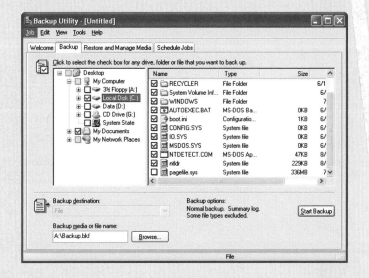

Click some of the folders on drive C:, and notice that you can move around in them, much as you can in My Computer, selecting and deselecting folders to include in a backup. When you have explored the folders, close the Backup Utility.

Create Restore Points for System Restore

Windows XP has a great System Restore, which solves some major problems with a few mouse clicks. If you make a change to a Windows XP computer that results in problems, you can restore it to its previous state, as long as you can start Windows—either normally or in Safe Mode (we describe Safe Mode in Chapter 7). System Restore saves complete Windows configuration information from discrete points in time. Each of these discrete points is a restore point. Some restore points are set automatically. For instance, by default, every time you install new software, System Restore creates a restore point. Thus, if installation of a program causes your computer to malfunction, simply restore the system to a point before that installation and the computer should work.

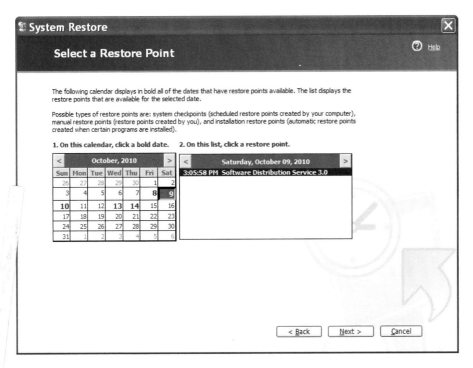

FIGURE 5–23 Selecting a restore point

During the restore process, only settings and programs are changed. No data is lost. Your computer will include all programs and settings as of the restore date and time. This feature is invaluable for overworked administrators. A simple restore will fix many user-generated problems.

To restore to a previous point, you start the System Restore wizard by choosing Start | All Programs | Accessories | System Tools | System Restore. Select the first radio button, Restore My Computer To An Earlier Time, and then click Next.

The second screen shows a calendar with restore points. Any day with a boldface date has a restore point. These points are created after you add or remove software, or install Windows updates, and during the normal shutdown of your computer. Figure 5–23 shows a program installation restore point. Select a date to restore to and click Next.

The last screen before restoring the system is a warning. It advises you to close all open programs and reminds you that Windows will shut down during the restore process. It also states that the restore operation is reversible. Thus, if you go too far back in time, you can restore to a more recent date.

You don't have to count on the automatic creation of restore points. You can open System Restore at any time and simply select Create A Restore Point. This is something to consider doing before making changes that might not trigger an automatic restore point, such as directly editing the registry.

System Restore turns on by default and uses some of your disk space to save information on restore points. To turn System Restore off or change the disk space usage, open the System Properties applet in Control Panel, and select the System Restore tab, where you will find these settings. Disabling System Restore is now a common part of cleaning off many virus infections to make sure that a virus isn't hiding in the restore

> Learn more about the registry in Chapter 7.

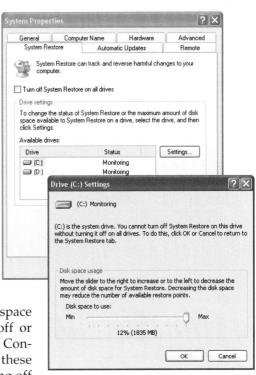

System Restore settings

files, but be warned that turning System Restore off, even for a moment, deletes all old restore points.

The Blue Screen of Death (BSOD)

The Stop screen, often referred to as the Blue Screen of Death (BSOD), will appear if the OS detects that a fatal error has occurred. A fatal error is one that causes too much instability to guarantee the integrity of the system and still prevent loss of data in open files. A stop error is such an event.

Preparing for Stop Errors in Windows XP

To prepare for a BSOD, you should decide how you want your computer to behave after a stop error. You do this by modifying the System Failure settings on the Startup and Recovery page. These settings can be found by opening the System applet in Control Panel, selecting the Advanced tab, and clicking the Settings button under Startup And Recovery.

- *Write An Event To The System Log* causes Windows to write an event to the system log, which is one of several log files you can view using Event Viewer (found under Administrative Tools). We highly recommend this setting because it means that even if the computer reboots after a Stop screen, you can read the stop error information that was on the screen in the system log.

- *Send An Administrative Alert* is a setting that sends an alert message to the administrator that will appear on the administrator's screen the next time the administrator logs on. This is a useful setting to alert a domain administrator if your computer is part of a domain.

- *Automatically Restart* is a setting we recommend, as long as you have also selected the first option, which preserves the stop error information in the system log file.

- *Writing Debugging Information* contains one drop-down list, a text box, and a check box. The drop-down list allows you to control the existence and the size of a dump file that will contain debugging information. The

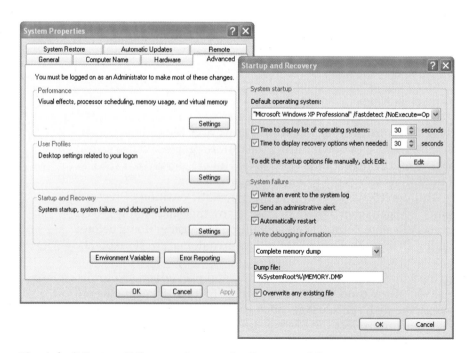

The default System Failure settings on the Startup and Recovery page settings include None, Small Memory Dump (64 KB), Kernel Memory Dump, and Complete Memory Dump. A complete memory dump contains an image of the contents of memory at the time of the fatal error. You can send this file to Microsoft for evaluation of a problem, but this amount of effort and cost (Microsoft charges for these services) is normally only expended on a critical computer, such as a network server. For a desktop computer, select None. This will gray out the second text box, the location of the dump file, and the check box labeled "Overwrite any existing file."

Troubleshooting a Stop Error

Eric, a colleague of ours, experienced a stop error in Windows XP. He was present when it occurred and he scanned the first few lines on the screen for a clue. The system rebooted while he was viewing the screen, but this was not a problem to him. After the reboot, he logged on and opened the system log in Event Viewer. He saw the message "STOP [several sets of numbers in the form 0x00000000] UNMOUNTABLE_BOOT_VOLUME." A search of support.microsoft.com using just the last part of this message (UNMOUNT-ABLE_BOOT_VOLUME) described how to determine the cause and the action to take by examining the values that preceded it. Eric discovered that the solution to his problem was to restart Windows using the recovery console and to run a command from the command line.

An Old Application Will Not Run

You have a new Windows XP computer. You need to run a program that worked nicely on your now-defunct Windows 95 computer. However, when you start the program in Windows XP, it doesn't perform correctly. Maybe the screen doesn't look quite right, or perhaps the program frequently hangs. To solve this problem, Windows XP allows you to trick the program into thinking that the OS is actually Windows 95 by using compatibility options. You

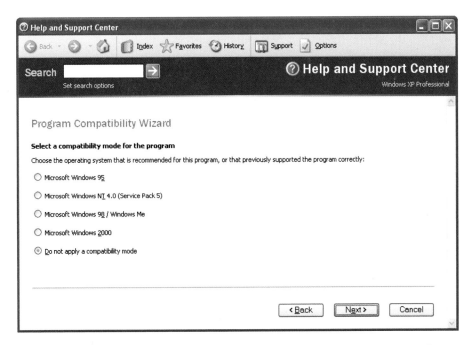

The Program Compatibility wizard walks you through assigning settings to allow an older program to run under Windows XP.

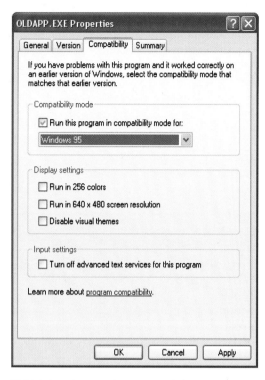

FIGURE 5–24 Use the Compatibility page to make manual settings.

can set these options by running the Program Compatibility wizard from the Help and Support Center or by setting the options manually from the properties of the shortcut or program file.

To run the Program Compatibility wizard, select Start | All Programs | Accessories | Program Compatibility Wizard. Following the instructions, you may choose to have the wizard display a list of all installed programs from which you can select your problem program. Then you can move through the wizard, selecting settings for emulating earlier versions of Windows and/or modifying the display settings for the program. Then test the program to see if there is an improvement.

Alternatively, you can set compatibility settings manually. On the Start menu, locate the shortcut for the offending program. Right-click and select Properties. Select the Compatibility tab. On this page, place a check in the box under Compatibility Mode, and then select Windows 95 in the drop-down list below it (see Figure 5–24). Click OK and test the program. If it still has problems, go back to the Compatibility page, and tweak the Display Settings and/or turn off advanced text services. If you need help, click the Program Compatibility link at the bottom of the page.

Chapter 5 REVIEW

Chapter Summary

After reading this chapter and completing the Step-by-Step tutorials and Try This! exercises, you should understand the following facts about Windows XP.

Windows XP Professional Benefits, Features, and Weaknesses

- The Windows XP editions include
  - Windows XP Professional
  - Windows XP Home Edition
  - Windows XP Media Center Edition
  - Tablet PC
  - Windows XP Embedded
  - Windows XP 64-bit Edition
- Windows XP Professional features and benefits include
  - Security, including the required logon, and security features in the NTFS file system
  - Stability and compatibility
  - Automatic updates
  - File system support of NTFS5, FAT32, and FAT16 on hard drives

- Recovery tools, including Last Known Good Configuration start-up option; Task Manager; Recovery Console; Safe Mode start-up options; Device Manager; System Restore; and Automated System Recovery

Installing Windows XP Professional

- No Setup start-up floppy disks are included with Windows XP. If you need to make them, you must connect to the Microsoft Web site and create them from a program available there.
- To combat software piracy, Microsoft requires that you activate Windows XP within 30 days of installation. Registration is still optional.
- Soon after installing Windows XP, you should verify network access and install new updates.

Managing Windows XP Professional

- To create and manage disk partitions, use Disk Management in the Computer Management console.

- When you install new programs in Windows, you will often use an installation program that comes with the new application.
- To uninstall a program, use the Add Or Remove Programs applet in Control Panel.
- Programs should be removed correctly using an uninstall program.
- To add or remove a Windows component, use the Windows Components wizard from the Add Or Remove Programs applet in Control Panel.
- Use the Display applet in Control Panel to ensure that the screen resolution is set properly.
- Save data files in folders you create below the My Documents folder.
- Windows XP supports both plug-and-play and non-plug-and-play printers.

Securing Windows XP Professional

- Windows XP Professional security features include required logon, the security features of the NTFS file system, code signing/driver signing, and security accounts.

- Use the User Accounts Control Panel applet for simple account management at home or in a very small business that has low security requirements.
- Use the Local Users and Groups node of the Computer Management console for more advanced account management.
- Windows XP Professional allows the currently logged-on user to create a Password Reset disk to use in case of a forgotten password.

Troubleshooting Common Windows XP Problems

- Help and Support Center is the Windows XP help program containing a large menu of options.
- Proactive tasks include creating backups and automated system recovery disks plus creating restore points for System Restore.
- If an old application will not run, or causes problems with the display, locate the executable file for the application, and select options in the Compatibility page of the file's properties dialog box.

Key Terms List

activation *(152)*
Add Printer wizard *(166)*
Automated System Recovery (ASR) *(149)*
Automatic Update *(148)*
Backup Utility *(182)*
clean installation *(151)*
Device Manager *(149)*
dump file *(186)*

image *(151)*
Last Known Good (LKG) Configuration *(149)*
Microsoft Product Activation (MPA) *(152)*
personal folders *(167)*
Program Compatibility wizard *(188)*
Recovery Console *(149)*

restore point *(149)*
Safe Mode *(149)*
Shortcut *(147)*
System Restore *(149)*
Task Manager *(149)*
Upgrade Advisor *(150)*
Windows Update *(148)*

Key Terms Quiz

Use the Key Terms List to complete the sentences that follow. Not all terms will be used.

1. When unsure about hardware and software compatibility before upgrading, use the Windows XP CD to run the Windows XP _____ on the computer.

2. _____ allows you to return your computer to a previous working state.

3. A/an _____ belongs to just one group, Local Users.

4. Windows creates _____ for each user for storing desktop configuration and

preference information as well as data created by the user.

5. _____ is a character-mode boot-up environment that has a command-line interface where you can enter advanced command-line commands to attempt to recover from a major OS failure.

6. You can find a recovery tool that backs up the system partition in the Advanced Mode of the Windows XP _____.

7. If a program written for an older version of Windows does not run under Windows XP, use the _____.

8. For _____ to work, you must have a set of disks that includes a system backup to back up media and a special floppy disk that can boot up the computer and start the new recovery.

9. A _____ is like a snapshot of Windows XP settings at a certain point in time.

10. Registration is optional, but _____ is mandatory.

Multiple-Choice Quiz

1. Which version of Windows XP is for general business users?
   a. Windows XP Home Edition
   b. Windows XP Media Center Edition
   c. Tablet PC
   d. Windows XP Professional
   e. Windows XP 64-bit Edition

2. How can you remove Windows components?
   a. Run the Uninstall program.
   b. Use the Display applet.
   c. Use the Windows Components Wizard.
   d. Run System Restore.
   e. Activate the component.

3. When did Microsoft introduce Windows XP as a new product?
   a. 1998
   b. 2001
   c. 2004
   d. 2005
   e. 2006

4. What is the correct term for what we know as the Blue Screen of Death (BSOD)?
   a. ASR
   b. LKG
   c. Recovery Console
   d. Safe Mode
   e. Stop screen

5. Which term best describes the logon to Windows XP Professional?
   a. Insecure
   b. Optional
   c. Mandatory
   d. Customary
   e. Character-mode

6. Which of the following is an NTFS permission that only applies to folders?
   a. Read
   b. Modify Folder
   c. Modify
   d. Full Control
   e. List Folder Contents

7. Why must you activate Windows XP after installation?
   a. This is how you register your product.
   b. It won't start up after installation unless you activate it.
   c. To detect computer viruses.
   d. Microsoft requires it to protect itself against software piracy.
   e. To create limited users.

8. Why should you install updates for Windows XP?
   a. To install new applications.
   b. To create a new computer administrator account.
   c. To correct general problems and security problems with the program code.
   d. To install new games.
   e. To be kept up-to-date on the latest Windows products.

9. Why would you use the ClearType option in Display Properties | Appearance | Effects?
   a. To make the text on the screen translucent.
   b. To smooth the edges of screen fonts.
   c. To personalize your desktop.
   d. To make printed documents more readable.
   e. To select the Bliss wallpaper.

10. What should you do ahead of time to help you recover in the event you forget your Windows XP password?
    a. Write the password on a note taped to your computer.
    b. Create a Password Reset disk.
    c. Create a restore point.
    d. Install the Recovery Console on the computer.
    e. Create an ASR backup.

11. The Manage Documents printer permission allows all but one of the following actions on a printer. Which one is not allowed?
    a. Pause
    b. Print
    c. Restart
    d. Cancel
    e. Resume

12. What mode, selectable from the properties of a shortcut or program file, allows you to run an old program in an environment that emulates an older version of Windows?
    a. Compatibility mode
    b. Safe mode
    c. Real mode
    d. Protected mode
    e. Standard mode

13. Last Known Good (LKG) only works within a narrow window of time that ends when the following occurs:
    a. An administrative alert is sent.
    b. Any user logs on.
    c. The computer reboots.
    d. The disk is defragmented.
    e. A new partition is created.

14. You have just installed Windows XP Professional and did not choose to activate it when prompted to do so during the installation process. How long do you have to activate it before Windows XP stops working?
    a. 10 days
    b. 120 days
    c. 6 months
    d. 30 days
    e. Indefinitely

15. You installed Windows XP Professional on a 15 GB partition created during installation. You are now creating a second partition in the remaining 65 GB of available space on the hard disk. The computer is not configured for dual-boot. What type of partition and which file system should you choose (is preferred) for this new partition?
    a. Extended partition with FAT32
    b. Primary partition with FAT16
    c. Extended partition with NTFS
    d. Primary partition with NTFS
    e. Primary partition with FAT32

Essay Quiz

1. What methods are available for booting into the Windows Setup program on a stand-alone PC?

2. In your own words, describe the difference between activation and registration. Be sure to explain which one is mandatory, and why Microsoft uses each.

3. Briefly describe why you might partition a very large hard disk into two or more partitions.

4. Why does Windows XP Professional have the two recovery tools—System Restore and Automatic System Recovery? Isn't one enough?

5. What feature of Windows XP do you like best? Why?

Lab Projects

LAB PROJECT 5.1

Currently your Windows XP Professional computer is working just fine, but you would like to prepare for a disaster—such as an unrecoverable hard disk failure in which you need to replace the hard disk and get yourself up and running as quickly as possible with your computer restored to its previous state before the failure.

You will need the lab computer on which you installed Windows XP Professional in Step-by-Step 5.01.

Then do the following:

1. Given the available drives and media, determine what recovery tools, from those featured in this chapter, are available to you. You will need to research beyond the information about these tools provided in this chapter.

2. Write a plan for using the recovery tools or tools that would be appropriate for the scenario described. Explain why each of the featured recovery tools will or will not work.

3. Do any proactive work that is possible to do on your computer to prepare for the chosen recovery tool.

4. Present your plan to your fellow students, and describe the proactive steps you have taken on your lab computer.

LAB PROJECT 5.2

Windows XP Professional is running on an older computer. You want to increase its speed by turning off extraneous animation and features in Windows XP.

You will need the following:

- A computer running Windows XP.
- The administrator password for this computer.

Then do the following:

1. Go to the Performance tab of the My Computer icon.

2. Turn off all video enhancements.

3. Set a dedicated virtual RAM size. A good formula is 1.5 times the size of your RAM.

LAB PROJECT 5.3

At this writing Microsoft no longer sells Windows XP as a retail product, nor does it allow OEM distribution. What is its status at the time you read this chapter? Do an Internet search and see if you can determine the percentage of PCs that are still running Windows XP. Also search to see if you can buy Windows XP from any source, including eBay.

6 Today's Windows— Windows Vista and Windows 7

"Windows 7 PCs are the fastest selling PCs in history, selling over 7 copies a second. They now represent more than 20% of the PCs connected to the Internet."

—Microsoft CEO Steve Balmer
Keynote Address at 2011 Consumer Electronics Show (CES) January 5, 2011

Microsoft released Windows Vista retail editions early in 2007, but Vista was not widely adopted. In fact, most institutional and individual users stayed with Windows XP rather than upgrade to Windows Vista. The resistance to moving to Windows Vista was so strong that Microsoft prolonged the life of Windows XP, allowing sales of new PCs with OEM (original equipment manufacturer) Windows XP installed up until October 2010. This was one year after the release of Windows Vista's successor, Windows 7, and nine years since the introduction of Windows XP. Therefore, this chapter is primarily about Windows 7 as the ascending Windows desktop OS, with a lighter treatment of Windows Vista as the less successful, but still present Windows OS. We'll begin with a comparison of these two OSs and an overview of features. We'll then consider the issues of installing today's Windows, followed by the basics of managing an installed OS. Finally, we'll explore issues for managing local security in Windows 7 and Windows Vista. ✸

Learning Outcomes

In this chapter, you will learn how to:

LO **6.1** Compare Windows 7 and Windows Vista.

LO **6.2** Install and configure Windows 7 and Windows Vista.

LO **6.3** Manage Windows 7 and Windows Vista.

LO **6.4** Manage local security in Windows 7 and Windows Vista.

LO 6.1 | Windows Vista and Windows 7 Overview

Windows Vista and Windows 7 possess major differences. These differences are in the core components of the operating systems, as well as in a distinctive and unifying look to the GUI. But Windows Vista and Windows 7 also have many similarities. Predictably, Windows 7 has important improvements and enhancements required to lure desktop users away from their dependence on Windows XP. As with earlier versions of Windows, Microsoft sells each of these versions as several separate products, called editions. We'll begin with a high-level comparison of these two Windows versions, and then look at the editions and some of the features available for each.

Comparison of Windows Vista and Windows 7

Although we expect a new version of the Windows OS to be an improved new generation, Windows 7 is not so much the child of Windows Vista as the younger sibling who succeeds in outdoing his older brother. The areas in which Windows 7 shows improvements are in the enhanced user interface, improved speeds in just about everything in any way you would want to measure an OS, and, if not lower hardware requirements, nearly identical hardware requirements as far as processor speed, video graphics, and hard disk space.

Windows Vista and Windows 7 Editions

Keep in mind that all editions of a single version of Windows have the same kernel and other core components. The differences among editions are mainly in the included components, targeted to specific types of users, and the more features, the more expensive the edition. Microsoft sells some Windows editions at retail, meaning you can buy a package containing the Windows disc. Other Windows editions are bundled with hardware as OEM Windows (with or without the accompanying disc), while the Enterprise Edition of any version of Windows is not available at retail, but sold only to customers of the Microsoft Software Assurance plan, a distribution channel for bulk licensing to organizations. The Enterprise editions have added features desirable to a large enterprise. These features include support for mass distribution, linking with enterprise security, compliance, collaborative productivity, and more.

Windows Vista and Windows 7 also come in two scaled-down editions called Starter and Home Basic. The Starter edition is an OEM edition that has many features removed or disabled, including the ability to change the desktop wallpaper or join a Windows domain. The Home Basic edition targets emerging markets and is not available in the United States, most of Europe, the Middle East, Australia, New Zealand, and Japan. Windows Vista and Windows 7 each come in three retail editions, listed in Table 6–1.

Windows Vista Features

Despite a long list of new features and improved old features, Windows Vista was not a successful product; the majority of users—both institutional and

> Presently, when you purchase one of the three retail editions of Windows Vista or Windows 7, you receive two discs—one 32-bit and one 64-bit. Further, each of these discs contains all three retail editions. The edition that installs depends on the edition you purchased. If you look carefully on the discs, you will see "Includes Windows Anytime Upgrade." This means that if you purchased and installed one of the lesser editions, you can contact Microsoft and, for a fee, receive a security key to upgrade to a higher edition.

TABLE 6–1 Windows Vista and Windows 7 Retail Editions	
Windows Vista	**Windows 7**
Home Premium	Home Premium
Business	Professional
Ultimate	Ultimate

TABLE 6–2 Windows Vista Features in the Retail Editions

	Home Basic	Home Premium	Business	Ultimate
Windows Defender and Firewall	✓	✓	✓	✓
Instant Search and Internet Explorer 7 (an upgrade to IE 8 is free)	✓	✓	✓	✓
Network and Sharing Center for making and managing network connections	✓	✓	✓	✓
Windows Aero desktop with transparent menu bars, Windows Flip 3D, and Live thumbnails		✓	✓	✓
Windows Mobility Center and Tablet PC support		✓	✓	✓
Windows Meeting Space for collaboration and document sharing		✓	✓	✓
Windows SideShow for extending the display to other devices		✓	✓	✓
Windows Media Center and Media Center Extenders		✓	✓	✓
Schedule Backup		✓	✓	✓
Windows DVD Maker		✓		✓
Premium games: Chess Titans, Mahjong Titans, and Inkball		✓		✓
Windows Movie Maker in HD			✓	✓
Windows Complete PC Backup and Restore			✓	✓
Windows Fax and Scan			✓	✓
Windows Ultimate Extras				✓
Windows BitLocker Drive Encryption				✓

individual—remained with Windows XP. They even went out of their way to buy new computers with Windows XP installed rather than Windows Vista. Table 6–2 compares the features in the various retail versions of Windows Vista available in normal retail markets, followed by a short overview of some features introduced in Windows Vista.

> There are many contributing factors for Windows Vista's lack of success. Perhaps the most important one was that when it was released in 2007, it was not compatible with a significant amount of existing software and hardware. Therefore, IT managers refused to upgrade to it or purchase new machines with Vista preinstalled.

Windows Aero

Windows Aero is Microsoft's name for a group of GUI desktop features and visual themes introduced in Windows Vista that include glass-like transparent windows (referred to as "Glass"), Windows animations, and Flip 3D.

Flip 3D lets you switch through your open windows as if they were a in a stack of cards or photos. Figure 6–1 is an example of the Windows Vista desktop with Aero enabled. Use the Windows Key + Tab combination to use Flip 3D, as shown in Figure 6–2. Windows Aero is not in the Starter editions and has some capabilities disabled in Windows Vista Home Basic edition. It also requires a video card that supports (at minimum) DirectX 9.0 and Shader Model 2.0. Although not written as an acronym with all caps, Aero purportedly stands for Authentic, Energetic, Reflective, and Open. Figures 6–1 and 6–2 also show one of the desktop themes available with Windows Vista.

User Account Control

An important security feature introduced in Windows Vista and included in all editions is User Account Control (UAC), as described in Chapter 2. While

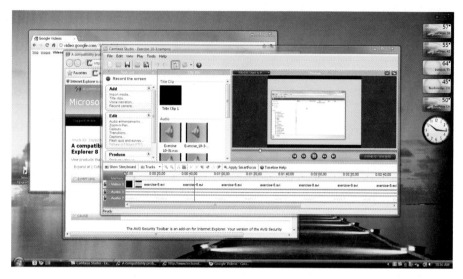

FIGURE 6–1 Windows Vista with Aero enhancements, including transparent Glass

FIGURE 6–2 Using Flip 3D in Windows Vista

this feature solved a significant security problem, many people found it very annoying and disabled it, which removed the protection Microsoft sought to provide. We'll look at UAC enhancements later in this chapter.

Windows 7 Features

Windows 7 comes with many new and improved features. Table 6–3 lists Windows 7 features and the products in which each feature is included. We will examine just a few of these features in the following sections.

Desktop Enhancements

Two areas of improvement on the desktop are enhancements to Aero and the use of Jump Lists and pinning on the Start menu and taskbar.

Aero. Windows 7 continues support for Aero (see Figure 6–3), along with transparent windows and Flip 3D (see Figure 6–4). New features in Windows 7 include Aero Snap and Aero Shake. **Aero Snap** lets you manipulate windows quickly. For instance, to maximize a window, drag it until its title bar touches

TABLE 6–3 Features in the Windows 7 Retail Editions

	Home Premium	Professional	Ultimate
Improved desktop navigation features (Shake, Peek, and Snap)	✓	✓	✓
Improved Instant Search (organized into categories, searches external hard drives, networked PCs, and libraries)	✓	✓	✓
Internet Explorer 8 (faster Web page access, easier to use, more secure)	✓	✓	✓
Windows Media Center (a TV tuner and other hardware required for some functions)	✓	✓	✓
HomeGroup for easy file-and-print sharing on a home network (requires a network and PCs running Windows 7)	✓	✓	✓
Windows XP Mode for running Windows XP programs		✓	✓
Windows Touch (requires a touch-sensitive screen)	✓	✓	✓
Domain Join wizard for joining a Windows domain		✓	✓
Backup to a home or business network		✓	✓
BitLocker			✓
Switch among 35 languages			✓

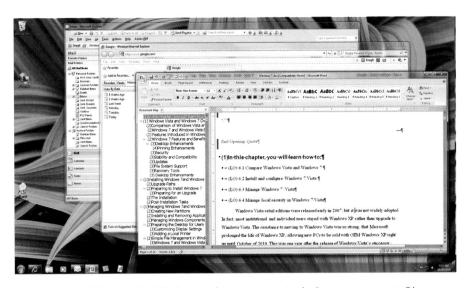

FIGURE 6–3 Windows 7 with Aero enhancements, including transparent Glass

FIGURE 6–4 Using Flip 3D in Windows 7

FIGURE 6–5 A Jump List for Microsoft Office Publisher

the top edge of your display. Restore a maximized window by dragging it away from the top of the display. **Aero Shake** lets you quickly minimize all but one window by giving that window a quick shake.

Jump Lists and Pinning. Windows 7 improves the Start menu and taskbar by the use of Jump Lists and pinning. The old pinned area of the Start menu is available, and programs are often pinned here, but you can also pin items on the taskbar. When you right-click on a program on the Start menu or taskbar, a Jump List displays, as in Figure 6–5. This is a list of recently opened items such as files, folders, and Web sites. It lists only the recently opened items automatically, but you can select an item and "permanently" pin it to a Jump List. Practice pinning items in Step-by-Step 6.01.

Pinning replaces the Quick Launch toolbar and the pinned area of the Start menu. It allows you to place icons for applications and destinations on the taskbar and Start menu. Once pinned, an item's icon remains on the toolbar regardless of whether the program is open or closed. Simply click it to open the application or destination. When a program is running, its icon appears as a square button on the toolbar, as demonstrated by the Microsoft Outlook button on the toolbar in Figure 6–6, which shows a portion of a Windows 7 taskbar with the various icons labeled.

Figure 6–7 shows the Jump List for Microsoft Word that includes both Word documents and other types of files, such as the recently embedded TIF files in Word documents.

Pin a program and then use that program's Jump List to pin several data files to the one program. When you pin a program to the taskbar, you use that one icon to open the program and switch to the program, and then you can select an item from the program's Jump List, which, like most pinned items, carries an automatically generated list of recently opened files for that item, but you can also add items to this list. There are several ways to pin programs. Learn more about pinning and Jump Lists in Step-by-Step 6.01.

FIGURE 6–7 Right-click a pinned item to view its Jump List

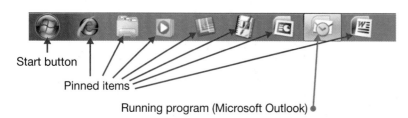

FIGURE 6–6 Pinned items on a taskbar, along with the button for a running program

Step-by-Step 6.01

Pinning Items

Practice pinning programs and then pinning files within a program's Jump List. In this step-by-step exercise, you will need the following:

- A computer with Windows 7 installed—either a conventional installation or an installation in a VM.

Step 1

Start a program, such as Microsoft Word. Then right-click the program's taskbar icon and select Pin This Program To Taskbar. The running icon will appear the same, but when you close the program, a pinned icon will remain.

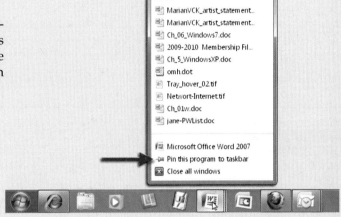

Step 2

You can also pin a program to the taskbar by dragging it. Open the Start menu and browse through the All Programs menu until you locate the icon for a program you wish to pin. Then drag and drop the program icon onto the taskbar.

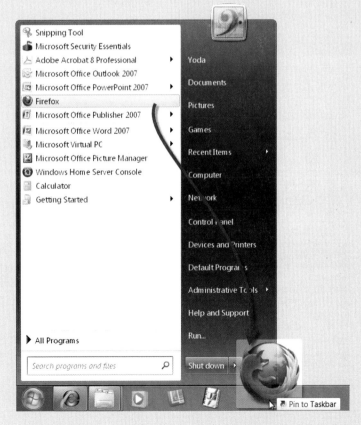

Windows 7 automatically generates Jump Lists, but you can ensure that an item stays on a Jump List by pinning it. To pin an item, right-click an icon on the Start menu to display the Jump List. Then hover the mouse cursor over an item in the list until the pushpin icon displays. Click the pushpin icon to pin the item.

Now you can see the distinction between the items Windows 7 automatically pins to the Jump List and those you choose to pin. Items automatically pinned are listed under the "Recent" heading, while those you select to pin are listed under the "Pinned" heading.

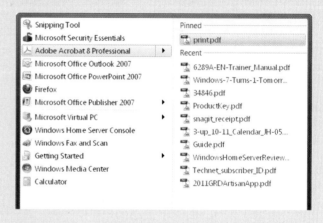

The hidden status icons revealed by clicking the Show hidden icons button

Notification Area. The notification area, also called the system tray, is not new in Windows 7, but it is greatly improved. The notification area holds status indicators and pop-up menus for a variety of devices and programs installed on your computer. It is so handy that many installation programs—both by Microsoft and by other software publishers—insert their own handy icons here. Before Windows 7, this practice resulted in clutter that detracted from the value of this feature. Windows 7 changed all that. To begin with, it does not display as many icons here itself and, best of all, it changed how icons appear and behave. Further, all those additional status icons are tucked away, but readily available with a click on the Show Hidden Icons button, as you see here.

Figure 6–8 identifies the objects in the notification area. The Network icon shown indicates an Ethernet (wired) network, whereas an icon with five vertical bars in graduated sizes indicates a wireless network. If the network adapter is disabled or a cable disconnected, a red *x* will appear on the icon. If there is another problem with the network, it will have a yellow

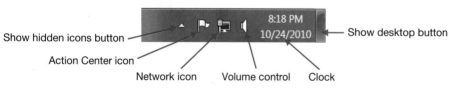

Show hidden icons button
Action Center icon
Network icon
Volume control
Clock
Show desktop button

FIGURE 6–8 The new and improved notification area

triangle with a black exclamation mark. Pause the mouse cursor over an icon to see a brief description. Right-click to display a context menu, and click on the icon to open the related program.

Action Center. The Windows Action Center, represented by the small flag icon, will briefly display a message balloon when there is a problem with your security programs and backup. Then it will quietly sit there with a white *x* against a red circle until you resolve the problem. A single click opens a message box, as shown here, and to open Action Center (see Figure 6–9) click on the Open Action Center link in the message box.

Libraries. Windows 7 has a new feature called libraries. A library looks like a folder, but it is not a folder, even though the four default libraries in Windows 7 carry the names of special folders in Windows Vista. These are Documents, Music, Pictures, and Videos. While a folder is a container for files and other folders (called subfolders), files and folders do not directly exist in a library; only links to the locations of those files and folders do.

A library stores information about the locations of folders and files, displaying them as if they were all in one location, thus making it easier for you to find related information or types of files. For instance, in our example, the Documents library shows two default locations: My Documents (in this case D:\Yoda\Documents) and Public Documents (D:\Users\Public\Documents), as shown in Figure 6–10 on the next page. Locations can be on the local computer or on shared locations on a network.

File System Support

As described in Chapter 1, Windows 7 supports the file systems previously supported in Windows Vista, including the various FAT file systems (FAT12 for floppy disks, FAT16, and FAT32), exFAT (for embedded systems), file systems for optical discs, and special file systems for working over networks. The NTFS file system is the preferred file system because it includes support for very large hard disks and for file and folder permissions, as well as encryption. Windows 7 also supports FAT32, but you should mainly use it on USB flash drives. Only use it on local hard drive partitions if you wish to multi-boot to an OS that does not recognize NTFS, such as Windows 95, Windows 98, or Windows Millennium Edition.

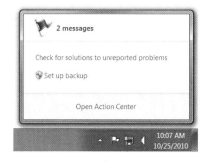

The Action Center message box appears after a single click of the Action Center icon.

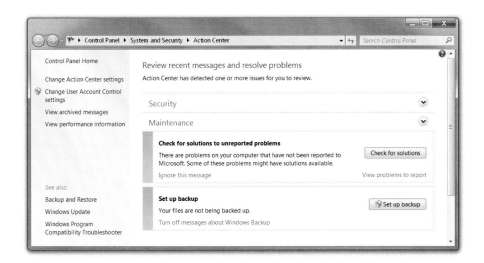

FIGURE 6–9 Open the Windows 7 Action Center by clicking on the Action Center link in the message box.

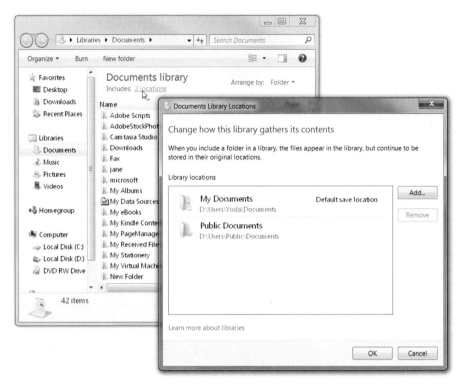

FIGURE 6–10 The two default locations for the Documents library

Security

In Windows 7, Microsoft improved existing security features such as User Account Control, BitLocker, and Windows Defender.

Improved User Account Control. User Account Control, introduced in Windows Vista, is less annoying in Windows 7, with fewer tasks requiring user intervention and use of an elevation prompt. Additionally, if you log on with an account with administrative privileges, you can adjust the User Account Control elevation prompt behavior.

BitLocker and BitLocker To Go. Introduced in Windows Vista Enterprise and Ultimate editions, BitLocker in Windows 7 is still limited to the Enterprise and Ultimate editions. In Vista you could only use BitLocker to encrypt the entire boot volume, the volume that contains Windows. In Windows 7, a feature called BitLocker To Go lets you encrypt other volumes, including USB storage devices. We'll look more closely at BitLocker later in this chapter when we discuss how to secure a Windows 7 computer.

AppLocker. You can use AppLocker, a new feature in Windows 7, to control which applications each user can run, reducing the chance of malware running on the user's computer. You administer AppLocker with Group Policy, which you can centrally manage through a Windows Active Directory domain.

Windows Defender. Introduced in Windows Vista, Windows Defender is an improved free built-in anti-spyware utility integrated into the Windows 7 Action Center where you can configure spyware scanning and updates.

Compatibility

If you need to run an old application that does not work well in Windows 7, you can first try tweaking the compatibility settings for that application. If the application still will not run, download and install Windows XP Mode, which is actually Windows Virtual PC with a free and legal Windows XP VM preinstalled. Then install the application into the Windows XP VM. Windows 7 will even allow you to create a shortcut on the Start menu to an application installed in Windows XP Mode.

Recovery Tools

With each version of Windows, Microsoft has enhanced the recovery tools for repairing damage to the operating system. You can access some of these tools while Windows is up and running, but in case a serious problem prevents Windows from starting, you can access an entire menu of tools by booting your system from the Windows Vista or Windows 7 disc. Choose the language settings, click Next, and click the option Repair Your Computer. Select the OS you want to repair (if you installed more than one), click Next, and the System Recovery Options menu will display (see Figure 6–11). The following tools are available from this menu:

- Startup Repair will scan for problems with missing or damaged system files and attempt to replace the problem files.
- System Restore will allow you to restore Windows to a previous point in time, providing it finds one or more restore points.
- System Image Recovery will let you restore a complete PC Image backup, providing you created one. This is a replacement for the Automated System Recovery (ASR) tool previously found in Windows XP.
- Windows Memory Diagnostic Tool tests the system's RAM because RAM problems can prevent Windows from starting normally. If this tool detects a problem, replace the RAM before using any other recovery tool.
- Command Prompt replaces the Recovery Console found in Windows XP. It provides a character mode interface in which you can use command-line tools to resolve a problem.

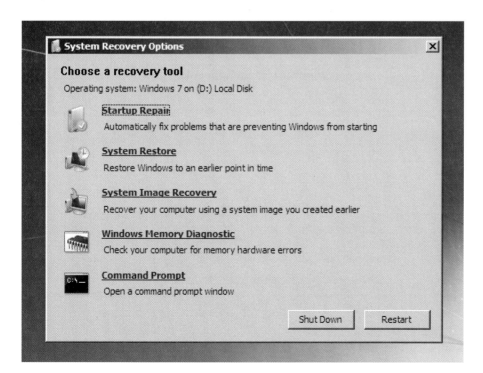

FIGURE 6–11 The Windows 7 System Recovery Options

LO 6.2 | Installing Windows

As you learned in the previous section, Windows Vista and Windows 7 are closely related, with many improvements in Windows 7. If you know how to install Windows Vista, you know how to install Windows 7. Since Windows 7 is the new and improved version, we will concentrate on concerns for installing Windows 7.

Upgrade Paths

An upgrade of an operating system, also called an in-place installation, is an installation of a newer operating system directly over an existing installation. An upgrade has the benefit of saving you the trouble of reinstalling all your programs and re-creating all your preference settings. You would have to do all this after a clean installation, which is an installation on a blank or "clean" hard drive partition. An upgrade also has its risks, since you end up with a new OS on an old computer with the potential limits of the older hardware, but that is your choice.

Upgrade paths to Windows Vista from Windows XP are edition-specific, as shown in Table 6–4, in which an "X" indicates an in-place installation (upgrade) is possible. Blank squares indicate that you must do a clean installation. We don't include upgrade paths for Windows 2000 and Windows XP Professional ×64 in this chart because they both require a clean reinstall.

You cannot directly upgrade from Windows XP or older versions to Windows 7. Table 6–5 lists the direct upgrade paths to Windows 7, and, as in Table 6–4, blank fields indicate that you must do a clean install.

Recommended System Requirements

The recommended system requirements for Windows Vista and Windows 7 are nearly identical (see Tables 6–6 and 6–7). When Microsoft introduced Windows Vista, people gave the hardware requirements as a reason they did not

TABLE 6–4 Upgrade Paths to Windows Vista

	Windows Vista Home Basic	Windows Vista Home Premium	Windows Vista Business	Windows Vista Ultimate
Windows XP Professional			X	X
Windows XP Home	X	X	X	X
Windows XP Media Center		X		X
Windows XP Tablet PC			X	X

TABLE 6–5 Upgrade Paths to Windows 7

	Windows 7 Home Basic	Windows 7 Home Premium	Windows 7 Professional	Windows 7 Enterprise	Windows 7 Ultimate
Windows Vista Business			X	X	X
Windows Vista Enterprise					X
Windows Vista Home Basic	X	X			X
Windows Vista Home Premium		X			X
Windows Vista Ultimate					X

TABLE 6–6 Windows Vista Recommended System Minimums

	Windows Vista Home Basic	Windows Vista Home Premium	Windows Vista Business	Windows Vista Ultimate
Processor	1 GHz 32-bit ×86 or 64-bit ×64 processor	1 GHz 32-bit ×86 or 64-bit ×64 processor	1 GHz 32-bit ×86 or 64-bit ×64 processor	1 GHz 32-bit ×86 or 64-bit ×64 processor
System Memory	512 MB	1 GB	1 GB	1 GB
Available Hard Drive space	20 GB	40 GB with 15 GB or greater available	40 GB with 15 GB or greater available	40 GB with 15 GB or greater available
Support for DirectX 9 graphics with WDDM driver	X	X	X	X
Graphics Memory	32 M	128 MB	128 MB	128 MB
Audio Output	X	X	X	X
Internet Access	X	X	X	X

TABLE 6–7 Windows 7 Minimum Requirements

	Windows 7 32-bit Editions	Windows 7 64-bit Editions
Processor	1 GHz 32-bit ×86	1 GHz 64-bit ×64 processor
System Memory	1 GB	2GB
Available Hard Drive Space	16 GB	20 GB
Support for DirectX 9 graphics with WDDM 1.0 or higher driver (DirectX 10 required for certain games)	X	X
Graphics Memory (to support Aero)	128 MB	128 MB
Audio Output (if desired)	X	X
Internet Access (best for keeping the OS updated)	X	X

upgrade their Windows XP computers to Windows Vista. However, in the years since then, hardware has continued its trend toward more power for less money, and today these same requirements seem very reasonable. It's almost as if Microsoft had reduced the hardware requirements. Further, Microsoft designed Windows 7 to provide better performance and to be more reliable on the same hardware required by Windows Vista. Windows 7 boots faster than Windows Vista and takes up less memory.

All versions of Windows have memory maximums—the maximum amount of memory the OS can address, as listed in Table 1–1 in Chapter 1. In brief, the maximum RAM for 32-bit Windows Vista or Windows 7 is 4 GB, and the maximums for the 64-bit versions vary by edition. For instance 64-bit Windows Vista Ultimate and Enterprise both have a 128 GB limit, while 64-bit Windows 7 Ultimate and Enterprise can work with up to 192 GB of RAM. In both versions 64-bit Home Basic has an 8 GB limit and Home Premium is limited to 16 GB.

> **WARNING!**
>
> If you plan to run Windows XP Mode, Microsoft recommends a PC with Intel-VT or AMD-V enabled in the CPU, plus you will need a minimum of 2 GB of memory and an additional 15 GB of free disk space.

Preparing to Install Windows 7

The preparation steps for installing Windows 7 vary based on whether you are doing an upgrade from Windows Vista, a side-by-side (dual-boot) installation, or a clean installation. Here is a brief overview of each of the installation types:

- **Upgrade** installs directly into the folders in which the previous version of Windows installed, preserving all your preferences and data. In a new twist on upgrading, Windows 7 Setup manages to preserve the old settings, while removing the old OS before installing the new OS, thus avoiding inheriting any problems in the old OS. You can only upgrade from a Windows Vista edition that is upgradeable to the edition of Windows 7 you plan to install (see Table 6–4). However, if you simply aren't quite ready to break all ties with your old installation of Windows Vista, then consider the next option.

- **Multi-boot** installation leaves an old OS in place, installing a new OS in a separate partition or hard disk. This allows you to select the OS you wish to boot into every time you start the computer, and it is what we did on Jane's computer because she still wanted an installation of Windows Vista for screen shots and comparison while writing about both Windows Vista and Windows 7. She also decided to multi-boot to have access to a few programs the Upgrade Advisor flagged as incompatible for Windows 7. This was a temporary arrangement because she soon found replacements for the programs, or found upgrades to them that worked better in Windows 7. To install Windows 7 to multi-boot, you do a clean installation on a separate partition or hard disk, which means you will select the Custom installation choice. Windows 7 Setup will preserve the earlier version of Windows and create a Windows Boot Manager menu, as Figure 6–12 shows.

- Clean installation takes the least amount of disk space and is a new beginning for the new OS installation. You most often do a clean installation on a totally clean hard drive, although, in the case of a multi-boot installation, you can direct Windows 7 Setup to install as a clean installation on a different partition or drive from that of the existing OS. To start a clean installation you will select the Custom installation choice.

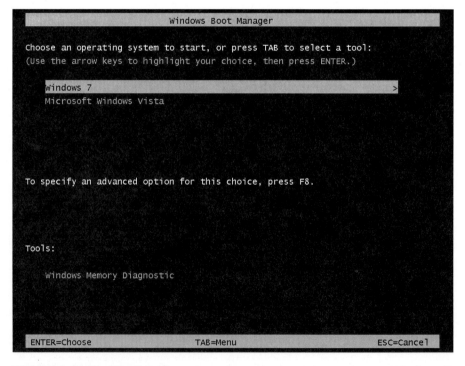

FIGURE 6–12 The Windows Boot manager menu showing two choices: Windows 7 and Windows Vista

Whether you are doing an upgrade or a clean install, you must ensure the hardware minimums are met, verify hardware and software compatibility, determine how to boot into the Windows setup program, and decide if you will activate immediately or later and if you wish to register the product with Microsoft. You can verify that your computer meets the recommend minimums by comparing the system configuration with Table 6–6 (Windows Vista minimums) or Table 6–7 (Windows 7 minimums).

Run Windows Upgrade Advisor

If you are preparing to upgrade Windows Vista to Windows 7, first run the Windows 7 Upgrade Advisor, which you can download from the Microsoft Web site and install. You will need administrative access to install it, and after you run it, the result will be a report of any hardware or software incompatibilities found, as shown here. Read the report carefully, because it will suggest actions to take, such as searching for updated drivers for a device or disabling a program just for the duration of the installation.

Download and Run the Windows 7 Upgrade Advisor

Download and run the Windows 7 Upgrade Advisor. Try this:

1. Point your browser to www.microsoft.com and then search on "download upgrade advisor." Navigate to the download page for the Windows 7 Upgrade Advisor.
2. Download the Upgrade Advisor. Once you have downloaded it, open the folder in which you saved it and run the installation program.
3. After the Upgrade Advisor installs, start it from a shortcut on the desktop or on the Start menu. It will take a few minutes to complete, and then it will display a report.
4. Print out the report and take any suggested action before installing Windows 7.

try this!

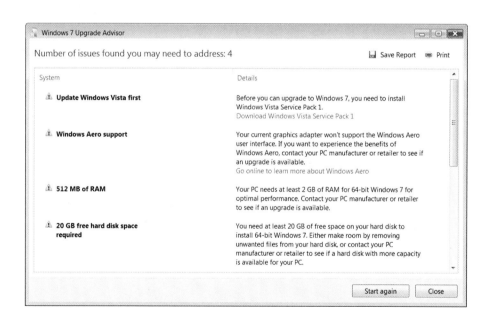

Prepare to Transfer Settings and Data

No matter what method you are using to move to Windows 7, you will want a way to transfer your data, e-mail, and settings for the Windows desktop and your applications. Microsoft provides a utility that will do this for you, whether you are planning to dual-boot between an older version of Windows and Windows 7, doing a clean installation, or purchasing a new computer with Windows 7 preinstalled. You can download this utility, Windows Easy Transfer (WET) from the Microsoft site where you will find versions for transferring files and settings from Windows XP or Windows Vista (both 32-bit and 64-bit editions).

FIGURE 6–13 Windows Easy Transfer for Windows 7

From your Windows XP or Windows Vista computer connect to www.microsoft.com and download the correct version of Windows Easy Transfer. Before you run it, make sure you have an appropriate location to which to copy the files you want to transfer. This can be directly to a new computer, providing you have a special cable to use or a network connection between the two computers. However, you are most likely to do this using an external hard drive or USB flash drive. Just make sure you are prepared to provide this, and that the location has plenty of free space for the files you will transfer. After you select the location, the next page asks "Which computer are you using now?" You will click the choice labeled "This is my old computer."

Then, when you have your Windows 7 computer ready, you run the Windows Easy Transfer utility, which you can find by entering "easy transfer" in Start | Search programs and Files. You will need to point Windows Easy Transfer to the location for the files, and then identify your computer by selecting "This is my new computer." Then follow the instructions to transfer the files. Figure 6–13 shows the Welcome screen to Windows Easy Transfer, describing the types of data that it can transfer.

A special USB cable, called an Easy Transfer Cable, can be used with Windows Easy Transfer. This is not a standard USB cable, but is available from electronics stores and other sources of computer cables, such as www.belkin.com.

The Installation

When you start the Windows 7 (or Windows Vista) start-up program the Windows Preinstallation Environment (PE) starts. This is a scaled-down Windows operating system. Much like the old Windows Setup program, it has limited drivers for basic hardware and support for the NTFS file system, TCP/IP, certain chipsets, mass storage devices, and 32-bit and 64-bit programs. Windows PE supports the Windows Setup GUI, collecting configuration information. Both Windows Vista and Windows 7 installation programs require very little user input near the beginning and the end of the process. Step-by-Step 6.02 will walk you through the steps for performing a clean installation.

Step-by-Step 6.02

Installing Windows 7

In this step-by-step exercise, you will do a clean installation of Windows 7. To complete this exercise, you will need the following:

- A Microsoft/Intel standard personal computer (desktop or laptop) compatible with Windows 7, with at least the recommended minimum hardware and configured to boot from DVD, and an unpartitioned hard disk (disk 0, the first hard disk) or a virtual machine you have prepared before beginning the Windows 7 installation (see Chapter 3).

- The Windows 7 DVD.
- The Product ID code. If you are using a retail version, look for this on the envelope or jewel case of your Windows 7 DVD. If you are not using a retail version, your instructor will provide a Product ID code or other instructions.
- A 15-character (or less) name, unique on your network, for your computer.
- A strong password for the user account created during Setup.

Step 1

Insert the Windows DVD and boot the computer. Watch the screen for instructions to boot from the optical drive. A plain black screen will briefly flash, followed by a black screen with the message: "Windows is loading files…" while Windows Preinstallation Environment is loaded and started. The Starting Windows screen signals that Windows PE is starting and will soon load the GUI for Windows 7 setup.

Step 2

On the first Install Windows page, select a language, time, and currency format, and keyboard input methods and select Next.

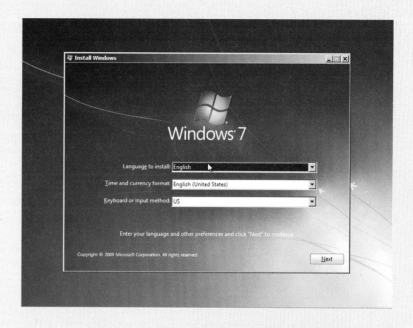

Step 3

The most prominent feature of the next screen is the Install Now button, but you should notice two important links. One is labeled What to know before installing Windows; click on it to see if you have overlooked a preparation step. The second link, labeled Repair your computer, is an important one to remember. If at any time after you install Windows 7, your system will not start, and if it also will not start in Safe Mode, pull out your Windows 7 DVD, boot from it, and select Repair your computer.

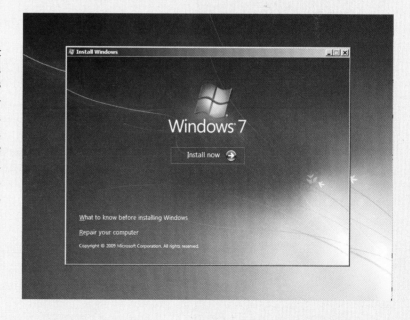

Step 4

On the license page read the Microsoft Software License Terms, click to place a check in the box labeled "I accept the license terms" and click the Next button.

Step 5

On the next page you are asked, "Which type of installation do you want?" Select Custom to perform a clean installation.

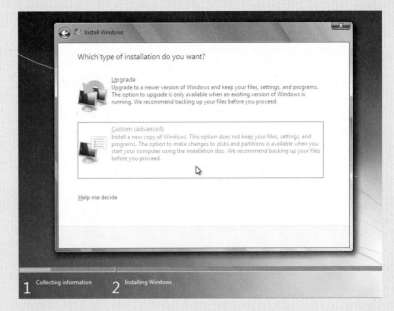

Step 6

On the next page, you need to select the target drive for the installation. On most systems, this page will show a single disk, and you will simply click Next. In this illustration, although it is not obvious, the target is a virtual hard drive in a virtual machine, and the virtual hard drive is smaller than we would normally choose for Windows 7, but the virtual hard disk is expandable.

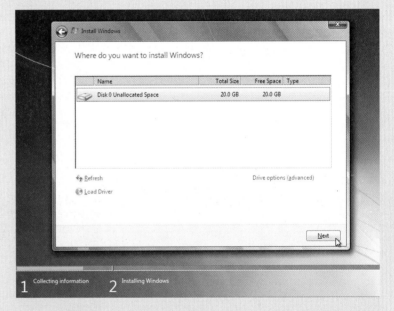

Step 7

Now relax while Windows 7 Setup goes through the phases of the installation, restarting several times, returning to this page that displays the progress with a green check by each completed phase.

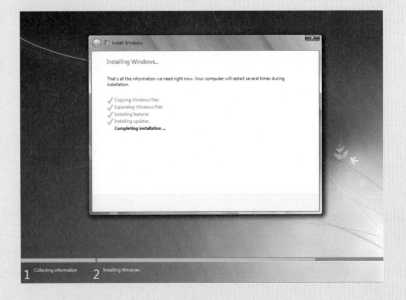

Step 8

When it reaches the Completing installation phase, the message "Setup will continue after restarting your computer" displays. After this, as Windows 7 restarts, the message "Setup is checking video performance" displays. Then you will need to enter a user name for the first user (a Computer Administrator type, although that detail is not mentioned) and a name for the computer.

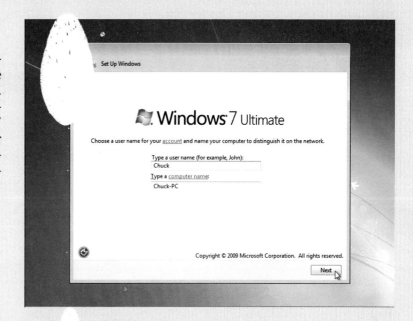

Step 9

Next create the password for the user account, entering it twice, and type a password hint that will help you to recall the password, but not reveal it to others. The password hint will display anytime you enter an incorrect password when logging on.

Step 10

On the next page you will need to enter the 20-character Product Key. Notice the check box labeled "Automatically activate Windows when I'm online." Already checked by default, this means it will activate automatically if your computer connects to the Internet. You must activate Windows within 30 days of installation. After that it will stop functioning. Click Next to continue the final configuration steps.

On the next page configure the Automatic Update Settings. Unless told otherwise, click the first option: "Use recommended settings." Windows Setup will then continue. On the next page select your time and date settings, and click Next.

Now select your computer's current location. If you are at home, select Home Network; if you are at school or work, select Work Network; if your computer has mobile broadband or you are using a public Wi-Fi network select Public Network. There will be a short delay while Windows connects to the network and applies settings.

The Welcome page displays, followed by a message: "Preparing your desktop..." Soon after the desktop displays and, depending on the setting you selected for updating and if you have an Internet connection, you will see a message that Windows is downloading and installing updates. Some updates require restarting Windows to complete installing the update.

If the network status icon displays a red x, it often indicates that the network cable is disconnected. Reconnecting the cable should solve that problem.

Post-Installation Tasks

After you install Windows 7, perform the necessary post-installation tasks. They include verifying network access (assuming you connected to a network) and installing at least the critical updates, including Service Packs. You should complete these tasks before moving on to customizing the desktop for yourself or another user and performing other desktop management tasks.

Verifying Network Access

Once you have completed the installation, look for the network status icon on the taskbar. If it does not show a red *x* then you have a network connection. If it shows a yellow exclamation mark, you have a local network connection, but do not have a connection to the Internet, although a router is present. Hover the mouse cursor over the icon. In the example shown here, the icon indicates a connection to a network named "ShortMoose" as well as to the Internet. If the network has no name, the top line will simply say "Network." In reality "ShortMoose" is the name of a wireless broadband router to which this computer connects via Ethernet. In Chapter 10 you will learn more about connecting your Windows computer to a private network as well as to the Internet.

The network status icon

Installing Security Software

It's difficult to say which is more important: downloading and installing the all-important updates or installing a security package. We opt to install the security program before completing all the updates. If you do not have another program available to use, consider the free Microsoft Security Essentials, shown in Figure 6–14, available at www.microsoft.com/security_essentials. It includes general malware protection and free, automated updates. If you do not have another preferred security program, download and install this easy-to-use package as soon as possible.

Installing Updates

Now that you have verified network access and installed security software, your next task is to install updates. Although some updates do install at the end of the Windows Vista and Windows 7 installation, you will need to ensure that additional updates install. How you actually obtain updates will depend on the organization (school or business) where you install Windows. In some organizations, the IT department may distribute updates for new installations on CD even before

Configure Windows Update

To configure Windows Update, try this:

1. Open the Start menu, in the Search Programs and Files box type "Windows Update," and select Windows Update from the results list.
2. In the task pane of Windows Update click Change Settings.
3. Using the drop-down lists and the check boxes, select the desired settings.
4. Click OK to close the Windows Update Change Settings box. Close Windows Update.

try this!

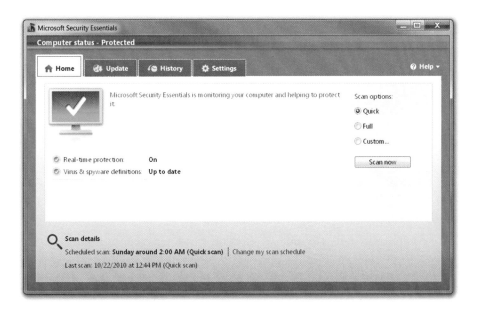

FIGURE 6–14 Microsoft Security Essentials

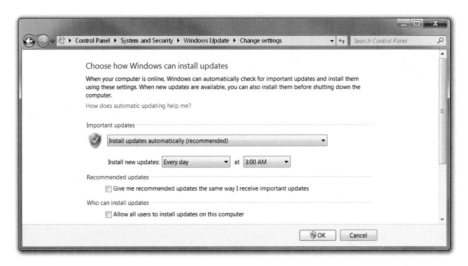

FIGURE 6–15 Options for Windows Update

connecting a computer to a network. Other organizations may make them available on a shared folder on the private network. In most cases, if you have an Internet connection, you will configure Windows Update to automatically download and install updates. Figure 6–15 shows the options for configuring Windows Update. We prefer to set it to install important updates automatically, and we clear the boxes for recommended updates and for who can install updates. These settings mean we will receive the important security updates, but we will have to view and select from the list of recommended updates. You can then browse through these updates and decide if you wish to install them.

If, during setup, you configured updates to download and install automatically, you can let nature take its course. But we like to be more proactive, because it can take Windows Update a few days before it downloads and installs all the updates for a new installation, especially as Microsoft continues to create more updates for a maturing Windows version. Therefore, even with Windows Update configured, we recommend you use the Windows Update program to manually access the updates immediately after upgrading or installing Windows. This will still take several iterations, but you will bring it up-to-date sooner this way.

Virtual Machine Additions

If you installed Windows Vista or Windows 7 into a virtual machine, be sure to install the virtual machine additions for Windows. Whatever hypervisor you are using will remind you to do this, usually when you start the newly installed OS in the virtual machine. The name for these additions, and how you start the installation of them, varies by hypervisor product. You may simply need to respond to a pop-up window or look in one of the menus on the window surrounding your virtual machine.

LO 6.3 | Managing Windows

Once you have installed Windows Vista or Windows 7, configured the OS to work with your network, and installed updates and service packs, it's time to customize Windows for the user. In this section, you will practice some of the common procedures for customizing and managing Windows Vista or Windows 7, using Computer Management tools for a variety of tasks, installing and removing applications, managing Windows components, and

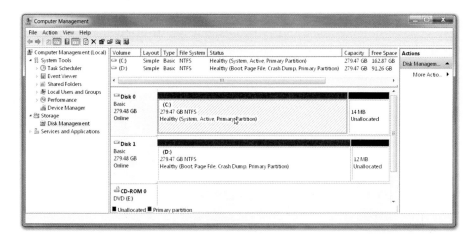

FIGURE 6–16 The Disk Management node in the Computer Management console

preparing the desktop for users, including modifications to display settings and adding a printer.

Computer Management

After you installed Windows 7, if you add a new hard drive to your computer and need to partition it or do any other maintenance, open the Computer Management console and expand the Disk Management node. Figure 6–16 shows the disks on our Windows Vista/Windows 7 dual-boot computer. Windows Vista is installed on Disk 0 (drive C:) and Windows 7 is installed on Disk 1 (drive D:).

If you add a hard drive—internal or external—use Disk Management to partition and format the drive, if necessary. New external drives often come pre-formatted with FAT32, which does not provide security and cannot automatically repair damage to the disk. Therefore, open Computer Management, and reformat your new drives if you wish to use the NTFS file system. This will destroy all data on the target partition. There is also a method for converting a FAT partition to NTFS from the command prompt, which it will do without losing data. To do this conversion, open a command prompt and enter "convert *d:* /fs:ntfs" where *d:* is the letter of the target partition you wish to convert to NTFS.

Preparing the Desktop for Users

In the decades we have worked with PCs running Windows OSs, we have noticed one phenomenon: A user who would have to have someone show him or her where the on/off button is will quickly figure out how to personalize the desktop. It seems like one day we help unpack the PC and a week later we come back to see dozens of shortcuts arrayed over desktop wallpaper of a child's crayon drawing. Whenever possible, we encourage such personalization because it means the person is making the computer his or her own and learning how to move around in Windows at the same time. So, whether you are preparing a PC for yourself or another user, there are some items to do after you complete the immediate post-installation tasks and before you install the necessary everyday applications. These include customizing the display settings—mainly the resolution—and adding a local printer.

Customizing Display Settings

After installing Windows Vista or Windows 7 you may need to customize the display settings for resolution and (if you are lucky) for multiple displays.

Display Resolution. Windows Vista and Windows 7 installation programs are very good at quickly installing Windows, but we still find that we need to tweak the display resolution settings because, during installation, Windows setup may install a generic display driver that may leave the display adapter at a lower resolution than it should be set to. This is especially true when you install into a virtual machine. In that case, you will install the virtual machine additions appropriate for the hypervisor and installed version of Windows, which will include better video adapter support. Then you will be able to select a higher resolution for the virtual display.

When you have installed Windows Vista or Windows 7 on a desktop computer with a flat panel display, if it installed the appropriate driver for the video adapter and the display, then resolution should be appropriate. A flat panel display has one native resolution, which will show as the recommended resolution.

A related issue is that because today's display systems (the video adapter and display combined) are capable of very high resolution, you may need to enlarge icons and other objects to make them more visible on the desktop. In fact, when you increase the resolution, it will prompt you to "Make it easier to read what's on your screen." This is where you change the size of items on your screen. Practice adjusting screen resolution in Step-by-Step 6.03.

Step-by-Step 6.03
Adjusting the Display Resolution

In this step-by-step exercise, you will familiarize yourself with the Windows 7 Appearance and Personalization applet and make a few changes to the desktop. We wrote the steps for Windows 7, but they are very similar to those for Windows Vista. To complete this task, you will need the following:

● A PC with Windows 7 installed.

Step 1

First change the screen resolution. A quick way to open the Screen Resolution page of the Appearance and Personalization applet is to right-click on an empty area of the desktop and select Screen Resolution from the context menu.

Click on the down arrow in the drop-down list labeled Resolution, look for a recommended resolution, and select it. Click OK.

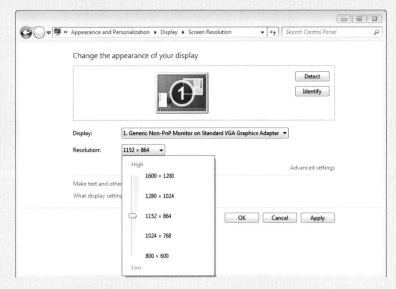

If you have increased your resolution, you will see this page, on which you can select the size of the text and other screen objects. This page is also available from the Screen Resolution page by clicking the link labeled "Make text and other items larger or smaller." Watch the Preview as you select a different size.

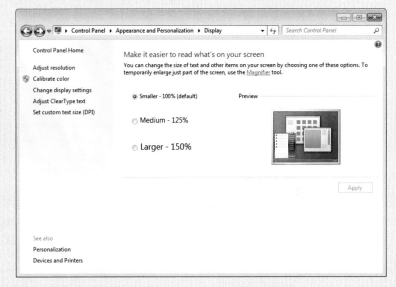

If you changed the text and object size, you will need to log off and then log on again for the change to take effect.

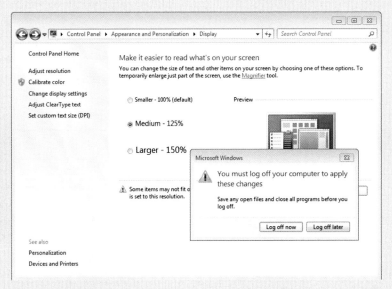

Multiple Displays. While most PCs today only have a single display, more and more jobs require the increased desktop real estate of multiple displays. Windows has supported multiple displays for several versions. All you need to add more display space to a typical desktop PC is a dual-headed video adapter and a second display. For most laptops the only cost is for a second display, since laptops usually come with a display connector for an external display that you can use simultaneously with the built-in display. We have worked with dual displays for several years on our computers and we found that the most ideal situation is identical displays. It can be a bit weird to work with multiple displays of different sizes.

When you have multiple displays, you can configure how Windows uses these displays on the Screen Resolution page. Our preferred mode is "Extend these displays," which leaves the taskbar on the primary display (labeled 1 in Figure 6–17) and extends the desktop to the secondary display. It is great to have a document open on one display and an Internet browser open on the other, for instance. The setting "Duplicate these displays" shows the same desktop on both displays. You might use this if your laptop connects to a projector on which you wish to show the desktop. The remaining setting "Show desktop only on 1" and "Show desktop only on 2" will leave the display you do not select blank.

Click the Identify button to have a number display on each physical display (see Figure 6–18) so that you can confirm that you have the displays oriented left to right as they are in the Screen Resolution page. If they are not, click and drag the display images on the Screen Resolution page to place them in the correct order.

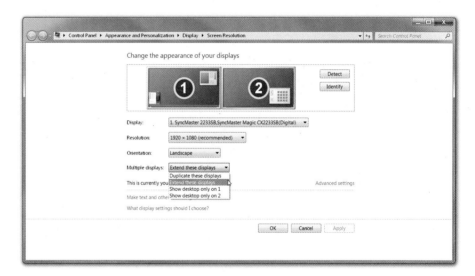

FIGURE 6–17 Select how you want the desktop to appear on multiple displays.

> Figure 6–18 is a screenshot captured on a dual-display with a window positioned to overlap both displays.

FIGURE 6–18 When you click the Identify button a numeral will appear briefly on each display.

Desktop Gadgets

Windows Vista had a feature called the Sidebar in which you could configure one or more small programs called gadgets. The Sidebar is gone from Windows 7, but the gadgets remain; now you can position them anywhere you wish on the desktop. Each gadget performs some small function—usually involving keeping information handy in a small screen object. This information may be the date or time, stock quotes, weather in a certain city, and much more. To find gadgets, first right-click on an empty area of the desktop and select Gadgets from the context menu. (See the illustration in Step 1 of Step-by-Step 6.03.) The Gadgets page displays, as shown here.

The gadget control panel

Simply double-click a gadget to install it onto the desktop. After installing a gadget on the desktop, pass the mouse over the gadget and note the button bar that appears beside the gadget, as seen in Figure 6–19. The button with a wrench icon allows you to modify options for the gadget. For instance, Options for the Weather gadget include selecting the city whose weather you wish to monitor.

FIGURE 6–19 Click the Options button for a gadget.

Adding a Local Printer

Installing a new printer in Windows should be a nonevent because Windows is a plug-and-play OS, and new printers are plug-and-play. Therefore, you simply follow the setup guide for the new printer. In many cases, Windows will already have the printer driver and will install it without requiring a disc from the manufacturer, but there can be another reason to run a setup program from the printer manufacturer. A new printer, especially one that includes other functions—primarily document scanning, copying, and faxing—will also include special software beyond the standard printer driver. Most common is software for scanning and organizing your documents.

Before connecting a printer, be sure to read the printer's setup guide—usually a hard-to-miss oversize sheet with the basic instructions for setting up the printer. Often, a printer setup guide will instruct you to install the printer's software before connecting it, especially if it connects via USB. It will also guide you through making both the power connection and the connection to the computer. How will your printer connect to the computer? The most common printer interface is USB, but modern printers also use IEEE 1394 (FireWire), Bluetooth, or Wi-Fi. If the printer uses a cable (USB or IEEE 1394) you will first connect the printer, and then turn it on. If it connects via a

FIGURE 6–20 Devices and Printers applet

In the example in Figure 6–20, not all devices in the Printers and Faxes categories are physical printers or faxes. Some are software "printers" such as Adobe PDF and Snagit 9, which take files from one format (a Word document or a graphic file) and "print" it to a file in a new format, such as Adobe PDF, a file format that is commonly used for distributing documents over networks.

wireless method, you will turn on the printer and establish the wireless connection. Once Windows detects a printer, it installs the driver and configures the printer for you. It will be added to the Devices and Printers applet, shown in Figure 6–20, and be available to all applications that can use a printer. The printer with the white check mark on a green circle is the default printer that it will use unless you select a different printer. Double-click on a printer icon to open the printer page with status information and links to the printer properties, print queue, and other pages for managing and controlling the printer and its features.

Connecting to a Network Printer

If a printer is available on your network, and an administrator has configured it with appropriate permissions so that you can connect and print to it, you can do just that. To do so, open Devices and Printers (Windows 7) and click Add a printer. In the Add Printer dialog select "Add a network, wireless or Bluetooth printer." It will take time to search for all available network printers and then display them in the box. Select the Printer Name of the printer you wish to connect to, click Next, and follow the instructions. This will install the appropriate printer driver on your computer so that Windows can format each print job before sending it to the network printer.

Installing and Removing Applications

By now, you are ready to install applications into Windows to make your computer the tool you need for work, home, or school. If you purchased a computer with Windows preinstalled, you may also need to remove some of those pre-installed applications you have no desire or need to use.

Installing Applications

Today, all mainstream applications come with their own installation program that will walk you through the installation process. Some offer you few options, installing with very little user input, while others will give you the option to do a custom install, in which you select the components to install

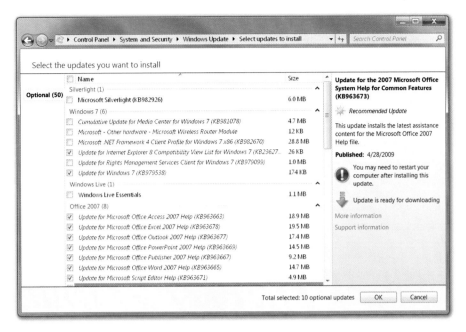

FIGURE 6–21 You can update Microsoft Applications through Windows Update.

and the location for the installed files. These programs copy the application files and make necessary changes to Windows, such as associating one or more file types with the application so that when you double-click on, say, a file with a DOCX extension, it knows to open Microsoft Word.

After completing an application installation, you should make sure to update the application. If you have an Internet connection, most applications will check for updates. This is very important today when malware targets even our business productivity software. If your applications are from Microsoft, you can update them through Windows Update, which will list updates under Optional Updates, as shown in Figure 6–21.

A quick method for opening the Control Panel is to click on the Start button and in the Search box enter **control**.

Removing Applications

When it comes time to remove an application, you should first look for an uninstall program for the application. If the application has a submenu off the Start menu, it may include the uninstall program, which is usually the best choice for uninstalling. You can also search the folder in which the application installed for an uninstall program. If you cannot find such a program for an application you wish to uninstall, open Control Panel, locate Programs, and click Uninstall A Program. It may take a few seconds for the list of installed programs to display in the Programs and Features page. Locate the program you wish to uninstall and double-click it. You

try this!

Use Add or Remove Programs

Become familiar with the list of programs installed on your computer. In addition to applications, the Programs and Features applet lists the installed Windows updates. Try this:

1. Open the Control Panel. Under Programs, click on Uninstall A Program. Wait for the list to display. Browse through the list of Currently Installed Programs.

2. If you find a program that you want to remove, click the program, and then click the Uninstall button in the bar above the list to begin the uninstall process. Sometimes you must provide the installation CD before you can remove the program!

3. In the task list on the left, click View Installed Updates to see a list of installed Windows updates. If you have a good reason to uninstall an update, this is the place to do it. We don't recommend uninstalling updates unless you are sure it is necessary.

4. When you have finished exploring, close the open windows. If you uninstalled an application, you may need to allow the uninstall program to restart the computer.

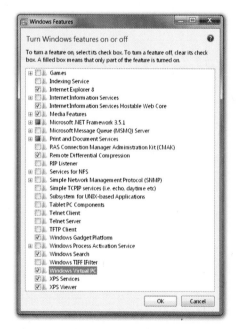

FIGURE 6–22 Uninstall unwanted programs

Turn Windows Features On or Off

The default installation of Windows 7 does not turn on Windows Virtual PC, including Windows XP Mode. If you need it you can turn it on. Try this:

1. Open the Control Panel and click Programs. Click the link labeled Turn Windows Features on or off.
2. Locate Windows Virtual PC in the list. If there is no check in the box by this choice, click to turn it on. If it is already checked and turned on, select another feature, such as Games.
3. Enabling Windows Virtual PC will require a restart of the computer. Close the open windows and restart your computer.
4. Open Start | All Programs and see if the feature you enabled is listed in the menus.

will see a warning, as shown in Figure 6–22. Follow the instructions to complete the operation.

Managing Windows Components

Windows Vista and Windows 7, like previous versions, include many Windows components beyond the basic operating system files. You can view the list of Windows features and simply click a check box to turn individual features on or off, as shown here.

Simple File Management

As with any operating system, file management in Windows Vista and Windows 7 is mainly about organizing data files so that you can easily find the files you need when you need them. Windows provides a set of folders for just this purpose. Before you use them, get a basic understanding of the default file hierarchy in whatever version of Windows you are using. Then learn how to work with not just files and folders, but also the libraries that Windows 7 introduced. Finally, learn about the Windows file systems for optical discs and the ones that allow you to copy files to CD or DVD as easily as you copy them to a hard drive or flash drive.

Windows Vista and Windows 7 Default File Hierarchy

All versions of Windows create one set of folders for the operating system, another set for application program files, and an additional set for each user account to hold user data files. This folder structure is nearly identical in Windows Vista and Windows 7. The 32-bit and 64-bit distributions of each differ only in the location in which they store programs. The 32-bit distributions of both Windows Vista and Windows 7 store all programs in the Program Files folder, while the 64-bit distributions store only 64-bit programs in this folder and store 32-bit programs in the folder named Program Files (×86). Figure 6–23 shows the folder hierarchy for

Use the check boxes to turn Windows features on or off.

a 64-bit installation of Windows 7. The default location for the majority of the Windows operating system files is in C:\Windows.

The default location for user data is C:\Users\<username> where <username> is the log-on user name. In Figure 6–24, note the folder for the user Jade. Within this folder are several folders created by Windows to hold various types of data or, as in the case of the Desktop folder, to hold files from a certain location. The Downloads folder holds files you download with your Internet browser.

try this!

Explore Windows Folders

If you are sitting at a computer with Windows Vista or Windows 7, explore the folder hierarchy. Try this:

1. Click Start | Computer.
2. In Windows Explorer double-click the icon for the Local Disk (C:). Note the folders in the root of drive C:.
3. Double-click the icon for Program Files and note the folders under Program Files. If you have a 64-bit installation of Windows, double-click the icon for Program Files (×86) and note the folders in this folder.
4. Now browse to the Users folder and open the folder for the account with which you logged on and explore the contents of this folder.

Navigating Windows Explorer

There are several ways to manage your files in Windows. The primary tool for saving files is the individual application you use to create and modify files of a certain type: for instance, a word processing program, spreadsheet program, photo editing program, or other application. When you issue the command within an application to save a file, you can navigate to the location of

Open Windows Explorer quickly by pressing the Window key and "e" keys together.

FIGURE 6–23 The Windows 7 64-bit default folder hierarchy

FIGURE 6–24 Windows 7 default folders for the user Jade

your choice and either save the file in an existing folder or create a new folder before saving. Similarly, when you decide to open an existing file from within an application, you can navigate to a location and open the desired file.

Although, you can also do many file management tasks within an application, the primary tool for copying, moving, renaming, and deleting files is Windows Explorer. Microsoft has added some new features to the Windows Explorer folder windows, which we will highlight here. Figure 6–25 shows the anatomy of a Windows Explorer folder window. By default, the Menu bar appears only when you press the ALT key, and you can use the Organize button and other buttons on the toolbar to modify the appearance and functionality of the Windows Explorer folder windows.

Navigate through Windows Explorer with mouse operations. When you hover the mouse over the navigation pane, small clear triangles appear next to each folder object that can be expanded. Click the triangle and it turns solid black and points down to the right in the navigation pane at the now-visible objects contained in the original folder. Click an object's icon in the navigation pane to open it in the contents pane. If you wish to open objects (folders, files, etc.) in the contents pane, you will need to double-click on the object. You can move files and folders from one location to another by dragging and dropping the object you wish to move. Right-click on an object to access other possible operations.

By default, Windows Explorer hides extensions for known file types, an inconvenience for power users. To make file extensions visible, open Windows Explorer and press Alt-T to open the Tools menu, select Folder Options, then click the View tab. In Advanced Settings clear the check box labeled Hide extensions for known file types. Click OK to close Folder Options.

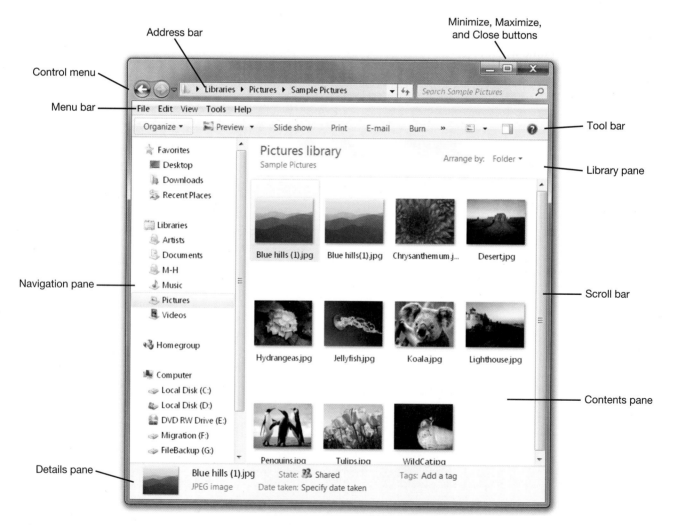

FIGURE 6–25 A Windows Explorer folder window

Libraries

Recall what you learned earlier in this chapter about libraries. A library points to one or more locations. Familiarize yourself with libraries by clicking the libraries pinned icon on the taskbar (it looks like a bunch of folders in a stand) and clicking on any library in the navigation pane. For instance, when you do this to the Documents pane, its contents appear in the contents pane and above that pane is the library pane. The word *Includes* appears in the Library pane, and after that appears the number of locations. But this also is a link— click it to open the Documents Library Locations window.

You can add locations to a library and create libraries of your own. This is very handy if you want to organize all the files related to a project but those files are stored in folders in various locations on your local hard drive, external hard drives, or network servers. You can back up data in a library as if it were stored in one location. To add a location to the Documents library, simply click the Add button, which opens the Include Folder in Document window. Use this to browse to the folders you wish to add, select the folder, and click the Include Folder button. Windows then adds the new location to the library.

Notice the words *Default save location*. When you save files into this library, you are putting them in the default location for saving files. To change the default save location, first you need more than one save location in a library. Then all you need to do is right-click the desired location and select "Set as default save location."

To create a new library, first click on Libraries in the navigation pane, then notice the New Library tool that appears on the toolbar. Click New Library, which will create a new library folder, ready for a name and locations. If you missed entering the name when you created it, right-click on the New Library, select rename, enter the name, and press ENTER. With the new library selected in the navigation pane, the contents pane will indicate that the library is empty. Click the "Include a folder" button to begin adding locations to this new library. You can continue to add locations. Network locations must already be indexed. If you see an error that it cannot add a location because it has not been indexed, use Windows Help and Support to solve this problem. Figure 6–26 shows a new library named M-H with two locations—one on a network server named HTC-SERVER.

Working with Optical Discs

Even most inexpensive consumer-grade PCs come with optical drives capable of burning (writing data, music, or videos to disc), and optical discs are great for those files you wish to remove to make more room on the computer's hard drive. Whatever your need for burning CDs or DVDs, you should first understand the two formats Windows 7 uses when it burns discs: the ISO Mastered format and the Universal Disk Format (UDF) Live File System.

Use the Mastered format when you want to be able to use a CD or DVD in a conventional CD or DVD player or in any computer (older Apple Macs or PCs). The trouble with using this format is that each item you select

FIGURE 6–26 A new library with two locations

to copy to the PC is stored temporarily in available hard disk space (in addition to the space used by the original file) until you finish selecting all you wish to copy, and then they are copied in one operation. This makes it difficult to copy files from a hard drive when you have very little free hard drive space on any hard drive in your computer.

Use the Live File System to burn a disc when you will only use the disc on newer Apple Macs and newer PCs (Windows XP and newer support it, but older PCs may not). Using Live File System you can directly copy items to the drive without requiring extra hard drive space. You can copy items individually, over time—either by leaving the disc in the drive or reinserting the disc multiple times. If all the systems in which you plan to use a disc are newer PCs or Macs, then keep the default setting, which uses the Live File System. Step-by-Step 6.04 will walk you through copying files to an optical disc using the Live File System format.

Step-by-Step 6.04

Burning a CD or DVD

In this step-by-step exercise, you will burn a DVD using the Live File System, which allows you to copy files much as you would to any hard drive or flash drive. We wrote the instructions based on the assumption that AutoPlay is on, meaning that certain actions occur when you insert a disc. When you insert a blank disc, the Autoplay dialog offers choices for burning the disc. To complete this exercise, you will need the following:

- A computer with a DVD/CD drive and with Windows 7 installed—either a conventional installation or an installation in a VM.
- A blank CD or DVD.

Step 1

Insert a blank disc into the optical drive. When the Autoplay dialog opens, you must choose between burning files (data), an audio CD, or a DVD. The choices shown here depend on the type of disc used. Select Burn Files to Disc.

Step 2

In the Burn a Disc dialog, provide a title for the disc (the default is the current date), enter a name, and then click Next.

Live File System format ——

Mastered format ——

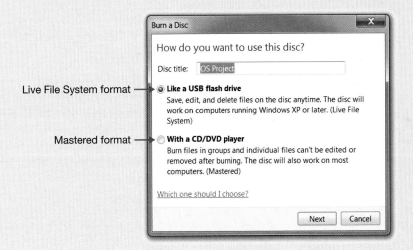

Step 3

Windows formats the disc.

Step 4

After the disc is prepared, this message displays. You can now copy files to the disc from Windows Explorer—either click the button labeled "Open folder to view files" (just one way to open Windows Explorer), or close the box and continue working, copying files to the disc as you would normally copy files to a hard disk or USB drive.

Step 5

For instance, you can drag and drop folders and files to the disc, as we have done here with the folder titled "06-A+SG_7E." When you use the Live File System, you can continue to add files to the disc as long as it has available space. You can do that now, or add files to it later.

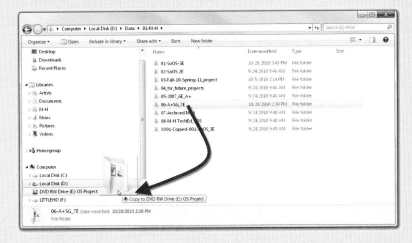

LO 6.4 | Managing Local Security in Windows

If your Windows computer is on a corporate network, the company will centrally manage it, including the security issues. A computer that is not part of a corporate network depends on the knowledge of the user for its security. Security implemented solely on a desktop or laptop computer is local security. Here we will look at administering local user accounts, local security for files and folders, Windows BitLocker drive encryption, Windows Defender antispam protection, and Windows Firewall.

Administering Local User Accounts

Local user accounts, as described in Chapter 2, reside in the local accounts database on a Windows computer. You use a local account to give someone access to the Windows computer and local data. More than one person can log on to a Windows desktop computer as an interactive user, thanks to a feature called Switch Users, but only one person at a time can physically use that Windows desktop computer's mouse, keyboard, and display. Only one interactive user ever uses the typical desktop computer. Therefore, most users have little or no experience managing local accounts—other than their own, and those same users rarely have need to make any changes to their own account. This section gives you a chance to create and manage a local user account. The tasks and the administrative tool for managing local user account in Windows Vista and Windows 7 are nearly identical. Therefore, for the sake of simplicity, we will focus on Windows 7.

User Accounts Applet

The primary tool for administering local user accounts is User Accounts, a Control Panel applet. Either browse to it from Start | Control Panel or enter "user accounts" in the Start menu Search box and select User Accounts from the list of results. In the example shown here, the user Yoda is an Administrator and the account is password protected. Keep User Accounts open because we will use this tool to explore local accounts.

Working with User Accounts in Windows

You must log on as an Administrator to see all the local user accounts on your computer. Do this by opening User Accounts and clicking Manage Another Account. The Manage Accounts folder will show the existing accounts. In this

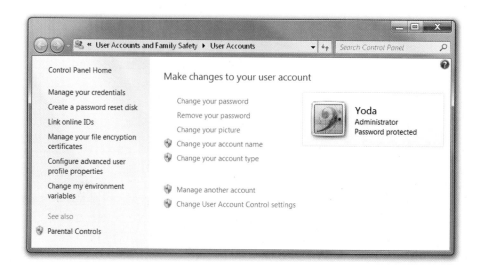

example there are only two accounts: Yoda and Guest; the Guest account is off, which is the default for this account, as described in Chapter 2.

Windows 7 also has a local account named Administrator, disabled by default during a clean installation and an upgrade. The exception to this is when you upgrade a Windows Vista installation that only has the Administrator and has no other active local account that is a member of the local Administrators group, which would be a rare occurrence. In that case, the local Administrator account is enabled, so it would be visible in Local Users when an administrator selects "Manage another account." When you are performing an upgrade to Windows 7 on a Vista PC in a Microsoft Active Directory Domain, it will disable the local Administrator account regardless of the contents of the local accounts database. You can enable this account after installation, but we strongly recommend that you not do it because *this* account is all-powerful and immune to the User Account Control (UAC) security feature, while other accounts that are simply members of the local Administrators group are not immune to UAC. Therefore, while the Administrator account is logged on, the computer is more vulnerable to a malware attack.

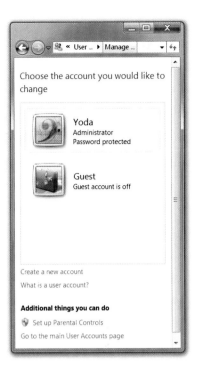

Step-by-Step 6.05
Creating a New Account in Windows 7

In this step-by-step exercise, you will create a new Standard user account. To complete this exercise, you will need the following:

- A computer or virtual machine with Windows 7 installed. You may use Windows Vista, keeping in mind that the screens will not exactly match the illustrations in the steps.

- To log on using an Administrator account (not necessarily *the* Administrator account).

Step 1

Open User Accounts, using one of the methods described earlier. In the User Accounts folder, click Manage Another Account. Enter a name for the account, read the descriptions of the Standard user and Administrator user account types, but leave Standard user selected and click Create Account.

Step 2

The Manage Accounts folder opens with the new user added.

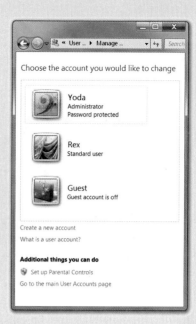

Step 3

The new account does not have a password. To password protect the account, you can either allow the user to log on and create a password, or you (as an Administrator) can create a password that the user will need to use when logging on. To create a password for this account, double-click on the account icon and click Create a Password.

Step 4

In the Create Password folder, enter the new password twice in the New password and Confirm new password boxes. It is optional to enter a password hint, but we recommend you do that. Then click the Create Password button.

Step 5

The new user account appears in User Accounts as a Standard user account and is password protected. Close all open windows. Notice the other changes you can make to this account. When you are finished, close User Accounts.

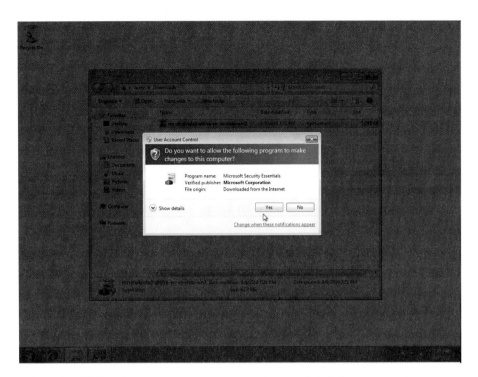

FIGURE 6-27 The Consent Prompt appears when an Administrator needs to provide consent for certain actions.

User Account Control

Recall from Chapter 2 that User Account Control (UAC), introduced in Windows Vista and improved in Windows 7, is designed to protect the computer from having malware installed. In Windows XP and earlier versions, if you logged on with an Administrator account, malware could install and have full access to your computer without you being aware of it. UAC prevents that from happening. In Vista or Windows 7, even if you log on as an Administrator, UAC will inform you that a program is trying to perform something for which it needs elevated permissions (administrator). In that scenario, the screen will go gray and the Consent Prompt, shown in Figure 6–27, displays. If you intended to run the program and you trust the source, click Yes to allow it to run. If you have logged on as a Standard user, the Credentials Prompt will display, requiring that you provide an Administrator password.

Windows 7 has eliminated many of the events that would have triggered UAC. For instance, if you are logged on with an Administrator type account you will not see the Consent Prompt appear for certain advanced administrative tasks, such as opening the User Account Control Settings window. A Standard user will need to provide credentials, as shown in Figure 6–28.

Local Security for Files and Folders

Windows Vista and Windows 7 both support the use of permissions to protect files and folders on local NTFS volumes. Additionally, they both offer encryption on NTFS volumes, allowing you to turn on encryption for a folder, as described in Chapter 2. This folder-level encryption on an NTFS volume is different from another feature in Windows Vista and Windows 7 called BitLocker Drive Encryption, which encrypts an entire physical disk. You will learn about Bitlocker later in this chapter. In this section, we will look at applying permissions on local NTFS volumes.

FIGURE 6-28 The Credentials Prompt will display when something requiring an Administrator occurs while a Standard user is logged on.

The NTFS file system allows you to control who has access to specified files and folders by assigning permissions. These permissions restrict access to local users and groups as well as to those who connect to these resources over the network. Although, in the case of those connecting over a network, the share permissions (not related to NTFS permissions) take effect first and may block access to the underlying files and folders. Only NTFS volumes allow you to assign permissions to files and folders directly. In this section, we will focus on the security features of NTFS, including file and folder permissions. We discussed NTFS encryption in Chapter 2.

File and Folder Permissions

On a volume formatted with the NTFS file system, each folder and file has a set of security permissions associated with it using the following mechanism. Each file and folder on an NTFS volume has an associated **Access Control List (ACL)**, which is a table of users and/or groups and their permissions to access the file or folder. Each ACL has at least one **Access Control Entry (ACE)**, which is like a record in this tiny ACL database that contains just one user or group account name and the permissions assigned to this account for that file or folder. An administrator, or someone with Full Control permission for the file or folder, creates the ACEs. To view the ACEs in an ACL for a file or folder, open the Properties dialog box and select the Security tab. Figure 6–29 shows the Security page for a folder named Jade, which is the top-level personal

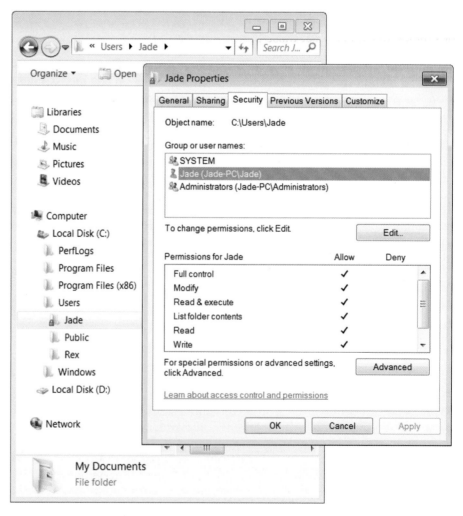

FIGURE 6–29 The list of permissions Windows creates on a user's personal folder

folder automatically created by Windows the first time the user Jade logged on. Notice the list of permissions for the user Jade. This is an ACE. These are the default permissions set by Windows on the user's personal folders.

Change the permissions on a folder or file by opening its Security page and clicking the Edit button to reveal the page shown here where you can add a user or group, remove a user or group, and specify the permissions assigned to the file or folder for each user or group. Table 6–8 compares the standard permissions on folders versus those on files.

These permissions apply to files and folders on an NTFS volume and protect those resources from both locally logged-on users and those who may connect over a network. Windows only assigns network shares to folders, so you must assign the permissions to the shared folder. This entirely different set of permissions is applied before a user accesses the NTFS folder and file permissions. We will explore sharing files on a network and setting share permissions in Chapter 10.

NTFS Permission Inheritance

The folders and files on a disk volume are in a hierarchy, with the drive itself at the top, followed by the root folder and subfolders. Every subfolder and its contents inherit these permissions. If you wish one of the subfolders to have different permissions, you must first navigate to it and open its Properties dialog to explicitly set those permissions on the Security page. When you view permissions on a file or folder, the permissions inherited from the parent are visible but unavailable, as shown by the gray checks and lack of boxes, and you will not be able to modify those permissions at that level. New permissions can be assigned, but inherited permissions cannot be altered. You can modify them in the folder in which they originated or you can choose to block inheritance on a folder or file to which you wish to assign different (usually more restrictive) permissions. To do this, you must access the Advanced Security Settings, then click the Change Permissions button, and deselect the check box labeled Include inheritable permissions from this object's parent.

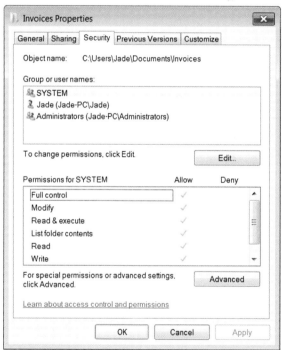

BitLocker Drive Encryption

If you have very high security needs and have either the Ultimate or Enterprise version of Windows Vista or Windows 7,

Inherited permissions are grayed out.

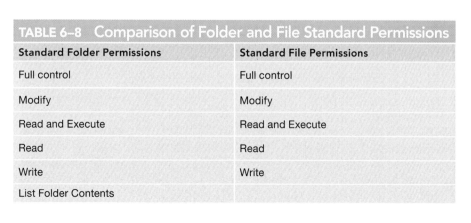

TABLE 6–8 Comparison of Folder and File Standard Permissions	
Standard Folder Permissions	**Standard File Permissions**
Full control	Full control
Modify	Modify
Read and Execute	Read and Execute
Read	Read
Write	Write
List Folder Contents	

consider enabling BitLocker Drive Encryption. Microsoft introduced it in Windows Vista as an optional feature for encrypting only the drive on which the Windows OS resides. It was enhanced in Windows 7 to include drives beyond the system drive, including internal hard drives and externally attached drives. This last feature is called BitLocker To Go.

BitLocker is off by default. When you enable it, it encrypts the entire contents of a drive, storing an encryption and decryption key in a hardware device that is separate from the encrypted hard disk. To do this, the computer must have either a chip with Trusted Platform Module (TPM) version 1.2 or higher or a removable USB memory device (USB flash drive). When you use TPM, the drive and computer are married because the chip resides in the computer.

To encrypt the drive on which Windows is installed, BitLocker requires a hard drive with at least two partitions: one that contains Windows (the "system" partition), and a second partition (the "boot" partition) created by BitLocker and not directly usable by the user. When you perform a clean installation of Windows 7 it creates the hidden boot partition. One of the improvements in Windows 7 is that this second partition is 100 MB, which is much smaller than in Windows Vista. This partition is critical to booting up your computer and without it, Windows cannot be started from the encrypted partition.

In Windows 7, when you wish to encrypt a drive—either internal or external—you simply open Windows Explorer, right-click a drive and select BitLocker from the context menu, as shown here. The existence of this choice on the menu indicates that the selected drive supports BitLocker.

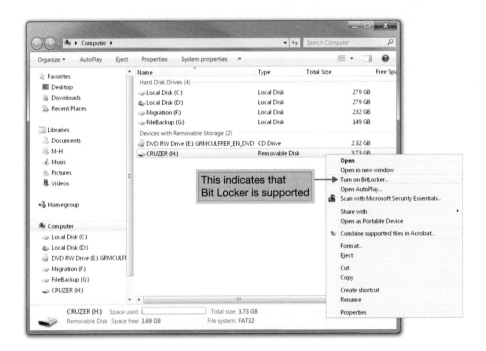

Right-click a drive and look for the option Turn on BitLocker.

BitLocker To Go may be the Bitlocker feature most ordinary folk will use because many people carry flash drives, and when they have confidential information, such as medical records, it is important to protect that data. However, you will be able to access the data only on the drive on the computer on which you encrypted it or on a computer where you can make the keys available, which is limited to computers running Windows 7.

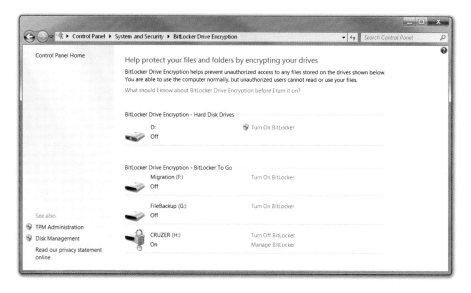

BitLocker is turned on for Drive H:.

The tool for managing Bit-Locker for all your drives is the BitLocker Drive Encryption control panel shown above. Notice the lock and key on the encrypted drive. Once you encrypt a drive with BitLocker, Manage BitLocker becomes a choice on the context menu for that drive in Windows Explorer, so you can access the management options for the drive from either location.

View the BitLocker Status of all Drives at Once

Quickly view and manage the BitLocker status of your drives on a Windows 7 computer. Try this:

1. Select Start | Control Panel | System and Security | BitLocker Drive Encryption or simply enter "bitlocker" in the Start | Search box.
2. Click the link labeled TPM Administration to see if your computer supports TPM.
3. If you have a flash drive and have permission to do so, insert it into your computer and turn on BitLocker for the drive.

Windows Defender

Windows Defender is free anti-spyware software included with Windows. To see if Windows Defender is running on your computer click Start, type "defender," and select Windows Defender from the results list. If you see this message, Windows Defender is off, and if no other anti-virus is enabled, click the link Click here to turn it on. However, if you have Microsoft Security Essentials, or almost any third-party security software installed, it will include anti-spyware software, but you should check to be sure if you find that Windows Defender is turned off.

Windows Defender is turned off.

Windows Firewall

We strongly recommend that you use a personal firewall on your PC if it connects to any network. Most security software suites come with a personal firewall, and, as described in Chapter 2, Windows Firewall has been a feature of Windows since Windows XP Service Pack 2. Windows Vista and Windows 7 added their own enhancements to this personal firewall. So, there is really no excuse for not using a personal firewall on your PC.

To open the Windows Firewall control panel click Start | Control Panel | System and Security | Windows Firewall. The example shown in Figure 6–30

FIGURE 6–30 On this page "Public networks" refers to public Wi-Fi networks and other untrusted public networks.

is on a computer connected to a private network. Notice that it shows we are not connected to a public network, which refers to an open Wi-Fi network like you would encounter if you used your laptop in an airport terminal or at your favorite coffee shop. The computer in question actually is connected to the biggest public network in the world—the Internet, but a firewall on a router guards our connection to the Internet.

Chapter 6 REVIEW

Chapter Summary

After reading this chapter and completing the Step-by-Step tutorials and Try This! exercises, you should understand the following facts about Windows Vista and Windows 7.

Windows Vista and Windows 7 Overview

- Windows Vista was not a successful operating system because it had problems that prompted people to stay with Windows XP. Windows 7 corrects many of the problems with Windows Vista.
- Windows Vista and Windows 7 both are bundled as several products called editions. Two scaled down editions of each of these Windows versions, Starter and Home Basic, are not considered mainstream editions.
- Windows Vista and Windows 7 each come in three retail editions. Both have a Home Premium edition and an Ultimate edition. Windows Vista has a Business edition, while Windows 7 Professional is its equivalent. The included features distinguish the Windows editions.

- Windows Vista introduced Windows Aero, and the desktop is enhanced with such features as Jump Lists and pinning.
- Security features such as User Account Control, BitLocker, and Windows Defender are improved in Windows 7, and BitLocker To Go and AppLocker have been added.

Installing Windows

- You cannot directly upgrade Windows XP to Windows 7. The ability to upgrade from Windows Vista to Windows 7 depends on the editions involved in the upgrade—both for Windows Vista and for Windows 7.
- The Windows 7 system requirements are nearly identical to the requirements for Windows Vista, but while the requirements described an upscale computer at the introduction of Widows Vista, today they describe a common, affordable computer.
- You must decide on the type of installation: upgrade, multi-boot, or clean installation. You

achieve the latter two by using the Custom option in the Windows setup program.

- Windows Vista and Windows 7 installation programs require very little user input.
- Immediately after installing Windows, verify network access, install security software, and finish updating Windows.

Managing Windows

- Familiarize yourself with the tools in the Computer Management console, especially the Disk Management node, which will allow you to perform a variety of tasks on disks.
- If necessary, adjust the display resolution, and change the text and object size.
- If a computer has multiple displays, use the Display Resolution control panel to configure the displays for the way the user will use them.
- Install and uninstall a program using the program's own installation program. Some programs do not come with an uninstall option. In that case, use the Programs applet in Control Panel to uninstall the program.
- Turn Windows features on and off in the Control Panel Programs applet.
- During installation, Windows creates a default folder hierarchy into which it installs operating system files and program files.
- The first time a user logs on, Windows creates the user's personal folders under the Users folder at the root of the drive on which Windows installed. If this is an NTFS volume, Windows will set permissions for the user's personal folders.
- Libraries appear to be folders when viewed in Windows Explorer, but a library is not a folder—it is an object that keeps track of one or more locations where certain folders and files are stored. There are four default libraries in Windows 7, and you can create custom libraries.

- If you burn an optical disc with the Mastered format you will able to use it in a conventional CD or DVD player, or in any computer, including older Apple Macs or PCs, but the burn process for this format requires hard drive space to temporarily store the files before burning to disc.
- If you burn an optical disc with the Live File System you will only be able to use the disc on newer Apple Macs and newer PCs (Windows XP and newer support it, but older PCs may not). This format allows you to directly copy items to the drive without requiring extra hard drive space. You can also add files to a disc formatted with the Live File System.

Managing Local Security in Windows

- Local user accounts reside in the local accounts database on a Windows computer, and the User Account Control Panel applet is the primary tool for managing these accounts.
- You must log on as an Administrator to see all the local user accounts on your computer.
- User Account Control (UAC) has been improved in Windows 7 with few events that trigger UAC prompts.
- Whether you log on as an administrator or standard user, UAC will not allow you (or malware) to attempt any task that requires administrator privileges. When it detects such an event, it grays out the desktop and displays either a Consent Prompt (for an administrator) or a Credentials Prompt (for a standard user) before proceeding.
- BitLocker in Windows Vista can only encrypt the boot volume (the volume on which Windows resides). In Windows 7, BitLocker can encrypt other disk volumes, as well as external disks. This last feature is called BitLocker To Go.
- Windows Defender is a built-in anti-spam utility. Windows Firewall is a personal firewall that comes with Windows.

Key Terms List

Windows Memory Diagnostic
Tool *(203)*

Windows Preinstallation Environment
(PE) *(208)*

Windows 7 Upgrade Advisor *(207)*

Windows XP Mode *(203)*

Key Terms Quiz

Use the Key Terms List to complete the sentences that follow. Not all terms will be used.

1. Each version of Windows comes in several _____, which differ mainly in the included components, with each targeted to specific users.

2. _____ is the name for a group of GUI desktop features and visual themes in Windows Vista and Windows 7.

3. _____ is a feature that lets you switch through your open windows as if it were a stack of cards or photos.

4. A/an _____ folder contains pointers to multiple locations on your local computer and network, allowing you to work with these files as if they were all stored in a single location.

5. _____ is a scaled-down Windows operating system that supports the Windows Setup GUI.

6. A/an _____ is a small program that performs some small function, usually displaying information in a small screen object.

7. Use the _____ format when you burn a disc to be used in a conventional CD or DVD player or in any computer including old Apple Macs or PCs.

8. Use the _____ to burn a disc when you will use the disc only on newer Apple Macs and newer PCs (Windows XP and newer support it, but older PCs may not).

9. When an administrator attempts to do something requiring administrator-level privileges, a/an _____ will display, requiring the user to click Yes.

10. When a standard user attempts to do something requiring administrator-level privileges, a/an _____ will display, requiring the user to provide the credentials for an administrator.

Multiple-Choice Quiz

1. What retail edition of Windows 7 includes BitLocker?
   a. Enterprise
   b. Home Basic
   c. Home Premium
   d. Professional
   e. Ultimate

2. What is the name for the desktop feature in Windows 7 that allows you to quickly minimize all but the current window with a simply mouse movement?
   a. Aero Snap
   b. Flip 3D
   c. Aero Shake
   d. AppLocker
   e. UAC

3. This Windows Vista and Windows 7 feature requires a video card that supports (at minimum) DirectX 9.0 and Shader Model 2.0.
   a. BitLocker
   b. Aero

   c. Instant Search
   d. Windows Defender
   e. Windows XP Mode

4. What alternative term correctly describes an upgrade of an operating system?
   a. Clean installation
   b. In-place installation
   c. Multi-boot
   d. Optional installation
   e. Managed installation

5. After you complete a multi-boot installation, you will see this special menu at every restart.
   a. Select OS
   b. F8
   c. System
   d. Windows Boot Manager
   e. Computer Management

6. You have Windows Vista Ultimate edition and want to upgrade to Windows 7. Which of the following editions is your only choice for doing

an in-place installation of Windows Vista Ultimate?

a. Ultimate
b. Home Premium
c. Home Basic
d. Enterprise
e. Business

7. For either a multi-boot or clean installation, select this installation type choice in Windows setup.

a. Upgrade
b. Custom
c. Dual-boot
d. In-place
e. Advanced

8. The Disk Management node exists in this console utility.

a. Administrative Tools
b. Control Panel
c. Windows Explorer
d. Computer Management
e. System and Security

9. If you are setting up a multi-monitor system, which Display option will let you put different windows and other objects on each multiple display, giving you more work space?

a. Landscape
b. Extend these displays
c. Show desktop only on 1
d. Duplicate these displays
e. The recommended resolution

10. Clock, Weather, Calendar, and CPU Meter are all examples of what types of desktop programs in Windows 7?

a. Sidebar
b. Widgets
c. Gadgets
d. Taskbar
e. Multimedia

11. What new feature of Windows 7 appears to be something it isn't, but allows you to organize and work with data from various locations as if they were together in one place?

a. Aero
b. Meeting Space
c. Library
d. SideShow
e. Instant Search

12. What all-powerful user account built into Windows is disabled by default?

a. Administrator
b. Standard
c. Local
d. Guest
e. Parental

13. During Windows Setup one account is created for the user of that computer, and you provide a name and password for it. What type of account is this?

a. Standard
b. Computer Administrator
c. Parental
d. Local
e. Guest

14. What is the term used in the Windows Firewall control panel to refer to Wi-Fi networks at coffee shops and other retail locations?

a. Private networks
b. Work networks
c. Home networks
d. Public networks
e. Internetworks

15. What anti-spyware program comes bundled with Windows?

a. Microsoft Security Essentials
b. UAC
c. BitLocker
d. BitLocker To Go
e. Windows Defender

Essay Quiz

1. Describe Flip 3D, including what it does and how to use it.

2. Your Windows XP computer is a newer PC that is more than adequate for Windows 7. You would like to do a clean installation of Windows 7, discarding your old Windows XP installation, but after running Windows 7 Upgrade Advisor you found that while all the hardware is compatible, one critical old application is incompatible and will not run in Windows 7. What is your best

option for continuing to use this old application on a Windows 7 computer until you find a compatible replacement? Describe both the best solution and one other option, including the type of installation of Windows 7 required for each, and any other requirements beyond the minimums.

3. Windows setup now includes updating Windows. Does the inclusion of this step mean that you will not have to update immediately after installing

Windows? Your answer must be more than a "yes" or "no." Include why your answer is true.

4. Describe how you would use a new feature in Windows 7 to keep track of all the files you are using for a project called Management Training, even though some of those files are on your local PC and some are on a network server. Name the feature and describe the general steps you would take to set this up.

5. Describe how UAC works to protect your computer from malware.

Lab Projects

LAB PROJECT 6.1

Is there Windows after Windows 7? Has a new version of Windows been introduced? Is a new one on its way?

Use whatever sources are at your disposal to answer these questions.

LAB PROJECT 6.2

How successful is Windows 7? What is the latest information on the global operating system market share for Windows 7? What is the latest information on the global operating system market share for Windows XP? Is Windows 7 more successful or less successful than Windows XP? Research the answers to these questions and write about your findings.

LAB PROJECT 6.3

Use the Internet to research the conditions under which you read a flash drive on a Windows XP PC after the flash drive has been encrypted with Bit-Locker To Go on a Windows 7 computer, then test it: Prepare the flash drive as necessary. Copy data onto the flash drive. Then use BitLocker To Go to encrypt the drive, using the option to create a password (be sure to remember the password). Then take the flash drive to a Windows XP computer and insert the drive. Are you prompted to supply a password? Are you able to access the data on the drive? Describe how you prepared the flash drive and the results.

7 Under the Windows Desktop

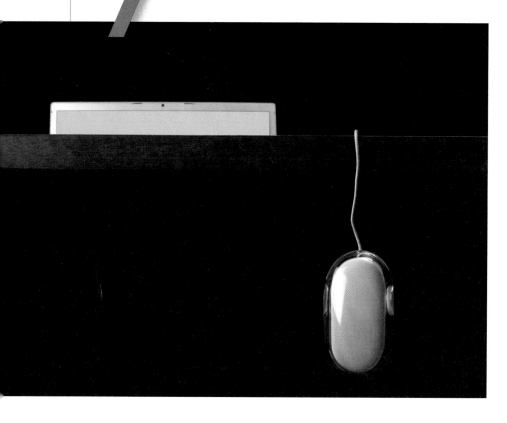

"Computing is not about computers any more. It is about living."

—**Nicholas Negroponte**
Founder and Chairman Emeritus of Massachusetts Institute of Technology's Media Lab and founder of the One Laptop per Child Association

When IBM introduced the IBM PC in 1981, the computer had a mostly open architecture. Because of this open architecture, computer users came to expect that they could make a personal computer into the tool they needed by adding the right mix of software and hardware. Today, we have even greater expectations. To many, a PC is an office automation tool with office productivity software, a printer, and maybe a scanner and Internet connection. Others may make it their video workstation with the addition of elaborate video editing and movie production components. A PC might be the uniting component in a music studio. It may run manufacturing equipment, or auto test equipment.

For the PC to be such a versatile machine, it must first have a hardware architecture that allows you to add your choice from a huge variety of hardware components. You also must have an operating system that you can configure to control all the devices you choose to plug in. And you probably want a visually pleasing, easy-to-use GUI operating system, along with GUI applications that are compatible with the OS and that complement your master plan for the PC.

Learning Outcomes
In this chapter, you will learn how to:

LO 7.1 Define the role of the registry in Windows, and back up and modify the registry when needed.

LO 7.2 Describe the Windows startup process.

LO 7.3 Install and manage device drivers.

LO 7.4 Troubleshoot common Windows problems.

Windows is just such a configurable operating system—but there is a price to pay for having so much variable potential in an operating system: complexity. This chapter looks under the Windows desktop at some of that complexity, including the registry, the device drivers, the Windows startup procedure, and the methods for troubleshooting common Windows problems. ✸

LO 7.1 | Understanding the Registry

The registry, introduced in Windows 95, is one of several technical features that has made Windows easier to configure and support than the earlier Microsoft operating systems. Ironically, it is also one of the most complicated and least understood features of Windows. In this section you'll learn about the registry—its role in Windows and how to modify it when needed.

The Registry Defined

The Windows **registry** is a database of all configuration settings in Windows. It includes settings for:

- Device drivers
- Services
- Installed application programs
- Operating system components
- User preferences

Windows creates the registry during its installation, and it continues to make modifications to it as you configure Windows and add applications and components. During startup, Windows depends on the registry to tell it what services, drivers, and components to load into memory, and how to configure each component. The registry remains in memory while Windows is active.

Automatic Registry Changes

The Windows registry will automatically change when:

- Windows starts up or shuts down
- Windows Setup runs (which occurs more often than you may think)
- Changes are made through a Control Panel applet
- A new device is installed
- Any changes are made to the Windows configuration
- Any changes are made to a user's desktop preferences
- An application is installed or modified
- Changes are made to user preferences in any application

Registry Files

Although considered only a single entity, the registry is actually stored in a number of binary files on disk. A **binary file** contains program code, as opposed to simple text. The Windows registry files include the following:

- DEFAULT
- NTUSER.DAT
- SAM
- SECURITY
- SOFTWARE
- SYSTEM

We call the portion of the registry represented in one of these registry files a **hive**—someone decided the registry structure resembled a beehive.

> Remember that the registry contains only settings, not the actual device drivers, services, or applications to which the settings apply. Windows will not work as you expect it to if these other components are damaged or not available.

> When you work on a computer—whether you are configuring a new installation or troubleshooting a problem, keep a journal of any changes you make. This can be in the form of a notebook or word processing document. The advantage of the first method is that it will be available to you if Windows becomes unstable. The advantage of using a word processor, such as Microsoft Word, is that you can take screen shots and copy them into the document. While we discourage you from making permanent changes to your Windows settings, accidents happen and/or you simply decide to experiment. A record of the changes will help you return stability to your computer.

Adding a new device creates changes in the registry.

These are the permanent portions of the registry, with all the changes saved from use to use. With the exception of NTUSER.DAT, these registry files are in a disk folder named CONFIG, located below C:\WINDOWS\SYSTEM32. Figure 7–1 shows the contents of the CONFIG folder in Windows 7. Look for the files that match the list above (except NTUSER.DAT). Notice that the registry files listed in the CONFIG folder have file names without file extensions. If you have Windows Explorer configured to show hidden files, you

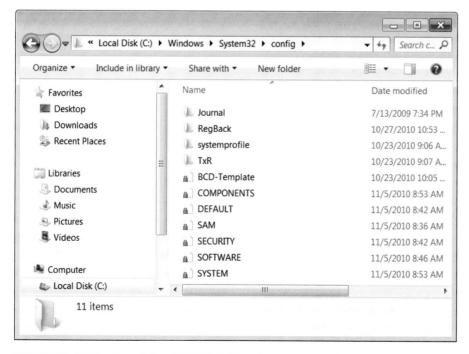

FIGURE 7–1 This view of the CONFIG folder shows registry files.

will see other files, including files with LOG extensions that have file names that match the registry files. The operating system uses LOG files for logging transactions to the registry files. Other hidden files with matching file names and SAV extensions are backup copies of registry files created at the end of the text mode stage of setup.

SYSTEM

The SYSTEM hive contains information used at startup, including device drivers to load as well as the order of their loading, and configuration settings, instructions for the starting and configuring of services, and various operating system settings.

SOFTWARE

The SOFTWARE hive contains configuration settings for software installed on the local computer, along with various items of miscellaneous configuration data.

SECURITY

The SECURITY hive contains the local security policy settings for the computer, including rules for password complexity and for how the system will handle numerous failed attempts at entering a password.

SAM

The SAM hive contains the local security accounts database; SAM is an acronym for Security Accounts Manager.

DEFAULT

The DEFAULT hive contains user desktop settings, called a user profile, used when no user is logged on. You do need desktop settings for the GUI even before you log on. You'll see evidence of this profile in the desktop settings used for the Logon screen shown in Figure 7–2.

FIGURE 7–2 The default user profile used until a user logs on

NTUSER.DAT

The NTUSER.DAT hive file contains the user profile for a single user. These settings include application preferences, screen colors, network connections, and other personal choices. Each user who logs on to the computer has a separate NTUSER.DAT file. During startup, Windows uses the other registry hives to load and configure the operating system. One of the last tasks of the operating system at startup is to request a user logon. When a user logs on, the settings from that user's NTUSER.DAT file apply and become part of the current registry. The first time a user logs onto a computer, Windows uses the NTUSER.DAT file from the DEFAULT USER folder to create the initial profile for the user. It saves the NTUSER.DAT file in the top-level personal folder for that user, and it is hidden so it is only visible if your Folder Options are set to Show hidden files, folders, and drives.

> We described personal folders in Chapter 6.

The Permanent Portions of the Registry: Registry Hives. Earlier you learned about the files used to store portions of the registry. Table 7–1 shows the registry hive files and their location in the registry.

The Temporary Portion of the Registry. The information stored in HKEY_LOCAL_MACHINE\HARDWARE is temporary information, gathered during the hardware detection process of the detect-and-configure-hardware phase of Windows startup. Windows does not save it to disk in a file, as it does other portions of the registry.

Viewing and Editing the Registry

You view and edit the hierarchical structure of the registry using the Registry Editor utility, usually called Regedit. Its executable file, REGEDIT.EXE, is located in the folder in which the operating system is installed (by default that is C:\WINDOWS), but it does not have a shortcut on the Start menu. This is for a very good reason: It should not be too handy. Because Microsoft doesn't want to make it too easy for us to casually run Regedit, we must start it from either the Start menu Search box or the Run box. It will aid your understanding of the registry if you open the Regedit program now and refer to it as you read the following descriptions of the registry components.

> **WARNING!**
>
> Do not directly edit the registry with a tool like Regedit unless it is absolutely necessary; there are many safer ways to make a change to the registry. For example, when you change settings in a Control Panel applet, that applet in turn modifies the registry because that is where Windows maintains and uses the settings.

try this!

Start Registry Editor

Open Registry Editor and explore the contents of the registry. Try this:

1. Click the Start button and enter "regedit" in the Search box. Then select REGEDIT.EXE from the results list.
2. Do not make any changes, but browse through the registry structure, much as you would navigate in Windows Explorer.
3. Notice the folders in the navigation pane and the various folders and settings in the contents pane. Keep Registry Editor open as you read this chapter section.

TABLE 7–1 Locations of the Hives within the Registry

Hive File	Registry Location
SYSTEM	HKEY_LOCAL_MACHINE\SYSTEM
SOFTWARE	HKEY_LOCAL_MACHINE\SOFTWARE
SECURITY	HKEY_LOCAL_MACHINE\SECURITY
SAM	HKEY_LOCAL_MACHINE\SAM
DEFAULT	HKEY_USERS\.DEFAULT
NTUSER.DAT (of the currently logged on user)	HKEY_CURRENT_USER and HKEY_USERS

To describe a registry location, use a notation that shows the path from a root key down through the subkeys similar to that used to describe file and folder locations on disk: HKEY_LOCAL_MACHINE\SYSTEM\CURRENTCONTROLSET\CONTROL.

The first time Regedit runs on a computer, it looks like Figure 7–3. Each folder represents a **key**, an object that may contain one or more settings as well as other keys. The top five folders are **root keys** (also called subtrees in Microsoft documentation). Each of these root keys is the top of a hierarchical structure containing more keys. Each key may contain one or more settings as well as other keys. A key that exists within another key is a **subkey**. Each setting within a key is a **value entry**. When you click on the folder for a key, it becomes the active key in Regedit, its folder icon "opens," and the contents of the key show in the right pane, as you see in Figure 7–4. Table 7–2 gives an overview of the information stored within each root key of the registry.

In Regedit, each value entry appears in three columns labeled: Name, Type, and Data. The Type column shows a label that describes the format of the data in that registry value, also called **data type**. There are many data types in the registry; take a few minutes to study Table 7–3, which shows just a few registry data types, to give you an idea of how diverse the data in the registry can be.

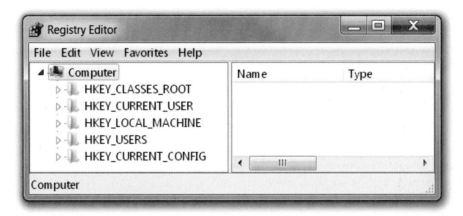

FIGURE 7–3 The registry root keys

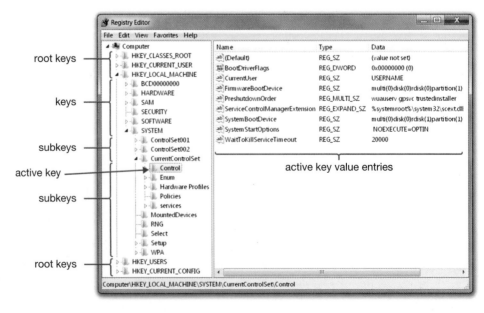

FIGURE 7–4 Registry components

TABLE 7–2 Contents of Registry Root Keys

Root Key	Description
HKEY_CLASSES_ROOT	Shows relationships (called associations) between applications and data file types defined by file extension. Thanks to the information in this key, you can double-click on a data file and the correct application will open and load the file. This root key is actually all the information located in HKEY_LOCAL_MACHINE\SOFTWARE\Classes.
HKEY_CURRENT_USER	Contains the user profile for the currently logged-on user, storing all the user settings that affect the desktop appearance and the default behavior of installed applications.
HKEY_LOCAL_MACHINE	Contains the system information, including detected hardware, application associations, and information for hardware configuration and device drivers.
HKEY_USERS	All user profiles for all local user accounts, including the profile of the currently logged-on user (also shown under HKEY_CURRENT_USER), the default profile, and profiles for special user accounts used to run various services. Except for the default profile, each is labeled with a security ID (SID), a unique string of numbers preceded by S-1-5 that identifies a security principal in a Windows security accounts database, such as users and groups.
HKEY_CURRENT_CONFIG	Contains configuration information for the current hardware profile, which is a set of changes (ONLY changes) to the standard configuration in the Software and Systems subkeys under HKEY_LOCAL_MACHINE.

TABLE 7–3 Windows Registry Data Types (The Short List)

Data Type	Description
REG_BINARY	Raw binary data. Ironically, Regedit shows binary data in hexadecimal and it might look like this: ff 00 ff ff 02 05.
REG_DWORD	A four-byte-long number (32-bits), stored in binary, hexadecimal, or decimal format. It may look something like this in hexadecimal: 0x00000002.
REG_EXPAND_SZ	A single string of text including a variable. A variable is a value that an application will replace when calling it. An example of a common variable is *%systemroot%*, which, when used by Windows, is replaced by the path of the folder containing the Windows system files. Example: a registry entry containing *%systemroot%*\regedit.exe becomes c:\windows\regedit.exe.
REG_MULTI_SZ	Multiple strings of human-readable text, separated by a special NULL character that it does not display. Example: wuauserv gpsvc trustedinstaller
REG_SZ	A sequence of characters representing human-readable text. The registry may use this data type when the data is quite simple, such as a string of alphanumeric characters—for example, ClosePerformanceData—or to represent an entire list: comm.drv commdlg.dll ctl3dv2.dll ddeml.dll.

Backing Up the Registry

It is very important to remember that the last thing you should consider doing, even if your best friend or brother-in-law insists you do it, is to directly edit the registry using Regedit or a third-party registry editing tool. We are even a bit squeamish about the registry cleaning tools promoted all over the Internet. But even though you should rarely if ever edit the registry, you should know how to back up the registry. Here are two methods for backing up the registry. The first, using System Restore, is a very broad approach that backs up the entire registry and more. The second method, backing up a portion of the registry with Regedit, is a more targeted approach.

> Any software that "cleans" the registry is modifying or deleting entries from the registry.

Creating a Restore Point

Our favorite method is to simply create a restore point using System Restore. While Windows creates restore points on a regular basis, you can create one any time you wish. Step-by-Step 7.01 will walk you through this process.

Step-by-Step 7.01

Creating a Restore Point in System Restore

In this step-by-step exercise you will create a restore point. For this exercise you will need a computer running Vista or Windows 7. The steps are written specifically for Windows 7, but are very similar to those for Windows Vista. In both cases, you will need to respond to a User Account Control (UAC) prompt. If you logged on as a standard account, you will need to enter an administrator password.

Step 1

Type "create restore" in the Search box and select Create a restore point in the results list.

Step 2

This brings up the System Properties dialog open to the System Protection page. Click the Create button.

Step 3

Type a descriptive name for the restore point. Then press the Create button.

Step 4

It will take a minute or two, during which a progress message will display in the System Protection box. When Windows has created the restore point, this message will display. Click the Close button.

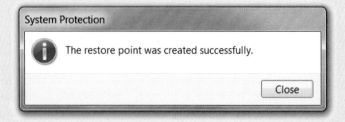

The System Properties dialog box will remain open. To see the restore points, click the System Restore button. If the page shown here displays with a recommended restore point, click Choose a different restore point. Then click the Next button. If a simpler page without the recommended restore point displays, simply click Next.

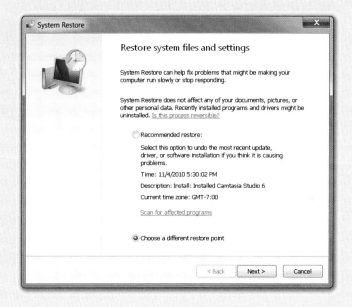

Caution: you want to view only the existing restore points—you do not want to actually roll back to a previous restore point. Simply view the list of restore points, noticing the descriptions. In the example, the top one is the only one we manually created. Windows created the others and gave an appropriate description at the same time. Press Cancel to exit from System Restore. Press Cancel again in the System Properties dialog.

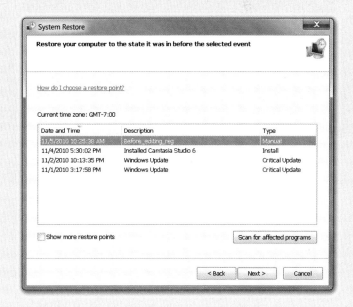

Use REGEDIT to Back Up the Registry

Despite knowing the danger of directly editing the registry, you might find yourself in a position in which editing the registry is the only way to solve a problem. Do this only after attempting all other avenues, including using system restore to restore your computer to a previous state or doing a total restore of your computer from a complete backup set. But if all else fails, and you know the exact change that you must make to the registry, then before you attempt to edit the registry, use REGEDIT to back up the portion of the registry you plan to edit. To back up a registry key, right-click on the folder for the key in Registry Editor and select Export, as shown in the illustration on page 250. Provide a location and name for the file, and REGEDIT will create a .REG file. If you need to restore the file, simply double-click on it.

When would you need to directly edit the registry? The short answer is "rarely." Here are a few scenarios: Sometimes even after using antivirus software to remove a virus, a reliable source, such as a security expert, may advise you to edit the virus to remove some remnant of its malicious code. Or you may need to edit the registry to remove leftover entries from a program you uninstalled.

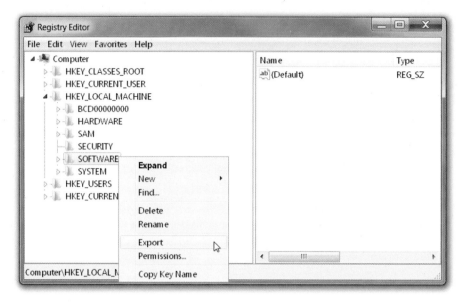

Back up a registry key and all its subkeys and values.

LO 7.2 | The Windows Startup Process

Before you can interpret Windows operating system startup failure symptoms, you must understand the normal Windows startup sequence and learn the role of each boot and system file in this sequence so you can determine at what point Windows startup fails. Then you will learn to modify startup options.

Phases of the Startup Process

The Windows startup process has several phases on a typical desktop PC:

1. Power-on self-test
2. Initial startup
3. Boot loader
4. Detect and configure hardware
5. Kernel loading
6. Logon

In the first two phases, the hardware "wakes up" and BIOS searches for an operating system. Through the remaining phases, the operating system builds itself, much like a building, from the ground up, with more levels and complexity added at each phase. You will learn about these phases in the order in which they occur.

Power-On Self-Test

The power-on self-test phase is common to all PCs. It starts when you turn on or restart a computer. The CPU loads the BIOS programs from a special read-only memory (ROM) chip, called ROMBIOS. The first of these programs includes the power-on self-test (POST). The POST tests system hardware, determines the amount of memory present, verifies that devices required for OS startup are working, and loads configuration settings from CMOS memory into main system memory. During the POST, the BIOS briefly displays information on the screen as it tests memory and devices. This black screen with white text flashes past very quickly.

Initial Startup

The initial startup phase is also common to all PCs. In this phase, the following occur:

- The BIOS startup program uses CMOS settings to determine what devices can start an OS and the order in which the system will search these devices while attempting to begin the OS startup process. One common order is A:, then a CD drive, then C:, in which case, the system will first look for a bootable floppy disk in drive A:. If one is not there, it will try to boot from a bootable optical disk (if present). If a bootable optical disk is not present, the startup code will try to boot from the hard disk and load the code in the master boot record (MBR)—the first sector on a hard disk—into memory.

- The BIOS loads the executable code from the MBR, giving control of the system to this code, which then uses information in the partition table (also located in the MBR) to find the boot sector—the first sector of the active partition—which is loaded into memory and called the boot code. The job of the Windows boot code is to identify the file system on the active partition, find the boot loader file, and load it into memory.

> Where does the boot code come from? Formatting the disk volume places it on the first sector of a disk partition.

Boot Loader

The OS takes control during the boot loader phase, switches the processor to protected mode, starts the file system, and discovers the location of the Windows OS files that need to be loaded into memory to start Windows. Microsoft made major changes in how the boot loader phase is handled beginning in Windows Vista. Therefore, we will look first at the Windows XP boot loader phase and then at the way this phase works beginning with Windows Vista.

Windows XP Boot Loader Phase. The boot loader in Windows XP is NTLDR. During the boot loader phase, NTLDR takes control of the system, switches the CPU to protected mode, starts the file system (the in-memory code that can read and write an NTFS or FAT volume), and reads the BOOT. INI file. In some cases, it then displays the OS Selection menu, but only if there is more than one operating system listed, as is the case in a dual-boot configuration.

> Up to this point, the CPU is in a very limited mode called "real mode." This was the only mode of the Intel 8088 in the first IBM PCs (circa 1981). Only when the CPU switches to protected mode can it access memory above 1 MB and support both multitasking and virtual memory.

If this is a multi-boot computer, and the newest OS is Windows XP, then, when you select Windows 9x or DOS from the OS Selection menu, NTLDR loads the boot sector file called BOOTSECT.DOS, and NTLDR is out of the picture for this session. BOOTSECT.DOS contains the boot code for DOS or early Windows versions up through Windows 9x.

When Windows XP is selected from the OS Selection menu (either automatically as the default, or manually), NTLDR moves to the next phase in the Windows startup process. But before we move to that step, let's look at how Windows Vista and Windows 7 handle things up to this point.

Windows Vista and Windows 7 Boot Loader Phase. The boot loader for Windows Vista and Windows 7 is BOOTMGR, which loads the Boot Configuration Database (BCD), an extensible database that replaces the old BOOT.INI file. BCD then loads WINLOAD.EXE, the OS loader boot program. Together, BOOTMGR and WINLOAD.EXE replace the major functions of NTLDR and complete the startup phases for Windows Vista and Windows 7. These two OSs do not need the files NTLDR, BOOT.INI, and NTDETECT.COM, but BOOT.INI and NTDETECT.COM will be present on a multi-boot computer that needs to start an older version of Windows requiring these files. Now we will briefly discuss the remaining startup phases.

Detect and Configure Hardware

The detect and configure hardware phase includes a scan of the computer's hardware and creation of a hardware list for later inclusion in the registry.

Kernel Loading

During the kernel loading phase the Windows kernel, NTOSKRNL.EXE (on both old and new Windows systems), loads into memory from the location indicated in either the BOOT.INI file (old Windows versions) or the BCD. During kernel loading, the Windows logo will display as seen here.

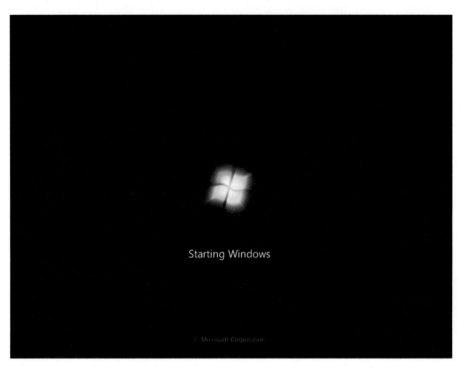

Starting Windows

© Microsoft Corporation

This Windows 7 screen displays during kernel loading.

Hardware information passes on to the kernel, and the hardware abstraction layer (HAL) file for the system loads into memory too. The System portion of the registry loads, and the drivers that are configured (through registry settings) to load at startup are now loaded. All of this code is loaded into memory, but not immediately initialized (made active).

Once all startup components are in memory, the kernel takes over the startup process and initializes the components (services and drivers) required for startup. Then the kernel scans the registry for other components that were not required during startup, but are part of the configuration, and it then loads and initializes them. The kernel also starts the session manager, which creates the system environment variables and loads the kernel-mode Windows subsystem code that switches Windows from text mode to graphics mode.

The session manager then starts the user-mode Windows subsystem code (CSRSS.EXE). Just two of session manager's other tasks include creating the virtual memory paging file (PAGEFILE.SYS) and starting the Windows logon service (WINLOGON.EXE), which leads us to the next phase.

Logon

More things happen during the logon phase than a simple logon, and they happen simultaneously.

Have you ever wondered why Windows seems busy after you see the logon screen and even after you log on? This busy status is evident by disk activity and sometimes the mouse pointer displays the busy (usually the hourglass) icon. This is because the Begin Logon dialog box appears before the service controller finishes loading services. This also means that after you log on, you might see an error message indicating that a service didn't load properly.

The actual screen or dialog box that appears before you log on varies with the configuration of your computer. If your computer connects to a corporate network with a Microsoft Active Directory domain, you will have a security logon dialog box. At home, or in a very small business, you may not have to enter a user name and password, or you may only need to select a user name from a list.

FIGURE 7–5 Log on to Windows 7.

User Logon. The key player in this phase is the Windows Logon service, which supports logging on and logging off, and starts the service control manager (SERVICES.EXE) and the local security authority (LSASS.EXE). At this point, depending on how your computer was configured, you may first see the Welcome To Windows screen, requiring that the user press CTRL-ALT-DELETE before the Log On To Windows dialog box or screen appears. A user then enters a user name and password, which the local security authority uses to authenticate the user in the local security accounts database. Figure 7–5 shows just one possible logon screen that you may see in Windows 7.

Program Startup. A lot of other things happen during the logon phase. Logon scripts run (if they exist), startup programs for various applications run, and noncritical services start. Windows finds instructions to run these programs and services in many registry locations.

Plug and Play Detection. During the logon phase, Windows performs plug and play detection, using BIOS, hardware, device drivers, and other methods to detect new plug and play devices. If it detects a new device, Windows allocates system resources and installs appropriate device drivers.

Modifying System Startup

You can modify the system startup on your Windows computer in many ways. First determine if you can make the change you wish through the GUI, such as the Advanced System Settings page. As a last resort, you can directly edit these settings using the correct tool for the version of Windows in question. We'll look at modifying system startup for Windows XP and for Windows Vista or Windows 7. In both cases, we look at settings for choosing the default OS that is started on a multi-boot system and the length of time the selection menu displays.

Learn about special startup modes for troubleshooting later in this chapter.

Modifying System Startup for Windows XP

In Windows XP the BOOT.INI file holds important information used by NTLDR to locate the operating system and, in the case of a multi-boot

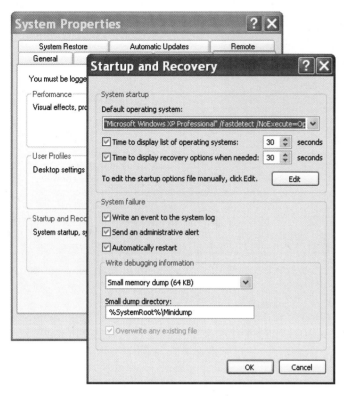

FIGURE 7–6 The Advanced System Settings in Windows XP

Even though the Edit button will open Notepad with the Windows XP BOOT.INI file loaded, you will not be able to save changes you make unless you remove the read-only attribute from this file before attempting to edit it. Do this by navigating to it using Windows Explorer, then right-clicking on the file and turning off Read only.

Still curious? Learn more about the BOOT.INI file and an alternative way to edit it. Point your browser to **www.microsoft.com** and search for the article "How To: Edit the Boot.ini File in Windows XP." Learn more about BOOT.INI switches in another article on the Microsoft site: "Available Switch Options for the Windows XP and the Windows Server 2003 Boot.ini Files."

configuration, to display an OS selection menu. You can edit this file directly, but it is an advanced task performed by system administrators. However, you can edit this file indirectly through the GUI if you have administrative access. Right-click Computer and select Properties. Then select the Advanced tab and click Startup and Recovery. The settings that modify the BOOT.INI file are in the top of this dialog box, in the System startup section, shown in Figure 7–6.

A drop-down list lets you choose the default OS in a dual-boot system and another setting allows you to set the length of time the OS selection menu displays. Yet another setting controls the length of time it displays recovery options, when needed. Plus you have an Edit button that opens Notepad with the BOOT.INI file loaded in it for editing. We strongly recommend that you do not directly edit the BOOT. INI file without a great deal of preparation and/or expert advice.

Here is an example of a BOOT.INI file for a multi-boot installation in which Windows 2000 is booted from the first partition on the hard disk (C:) and Windows XP is booted from the second partition on the hard disk (D:).

```
[boot loader]
timeout=30
default=multi(0)disk(0)rdisk(0)partition(1)\WINDOWS
[operating systems]
multi(0)disk(0)rdisk(0)partition(1)\WINDOWS="Windows XP
Professional"/fastdetect
multi(0)disk(0)rdisk(0)partition(2)\WINNT="Windows 2000
Professional"/fastdetect
```

The lines beginning with "multi" do not refer to "multi-boot." They provide the location information to NTLDR in a format called an ARC path, "multi (0) disk (0) rdisk (0) partition (1)." In brief, this identifies the disk controller ("multi"), the hard disk on that controller ("disk" or "rdisk"), the partition on that hard disk ("partition"), and finally, the folder in that partition in which the OS is located. The words that appear in quotes on these lines will display on the OS selection menu; anything after the quotes is a switch that affects how Windows starts. For instance, the /fastdetect switch is the default switch used with Windows 2000 and Windows XP. It causes NTDETECT to skip parallel and serial device enumeration. While there are many other BOOT.INI switches, you should not normally need to manually add any to your desktop installation of Windows.

Modifying System Startup for Windows Vista and Windows 7

In Windows Vista and Windows 7, the new Boot Configuration Database is actually a hidden part of the registry, stored in a registry file named BCD, located in C:\BOOT. The basic information stored in BCD provides locale information, the location of the boot disk and the Windows files, and other information required for the startup process. View the contents of BCD using the BCDEDIT program, a utility that needs to run from a Command Prompt with elevated privileges, meaning that it runs with the privileges of a local administrator, as described in Step-by-Step 7.02.

As with Windows XP, if you wish to change the startup settings, the safest method is to use the Startup and Recovery page of System Properties. Step-by-Step 7.02 will walk you through making a change to BCD using the Startup and Recovery page, and then you will use BCDEDIT to view the contents of BCD.

Step-by-Step 7.02

Modifying System Startup for Windows 7

In this step-by-step exercise you will modify the system startup for Windows 7 using the Startup and Recovery page of System Properties. The steps are written specifically for Windows 7, but are very similar to those for Windows Vista. You will need a computer running Windows Vista or Windows 7.

Step 1

A quick way to open the System Properties dialog is to click Start and enter "advanced" in the Search. Then locate and select View advanced system settings from the results list.

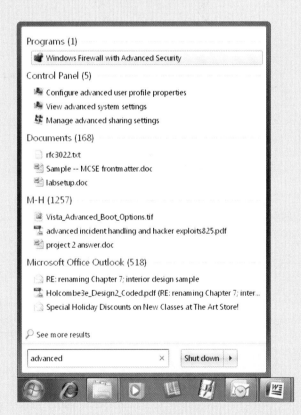

Step 2

On the Advanced tab of System Properties locate the Startup and Recovery section near the bottom and click the Settings button to open the Startup and Recovery page. If your computer is a multi-boot computer you can choose the default operating system that it will select if you do not respond to the menu during the time that it displays the list of operating system. Notice the time selected is 30 seconds.

255

Step 3

Change it to 35 seconds and click OK to close the Startup and Recovery page. Click OK again to close System Properties. Windows will save the changes in BCD and they will take effect the next time you restart.

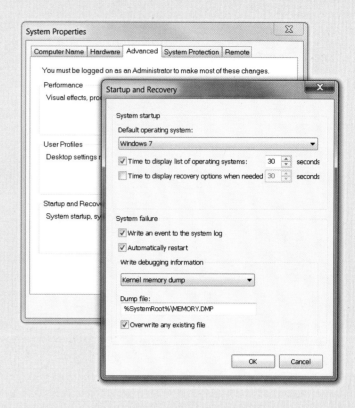

Step 4

Now prepare to run BCDEDIT to see the contents of BCD. To do this, you first need to locate the Command Prompt icon in Start | All Programs | Accessories. Then right-click, and select Run as administrator from the context menu, as shown here.

Respond to the User Account Control (UAC) prompt (if required). The Command Prompt will then open. Type "bcdedit" at the command prompt and press ENTER. The result should look something like the example here. Notice the Timeout setting, which you changed in the earlier steps.

```
Administrator: Command Prompt

Microsoft Windows [Version 6.1.7600]
Copyright (c) 2009 Microsoft Corporation.  All rights reserved.

C:\Windows\system32>bcdedit

Windows Boot Manager
--------------------
identifier              {bootmgr}
device                  partition=\Device\HarddiskVolume1
description             Windows Boot Manager
locale                  en-US
inherit                 {globalsettings}
default                 {current}
resumeobject            {fb9eed44-dbb2-11df-bdc6-cc8b6bde82b2}
displayorder            {current}
toolsdisplayorder       {memdiag}
timeout                 35

Windows Boot Loader
-------------------
identifier              {current}
device                  partition=C:
path                    \Windows\system32\winload.exe
description             Windows 7
locale                  en-US
inherit                 {bootloadersettings}
recoverysequence        {fb9eed46-dbb2-11df-bdc6-cc8b6bde82b2}
recoveryenabled         Yes
osdevice                partition=C:
systemroot              \Windows
resumeobject            {fb9eed44-dbb2-11df-bdc6-cc8b6bde82b2}
nx                      OptIn

C:\Windows\system32>
```

To close the Command Prompt windows type Exit and press ENTER.

LO 7.3 | Installing and Managing Device Drivers

A huge number of devices work in Windows. There are the ones we take for granted, such as hard drives, flash drives, keyboards, mice and other pointing devices, video adapters, network interface cards, displays, sound cards, and joysticks. Then there are others, such as cameras, scanners, and video capture cards. In this section learn about locating appropriate or updated device drivers, installing device drivers, and managing installed device drivers.

Finding Device Drivers

A new device normally comes with a disc containing an installation program and device drivers for one or more operating systems. But these discs have a way of disappearing soon after you open the packaging. Or, you wish to install an old device into a new OS, but cannot find the driver files on disc for the new OS. In either case, connect to the Web site of the manufacturer of the device and look for a link titled "Downloads" or "Device Drivers." Then search for the model name or number of your device and the OS version you need. Figure 7–7 shows a list of drivers for one device. Notice the version numbers. When presented with a list like this, you would normally select the latest version, unless you have some knowledge of a problem with the newest version.

Locate a Device Driver on the Web

Assume you are looking for a Windows 7 device driver for a Wacom Intuos4 digitizer. Try this:

1. Point your Web browser to **www.wacom.com**. Select a location and language. On the main page select Downloads.
2. On the Downloads page select Hardware Drivers. Then open the list box labeled "Select your tablet model" and select Intuos4 (PTK), and use the list box labeled "Select your operating system" and choose your operating system.
3. View the results list for the device you selected. Unless you actually need this device driver, do not download it.

try this!

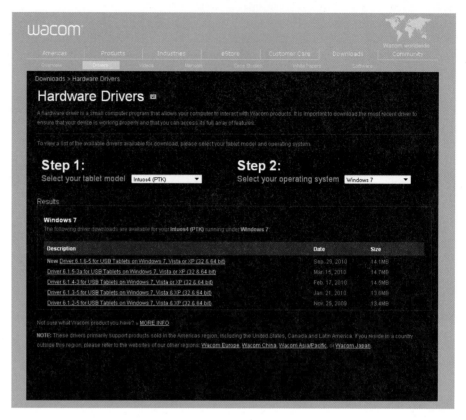

FIGURE 7–7 A list of drivers for a device

Installing Device Drivers

All devices need device drivers, and the latest versions of Windows (especially Windows 7) come with huge caches of device drivers. Windows and virtually all devices for PCs are plug and play. **Plug and play** is the ability of a computer and OS to automatically detect and configure a hardware device. To work, the computer, the device, and the OS must all comply with the same plug and play standard so when you connect a device, Windows recognizes it, and finds and installs the appropriate driver.

But there are exceptions. For example, in some cases, even though the device is plug and play, you need to install the driver (and with it the companion software) before connecting the device. There is also the issue of when you power on an external device. Some require that you power up the device before connecting it to the PC while others require that you connect the device, and then power it up. The supreme authority for each device is the manufacturer, and so you really need to read the manufacturer's quick start guide or user manual before connecting a new device.

Permissions

Regardless of where you find the device driver and how easily it installs, you need administrator privileges to install or uninstall a device. In Windows XP you must log on as Administrator or a member of the Administrators group to install any device driver. If you attempt to install a new device while logged on with a non-administrator account you will see the message similar to that shown in Figure 7–8.

In Windows Vista and Windows 7 you can install a device driver while logged on as either a computer administrator or as a standard user. In the former you will simply need to click Yes in the UAC Consent prompt box, while a standard user will need to provide the credentials for a computer administrator.

Fortunately, unplugging a device does not uninstall the driver from your computer—it just gives the device a status of "not present." Therefore, any local users may disconnect and reconnect the device without restriction and it will operate.

FIGURE 7–8 This Windows XP message shows that you have insufficient security privileges to install or uninstall a device

Working with Signed versus Unsigned Device Drivers

Because a device driver becomes a part of an operating system, a poorly written device driver can cause problems, including system crashes. For this reason bad device drivers have long been the top cause of operating system instability. To help users avoid badly written program code, Microsoft added several features beginning in Windows 2000 and Windows XP.

The central feature is code signing, the use of a digital signature provided by Microsoft as its seal of approval on program code. A Microsoft digital signature is encrypted data placed in the file. Windows decrypts the digital signature by a process called file signature verification. The digital signature includes information about the file so that the operating system can detect any alterations to the file. Driver signing is simply code signing of device drivers that indicates the integrity of the file or files, and that the device driver has passed Microsoft's test for compatibility. This does not mean all non-digitally-signed device drivers are bad. What it does mean is that Microsoft has provided a process that manufacturers can choose to use to have their device drivers tested and signed by Microsoft. This is part of the process of having a device added to Microsoft's compatibility list.

If you attempt to install a program that contains unsigned code, you may get a warning. It is then up to you if you want to continue using the unsigned code. If you trust the source, continue. You cannot install unsigned drivers in 64-bit Windows 7; the installation will simply fail.

> **try this!**
>
> **Install a Plug and Play Device**
>
> Locate a plug and play USB device never before installed on your computer, such as a printer or wireless NIC. Try this:
>
> 1. Read the documentation for the device. If required, install the device driver before connecting the device.
> 2. Follow the instructions for the order in which you must power on and connect the USB device to a USB port. You may see a balloon by the notification area as Windows automatically recognizes it.

Managing Installed Devices

There are several utilities for managing devices. You use one small utility, Safely Remove Hardware, when disconnecting certain devices. Two other utilities are (1) Devices and Printers and (2) Device Manager.

Disconnecting Devices

Windows plug and play support allows you to disconnect USB and IEEE 1394 external plug and play devices without first powering down the computer, but Windows would like a warning about the change! In Windows terminology you are *removing* the device, and you notify Windows of your intention by using the Safely Remove Hardware icon located in the notification area of the taskbar, as shown here. Figure 7–9 shows the Safely Remove Hardware dialog box, listing the devices that you may remove, and the Stop a Hardware Device box, which opened when one of the devices was selected.

Windows 7 has added the ability to eject removable media, so the applet has been renamed Safely Remove Hardware and Eject Media. This is a long

The Windows XP Safely Remove Hardware icon

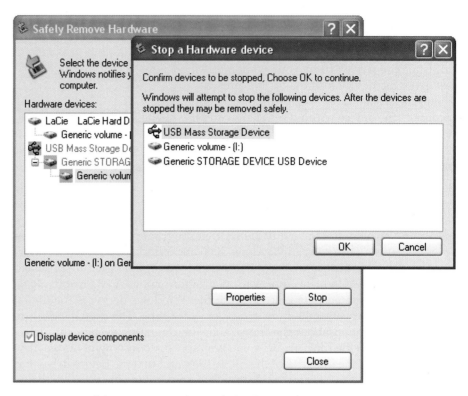

FIGURE 7–9 Safely Remove Hardware dialog box

name for the tiny icon in the Hidden Icon control. You access it by clicking the Hidden Icon button (the one with a small white triangle) in the notification area of the taskbar as shown in Figure 7–10. A single click on this icon gives you a list of choices, including Open Devices and Printers, and a list of the attached removable devices, as shown in Figure 7–11. Click on the device you wish to remove and when the message shown in Figure 7–12 appears, you may disconnect the device.

Devices and Printers

You can manage most devices through the user-friendly Devices and Printers Control Panel applet, as shown in Figure 7–13. This gives you an overview of the most obvious devices attached to your computer. From here you can access the Properties dialog and other appropriate applications and actions by double-clicking on the device (for the default action) or right-clicking and

FIGURE 7–10 Select Safely Remove Hardware from the hidden icons.

FIGURE 7–11 Select the device you wish to disconnect.

FIGURE 7–12 Now it is safe to disconnect the hardware.

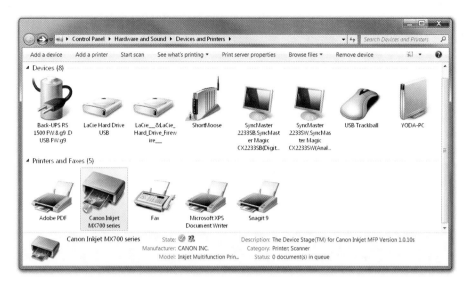

FIGURE 7–13 The Devices and Printers page

selecting an action from the context menu. For instance, double-clicking on the Fax object will open Windows Fax and Scan. If you have installed special faxing and scanning software from the manufacturer, that will open in place of Windows Fax and Scan. Further, expect newer devices to have a special "home page" that is part of Windows 7's new **Device Stage** feature. For instance, in previous versions of Windows, double-clicking a printer's icon brought up the printer's print queue. That still happens in Windows 7, but only if your installed printer does not have the Device Stage feature. If it has Device Stage, double-clicking on it will bring up a new page from which you can make many choices for managing the device, and it often includes an accurate image of the device. Figure 7–14 shows the Device Stage page for a printer.

Using Device Manager to Manage Device Drivers

Device Manager is a tool that allows an administrator to view and change device properties, update device drivers, configure device settings, uninstall

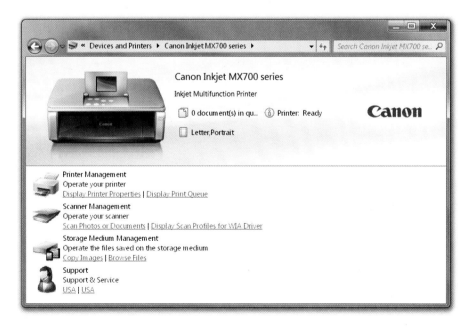

FIGURE 7–14 The Device Stage page for a printer

devices, and roll back a driver update. Rollback is quite handy for those times when you find the new device driver causes problems. You can find Device Manager through the System applet by selecting the Hardware tab, and then clicking the Device Manager button. It is a Microsoft Management Console (MMC) snap-in, opening into a separate console window. Alternatively find the Device Manager node in the Windows Management console (a preconfigured MMC), available by right-clicking on the Computer icon on the Start menu. Our favorite method for opening Device Manager is by simply entering "device manager" in the Windows Vista and Windows 7 Search boxes. But when you are working with Device Manager repeatedly on the same computer, consider making a desktop shortcut, as described in Step-by-Step 7.03.

Step-by-Step 7.03

Getting to Know Device Manager

In this step-by-step exercise you will create a shortcut to Device Manager on the desktop to make it more convenient to open. You'll then examine the information shown in Device Manager. We wrote this exercise for Windows 7, but the steps are identical in Windows Vista and nearly identical in Windows XP. You will need a computer running Windows Vista or Windows 7.

Step 1

Right-click on an empty area of the Desktop, select New | Shortcut. In the Create Shortcut wizard, a text box prompts you to enter the location of the item. Simply enter the file name and extension for the Device Manager console: devmgmt.msc. Click the Next button.

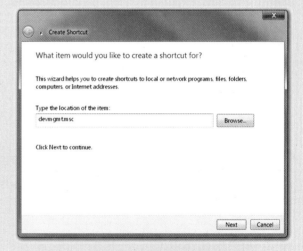

Step 2

In the text box labeled "Type a name for this shortcut," type "Device Manager," and click the Finish button. The new shortcut will appear on the desktop.

The Device Manager shortcut

Test your new shortcut by double-clicking on it to open Device Manager. Use the View menu to experiment with various ways of changing how it can display information—you have two options for viewing devices and two options for viewing resources, which you can choose from the View menu. You will normally view devices by type because this approach is simpler and more understandable.

When viewing devices by type, there is a node for each device type, such as Computer, Disk drives, and so on. Familiarize yourself with Device Manager by opening the nodes. Notice that the buttons on the button bar change as you click on the top node (the computer itself), then click on a type node (such as Display Adapters), and then click on a device under a type node. The buttons give you access to appropriate actions for the selected item.

To open the properties of the device, double-click on a device name, such as a network adapter, under the Network Adapters node. The tabs in the Properties dialog will vary by device. Look through the tab pages, but the Driver tab is where you will go to manage a device (some of these actions are available from the button bar). Do not make any changes, and when you are finished, close all open windows. You will use other features of Device Manager in the troubleshooting section of this chapter.

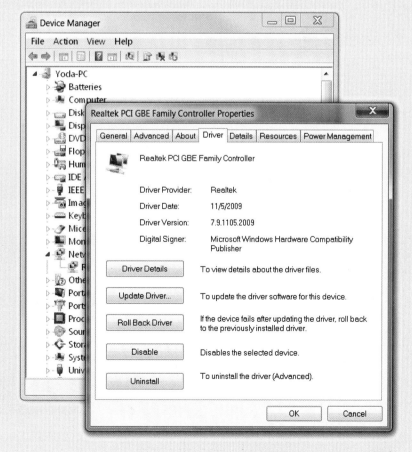

LO 7.4 | Troubleshooting Windows Problems

A short list of the handiest and most effective tools for troubleshooting Windows problems includes the various options on the Startup options menu, the System Configuration utility, and Device Manager. Explore these tools in this section.

Troubleshooting with Modified Startups

As you work with Windows computers, you may run into computers that fail to start normally or that behave oddly after startup. Windows offers a number of methods for starting Windows with certain components disabled. Some of these are available through a special menu of startup options, and others (including some of the same methods) are available through the System Configuration utility.

The Advanced Boot Options Menu

To access a list of startup options, restart the computer and press F8 before the graphical Windows start screen appears. This will bring up a special menu of startup options titled "Windows Advanced Options Menu" in Windows XP or "Advanced Boot Options Menu" in Windows Vista and Windows 7. Figures 7–15, 7–16, and 7–17 show these menus as they appear in Windows XP, Windows Vista, and Windows 7 respectively. Following are brief descriptions of these options.

Repair Your Computer (Windows 7 Only). If you select this option, Windows PE (the environment used by Windows setup) loads and first requires that you supply a keyboard input method, then requires that you log on, and finally displays the System Recovery Options shown in Figure 6–11 in Chapter 6. From here you can select one of the following recovery tools:

- Startup Repair
- System Restore
- System Image Recovery
- Windows Memory Diagnostic
- Command Prompt

Safe Mode. Safe Mode is a mode for starting Windows with certain drivers and components disabled. If Windows will not start normally, but starts

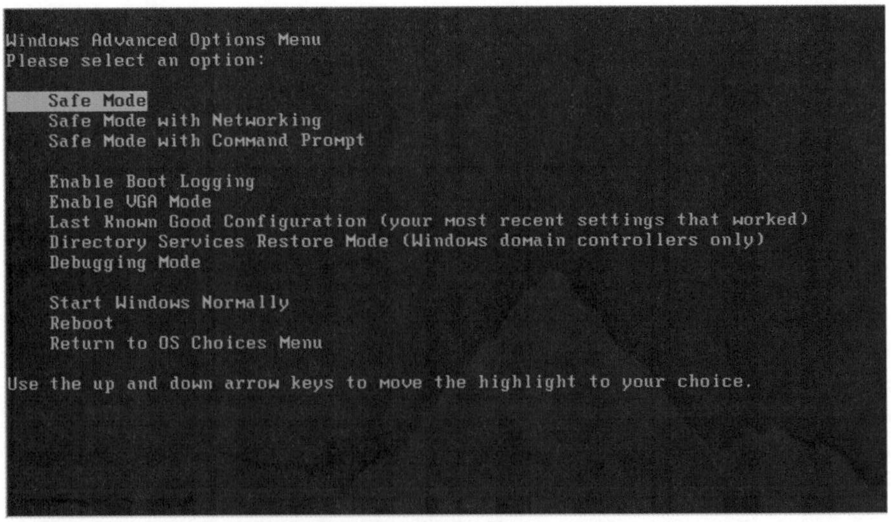

FIGURE 7–15 The Windows Advanced Options Menu for Windows XP

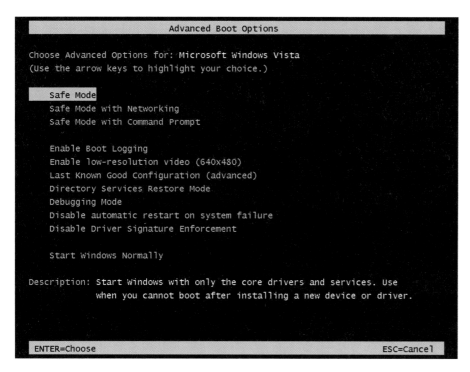

FIGURE 7–16 The Windows Vista Advanced Boot Options menu

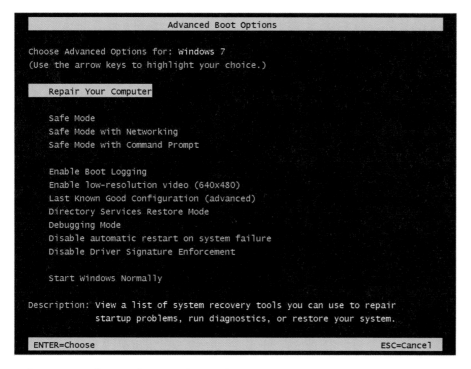

FIGURE 7–17 The Windows 7 Advanced Boot Options menu

just fine in Safe Mode, use Device Manager within Safe Mode to determine if the source of the problem is a faulty device. In Windows Vista and Windows 7, you can run System Restore while in Safe Mode and roll back the entire system to a restore point from before the problem occurred. Safe Mode does not disable Windows security. You are required to log on in all variants of Safe Mode, and you can access only those resources for which you have permissions.

Three Safe Mode variants are available:

- Safe Mode starts without using several drivers and components that it would normally start, including the network components. It loads only very basic, non-vendor-specific drivers for mouse, video (loading Windows' very basic VGA.sys driver), keyboard, mass storage, and system services.
- Safe Mode with Networking is identical to plain Safe Mode, except that it also starts the networking components. Use the following debug sequence with Safe Mode with Networking:
  - If Windows will not start normally but starts OK in plain Safe Mode, restart and select Safe Mode with Networking.
  - If it fails to start in Safe Mode with Networking, the problem area is network drivers or components. Use Device Manager to disable the network adapter driver (the likely culprit), then boot up normally. If Windows now works, replace your network driver.
  - If this problem appears immediately after upgrading a network driver, use Device Manager while in Safe Mode to roll back the updated driver. When an updated driver is available, install it.
- Safe Mode with Command Prompt is Safe Mode with only a command prompt as a user interface. In a normal startup, Windows loads your GUI desktop, but this depends on the program EXPLORER.EXE, the GUI shell to Windows. In place of this GUI shell, Safe Mode with Command Prompt loads a very limited GUI with a command prompt (CMD.EXE) window. This is a handy option to remember if the desktop does not display at all. Once you have eliminated video drivers as the cause, corruption of the EXPLORER.EXE program may be the problem. From within the command prompt, you can delete the corrupted version of EXPLORER.EXE and copy an undamaged version. This requires knowledge of the command line commands for navigating the directory structure, as well as knowledge of the location of the file that you are replacing. You can launch programs, such as the Event Viewer (eventvwr.msc), the Computer Management console (compmgmt.msc), or Device Manager (devmgmt.msc) from the command prompt.

Enable Boot Logging. While boot logging occurs automatically with each of the three Safe Modes, selecting Enable Boot Logging turns on boot logging and starts Windows normally. Boot logging causes Windows to write a log of the Windows startup in a file named NTBTLOG.TXT and save it in the *systemroot* folder. This log file contains an entry for each component in the order in which it loaded into memory. It also lists drivers that were not loaded, which alerts an administrator to a possible source of a problem.

Enable Low-Resolution Video (640x480). Titled "Enable VGA Mode" until Windows Vista, this option starts Windows normally, except the video mode is changed to the lowest resolution (640×480), using the currently installed video driver. It does not switch to the basic Windows video driver. Select this option after making a video configuration change that the video adapter does not support and that prevents Windows from displaying properly. Then, while in this mode, reverse the change you previously made.

Last Known Good Configuration. Last Known Good Configuration is a startup option that will start Windows normally and select the configuration that existed at the last successful user logon (the "last known good configuration"), ignoring changes made after the last logon. This works if you made changes that caused obvious problems. On the very next restart, selecting this option will discard the changes. But if you have logged on since the changes occurred, those changes will be part of the last known good, so this troubleshooting option won't work. This rather crude system restore method only works if you did not restart and logon since making the change.

Directory Services Restore Mode. This option only works on Windows Servers acting as domain controllers.

Debugging Mode. This is a very advanced, (dare we say) obsolete, option in which Windows starts normally and information about the Windows startup is sent over a serial cable to another computer that is running a special program called a debugger.

Disable Automatic Restart on System Failure (Windows Vista and Windows 7). The default setting for Windows is for it to restart after a system crash. However, depending on the problem, restarting may simply lead to another restart—in fact you could find yourself faced with a continuous loop of restarts. If so, press F8 at the next restart and select the Disable automatic restart on system failure option. Windows will attempt to start normally (just once for each time you select this option) and may stay open long enough for you to troubleshoot. Do not attempt to work with any data file after restarting with this option because the system may be too unstable. If you are not able to solve the problem, then you will need to restart in Safe Mode to troubleshoot.

Disable Driver Signature Enforcement (Windows Vista and Windows 7). If you are unable to install a driver due to Driver Signing, and you trust the manufacturer, select this option, which will start Windows normally, disabling driver signature enforcement just for that startup.

Start Windows Normally. Use this option to start Windows normally with no change in behavior. You would use this after using F8 to view the Advanced Options menu and deciding to continue with a normal startup. It does not restart the computer.

Reboot (Windows XP only). This option restarts the computer, acting like a warm reboot (CTRL-ALT-DELETE) from MS-DOS or Restart Windows from the Windows Shut Down menu. You may then choose to allow Windows to start normally or to open the Advanced Options menu with the F8 key.

Return to OS Choices Menu (Multi-Boot Only). Selecting this option on a multi-boot computer will return to the OS Choices Menu (OS Loader menu).

Step-by-Step 7.04

Using Windows in Safe Mode

In this step-by-step exercise you will start Windows in Safe Mode. Although we will use Windows 7 in the steps, you can use Windows XP or Windows Vista. The screen will not be identical, but you can experience Safe Mode in any of these OSs. Be prepared to provide credentials to access Safe Mode because security is still in place when you access Safe Mode. Once in Safe Mode you can run most Windows troubleshooting tools just as you would after a normal start.

Step 1

Restart the computer, pressing F8 as soon as the power down completes and before the splash screen appears. On the Advanced Boot Options menu use the up and down arrows to move the cursor around. Position the cursor on Safe Mode and press Enter.

When prompted, provide credentials. Safe Mode loads with a black desktop background and the words *Safe Mode* in the corners of the screen. It also opens Windows Help and Support to the page on Safe Mode. Browse through the help information and click on the link labeled "Diagnostic tools to use in safe mode."

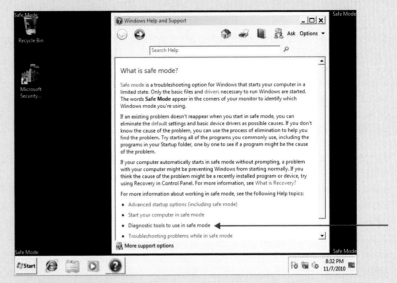

On the resulting page, locate links to start several very handy tools in Safe Mode. In the following steps, practice opening some of these utilities.

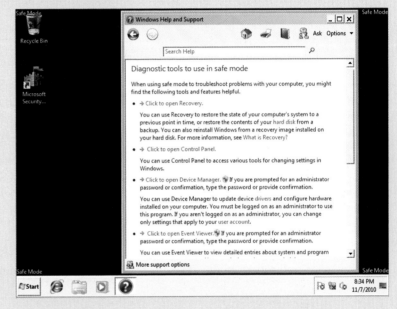

Click the link labeled "Click to open Recovery." On the Recovery page notice the links to other tools. Click the button labeled "Open System Restore." On the page labeled "Restore files and settings" click Next to see a list of the restore points on your computer. Click Cancel to leave System Restore and close the Recovery windows to return to Help and Support.

Next use the link that will open Control Panel. You can open most tools you would need from this page.

When you are finished exploring Safe Mode, close all open windows, and either shut down or restart Windows, allowing it to start normally.

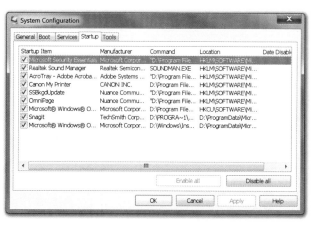

Troubleshooting with the System Configuration Utility (MSCONFIG)

The System Configuration Utility, more commonly known by its executable name, MSCONFIG, is a GUI tool for temporarily modifying system startup. It allows you to modify and test startup configuration settings without altering the settings directly. It gives you access to settings that are buried within the registry through a moderately friendly user interface, and it allows you to make the changes temporary or permanent (see Figure 7–18).

This utility is a great way to test startup "what if" scenarios. For instance, use it when you need to stop a program from launching at startup but do not want to search all the possible locations for starting programs and you are not yet ready to uninstall it. Temporarily disabling a program that normally starts with the OS is one way to see if that program is the source of a problem. Similarly, you can temporarily stop a service from starting. Further, if you are having a problem restarting a Windows Vista or Windows 7 computer in Safe Mode because you are unable to access the startup options menu, you can configure MSCONFIG to start Windows in Safe Mode.

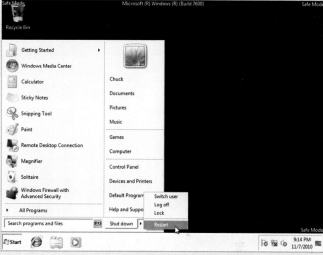

FIGURE 7–18 System Configuration (MSCONFIG) lets you test startup scenarios.

While System Configuration is listed in Administrative Tools, this menu is, by default, buried in the Windows GUI, or optionally on the Start menu.

269

Therefore, we prefer to launch this program from either the Search box (Windows Vista and Windows 7) or the Run box in Windows XP by simply typing "msconfig."

Troubleshooting Device Problems

You will quickly learn if Windows detects a problem with a device when you open Device Manager. You will see an expanded device type, and the problem device will have an exclamation mark on the icon, as Figure 7–19 shows. The problem may be with the device itself, its device driver, or the ability of the operating system to automatically configure it. In Figure 7–19, Windows has placed the problem device under Other devices because it does not have enough information about it. This usually means that no device driver is installed.

If you see the exclamation symbol on a device, double-click the device icon to open its Properties dialog box. You will see more information, as shown in the Windows 7 example in Figure 7–20. Follow the instructions in the Device Status box. In the example, it recommends running Update and provides the Update Driver button (not normally shown on this page). Clicking this opened the Update Driver Software page with two choices: Search automatically for updated driver software and Browse my computer for driver software. Select the second one if you have the driver disk or have the driver on your local computer or on a network share. Select the first choice to have Windows search on the Internet. In the scenario shown, we selected the first choice and it found the driver, downloaded it, and installed it with no more interaction from us. In our example, the device was recognized and placed under the Network Infrastructure Devices category, as shown in Figure 7–21.

> If you select the Safe option on the Boot page, it will also change settings on the General page. Therefore, any time you make changes, note the changes and be aware that before the system will restart normally, you will need to return to the General page and select Normal startup.

try this!

Explore MSCONFIG

Open MSCONFIG and explore the option pages. These steps are specific to Windows Vista and Windows 7. Try this:

1. Type "msconfig" in the Search box and select it from the results list.
2. Explore the five tabs (General, Boot, Services, Startup, and Tools) of the System Configuration dialog box.
3. If you make any changes, make sure you remember them. Click Apply, then OK and click the Restart button in the final message box.
4. After testing a modified restart, open MSCONFIG again and be sure to select Normal startup before restarting.

FIGURE 7–19 A problem with a device

FIGURE 7–20 The Device status box will describe the problem and recommend action to solve it.

For other Device problems, open Device Manager and check out the Driver page of the Properties for the device. For instance, if you update a device driver, and then find that the device fails or is not working as well as before the update use the Roll Back Driver button on the Driver page to remove the updated driver and return to the previously installed driver. This button is active only after you have updated a driver, as shown in Figure 7–22. You can also use this page to update a driver, disable it, or uninstall it. You might disable a driver to see if it relates to another problem. Uninstall it if you do not need a device or if you believe there was a problem with the installation and plan to reinstall the driver.

> If you log on as a non-administrative user in Windows XP and start Device Manager, you will receive a warning that you do not have sufficient privileges to install or modify device drivers. However, if you click the OK button on this warning box, Device Manager will open, allowing a non-administrative user to look but not touch!

FIGURE 7–21 After installing the device driver, Windows places the device under the Network Infrastructure Devices category.

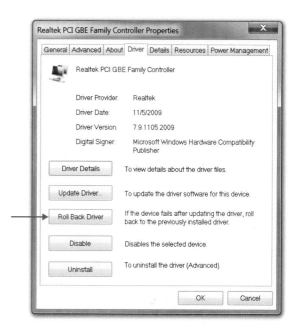

FIGURE 7–22 The Roll Back Driver button is active only after a driver update.

Chapter 7 REVIEW

Chapter Summary

After reading this chapter, and completing the Step-by-Step tutorials and Try This! exercises, you should understand the following facts about what is under the Windows desktop.

Understanding the Registry

- The registry is a database of all configuration settings in Windows. Avoid directly editing the registry because you can cause severe damage. The Control Panel applets provide a safe way to edit the registry.
- Windows creates the registry during setup and modifies it any time a setup or installation program runs after that and during startup and shut down. Windows also modifies it any time it

installs a device driver and whenever it configures any application, Windows component, or device.

- Most of the registry is in several files, called hives. They include SYSTEM, SOFTWARE, SECURITY, SAM, DEFAULT, and NTUSER.DAT. These are the permanent portions of the registry.
- You view the registry in a hierarchical folder structure in Registry Editor.
- A key is a folder object that can contain one or more sets of settings as well as other keys.
- There are five top-level keys, or root keys.
- A key that exists within another key is called a subkey.
- Settings within a key are value entries. Each value entry has a name, type, and data.

The Windows Startup Process

- The phases of the Windows startup process are
  - Power-on self-test
  - Initial startup
  - Boot loader
  - Detect and configure hardware
  - Kernel loading
  - Logon

- If necessary, modify system startup using the Startup and Recovery page in System Properties. You can also modify the BOOT.INI (Windows XP) and BCD (Windows Vista/Windows 7) files directly to modify startup, but only very advanced techs should do this.

Installing and Managing Device Drivers

- A device driver is program code, created by the device manufacturer, that allows an OS to control the use of a physical device. Look for device drivers on the disk that comes with a device or at the Web site of the manufacturer.

- You need Administrator privileges to install any device driver in Windows.

- Once a device is installed, a standard user may disconnect and reconnect the device without restriction—the driver will not be uninstalled.

- Code signing exists to avoid problems caused by badly written code. It involves a digital signature, provided by Microsoft, as a seal of approval of program code.

- Always read the manufacturer's documentation and follow the instructions before attempting to install a device driver, whether it is plug and play or not.

- When an administrator installs or connects a plug and play device to a Windows computer, the computer will automatically detect the device, and install and configure the driver with little or no interaction from the user, except to provide the device driver disk if requested.

- Plug and play devices connected to USB or IEEE 1394 (Firewire) can be disconnected without restarting Windows, but you should use the Safely Remove Hardware applet before disconnecting.

- Device Manager is the Windows tool for managing and troubleshooting device problems.

Troubleshooting Windows Problems

- Windows offers a variety of startup options, and some are well suited for troubleshooting. These include the Advanced Boot Options menu and the System Configuration utility. Both allow you to select from several options for restarting Windows.

- Device Manager is the primary tool for troubleshooting device problems. A yellow exclamation mark on a device in Device manger indicates a problem. Open the properties dialog box to see an explanation.

- Use Device Manager to uninstall, update, and remove device drivers. You can also use it to disable a device without removing the driver.

Key Terms List

binary file *(242)*

boot code *(251)*

code signing *(259)*

data type *(246)*

Device Stage *(261)*

digital signature *(259)*

driver signing *(259)*

file signature verification *(259)*

hive *(242)*

key *(246)*

master boot record (MBR) *(251)*

MSCONFIG *(269)*

plug and play *(258)*

registry *(242)*

root key *(246)*

security ID (SID) *(247)*

subkey *(246)*

value entry *(246)*

Key Terms Quiz

Use the Key Terms List to complete the sentences that follow. Not all terms will be used.

1. A/an _____ is a portion of a registry, containing a hierarchy of keys, that is saved in a registry file.

2. _____ is a new feature in Windows 7 that provides a special home page for a device. This home page contains many choices for managing the device.

3. When viewed with a registry editor, a/an _____ is a registry key located at the top level.

4. A/an _____ is an object in the Windows registry that contains one or more settings.

5. _____ is the use of a digital signature provided by Microsoft as its seal of approval on program code.

6. _____ is the ability of a computer and OS to automatically detect and configure a hardware device.

7. A/an _____ contains program code.

8. The _____ utility is very handy for troubleshooting startup problems, allowing you to temporarily disable programs you suspect are causing problems.

9. _____ is a startup mode for starting Windows with certain drivers and components disabled.

10. The _____ is a database of all the settings in your installation of Windows.

Multiple-Choice Quiz

1. Which of the following will you not find in the registry?
   a. Device driver settings
   b. Services settings
   c. User data files
   d. User preferences
   e. Application program settings

2. Any change to Windows or an installed application results in a change to this special database.
   a. Microsoft SQL Server
   b. Microsoft Excel
   c. NTUSER.DAT
   d. Registry
   e. DEFAULT

3. Most of the Windows registry files are in this location.
   a. *systemroot*\SYSTEM32\CONFIG
   b. D:\WINDOWS
   c. *systemroot*\SYSTEM32\REGISTRY
   d. *systemroot*\WINDOWS
   e. *systemroot*\WINNT

4. The source of the user profile settings used until after a user logs on to Windows.
   a. NTUSER.DAT
   b. USER.DAT
   c. SYSTEM.DAT
   d. DEFAULT
   e. SYSTEM

5. During this phase, programs start and plug and play devices are detected.
   a. Kernel loading
   b. Logon
   c. Initial startup
   d. POST
   e. Boot loader

6. Which statement is true?
   a. Only the Administrator may disconnect or reconnect an installed device.
   b. Only members of the Administrators group may disconnect or reconnect an installed device.
   c. Only members of the Guests group may disconnect or reconnect an installed device.
   d. Any member of the local Users group may disconnect or reconnect an installed device.
   e. No one may disconnect or reconnect an installed device.

7. Which statement is true?
   a. Not all unsigned drivers are bad.
   b. You can easily install unsigned drivers into 64-bit Windows 7.
   c. Only a manufacturer can install an unsigned device driver.
   d. You should never install unsigned device drivers.
   e. Unsigned device drivers are always dangerous.

8. Which of the following is a Device Manager feature introduced in Windows XP and still in today's Windows?
   a. Uninstall driver
   b. Roll back driver
   c. Disable driver
   d. Update driver
   e. Remove driver

9. What two files in Windows Vista and Windows 7 replace the functionality of the Windows XP NTLDR file?
   a. BCD
   b. WINLOAD.EXE
   c. BOOTMGR
   d. NTOSKRNL.EXE
   e. WINLOGON.EXE

10. Where in the Windows GUI for Windows XP, Windows Vista, and Windows 7 can you modify the length of time the OS selection menu displays during Windows startup?
    a. Startup and Recovery
    b. Device Manager
    c. BCDEDIT
    d. Local Security Policy
    e. Computer Management

11. What choice on the Windows 7 Advanced Boot Options menu gives you a selection of tools that includes Startup Repair, System Restore, System Image Recovery, Windows Memory Diagnostic, and Command Prompt?
    a. Safe Mode with Command Prompt
    b. Debugging Mode
    c. Directory Services Restore Mode
    d. Last Known Good Configuration
    e. Repair Your Computer

12. Which of the following startup options will not do you any good if you have restarted and logged on after making a change that caused problems in Windows?
    a. System Restore
    b. Repair Your Computer

c. Enable Boot Logging

d. Safe Mode with Command Prompt

e. Last Known Good Configuration

13. The first file to be loaded into memory during Windows XP boot-up is:

a. NTBOOTDD.SYS

b. NTLDR

c. BOOT.INI

d. NTDETECT.COM

e. NTBIO.SYS

14. You upgraded a device driver, and Windows immediately failed and restarted. The problem is that it seems to be in a continuous restarting loop. What boot startup option will restart normally and give you an opportunity to try to troubleshoot the problem after a normal reboot?

a. Debugging mode

b. Enable boot logging

c. Safe Mode with command prompt

d. Disable automatic restart on system failure

e. Safe Mode with networking

15. Which of the following is the executable name for the GUI utility that allows you to temporarily modify system startup?

a. SYSCON

b. MSCONFIG

c. SYSEDIT

d. REGEDIT

e. BCDEDIT

Essay Quiz

1. Name at least five actions that will automatically change the Windows registry.

2. Your Windows 7 computer is having display problems when starting. You suspect that the cause is a video driver update that you installed. You managed to log on at the first restart after the update, despite being barely able to see the distorted logon dialog box. Then you found that, even though you had logged on, it was hopeless to try to work with the GUI. Describe how you would confirm that the problem is the video adapter and how you will correct the problem.

3. Describe and contrast two tools for modifying Windows startup: the Advanced Boot Options menu and System Configuration.

4. A fellow student asked for your help in diagnosing a problem with a Windows XP computer. He believes there is a problem with the network adapter. He works in a small office and does not know the credentials for the Administrator account on that computer. The person who does know is out of town and is unwilling to give him the password until he can convince her that there truly is a problem. He wants to use Device Manager to see the status of the network adapter. What advice can you give him?

5. Describe what boot logging does and how you would use it as a troubleshooting tool.

Lab Projects

LAB PROJECT 7.1

Your Windows 7 computer will not start, and you believe the cause is a network card you recently installed.

1. Describe the steps you will take to isolate the problem.

2. Demonstrate how you will do this.

LAB PROJECT 7.2

A fellow student asked for your help with a problem that is keeping his Windows XP laptop from starting.

A black screen appears with a message that NTLDR is missing. Research how to solve this problem and describe the steps you would take.

LAB PROJECT 7.3

You are having a problem with your Windows computer that is isolated to a single graphics editing program that you use every day in your work. When you described the problem to the customer service support person for this product, she told you that the only fix for it is to edit a key under HKEY-LOCAL_ MACHINE\SOFTWARE. She has assured you that this fix will work without causing any problems, but you are wary of doing this.

1. Describe the steps you will take *before* making the suggested registry changes.

2. Demonstrate only the steps you would take before modifying the registry. Do not actually modify the registry.

chapter

8

Linux on the Desktop

"But at the end of the day, the only thing that matters is actual code and the technology itself and the people who are not willing to step up and write that code, they can comment on it and they can say it should be done this way or that way or they won't, but in the end their voice doesn't matter. The only thing that matters is code."

—Linus Torvalds

In an interview conducted by Jim Zemlin, executive director of the Linux Foundation, January 2008

L inux, a free operating system with many of the same qualities as UNIX, has the potential to save corporations millions of dollars. To grasp how important a free operating system is, compare Linux to the engine in your car. An engine costs thousands of dollars, but if a company started making and distributing free engines, the cost of your new car would drop dramatically.

In this chapter, you'll learn the basics of Linux on the desktop. Linux is far too broad a topic to give a detailed exploration here, but you will learn why Linux is growing in popularity. You will learn how to install and customize Linux, and how to work in a Linux environment. If you have never worked with Linux before, this chapter will serve as an introduction to this OS and perhaps inspire you to study it further. ❁

Learning Outcomes

In this chapter, you will learn how to:

LO **8.1** Describe Linux.

LO **8.2** Install Linux.

LO **8.3** Demonstrate basic skills for using Linux.

LO **8.4** Manage Linux files and directories with shell commands.

LO **8.5** Secure a Linux desktop.

LO **8.6** Troubleshoot common Linux problems.

LO 8.1 | Linux Overview

In this section you will discover why you should learn Linux, the features and benefits of Linux, and how and why Linux is used today.

Why Learn Linux?

Linux is very important—in fact, learning Linux can be very beneficial to your future career because of its growing importance on all types of computers. Like Windows and Mac OS X, you will find Linux on both desktops and servers. However, it is not as easy to use as these more common operating systems with their native GUI environment. Even with the new, improved GUI shells for Linux, if you implement Linux as your desktop OS, be prepared to spend a lot of time configuring Linux and providing training for other users who might need to use your computer.

Qualifying for a Job

The first reason to learn Linux is to help you get a job. If your résumé reflects that you understand Linux or UNIX, long regarded as the "difficult" operating systems, you are advertising your intelligence, initiative, and computer ability. Organizations reviewing your résumé would see Linux knowledge as a big plus. Their reasoning is simple—if you can learn Linux, then you should quickly learn the idiosyncrasies of an organization's internal computer systems.

Improving Your Skills

Another reason to learn Linux is to improve your computer skills for working in a non-GUI environment, thus forcing you to be precise. Any OS is unforgiving when given the wrong instructions, but it doesn't take precision to browse a GUI and select the correct graphical object, which is how a GUI buffers users from the precision required from a command prompt. Although there are great GUI options for working in Linux, much of the real work of supporting and managing Linux is still done from the command prompt, forcing you to be precise when entering commands. Acquiring the habit of being precise now will help you succeed in future computer work.

The Evolution of Linux

In the early 1970s, Ken Thompson, a developer working at Bell Labs, was criticized for playing a computer game on company equipment. Thompson's response to the criticism was to find an unused computer and write an operating system that would run his game. This operating system became the foundation of UNIX, which has gone on to power the computers of most of the universities, corporations, and governments of the world. UNIX has become a powerful, stable, and fast system.

In 1984, interested persons created the **GNU** organization to develop a free version of a UNIX-like operating system (GNU is a recursive acronym for GNU's Not Unix). Since its founding, GNU members have developed thousands of applications that run on UNIX and Linux platforms—many of which are bundled with distributions of Linux.

In 1988 a group of UNIX licensees formed the Open Systems Foundation (OSF) to lobby for an "open" UNIX after AT&T formed a partnership with Sun Microsystems to develop a single UNIX with the best features of many versions. In response, AT&T and other licensees formed UNIX International to oppose the OSF. The trade press called the maneuverings of these two groups the "UNIX wars."

Learn more about GNU at www.gnu.org.

In 1991, Linus Torvalds started a new hobby that resulted in Linux, an open source operating system based on UNIX. Torvalds wanted to write a better, open-source version of MINIX, a UNIX-like operating system. Open source software is distributed with all of its source code, allowing developers to customize the software as necessary. In turn, developers must also freely distribute the modified code. Torvalds and a team of programmers succeeded in his original goal, but he receives no direct financial gain because he does not own Linux—just the name, and the open source community could easily decide to rename it. But that won't happen.

Because the software was open source, many individuals and several companies modified the kernel. Two of the versions available in 1994 were the Slackware and Red Hat kernels. Both included the C++ language, TCP/IP functionality, and primitive Web servers. Of course, the code for the kernels was available as well. To obtain a copy, you simply went to an Internet site and selected the products to download. This is true today, with many more sources for the code.

> The kernel is the core of the operating system. It contains all of the programs needed to allow the user to interact with the computer. The Linux kernel's code is freely available to any who wish to download it. Along with a great deal of other information, you can find the latest version of the Linux kernel at www.kernel.org.

Linux Today

The open source movement has gained credibility, in part because vendors such as Novell and IBM have integrated open source software into their product mix. The notion of free and open software, with no one entity owning the source code, thrives today and has the support of many organizations that previously opposed it. Linux is the best example of this phenomenon and its popularity is growing. Manufacturers have added Linux to their server lines that previously featured mostly UNIX servers. These vendors offer inexpensive Web servers running Apache Web Server on Linux. Apache is one of the most popular servers due to its stability, security, and cost. Linux is the fastest growing operating system in the world.

> **try this!**
>
> **Research the Open Source Debate**
> View the current arguments in the open source debate. Try this:
> 1. Use your favorite Internet search engine to find recent articles on "open source debate."
> 2. Look at the arguments on the pro-open-source side and the anti-open-source side.
> 3. Who appear to be the major players on each side?

Features and Benefits of Linux

There are several benefits to using Linux on your desktop computer.

Linux Is Free or Inexpensive

The first benefit of Linux is cost. You may freely download many versions of Linux from the Web. Many sites, such as www.linuxlookup.com, offer Linux distributions in convenient ISO images. An ISO image is a copy of the entire contents of an optical disc that you can easily transfer to a writable disc using ISO image copy software. If you don't want to download these distributions, you may purchase prepackaged versions of Linux online or in computer stores for modest cost. In addition, you may legally share the software with your friends.

> Terminology for Linux is a little different from other OSs. When you buy or download a version of Linux you get a distribution, sometimes called a "distro." This is the whole set of programs that work together to make a functioning version of Linux. There are *many* distributions of Linux!

The savings for a company can be dramatic. Imagine an IT manager who needs to roll out 1,000 desktop computers. Rolling out 1,000 Linux computers could cost the company nothing in licensing fees for the operating system software, but rolling out 1,000 Windows 7 workstations would be in the tens of thousands of dollars, depending on the terms of the company's site license. In addition, when the time to upgrade the operating system comes, the Linux upgrade would still be free, whereas there would be a significant upgrade cost for the Windows solution. Of course, licensing costs are only a small part of the picture. The long-term cost of using and supporting Linux versus Windows on the desktop is still a hotly debated topic, with convincing arguments on both sides.

Linux Can Run on Old Equipment

In addition to being free or inexpensive, Linux can run on old equipment. A nonprofit organization could provide computers for its employees with donated or very inexpensive equipment. There are countless situations in which computers too underpowered to run even an outdated version of Windows continue to run reliably for years—as Web servers!

Linux Is Fast

While Linux runs respectably well on old computers, it is even faster on newer computers. This is because Linux programs are very lean and efficient. They use as few resources as possible, and, unlike Windows, graphics use in Linux is optional, and many Linux applications use few, if any, graphics. Graphics can slow a system's response time, making it seem slower than it truly is.

Linux Can Have a GUI

A shell is the user interface to an OS that accepts commands and displays error messages and other screen output. The traditional Linux shell is a command line interface (CLI), such as the BASH shell. A GUI shell standard for Linux, X Window System, has been around for many years, developed in1984 at MIT. An interested group formed the X Consortium in 1986 to continue the development of X Windows System (alternatively called "X Windows" or simply "X"). The Open Group then furthered the work, beginning in 1997. The most common implementation of X Windows is GNOME (GNU network object model environment), which was improved over the years and is as easy to work with as Microsoft Windows or Mac OS X.

Linux Is Stable

Linux code is well written, which increases the speed at which Linux runs and improves the stability of the operating system. Linux is next to impossible to crash. If an application crashes, you can simply remove the program from memory. This is why people use Linux on Web servers where stability is crucial. With Linux, Web hosting providers can guarantee 99.9 percent (or better) uptime.

Linux Is Secure

Linux is a secure operating system with all the appropriate security options, as well as the benefit of not being a target in the manner of Windows operating systems. As open source software, Linux has the advantage of legions of programmers working to make it a better and more secure OS.

Linux Is Open Source

Finally, Linux is open source software. This means users can read the source code and modify it as needed. This probably means little to the average user of the final version of a Linux kernel. However, during development, "beta" releases of the kernel are available to developers who will download the code and test it thoroughly. When possible, they will find any problems and correct the code. This process helps to ensure an as-well-written-as-possible final release of the kernel.

Once they release a final version, developers can adjust the kernel as needed. We know a developer who modified his kernel to be more usable for visually impaired users. He added better support for large-print output and a command-line narrator that reads the information on the command line. Open source allowed the developer to modify his code to suit his needs.

Drawbacks of Linux

Even though Linux is widely used on corporate servers, Web sites, and large-scale networking environments, you still won't find many people using it on their desktop computers or workstations at home. There are several reasons for this.

Lack of Centralized Support

No system is 100 percent secure; however, Microsoft products do have extensive documentation and support. Microsoft releases service packs and frequent updates to fix discovered vulnerabilities. Linux does not have this centralized support. When you purchase Linux from vendors it is often supported by vendor-provided documentation and user groups, but support and documentation for free Linux can be spotty. A user who downloads Linux from the Internet may receive only a downloadable manual and access to online help pages. It is true that the Linux community is growing, and there are many active user groups, but one must search them out and expend considerable time and effort to get questions answered.

Limited Software Selection

People purchase computers to run applications—whether for business or for pleasure. There are important titles for Windows that are not available for Linux, so you need to check the software selection before moving to Linux on the desktop. But more titles are available for Linux every year—even some very well-known titles. For example, consider Internet browsers. The most popular browsers, Mozilla Firefox, Google Chrome, and Microsoft Internet Explorer are available for Linux. In addition, other browsers are also available in Linux versions.

You are also limited in your choice of word processors. The most popular word processor is Microsoft Word. Chances are good that every Windows PC in your school uses Word. But Word is not available for Linux, although there are open source programs that allow Word to work under Linux in certain circumstances. Various distributions of Linux have bundled excellent substitutions, including StarOffice and OpenOffice. Each of these is an applications suite that contains a word processor and other office productivity tools. However, although both are very nice products, a proficient Microsoft Office user would have to learn how to use StarOffice or OpenOffice with the same level of proficiency.

Limited Hardware Support

Not all popular software runs on Linux and not all hardware products work with Linux, but we see this improving. Linux vendors work very hard to support the more common devices by providing drivers for them. Having the correct driver is crucial. If you have a new or unusual device, you may need to search the Internet for a driver. Maybe the vendor has not created a Linux driver for your new device, but there is great support among Linux users who create drivers and make them available on the Internet.

If you have a recent distribution of Linux with the Linux GNOME desktop, look for accessibility options listed under Assistive Technologies Preferences on the System menu.

Several browsers for Linux are available; however, if you want to see animation, find out if a browser supports JavaScript (which powers much of the animation on the Web) before installing it into Linux. Use your favorite search utility to find Web sites that have more information on Linux browsers and other available software for Linux.

We solved a printer problem by using an older driver for another, similar printer. Not all its features are available, but we can print successfully.

Complexity

The last block in the wall between Linux and greater success is Linux's difficulty of use at the command shell, meaning that only a limited subset of users care to invest the time and effort to learn its intricacies. Linux, like UNIX, assumes that you know what you are doing, and it assumes that you know the consequences of every command you type.

For a beginning user, Linux can be frightening to use; entering the wrong command can have serious consequences. It doesn't help that Linux is also case sensitive, so you must enter the commands in lowercase, and be very careful to use the correct case for each option you use with the command. Upper- and lowercase often result in different actions. Case sensitivity in a password is a security benefit. Case sensitivity in command syntax adds complexity and increases the level of difficulty in learning Linux. However, experienced Linux users find case sensitivity in command line options makes sense. For instance using the command **ls** lists information about files in the current directory. Adding the option **-a** (**ls -a**) lists all entries, including directory entries (their names begin with a dot (.)), while using the **-A** option lists "nearly all," excluding the entries beginning with a dot (.) or three dots (...).

Don't let this frighten you, however. By now, you have spent sufficient time working with operating systems so that you know the basic theory. You'll do fine in Linux.

Acquiring Linux for the Desktop

There are many distributions of Linux, and many sources for them. The most important criteria to keep in mind before selecting one is the role you wish the Linux computer to play—will it be a server or a desktop. When selecting a source, select one that meets your support needs. We looked for desktop (or workstation) versions, and the top three (in our opinion) are Canonical's Ubuntu, Fedora, and openSUSE. Learn more about each of these distributions at the following Web sites:

- Ubuntu (www.ubuntu.com)
- Fedora (fedoraproject.org)
- OpenSUSE (www.opensuse.org)

Ubuntu Desktop Edition is our choice for this chapter because the Canonical download includes a LiveCD distribution. Recall from Chapter 4 that a LiveCD is a CD or DVD from which you can boot an OS without requiring any part of the OS to be resident on a hard disk. Further, the version available today includes a complete software bundle including the GNOME GUI desktop and a number of GUI applications including Open Office, Firefox, and software selections for many other functions, such as e-mail, chat, social networking, music streaming, photo management and editing, and more. The download for this edition is 700 MB, so if you do not have a fast Ethernet connection, you may want to find a smaller distribution.

The various versions of Linux have many things in common, so what you learn about one version will carry over to another version.

You may call each character or group of characters you use following a command on the same command line an *argument*, *option*, *parameter*, *switch*, and so on. In this chapter we will use the term "option" because that is the term used in one of the handiest Linux command-line references. You'll find it at **http://ss64.com/bash/**. Whatever you call it, an option is an instruction to the command, altering its behavior.

In discussions of Linux distributions, people often mention FreeBSD, but it is not a version of Linux. FreeBSD is an operating system based on the Berkeley UNIX distribution, and primarily used on servers, whereas Linux was designed for and focused on desktop architectures.

Step-by-Step 8.01

Downloading Linux and Creating a LiveCD

This step-by-step exercise takes you through downloading a distribution of Linux and creating a LiveCD, which you will use in the remainder of the class. The instructions and illustrations are for Ubuntu Linux, a free distribution in the form of an ISO file that you can use to create a LiveCD and as a source for installing on a hard drive. We found that the size of the ISO file was a tad larger than the capacity of a CD disc, so we used a DVD. To complete this exercise you will need:

- A computer that has Internet Access and has an optical drive capable of burning discs.
- A blank disc.

Step 1

Use your browser to connect to **www.ubuntu.com**. Browse to the Download page by clicking the **Download Ubuntu** link on the home page. If the Web site has changed and no longer shows this link, search for an appropriate link.

Step 2

On the Get Ubuntu Desktop Edition page click **Start Download**.

Step 3

Now choose to save the ISO file and click OK. It may prompt you for a location. If so, supply a location, such as the desktop. Otherwise, it will save it in Downloads.

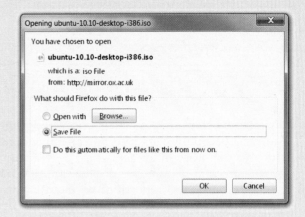

Step 4

Next burn the disc by using the ISO image you downloaded. If you need help doing this, click the **Show me how** button. You can also choose to create a USB drive that will boot into Ubuntu by selecting the appropriate option. Be sure to select the OS that is running on the computer on which you are creating the LiveCD or bootable flash drive.

Step 5

Now test the installation by rebooting the computer with the disc or flash drive inserted. After a brief delay you should see this page.

Step 6

To run Ubuntu from the disc or flash drive without installing it on your hard drive click **Try Ubuntu**. After a delay, Ubuntu loads with the GNOME desktop. Click on the items in the menu bar to open the various menus. Notice that there is a shortcut labeled Install Ubuntu. In Step-by-Step 8.02 you will install Ubuntu Linux. For now, if time permits explore the desktop.

When you are finished, click the shutdown button on the far right of the menu bar. Then click Shut Down in the Shut Down box.

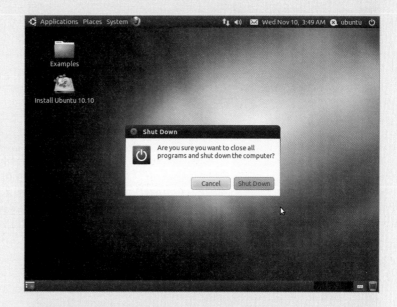

You will then see a text mode screen prompting you to remove the installation media and press ENTER. The computer will then power down.

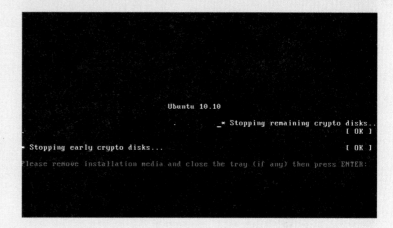

LO 8.2 | Installing Linux

When you encounter a new operating system, nothing makes you feel more in control than completing a successful installation. However, it is important to make certain preparations before beginning an installation.

Preparing for Linux Installation

Before installing Linux, review the installation documentation and decide how you wish to install. Do you plan to dedicate a computer to Linux? Do you have a single Windows computer and wish to be able to boot between the two operating systems? Or do you plan to install Linux into a virtual machine? Whatever the scenario, you should keep your installation as simple as possible and know the hardware requirements.

Keep Your Linux Installation Simple

As is true when installing any operating system, keep it simple by accepting the detected devices to allow a basic installation, and wait to fine-tune the specific devices until after the installation.

Prepare a Password

Recall what you learned in Chapter 2 about creating strong passwords and be prepared to create a unique strong password that is not easy for others to guess.

Hardware Requirements

There are versions of Linux for several computer platforms, including those based on Intel, AMD, and other processors. Linux memory requirements are small compared to Windows operating systems. If you do not plan to run GUI applications, you can install most versions of Linux on a system with as little as 8 MB of RAM, but a recommended minimum is 16 MB, and 256 MB is more than generous for most Linux desktop installations. In addition, you should plan to have additional free space for your data. Remember, you cannot have too much hard disk space! However, the Ubuntu Desktop Edition targeted as a Windows desktop replacement (with many bundled applications) that we use as an example in this chapter has both minimum requirements as well as a *recommended* system configuration that allows for installing additional software and storing user data (see Table 8–1).

Many distributions come with a large number of packages (Linux-speak for "programs"), and selecting some of these packages will greatly increase your disk space needs. Check the documentation of the version of Linux you plan to install.

Linux supports a number of hard disk controllers, but plan to read the documentation to verify that Linux will install on your computer before beginning an installation. Linux also supports optical and flash drives and all the standard video graphics adapters and monitors, but generally supports the use of a mouse only in graphic interfaces. In addition, Linux supports many printers, modems, and network adapters. Of course, Linux is free, so you can save yourself time and simply download it and try it on your computer.

Clean Installation versus Dual Booting

When you install Linux on a computer that already has another operating system, you have the option to create a clean installation (called a standard installation) or a dual-boot installation. When planning for a dual-boot configuration, plan for each operating system having its own hard disk partition. This is a very common installation for someone who is currently running Windows and wants to learn about Linux, but does not have a spare computer to devote to Linux. However, you will need unpartitioned disk space before you begin. The result will be a dual-boot installation that will allow you to select which operating system you boot into when you restart your computer.

TABLE 8–1 Ubuntu Linux *Minimum* Requirements versus *Recommended* System Configuration		
	Minimum	Recommended
Processor	700 MHz ×86	1GHz ×86
System RAM	256 MB	1 GB
Hard drive space	3 GB	15 GB
Display system resolution	1024 × 768	1024 × 768
Network	Internet helpful for updating	Internet helpful for updating

The Ubuntu setup program lets you choose the type of installation. On the Allocate drive space page of version 10.10 you have the following options:

- Erase and use the entire disk (clean installation).
- Specify partitions manually (advanced: either type of installation).

Booting into the Linux Installation Program

If you have a Linux distribution on a bootable optical disc or flash drive, you can boot into the Linux installation program. If you do not have bootable media, or if your computer will not boot from the optical drive or flash drive, and if you have a floppy disk drive in your computer, use a bootable floppy disk that you can create with a utility, sometimes called a raw write, that once came with most distributions of Linux. This utility places a boot image on a floppy disk, which will allow you to boot into Linux and begin the Linux installation program.

You will need to research which distributions have this available now and find documentation for using it. Once you create this floppy disk, you insert it and the optical disc into the computer on which you wish to install Linux, and restart the computer to begin the installation.

Performing the Installation

Once the Linux installation program begins, it guides you through the process by presenting successive pages providing choices. Many Linux installation programs, such as Ubuntu, provide a GUI with online help. Step-by-Step 8.02 describes the installation of Ubuntu Linux.

Step-by-Step 8.02

Installing Linux

This step-by-step exercise includes the steps for a clean installation of Linux—either as the only OS on a computer or into a virtual machine. The instructions and illustrations are for Ubuntu Linux, a free distribution. The steps describe many but not all pages that display. We strongly suggest that you accept the defaults. To complete this step-by-step you will need:

- A computer or virtual machine that meets or exceeds the minimum hardware requirements for the version of Linux you are using and that will boot up from the CD/DVD drive.
- A bootable CD/DVD distribution of Linux, with an installation program that guides you through the steps.

Step 1

Insert the Linux distribution disc into the CD/DVD drive and start or restart your computer. You will see several screens, mostly text on a black background while Ubuntu automatically starts from CD with the GNOME GUI. You may use a mouse or keyboard to move through the choices and make selections. When the Welcome screen appears, as shown in Step 5 of Step-by-Step 8.01, select Install Ubuntu.

On the Preparing to install Ubuntu page, stop to ensure that you meet the minimum disk space requirements. The recommendation to plug the computer into a power source is obviously referring to portable computers because it isn't wise to attempt a power-devouring task such as installing an OS on a computer running on battery. If the computer is connected to the Internet, click to select **Download updates while installing**, and then click Forward.

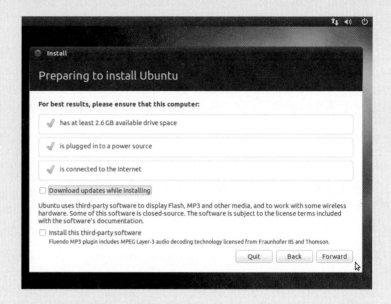

On the Allocate drive space page select **Erase and use the entire disk** (unless an instructor tells you otherwise) and click Forward.

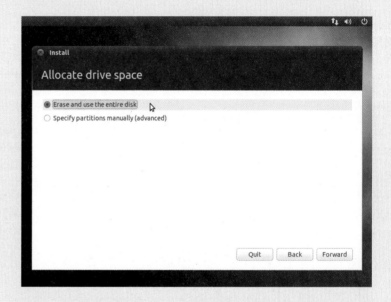

On the second Allocate drive space page, if it selected the wrong drive, select the correct drive. Once you select the correct drive, click Install Now. At this point a progress bar appears on the bottom of the page and you will not be able to move from this page until it creates the file system and prepares the disk for use.

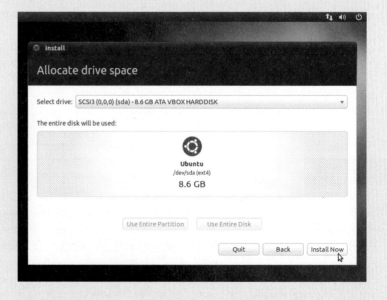

Step 5

On the Where are you? page, select your location and click Forward.

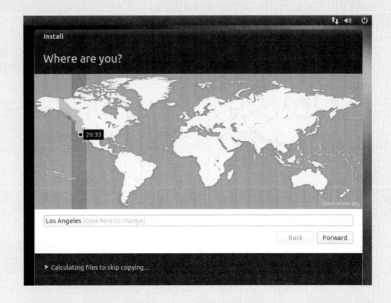

Step 6

On the Keyboard layout page select the appropriate layout and click Forward.

Step 7

On the Who are you? page enter your information, as well as a password. As you enter your password, notice that Ubuntu rates it according to its strength. It rated the one we entered as "good," which would not be good enough for a high-security environment. When you have completed this page select **Forward**—there will be a delay while files are copied.

Step 8

The Welcome page appears, displaying a progress bar along the bottom while the installation completes. This will take several minutes, during which you can use the arrows on the right and left of this page to scroll through a slide show about Ubuntu, the software, and other features of this distribution.

Step 9

When the installation is complete this box will appear. Click Restart Now.

Step 10

You will now see several screens—mostly text on a black background. One will prompt you to remove the disc from the drive. Then the new installation of Ubuntu starts and displays the logon dialog box, which includes the name of the computer (chuck-linux in this case), the name of a user you created during setup, and the choice **Other** for accessing a different account. Click the user name you created and enter your password.

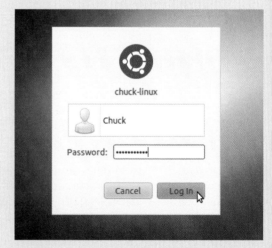

Step 11

The Ubuntu GNOME desktop will appear. You have successfully installed Ubuntu Linux.

LO 8.3 | Linux Basics

There are some basic Linux skills and concepts that everyone working with Linux should know. In this section you will practice these skills, including logging on and off, working with Linux commands at the Linux prompt, and shutting down the computer. Although we installed Ubuntu Linux, the examples in this section will include screenshots from a bare-bones Linux installation, as many people will also work with that type of installation.

Logging in to Linux

Just as in other OSs, Linux requires authentication of each user with a valid user name and password from a user account. If you configured your Linux computer for a command-line login, when it starts it will display the login prompt, which consists of the name of the computer, followed by a space and the word *login*, followed by a colon and a blinking cursor as shown in Figure 8–1. Once you type in your user name at this prompt and press Enter, it will prompt you for the password. Type your password (it will not be displayed, and the cursor will not move to indicate that you entered anything) and press Enter.

If the user name and password are correct, you will see information about the last time you logged on, followed by the standard command line prompt. This prompt, shown in Figure 8–2, consists of your user name and the computer name (host name) separated by an @ sign and followed by your user name again. All this is contained within square brackets and followed by a $ sign, which is the traditional end of a Linux prompt for an ordinary user. This entire assemblage is often called the $ prompt. The second instance of your user name indicates the current directory. When you create a user account, Linux creates a directory for that user, names it with the user name, and that directory is made current every time that user logs on. Other users cannot easily access a user's directory because it has permissions set for the specified user.

When you are through working in Linux, you will normally log out so that someone else can use the computer. Logging out allows you to leave Linux without shutting it down. Typing **exit** at the $ prompt, or pressing Ctrl-D, logs you out of Linux, which is similar to the Log off option in Windows.

Shutting Down Linux

The root account, often simply called "root," is the most powerful account on a Linux (or UNIX) computer, and, like the Administrator account on a Windows computer, it is capable of doing anything. In a conventional non-GUI installation of Linux only someone logged on as the root user can shut down Linux from the command line. You accomplish this with the shutdown command, which has many options that change the outcome of a command. Entering **shutdown -h now** tells Linux to shut down immediately and then to halt after shutting down. The process will take a few minutes. The shutdown command has several other options that you can use in place of the **-h** and **now** options. One option is the **-r** option. This will reboot the system after the shutdown. For a complete list of options, type **man shutdown** at a Linux prompt.

When working in a GUI in Linux, an ordinary user can shut down Linux. An administrator using the root account can disable this option that a GUI

FIGURE 8–1 The Login prompt

Whether you are logging in from the command shell or a GUI, a Linux password never shows on the screen, and the cursor does not move while you type in the password.

When the all-powerful root user (described later) logs in at the command shell, the prompt ends with a # sign.

FIGURE 8–2 The $ prompt shows user name, computer name, and current directory.

Log In and Log Out

If you have a Linux computer configured for a command-line login, log in using the account provided for you. Try this:

1. Start Linux (if necessary). At the login prompt type your user name and then press Enter. It will prompt you for a password. Type your password and press Enter. If all is correct, you will see the Linux prompt.
2. To log off type **exit** at the $ prompt.

try this!

Shutting Down a Linux Computer

If you want to turn off your computer when working at the command line in Linux, you should shut down Linux correctly. Try this:

1. To shut down a Linux computer when working at the command line when you logged in as an ordinary user, log out, and then log in again as root.

2. After logging in as root, issue the command: **shutdown -h now**

often turns on by default, but it is an advanced task. If someone is using a GUI on a desktop computer, he should be able to shut down the system without logging on as root. In Ubuntu 10.10 with GNOME, simply select the shutdown button on the far right of the menu bar and then select **Shutdown**.

Ubuntu Linux 10.10, which we are working with, locks the password for root by default.

The Ubuntu GNOME Terminal Window

If you installed Ubuntu with the GNOME desktop or if you are running Ubuntu from a LiveCD, you can open a terminal window, the equivalent of a Windows Command Prompt window, where you can try many of the commands we discuss in this chapter. Some will not be available to you. It is simple to open a terminal window from the GNOME Applications menu, shown here. The resulting terminal window will look like Figure 8–3.

> The numerous illustrations and figures used to demonstrate the Linux shell commands in this chapter are screenshots taken from both an Ubuntu terminal window (dark purple background) and a more classic Linux BASH shell (black background).

Working with Linux Commands

Your experience with DOS, or the Windows command prompt, will be very helpful in your initial explorations of Linux because of the many similarities between them. In this section we'll explore working at the famous non-GUI command-line interface (CLI) of Linux. First we will consider the Linux CLI, and help you understand the syntax for working with commands. Then we'll show you some characteristic shell commands, the commands that only execute at the CLI.

The Command Line Interface Shell

The most common Linux command line interface (CLI) shell is BASH, an acronym for Bourne Again Shell. This is an example of Linux humor because

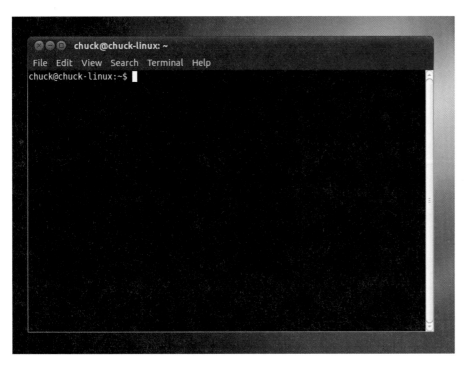

FIGURE 8–3 A GNOME terminal window

the original Linux shell was the Bourne shell. The Bourne developers added several features to improve the shell, thus the Bourne shell was "born again." Don't worry if you're not laughing—it takes a true Linux aficionado to appreciate much of Linux humor. A CLI shell processes commands, issues error messages, and provides other limited feedback. We call commands used at the CLI shell commands.

The Command Syntax

When working at the CLI, the Linux command syntax is pretty basic. All lines start with a Linux command (the first string of characters). Then, separated by spaces, are options specific to that command that modify its behavior. Order is usually of little importance for command options, but the space between the command and each option is crucial. Certain (but not all) options are preceded by a hyphen (-), and if you want to use multiple options for a command, you can combine them into one long option with a single hyphen at the beginning. Then there is the parameter, which is often a file name, directory, or device name. We usually place the parameter at the end of the command line. In general, the command syntax in Linux follows this format:

```
command -option parameter
```

For example, consider the Linux command **ls**, which lists files in a directory. The **ls** command has several options, two of which are **a** and **l**. To use **ls** with the **a** option, enter **ls -a**. To use both options, enter either **ls -al** or **ls -la**—either will work. If you want to use an option and list the /etc directory, you can enter **ls –a etc**. *In all cases, spaces separate the items on the command line.*

A case-sensitive operating system treats *A* differently than *a*. DOS and the Windows command prompt are *case insensitive*. Thus, **DIR** is the same command as **dir**. Linux is *case sensitive*. The command **exit** is much different than **EXIT** (which is not a command) and will cause an error message. Figure 8–4 shows the result of

In this chapter we can only hope to whet your appetite to learn more about Linux, and we recommend *The Linux Command Line* by William Shotts Jr., a free .pdf download at **http://linuxcommand.org/tlcl.php**. This 522-page book goes beyond a command reference, providing elegant explanations for Linux concepts including both the "whys" and the "hows."

```
chuck@chuck-linux:~$ MAN LS
MAN: command not found
chuck@chuck-linux:~$
```

FIGURE 8–4 Entering this command in all caps resulted in an error message.

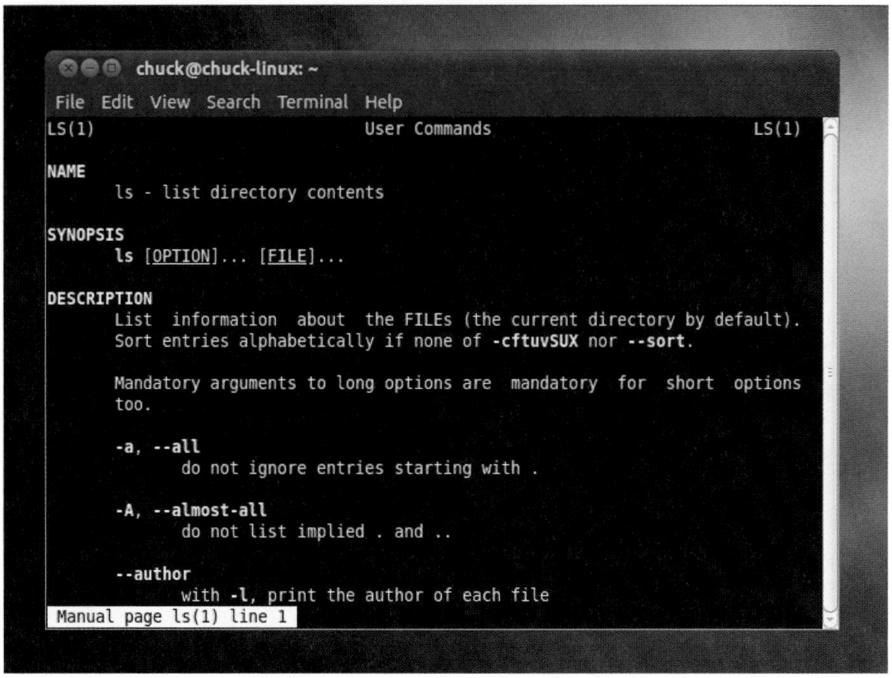

FIGURE 8–5 Entering the previous command in lowercase resulted in running the correct command, showing the user manual entry for the **ls** command.

using the wrong case, while Figure 8–5 shows the result of entering the same command in the proper case.

Command Line History

Linux saves the shell commands you enter during a session for the duration of the session, and you can scroll through these old commands while at the $ prompt. Simply use the up and down arrow keys to move through the history. When you find a command you would like to use, you can edit the command by moving back and forth through it with the left and right arrow keys. When you are ready to use the command, simply press ENTER. Linux saves these commands in a file called bash_history, but you do not need to know anything about this file to take advantage of this feature.

Command Completion

As you enter a command at the $ prompt, experiment with the command completion feature. Enter the command name and a few more characters of the options, then press the TAB key. BASH tries to guess what you wish to type, and is especially clever at doing this when it looks like you are entering a directory name, indicated by the forward slash (/), but you need to give it more information than just the forward slash. For instance, if you enter **cd /e** and then press the TAB key, it will guess that you intended to type "**etc/**" and will complete it that way.

The Help Manual

Help is always at hand in the form of the online user manual, accessed with the **man** command. The simple syntax for the **man** command is **man** *command* where *command* is the shell command you wish to view. You can even see the

> Recognizing that many users of Linux are (or were) users of DOS, distributions of Linux include some commands with names identical to those used in DOS—if only as aliases for Linux commands. In particular, the **dir** command works in Linux—because it is an alias (or substitute) for the **ls** command, you can use **dir** instead of **ls**. However, you will need to use the appropriate options for **ls**, rather than the DOS **dir** options.

try this!

Test Case-Sensitivity in Linux

If you have access to a computer with Linux configured to run at the shell, test its case-sensitivity. Try this:

1. Log in to Linux and enter the following command in all caps:

   MAN LS

2. Notice that you get an error message.

3. Now reenter the command in all lowercase. The result is that the Linux user manual will open to the page for the command **ls**, which is the **list directory contents** command.

documentation for the **man** command itself by entering **man man** at the $ prompt. Figure 8–6 shows the results of doing this. Even very simple commands have extensive help pages.

Use of Spaces

Another characteristic of Linux syntax is the use of spaces. In Linux, you must separate each part of a command line entry by a space. For example, neither of these commands will work in Linux:

```
shutdown-h  now
shutdown  -hnow
```

If you are working from the BASH shell, you will see a BASH error, as in Figure 8–7. If you are working from a GNOME terminal window, you will see an error similar to the one in Figure 8–8, which also provides some helpful information.

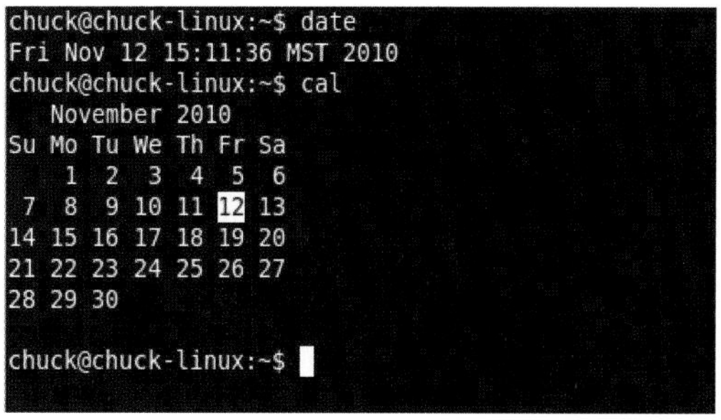

Paths

Another characteristic of Linux is the way you build the paths. In DOS and Windows, a full path to a file or directory begins with the drive designator (letter plus colon) and you build it using the backslash (\) character as separators between the drive and root directory (first backslash) and each of the subsequent directories in the path. Thus, a valid DOS or Windows path is C:\Winnt\System32. In Linux, you do not use a drive letter and you use the forward slash (/) character to separate directories. A valid path is **/etc/gtk**. Also, you show each drive and other device simply as a part of the file system and give it a path that begins at the root of the file system (/). Drives and other devices are given names, such as **/dev/sda0** (the first hard drive on a SCSI interface) or **/dev/hda1** (the first hard drive on an IDE interface).

> ### What Time Is It?
> Practice entering the date and calendar commands. Try this:
> 1. Type the command **date** and press ENTER. This will display the date.
> 2. Now type the command **cal** and press ENTER. This will display the current month's calendar.

The **date** and **cal** commands

> Simply press **q** to exit the Linux online manual. This works in other commands, too.

> ### Using the Linux Online Manual
> Use the online manual to view the documentation for the **ls** command. Try this:
> 1. Log in to Linux and enter: **man ls**
> 2. The **man** command displays the help screen for the **ls** command, a command analogous to the dir command in DOS.
> 3. Scan through the options for the **ls** command displayed on your screen, and then press the space bar to move to the next page. Continue pressing the space bar until you reach the end. You will know you are at the end by what you see at the bottom left of your screen.
> 4. When you reach the end press **q** to exit the manual.

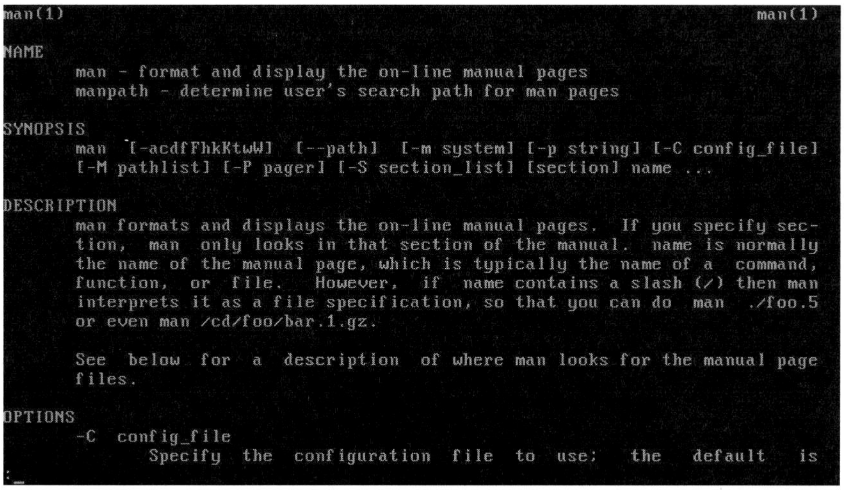

FIGURE 8–6 The **manual** command documentation

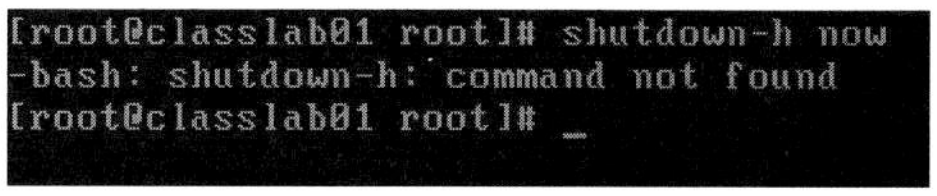

FIGURE 8–7 Example of a BASH error for an unrecognized command

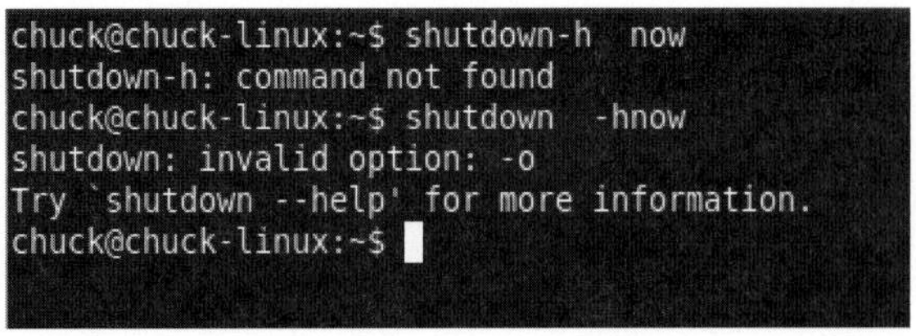

```
chuck@chuck-linux:~$ shutdown-h  now
shutdown-h: command not found
chuck@chuck-linux:~$ shutdown  -hnow
shutdown: invalid option: -o
Try 'shutdown --help' for more information.
chuck@chuck-linux:~$ █
```

FIGURE 8–8 An unrecognized command in a GNOME terminal window

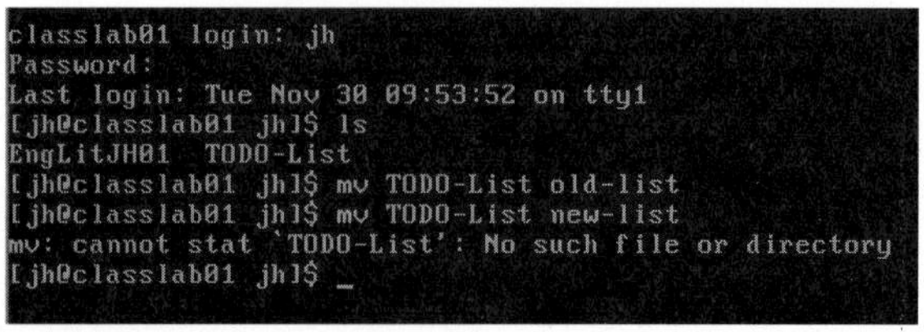

```
classlab01 login: jh
Password:
Last login: Tue Nov 30 09:53:52 on tty1
[jh@classlab01 jh]$ ls
EngLitJH01   TODO-List
[jh@classlab01 jh]$ mv TODO-List old-list
[jh@classlab01 jh]$ mv TODO-List new-list
mv: cannot stat 'TODO-List': No such file or directory
[jh@classlab01 jh]$ _
```

FIGURE 8–9 Linux error messages are not very helpful.

Linux Feedback

In the area of feedback, Linux commands are actually similar to DOS commands and Windows shell commands (those that run at the command prompt) in that they all provide cryptic feedback, communicating with you only if there is a problem. They will not report that they are successful, though you'll get a warning if the command is incorrect. Figure 8–9 illustrates this Linux trait. We ran this series of commands on yet another Linux system in the BASH shell, but the results would be very similar in a terminal window. The command **mv TODO-List old-list** successfully renames a file. Notice that no message returns to the user. The command **mv TODO-List new-list** attempts an operation on a file that no longer exists, thanks to the previous operation. Linux returns an error message. This is helpful, although cryptic, information.

```
login: jh
Password:
Last login: Tue Nov 30 10:08:39 on tty1
[jh@classlab01 jh]$ ls
EngLitJH01  old-list
[jh@classlab01 jh]$ ls -l
total 4
-rw-r--r--    1 jh       jh              0 Nov 29 22:49 EngLitJH01
-rw-r--r--    1 jh       jh             20 Nov 29 22:26 old-list
[jh@classlab01 jh]$ _
```

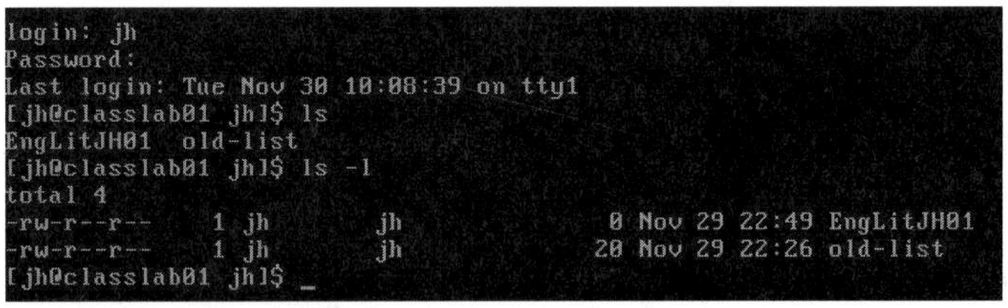

FIGURE 8–10 Output from the **ls** and **ls -l** commands

In addition to providing little feedback, Linux provides only the bare minimum output. For example, Figure 8–10 shows the result of running the **ls** command twice, once without an option and once with the **-l** option. Notice that running this command without an option gives minimal information, but running it with the **-l** option results in a listing with more information.

LO 8.4 | Managing Files and Directories with Shell Commands

File management is one of the most important tasks to learn for any operating system. Learning how to create, manipulate, and use files is crucial to your development as a Linux user because everything in Linux is a file. That is, in addition to files as containers of data or programs, Linux represents every hardware component by a discrete file. This section begins with an overview of Linux shell commands used for file and directory management. You will practice using the **ls** command, with its most common options, and then you will create a file using a text editor and use commands to copy, move, and delete a file. Finally, you will learn how to create a directory and protect the contents of that directory.

To learn the commands, you must enter them at a Linux prompt. Sit at a Linux computer while reading the following sections because, as we examine various commands, you will have frequent opportunities to try most of them. Feel free to also experiment on your own. Note that your screen may not look exactly like the ones shown in this book. This is OK.

Working with Directories in Linux

Like Windows, Linux relies heavily on a directory structure that has several predefined directories created by default during installation. Some hold

> The terms *folder* and *directory* are synonymous in Linux, as they are in Windows. However, it is customary to use the term *folder* in a GUI and *directory* in a command line interface. Suit yourself!

important system files, and others hold user data. Linux is very similar. It has several directories for system files and a home directory for each user.

Linux Directory Hierarchy

If you want to work with Linux, you will have to understand the default Linux directory hierarchy, which contains directories that we can categorize into two types. The first type consists of directories in which an ordinary user can make changes. We call these home directories. Every user has a home directory, the one place in Linux where a user has full control over files without requiring root privileges. By default the other category consists of directories that you cannot change. These are often system directories, such as **/etc** and **/bin**, or other users' home directories.

When you log in to Linux, your home directory becomes your current (or working) directory. If you installed Linux with the defaults, your home directory path is **/home/*username*. A shorthand for this path in a shell command is ~. The default installation includes several other directories. The **/bin** directory within your home directory contains many of the Linux commands. The **/etc** directory contains settings and configuration data for your Linux computer. Do not change anything in these directories unless you know what you are doing.

The **/etc** and **/bin** directories are not the only directories included with a Linux installation. After learning how to use the **ls** command in the next section, spend some time exploring your Linux computer to see others. Some have rather strange names. Table 8–2 shows some of the default directories created during a Linux installation.

Now that you know something about the directory structure on your Linux computer, you will learn how to use shell commands to work with files and directories on your computer. Table 8–3 provides a list of basic file management commands for your reference.

Listing the Contents of a Directory. The **ls** command is the Linux equivalent of the DOS command DIR. The **ls** command lists the contents of a directory. By default, ls provides only the names of visible files in the current directory.

TABLE 8–2   Linux Default Directories

Directory	Purpose
/	The top, or root, directory
/bin	Linux commands
/boot	Files to be loaded during Linux boot-up
/dev	Device files
/etc	Linux system configuration files
/home	Contains each user's home directories
/lib	Shared libraries for programs and commands to use
/mnt	Mount points for removable devices such as floppy diskette drives, thumb drives, and CD-ROMs
/opt	Optional (add-on) software packages
/sbin	System commands and binary files
/tmp	Temporary files
/usr	Secondary hierarchy
/var	Several directories containing variable data

TABLE 8–3 Basic Shell Commands for File Management

Command	Description
cd	Changes current directory
chmod	Changes the mode or file permissions
cp	Copies a file
head	Displays the first 10 lines of a file
ls	Lists contents of a directory
mkdir	Makes a directory
more	Displays a text file, one screenful at a time
pico, vi, vim, or emacs	Creates or edits a text file
pwd	Prints the working directory
rm	Deletes a file

TABLE 8–4 Commonly Used Options for the ls Command

ls SwitchOption	Description
-a	Lists all files in the directory, including the hidden files. Files are hidden in Linux by making the first character a period, like this: **.bash_profile**
-l	Displays a long listing of the directory contents with all file attributes and permissions listed
-F	Classifies the listed objects. In particular, directory names have a / character after the name
-S	Sorts the output by size
-t	Sorts the output by time

When you work at the CLI one directory has the focus, meaning that if you enter a file management command without specifying a directory path, the command will act on that directory. When describing the directory that has the focus, we use two terms interchangeably: "current" and "working." For example, In Table 8–3 the term word "current" is used in describing the **cd** command and the word "working" is used in the description of the **cwd** command.

Table 8–4 lists the commonly used options for **ls**. For a complete list of options, enter the following: **man ls** (see Figure 8–5).

- **Simple Directory Listings:** If you enter the command **ls**, you will get a list of all files in the current directory. Figure 8–11 shows the result of typing **ls /etc**. In this listing of the etc directory, different colors

```
gnome                minicom.users      skel
gnome-vfs-2.0        modules.conf       slrn.rc
gnome-vfs-mime-magic modules.conf~      smrsh
gpm-root.conf        motd               snmp
group                mtab               sound
group-               mtools.conf        ssh
grub.conf            Muttrc             sudoers
gshadow              nscd.conf          sysconfig
gshadow-             nsswitch.conf      sysctl.conf
gtk                  ntp                syslog.conf
gtk-2.0              ntp.conf           termcap
host.conf            oaf                updatedb.conf
hosts                openldap           updfstab.conf
hosts.allow          openoffice         updfstab.conf.default
hosts.deny           opt                vfontcap
hotplug              pam.d              vfs
htdig.conf           pam_smb.conf       warnquota.conf
im_palette.pal       pango              wgetrc
im_palette-small.pal paper.config       X11
im_palette-tiny.pal  passwd             xinetd.conf
imrc                 passwd-            xinetd.d
info-dir             passwd.OLD         xml
init.d               pbm2ppa.conf       xpdfrc
initlog.conf         pcmcia             yp.conf
[jh@classlab01 jh]$ _
```

FIGURE 8–11 File listing of the /etc directory

have different meanings. White files are simple files, dark blue files are directories, green files are either programs that you can run at the command prompt or binary data files such as jpegs. Light blue files are like Windows shortcuts; they are links to files in a different directory.

- **Fancy Directory Listings:** You might notice that when you enter the **ls** command without any options, it omits details such as date of creation and length from the output. You must tell **ls** that you want these details, which requires an option. To view more detail of the **/etc** directory enter the command **ls -l /etc**; the output will be similar to that shown in Figure 8–12. The first column lists the attributes on the file or folder, which you will examine a little later in this chapter. The next column indicates the type of file. The number 1 indicates a normal file, and 2 indicates a directory. Higher numbers indicate that the file is either a special system file or a link. The next two columns list the owner (normally the user who created the file) and last modifier of the file, respectively. The next number indicates the size of the file. The next columns indicate the file creation date and time. Lastly, it shows the name of the file. If a file is a link (shown in light blue), it next lists the link location; the file after the arrow is the original file, and the light blue file name in this directory is a shortcut to the original file.

> **Finding Hidden Files**
>
> View the hidden files in the current directory. Try this:
>
> 1. Enter **ls -a** to see only the hidden files and directories in the current directory.
> 2. Practice using the **more** and **head** commands to display one of the files shown in white. Be sure to include the period in the file name. For instance, to display the file in which BASH saves a history of the commands you use in a session, type: **more .bash_history**.

try this!

Like all Microsoft OSs, Linux automatically hides certain files and directories. There are even files and directories hidden in your home directory.

Using the **ls** command with the **–a** option will reveal the entire contents of a directory, including hidden files, as shown in Figure 8–13. The period (.) preceding a file indicates that it is a hidden file. Notice that most of the hidden files in the listing are actually directories, evident by their blue color.

WARNING!

Whenever you need to use a shell command to perform an operation on a hidden file or directory, be sure to include the (.) that precedes the name.

```
-rwxr-xr-x   1 root     root       22476 Jul  9  2002 slrn.rc
drwxr-xr-x   2 root     root        4096 Aug 29  2002 smrsh
drwxr-xr-x   2 root     root        4096 Oct  4 17:52 snmp
drwxr-xr-x   3 root     root        4096 Aug 27  2002 sound
drwxr-xr-x   2 root     root        4096 Oct  4 23:14 ssh
-r--r-----   1 root     root         580 Jun 27  2002 sudoers
drwxr-xr-x   7 root     root        4096 Oct  4 23:30 sysconfig
-rw-r--r--   1 root     root         526 Sep  4  2002 sysctl.conf
-rw-r--r--   1 root     root         693 Jun 23  2002 syslog.conf
-rw-r--r--   1 root     root      737535 Jun 23  2002 termcap
-rw-r--r--   1 root     root         140 Jun 23  2002 updatedb.conf
-rw-r--r--   1 root     root          35 Sep  3  2002 updfstab.conf
-rw-r--r--   1 root     root         772 Sep  3  2002 updfstab.conf.default
lrwxrwxrwx   1 root     root          34 Oct  4 17:54 vfontcap -> ../usr/share
/VFlib/2.25.6/vfontcap
drwxr-xr-x   3 root     root        4096 Oct  4 17:58 vfs
-rw-r--r--   1 root     root         864 Sep  6  2002 warnquota.conf
-rw-r--r--   1 root     root        4022 Jul 24  2002 wgetrc
drwxr-xr-x  17 root     root        4096 Nov 29 20:11 X11
-rw-r--r--   1 root     root         289 Aug 15  2002 xinetd.conf
drwxr-xr-x   2 root     root        4096 Oct  4 17:52 xinetd.d
drwxr-xr-x   2 root     root        4096 Oct  4 17:54 xml
-rw-r--r--   1 root     root        4941 Aug 26  2002 xpdfrc
-rw-r--r--   1 root     root         361 Oct  4 18:17 yp.conf
[jh@classlab01 jh]$ _
```

FIGURE 8–12 File listing with more details

```
[jh@classlab01 jh]$ ls -a
                            .file-roller      .gtkrc-1.2-gnome2   .openoffice
                            .fonts.cache-1    .ICEauthority       .qt
.bash_history               .gconf            .kde                .rhn-applet.conf
.bash_logout                .gconfd           letter              .sversionrc
.bash_profile               .gnome            .mailcap            .Trash
.bashrc                     .gnome2           .metacity           Untitled 1
.DCOPserver_classlab01__0   .gnome2_private   .mime.types         .user60.rdb
.DCOPserver_classlab01_:0   .gnome-desktop    .nautilus           .Xauthority
.emacs                      .gphoto           .netscape           .xsession-errors
EngLitJH01                  .gqview           .netscape6
.esd_auth                   .gtkrc            old-list
[jh@classlab01 jh]$ _
```

FIGURE 8–13 A listing with all entries displayed

Using Multiple Options

Practice using **ls**. Run the command with a single option and then with multiple options. Try this:

1. Enter the command **ls /etc**.
2. Notice that **ls** defaults to column output.
3. To get a long listing of this directory, enter **ls -l /etc**. This runs the -l option on the /etc directory.
4. Now use multiple options. Enter **ls -la /etc**. This provides a long listing for all files, including hidden files, in the /etc directory.

Changing the Current Directory. As in DOS, the command to change the current directory in Linux is **cd**. The **cd** command requires just one parameter to run: the directory to change to. If the directory is a child of the current directory, then you only need the name to change to this directory. For example, suppose that in your home directory you have a child directory called private. To change to this directory, you enter **cd private**.

If the directory is not a child of the current directory, you will need to enter the path to the directory. Typically, the path will start with / (the root directory). Each directory in the path is listed after the / and separated by another /. For example, to change to the **sbin** directory under the **/usr** directory, you would enter **cd /usr/sbin**.

When you correctly use **cd** to change to a different directory, it rewards you with a change in your prompt. In Figure 8–14 the user started in the **jh** directory and changed to the sbin directory. The prompt changed to reflect the new directory. You can quickly change back to your personal home directory by entering **cd ~**. Figure 8–15 shows the result of entering this command.

Unfortunately, the Linux prompt does not (by default) show the entire path to the current directory. If you are unsure what path you are in, use the command **pwd,** which stands for *print working directory*. It does not send anything to your printer, rather it displays the path to the working (current) directory on your screen.

Using Relative Path Statements

A little practice with relative paths is helpful. Try this:

1. Type the command: **cd ..**
2. Return to your home directory by typing: **cd ~**
3. Now move to the /etc directory using a relative path: **cd ../../etc**
4. Return to your home directory by typing: **cd ~**

Relative Path. Linux allows you to use commands to navigate directories, using special symbols as shorthand for moving to directories that are relative to your current directory. For instance, the command **cd ..** will change the current directory to the next directory up in the hierarchy.

```
[jh@classlab01 jh]$ cd /usr/sbin
[jh@classlab01 sbin]$ _
```

FIGURE 8–14 Changing directories

```
[jh@classlab01 sbin]$ cd ~
[jh@classlab01 jh]$ _
```

FIGURE 8–15 Changing back to a home directory using the tilde (~)

If you are in your personal home directory, this command will move you to the home directory, one level up. You can also place the **..** characters between forward brackets (/) to move up additional levels. In addition, you can throw in a specific directory that exists at that level. For example, the command **cd ../../etc** moves up two levels and then to the etc directory. Be sure you know where you want to go, and remember, using one of these characters is supposed to save you typing. Rather than use the command string **cd ../../etc**, it is shorter to type **cd /etc**. Another special symbol is the single dot (.) which refers to the current directory. While you are first learning Linux, any path that gets you to the right place is the right path!

Wildcards. Linux supports the use of wildcards, symbols that replace any character or string of characters, at the command prompt. For instance, the use of the asterisk in a file name or directory name replaces all the characters from the point at which you place the asterisk to the end of the name. For instance bi* would include all files or directories that begin with "bi." Linux wildcard support is more flexible than that of DOS. You can enter a range of characters as a wildcard. For instance, if you enter **ls [c-d]*** the **ls** command will display all files in the current directory that begin with the letters *c* through *d*. The [] symbols are part of a Linux feature called regular expressions. Linux also allows you to use the dollar sign ($) to represent a single character within a file name, a feature also supported by DOS. We considered ourselves very experienced DOS users (back in its heyday), and we found that the $ sign was rarely worth bothering with.

Using Wildcards

1. Change to the /etc directory.
2. Enter the command **ls e***. You'll see all files that begin with the letter *e*.
3. Now enter the command **ls [c-de]* /etc**.

try this!

```
[jh@classlab01 etc]$ ls e*
esd.conf   exports

ethereal:
diameters  manuf
[jh@classlab01 etc]$ ls [b-c]*
bashrc  cdrecord.conf  crontab  csh.cshrc  csh.login

bonobo-activation:
bonobo-activation-config.xml

cron.d:

cron.daily:
00-logwatch  0anacron  logrotate  makewhatis.cron  rpm  slocate.cron  tmpwatch

cron.hourly:

cron.monthly:
0anacron

cron.weekly:
0anacron  makewhatis.cron
[jh@classlab01 etc]$
```

Using wildcards

Creating Directories

You create a directory in Linux with the **mkdir** command, which requires at least one parameter: the name of the directory to create. For example, to create a directory called junk within the current directory, enter the command **mkdir junk**. Because Linux gives you no feedback after you create a directory, use **ls** to verify that it built the directory.

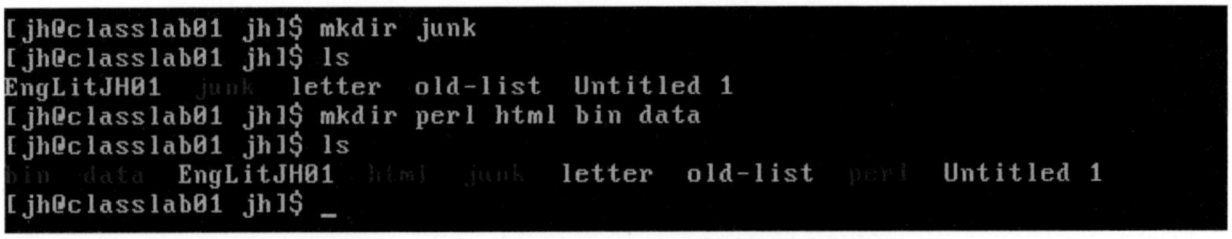

```
[jh@classlab01 jh]$ mkdir junk
[jh@classlab01 jh]$ ls
EngLitJH01    junk    letter   old-list    Untitled 1
[jh@classlab01 jh]$ mkdir perl html bin data
[jh@classlab01 jh]$ ls
bin  data    EngLitJH01   html  junk    letter   old-list    perl    Untitled 1
[jh@classlab01 jh]$ _
```

FIGURE 8–16 Using *mkdir* to create directories and *ls* to show them

try this!

Create Directories

Create directories in your home folder. Try this:

1. Enter the command **mkdir data**.
2. Use the **ls** command to confirm that it created the data directory.
3. Make several directories by entering the **mkdir** command followed by several names for new directories.
4. Use the **ls** command to confirm that it created the new directories.

If you list more than one parameter, then it will create a directory for each. Therefore, to create several directories at once, enter the command **mkdir perl html bin data** (see Figure 8–16).

Copying Files in Linux

Like DOS and Windows, Linux allows you to copy files. The command to copy files in Linux is **cp**. If you are wise, you will make a copy of a file before you change it. This allows you to recover from any changes you make.

The **cp** command requires two parameters. The first is the source file, which can be a file in the current directory or a file in another directory. The second parameter is the target, which can be a target location to copy to and/or a name for the file. Like the DOS copy command, this makes more sense after you practice using the command.

As you can see in Figure 8–17, the file ntp.conf was copied to the current directory (the period at the end represents the current directory). The file ntp.conf resides in the /etc directory. Notice that Linux does not report that it copied a file. The figure also shows that we used the **ls** command to verify a successful copy of the file.

WARNING!

A file you may want to copy is your **.bash_profile** file. This file runs when you log in to Linux. A mistake in this file can cause Linux to not work. By creating a copy of the file, you can recover if you make a mistake when changing this file.

```
[jh@classlab01 jh]$ cp /etc/ntp.conf .
[jh@classlab01 jh]$ ls
EngLitJH01    letter   ntp.conf   old-list    Untitled 1
[jh@classlab01 jh]$ _
```

FIGURE 8–17 Copying the ntp.conf file

Creating and Editing Files in Linux

In any operating system, there are times when it is useful to create and edit files with a text editor. A text editor works with plain text—that is, it works with a simple alphanumeric character set with just the minimal formatting codes reminiscent of old typewriters: carriage return (move to the beginning of the line) and line feed (move to the next line). There are also no special codes for formatting characters, as you find in word processing. You use text editors to create simple script files, programming code, and for any other occasion when you do not want extraneous code in a file. Many text editors are available for Linux. A few that you may encounter are Pico, vi/Vim, and Emacs. Learn how to use a text editor if you ever plan to write a script or program in Linux.

Using Pico. While not the most popular Linux text editor, Pico is a good one for a beginner because it has a few features that make it attractive to a new user:

- It provides a series of commands at the bottom of the screen.
- It allows you to use the keyboard as expected—Backspace and Delete work as usual.
- Text will wrap to the next line after you enter 80 characters (a feature we take for granted in a word processor, but one that is not always included in a text editor).

We use it here as an example of a text editor that runs on BASH, and because you will find that for anyone with even a little experience with a word processor, entering text into Pico seems to work as you expect it to. If you need help with spelling, you are in luck too, because Pico includes a spell checker, accessed by pressing CTRL-T, but you will quickly notice that the checker is not quite as nice as the spell checker in Microsoft Word.

Table 8–5 lists handy Pico commands. Figure 8–18 shows Pico with an open document. (Saying nice things to a teacher or instructor will rarely hurt your grade!)

Create a File

Use a Linux text editor to create a file. In this example we use Pico. Try this:

1. To use Pico to create a file named "instructor_letter" type the following at the $ prompt: **pico instructor_letter**. If you're not using Pico, substitute the name of the editor you are using.

2. Type a letter. When you are done, use the command to save a file. In Pico this command is CTRL-O.

3. Exit from the text editor. In Pico the command to exit is CTRL-X.

The Vi/Vim Text Editor. One of the oldest editors around is vi, which is a line editor. You essentially edit one line at a time. A group of programs designated Vim, or Vi Improved, has become the most popular Linux text editor. Ramesh Natarajan of www.thegeekstuff.com asked readers to name what they judged to be the best Linux editor. Of the 200 respondents, 137 named Vim. While it does show improvements over vi, Vim is still more difficult to use than Pico because it does not keep the basic commands visible to the

TABLE 8–5 Common Pico Commands

Pico Command	Description
CTRL-O	Saves the current file. If it is unnamed, it will prompt you to name it.
CTRL-R	Opens another text file. You will need to enter the name of the file you want to open.
CTRL-T	Spell-checks the current document.
CTRL-X	Exits Pico. If the current file is unsaved, it will prompt you to save the file.

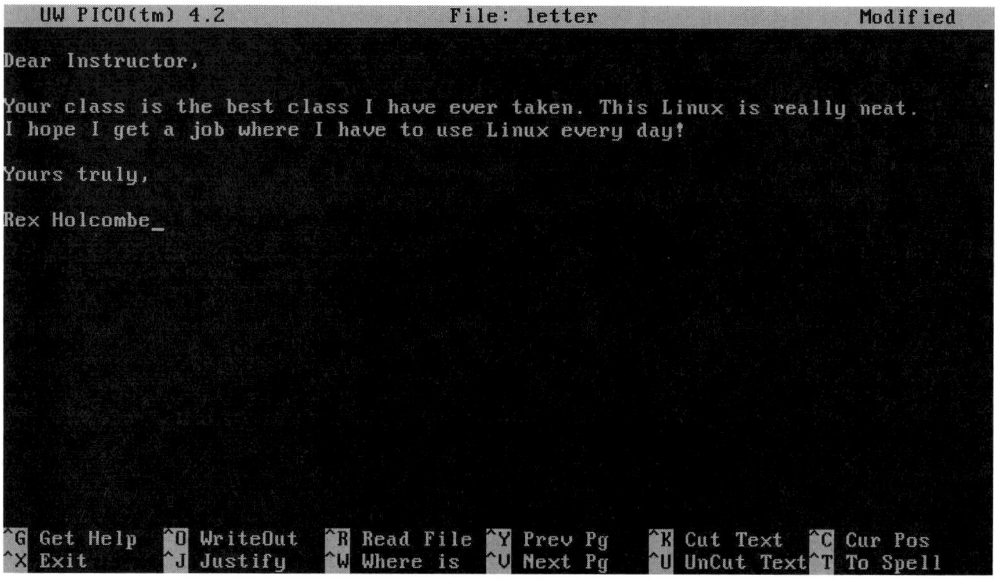

FIGURE 8–18 The Pico editor with an open document

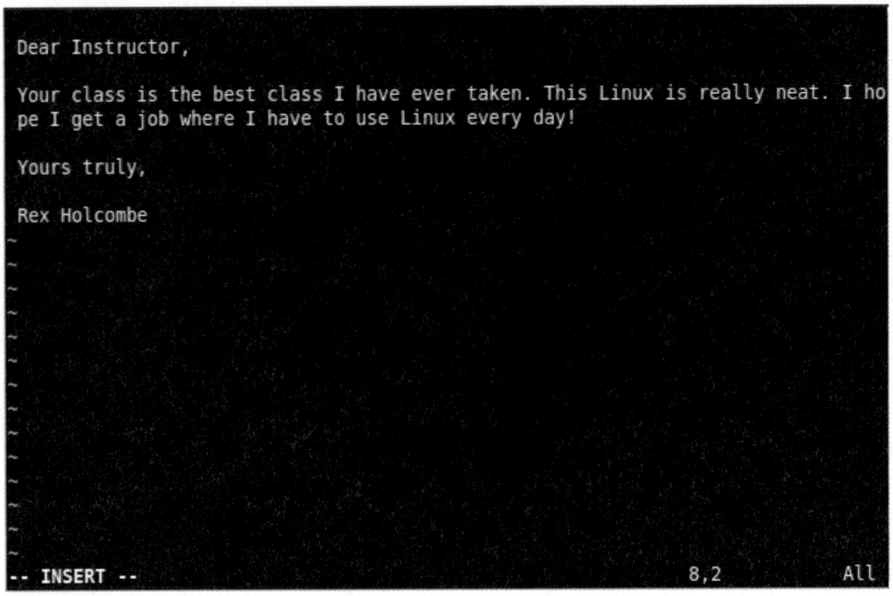

```
Dear Instructor,

Your class is the best class I have ever taken. This Linux is really neat. I ho
pe I get a job where I have to use Linux every day!

Yours truly,

Rex Holcombe

~
~
~
~
~
~
~
~
~
~
~
-- INSERT --                                                    8,2              All
```

FIGURE 8–19 The Vim user interface with a document open

user. Figure 8–19 shows the Vim interface. Notice that, while it does wrap the text at the end of the line, it breaks a word in a nonstandard way to do it.

The Emacs Text Editor. In that same informal survey mentioned above, Emacs was a distant second to Vim. Emacs has several features designed for programmers. One of these is called the Emacs dance. When you close a pair of quotation marks or parentheses, the cursor jumps back to the item that you are closing. This feature helps developers with complex code.

Deleting Files in Linux

When you find you no longer need a file, you should delete it to free disk space and to make life less confusing. The command to delete a file is **rm**. The **rm** command requires at least one parameter: the name of the file to delete. If you include more than one file name, it will erase each file. Figure 8–20 shows a listing of the home directory for jh, then we ran the **rm** command with the names of two files: letter and ntp.conf. Finally, another listing shows that those files no longer exist in the directory.

> **WARNING!**
>
> Linux does not have an undelete command. Only delete files that you created yourself and that you are certain the operating system or other programs don't need.

try this!

> **Deleting Files**
>
> Practice deleting files. Try this:
>
> 1. To delete the file you copied earlier, enter this command:
>   **rm ntp.conf.**
> 2. Enter **ls** to list your files to verify that the copy operation worked.

Renaming or Moving Files in Linux

The **cp** command allows you to have two versions of a file, which is a good thing to do before making changes to an important file. There are also times when you want to rename a file. The net result is one

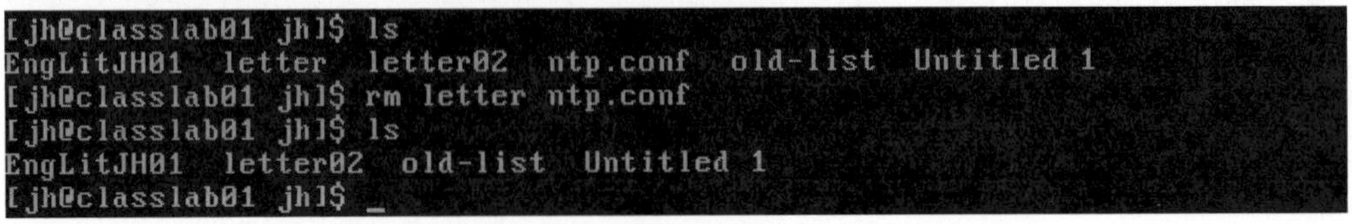

```
[jh@classlab01 jh]$ ls
EngLitJH01  letter  letter02  ntp.conf  old-list  Untitled 1
[jh@classlab01 jh]$ rm letter ntp.conf
[jh@classlab01 jh]$ ls
EngLitJH01  letter02  old-list  Untitled 1
[jh@classlab01 jh]$ _
```

FIGURE 8–20 Using the **rm** command to delete a file

instance of the file, not two instances like you get with the **copy** command. Copying the file and then deleting the original file can accomplish this, but it is handy to be able to do this in just one operation, which you can do with the **mv** command. The **mv** command can rename a file in the current directory, or move the file from the current directory to a different directory.

```
[jh@classlab01 jh]$ mv letter instructor_letter
[jh@classlab01 jh]$ ls
instructor_letter
[jh@classlab01 jh]$ _
```

Renaming a file with the **mv** command

The **mv** command requires two parameters: the name of the original file and the new name or location of the file. If the original file does not exist, then you will get an error message. If you cannot delete or change the original file, then **mv** will generate an error message.

Renaming a File

Practice renaming a file. Try this:

1. Log in as a regular user, not root. Use **mv** to rename your file. Enter the command **mv letter instructor_letter**.
2. Use the **ls** command to verify the name change.

try this!

Viewing the Contents of a File. A typical Linux directory contains many files. You often need to know what is in the files, so there are several Linux commands that let you view files. These include **more**, **head**, **less**, **tail**, and **cat**. These commands are viewers for text files. When you use one of these commands on a text file, you will see standard text characters. However, if you use one of these commands to view a program (binary) file, you will see mostly nonsense (techies call it garbage) on your screen.

- The **more** command displays the entire contents of a file page (or screenful) at a time. Press the space bar to view another page; press the ENTER key to see another line. The **more** command can be used on more than file contents. You can use the **more** command for those shell commands that put so much information on the screen that the beginning scrolls off before you can read it. When you get ready to enter a command that you believe will scroll off the screen, simply add "| more" to the end of the command line—without quotes, of course. For instance, the command **ls –a** will often produce more than a screenful of output, so add the **more** command: **ls –a | more.** The vertical bar is called a pipe symbol, and when used this way, you are "piping" the output of the first command to the **more** command, and it, in turn, displays the output from the first command, one page at a time (see Figure 8–21).

```
[jh@classlab01 jh]$ ls -a | more
.
..
.bash_history
.bash_logout
.bash_proback
.bash_profile
.bashrc
.emacs
.esd_auth
.fonts.cache-1
.gconf
.gconfd
.gnome
.gnome2
.gnome2_private
.gnome-desktop
.gtkrc
.gtkrc-1.2-gnome2
.ICEauthority
instructor_letter
.kde
.metacity
.mozilla
--More--
```

FIGURE 8–21 Using the **more** command.

- The **head** command displays just the first 10 lines of a file, which is helpful on occasions when you don't want to see the entire file, and the first few lines will suffice.
- The **less** command is nearly equivalent to the **more** command. The difference is that the **less** command allows you to move forward and backward in the file, whereas the **more** command only allows you to move forward. Thus, the **less** command has more features than the **more** command. (This is more Linux humor.)
- The **tail** command displays the last 10 lines of a file.
- The **cat** command displays the entire contents of a file. Be careful with the cat command because "catting" a large file can take some time.

LO 8.5 | Securing a Linux Desktop

It is important to know how to configure a computer for the needs of users. This includes managing user accounts and applying security to directories. These involve tasks that require the use of the root account. In this section you will learn a handy command and technique for using the root account while logged on as an ordinary user. Then you will work with user account management tasks, including creating new accounts, changing user passwords, and deleting user accounts.

Using the Root Account

The root account can access any file or program on a computer. It is also required to shut down Linux from the command line interface (CLI). Be very careful with your use of root. Log in as root only when you need to perform system maintenance tasks. Create a strong password for root and take steps to remember and protect this password. If you forget this password you will not be able to access administrative functions on your system, which will ultimately require entering the root password recovery process—which is something you will not enjoy!

In your encounters with Linux, you may see the term superuser. The superuser is not a comic book hero; superuser is simply another name for root. This name still appears in Linux or UNIX help pages and chat rooms, and if you're going to be surfing these Internet spots, you need to be savvy about the vocabulary.

Performing Administrative Tasks at the Command Shell or Terminal Window

As a rule, if you log on as an ordinary user and work at the CLI when you realize that you need to perform something that requires superuser capabilities, enter the command **su root** and then enter the root password. You will then have root permissions. The **su** command stands for substitute user, but if it helps you to remember the command, think of it as standing for superuser, although it allows you to substitute the current user with any other user. If you don't specify a user name, then Linux assumes that you are logging in as root. Figure 8–22 shows user jh logging in as root. The only clue you'll see that she logged in as root is the # prompt that indicates the root account.

The current Ubuntu distribution offers an alternative to the **su** command: the **sudo** command. The **sudo** command seems to have the same effect, but what it actually does is temporarily assign root account privileges to the currently logged on user, without having the user log out and log in again. During installation Ubuntu creates two user accounts: a primary user account and a root account. The primary user account works much like a standard

WARNING!

Be careful when logged in as root because you have the ability to do anything you want to the system— and if you are working with shell commands, you will not receive a warning when you attempt to delete a file—even if it is a critical one.

account in Windows with User Account Control enabled, so when you need to perform administrative functions, you do not log out as a primary user and log in as root. You temporarily use root account privileges for administrative tasks, such as installing or removing software, creating or removing users, and modifying system files. When you use **sudo** at the CLI, it will prompt you to enter *your* password (not the root password). So, if you want to open an editor with root privileges so that you can edit a file that a standard user would not be able to edit, open the terminal window, and, at the $ prompt, enter **sudo pico**. The output looks like the example shown here with a simple password prompt and blinking cursor. As soon as you enter the password, the command will complete. In this case, it will open the Pico text editor.

FIGURE 8–22 After logging on as *root* the # prompt displays.

The GNOME version of sudo is **gksudo**. When you run **gksudo** with the command you want to run with root privileges, it opens a graphic box requesting your password. So, to open the Pico editor with root privileges, open a terminal window and enter this command: **gksudo pico**. Figure 8–23 shows the GUI prompt that appears, requiring your password.

The **sudo** command prompts for a password before executing a command.

Performing Administrative Tasks in a GUI

In the GNOME GUI in Ubuntu whenever you attempt to do an administrative task, it will prompt you to supply your user password, as shown in Figure 8–24. This is sudo at work; it reminds you that you are performing an administrative task and requires that you supply your password before it will proceed.

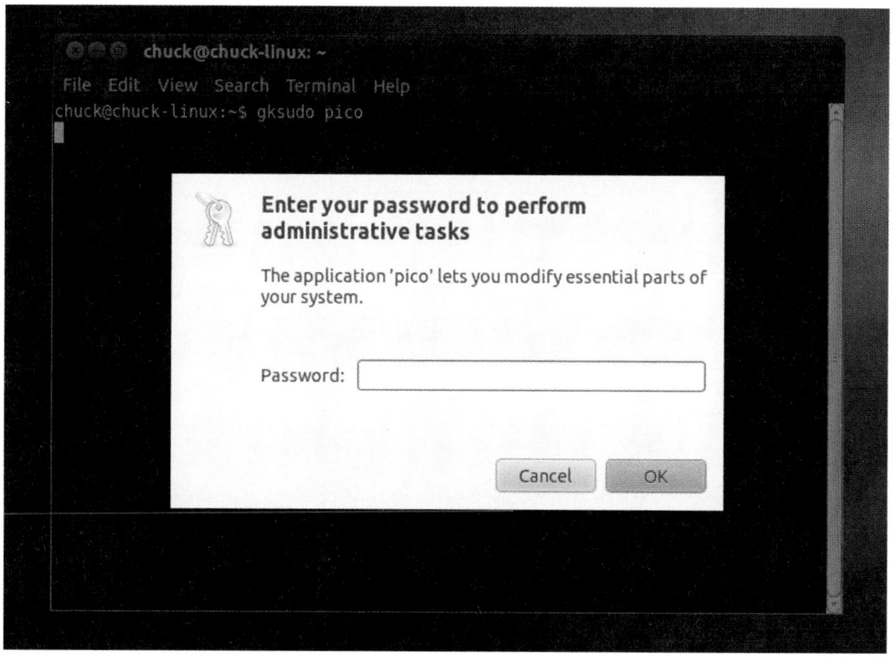

FIGURE 8–23 The **gksudo** command prompts you for the password of the current user—not the root account.

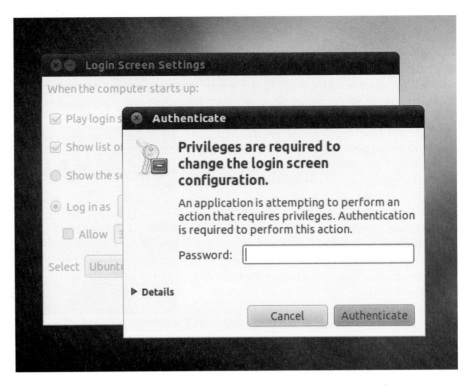

FIGURE 8–24 Supply your password to perform an administrative task.

Managing Users

Linux allows several users to use one computer, but each user should have a unique account. When you create a user account, Linux also creates a home directory for the new user in which that user can both save files and create new subdirectories. Users can further protect files from other users by changing the permissions on files and folders in their home directories.

Normally, the primary account created during installation and the built-in root account are all you need on a Linux desktop. However, if you plan to allow more than one user to use a Linux computer, you will need to learn how to create users, delete users, and change user passwords. You can create user accounts with command shell commands or from within a GUI, using a tool such as Users Settings, available in Ubuntu Linux from System | Administrations | Users and Groups (see Figure 8–25). Of course, when you attempt to make any changes, it will prompt you to authenticate.

Advanced Linux users find it faster to add and change users at the CLI than to do so using a GUI. We believe that if you need to create only a few users on a few computers, it is easier to work through the GUI. However, if you need to manage users on a Linux computer without a GUI, you will need to know how to work with shell commands. Table 8–6 lists useful commands for managing users from the command shell.

TABLE 8–6	Shell Commands for User Management
Command	**Description**
useradd	Adds a user to the system
userdel	Removes a user from the system
passwd	Changes a user's password
finger	Finds a user name

FIGURE 8–25 A GUI tool for user management

The **finger** command allows you to look up user information, but some installations of Linux (including Ubuntu) do not automatically install it. Therefore, if you want to experiment with the **finger** command, you must install the finger daemon using **sudo apt-get install finger**, which should result in the output shown here.

> A daemon is a program that runs in background until it is activated. Once installed, the **finger** daemon, is activated by running the **finger** command.

```
chuck@chuck-linux:~$ sudo apt-get install finger
[sudo] password for chuck:
Reading package lists... Done
Building dependency tree
Reading state information... Done
The following NEW packages will be installed:
  finger
0 upgraded, 1 newly installed, 0 to remove and 6 not upgraded.
Need to get 18.6kB of archives.
After this operation, 77.8kB of additional disk space will be used.
Get:1 http://us.archive.ubuntu.com/ubuntu/ maverick/main finger i386 0.17-14 [18
.6kB]
Fetched 18.6kB in 0s (19.8kB/s)
Selecting previously deselected package finger.
(Reading database ... 121069 files and directories currently installed.)
Unpacking finger (from .../finger_0.17-14_i386.deb) ...
Processing triggers for man-db ...
Setting up finger (0.17-14) ...
chuck@chuck-linux:~$
```

Installing the **finger** daemon

> **WARNING!**
>
> There is a good reason the **finger** command is not automatically installed. It is considered a security risk. However, you can choose to install it, and then disable it when you do not need it.

Creating User Accounts

Before creating user accounts, you develop at least an informal naming convention for creating user names—the names the users will use to log in. For ease of use, the user name should be short and, of course, it must be unique in the accounts database. A common rule is to use the first letter of the first name plus the last name, or a portion of the last name. From the command shell, use the **useradd** command to create a user. This command

```
[root@classlab01 root]# useradd aphoenix
[root@classlab01 root]# finger aphoenix
Login: aphoenix                         Name: (null)
Directory: /home/aphoenix               Shell: /bin/bash
Never logged in.
No mail.
No Plan.
[root@classlab01 root]# _
```

FIGURE 8–26 Using the **useradd** command to create a user

Creating New Users

Practice creating user accounts for Ashley Phoenix, Jose Martinez, Kiesha Olson, and Beverly Chung. The naming convention method you will use for user name logins is a combination of the first letter of the first name with the last name, so the user names will be aphoenix, jmartinez, kolson, and bchung. Try this:

1. Log into the system as root (or alternatively, precede each command with **sudo**). Start by creating one user, Ashley Phoenix.

2. Enter the command **useradd aphoenix**.

3. Confirm that Linux added the account by entering the command **finger aphoenix**.

4. Now add the remaining three names.

Change a Password

Create passwords for the accounts you created. If you did not log on as root, begin the first command with the **sudo** command. Try this:

1. Create passwords for Ashley Phoenix (aphoenix), Jose Martinez (jmartinez), Kiesha Olson (kolson), and Beverly Chung (bchung). Use the **passwd** command individually for each account.

2. If you logged on as root, change the password for the root account. Enter the command **passwd** with no user name. Be sure to memorize this password!

requires at least one parameter, the user name you want to add. For instance, to create an account for Ashley Phoenix using the user name of aphoenix, enter the command **useradd aphoenix**. To verify that it created the user account, use **finger aphoenix** (see Figure 8–26).

Changing User Passwords

Setting up a user without a password is a bad idea. The password proves that the correct user is logging in. Changing a user's password involves the command **passwd**. Entering **passwd** without any additional parameters will let you change your own password. Any user can change his or her own password, but only a user using root privileges can change the password on other user accounts. For example, entering **passwd aphoenix** will enable the root account to change the password for the aphoenix account. The user logged on as root does not need to know the current password for the account before changing it to the new one, but can simply enter the new password twice. Figure 8–27 shows a successful password change. Note that, as always, Linux doesn't display passwords.

```
[root@classlab01 root]# passwd aphoenix
Changing password for user aphoenix.
New password:
Retype new password:
passwd: all authentication tokens updated successfully.
[root@classlab01 root]# _
```

FIGURE 8–27 Using **root** to change another account's password

Note that selecting passwords can be difficult. Linux will force the password to be complex. If you have a problem coming up with an appropriate password, review the discussion on passwords in Chapter 2.

Deleting Users

In any organization, employees leave. For security reasons, you should remove these accounts from the system shortly after the employee leaves. The command **userdel** allows you to remove a user from a Linux account.

The syntax for userdel is similar to that for **passwd** and **useradd**. You use this format:

```
userdel username
```

For example, you can remove the aphoenix account with the command **userdel aphoenix**.

Recall that every user has a home directory in which to store his or her files. When you delete a user you do not remove this directory—you must remove these files manually. The long explanation for doing this is to delete the files contained in the home directory first; then delete the directory itself. However, if a directory has subdirectories, you first need to switch into each subdirectory and delete all files in those as well. Once you have deleted the files, you change the directory to one level above and use the **rmdir** command. The syntax for **rmdir** is as follows: **rmdir** *directoryname*.

Now, for the quicker method for deleting a directory and its contents, remember the **rmdir** command can only remove empty directories, but the **rm** command removes a directory and its contents. Use the **rm** command with the –r (remove) and –f (force); type **rm –rf** *directory-or-file-name* to remove a directory and everything below it. (Be careful!)

File and Folder Permissions

One of the benefits of Linux is the security. However, unless you implement the security features, anyone can access anyone else's directories and files on the Linux computer. To secure your files, you need to decide which files you want to secure.

To implement security for a file or folder, you must first understand Linux file and folder attributes. When you use the –l option with the **ls** command you will see the attributes listed in a column of 10 characters on the far left. Each character is significant in both its placement (first, second, etc.) and in what each single character represents. The first character at the far left indicates whether the entry is a file (-), directory (d), or link (l). The next nine characters show the permissions on the file or folder for three different entities. Figure 8–28 shows a listing of a directory using both the -a and -l options to show the attributes of all entries. To decode the permissions, use the following list:

r = read

w = write

x = execute

- = disabled

Notice the set of permissions for the link named awk. They repeat three times. Linux is not repeating itself; it is listing permissions for three different groups of people. The first set of three permissions applies to the user who owns the files (owner). Normally, if you create a file, then you are the owner.

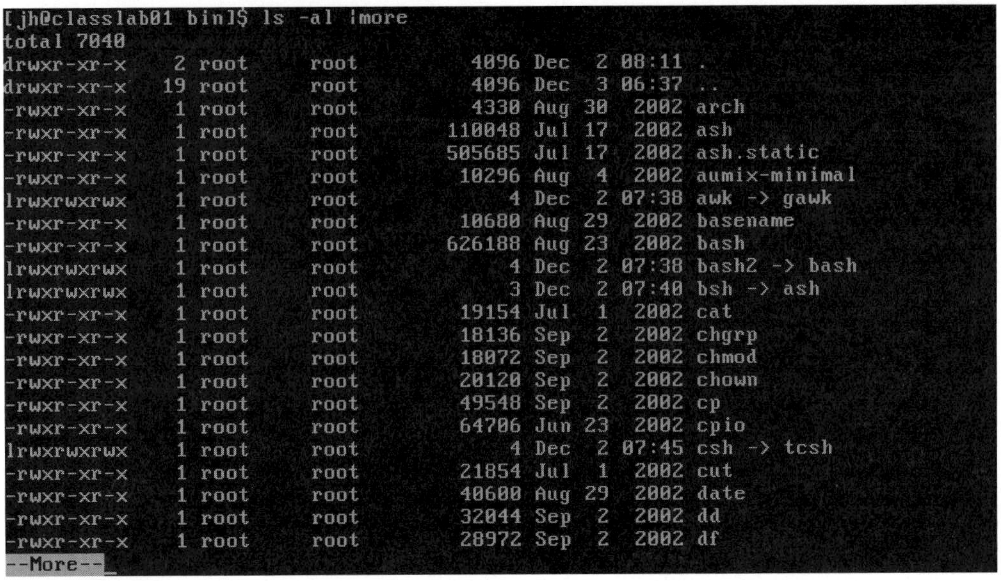

```
[jh@classlab01 bin]$ ls -al ¦more
total 7040
drwxr-xr-x    2 root     root        4096 Dec  2 08:11 .
drwxr-xr-x   19 root     root        4096 Dec  3 06:37 ..
-rwxr-xr-x    1 root     root        4330 Aug 30  2002 arch
-rwxr-xr-x    1 root     root      110048 Jul 17  2002 ash
-rwxr-xr-x    1 root     root      505685 Jul 17  2002 ash.static
-rwxr-xr-x    1 root     root       10296 Aug  4  2002 aumix-minimal
lrwxrwxrwx    1 root     root           4 Dec  2 07:38 awk -> gawk
-rwxr-xr-x    1 root     root       10680 Aug 29  2002 basename
-rwxr-xr-x    1 root     root      626188 Aug 23  2002 bash
lrwxrwxrwx    1 root     root           4 Dec  2 07:38 bash2 -> bash
lrwxrwxrwx    1 root     root           3 Dec  2 07:40 bsh -> ash
-rwxr-xr-x    1 root     root       19154 Jul  1  2002 cat
-rwxr-xr-x    1 root     root       18136 Sep  2  2002 chgrp
-rwxr-xr-x    1 root     root       18072 Sep  2  2002 chmod
-rwxr-xr-x    1 root     root       20120 Sep  2  2002 chown
-rwxr-xr-x    1 root     root       49548 Sep  2  2002 cp
-rwxr-xr-x    1 root     root       64706 Jun 23  2002 cpio
lrwxrwxrwx    1 root     root           4 Dec  2 07:45 csh -> tcsh
-rwxr-xr-x    1 root     root       21854 Jul  1  2002 cut
-rwxr-xr-x    1 root     root       40600 Aug 29  2002 date
-rwxr-xr-x    1 root     root       32044 Sep  2  2002 dd
-rwxr-xr-x    1 root     root       28972 Sep  2  2002 df
--More--
```

FIGURE 8–28 A sample listing showing attributes

To remember the order of the groups, think of the name UGO. UGO stands for User, Group, Other.

WARNING!

Always be sure the file owner has at least an access mode number of 6 for a file, which allows for read and write permissions. If the mode for the owner drops below 6, on some Linux installations any future access to this file is blocked. You should rarely have a file with permissions of 777 because it means that anyone can change the file.

The second set of three permissions applies to the group the user belongs to. We use groups to organize users, joining those with similar needs and access privileges. For example, a school may group all faculty members into a single group. This will allow instructors to create files that other instructors can read, but that students cannot read. The third set of three permissions applies to all others. So the read, write, and execute permissions on awk apply to the owner (root), the owner's group, and all others. The permissions on the file arch are set so that the owner has read, write, and execute permissions, but the owner's group and all others have only read and execute permissions, meaning only the owner can change or delete the file.

The command to change a file's permissions is **chmod** (called change mode). The **chmod** command requires two options. The first option is the access mode number. The second option is the file to change.

There is a small calculation to perform to determine the access mode number. In Figure 8–28, the file awk has access mode number 777, and arch has access mode number 755. You can calculate this number by using the values in Table 8–7. Determine the permission for each user or group by adding the values together. Thus, if the owner needs to read, write, and execute a file, the first number is $4 + 2 + 1 = 7$. If the group is to also read, write, and execute the file, the second number is also 7. If a user has permission only to read and execute a file, the value is $4 + 1 = 5$.

TABLE 8–7 Access Mode Numbers	
Permission	Value
Read	4
Write	2
Execute	1

Working with Directories

Imagine that a marketing firm that uses Linux as its primary OS hired you. You will work with a group of users. You will need to create a series of directories that the group can see as well as a private directory that no one else but you can see. Be sure that you log in as a regular user. The following steps will allow you to create directories and set permissions on the directories.

You will create these directories in your own home directory.

You will need the following:

- A Linux computer.
- An account on this computer.
- Read access to the /etc directory.

Step 1

First create the directories needed to work. Use **mkdir** to create two directories, called wineProject and private, entering this command: **mkdir wineProject private**.

Step 2

Use the command **ls –l** to verify that Linux created the directories and to view the permissions assigned to the directories by default.

```
[jh@classlab01 wineProject]$ ls -l
total 8
-rw-rw-r--    1 jh        jh              70 Dec  3 10:11 busplan2006
-rw-rw-r--    1 jh        jh             178 Dec  3 10:10 instructor_letter
[jh@classlab01 wineProject]$ cd ~
[jh@classlab01 jh]$ ls -l
total 216
-rw-rw-r--    1 jh        jh              70 Dec  3 08:14 busplan2006
-rw-rw-r--    1 jh        jh             178 Dec  2 19:51 instructor_letter
-rw-r--r--    1 jh        jh            9283 Dec  2 22:03 mailcap
-rw-r--r--    1 jh        jh             112 Dec  2 22:03 mail.rc
-rw-r--r--    1 jh        jh            4426 Dec  2 22:03 man.config
-rw-r--r--    1 jh        jh           36823 Dec  3 06:49 mime-magic
-rw-r--r--    1 jh        jh           99960 Dec  2 22:03 mime-magic.dat
-rw-r--r--    1 jh        jh           12786 Dec  2 22:03 mime.types
-rw-r--r--    1 jh        jh            1110 Dec  2 22:03 minicom.users
-rw-r--r--    1 jh        jh             311 Dec  2 22:03 modules.conf
-rw-r--r--    1 jh        jh             281 Dec  2 22:03 modules.conf~
-rw-r--r--    1 jh        jh               0 Dec  2 22:03 motd
-rw-r--r--    1 jh        jh             242 Dec  2 22:03 mtab
-rw-r--r--    1 jh        jh            1913 Dec  2 22:04 mtools.conf
drwxrwxr-x    2 jh        jh            4096 Dec  3 10:10 private
drwxrwxr-x    2 jh        jh            4096 Dec  3 10:11 wineProject
[jh@classlab01 jh]$ _
```

Step 3

You are now the owner of these directories. Set the permissions on the private directory so that only you can access it, and on the wineProject directory give yourself read, write, and execute permissions, only read and write permissions to users in your group, and no permissions for others. To set the permissions appropriately enter these two commands: **chmod 700 private** and **chmod 760 wineProject**.

Confirm the new permissions using **ls -l**.

```
[jh@classlab01 jh]$ chmod 700 private
[jh@classlab01 jh]$ chmod 760 wineProject
[jh@classlab01 jh]$ ls -l
total 216
-rw-rw-r--   1 jh       jh            70 Dec  3 08:14 busplan2006
-rw-rw-r--   1 jh       jh           178 Dec  2 19:51 instructor_letter
-rw-r--r--   1 jh       jh          9283 Dec  2 22:03 mailcap
-rw-r--r--   1 jh       jh           112 Dec  2 22:03 mail.rc
-rw-r--r--   1 jh       jh          4426 Dec  2 22:03 man.config
-rw-r--r--   1 jh       jh         36823 Dec  3 06:49 mime-magic
-rw-r--r--   1 jh       jh         99960 Dec  2 22:03 mime-magic.dat
-rw-r--r--   1 jh       jh         12786 Dec  2 22:03 mime.types
-rw-r--r--   1 jh       jh          1110 Dec  2 22:03 minicom.users
-rw-r--r--   1 jh       jh           311 Dec  2 22:03 modules.conf
-rw-r--r--   1 jh       jh           281 Dec  2 22:03 modules.conf~
-rw-r--r--   1 jh       jh             0 Dec  2 22:03 motd
-rw-r--r--   1 jh       jh           242 Dec  2 22:03 mtab
-rw-r--r--   1 jh       jh          1913 Dec  2 22:04 mtools.conf
drwx------   2 jh       jh          4096 Dec  3 10:10 private
drwxrw----   2 jh       jh          4096 Dec  3 10:11 wineProject
[jh@classlab01 jh]$ _
```

Populate the wineProject directory by copying two files into it from your home directory, using the **cp** command. For instance, to copy the file named "letter" type **cp letter wineProject.**

Change to the wineProject directory by entering the command **cd wineProject.** Confirm that the files are there and view the permissions on the files. They do not inherit the permissions of the directory. You will need to modify the permissions on the files if you wish permissions more restrictive than those assigned to the directory. However, any restrictive directory permissions will keep users from accessing the contents of the directory.

```
[jh@classlab01 jh]$ cp instructor_letter wineProject
[jh@classlab01 jh]$ cp busplan2006 wineProject
[jh@classlab01 jh]$ cd wineProject
[jh@classlab01 wineProject]$ ls
busplan2006  instructor_letter
[jh@classlab01 wineProject]$ ls -l
total 8
-rw-rw-r--   1 jh       jh            70 Dec  3 10:11 busplan2006
-rw-rw-r--   1 jh       jh           178 Dec  3 10:10 instructor_letter
[jh@classlab01 wineProject]$ _
```

LO 8.6 | Troubleshooting Common Linux Problems

This section describes typical problems you may encounter when using Linux and possible solutions.

Cannot Save File

You may sometimes see an error message similar to the one seen near the bottom of Figure 8–29: "Cannot open file for writing: Permission denied."

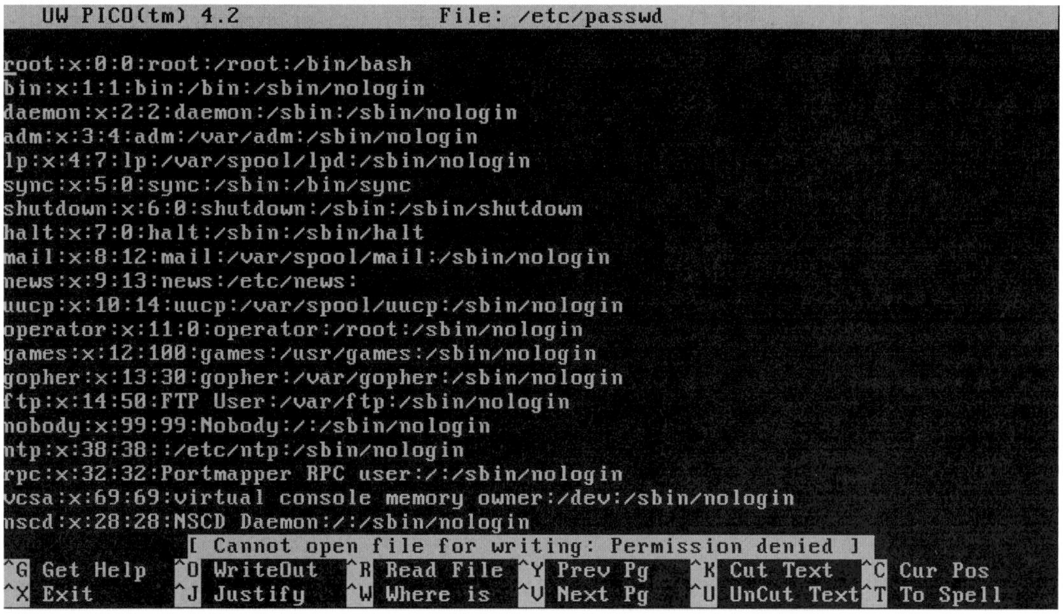

```
UW PICO(tm) 4.2                   File: /etc/passwd

root:x:0:0:root:/root:/bin/bash
bin:x:1:1:bin:/bin:/sbin/nologin
daemon:x:2:2:daemon:/sbin:/sbin/nologin
adm:x:3:4:adm:/var/adm:/sbin/nologin
lp:x:4:7:lp:/var/spool/lpd:/sbin/nologin
sync:x:5:0:sync:/sbin:/bin/sync
shutdown:x:6:0:shutdown:/sbin:/sbin/shutdown
halt:x:7:0:halt:/sbin:/sbin/halt
mail:x:8:12:mail:/var/spool/mail:/sbin/nologin
news:x:9:13:news:/etc/news:
uucp:x:10:14:uucp:/var/spool/uucp:/sbin/nologin
operator:x:11:0:operator:/root:/sbin/nologin
games:x:12:100:games:/usr/games:/sbin/nologin
gopher:x:13:30:gopher:/var/gopher:/sbin/nologin
ftp:x:14:50:FTP User:/var/ftp:/sbin/nologin
nobody:x:99:99:Nobody:/:/sbin/nologin
ntp:x:38:38::/etc/ntp:/sbin/nologin
rpc:x:32:32:Portmapper RPC user:/:/sbin/nologin
vcsa:x:69:69:virtual console memory owner:/dev:/sbin/nologin
nscd:x:28:28:NSCD Daemon:/:/sbin/nologin
                 [ Cannot open file for writing: Permission denied ]
^G Get Help   ^O WriteOut   ^R Read File  ^Y Prev Pg   ^K Cut Text   ^C Cur Pos
^X Exit       ^J Justify    ^W Where is   ^V Next Pg   ^U UnCut Text ^T To Spell
```

FIGURE 8–29 Error screen in an application indicating trouble saving a file

Typically, this appears when you try to save a file anywhere but in your home directory or in a subdirectory you have created in your home directory. You simply lack the permissions to write a file in the target directory. The solution is to direct the application in which you are working to save the file in a location within your home directory.

Screen Displays Gibberish

Does your screen display gibberish? This error usually occurs when you use the **head** or **cat** command on a file that contains non-text data. Figure 8–30 shows the results of entering a **head** command for a binary file.

FIGURE 8–30 Results of entering a **head** command for a.out

This is not an error—it is simply the result of trying to view executable or binary code. The code is in a language that your CPU can understand, but that you can't.

Often, after a gibberish display, your prompt and input will be messed up. Linux is now confused and displays the wrong characters. The last line of Figure 8–30 is an attempt to type **ls** at the $ prompt. The easiest way to fix this problem is to log out and then in again.

> Although the file used to produce the error in Figure 8–30 is a binary code, you see some recognizable characters because the value of each byte in the file is interpreted as text and other special characters as it is sent to the screen by the command.

Command Not Found Error

Working at the command shell almost guarantees that you will see the error "Command not found." The No. 1 cause of such an error is typos. Use the up arrow on the keyboard to move up through the command line history and double-check the string you entered. Use the left and right arrow keys to move through the line and correct your error. Press ENTER when you are ready to test the corrected command.

Chapter 8 REVIEW

Chapter Summary

After reading this chapter and completing the Step-by-Step tutorials and Try This! exercises, you should understand the following facts about Linux.

Linux Overview

- Linux, originally created by Linus Torvalds, is free, open source software that is like UNIX in stability and function.
- Many versions of Linux exist for all types of computers, and people often use Linux on Web servers.
- Linux benefits include cost (it is free or inexpensively bundled), the ability to run on old hardware, speed, and stability.
- Drawbacks of Linux include lack of centralized support, limited software selection, limited hardware support, and complexity.

Installing Linux

- Decide how to install—clean installation, upgrade, or dual boot. Keep the installation simple and fine-tune it later, especially as far as undetected devices go.
- Linux memory and hard disk space requirements are small compared to Windows operating systems.

- Linux supports all standard video graphics adapters and monitors; supports the use of a mouse, primarily in graphics interfaces; and supports many printers, modems, and network adapters.
- Be prepared to work with the root account (superuser) before installing Linux; give this account a strong password, and only use it when you need to perform system maintenance tasks.
- Many Linux installation programs now run in GUI mode, providing online help in a pane on screen throughout the process.

Linux Basics

- Linux requires authentication via a login—either in the command shell or in a GUI.
- The Linux shell is called BASH.
- The $ (dollar) prompt appears when an ordinary user logs in to the command shell. It consists of the user name and the computer name (host name) separated by an @ sign, followed again by the user name (this last indicates the name of the current directory).
- When the root account logs in at the command shell, the prompt is similar, but ends with a # sign.

- Log out of Linux by typing **exit** at the prompt, which allows you to leave Linux without shutting down.
- Only root can shut down Linux from the command line. You accomplish this with the shutdown command, which has many options (that change the outcome of a command).
- Linux is case sensitive, while DOS and the Windows command prompt are case *in*sensitive.
- An option is a subcommand that changes the outcome of a command. Many options are preceded by a hyphen (-).
- Linux requires that you separate each part of a command line entry with a space.
- In DOS, a full path to a file or directory begins with a drive letter, but Linux does not use drive letters.
- Linux shows each device as part of the file system as in **/dev/sda0** (the first hard drive on a SCSI interface).
- The **man** command gives you access to the Linux shell commands help manual.

Managing Files and Directories with Shell Commands

- Linux has several directories for system files and a home directory for each user.
- Your home directory is the only place you can save files, and when you log in this directory becomes your current (or working) directory.
- The /bin directory within your home directory contains many of the Linux commands.
- The /etc directory contains settings and configuration data for your Linux computer. There are many other directories created for the system's use, and an ordinary user cannot access these directories.
- You use the **ls**, **cd**, **more**, **mkdir**, **cp**, **rm**, and **mv** commands in file management.
- You can use the, **head**, **less**, **tail**, and **cat** commands to view files.

- You can use special symbols with the shell commands to navigate to directories that are relative to your current directory.
- Use the asterisk (*) wildcard to replace all the characters from the point where you place the asterisk to the end of the name. Use square brackets with the asterisk to include a range of characters to precede the wildcard.
- A text editor works with plain text. Pico, Vi, Vim, and Emacs are text editors that come with some distributions of Linux.

Securing a Linux Desktop

- You must use the root account to create and manage users, and to make system changes.
- When logged on as an ordinary user, use the **su** command to log on as another user (most often root).
- When logged on as an ordinary user in a GUI, any time you attempt to perform a root-only function you will automatically be prompted to provide the root password.
- Common commands for working with user accounts are **useradd**, **userdel**, **passwd**, and **finger**.
- Use permission attributes on files and folders to control access to them.
- The permissions include: **r** (read), **w** (write), **x** (execute), and **-** (disabled).
- Use the **chmode** command to modify attributes, based on mode number.
- Permission attribute modes are 1 (execute), 2 (write), and 4 (read).

Troubleshoot Common Linux Problems

- You must have permission to save a file in a directory.
- Trying to display a binary file results in garbage on the screen.
- The "Command Not Found Error" usually results from a typo at the command prompt.

Key Terms List

Key Terms Quiz

Use the Key Terms List to complete the sentences that follow. Not all terms will be used.

1. To access the command line in the GNOME GUI, you start a/an _____.

2. GNOME is an example of a/an _____ GUI.

3. When you log on as a user, you enter commands at the _____.

4. When you create a user in Linux, the OS creates a/an _____ on disk for that user.

5. If you cannot boot from an optical disc or bootable flash drive to begin the Linux installation, use the Raw Write utility to place a/an _____ onto a floppy disk.

6. While it sounds like a comic book character, _____ is simply another name for root.

7. The _____ organization was created in 1984 to develop a free UNIX-like operating system.

8. _____ are commands that you must enter at the command prompt.

9. _____ is distributed with all of its source code, which allows the purchaser to customize the software as necessary.

10. The most powerful account in Linux has the login name of _____.

Multiple-Choice Quiz

1. Linux is modeled on which operating system?
   a. Windows
   b. UNIX
   c. NT
   d. VMS
   e. CP/M

2. If the access mode number for the owner drops below this on some Linux installations, any future access to this file is blocked.
   a. 5
   b. 8
   c. 1
   d. 7
   e. 6

3. Who was the initial developer responsible for Linux?
   a. Ken Thompson
   b. Linus Torvalds
   c. Steve Jobs
   d. Dennis Ritchie
   e. Fred Linux

4. Which user has the most power and privileges in Linux?
   a. Administrator
   b. Admin
   c. Absolute
   d. Root
   e. Linus

5. What is the command a user invokes to leave (log off) when working at the Linux shell?
   a. exit
   b. shutdown
   c. bye
   d. log off
   e. quit

6. What is the Linux command to copy a file?
   a. cpy
   b. rm
   c. mv
   d. copy
   e. cp

7. What option for the **ls** command lists all files in a directory, including the hidden files?
   a. -S
   b. -F
   c. -l
   d. -a
   e. -t

8. What is the command to turn off a Linux computer from the shell?
   a. down
   b. shutdown
   c. exit
   d. off
   e. power

9. When you are using Pico, what is the key combination to save a file?
   a. CTRL-O
   b. CTRL-S
   c. CTRL-D
   d. CTRL-W
   e. CTRL-V

10. What command displays only the first 10 lines of a file?
    a. more
    b. begin
    c. tail
    d. top
    e. head

11. Which command displays a text file, one page at a time?
    a. mkdir
    b. more
    c. pwd
    d. pico
    e rm

12. Why is Linux fast?
    a. It uses resources efficiently.
    b. It only runs on Pentium III or newer.
    c. Linux is graphics-intensive.

    d. It has no security.
    e. It only runs in real mode.

13. Which Linux command would you use to change file permissions?
    a. cd
    b. ls
    c. cp
    d. chmod
    e. head

14. Why would you use the command line rather than the GNOME when you are creating and changing users?
    a. The command line is more intuitive.
    b. GNOME is too cryptic.
    c. The command line is faster.
    d. The command line is more secure.
    e. You cannot create users from GNOME.

15. If you see an error message when you attempt to save a file in a directory, what is the most likely cause?
    a. Invalid file.
    b. You are logged on as root.
    c. Typo.
    d. File too large.
    e. Lack of permissions.

Essay Quiz

1. List and explain the reasons that Linux has not yet taken over the desktop OS market.
2. Discuss how your school or work could use Linux.
3. Discuss how open source software can benefit an organization.
4. The Helping Hand, a charitable organization, has asked you to set up its computer systems. The organization has a very limited budget. Describe how Linux can allow users to be productive while costing very little.
5. Explain the merits of **sudo**, as implemented in Ubuntu Linux.

Lab Projects

LAB PROJECT 8.1

The GNOME GUI includes the Workspace Switcher, a tool not mentioned in this chapter. Research the GNOME Workspace Switcher and write a few sentences describing both the notion of workspaces in Linux, as well as how the Workspace Switcher works.

LAB PROJECT 8.2

When installing Ubuntu Linux you noticed an option on the Who are you? page—a suboption under **Require my password to log in** titled "Encrypt my home folder." Research this option, and describe another option you should not enable after you have selected this option, along with the reason not to.

LAB PROJECT 8.3

Research and describe the Suspend and Hibernate options available from the GNOME Shutdown menu (accessed from the icon on the far right of the menu bar).

9

Mac OS X on the Desktop

"Steve had this perspective that always started with the user's experience; and that industrial design was an incredibly important part of that user impression. And he recruited me to Apple because he believed that the computer was eventually going to become a consumer product. That was an outrageous idea back in the early 1980s because people thought that personal computers were just smaller versions of bigger computers."

—John Sculley

Former CEO of Apple discussing Steve Jobs in an October 2010 interview by Leander Kahney, editor and publisher of Cult of Mac (www.cultofmac.com)

We have been talking for eight chapters now about desktop operating systems, and we have discussed DOS, three versions of Microsoft Windows, and Linux. Now we will discuss Mac OS X from Apple.

In this chapter, you will explore the Macintosh OS X operating system, beginning with an overview and then learning how to install it, manage the desktop, and troubleshoot common Mac OS X problems. You'll also learn the basics of local security in Mac OS X on the desktop. There are 800-page tomes written about using Mac OS X, so we won't pretend to give you more than a survey of the OS and key facts and features. ✳

Learning Outcomes

In this chapter, you will learn how to:

LO **9.1** Describe Mac OS X features.

LO **9.2** Install Mac OS X.

LO **9.3** Manage Mac OS X on the desktop.

LO **9.4** Manage local security in Mac OS X.

LO **9.5** Troubleshoot common Mac OS X problems.

LO 9.1 | Mac OS X Overview

Let's explore the Mac OS, its history and place in the world of computing, and learn about the main features of Apple's Mac OS X.

Make a Mac OS X desktop suit your tastes and needs.

A Brief History

Apple Computer (now officially Apple Inc.) began April 1, 1976, when high school friends Stephen Wozniak and Steven Jobs began marketing the Apple I computer from a garage in Los Altos, California. The following year, the Apple II version debuted at a local trade show. It was the first personal computer to be in a plastic case and include color graphics, although it didn't have a graphical interface. In 1983, Apple launched the Lisa, the first production computer to use a graphical user interface (GUI), and in 1984 the company launched the Macintosh 128k, the first *affordable* personal computer with a GUI. The Macintosh brought with it a new operating system, and the name was shortened to **Mac** in more recent models of Apple computers.

Many credit these earliest incarnations with popularizing the personal computer beyond the world of techies, leading to today's popular iMac, Mac Pro, MacBook, MacBook Pro, MacBook Air, and other models, not to mention the iPod, iPhone, and iPad. Apple computers have had a profound impact on the computer industry and have inspired a strong community of proponents.

For many years the microprocessors and chipsets in Apple computers were very different from those used in standard PCs running Windows, and Apple computers would not run Windows. Apple abandoned this strategy in about 2006 when they adopted Intel compatible microprocessors and chipsets, so now these computers can run Windows and you can configure a new Mac to dual boot between Windows and Mac OS X using Boot Camp, as described in Chapter 3.

As for the operating system, the Mac OS, or "System," was born along with the Macintosh in 1984 and went through many changes in the original code over the years until Apple introduced **Mac OS X Server** 1.0 in 1999 and the desktop version, OS X 10.0 in 2000. OS X is an entirely new OS for the Mac, with a UNIX core, known as **Darwin**, which is a product of the open source development community, with all the advantages that brings.

As with the differences between Windows Server and desktop products, Mac OS X Server is, at its core, the same OS. Apple preinstalls Mac OS X Server in its server computers, the Xserve line. However, Server has many enhancements and services required for its role as a server. In this chapter we will discuss only the desktop versions of Mac OS.

Mac OS X Versions

OS X (referred to as OS ten) seems always to be a work in progress, as Apple has issued new major releases beginning with the initial release for the desktop, 10.0, code named Cheetah. During development, each version of OS X has had a code name of a cat, and, while Apple did not publicly use this code name for 10.0 and 10.1, for subsequent versions it tied the code name to the product, using it heavily in marketing and packaging. At the time of this writing, the most recent release of OS X is version 10.6, OS X Snow Leopard, the seventh major release, which was touted as not adding new features to its predecessor, Leopard, but improving on it with a speed increase and a size decrease in memory usage and required disk space. Apple announced the next version, Mac OS X Lion (10.7), at Apple's "Back to the Mac" event in October 2010. Apple plans to release this product in the second quarter of 2011. Between the major releases have been minor releases (10.0.1, 10.0.2, etc.).

We used two minor releases for the screenshots in this chapter: 10.6.4 and 10.6.5, although the differences between the two are not evident in the figures. Each major release has added a variety of improvements and new features, and, as you may notice while comparing the illustrations in this book to OS X on your lab computer, you always have the ability to customize the look so that no two installations need to be identical. The screenshots you see in this chapter all use either the default Aurora background or a white background for ease of viewing the captured windows and message boxes. Table 9–1 lists the major releases, their names, and release dates.

At the time of this writing, the list price for the OS X Snow Leopard single user upgrade is $29, while an upgrade Family Pack with five licenses is $49.

try this!

Determine the Installed Version of the Mac OS

It is simple to check the installed version of the Mac OS. Try this:

1. Log on to a Macintosh computer and click an empty area of the desktop.
2. Click the Apple menu in the top left corner of your desktop and select *About this Mac*. The screen that pops up shows the installed version of the Mac OS.

Mac OS X Features

One quirk of Apple's history is that, barring one experiment lasting from 1993 to 1997, Apple has never licensed its OS to any other hardware manufacturer, thus irrevocably binding together the OS and the boxes it comes in. This has tended to make the Mac "the sum of more than its parts" in the minds of its dedicated users.

Apple OSs still account for a smaller market share than Microsoft Windows, but because of its fine hardware and hallmark ease-of-use OS, Apple has disproportionately penetrated niche markets, and its overall share of the desktop market is growing.

TABLE 9–1 Release Dates of Major OS X Versions

Major OS X Release	Release Date
10.0 Cheetah	March 2001
10.2 Jaguar	August 2003
10.3 Panther	October 2003
10.4 Tiger	First half 2005
10.5 Leopard	October 2007
10.6 Snow Leopard	August 2009
10.7 Lion	Projected for 2011 second quarter

Apple MacBook and iMac
Courtesy of Apple

With its current line of operating systems, Apple has further refined its user interface while placing it on top of a UNIX system, offering increased stability, networking potential, and security. In this chapter we will focus on OS X Snow Leopard (version 10.6). As with other GUI operating systems, Macintosh operating systems share such common metaphors as the desktop, files and folders, and the trashcan. Similarly, hardware falls into certain types.

Built-in Multimedia Hardware and Software in the Mac OS

Apple's standard inclusion of hardware historically considered by other manufacturers to be *optional* multimedia elements has tended to make Mac users low maintenance insofar as their technical needs are concerned when compared with users of other operating systems. This has changed with the addition of multimedia devices standard to most consumer-grade PCs.

The developers of Mac's operating systems have typically had to consider only a few hardware platforms, built with the same basic architecture, making problems such as component/software conflicts less likely to be issues than they are with Wintel machines that require the operating systems be designed to work on hardware manufactured by a host of other companies.

Macs included sound cards, the hardware interface that allows your computer to accept and output high-fidelity audio, from surprisingly early in their history. In fact, if you mention the phrase "sound card" to Mac users, many will not understand what you're talking about because a sound card was never an option when purchasing their computers, but was included as standard.

The standard hardware and software configurations that Macs include are sufficient to organize a music or photo collection, edit home video, or burn CDs and DVDs. Apple raised the bar and the personal computer industry followed suit, making multimedia features and support for writable CDs and DVDs standard on most consumer Windows desktops. Ultimately, the computer you choose these days, whether Apple or PC, matters less and less, as companies rush to match and better their competitors, usually within a matter of months.

Ease of Use of the Mac OS

The Mac OS interface is as simple as possible, involving users with as little of the backend functionality as possible. In hardware terms, this has meant delivery of a minimum system configuration of computers that contains many extras as standard.

In software terms, the Mac OS has tended to minimize user intervention as much as possible. You know when you buy new software that all you have to do is insert the disc, and the program will install automatically with very little intervention while asking you the fewest questions needed to complete the task.

Macs—with their single-source hardware, operating system, and software—tend to break only when they're actually broken, rather than because someone did something to something while adding a new component or installing software. This is an advantage of single-source hardware and software manufacturers.

Mac OS X Snow Leopard Enhancements

The most important enhancements to Snow Leopard are under the hood, such as improved code that runs faster and an installed size that takes half the disk space of the previous version. However, what you see is also important, and experienced Windows users are relieved to see the same basic metaphors visible on the OS X desktop: a trash can (now sitting on the Dock), menu bars, icons that represent programs, data files, and other objects, and a customizable background for displaying either static "wallpaper" or personal photos. Here is a short list of enhancements found in Mac OS X Snow Leopard, followed by descriptions and illustrations of just a select few of the GUI enhancements.

- Boot Camp, introduced in Mac OS X Leopard (10.5) and improved in Snow Leopard, is a utility that allows users to install Microsoft Windows or Linux in a dual-boot configuration beside an installation of Mac OS X.

- Finder, the users' main interface to programs, data, and other objects, was rewritten to work with new features in Snow Leopard.

- Apple introduced Version 4 of the Safari Internet browser with Snow Leopard. It has since been upgraded to version 5.

- Support for Apple's backup service, Time Machine, was improved to speed up the initial connection as well as the backup.

- User interface features were enhanced. These include Exposé, the Dock, windows, and many menus.

- The operating system code was improved for speed and stability. Reviewers saw speed improvements in the built-in Mac apps as well as in startup and shutdown.

The Default OS X Snow Leopard Desktop. For the user, Finder is the foundation of the Mac OS GUI and the equivalent to Windows Explorer, the Windows file management tool. Where early versions of Mac OS used the Finder as a task switcher, OS X delegates this task to the Dock, an area that holds icons for commonly used programs, as well as icons for open applications. A divider that resembles the dotted line on a highway separates program icons from icons representing disks, folders, and documents. Where Windows has a menu bar at the top of every open window, Mac OS X has a menu bar at the top of the screen containing the menu for the current (active) window; the Finder menu is the current menu when you have closed or minimized all other windows. The menu bar also contains the icon for opening the Apple menu, a notification area with day and time (on the right), and an icon that opens Spotlight Search. Figure 9–1 shows the key

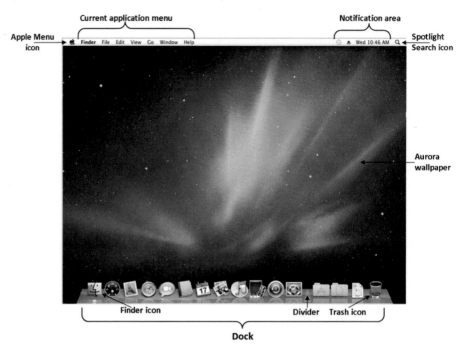

FIGURE 9–1 Key features of the default Mac OS X Snow Leopard desktop

features of the Mac OS X Snow Leopard desktop. All of this is configurable to match your tastes and work habits.

The Dock. The Dock is an area on the desktop, resembling a floating bar or shelf, that holds a group of icons representing shortcuts to programs for fast launching. When you launch a program, a small dot appears under the icon to show that it is running, an icon also displays for each open window, and you can click one of these icons to switch between tasks. And we can't forget the Trash icon, which sits on the Dock waiting for you to drop unneeded files into it for erasing. Customize the Dock by dragging and dropping programs onto it. The Dock is not new, but in Snow Leopard it looks like a strangely translucent aluminum shelf in its default location, but turns into dark smoked glass when moved to the left or right of the screen. With the 16:9 ratio of today's displays, we prefer to keep the dock on the side, as shown here, which leaves more height for open windows.

Exposé. While not new in Snow Leopard, Exposé has a new look and more options. Exposé serves the same purpose as Windows' Flip 3D—allowing you to select an open application from an array of miniature graphical Windows. If your desktop looks like Figure 9–2, and you want to switch to another window, you can add Exposé to your methods for switching among open windows. With Exposé simply press F3 to change a mess like Figure 9–2 to something like Figure 9–3. Press F3 (on new models with the aluminum keyboard or F9 on older plastic keyboards) again to close Exposé. In Exposé you can quickly bring a window of your choice to the foreground by simply clicking on it. You can also navigate the Exposé view by using the arrow keys. Notice the blue outline around the currently selected window, as shown in Figure 9–3. Press the RETURN key to open the current window. In Snow Leopard, Exposé has a new look with windows of proportional sizes, rather than all the same size as they were in previous versions. Exposé has three modes in which it functions. Learn more about Exposé by searching on "Exposé" in the Apple Help menu.

The Dock on the right side of the screen

FIGURE 9–2 A cluttered desktop

FIGURE 9–3 Exposé in action

LO 9.2 | Installing Mac OS X

This section details the process of installing and configuring Mac OS X, including the minimum hardware and software requirements, the installation process, and the post-installation task of updating software. If you purchase a new computer with Mac OS X preinstalled, the OS will come installed but not configured. In that case, the first time you power up your new computer the **Mac OS X Setup Assistant** prompts you for the user preferences information that begins with Step 11 in Step-by-Step 9.01.

Preparing to Install Mac OS X

Anyone purchasing a new Apple Mac computer will have Mac OS X preinstalled, but people with existing Macs will probably upgrade to this greatly improved OS, so we will begin by discussing the minimum hardware requirements for upgrading to OS X.

Mac OS version information from the Apple menu

Checking the Version Before Upgrading

Verify the version of the Mac OS running on a computer before upgrading because if your Mac OS is too old you may not be able to upgrade. Simply open the Apple menu and select About this Mac and the version information will display, as shown here. Click the More Info button to see an exhaustive list of the installed components and software. You can browse through this list, as shown in Figure 9–4.

To upgrade to a new version of Mac OS X, insert the DVD, and when the folder appears, select Install Mac OS X to see the window shown in Figure 9–5. The installation program will detect the installed OS and guide you through an upgrade (see Figure 9–6).

Hardware Requirements

Mac OS X Snow Leopard breaks with tradition by dropping support for the PowerPC architecture, which Apple supported in Macs since System 7.1.2. This is not a big surprise, since the Apple Mac product line has focused on Intel-based systems for several years. Table 9–2 shows the minimum hardware requirements for installing Mac OS X on a Mac desktop or laptop. We view these requirements as fine for basic use, but you will want to beef up the memory and hard disk space if you plan to regularly undertake image or video editing with your computer.

FIGURE 9–4 The More info button provides an extensive list of installed hardware and software.

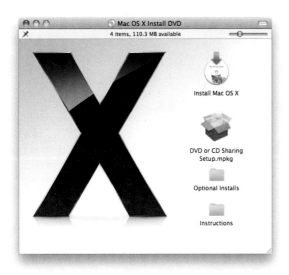

FIGURE 9–5 The menu from the Mac OS X installation DVD

FIGURE 9–6 From here the Mac OS X Setup Assistant will guide you through the upgrade.

TABLE 9–2	Minimum Hardware Requirements for OS X
Computer	Mac computer with an Intel processor
Hard disk	5 GB of available disk space
RAM	1 GB
DVD drive	Required for installation

The Installation

There are rarely surprises with Mac OS X installations—mainly because the installation is usually an upgrade because one can legally license this OS only on Apple Mac computers. You won't run into the incompatibility problems with strange hardware that you can encounter during a Windows installation.

Even when you buy a new Apple computer, which always has the OS pre-installed, you get to experience the final stages of the installation (steps 11 through 15 in Step-by-Step 9.01) the first time you start the computer.

> Before creating passwords, review the information on creating strong passwords in Chapter 2.

Step-by-Step 9.01
Installing Mac OS X

In this step-by-step exercise, you will install Mac OS X and create a configuration necessary for a typical user. If you have an Apple Mac that meets the hardware requirements but is using an older OS version, you can perform an upgrade during this exercise. If you have the current version of the Mac OS installed on a computer, you may want to download and install a hypervisor, such as the free Sun Virtual Box, create a virtual machine for Mac OS X, and use a Mac OS X DVD to install into the virtual machine. Start this exercise with either Step 1 or

Step 2 depending on what you want to do. To complete this exercise, you will need the following:

● An Apple Mac that meets the hardware requirements.

● A preconfigured virtual machine if you want to try that option.

● A user name and password that will allow you to log on to your computer.

● The OS X installation DVD disc.

Step 1

Virtual Machine Option: In a new virtual machine, first ensure that the virtual machine will capture the optical drive, then insert the OS X disc and start the virtual machine. While the installation program loads you may notice text screens such as this before the GUI loads. Once the GUI starts, you will see the screen shown in Step 3. Skip to Step 3.

```
efiboot loaded from device: Acpi(PNP0A03,0)/Pci(1|1)/Ata(Secondary,Master)/CDROM
(Entry0)
boot file path: \System\Library\CoreServices\boot.efi
.Loading 'mach_kernel'...
....................
root device uuid is '7CD816BE-C4C9-3535-B022-F1E7F2B1C7BD'
Loading drivers...
Loading System\Library\Caches\com.apple.kext.caches\Startup\Extensions.mkext...
.......
```

Step 2

Upgrade Option: From the OS X desktop insert the OS X disc, and when the disc's folder opens double-click the Install Mac OS X icon.

Step 3

The OS X installer loads; select the main language for the user interface, then click the arrow button in the lower right corner.

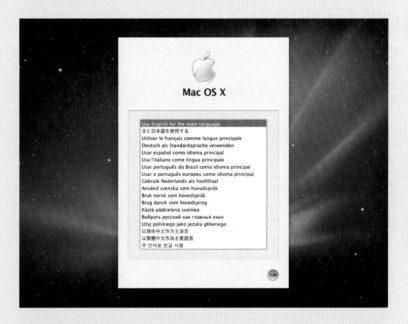

Step 4

The Preparing Installation page displays with a progress bar.

Step 5

Notice the appearance of the Mac OS X Installer menu bar at the top of the screen. The flag indicates that the primary language will be U.S. English. For now click Continue.

Step 6

Read the license agreement and click Agree to continue.

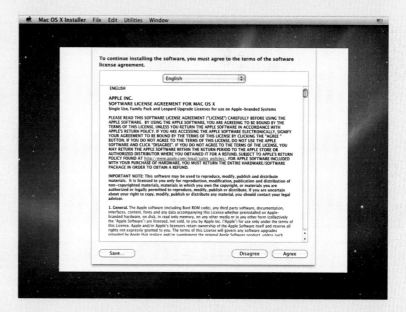

Step 7

Select the disk where you want to install Mac OS X. The green arrow indicates that you have selected a disk. After selecting a disk click Install.

Step 8

A progress bar will display while OS X installs.

Step 9

The Additional Information page (not shown) advises that if you erased and reinstalled Mac OS X, you should use the Applications installation disc to reinstall the iLife applications. This is just an informational page. Click Continue.

Step 10

On the Install Succeeded page click Restart.

Step 11

On the Welcome page select the country or region and select Continue. On the Select Your Keyboard page select the country layout and click Continue. The Do You Already Own a Mac? page will help you move information from another installation of the Mac OS including network settings, user accounts with preferences and e-mail, documents, and applications. Click Continue to finish the installation.

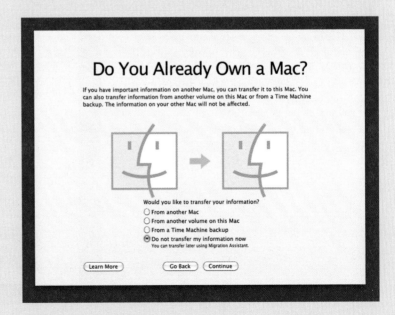

If you have an Apple ID, enter it on the Enter Your Apple ID page. Otherwise, click Continue. The Registration Information page is also optional, so you can click Continue if you don't wish to complete it at this time. Don't be daunted by the message and arrows that appear on the page (shown here). You can continue without completing this page.

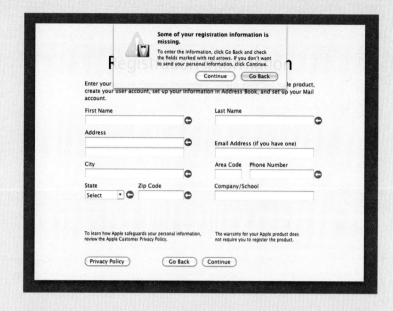

You must complete the Create Your Account page with your name and account name. It will remove the spaces from your name and offer that as an Account Name, but you can provide a different account name if you wish. Be sure to provide a password hint to help you *when* you forget your password. Click Continue.

Enter the closest major city into the Select Time Zone page, and then click Continue.

The Thank You page signals the end of the installation. Click Go to open the desktop. If the OS has not recognized your keyboard you may see this message. If so, click Continue and follow the instructions to press certain keys on the keyboard. This should enable it to recognize the keyboard. On the final page of the Keyboard Setup Assistant click Done and it will close. If you have not already done so, remove the installation disc by right-clicking and selecting Eject. If right-clicking is not turned on, then press the eject button on your keyboard.

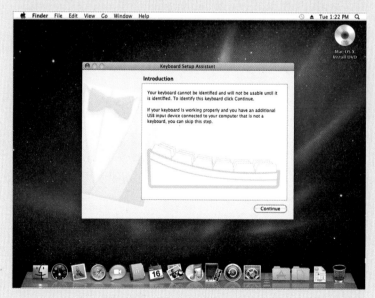

Software Update

Software updates for your computer are ready to be installed. Do you want to install them now?

You must restart your computer after the updates are installed.

Note: Use of this software is subject to the original Software License Agreement(s) that accompanied the software being updated. A list of Apple SLAs may be found here: http://www.apple.com/legal/sla/

Show Details   Not Now   Install and Restart

FIGURE 9–7 If you have an Internet connection, this message will appear soon after you complete a new installation.

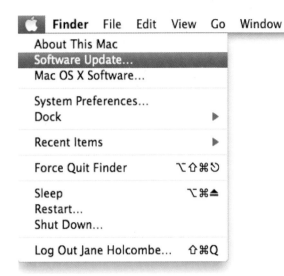

FIGURE 9–8 Open Software Update from the Apple Menu

Post-Installation Tasks

As with a new Windows installation, you should ensure that you update your operating system soon after installing it (or in the case of a new Mac, initializing it). Don't start working and creating new data on your computer until you do update it. If you have connected to the Internet, within hours, if not minutes, of installing Mac OS X you will see a Software Update message similar to that shown in Figure 9–7. You don't need to wait for the Software Update box to initiate an update. Simply select Software Update from the Apple menu, shown in Figure 9–8. The Checking for new software message will display with a progress bar while it connects to the Apple site looking for updates to your OS and other Apple software.

Click the Show Details button to view a list of the updates. If you wish to postpone installing updates (not a good idea), select Not Now. The wise choice is to click Install and Restart.

try this!

Install Software Updates

It is simple to install updates. Try this:

1. Click the Apple menu in the top left corner of your desktop and click Software Update. A progress bar will display while it connects and checks for updates.
2. In the Software Update box click Install and Restart.
3. Click Agree on any License Agreement page that displays (if you agree, of course). There may be several.
4. Click Restart.
5. It can take several minutes for the updates to install, especially the first time you update after installing Mac OS X.

LO 9.3 | Managing Mac OS X on the Desktop

Managing Mac OS X is much like managing the Windows desktop. Tasks include customizing the desktop, installing and removing applications, and adding a printer. You will learn how to set up system preferences, manage files, print, and create and manage user accounts.

Finder

The Finder menus in OS X—Finder, File, Edit, View, Go, Window, and Help—offer a variety of file management and power-on or off tools. The Window menu arranges window views, and the Go menu offers shortcuts to folders used for storage both on the computer and on the Internet.

Finder window with Applications folder open

Apple Menu

Click on the small Apple icon on the left of the menu bar to open the Apple menu, a drop-down menu that includes the items shown in Figure 9–9. This is where you go to find the version information (and details of the hardware and software), initiate a Software Update, connect to the Apple Web site (via the Mac OS X Software option), put the computer into Sleep mode, restart the computer, shut down, and log out.

Changing System Preferences

Open System Preferences from the Apple menu or from the Dock where its icon is a gray box filled with gears. This is the Mac OS X equivalent of the Windows Control Panel. Figure 9–10 shows the main System Preferences

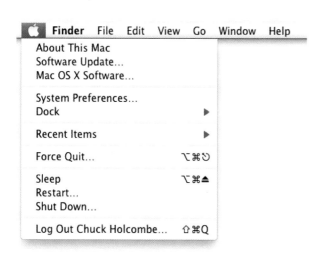

FIGURE 9–9 The OS X Apple menu

FIGURE 9–10 The content of System Preferences varies by system configuration.

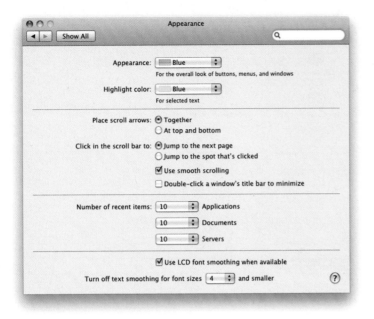

Appearance preferences

If you work with a large number of documents and applications and want a simple way to find them without maintaining a complex set of aliases and Dock items, just increase the number of recent items in the Appearance preference pane. Files and applications can be set separately with a maximum setting for each at 50. These are then accessible from Apple Menu | Recent Items.

window. Notice the Show All button in the title; this will always return you to the main System Preferences window. The icons are in rows by categories. The actual icons in each row depend on the installed hardware. In the following we'll explore common system preferences (we call each preference window a preference pane). Many of the settings in these panes can be modified by any user, but some are secure system preferences panes, requiring a password to unlock some or all settings in the pane.

Personal Preferences

The preferences found in the row labeled "Personal" are settings that control visual and security preferences for the currently logged-on user.

Appearance. The Appearance preference allows you to alter the color of buttons, menus, windows, and text highlight. You can also choose the location and behavior of scroll arrows and the scroll bar and determine the number of applications and documents that appear in the Recent Items (both applications and documents) submenu of the Apple menu (choose from 5 to 50).

Desktop and Screen Saver. The Desktop and Screen Saver preference allows you to select a background and screen saver for your desktop. Click on Desktop to view the desktop settings and click on Screen Saver to view the screen savers available on your Mac. In the Desktop settings, to select a different group of images, choose another folder from the list on the left. Clicking on the Screen Saver button presents more preferences including a selection of screen savers and settings for the selected screen saver.

The Desktop Preferences

Dock. The Dock preference allows you to control the size and position of your Dock. Slider controls allow you to control the Dock size and magnification. Radio buttons allow you to position the Dock on the left, bottom, or right, while a box gives choices for the Minimize effects. You can also control the appearance of applications as they close and open. It does not allow you to customize the color of the Dock.

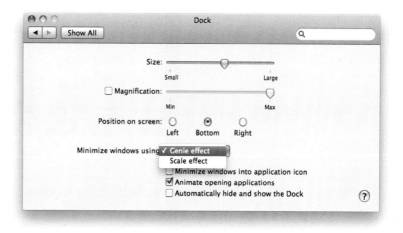

Exposé and Spaces. The Exposé and Spaces preferences pane is really two related features.

The Dock preference

- Opening the Exposé preferences greets you with the Active Screen Corners settings that are also available through the Hot Corners button in Screen Savers. But Exposé is really about letting you assign actions to certain keys or mouse buttons that will expose all open windows at once, or just application windows, or the desktop. This is very handy when you are working in one application and need to quickly get to another application or the desktop.

- The Spaces feature is very similar to the Linux notion of workspaces. We like Spaces for separating work, play, and community service projects because it lets you configure several virtual display screens that exist as separate areas. To do this, you must enable Spaces in the Spaces pane and assign one or more applications to each space. Then, when you start

WARNING!

Keep the Dock out of your way! Don't get carried away with the magnification feature because it can get in the way when you are moving your mouse around and cause you to open application windows. There is a simple solution: Turn off magnification and reduce the size of the floating launch bar.

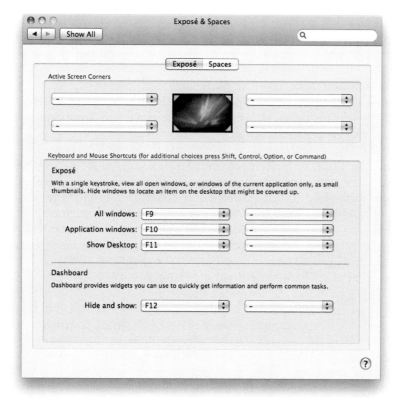

Use the Exposé pane to assign keys or mouse buttons to actions that will quickly reveal all open windows.

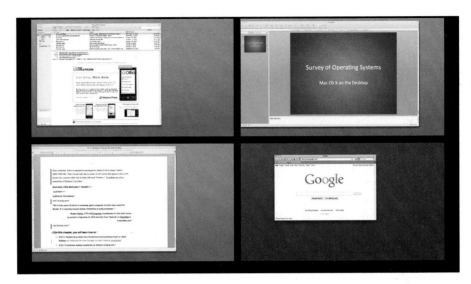

FIGURE 9–11 Select a space.

FIGURE 9–12 Yet another way to move among the spaces.

one of the assigned programs, it loads into its assigned space. Figure 9–11 shows the selection screen with four spaces occupied with running programs. Simply click in one of the spaces and it expands to cover the desktop. When you wish to move to another space, simply press the F8 key (or Fn+F8) to see the image similar to Figure 9–11. This is a rather dramatic way to switch between spaces, and it is handy to demonstrate spaces. However, if you decide to work with spaces, enable the Show Spaces in menu bar option in the Spaces pane. Then the menu bar will contain a small icon indicating the current space. To move among the spaces, click this menu bar to open a drop-down menu and select a space (see Figure 9–12). You can explore more subtleties and capabilities in Spaces on your own by turning it on and experimenting.

Language and Text. The Language and Text preference allows you to choose the language that appears in application menus and dialog boxes and the text behaviors of languages; date, time, and numbering conventions; and the keyboard layout.

Security. The Security preference includes, as you might expect, security settings. Here you can configure a password requirement for waking the computer from sleep or screen saver, and determine systemwide settings to enable or disable automatic login (only enable this in an extremely safe environment). You can require a password to unlock each secure system preferences pane, configure an automatic log out after a predetermined period, and enable Secure Virtual Memory. You may also turn on and configure FileVault, the file encryption feature, and set a Master Password that allows you to unlock any account on the computer. Figure 9–13 shows the General pane of Security preferences; notice the lock icon on the bottom left. Up to this point in our review of Personal preferences, there has been no restriction on your ability to modify the settings. That changes with Security preferences, which require credentials before you can make changes.

Spotlight. As with many Mac OS X features, Spotlight merits a full chapter in some books, but not this book since we are trying to present a survey of each operating system. **Spotlight** is a search utility that, much like Search in Windows, is a live search, meaning it starts presenting results as soon as you start typing. To open Spotlight, press the COMMAND key plus the space bar or simply click the magnifying glass icon on the top right of the menu bar. Figure 9–14 shows the results list that displayed after we entered "ch." Notice the variety of data files and programs listed. Clicking any of these items will launch the appropriate program and, when appropriate, the selected data file.

Hardware Preferences

The Hardware row contains panes for setting preferences for such hardware areas as CDs and DVDs, Displays, energy saving (power management), keyboard, mouse, trackpad (if on a MacBook), printers and faxes, and sound.

CDs & DVDs. The CDs & DVDs preference allows you to select the action that should occur when you insert a blank CD or DVD (separate actions), a music CD, a picture CD, or a video DVD.

Displays. The Displays preference allows users to customize the resolution, number of colors, refresh rate, and display profiles for each supported monitor connected to the computer. You can also calibrate the monitor using the Color option within the Displays preference. The calibration includes a ColorSync component, which enables you to specify the ColorSync profile for displays and printers for better screen rendering and print output.

Energy Saver. The Energy Saver preferences pane, shown here, offers options for putting your system, display, or hard disk to sleep after a defined period of inactivity and defines situations that will wake the sleeping computer. On laptops, it is possible to select different values for when you are powering the laptop from its battery or from a power supply. Changing settings in this pane requires credentials. When you have finished your selection, click the lock icon to secure these settings.

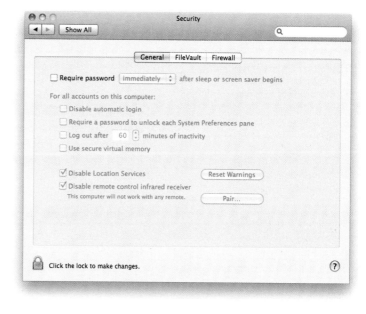

FIGURE 9–13 General pane on Security preferences

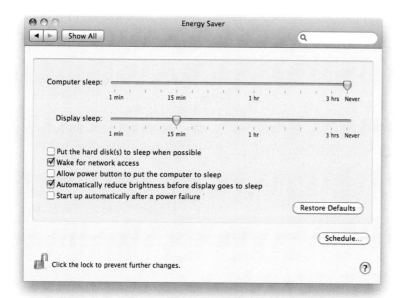

The Energy Saver pane requires credentials to make changes.

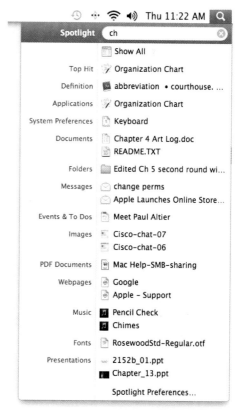

FIGURE 9–14 An example of Spotlight's live search results after entering only "ch"

Everyone types differently. Some people type faster and therefore require a higher key repeat rate than others, and others are frustrated when their slower key presses result in too many of the same letters. On the Settings tab of the Keyboard preference pane, adjust the Key Repeat Rate and Delay Until Repeat slider bars until you are comfortable with the results.

Keyboard. The Keyboard preferences pane includes both a Keyboard page and a Keyboard Shortcuts page. The Keyboard page allows keyboard behavior customization. The Keyboard Shortcuts pane allows modification of keyboard shortcuts, which are key combinations to perform a variety of functions.

Mouse. The Mouse preferences pane lets you customize mouse tracking, scrolling, and double-click speed. It also allows you to modify settings for special features of the pointing device connected to your computer. For instance, as shown here, Mouse preferences on our iMac includes settings for the wireless Magic Mouse, along with an animated tutorial for setting up the mouse.

Print & Fax. The Print & Fax preferences pane contains settings for both printers and faxes. Open the Printing page to add or remove a printer, determine the printer selected in the Print dialog, select a default paper size, and share locally attached printers. Open the Faxing page to configure settings for faxing, such as the sending phone number, and actions to take when a fax arrives.

Mouse preferences for the wireless Magic Mouse

Sound. The Sound preference permits users to select system alert sounds and the alert volume, main volume, and speaker balance and to choose between connected devices for sound input and output.

Internet and Wireless

The Internet and Wireless row contains preferences that apply to networking.

MobileMe. The MobileMe preferences pane allows a user to set up a MobileMe account for synchronizing the data on a Mac, PC, iPhone, iPod touch, or iPad. Apple charges for this service, but Snow Leopard 10.6.5 on our new iMac has a 60-day free trial accessible from this pane.

try this!

Changing the Alert Sounds

Not every sound is pleasing to every ear. We recommend how to change those sounds. Try this:

1. Go to the Sound preferences pane in OS X.
2. On the Sound Effects page, click the name of a sound other than the one currently highlighted.
3. You will hear the sound. Repeat this process until you find a sound you like; then close the panel.

Network. The Network preferences pane, shown on the next page, allows you to configure an AirPort, Ethernet, or FireWire connection. The Location setting is a function more appropriate to laptops. On a desktop configure this to Automatic. By default, Mac OS X will attempt to discover if a network device is connected and automatically configure it, as it did in the example shown.

Bluetooth. Modern Macs have a Bluetooth short-range wireless transceiver built-in, and some models, such as the iMac, come with Bluetooth devices. Figure 9–15 shows the Bluetooth preferences pane with two discovered devices. The Bluetooth preferences pane allows you to configure the connected Bluetooth devices.

Sharing. The Sharing preferences pane is another secured pane. It allows you to configure sharing of a long list of local resources over a network. These local resources (listed as services) include DVD or CD, files, printers, scanners, Web, remote login, remote management, remote Apple Events, Xgrid, Internet, and Bluetooth. For each resource, you can assign permissions to specific users and configure other appropriate settings.

System

The preferences in the System row include non-hardware settings common to all users of the computer.

Users/Accounts. Another pane that requires authentication is the OS X Users preference pane, which allows you to add, delete, and edit users from your computer. In addition, this pane allows a variety of login options, including the password, a password hint, and selecting a picture to use when logging in. You can also set Parental Controls on each user.

The Network preferences pane

Date and Time. Although the Date and Time preference has seemingly limited functionality, in fact it lets you perform a variety of functions. Obviously, it allows you to set the date and time, but the panel also lets you control the appearance and specifics of the menu bar clock, specify your time zone, and synchronize with a global network time server so that your computer clock is regularly adjusted to the global standard time.

Parental Controls. If you are setting up a Mac for a child or vulnerable adult, assign that person a standard account and then configure Parental Controls.

FIGURE 9–15 The Bluetooth preferences pane shows discovered Bluetooth devices.

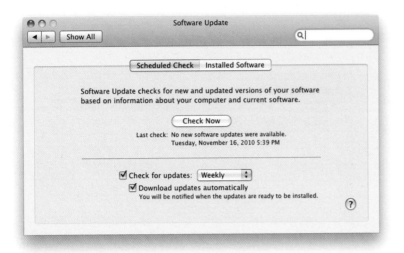

Software Update pane

Software updates have an order. Some software updates are visible only when previous updates are installed. If you are installing a system from an older version of OS X, be sure to click the Update Now button in the Software Update preference pane after each new update is installed to check for these stacked updates. Only when your Mac tells you that no further updates are available do you know that your work is truly complete!

This allows you to place many restrictions on an account, including specifying the hours of the day during which the user may be logged in, restricting the people with whom a child may exchange e-mails or instant messages, and much more.

Software Update. Software Update is a utility that automatically or manually checks for system security and other bug-fix upgrades and new versions of common software programs, downloads them when you agree to installation, and keeps track of what you've downloaded and installed and what you haven't.

In OS X, the utility proves to be more useful as Apple releases bug fixes and does feature tweaking. We recommend that you set the update option in Software Update to Automatic rather than Manual so that it regularly checks for and downloads updates.

Speech. Speech is a System preference pane that can enable the use of spoken commands for your computer and offers a place where you can customize the voice with which your computer speaks back. This feature is among many that make a Mac an attractive and easy-to-use computer for people who do not type fast or require other enhancement of the OS.

Startup Disk. As a Mac starts up it looks in a certain location for the System folder. This location is known as the startup disk, and it can be an optical disc, a hard disk, or a network volume. The System folder contains the operating system files that must load into memory at startup. You will not change the Startup Disk preference on most Mac desktops or laptops because, by default, most Macs only have one System folder from which it starts. If your computer has more than one source of a System folder, such as another operating system located on a second hard drive, the Startup Disk preference allows you to select the default operating system that boots up the computer on restart. If your computer is configured with more than one System folder or operating system, you can also change the startup disk temporarily by pressing and holding the OPTION key as you restart the computer. When the available startup disks display, select the one you wish to use.

Time Machine. Time Machine is an automatic system backup feature that requires a second hard drive larger than the drive you are backing up. It is simple to configure.

Universal Access. The Universal Access preferences pane contains various pages that give users a large selection of options to aid people in using their computer. These include settings for seeing and hearing as well as settings to make one-handed mouse and keyboard usage possible.

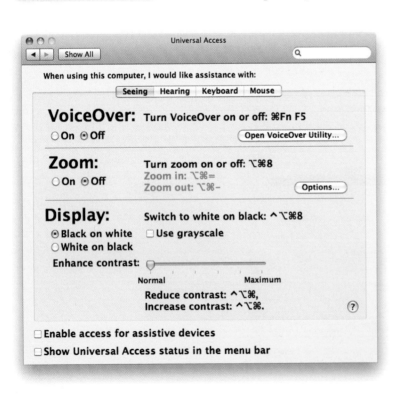

The Universal Access preferences pane

Adding Objects to the Dock

If you want to put a file, folder, application, or Internet bookmark in the Dock, just drag it on. If you want to remove something that's on there, just drag it off the Dock and onto the desktop and let go. It will disappear in a puff of smoke.

Terminal Windows in Mac OS X

If you have a desire to get in touch with your "inner geek," launch Terminal, found in Utilities under the Applications folder. This gives you a doorway to the UNIX underpinnings of OS X via a BASH shell complete with the

try this!

Add an Icon to the Dock

Add a shortcut icon to the Dock. Try this:

1. Use Finder to select something you would like to call up quickly from the Dock.
2. Click the item's icon and drag it onto the Dock. Before letting go of the mouse button, move the icon over the Dock to position it between existing Dock icons. Depending on the type of icon, you will be able to position it to the right or left of the divider.
3. Release the mouse button when you are satisfied with the position of the icon.
4. Reposition the Dock to the left or right and notice the change in appearance as well as the orientation of the icons.
5. To remove the icon, simply drag it to the desktop and it will disappear in a puff of smoke.

$ prompt you learned about in Chapter 8. You can use many of the same commands in both UNIX and Linux. As with Windows, working from a command line interface (CLI) does not allow you to bypass OS X security. Figure 9–16 shows a Terminal window in which two commands were run: **ls** and **man ls**. The beauty of working with Terminal in a GUI environment is that you can have more than one Terminal window open at a time. For instance, open a Terminal window and examine the manual page for a command (remember **man** command). Then open a second Terminal window and use the first window as a reference while using the command and its switches. Open a Terminal window and experiment with the commands you learned in Chapter 8.

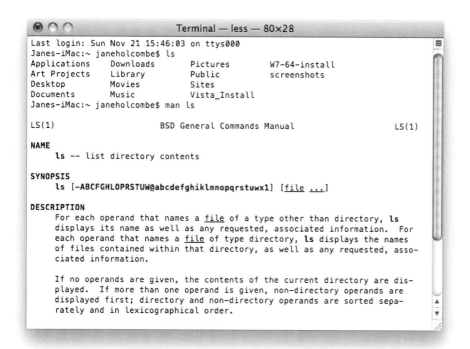

FIGURE 9–16 A Terminal window showing the result of running two commands

Managing Files in Mac OS X

The Finder is your navigation tool in OS X, and in the following sections we will look at the Finder views, then practice creating folders, and learn other file management tasks.

Finder Views

Finder has four views, or ways of displaying objects: Icon, List, Column, and Cover Flow. The Finder saves the preferred view of the first folder or disk opened in a new Finder window. The unifying factor in all four viewing modes in OS X is the ability to navigate the file and folder structure of your disks and to open files and folders by double-clicking them. Figure 9–17 shows a Finder window open in Cover Flow view. If you are sitting at a Mac, open Finder while reading the following paragraphs describing the four views. You can set view options from the View menu of the Finder and, alternatively, from the View toolbar of any open folder or disk.

Sorting Files in List View

In List view, four columns offer information about your files: Name, Date Modified, Size, and Kind. The default view is an alphabetical sort by name. You can change that order. Try this:

1. Double-click a folder or hard disk.
2. Click the title of any of these columns, and you will see your files sorted by that attribute. Sorting based on the Kind column is useful when you want to recover hard disk space. Look for big, obsolete files this way.
3. Click the same title again to see the files sorted by that attribute in reverse order. Used most often with the Date column, this technique is effective when you want to search for recently changed or out-of-date files.

Icon View. In Icon view you select an item by clicking it once, and you open it by double-clicking it to open it in a new window. You can set an option so that a folder opens in the same window when you double-click, and it works in all four viewing modes. You can turn this option on and off in the Finder preferences (Finder | Preferences).

List View. List view displays content in an indented outline format that allows you to see the contents of enclosed folders. This is a powerful means of viewing and organizing your folders and files without having to open new windows for each subfolder, a process that can make your virtual desktop as messy as a real one!

FIGURE 9–17 A Finder window in Cover Flow view

To open a folder, click the triangular icon to the left of the folder icon. To close the folder, simply click the icon again to hide the contents of that folder. The List view offers a wealth of information about folders and files such as date modified, size, and kind (for example, application or file). If you double-click a folder, that folder opens inside itself, as in the other two view options.

Column View. In Column view, when you select a file by clicking it once, the file's icon or a preview of its contents, either text or graphics, is displayed in a column to the right. If you click on a folder, the contents display in the column to the right, and if you click on a subfolder, yet another column opens with that folder's contents. When a window is in Column view, you can change the size of columns by dragging the bottom of the column divider.

Cover Flow View. Cover Flow view opens a pane containing small images of each object in the currently selected folder. Below this pane is a list pane. Select a file or folder in this list and it will appear in the center of the Cover Flow.

Creating Folders in the Finder

With folders, you can organize your documents and applications in the contents pane. Create a new folder by choosing New Folder from the File menu in the Finder or by right-clicking an area of the contents pane and selecting New Folder.

Copying, Pasting, and Deleting Files and Folders

You can copy and paste files and folders into the same or a different document or folder.

- To copy, select the item and choose Copy from the Edit menu (or press COMMAND-C).
- To cut, select the item and choose Cut from the Edit menu (or press COMMAND-X).
- To paste, first either copy or cut a file or folder. Then open the destination folder and select Paste from the Edit menu (or press COMMAND-V).
- To delete, choose Delete from the Edit menu (or press COMMAND-DELETE). This moves the file or folder into the Trash. To empty the Trash, select Empty Trash from the Finder menu (or press COMMAND-SHIFT-DELETE).

Copying a file

Moving and Renaming Files and Folders in Finder

Moving files and folders between locations on the same disk is as simple as selecting the item with your mouse, dragging it into the desired new location, and letting go. You may also select an item, and use the cut and paste option described in the preceding section. To copy a file, hold down the OPTION key as you let go of the file or folder.

There are two ways to rename a file:

- Open Finder and locate the desired item to rename; then, with a short pause between the clicks, click twice. This will highlight the name of the item and you will be able to edit the file name. When you are ready to save the item with the new name, either click away from the item or press RETURN.

- Right-click the file or folder in Finder, choose File and then Get Info (formerly File Info) or press COMMAND-I. This will bring up the information window. In the pop-up menu that displays General Information by default, select Name and Extension. In the box, replace the name and extension with whatever new name you want and then close the window.

Step-by-Step 9.02

Creating a New Folder to Organize Files

In this exercise, you will create a folder within an existing folder, rename it, and move files into it. To complete this exercise, you will need the following:

- A Mac computer with Mac OS X installed.

- A user name and password that will allow you to log on to your computer.
- Files in at least one of the folders of your home directory.

Step 1

Open Finder by clicking its icon on the Dock (the square, blue icon with a face image). Finder will open your home folder.

Step 2

Create a new folder. Press COMMAND-SHIFT-N or select New Folder from the Finder's File menu. A new folder, called "untitled folder," will appear in the list of files and folders.

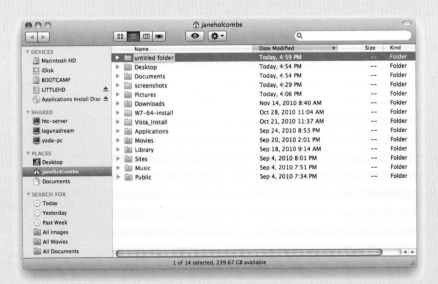

Step 3

Begin typing a new name for the folder; or click the folder once, pause and then click it a second time to highlight its name, and then type a new name.

Step 4

Double-click on the new folder so that the contents pane opens on the empty folder.

Step 5

On the menu bar, select New Finder Window. Position the new window next to the window for the new folder. In the newly opened window, navigate to a folder containing files or folders you wish to move to the new folder.

Step 6

Select a file or folder that you want to place into this folder by clicking it once. If you want to select multiple files or folders to drag into the folder, hold down the SHIFT key while clicking them.

Step 7

When you are finished selecting items you want to put into the new folder you have created, select one of the highlighted items, drag it to the contents pane for the new folder you created until the folder highlights, and then let go. The file moves into the new folder.

Printing in Mac OS X

No matter what type of printer you have, almost every OS X application manages the printing process in the same way, including giving you the ability to create an Adobe PDF document from any Print menu.

Installing a Printer

Installing a printer in OS X is a nonevent. You simply connect the printer, power up, and it installs without any fuss or obvious activity. In previous versions of OS X this was because a great deal of disk space was taken up with print drivers, but Snow Leopard installs only the drivers for the printers detected during installation, including network printers. Therefore, after you connect and power on a printer, OS X quietly goes searching for the driver, downloading it from the Internet if the computer has an Internet connection.

To verify that the printer installed, select the Print command from the File menu of an OS X application. Printer names appear in this dialog box when you install printer drivers. If your new printer is not listed, then use the scroll arrows on the Printer box and select Add Printer, from the pop-up, as shown in Figure 9–18. The OS will attempt to detect the printer and display all detected printers in the list on the Add Printer page.

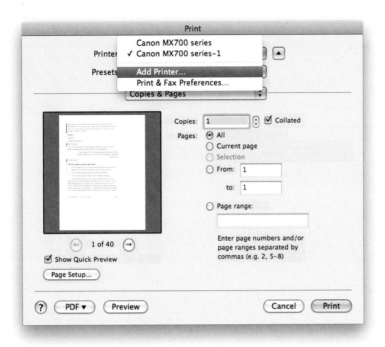

FIGURE 9–18 The Add Printer pop-up menu in the Print dialog box

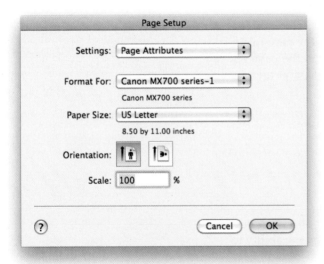

The Page Setup dialog box

Security

Most of your printer interaction takes place within the Print dialog box within applications. During printing, the Print Center icon appears in the Dock, allowing you to view, hold, or delete jobs.

Setting Printing Options

Most printers have a variety of configurable options, which you may modify from the Print menu in any application's File menu. In the Print dialog box you will have access to a variety of configurable options from pop-up menus. These options are specific to the printer model. You should explore these options for your own printer so that you are aware of the capabilities and can plan to take advantage of them.

Click the Page Setup button near the bottom left of the Print dialog box to make changes.

Where to Find the Print Queue

When you are ready to send a job to the Printer, simply open the Print dialog box, select the printer, and click the Print button. While a job is printing, an icon displays on the Dock, and if you're fast, you can open it in time to see the print queue, which closes when the print job is finished. Otherwise, you can find the Print Queue for an individual printer by calling up the Print and Fax pane from System Preferences. Select a printer from the list on the left and double-click on any printer or click the Open Print Queue button to view its print queue.

LO 9.4 | Managing Local Security in Mac OS X

We recently purchased an iMac at an Apple Store and once again heard the mantra that Macs don't need third-party security software. Well, while most malware attacking desktop computers target Microsoft Windows, Mac OS X is not impregnable, but Apple has built in many security features that are turned on by default because everyone is targeted, especially if you connect to the Internet. There are several steps to take to maintain a secure system. This includes installing antivirus software, as even Apple's Web site subtly recommends, advice we found at the end of a Web page titled "Mac OS X has you covered" at www.apple.com/macosx/security/. See Figure 9–19.

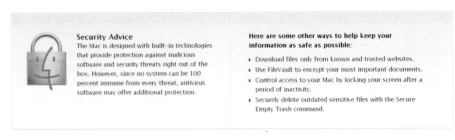

FIGURE 9–19 Advice from Apple

So where do you begin? Every day, as you work on your Mac, follow Apple's advice (see Figure 9–19). But start your relationship with your Mac by securing your Internet connection, allowing Mac OS X to receive and install updates regularly, managing local user accounts, and installing antivirus protection. We'll discuss all of these options in the following section.

Securing an Internet Connection

How does your Mac connect to the Internet? Is it through a broadband router at home, through a Wi-Fi hotspot at the school cafeteria or the local coffee shop? However your computer connects—whether it is a network you trust (at home or school) or an untrusted network, such as many of the public Wi-Fi hotspots, you need to ensure that you have the OS X Firewall turned on. While the most recent versions of OS X turn it on by default, you should check it out and familiarize yourself with it.

To view and modify Firewall settings, open the Security pane in System Preferences and click on Firewall. Ensure that the firewall is on. If it is not, turn it on. You may need to click on the lock icon on the lower left of the windows to unlock the settings; if so, you will need to provide your password. Then click Start to turn the firewall on—the little "led light" should now be green, as shown in Figure 9–20.

After ensuring that the firewall is on, click the Advanced button to view the settings. Figure 9–21 shows the default setting when we turned on the

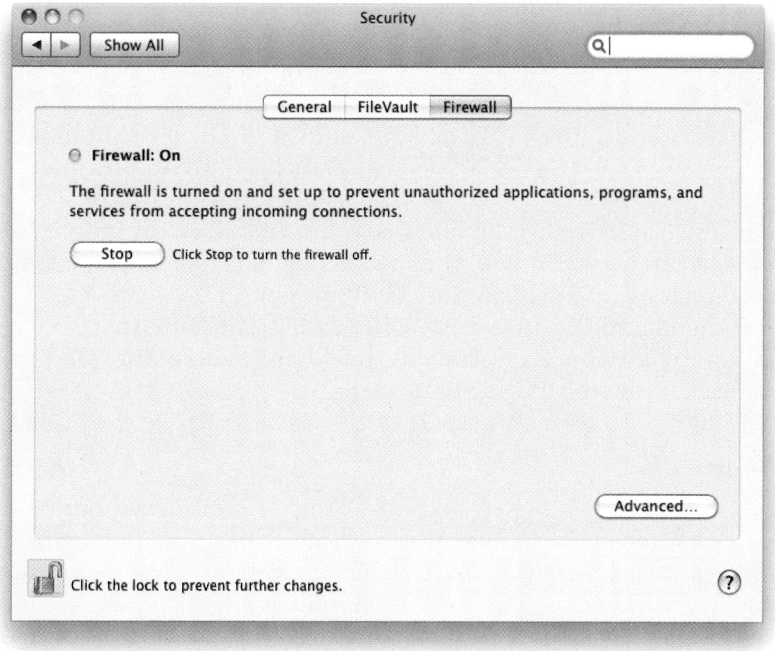

What Does Apple Say About Security Today?

We had heard that Mac OS X Snow Leopard includes antivirus software, but if it is there, we have not found mention of it as "antivirus" at the Apple Web site. As we described in the introduction to this chapter, the Mac OS X security page recommends antivirus software, but did not name any; nor did it state that any was included in the OS. Find out what Apple says about security today. Try this:

1. Point your Internet browser to **www.apple.com/macosx/security/**. If the page is no longer at this address, do a search of the site on "OS X security."
2. Read the contents of the resulting page.
3. Look for a link to a recent security brief, and retrieve it and read it.
4. Come to your own conclusions about the security of your Mac and discuss it with classmates.

WARNING!

Any time you unlock a settings pane, be sure to lock it again when you finish.

FIGURE 9–20 Firewall turned on

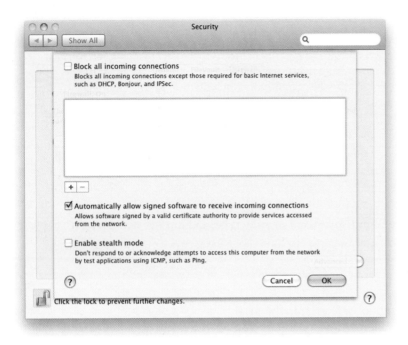

FIGURE 9–21 This setting is necessary if you are using any sharing services on your Mac.

firewall on a new installation of Mac OS X Snow Leopard. This requires some explanation. You could block all incoming connections if all you are doing is simple Web browsing and sending and receiving e-mail. During these operations you initiate the connection to a Web server or mail server. The traffic that comes to your computer because of these actions is not seeking to initiate a connection to your computer; it is simply responding to your request for Web pages or e-mail messages. Therefore, you could block all incoming connections, but still browse the Internet and send and receive e-mail.

You may wonder why you would want to allow someone from the Internet or even from your private network to initiate a connection to your computer. If you want to share anything from your computer, you need to select the setting shown in Figure 9–21. That includes files or printer sharing, screen sharing, iChat Bonjour, and iTunes music sharing. However, if you do not plan to do any type of sharing, select Block all incoming connections. When you do this, the third option, Enable stealth mode, automatically turns on. If later you wish to use a sharing service change the setting back.

Antivirus and Antispyware

Because the Mac OS has been a minority operating system, Macs have not been severely plagued by viruses, unlike Windows systems. OS X's insistence on an administrator password before installing new software offers an additional barrier of protection. Nonetheless, we recommend you install antivirus software. There are commercially available antivirus programs such as Norton AntiVirus (www.norton.com) and avast! antivirus Mac Edition as well as free antivirus programs, such as ClamXav. Similarly, you will find a selection of commercial anti-spyware products, such as Internet Cleanup 4.0 from Smith Micro and MacScan 2.5 from SecureMac, and an Internet security suite from NetBarrier X5 includes anti-spyware. As Mac sales expand, the likelihood of becoming more vulnerable to attacks will probably increase.

FileVault

FileVault is Mac OS X's file encryption feature. When turned on for a user account, FileVault encrypts that user's Home folder using a sophisticated encryption scheme. Previously, even though permissions were set on a user's Home folder, there were many schemes for accessing those files even when the user was not logged on. With FileVault turned on, your files are accessible only while you are logged on. Unless someone has access to your password, or you walk away from your computer without logging out, no one can open

WARNING!

Don't forget the Master Password. If a user forgets the login password, the Master Password is the only way to access that user's FileVault-protected Home folder.

files in your Home folder. An administrator
can turn FileVault on for a user when creating
an account, or the user can turn on FileVault
after logging in, using the Security preferences pane, as shown in Figure 9–22. The Master Password must be set by an administrator
because this is the unlocking password for
all FileVault-compressed Home folders on the
computer—a fail-safe for when a user forgets
a login password. A Master Password needs
to be set only once on each computer, but an
administrator can also change this password.

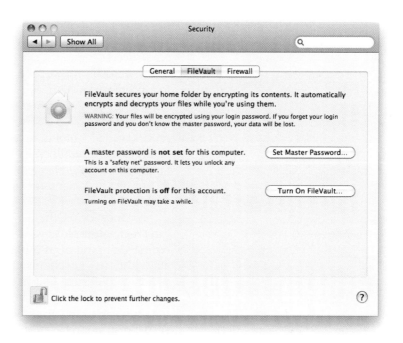

Secure Virtual Memory

Mac OS X uses a swap file, much as Windows
does. The swap file is disk space the OS uses
as if it is memory. Therefore, this is called
virtual memory. All multitasking operating
systems use virtual memory to allow you to
have several applications open. While you
are actively using your word processor, most

FIGURE 9–22 The Security
preferences pane with FileVault
settings

other open applications are just waiting for you to switch back to them. Therefore, it temporarily saves at least part of the code and data for these other apps
to the swap file. Clever hackers can access the swap file, so Apple has added a
feature called Secure Virtual Memory, which encrypts the swap file. Turn this
on if you work with data that you must protect from snooping. The downside
is that you may (or may not) notice a slight delay when switching programs
because that is when the contents of the swap file are decrypted and brought
back into memory. Enable Secure Virtual Memory on the General page of the
Security preferences pane.

Securing System Preferences Panes

You may recall that certain System Preferences panes can be locked and unlocked. This
is a good thing. However, the default setting
for this behavior is that if you unlock one
pane, all the others are unlocked. Of course,
this means that if you lock one the others lock
also. If you want to ensure that the panes must
be unlocked and locked individually, open the
Security preferences pane and click to place a
check in the box labeled "Require a password
to unlock each System Preferences pane," as
shown here.

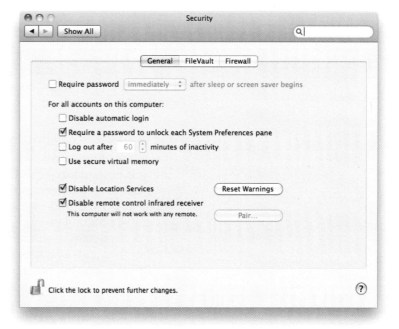

Keychain

The keychain is part of a credentials management system using the word "keychain" as a
metaphor for a physical keychain. The password to the keychain gives the user access to
all the passwords or "keys" on that keychain.
Each keychain is a secure database of a user's
passwords. Two default keychains, System and System Roots, belong to the
OS. By default, Mac OS X creates a keychain, called login, for you the first

Make System Preferences panes
more secure.

time you log in, using your account password as a master password for the keychain. Then as you go about your business, logging in to various servers to access e-mail and access other resources, as well as various Web sites, the credentials you supply are saved in your keychain, provided you respond to a prompt asking if you want to save the password. While some Web sites have login programs that will not allow this, many do, and if you save the password for a Web site in your key chain, it will complete the login boxes (a process called AutoFill in Safari) each time you reconnect to one of these sites. Safari turns AutoFill on by default, and you can turn it off, if you do not want keychain to remember your credentials. Look for a setting similar to Auto-Fill, or one that mentions remembering passwords in any Internet browser to enable keychain with that browser.

For most of us, the login keychain is sufficient for all our needs, but you can create multiple keychains, each with a separate purpose, such as for your online shopping or as a place to save your personal credit information. Create additional keychains if you need varying security levels. For instance, you can configure one keychain so that the keychain locks if there is idle time over a certain threshold. This is where you keep your keys for accessing online banking accounts. Then create another keychain that will not have such a restriction because it is for low-security activity, such as a Web site you access purely for entertainment, such as Pandora, or for your instant messaging account. To create multiple keychains for various purposes, use Keychain Access, found in Finder | Applications | Utilities.

Managing Local User Accounts

Mac OS X supports multiple local user accounts. At home, school, or work, you can set up a single computer with multiple accounts so that each person is restricted to his or her own home folder, preserving preferences from one session to another. As in Microsoft Windows, two users can log in to the same computer at the same time, but only one can have control of the "console," the keyboard, screen, and mouse at any given time. Mac OS X preserves each account's session in memory and users can switch back and forth using something called fast user switching. As a rule, users log in and log out when they finish working.

When multiple user accounts exist, you will see a login prompt similar to Figure 9–23. To log in you simply click on your user name and supply the password. In this section we will describe the types of users, something called Automatic login, and a security feature called File Vault, which you can enable for each individual user. Then you can practice creating a user account.

Types of Users and Privileges

There are three types of user accounts—two, administrator and standard, are self-explanatory. The third, root, is an account type that offers UNIX root access to your computer and file system, and which you should implement only if you understand the restrictions (or lack of them) placed on these accounts. Changing things on your computer in this account mode can result in serious system dysfunction and lost data. Do not implement it unless you are familiar with UNIX.

We describe the main functionality of the three account types here.

Administrator Account. The administrator account type, also simply called admin, is for advanced users or for the person who will administer this computer, adding more users, installing software, and the like. The first account created during installation is an administrator. Open the Accounts preferences pane from System Preferences and view the local accounts on a Mac.

> Remember that the basis of OS X is UNIX, so references in the text to UNIX are not mistakes!

FIGURE 9–23 A multiuser login prompt

Right after installation, it should have only one active account, the account created during installation. Notice the description, Admin under the account name in Figure 9–24. This level allows you to:

- Change all system preference settings and install software in the main application and library folders.
- Create, modify, and delete user accounts.

Standard Account. This account type is for ordinary users, those whom you typically need to save from themselves on a regular basis. This account level will minimize those desperate tech support calls! This level has the following restrictions:

- File access is limited to only the user's Home folder and the shared folder (/Users/Shared/).
- Access is denied to higher-level system preferences, such as network settings, sharing, software update settings, user setup, and date and time settings.

Root Account. The root account exists but is not enabled in the standard installation of Mac OS X. Root is only for people familiar with the inner workings of UNIX. It is not for normal software installation or most administrative tasks. Root does the following:

- Gives you complete control over all folders and files on the Mac
- Is seldom needed for normal use

FIGURE 9–24 The Accounts preferences pane

You rarely will require the amount of control over OS X system files that the root account allows. Apple specifically organized OS X to limit the need to change the system files and folders. The files that most users will want to change are located in the main Library folder (administrator access required) or in the user's private Library folder (/Users/*YourUsername*/Library/), where the ordinary user has access.

Even if you decide to do a task that your admin account cannot perform, it is also likely to be a task you will do at the Terminal. Therefore, you can open a Terminal window and use the **sudo** command (see Chapter 8) to temporarily borrow root privileges to complete a task.

If you are still determined to enable the root, be sure you are prepared to give it a strong password. Then, open the Help menu and type "enable root user" in the Spotlight Search box. Select the result titled "Enabling the root user" and follow the instructions. If you enable the root, only log in when you need to use it and log out immediately after. You should log in for normal work with either a standard or admin type account.

Automatic Login

Automatic login bypasses the login window during startup and logs into the designated user account when the computer powers on. With Automatic Login turned off, it prompts users to choose their individual accounts and passwords when the computer boots up. Depending on the version of OS X you are using, you will configure automatic login on the Login panel of System Preferences (old releases), or by using the Login Options in the Accounts preference.

Creating User Accounts

The first user account is set up when you install OS X. This account is automatically set up with administrator access. After the installation process is complete, you can create additional user accounts.

Step-by-Step 9.03
Adding a New User

In this exercise, you will add a new user to your computer. To complete this exercise, you will need the following:

- A Mac computer with OS X installed.
- An administrator account and password that will allow you to log on to your computer.

Step 1

Begin the process of creating a new user by choosing System Preferences from the Apple menu, clicking the Accounts preferences pane, and clicking the button with the Plus sign (or the New User button).

Step 2

Type a long and a short name in the corresponding boxes. Both are case sensitive, and the short name is limited to a maximum of eight characters with no spaces. OS X uses the short name for the user's home folder as well as to recognize the user during login processes. You can change the full name and password later, but the short name is permanent. The user can log in as either.

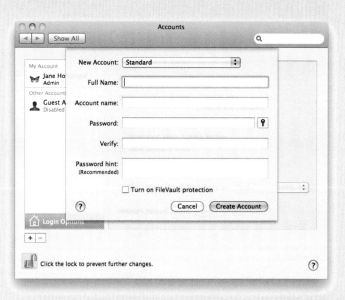

Step 3

Assign the user password. A password can be anything, even blank for any user not needing administrator access. For highest security, the password should contain, at minimum, upper and lower case alpha characters and one number or symbol: for example, 5$mUffins. If you are curious about how strong your password is, click the key button to open the Password Assistant. It will rate the "quality" of the password and suggest a strong password. Close Password Assistant once you have arrived at a password.

Step 4

Complete the New Account drop-down box, selecting Turn on FileVault protection, and then click the Create Account button. If you wish to make the system more secure, click to place a check in the box labeled "Use secure virtual memory." Click Create Account. If this is the first time you have turned on FileVault for any user on this computer, you will need to create a master password in the provided drop-down box. Do so and then click Continue. The Accounts pane will display with the new user listed.

Step 5

If you turned on secure virtual memory, you will need to restart the computer for it to take effect. If you did so, restart now; if you did not, then, as a test, log off and log back in as the new account.

LO 9.5 | Troubleshooting Common Mac OS Problems

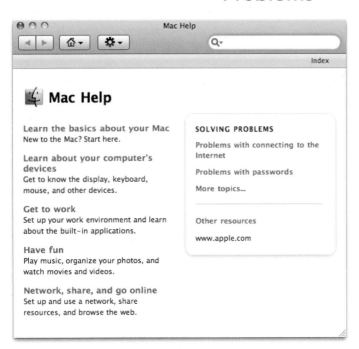

OS X Mac Help window with the Spotlight Search box on the top right

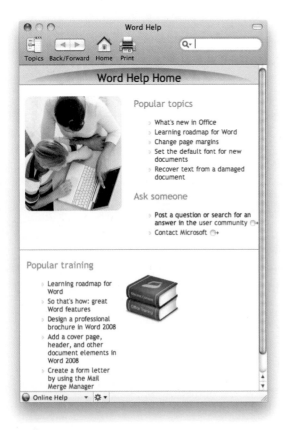

FIGURE 9–25 The Microsoft Word for Windows Help utility

In this section you learn where to find basic help and a guide to the system utilities and keyboard shortcuts that can help you get out of trouble. You'll also learn how to handle the larger files that you'll encounter in today's computing environment.

Where to Find Help

Where do you go to find general help in Mac OS 9 and OS X or from within an application?

Help with the OS

If you have questions about how the Mac OS works, the first port of call is the help facility built into the Mac OS. From the Finder, go to the Help menu and select Mac Help. Now either click one of the blue links or enter a keyword in the Spotlight Search box. If system help does not answer your questions and solve your problem, connect to the Internet and visit Apple's support center at **www.apple.com/support/**. Information there is well organized, and Apple's Knowledge Base, manuals, and related discussion groups are all fully searchable.

If self-help fails and your computer is still under warranty, contact Apple directly, using the information that came with your computer. Technical support is expensive if your computer is outside its warranty period. Novice users who use their computers enough to increase the likelihood of multiple requests for support should consider signing up for an AppleCare service and support package to keep technical support costs down. Find more information at **www.apple.com/support/products/**.

Alternatively, members of the network of Apple user groups around the world can get support from other users and learn more about their computers. Apple user groups are a useful and affordable way to increase your knowledge of your system and the software you choose and use. For more information, see **www.apple.com/usergroups/**.

Help within Applications

If a problem with an application persists, click the Help menu from the menu bar. In many cases, there will be a local help utility and an option to find online help for the application. Search through the help utility to find an answer to your problem. Figure 9–25 shows the Microsoft Word help utility.

When to Quit

If an open application is behaving strangely—maybe it freezes, displaying the "busy" icon for no apparent reason—quit the application and restart it. This will resolve many transient problems. To quit an open application, click its name in the menu bar and select Quit, as shown on the next page. Then, relaunch the application.

Sometimes an application will not politely quit; that's when you must use Force Quit—either from the Apple menu or with the key combination of OPTION-COMMAND-ESC. This will bring up the Force Quit Applications box, shown here. It shows you all the running applications, so you can select the correct one. A force quit allows you to safely remove an application from memory without requiring a restart of your computer and without adversely affecting the rest of the programs running in memory.

An application's Quit option

Select the application from the Force Quit Applications box

Failure to Quit

Sometimes, when you attempt to shut down, log off, or restart, you see a message that you haven't been logged out because an application has failed to quit, like the one shown here. This is another occasion to roll out the Force Quit tool. If the application still refuses to quit, do a hard power-down by pressing and holding the power button for several seconds.

Forgotten Password

The first-created user account on your computer is automatically designated an administrator. If you happen to forget or lose the administrator password, you can reset it by using the OS X installation DVD. To do this insert the DVD and from the Install screen choose Utilities | Reset Password. Select the hard drive that contains the System folder, and use the first pop-up menu to select the name of your account. Enter your new password twice. You should keep the DVD in a safe place, because anyone with the OS X DVD can gain complete access to your system.

Mac Help to the Rescue!

If you're in OS X and can't remember the keyboard shortcuts for escaping a program freeze, jog your memory with Mac Help. Try this:

1. Click the desktop to make sure you're in the Finder.
2. Move the mouse to the Finder's Help menu and select Mac Help or press COMMAND-SHIFT-?.
3. Type "Freeze" in the search field.
4. Click the Ask button.
5. Choose Shortcuts for Freezes.

try this!

Disappearing Sidebar Items

Our mantra is "Disaster is only a mouse-click away." We could write an entire book on the foibles of blithely moving objects around in any GUI. One

Control what appears in the Sidebar

> If your system is crashing a lot, one of the reasons may be damage to the hard disk. Running a diagnostic test with Disk Utility will reveal if there is damage.

minor, but annoying problem we have had in OS X that we feel is due to mousing around is the disappearance of Applications in the Finder Sidebar. Here is a simple solution to this problem, or if any other items disappear from the Sidebar: Simply open the Finder menu, select Preferences, and then click Sidebar in the button bar. In the list of items, ensure that all the items you wish displayed have a check mark, then close Finder Preferences.

Useful System Utilities

The utilities described here for OS X are useful for basic troubleshooting. As with any situation, if you find yourself in deep water, seek expert advice. Here is a quick guide to OS X's hard disk and network software utilities.

Disk Utility

Found in the OS X Utilities folder (Applications | Utilities), Disk Utility offers a summary and usage statistics for all volumes attached to the computer. The utility, shown below, also includes Disk First Aid, which enables you to verify or repair Mac OS Standard-, Mac OS Extended-, and UFS-formatted disks, including hard disks and CD-ROMs. The software also works as a one-stop shop for erasing and partitioning volumes.

Network Preferences

Have you ever had a problem with your home Internet connection and found yourself talking to a help desk person from your Internet service provider (ISP)? The help desk often wants you to provide information about your network connection, such as the IP address and other configuration settings. To do that in OS X Snow Leopard, open the Network pane in System Preferences, click the Advanced button, and click on the TCP/IP tab in the drop-down box, shown on the next page.

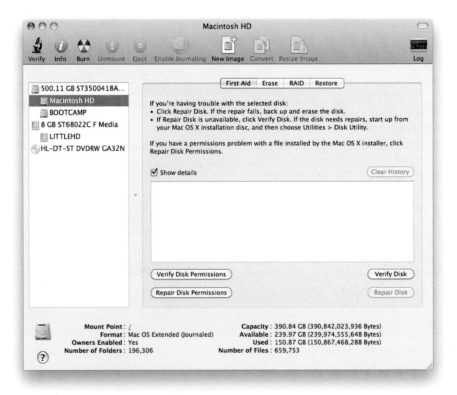

Disk Utility window

Similarly, if the help desk asks you for the physical address of your network adapter (also called a hardware address or MAC address), you will find this in the Network pane by clicking on the name that represents the hardware connection. For instance, if you are using AirPort Wi-Fi, the hardware address is at the bottom of the page titled "AirPort ID." If you are connected with Ethernet, click the Ethernet button to open the Ethernet panel where you will find the hardware address labeled "Ethernet ID." It shows both of these values as six sets of two-digit hexadecimal values separated by colons (:).

Network preferences pane

Chapter 9 REVIEW

Chapter Summary

After reading this chapter and completing the Step-by-Step tutorials and Try This! exercises, you should understand the following facts about Apple computers and the Mac OS.

Mac OS X Overview

- Apple Computer, now officially Apple Inc., began April 1, 1976 ,with the Apple I. The company introduced the Apple II one year later. In 1983 the Lisa was introduced, the first production computer with a GUI.
- Apple introduced the Macintosh in 1984, the first affordable personal computer with a color GUI.
- Apple's UNIX core, known as Darwin, is a product of the open source development community, with all the advantages that brings.
- Apple has introduced six major versions, announced a seventh, and had many interim minor versions of OS X. The most recently announced major version is Lion, projected to ship in the second quarter of 2011.

Installing and Configuring Mac OS X

- Mac OS X installations are on proprietary Mac hardware, which normally comes with the OS

preinstalled. Therefore, as a user, most people complete the installation with the help of the Mac OS X Setup Assistant.

- Before upgrading, check the version of the installed Mac OS.
- Hardware requirements have not increased between Mac OS X Leopard (10.5) and Mac OS X Snow Leopard (10.6).
- The most important post-installation task is bringing the Mac OS X installation up-to-date with the latest security and functionality updates. This will occur automatically, or you can initiate it through the GUI.

Managing Mac OS X on the Desktop

- In OS X, what were called Control Panels in OS 9 are now described as System Preferences.
- The Finder in OS X is the GUI face of OS X to the user. It offers a variety of file management tools.
- The Apple menu opens when you click the Apple icon in the upper left of the OS X window. Use this menu to shut down, restart, or log out, and a few other tasks.
- System Preferences is the Mac OS X equivalent of the Windows Control Panel.

- Drag icons on and off the Dock and configure it to be on the left side, right side, or bottom of the screen.
- Open Applications | Utilities and select Terminal to open a window with the $ prompt where you can enter UNIX commands.
- Most printers install automatically, appearing in any applications Print menu.
- If a printer does not automatically install, use the Print box and click Add Printer and it will attempt to detect the printer.

Managing Local Security in Mac OS X

- Ensure that you enable the OS X Firewall.
- While Mac OS X includes many security features, even Apple recommends that you install antivirus software.
- If you have important and sensitive information on your Mac, ensure that you securely encrypt your Home folder with FileVault. Additionally, use a strong password, and never leave your computer unattended without logging out.
- Turn on Secure Virtual Memory for added security.
- The keychain is a secure database of a user's passwords. By default, Mac OS X creates a keychain for you the first time you log in, using your account password as a master password for the keychain.

- Mac OS X supports multiple local user accounts.
- The first user account in the Mac OS X is automatically designated an administrator. If you forget the user name or password for this account, you can use the OS X installation CD to reset the password.
- The types of user accounts in OS X are administrator, standard account, and root.
- The administrator account type can create new accounts, change all system preference settings, and install software in the main application and library folders.
- The standard user account type can only access files in the user's home folder and the shared folder (/Users/Shared/).
- The root account has complete control over all folders and files on the Mac. This account is disabled by default.

Troubleshooting Common Mac OS Problems

- When you need help with Mac OS X, first search through Mac Help or the Help utility for an application if you have narrowed the problem to one application.
- If an application freezes, press COMMAND-OPTION-Esc to force it to quit. OS X handles this extreme measure very well.

Key Terms List

Apple menu *(333)*	Lion *(321)*	Secure Virtual Memory *(349)*
Darwin *(320)*	Mac *(320)*	Snow Leopard *(321)*
Dock *(324)*	Mac OS X Server *(320)*	Spotlight *(336)*
Finder *(323)*	Mac OS X Setup Assistant *(325)*	System Preferences *(333)*
keychain *(349)*	Master Password *(349)*	

Key Terms Quiz

Use the Key Terms List to complete the sentences that follow. Not all terms will be used.

1. Apple is the company, and _____ is the nickname for the line of computers dating from 1984 and continuing to today.

2. To search for files, the utility you need is called _____.

3. A user's login passwords for purposes of logging on to various servers and Web sites are saved in a secure database called the _____.

4. At the core of OS X is a powerful UNIX system called _____.

5. The 10.7 version of OS X is named _____.

6. _____ encrypts the Mac OS X swap file.

7. _____ is to Mac OS X as Windows Explorer is to Windows.

8. The _____ is a GUI object on the desktop that holds program icons for fast launching, as well as icons for open applications you can use for task switching.

9. Set a/an _____ and be sure to remember it because this is the only way to access a user's FileVault-protected Home folder after a user forgets his login password.

10. The _____, accessed through a small icon at the extreme top left of the Mac OS X screen, sounds like something you might be given as you are seated in a vegetarian restaurant.

Multiple-Choice Quiz

1. When did the first Mac OS appear?
   a. 1976
   b. 1983
   c. 1999
   d. 1984
   e. 2000

2. What major revision of Mac OS X did Apple announce in the fall of 2010?
   a. Leopard
   b. Cheetah
   c. Snow Leopard
   d. Tiger
   e. Lion

3. When you first power up a new Mac, what program starts automatically and prompts you for information?
   a. Dock
   b. Safari
   c. Mac OS X Setup Assistant
   d. iChat
   e. System Preferences

4. Complete this sentence: In OS X, forced quits of applications . . .
   a. often cause other applications to fail.
   b. always require a restart of the OS.
   c. require that you run a program from a Terminal window.
   d. usually cause a system crash.
   e. rarely affect the performance of the rest of the computer's functions.

5. Where will you quickly find version information for your Mac OS X installation?
   a. Recent items
   b. Window menu
   c. Help menu
   d. Apple menu
   e. Finder

6. Which of the following is one of the four views available when browsing Finder windows?
   a. Date
   b. Icon
   c. Reverse
   d. Finder
   e. Juke Box

7. The Applications folder has disappeared from the Finder Sidebar. Where in the GUI can you go to put the Applications folder back into the Sidebar?
   a. System Preferences | Appearance
   b. Utilities
   c. Sidebar | Preferences
   d. Finder | Preferences
   e. Windows | Restore

8. OS X's Date and Time system preference can be configured to keep the correct time by regularly comparing your system time with:
   a. GMT
   b. The BBC
   c. A network time server
   d. Your watch
   e. The DOS clock

9. Which account is disabled by default and yet is the most powerful account on a Mac OS X system?
   a. Standard
   b. Group
   c. Administrator
   d. Root
   e. Global

10. You have an external hard drive from another Mac, and you would like to remove all the data on it and use it as backup for your new Mac. What will you use to prepare this disk for use?
    a. Finder
    b. Boot Camp Assistant
    c. System Preferences
    d. Tools
    e. Disk Utility

11. What item should you keep safely stored because anyone who has it can gain complete access to your Mac system?
    a. Keyboard
    b. Keychain
    c. Mouse
    d. Bootcamp Assistant
    e. OS X installation DVD

12. What keyboard shortcut can you use to force an application to quit?
    a. COMMAND-POWER key
    b. SHIFT-ESC
    c. SHIFT-RETURN
    d. COMMAND-OPTION-ESC
    e. Press C during startup

13. Which of the following is the name of the command-line interface in OS X that allows you to run commands at the $ prompt?
    a. DOS Editor
    b. ResEdit
    c. Terminal
    d. End User
    e. iMonkey

14. Which of the following is not customizable in the OS X Dock?
    a. Size
    b. Position on the screen
    c. Magnification turned on or off

d. Color

e. Icons that appear on the Dock

15. Which of the following preference panes allows you to change the time zone?

a. Universal Access

b. Date and Time

c. World Time

d. Time Machine

e. Longitude

Essay Quiz

1. Write a few sentences describing the significance of the UNIX core of OS X.

2. Your Mac laptop has both personal financial information and files for all your in-process school projects, including data from research for a major project in one of your classes. This laptop is always with you at home, at school, and at work. Describe how you will ensure the security of your valuable data.

3. Your copy of Microsoft Word suddenly freezes in midsentence. Describe the best way to regain control of your Mac.

4. When you brought your new iMac home and completed the information in the Mac OS Setup Assistant, you did not have Internet access. You have signed up for Internet access and the setup instructions from your ISP requires the hardware address of your network card. Explain where you will find this information within the Mac OS X GUI and describe how it represents this value.

5. Describe the purpose of the Dock.

Lab Projects

LAB PROJECT 9.1

You support the Mac computers in your office and one of your coworkers, Helen Bandora, married Jon Moz and changed her name to Helen Moz. She has asked you to change her user account so that both the full name (the "long name") and the account name (the "short name") reflect her new name. She would also like her home directory, currently named *hbandora*, to be named *hmoz*.

You have agreed to make these changes for her.

You will need a computer with OS X installed on which you have administrator rights.

You will need to do the following:

1. Research the solution for setting up Helen with a correctly named account.

2. Find Helen's Home directory on the hard drive.

3. Implement your solution on the lab computer.

LAB PROJECT 9.2

The manager of your department has asked you to set up a Mac with two USB printers attached and to teach a user how to print something on each of the two printers.

You will need a computer with OS X installed on which you have administrator rights, plus two USB printers. To make this lab true to life, it would be useful if one printer were a black-and-white laser printer

and the other a color ink-jet so there's a good reason someone might switch between the two.

You will need to do the following:

1. Install and check that both printers are working on your lab computer.

2. Find a willing volunteer.

3. Show the volunteer how to use the Print menu from any application to switch between printers.

LAB PROJECT 9.3

If you ever find yourself the administrator of a large network, you would want to minimize your network's electricity consumption by instituting good energy practices.

You will need a computer with OS X installed and to do the following:

1. Go into the Energy Saver control panel and assess the various options you have for controlling the display and hard disk sleep features. Your goal is to reduce the display and hard disk sleep times to the minimum possible without causing the display to dim or the hard disk to spin down intrusively for users.

2. This is a chance to be creative and aware of the types of users of your network, and how they interact with the lab environment. Are computers used constantly, requiring a generous display or hard disk sleep time? Is the amount of RAM sufficient for working with files in memory or does the hard disk need to be accessed constantly? What kinds of software do your users use: processor and hard drive-intensive programs such as image manipulation and multimedia programs, or e-mail and word processing software?

chapter 10

The Client Side of Networking

"Several principles are key to assuring that the Web becomes ever more valuable. The primary design principle underlying the Web's usefulness and growth is universality. When you make a link, you can link to anything. That means people must be able to put anything on the Web, no matter what computer they have, software they use or human language they speak and regardless of whether they have a wired or wireless Internet connection."

—**Tim Berners-Lee**
Essay in Scientific American,
November 22, 2010

A stand-alone PC—one with no connection whatsoever to a network—is a rare thing today. Most of us can find some reason or need to connect to a network, whether it is a small home network, a corporate intranet, or the Internet. Without a network connection, a PC is like a remote island where the inhabitants have resolved to be isolated from civilization. And it does take resolve today to be so isolated because there are means by which a computer in even the most remote location can connect to the Internet or another network. The heart and soul of all networks are servers, the computers that provide the services we, as clients, seek on a network. These services are as simple as those that give us access to files and printers, Web pages, applications, and much more. Each of these services provides an important role on a network.

At work, at school, and at home, computer users depend on client software components to accomplish work—whether they are doing research over the Internet, playing an Internet game, using e-mail, or transferring files from a server to the desktop computer.

Learning Outcomes

In this chapter, you will learn how to:

LO **10.1** Configure a client for a TCP/IP network.

LO **10.2** Connect to the Internet.

LO **10.3** Work with basic Internet clients.

LO **10.4** Configure File and Print clients.

LO **10.5** Troubleshoot common network client problems.

In this chapter you will study the client side of networking. Because a client cannot interact with network servers unless you properly configure it to communicate on a network, we will begin with an overview of the TCP/IP protocol suite, the most popular set of rules for transporting information over all types of networks. You'll learn how to configure TCP/IP settings on a client computer, and learn about the file and print clients used most often on private networks. Then you will move on to the Internet, first examining methods for connecting to the Internet, and then examining the most common Internet clients. Finally, you will practice methods for troubleshooting common connection problems. ✳

LO 10.1 | Configuring a Client for a TCP/IP Network

TCP/IP is the underlying protocol suite of the Internet and nearly all private networks, regardless of the network medium (wired or wireless). Therefore, you must configure your computer to work with TCP/IP to communicate over these networks. In this section we will work at understanding the TCP/IP protocol suite so that you can easily configure your computer.

Understanding the TCP/IP Protocol Suite

TCP/IP is a suite of protocols that work together to allow both similar and dissimilar computers to communicate. You need this protocol suite to access the Internet and it is the most common protocol suite used on private intranets. It gets its name from two of its many protocols: Transmission Control Protocol (TCP) and Internet Protocol (IP)—the core protocols of TCP/IP. If, during Windows installation, Windows detects a network adapter it will install a driver for that adapter card and the TCP/IP protocol will automatically install.

TCP/IP is a subject of epic proportions! In the following sections, we offer only an introduction to TCP/IP in which we attempt to arm you with useful information, but not overwhelm you with detail. Our goal is to give you an overview of TCP/IP, and familiarize you with the settings that you may need to enter or modify for your Windows desktop computer.

Transmission Control Protocol (TCP)

Transmission Control Protocol (TCP) is the protocol responsible for the accurate delivery of messages, verifying and resending pieces that fail to make the trip from source to destination. Several other protocols act as sub-protocols, helping TCP accomplish this.

Internet Protocol (IP)

Internet Protocol (IP) is a protocol that packages your communications in chunks, each of which is called a **packet**. This protocol allows a logical address, called an IP address, to identify your computer on a simple network as well as an internetwork (a network of networks connected through routers). Special routing protocols can use a destination IP address to choose the best route for a packet to take through a very complex internetwork. IP also has sub-protocols that help it accomplish its work, but we will not discuss the sub-protocols. It is important for you to learn about IP addresses because you cannot participate on a TCP/IP network without a valid IP address.

If you want to learn more, check out the TCP/IP tutorials available on the Internet. The most entertaining is a video at www.warriorsofthe .net (also on YouTube). Be sure to watch the full version. Two more conventional tutorials are at www. learntcpip.com and www. learntosubnet.com. Pick one and spend a rainy Saturday learning about TCP/IP and binary math!

IP Addressing Fundamentals

In your first computer-related job, you might not have any responsibility for IP addressing on your network, so you might think this section is not necessary or you can ignore it. However, whether you're a junior networking associate or a power user in a company, or at home as a customer of an Internet service provider (ISP), you might have to look up an IP address on your own workstation or the workstation of others. Why? Because a network administrator (or technical support person at your ISP) may need the information, and you may be physically at the computer while the network administrator may not be. This means you should be familiar with IP addressing so that your encounters with networking staff are less stressful and more educational.

Let's now explore the basics of IP addressing. First, an IP address is not assigned to a computer but to each network adapter, whether wired (Ethernet) or wireless (Wi-Fi). Even a modem has an address when you use it to dial to the Internet. If your computer has multiple network connection devices connected to different networks, such as an Ethernet network adapter connected to a local area network (LAN) and a modem used as a dial-up WAN connection to a remote network, each has an address.

A desktop computer usually has only a single network device connecting it to a specific network, so that is the only address by which the network knows that computer. That is why you see the Internet Protocol as a component of a connection in Windows (see Figure 10–1). The Connect Using box near the top of the Local Area Connection Properties dialog box identifies the connecting device to which these settings apply. There are two Internet Protocols listed in Figure 10–1: Internet Protocol versions 4 (IPv4) and Internet Protocol version 6 (IPv6). We'll look at each of these in turn, but first we'll talk about IP addresses in general.

An IP address identifies a computer, a "host" in network terms, and the network on which the computer resides. This address, when added to a message packet as the destination address, allows the message to move from one network to another on the Internet. At the connecting point between networks, a special network device called a router uses its routing protocols to determine the route to the destination address, before sending each packet along to the next router closer to the destination network. Each computer that directly attaches to the Internet must have a globally unique IP address. Both versions of IP have this much, and more, in common. Following are short explanations of IPv4 and IPv6 addresses.

Internet Protocol Version 4 (IPv4). Internet Protocol version 4 (IPv4) and its addressing scheme have been in use for the past three decades. With 32-bit addressing, calculated by raising 2 to the 32nd power (2^{32}), IPv4 offers almost 4.3 billion possible IP addresses, but the way in which they were allocated in the beginning greatly reduced the number of usable addresses.

An IPv4 address is 32-bits long in binary notation, but it usually appears as four decimal numbers, each in the range of 0–255, separated by a period. See examples of IPv4 addresses in Figures 10–2, 10–3, and 10–4. Figure 10–2 shows the Windows 7 Network Connection Details with the address of the local connection being 192.168.1.134. The other IP addresses shown are to other network devices. In the Mac OS X Network preferences pane, shown in Figure 10–3, the AirPort WiFi device has an IPv4 address of 192.168.1.135. In the box in Figure 10–2 and the pane in Figure 10–3 are IP addresses. The Network Tools dialog box from Ubuntu shows an IPv4 address in Figure 10–4.

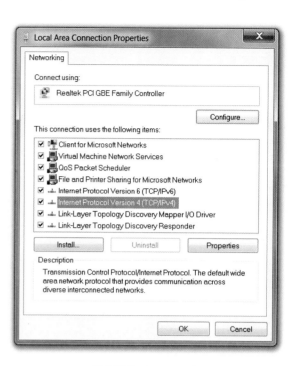

FIGURE 10–1 Windows 7 Local Area Connection Properties dialog box

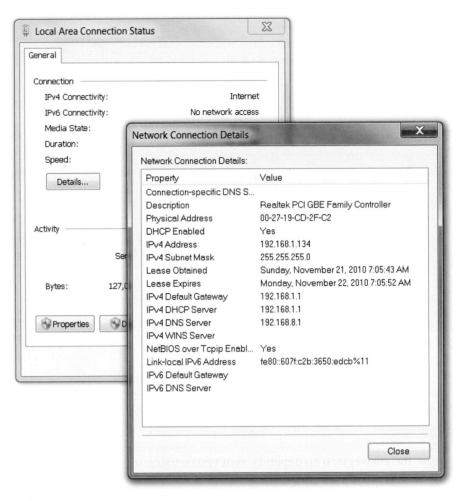

FIGURE 10–2 Windows 7 Network Connection Details box

FIGURE 10–3 Mac OS X Network preferences pane

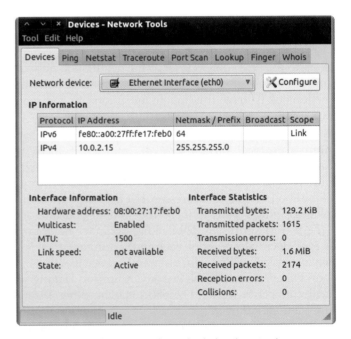

FIGURE 10–4 The Network Tools dialog box in the **GNOME** GUI in Ubuntu

Because this is a very simplified explanation, we will not go into the exact rules for these addresses, just an overview. And, as you can see, there is more to an IP configuration than the address of the device itself, but before we discuss these other settings we will first tell you more about IP addresses.

IPv6 Addresses. The Internet is currently transitioning to Internet Protocol version 6 (IPv6) with a new addressing scheme that provides many more addresses. For many years, manufacturers and standards organizations have worked toward the day when they can fully support IPv6 on the Internet. We aren't there yet, even though the last block of IPv4 addresses was assigned by the Internet Assigned Numbers Authority (IANA) on February 1, 2011. In preparation for the day when ISPs, the Internet routers, and networking applications are fully IPv6 ready, recent versions of operating systems and virtually all new networking equipment comes with support for IPv6 built in.

IPv6 has 128-bit addressing, calculated by raising 2 to the 128th power (2^{128}), which supports a huge number of unique addresses—340,282,366,920,938,463,463,374,607,431,768,211,456 to be exact. An IPv6 address appears in eight groups of hexadecimal numbers separated by colons, such as this: 2002:470:B8F9:1:20C:29FF:FE53:45CA. You will often see an IPv6 address shortened by eliminating leading zeros in a group, and if there are all zeroes between a set of colons, the zeros won't show and you will see two colons together. And, if two or more groups of all zeros are adjacent, there will still only be two colons. The IPv6 address shown in Figure 10–4 has two adjacent colons where two groups of all zeros exist in the address.

Which Addresses Can You Use?

There are billions of addresses, so how do you pick an address to use? Of course, the answer is: It all depends. Will you be using the address on a public network (the Internet) or on a private network? A central organization decides how to allocate all these addresses for use on the public Internet. They also understand that organizations need to use IP addresses within their private networks. Therefore, they have divided the possible IP addresses into two broad categories: public addresses and private addresses.

Public Addresses. Public IP addresses are for hosts on the Internet. In IP terminology a host is any computer or device that has an IP address. To communicate over the Internet, you must send your message from an IP address that is unique on the entire Internet, and your message must go to an IP address that is also unique. The centrally responsible organization for allocation of public IP addresses is the Internet Assigned Numbers Authority (IANA). This organization allocates numbers to various Regional Internet Registries (RIRs), which have the task of allocating IP addresses to Internet service providers (ISPs). The largest ISPs, in turn, allocate addresses to other ISPs. You, or your school or employer, receive addresses for each Internet connection from your ISP. The addresses provided are from selected portions of those billions of possible addresses specifically used on the Internet.

Private Addresses. A private IP address is an address from one of three ranges of IPv4 addresses designated for use only on private networks, so they are unusable on the Internet. All the IPv4 addresses in Figures 10–2, 10–3, and 10–4 are private addresses. In fact, many organizations use these addresses on their private IP networks, and you do not need to get permission to do so. If a computer with a private address connects to the Internet, the Internet routers that route packets based on their IP addresses are configured to not let packets with these addresses pass. Table 10–1 shows the three ranges used as private IPv4 addresses. All other IPv4 addresses either have

TABLE 10–1   IPv4 Private IP Address Ranges
Private IPv4 Address Ranges
10.0.0.0 through 10.255.255.255
172.16.0.0 through 172.31.255.255
192.168.0.0 through 192.168.255.255

specialized uses or are public addresses valid for computers and devices that are on the Internet.

If a computer user on a private network using private IP addresses wishes to connect to the Internet, a device between the local network and the Internet must intercept, repackage, and give a public IP address as its source address to each data packet before it goes onto the Internet. Then, if there is a response, each returning packet will go through the same process before returning to the private address.

If you are connecting to the Internet from home, or through your school or work, there is probably a device between your computer and the ISP that substitutes (or translates) your actual IP address to a unique Internet IP address. There are a couple of methods for doing this. One involves a special network service called a proxy server, and another involves a special service called network address translation (NAT), which a NAT router provides. These are services that your ISP or network administrator manages for your school or organization. Such services also exist in the common devices now sold in consumer electronics stores called broadband routers, which allow home or small office computers to connect to the Internet, usually through a cable or DSL connection.

How Does a Computer Get an IP Address?

A computer gets an IP address in one of two ways: static address assignment and automatic address assignment. Automatic is the most common method used today.

Static Address Assignment. A static IP address is manually configured for a host and can, therefore, be considered semipermanent—that is, it stays with the device until someone takes action to change it. Manually configuring an IP address involves manually entering the IP address and other necessary IP settings. Most organizations do static IP addressing only on servers, network printers, and network devices such as routers that are required to have permanent addresses.

Where will you find this information in the rare event that you are required to use a static address on your desktop or laptop computer? Actually, unless you are setting up your own TCP/IP network (a very advanced task!), you will be given the IP addressing information by a network administrator if you are connecting to a LAN or by your Internet service provider if you are configuring an Internet connection. But most ISPs automate all the configuration of home broadband connection.

If you find yourself having to do this, be sure to carefully enter the numbers given to you, and double-check them! In Windows, you will enter these in the TCP/IP properties found in the properties dialog box for the network connection.

Automatic Address Assignment (DHCP and APIPA). One nearly universal method is used for assigning IP addresses to computers: automatic IP addressing. Another method is used as a sort of failsafe on Microsoft Windows computers: Automatic Private IP Addressing (APIPA).

WARNING!

Incorrect IP configuration settings can make your network connection useless. Modify IP configuration settings only if told to, and if you have been provided with settings from a network administrator or from your ISP. Then take great care to be accurate!

- Most organizations use automatic IP addressing for their desktop computers. It requires a special server or service on the network, called a Dynamic Host Configuration Protocol (DHCP) server, which issues IP addresses and settings to computers configured to obtain an IP address automatically, thus making them DHCP clients. The news gets even better since the default configuration of TCP/IP on a Windows, Mac, or Linux (depending on the distribution) computer is to obtain an IP address automatically! Look at Figures 10–2 and 10–3 to see if you can tell if these dialog boxes indicate how it acquired the addresses, such as a reference to "automatic" or "DHCP." You will not find such clues in the Ubuntu GNOME Network Tools dialog box in Figure 10–4; you would need to click the Configure button, and bring up the Network Connections dialog box to see how a connection device receives an IP address.

- Do not confuse *automatic* with *automatic private*. Microsoft adds a twist to the DHCP client—Automatic Private IP Addressing (APIPA), whereby a DHCP client computer that fails to receive an address from a DHCP server will automatically give itself an address from a special range that has 169.254 in the first two octets of the IP address. If a computer uses this range of addresses, it will not be able to communicate with other devices on the network unless they also have addresses using the same network ID.

  APIPA allows a novice to set up a small TCP/IP network and not have to bother learning about IP addressing. Each computer would use APIPA to assign itself an address, first testing that no other computer on the LAN is also using that same host ID. Theoretically, two or more computers on the same network using this method could do file and printer sharing.

IP Configuration Settings

If you must manually configure IPv4, you will need to understand the other settings to enter in addition to the IP address. Refer to the Internet Protocol Version 4 Properties dialog box in Figure 10–5 while reading the following descriptions of the various IP settings.

Subnet Mask. When a network device gets an IPv4 address, it must also get a subnet mask. The subnet mask is as critical as the address itself because it takes what looks like a single address and divides it into two addresses by masking off part of the address. It is sort of like your house address. The house number gives the address on the street, but you also need the street name. For example, the address 192.168.100.2 has a mask of 255.255.255.0. The IP protocol now knows that this network device has the host address of 2 (its house number) on network 192.168.100 (its street address). The host portion is the host ID, or host address, and the network portion is the net ID, or network address.

Take a brief look at how masking works. Technically, it is done using binary math (base-2 math that uses only 0s and 1s), but you do not have to be a binary math whiz to understand the concept of masking; just look at the IP address and the mask in its binary form. You can use the scientific setting of the Calculator program that comes with Windows to convert each octet (a group of eight binary digits) of an IP address from binary to decimal or vice versa. If you convert the IP address 192.168.100.2 to binary, it looks like this:

```
11000000.10101000.01100100.00000010.
```

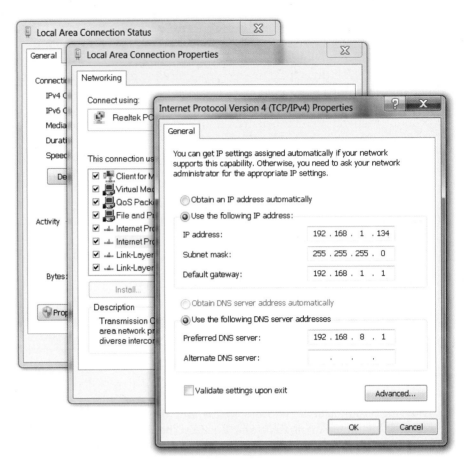

FIGURE 10–5 Manually configure TCP/IP in Windows using the Internet Protocol Version 4 (TCP/IPv4) Properties dialog box

If you convert the mask we are using, 255.255.255.0, to binary, it looks like this:

11111111.11111111.11111111.00000000.

If you lay the mask on top of the IP address, the ones cover (mask) the first 24 bits (short for binary digits). What falls under the ones of the mask is the network address, and what falls under the zeros of the mask is the host address. Figure 10–6 should make this concept clearer.

Default Gateway. The next entry is the default gateway. This is the IP address of the router connected to your network. The net ID of the gateway address should be identical to that of your NIC. The router is the network device that directs traffic to destinations beyond the local network. Without this, you will not get beyond your network. In our example, the router connects network 192.168.1 to other networks. Any time your computer has a packet destined for a network with an address other than 192.168.1, IP will send the packet to the gateway address.

DNS Servers. The last two settings are addresses of Domain Name System (DNS) servers. DNS is a distributed online database containing registered domain names mapped to IP addresses. Thousands of name

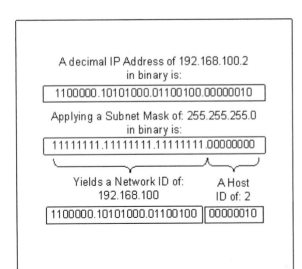

FIGURE 10–6 A subnet mask covers a portion of an IP address.

servers on the Internet maintain this distributed database. When you attempt to connect to a Web site, such as www.mcgraw-hill.com, your computer's DNS client queries a DNS server to determine the Web site's IP address.

You may enter two addresses in the Microsoft Properties dialog shown in Figure 10–5—a primary DNS server (sometimes called *preferred*) and a secondary DNS server (sometimes called *alternate*). The primary DNS server is the server your computer contacts any time you make a request to connect to a server using a domain name rather than an IP address. The DNS server will attempt to resolve the name to an IP address. It contacts the second DNS server only if there is no response from the first DNS server, but it does not use the second DNS server when the first DNS server responds that it cannot resolve the name. This is when you see an error similar to: "DNS query for www.*somedomainname*.com failed: host not found."

The Internet Corporation for Assigned Names and Numbers (ICANN), a California nonprofit corporation, currently oversees the Domain Name System, after having replaced an organization called InterNIC. The U.S. government sanctions ICANN, which reports to the U.S. Department of Commerce. Anyone wishing to acquire a domain name contacts one of the roughly 200 domain name registrars of top-level domains (.com, .org, .pro, .info, .biz, and so on) accredited by ICANN. Once registered with ICANN, each domain name and its IP address go on the Internet Domain Name Servers so that users can access Internet services offered under those domain names.

Step-by-Step 10.01

Examine a Connection's IP Configuration in a GUI

In this step-by-step exercise, you will examine a connection's IP configuration in the Windows 7 GUI. You will need:

- A computer with Windows 7.
- A user account and password for the computer.

Step 1

Open Control Panel and under Network and Internet click View network status and tasks. This opens the Network and Sharing Center.

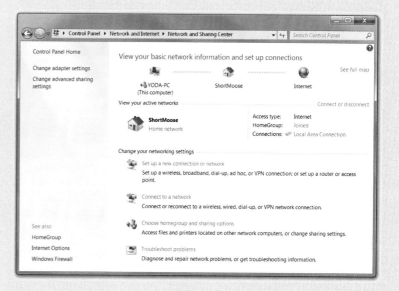

Step 2

In the Network and Sharing Center click Change adapter settings in the task list on the left. This opens the Network Connection window. Our example has only one network connection device, but you may have more than one listed.

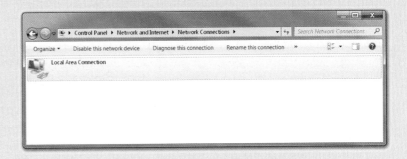

Step 3

Double-click on the bar containing the network connection you wish to examine. This opens the Status dialog box for the connection.

Step 4

Click the Details button. This will open the Network Connections Detail box, as shown in Figure 10–2. If you wish to make changes to the configuration, click the Close button to return to the Status dialog box. Then click the Properties button to open the properties for this connection.

Step 5

Keep in mind that only an advanced user should make changes to the network configuration. To look at the Properties dialog box for IPv4 for this connection double-click Internet Protocol Version 4 (TCP/IPv4).

Step 6

When you have examined the configuration, click Cancel to close each open box without making changes.

Viewing an IP Configuration from a Command Prompt

You can view the IP configuration of a Windows, Linux, or Mac computer from a command prompt using either IPCONFIG (Windows) or **ifconfig** (Linux and Mac).

In Windows use the IPCONFIG command without any command line switches to have it display only the IP address, subnet mask, and default gateway for each network interface. Using the command with the /all switch will display all the IP configuration information for each network interface on a computer. Figure 10–7 shows the result of running the IPCONFIG command in Windows with the /all switch.

The equivalent of the Windows IPCONFIG command in the Mac OS X Terminal window or a $ prompt in Linux or UNIX is the **ifconfig** command. Open a Terminal window in Mac OS X or access the $ prompt in Linux and enter the **ifconfig** command with the **–a** switch. The results for a Mac OS X Terminal window are shown in Figure 10–8 and from the $ prompt in Linux Ubuntu in Figure 10–9. Notice that the information is in an easier-to-understand presentation in Windows.

> ### View Your IP Configuration from a Windows Command Prompt
>
> Check out your current IP configuration using the IPCONFIG command. This will work in Windows XP, Windows Vista, and Windows 7. Try this:
>
> 1. Open a command prompt by selecting Start | Run, and in the Open dialog box, type "CMD" and press ENTER.
> 2. At the command prompt type "ipconfig."
> 3. After viewing the results of the command, type the command again with the /all switch: ipconfig /all.
> 4. Notice the additional information the /all switch provides.

try this!

LO 10.2 | Connecting to the Internet

A connection to the Internet is a wide area network (WAN) connection, and there are several WAN technologies to choose from. Some of these are wired technologies, and some are wireless. You must initiate some connections

```
D:\Windows\system32\cmd.exe

D:\Users\Yoda>ipconfig /all

Windows IP Configuration

   Host Name . . . . . . . . . . . . : Yoda-PC
   Primary Dns Suffix  . . . . . . . :
   Node Type . . . . . . . . . . . . : Hybrid
   IP Routing Enabled. . . . . . . . : No
   WINS Proxy Enabled. . . . . . . . : No

Ethernet adapter Local Area Connection:

   Connection-specific DNS Suffix  . :
   Description . . . . . . . . . . . : Realtek PCI GBE Family Controller
   Physical Address. . . . . . . . . : 00-27-19-CD-2F-C2
   DHCP Enabled. . . . . . . . . . . : Yes
   Autoconfiguration Enabled . . . . : Yes
   Link-local IPv6 Address . . . . . : fe80::607f:c2b:3650:edcb%11(Preferred)
   IPv4 Address. . . . . . . . . . . : 192.168.1.134(Preferred)
   Subnet Mask . . . . . . . . . . . : 255.255.255.0
   Lease Obtained. . . . . . . . . . : Sunday, November 21, 2010 7:05:43 AM
   Lease Expires . . . . . . . . . . : Monday, November 22, 2010 7:05:51 AM
   Default Gateway . . . . . . . . . : 192.168.1.1
   DHCP Server . . . . . . . . . . . : 192.168.1.1
   DHCPv6 IAID . . . . . . . . . . . : 234891033
   DHCPv6 Client DUID. . . . . . . . : 00-01-00-01-14-2D-C9-A0-00-27-19-CD-2F-C2

   DNS Servers . . . . . . . . . . . : 192.168.8.1
   NetBIOS over Tcpip. . . . . . . . : Enabled
```

FIGURE 10–7 The output from running the command IPCONFIG /all

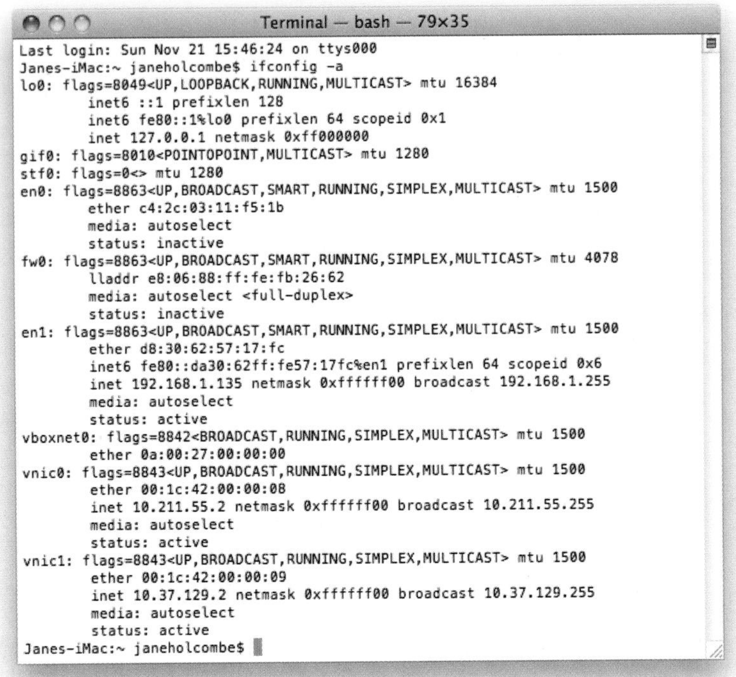

FIGURE 10–8 The result of running the **ifconfig -a** command in a Terminal window in Mac OS X

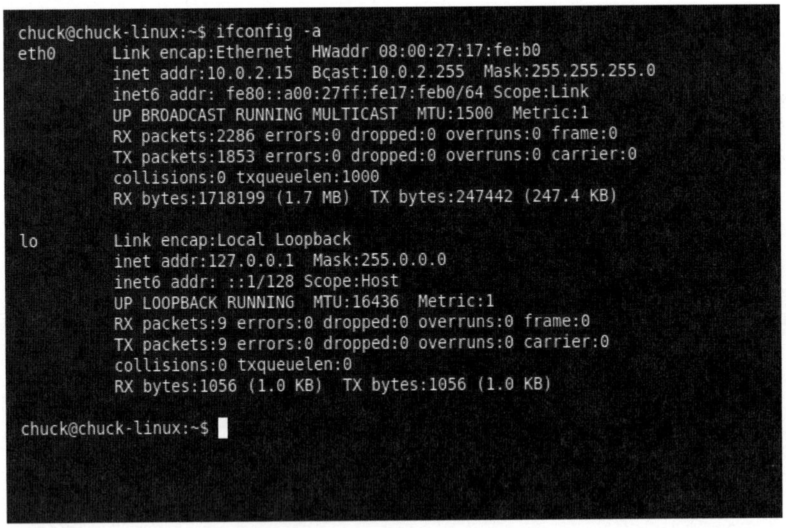

FIGURE 10–9 The result of running the **ifconfig -a** command at the $ prompt in Ubuntu Linux

every time you wish to connect to the Internet, while most connection methods remain available 24/7, in which case, Internet access is as simple as opening your browser or sending an e-mail. The connections include a wide range of speeds. In this section, we will compare the various means of connecting a network or computer to the Internet and discuss the most common methods for doing so from home or a small business so that you can make a decision for yourself. This will also help you to understand something about how you are connecting to the Internet from school or work, although we will not discuss the very expensive high-speed WAN services for connecting a large enterprise (commercial, government, or educational) to the Internet.

The choice of physical means of connecting to the Internet closely relates to your choice of an organization that will give you access to the Internet. Such an organization is an Internet service provider, and you will learn about these organizations first. Then you will consider the differences between a direct computer-to-Internet connection versus a computer-to-LAN-to-Internet connection. And finally, you will learn about the technologies used at the connection point to the Internet, regardless of whether it is a single computer or a LAN connection. Most of the screenshots used as examples in this section are Microsoft Windows 7, but all OSs surveyed in this book have capabilities similar to those described here.

Internet Service Providers

An Internet service provider (ISP) is an organization that provides individuals or entire companies access to the Internet. For a fee, an ISP provides you with this connection service and may offer other Internet-related services, such as Web server hosting and e-mail. Many ISPs provide proprietary software for Web browsing, e-mail management, and accessing other Internet services. Some ISPs specialize in certain connection types. For instance, Ground Control (www.groundcontrol.com) is an ISP that specializes in satellite Internet and mobile satellite Internet services; T-Mobile (www.tmobile.com) provides ISP services for its cellular customers; and your local telephone company may provide ISP services for dial-up, DSL, and even cable customers. Virtually all cable TV providers also provide Internet service.

> **Find Internet Service Providers**
>
> You can use the Internet to find ISPs you might want to use. Try this:
>
> 1. Use your Web browser to connect to your favorite search engine, search on "Internet Service Provider," and brace yourself for a *long* list of ISPs and sites related to ISPs.
> 2. Look for an option to search within the results. To find ISPs that specialize in satellite connections, for example, search within the previous search results for "satellite."
> 3. Then, further refine your search to just one country by entering a country name in the search by results box.

try this!

Computer-to-Internet versus LAN-to-Internet

A computer can have many types of connections, and some of them may lead to the Internet. Most methods for connecting a desktop computer involve a cabled connection between the computer's Ethernet card and some network device, but the path to the Internet can vary. For instance, it may have a direct connection to the Internet when a cable connects the computer's Ethernet network interface card (NIC) directly to a special device (usually a DSL or cable "modem") through which it makes a connection to the telephone or cable network and thence to the Internet. Or your computer's network card may be connected to a local area network (LAN) via an Ethernet switch. A computer that connects to a LAN may have access to the Internet through that LAN, if the LAN itself or another LAN to which it has a connection, connects to the Internet (see Figure 10–10). A computer connected to a LAN may also have a separate connection to the Internet—perhaps via an analog modem for a dial-up connection. So many choices! We will try to simplify this.

Wired Connectivity Technologies

Many wired WAN technologies for connecting to the Internet utilize the telecommunications infrastructure of the telephone system—either in its

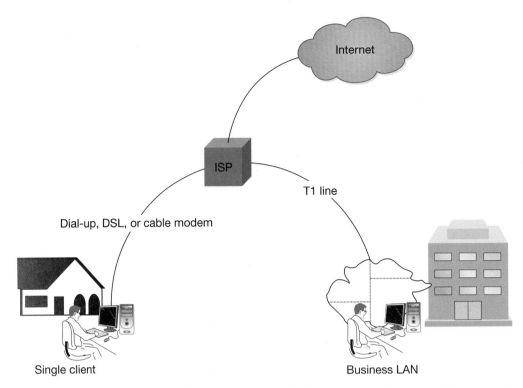

FIGURE 10–10 Connecting to the Internet from a single computer or from a LAN

traditional state or with upgrades and equipment added to that infrastructure. Another private network often used for wired Internet connections belongs to the cable TV companies, which in recent years added Internet access for their customers.

Dial-up Connections

A technology that clearly takes advantage of the traditional phone system is **dial-up**—an inexpensive choice available to anyone with a phone line and a standard analog modem. The long-time speed standard for dial-up is 56-kilobits per second (Kbps). Dial-up is very slow and only used when faster options are too expensive or not available. You also need to subscribe to an Internet connection service from an ISP.

The cost of the ISP subscription should be your only additional cost. There is usually no additional fee for using a modem on your voice line, but it is an either/or situation—you may either use the modem *or* use the phone *or* use a fax machine. You may not use the phone line for multiple purposes simultaneously when using an analog modem.

In a dial-up connection to the Internet, your computer uses its modem to dial a telephone number provided by the ISP (hence the term *dial-up connection*). One of many modems maintained by the ISP at its facility answers your computer's call; a server maintained by the ISP for authenticating customers authenticates you, and then the ISP routes traffic between your computer and the Internet for that session. Like a voice phone conversation, the connection is only temporary and ends when either your PC or the ISP's server ends the call. Many ISPs have discontinued dial-up service.

Furthermore, you can also use a dial-up connection to connect a remote computer to a private network at school or work. In this case, the modem that answers the call, and the server that authenticates the user, is located on a private network and allows the user to work on the network as if the user were

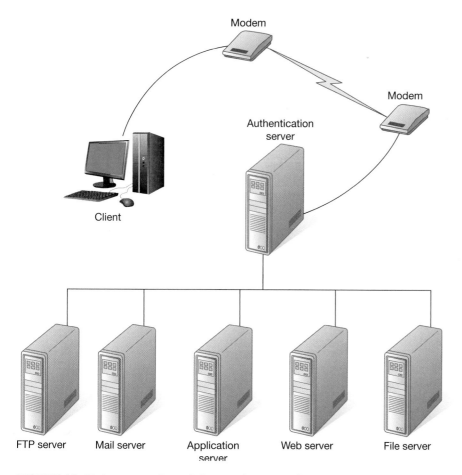

Modem

Modem

Authentication
server

Client

FTP server   Mail server   Application
server   Web server   File server

FIGURE 10–11 A remote client dials in to the network

physically at school or work, as shown in Figure 10–11. Note that the dial-up connection at 56-Kbps is very slow compared to a LAN running at 100 megabits per second (Mbps), or 1 gigabits per second (Gbps).

Installing a Modem. To prepare for a dial-up connection, first verify that you have a working modem. If the modem is an external modem, ensure that it is connected and powered on (an internal modem is by definition connected, and it gets its power from the computer). Then, assuming your modem is plug and play, it should automatically install into Windows or Mac OS X. Look for the device in the GUI. In Windows open the Phone and Modem applet in Control Panel and click on the Modems tab. Figure 10–12 shows the Modem page with one modem using COM1. In Mac OS X Snow Leopard, look for the modem listed in the Network preferences pane.

Creating a Dial-up Connection. Once you have configured a connection on your computer, you can initiate a dial-up session by using the connection applet for that specific connection. Certain applications, such as a browser or e-mail client, will automatically open an Internet connection whenever the application starts, so there is no need for the connection applet.

FIGURE 10–12 The Windows 7 Phone and Modem dialog box

Step-by-Step 10.02

Configuring a Dial-up Client

In this step-by-step exercise you will configure a dial-up client by creating a new dial-up connection. There are many ways to access the dialog boxes for this task, and we will take what seems like the long way through the GUI in order to explore the links for many network tasks. You will need:

- A computer with Windows installed (the steps are for Windows 7, but are similar in earlier versions),
- A modem that has been installed into Windows (you can manually install the driver without having a physical modem installed).
- The user name and password of an administrator for UAC prompts.

Step 1

Open Control Panel | Network and Internet | Network and Sharing Center. Take time to explore the links on this page, and then return to it before moving to Step 2.

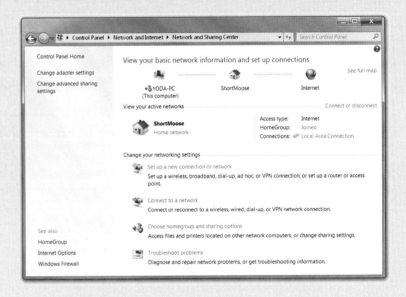

Step 2

Click the link labeled "Set up a Connection or Network." In the resulting dialog box click Set up a dial-up connection and click Next.

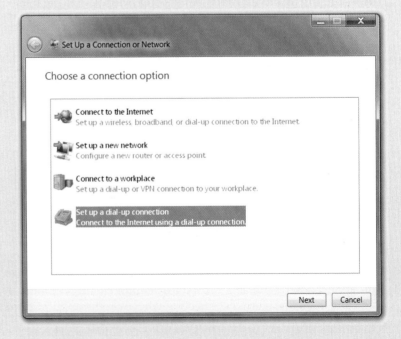

Step 3

On the Create a Dial-up Connection dialog box, enter the information for this connection. Notice the hints provided, and if you are just doing this as an exercise, use a fake phone number, such as 555-555-5555. Notice that you can share this dial-up connection with others on your LAN. When finished click Connect.

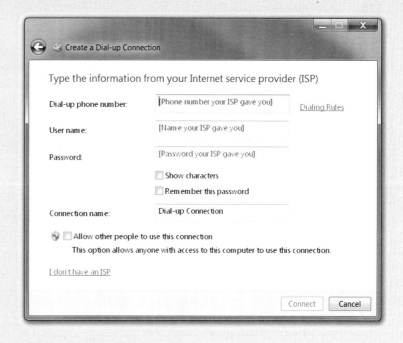

Step 4

It will attempt to connect using the phone number and credentials you provided.

Step 5

On the Completing the Network Connection Wizard page, review the list under the name of your connection. If you wish to make any changes, select Back, and make your changes. If you want a shortcut on the desktop, select the check box by that option. When done, click Finish.

Step 6

If the modem is real and the connections settings are valid, the connection should be successful and you will be able to browse the Internet, but it will be slow because this is dial-up. However, this connection is adequate for sending and receiving e-mail with, at most, small attachments.

High-Speed

You can share any type of Internet connection through a LAN, but if multiple users need to share an Internet connection, the connection between the network and the ISP must be adequate to carry the traffic created by all the users simultaneously at peak usage times. These WAN connections are categorized as high-speed WAN connections. High-speed options include some cellular services, ISDN, DSL, cable, T-carrier, satellite, and fiber.

Dedicated high-speed data circuits are available from telephone companies, cable network services, and other suppliers such as large networking companies and satellite service providers. We call these high-speed services broadband when they can handle multiple communications channels. Broadband connections communicate over media such as fiber optics, microwave, radio waves (wireless LANs), cable, and other technologies. In contrast, wired LAN technologies are usually baseband, with only a single communication channel. Here we will look at the wired broadband options of ISDN, DSL, cable, T-carrier, and fiber. Later we'll look at the wireless high-speed services.

> The traditional benchmark for broadband is anything faster than dial-up, but our need for speed makes many people somewhat disdainful of speeds under 1 Mbps.

Integrated Services Digital Network (ISDN). Integrated services digital network (ISDN) is a digital telephone service that simultaneously transmits voice, data, and control signaling over a single telephone line. ISDN service operates on standard telephone lines but requires a special modem and phone service, which adds to the cost. An ISDN data connection can transfer data at up to 128,000 bits per second (128 Kbps). Most telephone companies offer ISDN at a slightly higher cost than the modem dial-up service that it replaces. Rarely used in homes in the United States, it may be all that is available for a wired WAN connection in some areas, especially outside of the United States.

The benefits of ISDN (beyond the faster speed compared to a dial-up connection) include being able to connect a PC, telephone, and fax machine to a single ISDN line and use them simultaneously. Many ISPs and local telephone companies that offer Internet access services support ISDN connections.

However, ISDN is dropping out of favor because of the increasing availability of higher-performance broadband options, such as cable and DSL. In remote parts of the world, another optional broadband service, satellite communications, may be a more viable option than ISDN.

Digital Subscriber Line (DSL). Digital subscriber line (DSL) service is similar to ISDN in its use of the telephone network, but it uses more advanced digital signal processing to compress more signals through the telephone lines. Because you can use DSL only within a few miles of the central office, it requires component changes in the telephone network before they can offer it. Like ISDN, DSL service can provide simultaneous data, voice, and fax transmissions on the same line. It gives you a dedicated circuit from your home or office to the central office and the service can usually guarantee consistent upload and download speeds.

Several versions of DSL services are available for home and business use. Each version provides a different level of service, speed, and distance, and they normally provide full-time connections. The two most common are asynchronous DSL (ADSL) and synchronous DSL (SDSL). ADSL is the type of service normally available to home users. Others include high-data-rate DSL (HDSL) and very high-data-rate DSL (VDSL). The abbreviation often used to refer to DSL service in general begins with an *x* (*x*DSL), reflecting the varied first character in the DSL versions.

Across the DSL standards, data transmission speeds range from 128 Kbps for basic DSL service through 8.448 Mbps for high-end service. When describing DSL speeds, they usually refer to the speed of traffic flowing "downstream"— that is, from the Internet to your computer. For instance, ADSL's downstream speed (commonly 256 Kbps, 512 Kbps, or 768 Kbps) is much faster than its upstream speed, which may be as low as 16 Kbps. While SDSL provides the same speed in each direction, it is much more expensive and not widely available. Most home users require only the higher speeds for downloads (browsing the Internet, downloading multimedia files, and so on), so we recommend SDSL service for customers who must upload a great deal of data. If you had a Web server in your home, it would upload data every time an Internet user accessed it so it would benefit from SDSL service. Additionally, you would also want a static IP address for this server, a second expensive option. As a rule, if you require a Web site for a small business or hobby, the cheapest and most reliable way to do this is to use a Web hosting service which will host your Web site on their servers, providing a wide range of optional services.

Although the various Internet servers must upload a great deal of data in response to user requests, commercial Internet servers are normally hosted on much faster links than those discussed here.

Cable. Many cable television companies now use a portion of their network's bandwidth to offer Internet access through existing cable television connections. They call this Internet connection option cable modem service because of the need to use a special cable modem to connect.

Cable networks use coaxial cable, which can transmit data as much as 100 times faster than common telephone lines. Coaxial cable allows transmission over several channels simultaneously. Internet data can be on one channel while transmitting audio, video, and control signals separately. A user can access the Internet from his or her computer and watch cable television at the same time, over the same cable connection, without the two data streams interfering with one another.

The biggest drawback to cable modem service is the fact that the subscribers in a defined area share the signal. As the number of users in an area increases, less bandwidth is available to each user. Therefore, while cable providers advertise higher speeds than DSL, they cannot guarantee consistent speeds.

Wireless Connectivity Technologies

Like wired communications, wireless has moved from analog to digital over the years. Today, you can connect to the Internet through cellular networks, wireless wide area networks (WWANs), wireless LAN (WLAN) connections (if the WLAN ultimately connects to the Internet), and by satellite.

New wireless handheld devices take advantage of high-speed WWAN technologies, allowing users to surf the Internet from any location offering the required signal. Enhanced personal digital assistants (PDAs) have cellular communications features, Web browsing, and e-mail client software, but smartphones that have added many of the features of PDAs plus screens and software for working on the Internet are overshadowing them.

Wireless WAN (WWAN) connections

A wireless wide area network (WWAN) is a digital network that extends over a large geographical area. A WWAN receives and transmits data using radio signals over cellular sites and satellites, which makes the network accessible to mobile computer systems. At the switching center, the WWAN splits off into segments and then connects to either a public or private network via telephone or other high-speed communication links. The data then links to an organization's existing LAN/WAN infrastructure (see Figure 10–13). The coverage area for a WWAN is normally measured in miles (or kilometers) and it

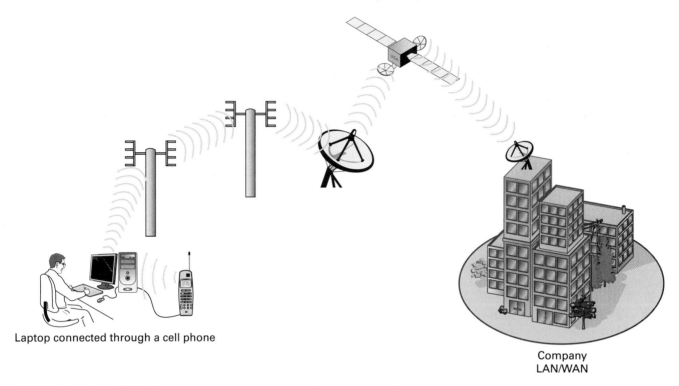

Wireless wide area network (WWAN) structure

Laptop connected through a cell phone

Company
LAN/WAN

FIGURE 10–13 A WWAN includes devices that retransmit the wireless signal

is therefore more susceptible to environmental factors, such as weather and terrain, than wired networks.

A WWAN is a fully bidirectional wireless network capable of data transfer at speeds in excess of 100 Mbps for a cost comparable with most DSL connections. Usually, basic WWAN services offer connection speeds between 1 and 10 Mbps. With dedicated equipment, the speeds can reach 100 Mbps. A WWAN system requires an antenna tuned to receive the proper radio frequency (RF).

A cellular Internet connection is an example of a WWAN. Many cellular services offer Internet access. That access may be directly from a smartphone, in which case, special software is included in the phone to provide a user interface. Some cellular providers also allow for the use of cellular modems with a desktop or laptop computer. Most cellular services sell a cellular modem card.

Satellite

Satellite connections are as suitable for large businesses as for small offices, cyber-cafés, individuals, homes, and the armed forces. Satellite is the WAN of choice when it is not possible or practical to use a wired connection and when cellular WAN services are not available or are too slow or costly. Satellite Internet providers offer several levels of service based on speed and they offer either stationary installations or mobile installations. The hardware cost for a mobile installation is considerably higher than that for a stationary installation, and the ongoing service fees are also higher.

Like ADSL, satellite data communication is usually faster downstream than upstream. The discrepancy can be huge, as we found when we had our own mobile satellite system installed on our motor home several years ago. We often achieved download speeds of 400 Kbps to 800 Kbps (and occasionally more), but upload speeds were only in the range of 25 to 45 kbps. While these speeds seem rather minimal compared to the mobile satellite options available today, the system worked well for us because, like most Internet users, our greatest need was for fast downloads as we browsed the Internet or downloaded files. Because of our mobile lifestyle and need to stay in touch with business associates, we needed a mobile solution. At the time, cellular service was slow or simply did not exist in most locations, and so we found a mobile satellite connection was the best solution as long as we were careful not to park under trees or other obstacles to the satellite signal.

Today, if you are willing to spend the money on the appropriate equipment and service, you can have mobile satellite speeds of up to 5 Mbps down and 2 Mbps up. However, satellite communications tend to have a higher latency, or lag. Think of the experience of watching a news broadcast that includes a foreign correspondent reporting over a satellite link. The news anchor in the studio asks a question, and you see the correspondent on the screen with a frozen smile while he or she waits to hear the question in its entirety. While it is barely noticeable when someone is reporting the news, such latency is very undesirable for real-time Internet applications, such as online games. Many IT professionals consider satellite connections unreliable, but it can be the best solution for Internet communications in remote areas.

When individuals or organizations contract with an ISP for satellite service, they install an Earth-based communications station. It usually includes three parts: a transceiver (a combined transmitter and receiver), and a device that we call a modem for simplicity and the satellite dish on its mount. You place the satellite dish outdoors in direct line-of-sight of one of several special data satellites in geostationary orbit around the Earth. The modem connects the other components to the computer or LAN. A mobile installation (on a land- or water-based vehicle) is generally much more expensive than a stationary installation because the mount must allow for moving the dish to align on the satellite, and therefore requires controlling circuitry and a costly motor-driven mount to achieve this with precision. The monthly service plans for mobile satellite communications are also more expensive than those for stationary installations.

A satellite traveling in a geostationary orbit moves at the same speed as the Earth's rotation and thus is sitting over the same place on the Earth—therefore you can align the dish precisely on the satellite. The satellite links the user's satellite dish to a land-based satellite operations center, through which the signal goes to the Internet (see Figure 10–14).

WLAN Connections

A wireless LAN (WLAN) is a local area network, usually using one of the standards referred to as Wi-Fi (for wireless fidelity). The Wi-Fi standards of the Institute of Electrical and Electronics Engineers (IEEE) include 802.11a, 802.11b, 802.11g, and 802.11n, listed from oldest to newest. AirPort is Apple's implementation of these standards. Usually we measure the distance covered by a WLAN in feet (or meters) rather than miles. Therefore, this is not a technology that connects directly to an ISP (as a WWAN or satellite connection will) but can be used to connect to another LAN or device with a WAN connection. This is the technology of Internet cafés and wireless notebooks. With enough wireless connect hubs, called access points, an entire community can offer wireless access to a shared Internet connection.

The latest IEEE 802.11 standards are both faster and more secure thanks to encryption technology. Therefore, we don't continue using old Wi-Fi devices that are not up to the new standards.

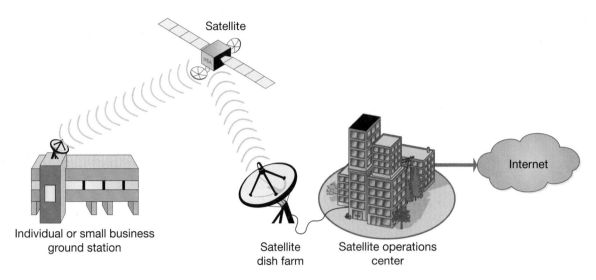

FIGURE 10–14 Accessing the Internet through a satellite WAN connection

Sharing an Internet Connection

You can share an Internet connection to your Windows computer much like sharing an Internet connection to a LAN—through a router. The difference is that when you turn on Internet Connection Sharing in Windows, your computer becomes the router to the Internet for other computers on your LAN or WAN. Windows Internet Connection Sharing (ICS) is the name of this service.

There are some negatives to using ICS. The ICS "router" PC must have two network cards—one that connects it directly to the broadband modem, and another that connects to the LAN or WAN where the other computers sharing the connection reside. And you cannot turn off or allow the ICS host computer to go into sleep mode while others require this connection. We used the earliest implementation of Windows ICS many years ago, but today we do not recommend it because the low cost and convenience of a broadband router outweigh the inconvenience of using ICS.

If you have the correct configuration for this—two network connections with one connected to a broadband modem or to dial-up connection you wish to share (this will be very slow)—enable ICS by opening Network and Sharing Center, clicking on Manage network connections, and then your two connections should display. Right-click the connection to share and open the Properties dialog in which you configure ICS. Once configured, you can share your Internet connection with other Windows clients as well as Mac and Linux clients.

Using a Virtual Private Network

Mobile users and remote offices often need to connect to a corporate intranet through the Internet using any of the connection technologies discussed earlier. You can make such a connection more secure by connecting through a **virtual private network (VPN)**, which you can make over an existing WAN connection. For individual users, this is called a remote access VPN (see Figure 10–15). When two networks connect by VPN, it is called a site-to-site VPN.

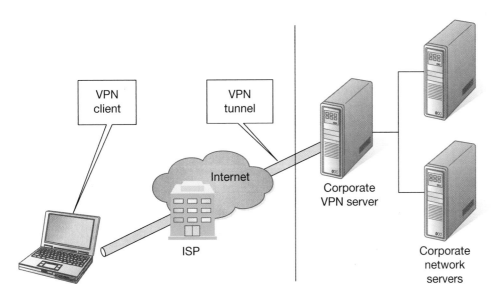

FIGURE 10–15 A remote access VPN

Think of a VPN as a simulated private network that runs inside a "tunnel" from end point to end point. One end may be a user's computer, while the other end is a VPN server in the private network. We achieve the tunnel effect by encapsulating each data packet sent at one end of the tunnel and removing it from the encapsulation at the receiving end. The encapsulation itself provides a very small amount of protection; we need to apply other measures to truly protect the data, such as encrypting the data, and requiring authentication of both ends of the tunnel.

LO 10.3 | Using Internet Clients

The growth of Internet services has increased the number of client types required to access those services. We will limit our discussion of Internet clients to Web browsers, e-mail clients, and FTP clients. Many services are accessible through Web browsers. E-mail may be the most important service on the Internet—many people, who have no other use for the Internet, use e-mail. And finally, the File Transfer Protocol (FTP) remains an important file transfer method on the Internet.

Web Browsers

While the World Wide Web (the Web) is just one of many services that exist on the Internet, it alone is responsible for most of the huge growth in Internet use that began after the Web's introduction in the early 1990s. Web technologies changed the look of Internet content from all text to rich and colorful graphics, and made it simple to navigate the Web by using a special type of client called a Web browser. The Web browser's ease of use hides the complexity of the Internet, as protocols help to transfer the content of a Web page to the user's computer. There the Web browser translates the plain text language into a rich, colorful document that may contain links to other pages—often at disparate locations on the Internet. Today, Web browsers offer versions for Mac OS X, Microsoft Windows, and Linux. Beyond the desktop, you'll find versions of these Web browsers with scaled-down screens for smartphones and other hugely popular mobile devices. In short, just about any electronic device that can connect to the Internet and has a display has some kind of browser.

Web browsers are free; Apple's Safari is bundled with OS X and Internet Explorer is bundled with Microsoft Windows. In its "2011 Internet Browser Software Review Product Comparisons," the Web site TopTenReviews (www. toptenreviews.com), ranks Mozilla Firefox, Google Chrome, and Microsoft Internet Explorer as the top three Web browsers. We'll look at all three of these after discussing their most important predecessor, Netscape Navigator.

Netscape Navigator

It is worth learning about Netscape Navigator because of its place in the development of great tools for browsing the Web. In 1994, Mosaic Communications (later renamed Netscape Communications) developed a Web browser called Netscape Navigator. It was to compete directly with a Web browser developed earlier at the National Center for Supercomputing Applications (NCSA). Mosaic's plan was to give the browser away and sell Web server software and other services.

When it released Netscape Navigator, the company announced that it intended to develop it into a platform-independent GUI, obviously to compete head-to-head with Microsoft. Although Netscape was then far from achieving that goal, it did get the attention of Microsoft, which eventually followed up with its own Web browser, Internet Explorer.

AOL purchased Netscape Communications in 1999, and continued to update the Navigator and offer it freely—while selling a variety of services and specialized server software. But in March 2008, AOL ended official support of Netscape (see the Netscape Archive at browser.netscape.com). This was in part due to the continued success of Microsoft's Internet Explorer and also due to the success of an open source browser that Netscape Communications began developing before the acquisition. Beginning in 2003, the nonprofit Mozilla Foundation (www.mozilla.org), sponsored in part by AOL, continued this work. The open source software developed by this group includes Firefox, a very popular Web browser today.

Mozilla Firefox

Mozilla Firefox, a product of the Mozilla Foundation, is rated No. 1 at TopTen-Reviews (see Figure 10–16). This is our favorite browser in all three OS platforms because we consider it a safer Web browser than IE and because a Firefox Add-on, FireFTP, is our workhorse FTP client (discussed later in this chapter).

Google Chrome

Google Chrome is a result of open source software from the Chromium open source project and other sources. It is in its seventh major version and has a distinctive look with file-folder-like tabs across the top and menus accessed from a wrench icon on the right of the folder. Figure 10–17 shows Google Chrome with the wrench menu open. We also recommend the online book currently featured on Chrome's welcome page titled, *20 Things I Learned about Browsers and the Web*. This charming animated book gives a compressed history of the Web and browsers while presenting a case for Chrome's superiority. It is a biased view, but educational.

Internet Explorer

In August 1995, in response to the introduction of the Netscape Web browser, Microsoft introduced its Internet Explorer (IE) Web browser when it launched the Windows 95 operating system. IE browser was included (or bundled) free

FIGURE 10–16 Mozilla Firefox

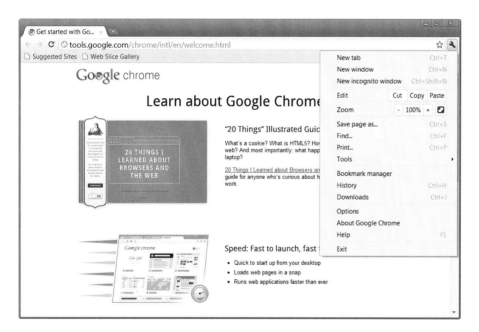

FIGURE 10–17 Google Chrome with the wrench menu open

with the operating system. IE is still bundled with Windows, and free updates to newer versions of IE for Windows and Mac OSs are available at the Microsoft Web site. Figure 10–18 shows the open Help menu for IE 9.

IE is primarily a Web browser; the Mail and News options found on the Tools menu will actually call up your default e-mail program and Outlook News Reader. Similarly, selecting the Windows Messenger option will call up the Windows Messenger applet. IE on Windows XP with Service Pack 2 includes a pop-up blocker and an add-on manager.

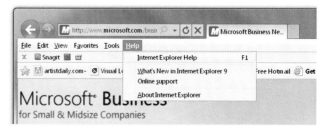

FIGURE 10–18 Microsoft Internet Explorer

The Opera Web browser logo

The Apple Safari browser logo

You can also open Internet Options from within Control Panel.

This discussion is based on Internet Explorer version 6, running on a Windows XP Professional computer with Service Pack 2 installed.

Others

While Firefox, Chrome, and IE are rated (at least at TopTenReviews) as the top three Web browsers, alternatives include Opera (www.opera.com) and Apple Safari (www.apple.com/safari) for Macs and Windows PCs.

Browser Configuration Options

Browsers are now full-featured applications that go beyond simple Web browsing and, as such, they have a multitude of configuration settings that range from GUI preferences to critical settings to protect your privacy and maintain security for your computer and personal data. We will use just two browsers—Firefox and IE—for this discussion of configuration options.

View Menu GUI Preferences. For both Firefox and IE, you access most, but not all, GUI preferences in the View menu on the menu bar. In both cases, open the View menu and select the components you wish to change. Figure 10–19 shows the Firefox View menu with the Toolbars submenu open. In Window's IE, press the ALT-V key combination to open the View menu, shown in Figure 10–20. Both of these have a large number of settings available from this menu.

Tools. The Tools menu in both Firefox and IE is the doorway to many settings for security, privacy, and much more. Figures 10–21 and 10–22 show these

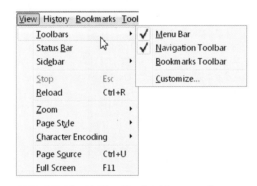

FIGURE 10–19 The Firefox View settings

FIGURE 10–20 Internet Options for Internet Explorer

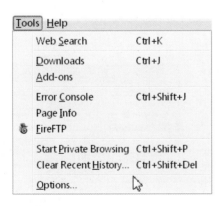

FIGURE 10–21 The Firefox Tools menu

FIGURE 10–22 The IE Tools menu

menus. The Options choice on the Firefox Tools menu (see Figure 10–23) holds seven tabs of configuration options. The IE Tools menu is a bit cluttered, and some of the options here are duplicated in the Internet Options dialog box (see Figure 10–24) where you will find seven tabbed pages of settings. Compare the tabbed pages in both of these browsers side-by-side. Five have identical names. They are: General, Security, Content, Privacy, and Advanced. In addition, Firefox has a separate tabbed page named Tab, which contains settings for the behavior and appearance of the tabbed windows. This group of settings is on the General page in IE. So, while the browsers have similarly named tabbed pages in these dialog boxes, they don't include the same sets of configuration options. Table 10–2 on the next page compares these dialog boxes in the two browsers.

> Internet Explorer and the Windows operating systems have a very close relationship. That is why the settings in Internet Options go beyond Internet Explorer, as in the Programs settings for the programs Windows uses for Internet services other than Web services. This is also why Internet Options is an applet in Windows Control Panel.

Security and Web Browsers

Rather than dive into the details of every security setting in your Web browser, we'll define certain security threats and describe how to manage them through modern Web browsers.

Cookies. As you learned in Chapter 2, cookies are good—mostly. Under some circumstances people can use them for the wrong purposes, but for the most part, their benefits outweigh the negatives.

Normally, only the Web site that created the cookies can access them. However, some advertisers on Web sites have the browser create cookies, and then other sites that include this advertiser can use them. This is an example of the use of third-party cookies. Look for options to manage cookies when configuring a Web browser. Figure 10–25 on the next page shows the Firefox Privacy page with the settings for cookies. Notice that we configured it to only accept first-party cookies (those directly from a site). In IE, you need to dig a little deeper to find the settings for cookies. Open the Privacy page in Internet Options and click the Advanced button. On the Advanced Privacy Settings dialog box you can control management of first-party and second-party cookies, with options to accept, block, or prompt you for each type of cookie.

FIGURE 10–23 Firefox Options menu

FIGURE 10–24 IE Internet Options menu

TABLE 10–2   A Comparison of Options for Firefox and Internet Explorer

Tabbed Page	Firefox Options	IE Internet Options
Advanced	Accessibility Browsing (scrolling behavior; spell checker) System Defaults (default browser)	Rarely used settings Useful: Reset to IE defaults
Applications	How to handle various file types in FireFox	N/A
Connections (IE only)	N/A	The Setup button opens the Connection to the Internet wizard Dial-up and VPN settings LAN settings for connecting through a LAN to the Internet and configuring a proxy server
Content	Pop-up blocker configuration Handling of images JavaScript configuration Fonts and Colors Preferred language	Parental Control Content Advisor Certificates AutoComplete Feeds and Web Slices
General	Home page Downloads Manage add-ons	Home page Browsing history Search Tabs Appearance
Privacy	Manage browsing history Enable/configure private browsing Cookies Location Bar settings	Set a standard privacy level or customize based on the sites Pop-up blocker InPrivate browsing settings.
Programs (IE only)	N/A	Set default applications for Web browsing and other Internet services Set application for editing HTML code Manage add-ons
Security	Warn if sites try to install add-ons Block reported attack sites Password management Configure warning messages	Configure zones for various levels of security Enable protected mode
Tabs (Firefox only)	Configure tabbed browsing	N/A

FIGURE 10–25 The Firefox privacy page with settings to protect you while browsing

Browsing History and Passwords. Your browsing history is useful information to marketers and others who want to learn more about you. At the same time, this information also makes life a bit easier for you when you return to favorite sites. While your browser does not divulge this information, a system compromised by spyware or other malicious means could reveal this information to the wrong persons. Additionally, if you leave your computer unattended, but logged on with your account, anyone with access to your computer can look at your browsing history. Further, system administrators or others who have administrative access to your computer can do the same. Once again, your security needs may be at odds with your need for convenience on the Web. Therefore, Web browsers allow you to manage your browsing history. In Firefox, you can delete current browsing history from the Tools menu, and you manage browsing history settings on the Privacy page in the Options dialog box. In Chrome, click the Wrench button at top right, click History, and when the recent history list appears click Edit items at top right. You can then select individual items to delete or choose to Clear all browsing data. At the bottom of the page you can click Older to look at other items you browsed to. You can also clear all browsing data from both the Tools menu under the wrench button and the Options button.

In IE if you want to quickly delete all browsing history, open the Tools menu and select Delete browsing history. If you want to configure how long to save browser history, open Internet Options from the Tools menu and on the General tab click the Settings button under Browsing History. On this page you can set the number of days to save browser history as well as control how IE handles temporary Internet files.

Private Browsing. Private browsing is browsing without saving any history of the sites visited. Both Firefox and IE offer private browsing. To configure private browsing in Firefox open the Privacy page in Options. When you turn on private browsing decide how to manage the cookies.

IE's term for private browsing is InPrivate Browsing, and this setting is on the bottom of the Privacy page of Internet Options. When this is turned on IE opens a new window, and your protection exists as long as you remain in that window, even as you open new tabs within the window. However, if you inadvertently open a new browser window, it will take you out of InPrivate browsing. For instance, browsing to a new restaurant and clicking on the map link to get directions opens a new window. To protect yourself in these situations, turn on InPrivate Filtering, also available on the Privacy page.

Do you like to have your browser remember your password to Web sites or would you rather enter your user name and password every time you access a site? Configure password settings in Firefox on the Security page of the Options dialog box; in IE, password settings are accessible in the Internet Options Content page via the Settings button under AutoComplete. Figure 10–26 shows this page with saving these passwords turned off.

Bad Neighborhoods. Many Web sites are notorious for attempting to install all types of malware when users browse to them. Therefore modern Web browsers can detect and block this type of behavior as well as block sites known for attacking browsers. In both Firefox and IE, these settings are on the Security page of their respective options dialog boxes. Most of the settings for blocking sites in both browsers are straightforward, giving you options for how the browser handles known bad sites and when to warn you about suspicious behavior from a Web site. Both also allow you to provide domain names of trusted sites. IE goes a bit further, providing the notion of zones. IE uses zones to assign security settings for selectively restricting browsing. A zone may be an area such as the Internet or local intranet or a list of sites grouped together, as in trusted sites and restricted sites.

Pop-ups. We've all seen them. Those windows that pop up from a Web site advertising products, wanting to show you videos, or any number of excuses to get your attention and interrupt your stream of thought. They're called pop-ups, and not all pop-ups are bad. Some of our favorite Web sites use pop-up windows to open something we requested, such as a downloaded page or even a login page, but the latest standard for creating Web pages discourages pop-ups because they do not work on all platforms and they interfere with assistive browsing technologies. Therefore, the use of pop-ups should wane in coming years. For the foreseeable future software that blocks pop-ups is necessary, but it also needs to be configurable so you can block pop-ups from all but the

> **WARNING!**
>
> You put yourself at risk if you allow your browser to remember passwords because anyone who has access to the computer can find and use these stored passwords.

FIGURE 10–26 Password saving is off for IE in this dialog box.

sites you trust. Therefore, the major browsers have pop-up blockers. Configure Firefox's pop-up block on the Content page of the Options dialog box and configure IE's on the Privacy page of Internet Options. In Chrome, click the Wrench button, then Options, and on the Under the Hood tab click Pop-ups in the left column. You can then choose Allow or Do not allow any site to show pop-ups.

E-mail Clients

The scope of Internet e-mail has made several major jumps in the past few decades. This is mainly from use by academics and government workers, through the period when early PC users accessed services such as CompuServ, to today's casual PC users, numbered in the billions, who joined the Internet since the advent of the World Wide Web in 1991. Because of the explosion in the use of the Internet, e-mail has long been the most compelling reason to own a PC—but today you do not even need to use a PC to participate in personal e-mail. Now a plethora of handheld devices, including cell phones, smartphones, and PDAs, allow users to send and receive e-mail over the Internet. Many of these do not allow attachments, but most messages do not include attachments. Further, you do not even need to own the device you use for Internet access. Today you can visit your local library or Internet café to keep up with the travels of Uncle Alonzo.

An e-mail client used in a school or corporate network may be specific to the private mail servers the user connects to (Microsoft Exchange, IBM Lotus Domino, Novell GroupWise), or the client may be one of several that can be used for different types of mail servers. Many users have access to e-mail client software such as Microsoft Outlook, Windows Live Mail, Mozilla Thunderbird, Eudora, or Pegasus. Users that subscribe to Web mail, or free e-mail services such as MSN or Yahoo!, can use a Web browser rather than special e-mail client software. Regardless of the type of client software, they all accomplish the task of sending and receiving in the same way.

The client software will show a list of all of the messages in the mailbox by displaying information it reads from the message headers. The message header is information added to the beginning of the message that contains details such as who sent it and the subject, and also may show the time and date of the message along with the message's size. Then the user may click on a message to open it and read the body of the e-mail. Users can then respond to the message, save the message, create a new message, add attachments, and/or send it to the intended recipient.

E-mail clients have become much easier to use, even to the point of automatically detecting and configuring the underlying settings for connecting to an e-mail server, given your personal account information. They also will import your e-mail and contact information from other accounts.

Types of E-mail Accounts

There are three types of e-mail accounts: POP, IMAP, and Web mail. The first two are protocols, while the third describes e-mail that you access via the Web, and therefore, the protocol is HTTP. When you configure an e-mail client, you need to know the address and type of server, defined by the account type.

POP. Post Office Protocol (POP) is a protocol that enables e-mail client computers to pick up e-mail from mail servers, so that you can open it and read it in your e-mail client. When it picks up a message, it deletes it from the POP server. The current version is POP3. This has been very popular with ISPs because it minimizes the amount of disk space required on the e-mail server for each account. The user is responsible for maintaining and backing up messages. When the client computer does not connect to the e-mail server, the user can still access all the locally stored messages.

IMAP. Internet Message Access Protocol (IMAP) is a protocol that will allow users to maintain the messages stored on an e-mail server (usually on the Internet) without removing them from the server. This type of account allows you to log in and access your message store from any computer. Of course, the message store is not available to you when you are offline, and you may run out of allotted disk space on the mail server, at which point it rejects new messages.

Web Mail. Web mail is a generic term for the practice of using a Web browser to retrieve e-mail, replacing the traditional e-mail client, such as Microsoft Outlook. You can use Web mail to connect to Web-based e-mail services such as Hotmail, Gmail, and Yahoo! that keep your messages stored on the Internet. If you wish to connect to one of these services using an e-mail client, you will need to enable IMAP for your account before you can successfully add your account to the client. To do that, consult the Help utility at the provider.

> Most mail servers with POP accounts give you the option to connect using Web mail so that when you are away from your desktop computer and your e-mail client software, you can connect using any Web browser from any computer. Of course, you will need to authenticate using your e-mail address and password. If you are planning to do this, be sure to access it at least once beforehand to make sure you know how to use it!

Outlook

Outlook is Microsoft's e-mail client that is part of the Microsoft Office suite. You can use it as a client to any of the three types of accounts. It offers core e-mail features, such as an address book and folders for organizing mail, plus additional personal productivity features such as an appointment calendar, a to-do list, and scheduling. It supports the use of more than one e-mail account.

Windows Live Mail

Windows Live Mail, an e-mail client with calendar and newsreader, is bundled with Windows 7 and installed during Windows installation. It does not have all the features of the commercial Outlook product. For instance, you can only use it for Internet e-mail accounts, but like Outlook, Windows Live Mail will manage multiple e-mail accounts.

Configuring and Using an E-mail Client

Whether you use Outlook, Windows Live Mail, or one of many third-party e-mail clients, you will need to know the same information to configure your e-mail client. This includes:

- The type of mail server you are accessing (POP3, IMAP, or HTTP).
- Your account name and password.
- The DNS name of the incoming mail server.
- If you are preparing to connect to a POP3 or IMAP server, you will also need to know the name of an outgoing mail server.

If you do not have this information, ask your ISP, in the case of a private account, or network administrator if your mail server is a corporate mail server. ISPs often provide e-mail configuration information on their Web sites. Check this out before configuring your e-mail client because it will help you avoid certain pitfalls. For instance a client using a cell modem may have to configure it to authenticate to a certain mail server in the home service area.

Connecting a Client to an E-mail Account

To complete this step-by-step exercise you will need a PC with an Internet connection and Windows 7 with Windows Live Mail, although the basic steps are similar in other e-mail clients. To complete the exercise you will need the following information:

- The type of account.
- Your account name, password, and e-mail address.

- The DNS name of the outgoing and incoming mail server.
- The DNS name or IP address of an incoming mail server for POP3, IMAP, or HTTP.
- The DNS name or IP address of an outgoing mail server (SMTP).
- If using a provider, such as Gmail, you will need to enable IMAP first.

Step 1

Open Windows Live Mail and click on the link labeled "Add e-mail account."

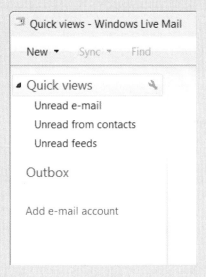

Step 2

In the Add an E-mail Account page enter the all the information for your account. If your information is correct, Live Mail will be able to automatically configure the account, so do not turn on the manual option shown at the bottom. Click Next.

Step 3

The next screen will confirm that the information entered successfully and may contain a message reminding you to enable IMAP for the account. If you enabled IMAP for the account before this, simply click Finish. If you have not already done that, open your Web browser, go to the account settings page, and enable IMAP. Then return to Live Mail and Click Finish.

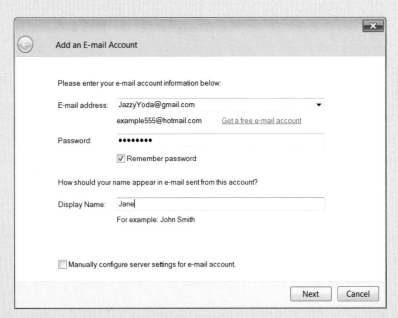

On the Show/Hide IMAP Folders you may select which folders are visible in Live Mail. For now, leave all visible until you decide what you wish to hide. Click OK.

Live Mail now displays your new account. Close the Windows Live Mail window when you are finished.

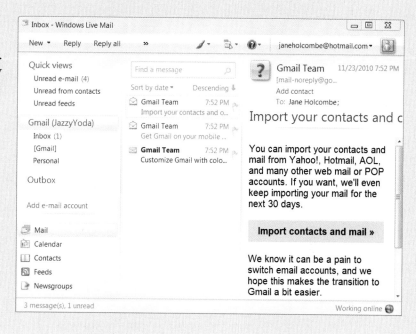

FTP Clients

File Transfer Protocol (FTP) is a protocol used to transfer files between a computer running the FTP server service and an FTP client. It is a preferred method of transferring files over a TCP/IP network, especially the Internet, because it is simple and fast. Before the advent of the World Wide Web and the use of GUI tools for working on the Internet, people used character mode FTP clients because that was all there was. Because of the tremendous growth in the number of Internet and Web users, we now have a variety of GUI FTP client programs. You can even use some of the popular Web browsers as FTP clients, although programs designed specifically as FTP clients are usually easier to use and allow you to save the settings for connecting, including (but not limited to) the URL for the site, user name, and password.

Anonymous FTP

If an FTP site does not require a user name and password, it is said to allow anonymous connection, which means that all users connecting are using the Anonymous account, which may mean they can only read and copy the files from the FTP site and cannot copy files to the site. We call an FTP site that allows anonymous connections an anonymous FTP site. It is simple to connect to such a site using your browser by entering the URL, including the protocol suffix. Once connected, navigate through the list of folders and files, much as you do your local folders and files. Then, to copy the

Find FTP Sites

Look for lists of FTP sites on the Internet. Try this:

1. Use your Web browser to connect to your favorite search engine and search on "FTP sites."
2. Browse through the results. Notice that many of the results are links to compiled lists of sites, often organized by topic.

try this!

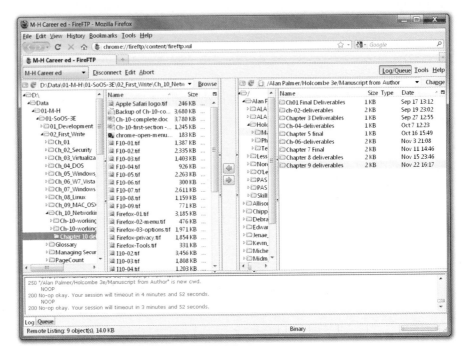

FIGURE 10–27 The user interface of FireFTP, an FTP client

item to your local hard drive, right-click on a file or folder and select the Copy to folder option.

Configuring an FTP Client

When connecting to a site that requires a user name and password, you can use a Web browser, and the site will prompt you to log in. A Web browser is fine for connecting to an FTP site you will visit only once, but when you wish to save the site settings, or manage settings for many FTP sites, you should find a free or commercial FTP client that suits your needs. A quick search of "FTP client" using an Internet search engine will yield a long list of clients. The free Mozilla FireFTP, an add-on to Mozilla Firefox, is a favorite of ours. To configure an FTP client you will need:

- The host name of the FTP server.
- A user ID and password (if applicable).

You may also need to know if the FTP server allows passive mode connections and/or secure (SSL) connections. Figure 10–27 shows FireFTP. The left pane is open to the local hard drive, while the right pane shows the contents of a folder on the FTP site.

LO 10.4 | Sharing Files and Printers

File and print sharing allows users to share and access files and printers over a network. All the OSs discussed in this book have methods for allowing file and print sharing. There are two sides to file and print sharing: the server side and the client side, and before you implement either side of this equation, take a few minutes to understand how they interact. Both sides must use complementary files and print services that can talk to each other. Then, you can implement sharing on the server side (even on a desktop computer) and users can access it from the client side. For our examples we'll use Microsoft Windows 7.

The Server Side of File and Print Sharing

Examples of file-sharing protocols used on the server side are Microsoft's Server Message Block (SMB) protocol; Novell's venerable NetWare Core Protocol (NCP); Common Internet File System (CIFS), a standard used by many OSs; the network file system (NFS) used in Linux and most Unix versions; and even the P2P file-sharing protocol used to share files over the Internet. Most of these file-sharing protocols include support for sharing a printer attached to the local server, and these services are also contained in dedicated network devices for sharing printers. On a Windows desktop computer, look for File and Printer Sharing for Microsoft Networks in the Properties dialog box for a network connection, as shown in Figure 10–1 on page 363.

The Client Side of File and Print Sharing

A file and print server (often simply called a file server), is a computer that gives client computers access to files and printers over a network. A file and print client includes both the user interface and the underlying file sharing protocols to access its matching file sharing server service on a network server. The client for Microsoft file and print sharing automatically installs and enables when installing a Windows operating system. With the client installed, you are able to use the Windows GUI to see those Microsoft computers on the network that have file and printer sharing turned on, whether they are using Microsoft's original SMB file sharing protocol or the newer CIFS protocol standard. You can see both dedicated Windows network servers and Windows desktops that have the server side of this—File and Printer Sharing for Microsoft Networks—turned on. Figure 10–28 shows the Properties dialog box of a network connection with both the Microsoft client and service enabled. You will be able to see Microsoft servers on your network in Windows Explorer, but your ability to connect to any shares on those computers depends on the permissions applied to each share. The top three icons in the right-hand pane have this service turned on, but only one, HTC-SERVER, is a dedicated server. Of the other two, one is Windows running in a VM on an iMac, and the other, Yoda-PC, is a PC with Microsoft Windows. The next two icons are computers running Microsoft's Media Server service, and the final icon, ShortMoose, is the broadband router.

With appropriate permissions, you will be able to browse to the shared folders on a server and perform file operations, such as copying, moving, deleting, and opening files in your locally installed applications.

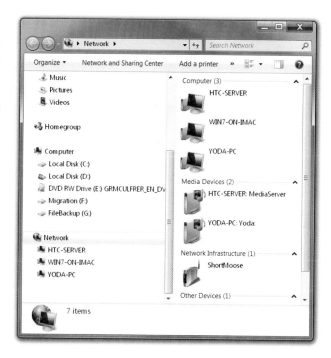

FIGURE 10–28 The first five icons in the right pane are computers with a server service turned on.

> As a rule, a desktop computer should not have File and Print Sharing turned on, especially if the computer is a member of a domain and connects to dedicated servers for file and print services. The exception to this is when a desktop computer is participating in a work group rather than in a domain and must share local files and printers with other computers in the work group.

Sharing Files and Printers in Windows 7

To illustrate how to share files and printers from your Windows desktop we will use Windows 7, which has three methods that range from ridiculously easy to a bit techie. The first is HomeGroup, a feature of Windows 7. The second is the sharing of the Windows 7 Public folder, and the third is manual file and printer sharing. We'll discuss these in turn.

---

try this!

Find Microsoft File and Print Servers

You can use Windows Explorer in Windows to look for the file and print servers on your network. Try this:

1. From the Start menu open Network.
2. View the icons in the contents pane. In Windows 7 the icons resembling a computer with a blue screen are file and print servers.
3. If any file and print servers are visible, double-click one to access it and browse. If you do not have permissions, you will see a Network Error message. If you have permissions to a server, you will be able to browse the folders to which you have permissions.

Sharing with Homegroups

HomeGroup, new in Windows 7, is an easy-to-configure implementation of Microsoft's file and print sharing, with only a single password protecting the HomeGroup shares on all Windows 7 computers that join a homegroup. You only have to enter the password once on every client in the homegroup when the client joins the homegroup. You can configure a Windows 7 computer running any edition of this OS to be a client in a homegroup, but only certain editions can create and host a homegroup. Those versions are Windows 7 Home Premium, Professional, Ultimate, and Enterprise editions.

You can belong to only one homegroup at a time, and computers that are part of a Windows Active Directory Domain cannot create a homegroup. Microsoft created HomeGroup to make it simple for people on a very small network to share their data with one another. It is ideal for a family or small business. Support for HomeGroup is turned on but a homegroup is not created when you select the Home network type versus Work or Public network. If you open the HomeGroup applet and are not on a Home network, you will see this message. If you change your network type to a Home network, you can participate in HomeGroup.

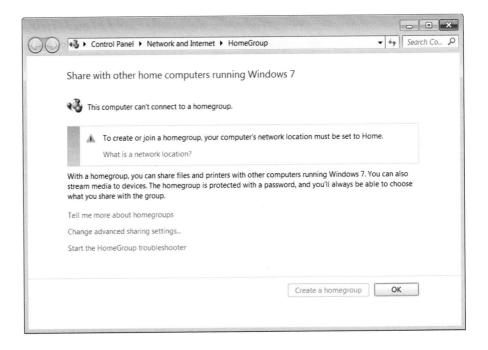

Step-by-Step 10.04

Creating and Joining a Homegroup

Create a homegroup to share your local files and printers with others on your home or small business network. To complete this exercise you will need the following:

- Windows 7 Home Premium, Professional, Ultimate, or Enterprise edition.

- The Windows 7 computer must be connected to a Home network (Open Network and Sharing Center to confirm).

From the Start menu enter HomeGroup in the Search box and select HomeGroup from the results list. On the HomeGroup page click Create a homegroup.

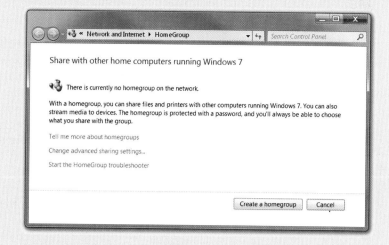

The first page of the Create a Homegroup wizard lists your personal folders and any local printer with checks for those that are shared and empty check boxes for those that are not shared. By default, Windows does not share your Documents folder. Select what you would like to share, and click Next.

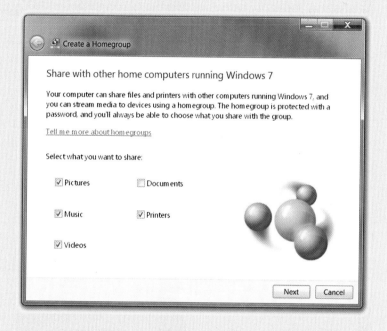

Windows will generate a password for your homegroup. Write it down or use the link to print the password and instructions. You will need to enter the password on the other computers on your network as you join them to the homegroup. After writing down or printing out the password, click the Finish button. Note, if you lose the password you can open HomeGroup and view it.

Go to another Windows 7 computer on your network, and from the Start menu enter "homegroup" in the Search box. Then click Join now and follow the instructions to enter the homegroup password.

FIGURE 10–29 The Public folder and its contents

FIGURE 10–30 The Public folders within each Library

Sharing the Public Folder

If you have a mix of Windows versions on a home or small business network, then HomeGroup is not an option if you want all the computers to participate. Two other options for sharing will work with disparate versions of Windows. First we'll look at the easier of these two, sharing the Public folder. Then in the next section we'll describe the more complex one, advanced sharing.

First look at the Public folders on a Windows 7 computer. The master Public folder is located under the Users folder on the drive on which Windows 7 is installed. This folder is, by default, shared to anyone on the network who has an account in the local accounts database. In fact, if a user on the network is logged on to a Windows computer using an account that matches the one you create on your "server" computer, then the user can connect to the Public share without going through a logon screen. The Public folder has several subfolders, shown in Figure 10–29. These folders have a special relationship with the default Libraries for each user.

By default, no user data resides in the Public folder. You have to copy or move files into the Public folder, and the way you do that in Windows 7 is through the Libraries. If you look at the contents of the Libraries on a Windows 7 computer, you will see that each Library has a Public folder, in addition to the base folder for that library, as shown in Figure 10–30. Recall what you learned about Libraries in Chapter 6. A library does not contain the folders that appear in the library, but rather pointers to the locations for those folders. So, the My Documents folder in the Documents library points to the currently logged-on user's Documents folder, located in a folder with that user's name, that holds the user's folders and preferences (also called the profile). Similarly, the Public Documents folder in the Documents library points to the Public Documents folder under the Public folder.

So, simply drop files and folders into one of these public folders in your libraries, and people on the network who have local accounts on your computer can connect and access these files and folders. Be sure to add the users to your local accounts by following the instructions in Step-by-Step 6.05 in Chapter 6. If the user name and password do not match the account with which a user logs on at her computer, she will need to supply a user name and password to access the Public folder.

Advanced Sharing

Advanced sharing is simply a term for managing shares the old-fashioned way—one share at a time—turning on sharing for a folder or printer and giving users access to that share. You can make this as complex as you want, but Windows 7 makes it a bit easier than it was in the past. An advantage of this method is that you can share any folder you wish. It is even easier if you have Windows 7 Home Premium, with simpler dialog boxes that protect you from some of the complexity you will see with Windows 7 Ultimate, the version we use for our example.

Open Computer and browse to a local folder you want to share. Right-click this folder and select Shared with | Advanced Sharing. This opens the Properties for the folder with the Sharing tabbed page active. On this page click the Advanced Sharing button. Click to place a check mark in the box labeled "Share this folder." In Figure 10–31 we turned sharing

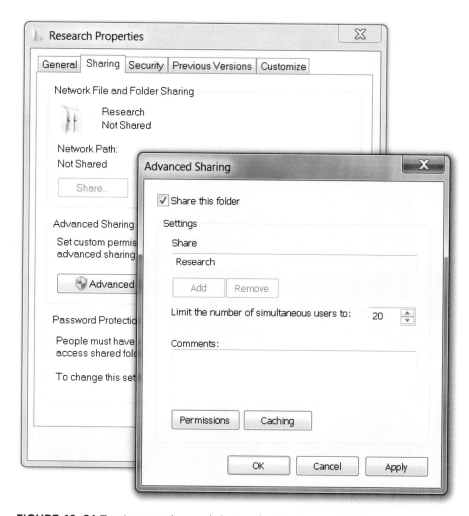

FIGURE 10–31 Turning on advanced sharing for the Research folder

on for the folder named Research. This created a share, or connecting point, to which network clients with the correct permissions may connect. It is visible as a folder over the network, but it is a separate entity from the disk folder to which it points. If you choose, you can give the share a separate name by entering it in the Share box. Whatever name you provide is the name users will see from the network, but local users see this disk folder by its folder name, not the share name. Do not close this box until you set permissions.

If you click OK in the Advanced Sharing dialog box, the share will be created with the default permissions giving the Everyone group (literally everyone who connects) only the Read permission. For most shares, the default permissions are both too much and too little—too much in that you have not narrowed it down to a single user or local group, and the Read permission may be too little if you want users to be able to save files into this share or modify the files in it.

To set permissions click the Add button to open Select Users or Groups. Then ensure that the location is the name of your local PC and click Advanced and then Find Now to list the accounts on your computer. Select each account, clicking OK after each selection, until you have selected all the accounts. Then click OK on the Select Users or Groups box. When you return to the Permissions dialog box, the accounts are listed. Click on each one in turn to apply the correct permissions. Before leaving this dialog box remove the Everyone group by selecting it and clicking the Remove button. The resulting Permissions dialog box should resemble Figure 10–32. These permissions are share

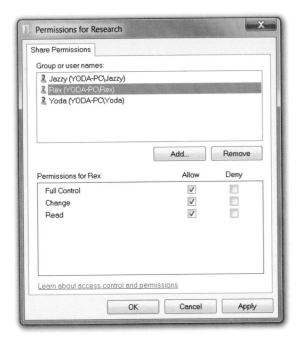

FIGURE 10–32 Custom permissions on a share

permissions set on the share; they are not NTFS permissions set on the folder itself. If you wish to set NTFS permissions, right-click on the folder, select the Security tab, and set permissions in a similar fashion to how you set them on the share.

LO 10.5 | Troubleshooting Common Network Client Problems

If you are unable to access another computer on the network, several command-line utilities will help in pinpointing the source of a problem and arriving at a solution. In this section you will learn to troubleshoot common client connection problems using each of these utilities, as required by the problem symptoms. Each utility provides different information and is most valuable when used appropriately. For instance, you should first view the IP configuration using the IPCONFIG utility and verify that it is correct for the network to which you are connected. If you discover any obvious problems when you view the IP configuration, correct them before proceeding. Then test the ability to communicate using the PING command. Here you will practice this procedure and a few others.

Built-in Network Diagnostics

Each of the operating systems surveyed in this book has a variety of utilities for diagnosing network problems. From the command-line utilities discussed later in this section to GUI tools that combine the functions of several tools into one broad-stroke diagnostics tool, each generation of OS brings improvements in these tools. In Windows 7, the Windows Network Diagnostics, shown in Figure 10–33, will diagnose the problem area (the broadband modem in this example) and instruct you on how to solve the problem. Similarly, if your Internet connection fails, the Network Diagnostics window will display and attempt to diagnose the problem.

The Network Utility in Mac OS X Snow Leopard, shown in Figure 10–34, requires more knowledge of the individual tools, but it does spare you from entering the commands from Mac OS X Terminal window.

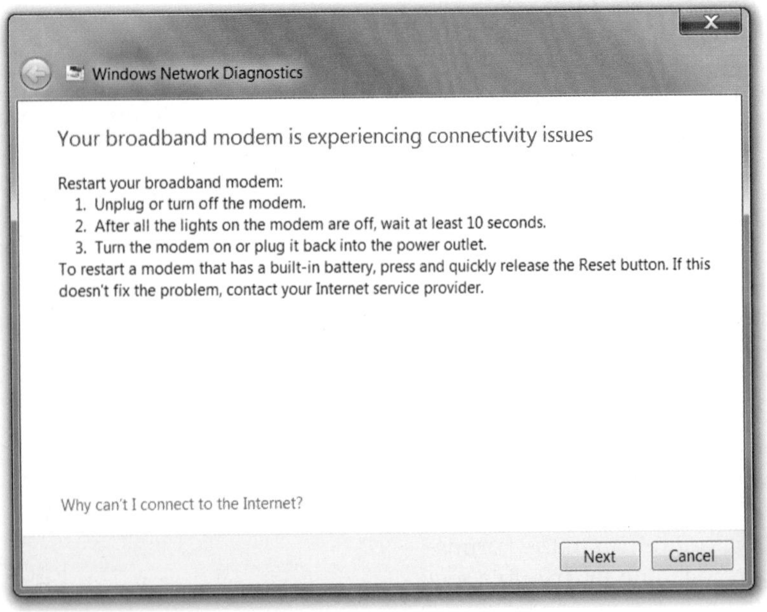

Testing IP Configurations and Connectivity

When the TCP/IP suite is installed on a computer, it includes many protocols and many handy little programs that network professionals quickly learn to use. You should learn two right away, for those times when you find yourself sitting at your computer and talking to a network professional while trying to resolve a network problem. These are commands you enter at a command line. In Windows these commands are IPCONFIG and PING. In Mac OS X and Linux they are **ifconfig** and **ping**. Learn about these commands below, and then do

FIGURE 10–33 The Windows 7 Network Diagnostics tool

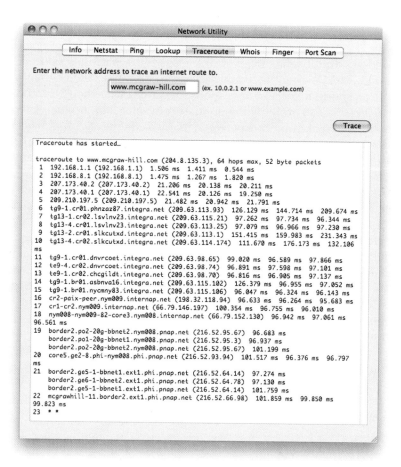

FIGURE 10-34 The Mac OS X Network Utility at work (notice the other utilities listed across the top)

Step-by-Step 10.05, in which you will use both of these commands to test a network connection.

Verifying IP Configuration with IPCONFIG

The IPCONFIG command will display the IP configuration of all network interfaces, even those that receive their addresses and configuration through DHCP. Using this command shows whether the IP settings have been successfully bound to your network adapter. *Bound* means that there is a linking relationship, called a binding, between network components—in this case, between the network protocol and the adapter. A binding establishes the order in which each network component handles network communications. When troubleshooting network connectivity problems on an IP network, always use the IPCONFIG command to verify the IP configuration.

If the IPCONFIG command reveals an address beginning with 169.254, it is a symptom of a failure of a Windows DHCP client to receive an IP address from a DHCP server (for whatever reason). Troubleshoot the DHCP server on your network (such as the DHCP service in a broadband router).

Troubleshooting Connection Errors with the PING command

The PING command is useful for testing the communications between two computers. The name of this command is actually an acronym for packet Internet groper, but we prefer to think (as many do) that it was named after the action of underwater sonar. Instead of bouncing sound waves off surfaces, the PING command uses data packets, and it sends them to specific

IP addresses, requesting a response (hence the idea of pinging). This is a great test to see if you can access a certain computer. To run this command, give it an IP address and it sends packets to the specified address and then it "listens" for a reply. Pinging the IP address of the computer's own network interface and receiving a successful response indicates that the IP protocol and the local address is working. Ping another computer on the same network to test the ability to communicate between the two computers; ping the gateway address to ensure that your computer can communicate with the router, and ping an address beyond your network, to test the router and the ability to communicate with a computer via the router.

Now that we have you excited about using the PING command, we'll give you the bad news. First, it's possible to configure a firewall to block specific types of traffic or configure an individual computer not to respond to a ping. Hence, you may not be able to ping a computer, even if you can communicate with that same computer in other ways such as Web browsing or downloading e-mail. The reason firewalls or individual computers block or ignore the requests from a PING command is because people can use this command in malicious ways—most notoriously in a denial of service (DoS) attack, also called ping of death (POD) attack. Such an attack may send a very large packet to a server, causing a "buffer overflow" problem with the server thus making the server unavailable to accept other traffic. Or someone will simultaneously send a large number of pings to a server, using up all the connections, so the server cannot respond to other legitimate client traffic. Nonetheless, it is still worth learning to use the ping command for testing a connection because it will often work and give you good information.

> For a more thorough treatment of this topic, search the Microsoft TechNet site for the article "How to Troubleshoot Basic TCP/IP Problems."

Step-by-Step 10.05

Testing an IP Configuration

In this step-by-step exercise, you will look at the IP configuration settings to determine whether they are automatic or static, then you will test the current configuration. The first test will let you confirm that you can communicate with a computer on your network, and the second test will confirm that you can communicate with a router on your network. The last test will confirm that you can communicate with a computer beyond your network. To complete this exercise, you will need the following:

- A computer with Windows.
- A working connection to the Internet.
- The IP address of another computer on your local network (use this when a step asks for *localIPaddress*).
- The IP address of a computer beyond your local network (use this when a step asks for *remoteIPaddress*).
- The user name and password of an account that is a member of your computer's Administrators group.

Step 1

Check out your current IP configuration using the IPCONFIG command. To do that, first open a command prompt by selecting Start | Run, and in the Open dialog box, type "CMD" and press ENTER. Type "ipconfig /all" at the command prompt.

```
C:\Documents and Settings\Jane>ipconfig /all

Windows IP Configuration

        Host Name . . . . . . . . . . . . : Wickenburg
        Primary Dns Suffix  . . . . . . . :
        Node Type . . . . . . . . . . . . : Hybrid
        IP Routing Enabled. . . . . . . . : No
        WINS Proxy Enabled. . . . . . . . : No

Ethernet adapter Local Area Connection:

        Connection-specific DNS Suffix  . :
        Description . . . . . . . . . . . : Realtek RTL8139/810x Family Fast Eth
ernet NIC
        Physical Address. . . . . . . . . : 08-00-46-A7-29-3B
        Dhcp Enabled. . . . . . . . . . . : No
        IP Address. . . . . . . . . . . . : 192.168.100.48
        Subnet Mask . . . . . . . . . . . : 255.255.255.0
        Default Gateway . . . . . . . . . : 192.168.100.1
        DNS Servers . . . . . . . . . . . : 192.168.100.1

C:\Documents and Settings\Jane>
```

Step 2

If the current settings show an IP address other than 0.0.0.0, IP has successfully bound an IP address to the network adapter. If the current settings include DHCP enabled = Yes, and shows an IP address for a DHCP server, then your network adapter is configured to receive an address automatically. If your DHCP Enabled setting equals No and your computer has a set of values for the IP address and subnet mask, then it has a static IP configuration that is successfully bound to the network adapter.

Step 3

Gather the information from the IPCONFIG command in the space provided below. You will need these addresses in the following steps.

IPaddress: _____

Default Gateway: _____

DNS Server: _____

Step 4

At the command prompt, enter **ping** *IPaddress*, where *IPaddress* is the address of your computer. You should receive four replies if your computer is properly configured. If you receive an error message or fewer than four replies, report this to your instructor.

Step 5

At the command prompt, enter **ping** *localIPaddress*, where *localIPaddress* is the address of another computer on your same network. You should receive four replies if your computer is properly configured and if the other computer is also on the network and properly configured. If you receive an error message or fewer than four replies, report this to your instructor.

```
C:\Documents and Settings\Jane>ping 192.168.100.48

Pinging 192.168.100.48 with 32 bytes of data:

Reply from 192.168.100.48: bytes=32 time<1ms TTL=128
Reply from 192.168.100.48: bytes=32 time<1ms TTL=128
Reply from 192.168.100.48: bytes=32 time<1ms TTL=128
Reply from 192.168.100.48: bytes=32 time<1ms TTL=128

Ping statistics for 192.168.100.48:
    Packets: Sent = 4, Received = 4, Lost = 0 (0% loss),
Approximate round trip times in milli-seconds:
    Minimum = 0ms, Maximum = 0ms, Average = 0ms

C:\Documents and Settings\Jane>_
```

If the last test was successful, and if your computer has a gateway address, test this address now. Return to the command prompt and enter **ping** Default Gateway, where Default Gateway equals the Default Gateway address recorded in Step 3. You should receive four replies if your computer is properly configured and if the default gateway is active on your network.

```
C:\Documents and Settings\Jane>ping 192.168.100.1

Pinging 192.168.100.1 with 32 bytes of data:

Reply from 192.168.100.1: bytes=32 time<1ms TTL=128
Reply from 192.168.100.1: bytes=32 time=1ms TTL=128
Reply from 192.168.100.1: bytes=32 time<1ms TTL=128
Reply from 192.168.100.1: bytes=32 time<1ms TTL=128

Ping statistics for 192.168.100.1:
    Packets: Sent = 4, Received = 4, Lost = 0 (0% loss),
Approximate round trip times in milli-seconds:
    Minimum = 0ms, Maximum = 1ms, Average = 0ms

C:\Documents and Settings\Jane>
```

If your IP configuration includes the address of a DNS server, you should test connectivity to the DNS server now. Return to the command prompt and enter **ping** *DNS Server*, where *DNS Server* equals the DNS Server address recorded in Step 4. You should receive four replies if your computer is properly configured and if the default gateway is active on your network.

If you were given the address of a computer beyond your local network, test this address now by returning to the command prompt and entering **ping** *remoteIPaddress*, where *remoteIPaddress* is the address of the remote computer.

> If you want to save a copy of the information displayed by a command-line command (such as TRACERT), you can send the screen output of this command to a text file, using the command-line redirection symbol (>). You can use any file name and any path to which you have write access. No output will appear on the screen.

Troubleshooting Connection Problems with TRACERT

You may have situations in which you can connect to a Web site or other remote resource, but the connection is very slow. If this connection is critical to business, you will want to gather information so that a network administrator or ISP can troubleshoot the source of the bottleneck. You can use the TRACERT command to gather this information. TRACERT is a command-line utility that traces the route taken by packets to a destination. When you use this command with the name or IP address of the target host, it will PING each of the intervening routers, from the nearest to the farthest. You see the delay at each router, and you will be able to determine the location of the bottleneck. You can then provide this information to the people who will troubleshoot it for you. Consider a scenario in which your connection to the Google search engine (www.google.com) is extremely slow. You can use the following to run TRACERT and save the results to a file:

```
TRACERT www.google.com >
tracegoogle.txt
```

try this!

Use TRACERT

You can use TRACERT to determine where a problem is occurring. Try this:

1. Open a command prompt.
2. Type TRACERT www.google.com
3. If the command runs successfully, you will see output similar to this, but with different intervening routers.

Troubleshooting DNS Errors Using PING, NETSTAT, and NSLOOKUP

Have you ever attempted to browse to a Web page, only to have your browser display an error message such as "Cannot find server or DNS Error?" This

```
C:\>tracert www.google.com

Tracing route to www.google.akadns.net [216.239.41.99]
over a maximum of 30 hops:

  1    <1 ms    <1 ms    <1 ms   192.168.100.1
  2    858 ms   810 ms   812 ms  hh1095067.direcpc.com [205.177.62.67]
  3    875 ms   819 ms   807 ms  dpc6682016181.direcpc.com [66.82.16.181]
  4    803 ms   746 ms   872 ms  dpc6682016073.direcpc.com [66.82.16.73]
  5    749 ms   820 ms   747 ms  so-5-1.hsa1.Washington1.Level3.net [63.215.128.129]
  6    806 ms   867 ms   879 ms  ge-9-2.ipcolo2.Washington1.Level3.net [4.68.121.172]

  7    815 ms   806 ms   760 ms  unknown.Level3.net [166.90.148.174]
  8    749 ms   812 ms   811 ms  216.239.47.69
  9    821 ms   805 ms   812 ms  216.239.47.154
 10    871 ms   747 ms   811 ms  216.239.48.77
 11    755 ms   867 ms   880 ms  216.239.41.99

Trace complete.

C:\>_
```

may be a name resolution problem, since the fully qualified domain name (FQDN) portion of a URL, such as www.google.com, must be resolved to an IP address before a single packet goes to the Web site.

One way to test if the problem is a connectivity problem or a DNS error is to first test for connectivity by either pinging (using the PING command) the IP address of the Web site or using the IP address in place of the FQDN in the universal resource locator (URL). If you cannot reach the Web site by using its IP address, then it is a connectivity problem that should be resolved by contacting your network administrator or ISP.

If you can reach the Web site by pinging the IP address but cannot access it through your browser, then it is a name resolution problem and a simple test of DNS name resolution is to ping the FQDN. Figure 10–35 shows the result of pinging the FQDN www.google.com. Notice that this displays the IP address of the Web site, confirming the DNS name-to-IP address resolution is working.

When you are troubleshooting networking problems, it is very helpful to have a second computer that does not display the same problems. Then you can use the second computer to discover the IP address of a Web site by using your browser to connect. Once connected, you can use the NETSTAT command, to discover the IP address of the Web site. NETSTAT displays network statistics, protocol statistics, and information about current TCP/IP connections. Figure 10–36 shows the result of running the NETSTAT command after connecting to a Web site with a browser. The IP address for this Web site, www.google.com, is shown under Foreign Address, and the protocol used to connect to the Web site, http, is shown after the colon.

Finally, the classic command for troubleshooting DNS, used for many years on the Internet and other TCP/IP networks, is NSLOOKUP. The NS in this command name stands for "name server." This command allows you to send queries to a DNS name server directly, and see the results. It is a very powerful command, but you can use it to test your DNS setting without learning all of its subcommands. Running NSLOOKUP in a command prompt

```
C:\>ping www.google.com

Pinging www.google.akadns.net [216.239.41.104] with 32 bytes of data:

Reply from 216.239.41.104: bytes=32 time=923ms TTL=245
Reply from 216.239.41.104: bytes=32 time=856ms TTL=245
Reply from 216.239.41.104: bytes=32 time=855ms TTL=245
Reply from 216.239.41.104: bytes=32 time=858ms TTL=245

Ping statistics for 216.239.41.104:
    Packets: Sent = 4, Received = 4, Lost = 0 (0% loss),
Approximate round trip times in milli-seconds:
    Minimum = 855ms, Maximum = 923ms, Average = 873ms

C:\>
```

FIGURE 10–35 Pinging the FQDN www.google.com reveals the IP address.

```
C:\>netstat

Active Connections

   Proto   Local Address          Foreign Address        State
   TCP     Wickenburg:1175        216.239.41.104:http    ESTABLISHED

C:\>
```

FIGURE 10–36 NETSTAT displays the IP address and protocol information of current connections.

To learn more about the NSLOOKUP command, search on "NSLOOKUP" in the Windows Help program.

without any additional command-line parameters will cause it to attempt to connect to the name server address in your IP configuration. Then it displays the NSLOOKUP prompt, a greater-than sign (>). You may enter subcommands at this prompt. If it cannot connect to the DNS server, it will display an error, as shown in Figure 10–37. If you see this error, contact your network administrator or ISP. Type "Exit" at the NSLOOKUP prompt to exit from the command. Then type "Exit" again to exit from the command prompt.

```
C:\>nslookup
*** Can't find server name for address 192.168.100.1: Non-existent domain
*** Default servers are not available
Default Server:  UnKnown
Address:  192.168.100.1

>
```

FIGURE 10–37 NSLOOKUP reveals a DNS problem.

Chapter 10 REVIEW

Chapter Summary

After reading this chapter and completing the Step-by-Step tutorials and Try This! exercises, you should understand the following facts about networking.

Configuring a Client for a TCP/IP Network

- TCP/IP is the protocol suite needed to access the Internet.
- Transmission Control Protocol (TCP) and Internet Protocol (IP) are the core protocols of TCP/IP.
- An IP address is assigned to a network adapter or modem in a computer that connects it to a network.
- IPv4 is a very old version of the protocol, slowly being replaced by IPv6. An IPv4 address is 32-bits long and usually expressed in dotted decimal form, such as 192.168.1.1. An IPv6 address is 128-bits long, expressed in eight groups of hexadecimal numbers separated by colons, such as 2002:2470:B8F9:1:20C:29FF:FE53:45CA.

- Public IP addresses are used for hosts on the Internet and each address must be unique on the entire Internet.
- A private IP address is one of three ranges of IP addresses designated for use only on private networks. They are not to be used on the Internet, and you do not need to obtain permission to use these addresses on a private network.
- Computers on a private network using private IP addresses get access to the Internet through a specialized device, usually a router.
- Each host on a TCP/IP network must have an IP address. A host receives an address by two general methods: automatically as a DHCP client via a network DHCP server (or a self-assigned APIPA address), or statically, which involves someone manually assigning an address to the host.

- In addition to the IP address there are several IP configuration settings including subnet mask, default gateway, DNS server, advanced DNS settings, and WINS settings.

Connecting to the Internet

- An Internet service provider (ISP) is an organization that provides individuals or entire companies access to the Internet.

- Common wired WAN technologies include dial-up, ISDN, DSL, and cable.

- ISDN is a digital telephone service that simultaneously transmits voice, data, and control signaling over a single telephone line and can transfer data at up to 128,000 bits per second (128 Kbps).

- Digital subscriber line (DSL) service is similar to ISDN in its use of the telephone network, but it uses more advanced digital signal processing to compress more signals through the telephone lines and so is much faster than ISDN.

- Many cable television companies now offer Internet access through existing cable television connections using special cable modems.

- Wireless options for connecting to the Internet include cellular networks, wireless wide area networks (WWANs), wireless LAN (WLAN) connections (if the WLAN ultimately connects to the Internet), and satellite.

- Mobile users and remote offices often need to connect to the corporate intranet through the Internet using any of the connection technologies discussed earlier, with the addition of a virtual private network (VPN) for security.

Using Internet Clients

- Web technologies changed the look of Internet content from all text to rich and colorful graphics, and made it simple to navigate the Web by using a special type of client called a Web browser.

- The top Web browsers are Mozilla Firefox, Google Chrome, and Internet Explorer.

- Firefox, Chrome, and IE have a large number of configuration settings that range from GUI preferences to settings critical to protecting your privacy and maintaining security for your computer and personal data.

- An e-mail service and client are defined by the protocols they use, which are POP, IMAP, and Web mail (HTML protocol).

- While some e-mail services require dedicated clients, some e-mail clients can interact with a variety of e-mail server types.

- To configure any e-mail client you need a specific set of information:
  - The type of mail server you are accessing (POP3, IMAP, or HTTP).
  - Your account name and password.
  - The DNS name of the incoming mail server.
  - If you are preparing to connect to a POP3 or IMAP server, you will also need to know the name of an outgoing mail server.

- File Transfer Protocol (FTP) is a protocol used to transfer files between a computer running the FTP server service and an FTP client. It is simple and fast.

- An FTP site that allows anonymous connections is an anonymous FTP site.

- If a site requires a user name and password, it will prompt you, whether you are using a Web browser to connect or an FTP client.

- A Web browser is fine for occasionally connecting to FTP sites, but use an FTP client to save settings for FTP sites you visit repeatedly.

- To configure an FTP client you will need:
  - The host name of the FTP server.
  - User ID and password (if applicable).
  - Account (if applicable).

Sharing Files and Printers

- A file and print client includes both the user interface and the underlying file sharing protocols to access a file sharing system on a network file and print server.

- File sharing protocols include Microsoft's SMB; Novell's NCP, CIFS, NFS used in Linux and UNIX; and the P2P file sharing protocol used to share files over the Internet.

- The client for Microsoft networks, installed when a Windows operating system is installed, allows users to see those Microsoft computers on the network that have file and printer sharing turned on, whether they are using SMB or CIFS.

Troubleshooting Common Network Client Connection Problems

- All the OSs surveyed in this book have GUI-based Network Diagnostics that combine many functions.

- Several command-line commands help in diagnosing and solving network client connection problems. These utilities include:
  - IPCONFIG
  - PING
  - TRACERT
  - NETSTAT
  - NSLOOKUP

Key Terms List

anonymous ftp site *(393)*

automatic IP address *(367)*

Automatic Private IP Addressing (APIPA) *(367)*

broadband *(378)*

Common Internet File System (CIFS) *(395)*

default gateway *(368)*

dial-up *(374)*

digital subscriber line (DSL) *(378)*

Domain Name System (DNS) *(368)*

Dynamic Host Configuration Protocol (DHCP) server *(367)*

file server *(395)*

file and print server *(395)*

File Transfer Protocol (FTP) *(393)*

fully qualified domain name (FQDN) *(405)*

host ID *(367)*

integrated services digital network (ISDN) *(378)*

Internet Protocol (IP) *(362)*

Internet service provider (ISP) *(373)*

net ID *(367)*

NetWare Core Protocol (NCP) *(395)*

octet *(367)*

packet *(362)*

private IP address *(395)*

public IP address *(365)*

router *(368)*

Server Message Block (SMB) *(395)*

share *(399)*

static IP address *(366)*

subnet mask *(367)*

TCP/IP *(362)*

Transmission Control Protocol (TCP) *(362)*

virtual private network (VPN) *(382)*

Web browser *(383)*

Web mail *(391)*

wireless LAN (WLAN) *(381)*

wireless wide area network (WWAN) *(379)*

zone *(389)*

Key Terms Quiz

Use the Key Terms List to complete the sentences that follow. Not all terms will be used.

1. _____ are used for hosts on the Internet.

2. SMB, NCP, and _____ are all file sharing protocols.

3. IE uses a/an _____ to assign security settings for selectively restricting browsing.

4. An IPv4 address beginning with 169.254 is a/an _____ address.

5. A/an _____ is not used for hosts on the Internet.

6. A/an _____ is an organization that provides individuals or entire companies with access to the Internet.

7. In an IPv4 address, each grouping of decimal numbers is called a/an _____ because it represents eight bits.

8. Among IP configuration settings the _____ is the IP address of the router used to send packets beyond the local network.

9. _____ service is a term for a group of wired broadband technologies offered through the phone company and capable of greater speeds than ISDN.

10. Most organizations use _____ to assign IP addresses to desktop computers.

Multiple-Choice Quiz

1. The IPv4 address 192.168.30.24 is an example of one of these.
   a. DNS server address
   b. Public IP address
   c. Private IP address
   d. Automatic private IP address
   e. WINS Server address

2. A computer requiring access to file and print services on a network server running a Windows operating system must have a Microsoft file and print client installed. Where can you find this?
   a. It is included with Windows and must be installed after setup.

   b. It is included with Windows and installed during setup.
   c. It is not included with Windows and you must download it from the Microsoft Web site.
   d. It can be downloaded from the Novell Web site.
   e. It must be installed and configured in the Connection properties dialog box.

3. In the chapter, which form of DSL is described as having the same speed upstream as downstream?
   a. ADSL
   b. *x*DSL

   c. VDSL
   d. HDSL
   e. SDSL

4. Your neighbor tells you that he has to initiate a connection to the Internet and complains that the connection is much slower than the connection he enjoys at work—and he is disconnected if there is a period of inactivity. From his description, which type of connection do you believe he has?
   a. ISDN
   b. Dial-up
   c. ADSL
   d. SDSL
   e. Cable

5. What appears in the Connect Using box in the connection properties dialog box?
   a. A connection device
   b. An ISP name
   c. A user name
   d. A password
   e. A phone number

6. Which of the following is obviously *not* a valid IPv4 address?
   a. 192.168.100.48
   b. 10.0.33.50
   c. 172.300.256.100
   d. 30.88.29.1
   e. 200.100.99.99

7. You have two e-mail clients installed on your computer. Where can you configure Windows to use one of them as your default e-mail client?
   a. Control Panel | Internet Options | Programs
   b. Control Panel | Network Connections
   c. Start | Run | CMD
   d. Control Panel | Internet Options | Advanced
   e. Start | All Programs | Outlook Express

8. What command can you use to view the status of current connections, including the IP address and protocol used for each connection?
   a. IPCONFIG
   b. CMD
   c. PING
   d. NETSTAT
   e. TRACERT

9. Which of the following is Microsoft's original file and print sharing protocol standard, used by more than one vendor?
   a. Common Internet File System (CIFS)
   b. NetWare Core Protocol (NCP)
   c. Network file system (NFS)
   d. Server Message Block (SMB)
   e. File and print sharing

10. Which command would you use as a test to see if a DNS server will respond to a request to resolve a name?
    a. PING
    b. NSLOOKUP
    c. IPCONFIG
    d. NETSTAT
    e. TRACERT

11. This IPv4 configuration setting defines the two parts of an IP address: the Host ID and the Net ID.
    a. Gateway
    b. Subnet mask
    c. DNS
    d. DHCP
    e. Host name

12. Where in Internet Options can you configure how IE manages cookies?
    a. General page
    b. Security page
    c. Tabs page
    d. Advanced Privacy Settings dialog box
    e. Exceptions button

13. Your neighbor, a retiree on a modest fixed income, has asked your help in acquiring an Internet connection for his computer, a desktop computer running Windows 7. His only interest in Internet access is to use e-mail to keep in touch with his children, who live in other states. He has a reliable phone connection. Based on this information, which service will you recommend?
    a. Cable
    b. ISDN
    c. Dial-up
    d. DSL
    e. Satellite

14. If you wanted to see the IP configuration from the $ prompt on a MAC, Linux, or UNIX system, which command would you use?
    a. ipconfig
    b. netstat
    c. nslookup
    d. ping
    e. ifconfig

15. What protocol is responsible for the accurate delivery of messages, verifying and resending pieces that fail to make the trip from source to destination?
    a. Internet Protocol
    b. Transmit Control Protocol (TCP)
    c. Secure Sockets Layer (SSL)
    d. File Transfer Protocol (FTP)
    e. Transmission Control Protocol (TCP)

Essay Quiz

1. Your computer was recently connected via a network adapter to a LAN that includes a router through which traffic passes to the Internet. You know the adapter was configured to use TCP/IP, and you need to test its ability to communicate with computers on the LAN and on the Internet. In your own words describe the steps you will take.

2. Your school uses an FTP site where each instructor posts documents, such as course assignments, white papers, and schedules for students to download. In addition, for each course, every student has a folder and is expected to upload class assignments to his or her folder. Each student has a user name and password to access the FTP site and must connect to a specific folder for each course. Would you use a Web browser or would you use an FTP client program? In your own words, explain your choice, including why it is the right choice for you.

3. A state agency that dispatches mobile units to disaster areas to monitor the disaster sites for hazardous chemical and biological contamination requires reliable Internet access for these units from any location in the state. They need to keep up-to-date with technical information via postings on federal Web sites and to upload their data to state and federal FTP sites. Which Internet connection option is the best fit for their needs? Explain your answer.

4. Describe Windows 7 HomeGroup.

5. Explain subnet masking in simple terms, including why a subnet mask is required when an adapter is configured with an IP address.

Lab Projects

LAB PROJECT 10.1

Survey your classmates, co-workers, and other acquaintances to determine the following:

1. What percentage of them have Internet access from home?

2. Of those who have Internet access from home, what percentage have had it for 10 years or more?

3. Of those who have Internet access from home, what percentage have had it for five years or more?

4. Of those who have Internet access from home, what percentage have had Internet access for less than one year?

5. Why is home Internet access important to those who have it?

6. Discuss the results with your classmates.

LAB PROJECT 10.2

This project requires the use of a Windows, Linux, or Mac computer that has Internet access. Using methods you learned in this chapter, find the answers to the following questions:

1. Does the lab computer have its own connection to the Internet or does it connect to the Internet through a LAN?

2. How is an IP address assigned to the lab computer?

3. Record the IP configuration settings for the lab computer below:
   a. IP address
   b. Subnet mask
   c. Default gateway
   d. DNS server

LAB PROJECT 10.3

Interview the IT staff at your school, place of work, or another organization and determine what Internet services they offer to students (Web pages, e-mail, FTP, etc.).

The list will usually go beyond the basic services studied in this chapter. Create a list of these services and the clients they require.

Glossary

The number at the end of the entry refers to the chapter where the term is introduced.

$ prompt (Pronounced "dollar prompt.") The Linux command prompt displayed in the BASH shell when you are logged on as an ordinary (nonroot) user. (8)

Access Control Entry (ACE) Each Access Control List has at least one Access Control Entry (ACE), which is like a record in this tiny ACL database that contains just one user or group account name and the permissions assigned to this account for that file or folder. (6)

Access Control List Each file and folder on an NTFS volume has an associated Access Control List (ACL), which is a table of users and/or groups and their permissions to access the file or folder. (6)

access mode number A value assigned to a file permission in Linux. The user (owner), group, and others each have a different access mode number calculated using the following values: read = 4, write = 2, and execute = 1. (8)

Action Center The Windows Action Center, represented by the small flag icon on the right of the toolbar, will briefly display a message balloon when there is a problem with your security programs and backup. Then it will quietly sit there with a white "x" against a red circle until you resolve the problem. (6)

activation A method of combating software piracy, intended to ensure that each software license is used solely on a single computer. Many vendors now use activation. Microsoft's implementation of activation is Microsoft Product Activation (MPA). (5)

Add Printer wizard A series of onscreen instructions that guide you through the installation of a printer's driver and utilities. (5)

address The processor uses each address in the address space to access a location in RAM or ROM. (4)

administrator account type An account type in the OSs surveyed in this book. A user logged on with an administrator account type can perform systemwide tasks such as changing computer settings and installing or removing software and hardware. (2)

adware A form of spyware software downloaded to a computer without permission. It collects information about the user in order to display targeted advertisements, either in the form of inline banners or pop-ups. (2)

Aero Shake A Windows Aero feature that lets you quickly minimize all but one window by giving that window a quick shake. (6)

Aero Snap A Windows Aero feature that lets you manipulate windows quickly. For instance, to maximize a window drag it until its title bar touches the top edge of your display. Restore a maximized window by dragging it away from the top of the display. (6)

anonymous FTP site An FTP site that does not require a user name and password, but allows anonymous connection, which means that all users connecting are using the Anonymous account. As such, a user only has the permissions assigned to the Anonymous account. (10)

Apple menu A pop-up menu opened by clicking on the Apple icon in the upper left of the Mac OS desktop. (9)

application Software that allows a computer user to perform useful functions such as writing a report or calculating a budget. (4)

application virtualization Virtualization of an application whereby a user connects to a server and accesses one or more applications rather than an entire desktop environment. (3)

AppLocker A new feature in Windows 7 for controlling which applications each user can run, reducing the chance of malware running on the user's computer. Administer AppLocker with Group Policy, centrally managed through a Windows Active Directory domain. (6)

authentication Validation of a user account and password that occurs before the security components of an OS give a user access to the computer or network. (2)

authorization The process of both authenticating a user and determining the permissions that the user has for a resource. (2)

Automated System Recovery (ASR) New in Windows XP, this replaces the Emergency Repair process of Windows NT and Windows 2000. ASR is available from the Windows Backup program (NTBACKUP.EXE). (5)

automatic IP addressing A method by which a host can be assigned an IP address and all the additional configuration settings automatically. (10)

Automatic Private IP Addressing (APIPA) A method by which a DHCP client computer that fails to receive an address from a DHCP server will automatically give itself an address from a special range that has the value 169 (base-10) in the first octet (eight binary digits) of the IP address. (10)

Automatic Update A Windows utility that you can configure to automatically connect to the Microsoft site and download updates. (5)

back door A way to bypass security and gain access to a computer. (2)

Backup Utility A utility that you can use to back up system data files. Beginning with Windows XP, you can also use the Windows Backup Utility (NTBACKUP.EXE) to create a set of disks for Automated System Recovery. (5)

BASH An acronym for Bourne Again Shell; the Linux component (shell) that provides the character-mode user interface for entering and processing commands, issuing error messages, and other limited feedback. (8)

batch file Text files that contain commands that you could type at the command prompt, but which you choose to put in a batch file. (4)

binary file A file that contains program code, as opposed to a file containing data. (7)

BitLocker A feature in the Enterprise and Ultimate editions of Windows Vista and Windows 7 for encrypting the drive on which the Windows OS resides and (beginning in Windows 7) other drives beyond the system drive. BitLocker is off by default. BitLocker works with a Trusted Platform Module chip in the computer so that if the drive is removed, it cannot be decrypted. (6)

BitLocker To Go An enhanced feature in Windows 7 BitLocker that includes encryption of removable devices. (6)

Bluesnarfing The act of covertly obtaining information broadcast from wireless devices using the Bluetooth standard. (2)

boot code Program code in the first sector of the active partition; this code identifies the file system on the active partition, finds the boot loader file, and loads it into memory. (7)

boot drive A drive containing the files required to load an OS into memory (the boot files). (4)

boot image A special file that contains a boot sector and all the files required to boot up an operating system. A boot image is in a format that can be placed on the disk sector by sector. (8)

bootstrap loader A small ROM-BIOS program that searches for a boot sector on disk. Once it finds one, it loads it into memory. The boot sector program then looks on the disk from which it was loaded for operating system files, which it will then load into memory. (4)

botnet A group of networked computers that, usually unbeknown to their owners, have been infected with programs that forward information to other computers over the network (usually the Internet). (2)

broadband High-speed data circuits that can simultaneously handle multiple communications channels. (10)

browser hijacking Malware installed on a computer that causes the Internet Explorer home page to always point to a specific site, often advertising something. Hijackers make it very difficult to defeat the hijack by modifying the registry so that every time you restart Windows or Internet Explorer the hijack reinstates. (2)

central processing unit (CPU) An integrated circuit (chip) that performs the calculations, or processing, for a computer. See also *microprocessor*. (1)

clean installation An installation of an OS onto a completely empty new hard disk or one from which all data is removed during the installation. (5)

client A software component on a computer that accesses services from a network server. (1)

code signing A practice introduced in Windows 2000 in which all of the operating system code is digitally signed to show that it has not been tampered with. See also *driver signing*. (7)

cold boot A method of starting up a computer by turning on the power switch. (4)

command-line interface (CLI) On a computer running DOS or Linux (without a graphical shell), this visual component consists of a character-based command line that provides only sparse amounts of information. (1)

Common Internet File System (CIFS) A file sharing protocol standard used by Microsoft, Novell, and many others. (10)

Consent Prompt In Windows Vista or Windows 7, if a program is trying to perform something for which it needs administrator permissions, and you are logged on as an administrator, a User Account Control consent prompt will appear asking if you trust the source. (6)

content filter In an Internet browser, software that blocks content. (2)

conventional memory In real mode, the first 640 KB of RAM that can be used as the workspace for the operating system, application programs, and data. (4)

cookies Very small text files an Internet browser saves on the local hard drive at the request of a Web site. Cookies may contain user preferences for a specific site, information entered into a form at a Web site (including personal information), browsing activity, and shopping selections made at a Web site. (2)

Credentials Prompt Similar to a Consent Prompt for those logged in as a standard user. The User Account Control Credentials Prompt will appear if a program is trying to perform something for which it needs administrator privileges and it will ask the user for an administrator password. (6)

cursor In a command-line interface (CLI), the cursor is merely a marker for the current position where what you type on the keyboard will go. In a GUI the cursor is sometimes replaced by a graphical pointer that can have a variety of shapes you can move around by manipulating a pointing device. (1)

Darwin The name of the core operating system on which Mac OS X is based. A product of the open source community, it allows OS X to provide vastly improved system performance over OS 9. (9)

data type In the Windows registry, a special data format. There are several registry data types, such as REG_BINARY, REG_DWORD, and so forth. (7)

data wiping The permanent removal of data from a storage device. (2)

default gateway The IP address of the router connected to your network. The net ID of the default gateway address should be identical to that of your NIC. The router is a network device that sits between networks and directs traffic to destinations beyond the local network. (10)

desktop virtualization The virtualization of a desktop computer into which you can install an operating system, its unique configuration, and all the applications and data used by a single person. (3)

device driver Software that is added to an OS to control a physical component (device). A component-specific device driver is needed for each unique hardware device connected to a computer. (1)

device management An OS function that controls hardware devices through the use of device drivers. (1)

Device Manager A Windows recovery tool that aids in troubleshooting device problems. This Windows Control Panel applet displays the list of hardware and the status and properties of each device. Use this to disable a device or to update or roll back a device driver. (5)

Device Stage A feature introduced in Windows 7 that, if the device supports it, will bring up a page from which you can make many choices for managing the device, and it often includes an accurate image of the device. (7)

dial-up An inexpensive WAN option available to anyone with a phone line and a standard analog modem (the longtime standard runs at 56 Kbps). (10)

digital certificate A special file stored on a computer that may hold a secret key for decrypting data. (2)

digital signature In Windows, encrypted data that can be unencrypted by Windows in a process called file signature verification. (7)

digital subscriber line (DSL) A WAN service similar to ISDN in its use of the telephone network, but using more advanced digital signal processing to compress more signals through the telephone lines. (10)

directory A special file that can contain files as well as other directories. This term is most often used with non-GUI operating systems, while *folder* is most often used when describing a directory in a GUI. (1)

distribution A bundling of the Linux kernel and software—both enhancements to the OS and applications—such as word processors, spreadsheets, media players, and more. (1)

DMZ A network between the internal network and the Internet with a firewall on both sides. (2)

Dock A floating bar on the Mac OS X desktop that gives access to a variety of system preferences, including location, Internet dial-up, and screen resolution. (9)

Domain Name System (DNS) A distributed online database containing registered domain names mapped to IP addresses. Thousands of name servers on the Internet maintain this distributed database. When you attempt to connect to a Web site, your computer's DNS client queries a DNS server to determine the IP address of the Web site. (10)

DOS prompt The user interface of DOS, also called the command prompt. It includes, at minimum, the current drive letter followed by a blinking cursor, indicating that the command interpreter is ready for input. (4)

drive-by download A program downloaded to a user's computer without consent. Often the simple act of browsing to a Web site or opening an HTML e-mail message may result in such a surreptitious download. A drive-by download may also occur when installing another application. (2)

driver signing Code signing of device drivers that indicates two things: the integrity of the file or files, and that the device driver has passed Microsoft's tests for compatibility. (7)

dumb terminal A terminal consisting of little more than a keyboard and display with a connection to a host computer (mainframe or minicomputer) and having no native processing power of its own. (3)

dump file In Windows, a file to which memory contents are copied (dumped) when a stop error occurs. You can use the information in a dump file when debugging stop errors. You can also send this file to Microsoft for evaluation of a problem. (5)

Dynamic Host Configuration Protocol (DHCP) server A server that issues IP addresses and settings to computers that are configured to obtain an IP address automatically, thus making them DHCP clients. (10)

editions Windows Vista and Windows 7 are versions of Windows with major differences between them. Microsoft sells each of these versions as several separate products, called editions. (6)

embedded systems ROM-based operating systems running on a computer embedded in a device such as a handheld computer or a smart kitchen appliance. (4)

Encrypting File System (EFS) An NTFS file encryption feature introduced with Windows 2000 and NTFS5. (2)

encryption The transformation of data into a code that can be decrypted only through the use of a secret key or password. (2)

environment A special area of memory used to store messages to DOS and other programs. (4)

extended partition A partition type that can contain one or more logical drives, each of which can use a portion of the partition. FDISK can create only two partitions on a physical drive; only one can be primary, and one can be extended. MS-DOS will boot from a primary partition, but not from an extended partition. (4)

external command A command program stored on disk, rather than within the operating system code that remains in memory. MS-DOS looks for an external command program on disk if it cannot find it in memory. (4)

file and print server A network server that gives client computers access to files and printers. Also simply called a file server. (10)

file attribute A component of file or directory entries that determines how an operating system handles the file or directory. In the FAT file system, the attributes are read-only, archive, system, hidden, volume label, and directory. (4)

file management An operating system function that allows the operating system to read, write, and modify data and programs organized into files. (1)

file server A network server that gives client computers access to files. (10)

file signature verification The process by which Windows unencrypts a digital signature and verifies that the file has not been tampered with. (7)

file system The logical structure used on a storage device for the purpose of storing files, as well as the code within an operating system that allows the OS to store and manage files on a storage device. (1)

File Transfer Protocol (FTP) A protocol used to transfer files between a computer running the FTP server service and an FTP client. It is a preferred method of transferring files over a TCP/IP network, especially the Internet, because it is simple and fast. (10)

FileVault A feature in Mac Os X that encrypts all the files in a user's home folder. (2)

Finder The foundation of the Mac OS GUI and the equivalent to Windows Explorer, the Windows file management tool. (9)

firewall A firewall is either software or a physical device that examines network traffic. Based on predefined rules, a firewall rejects certain traffic coming into a computer or network. The two general types of firewalls are network-based firewalls and personal firewalls that reside on individual computers. (2)

first-party cookie A cookie that originates with the domain name of the URL to which you directly connect. (2)

Flip 3D A Windows Aero feature that lets you switch through your open windows as if they were in a stack of cards or photos. (6)

folder A special file that can contain files as well as other folders. This term is most often used with GUI operating systems, while *directory* is most often used when describing a directory in a non-GUI. (1)

formatting The action of an operating system when it maps the logical organization of the file system to physical locations on the storage device (most often a conventional hard disk drive or solid state drive) so that it can store and retrieve the data. (1)

fully qualified domain name (FQDN) The human-readable TCP/IP name corresponding to the TCP/IP address of a host, as found on a computer, router, or other networked device. It includes both its host name and its domain name. (10)

gadget A small program represented by an icon on the Windows Vista Sidebar, or, in Windows 7, anywhere on the desktop. A gadget performs some small function—usually involving keeping information handy in a small screen object. (6)

GNOME An acronym for GNU network object model environment, a UNIX GUI that uses the Linux X Window System. (8)

GNU An organization created in 1984 to develop a free version of a UNIX-like operating system. GNU, a recursive acronym for GNU's Not UNIX, has developed thousands of applications that run on UNIX and Linux platforms. Many are distributed with versions of Linux. (8)

graphical user interface (GUI) A user interface that takes advantage of a computer's graphics capabilities to make it easier to use with graphical elements that a user can manipulate to perform tasks such as system and file management and running applications. (1)

group account A security account that may contain one or more individual accounts. In some security accounts databases, it may contain other groups. (2)

guest account A special account used when someone connects to a computer over a network but is not a member of a security account recognized on that computer. That person connects as a guest (if the guest account is enabled) and will only have the permissions assigned to the guest account. (2)

guest OS An operating system running within a virtual machine. (3)

hive The portion of the Windows registry represented in one registry file. (7)

home directory In Linux, a directory created for a user, using the user's login name, and located under the /home directory. This is the one place in Linux where an ordinary user account has full control over files without logging in as the root account. (8)

host ID The portion of an IP address that identifies the host on a network, as determined using the subnet mask. (10)

host key The virtual machine captures the mouse and keyboard, giving the VM the focus. To release the mouse and keyboard there is a host key, which varies in each hypervisor. In VirtualBox on a Mac, it is the left Command key, while in Virtual PC it is the right Alt key. You will normally see a message about the host key during the installation or the first time you run the guest OS. (3)

Host OS The operating system installed directly on the computer. (3)

hypervisor The software layer that emulates the necessary hardware for an operating system to run in. It is the hardware virtualization that lets multiple operating systems run simultaneously on a single computer, such as a network server. Each hypervisor normally emulates a computer separate from the underlying computer, but it must use a virtual processor compatible with that of the underlying machine—mainly either an Intel processor or an AMD processor. (3)

identity theft This occurs when someone collects personal information belonging to another person and uses that information to fraudulently make purchases, open new credit accounts, or even obtain new driver's licenses and other forms of identification in the victim's name. (2)

image An exact duplicate of the entire hard drive contents, including the OS and all installed software, that is used to install copies of an OS and associated applications on multiple computers. (5)

input/output (I/O) Anything sent into a computer (input); anything coming out of a computer (output). Every keystroke you enter, all files read in, and even voice commands are input. Output can include a printed page, what you see on the screen, and even sounds. (1)

integrated services digital network (ISDN) A digital telephone service that simultaneously transmits voice, data, and control signaling over a single telephone line. ISDN service operates on standard telephone lines, but requires a special modem and phone service, which adds to the cost. An ISDN data connection can transfer data at up to 128,000 bits per second (128 Kbps). (10)

internal command A command program within the operating system code that remains in memory. MS-DOS internal commands are stored within COMMAND.COM. (4)

Internet Protocol (IP) A core TCP/IP protocol that packages your communications in chunks, called packets. This protocol allows your computer to be identified on an internetwork by a logical address called an IP address. Special routing protocols can use a destination IP address to choose the best route for a packet to take through a very complex internetwork. IP also has sub-protocols that help it accomplish its work. (10)

Internet service provider (ISP) An organization that provides individuals or entire organizations access to the Internet. For a fee, an ISP provides you with this connection service and may offer other Internet-related services such as Web server hosting and e-mail. (10)

ISO image A copy of the entire contents of a CD or DVD that can be easily transferred to a writeable CD or DVD with ISO image copy software. (8)

job management An operating system function that controls the order and time in which programs are run. For example, an operating system's print program can manage and prioritize multiple print jobs. (1)

jump list In Windows 7, a list of recently opened items such as files, folders, and Web sites that appear when you right-click on a program on the Start menu or taskbar. (6)

kernel The main component of an operating system that always remains in memory while a computer is running. (1)

key In the Windows registry, a folder object that may contain one or more sets of settings as well as other keys. (7)

keychain A database in which OS X saves encrypted passwords. (9)

keylogger See *keystroke logger*. (2)

keystroke logger A hardware device or a program that monitors and records a user's every keystroke, usually without the user's knowledge. (2)

Last Known Good (LKG) configuration A Windows start-up option for start-up failures due to a configuration change. It lets you restore the system to a single restore point (not called that), and you only have a narrow window of opportunity in which you can use LKG—on the first reboot after making a configuration change, and *before* logging on. (5)

library A feature introduced in Windows 7, in which a library is a special folder with pointers to disk folders that

can be in many locations, but will all appear to be in the same library. (6)

limited account An account type in Windows XP that is a simplistic reference to an account that only belongs to the Local Users group. This is similar to a standard user account in newer versions of Windows and a standard account in Mac OS X. (2)

Linux An open source operating system based on UNIX that was developed by Linus Torvalds and others beginning in 1991. (8)

Lion The most recently announced version of Mac OS X (10.7), projected to ship in the second quarter of 2011. (9)

live CD A CD or DVD from which you can boot an OS without requiring any part of the OS to be resident on a hard disk. (4)

Live File System A file format used by Windows 7 to burn discs that will only be used on newer Apple Macs and newer PCs (Windows XP or newer OS). Using Live File System you can directly copy items to the drive without requiring extra hard drive space. You can copy items individually, over time—either by leaving the disc in the drive or reinserting the disc multiple times. (6)

local security The security options available and limited to a local computer. In Windows, this includes local security accounts and local security for files and folders, Windows BitLocker drive encryption, Windows Defender anti-spam protection, and Windows Firewall. (6)

logical drive A portion of a physical hard drive that is treated as a separate drive with a drive letter assigned to it. (4)

Mac The nickname for Apple's computers. (9)

Mac OS X Server The first of the Mac OS X line designed for Mac Server computers. It was introduced in 1999. (9)

Mac OS X Setup Assistant When you purchase a new computer with Mac OS X preinstalled, the OS will come installed but not configured, so the first time it is powered up, this program prompts you for the user preferences information. (9)

malware A shortened form of "malicious software" that covers a large and growing list of threats such as viruses, worms, Trojan horses, or spam. (2)

master boot record (MBR) The first sector on a hard disk, containing code that is loaded into memory by the BIOS startup program during the initial startup of a computer. (7)

Master Password On a Mac OS X system, the password set by an administrator that is the unlocking password for all FileVault compressed Home folders on the computer—a fail-safe for when a user forgets a login password. (9)

Mastered When burning a disc in Windows 7, use this option when you want to be able to use a CD or DVD in a conventional CD or DVD player or in any computer (older Apple Macs or PCs). The downside is that each item you select to copy to the PC is stored temporarily in available hard disk space (in addition to the space used by the original file) until you finish selecting all you wish to copy, and then they are copied in one operation. This makes it difficult to copy files from a hard drive when you have very little free hard drive space on any hard drive in your computer. (6)

memory The physical chips that store programs and data. There are two basic types: random-access memory (RAM) and read-only memory (ROM). (1)

memory management An operating system function that manages and tracks the placement of programs and data in memory. Advanced operating systems, such as Windows, Linux, and Mac OS X, use memory management to make optimal use of memory. (1)

microcomputer A computer built around a microprocessor. (1)

microprocessor An integrated circuit (chip) that performs the calculations, or processing, for a computer. Also called a processor or central processing unit (CPU). (1)

Microsoft Product Activation (MPA) Microsoft's method of combating software piracy, intended to ensure that each software license is used solely on a single computer. After installing Microsoft software, MPA will attempt to contact Microsoft's site to confirm the product is authentic. Normally, during activation the user is prompted to enter a product code, found on the packaging. Many other software vendors use activation. See also *activation*. (5)

motherboard The central circuit board of a computer to which all other devices connect. (1)

MSCONFIG The System Configuration Utility, a Windows tool for modifying system start-up, allows you to modify and test start-up configuration settings without having to alter the settings directly. It allows you access to settings that are buried within the registry and allows you to make the changes temporary or permanent. (7)

multi-boot An installation that leaves an old OS in place, installing a new OS in a separate location. This allows you to select the OS you wish to boot into every time you start the computer. (6)

multitasking Two or more programs (tasks) running simultaneously on a computer. (1)

net ID The network portion of an IP address, as determined through the subnet mask. (10)

NetWare Core Protocol (NCP) Novell's file sharing protocol, used in Novell's server products for many years. (10)

network virtualization A network addressing space that exists within one or more physical networks, but which is logically independent of the physical network structure. (3)

octet A group of eight binary digits. (10)

open source software Software distributed with all its source code, allowing developers to customize it as necessary. (8)

operating system (OS) A collection of programs that provides a computer with critical functionality, such as a user interface, management of hardware and software, and ways of creating, managing, and using files. (1)

operator A command line operator is a symbol, such as the vertical bar (|) and the greater-than sign (>), that affects the behavior of commands. (4)

owner In Linux, the user account that creates a file or directory. This term is also used in Windows. (8)

packet A piece of a message packaged by the Internet Protocol. In addition to the portion of a message, each packet is given a header that contains information including the source address (local host address) and the destination address. (10)

Parental Controls A feature in Internet Explorer that allows parents using a password-protected administrator account to protect their children from harm by setting specific Parental Controls for a child's user account. (2)

parse Used in the context of an operating system's treatment of a command entered at the command line, *parse* means to divide the command into its components. DOS's command interpreter parses an entry based on special delimiter characters, such as the space character. (4)

partition (n.) An area of a physical hard disk that defines space used for logical drives. (v.) To define the space used for logical drives using a program such as the MS-DOS FDISK program. (1)

password A string of characters that a user enters (along with a user name) in order to be authenticated. (2)

password cracker A program used to discover a password. (2)

permission A level of access to an object, such as a file or folder, that is granted to a user account or group account. (2)

personal computer (PC) A microcomputer that complies with the Microsoft/Intel standards. (1)

personal folders In Windows, a set of special folders saved on disk for each user who logs on. (5)

phishing A fraudulent method of obtaining personal financial information through Web page pop-ups, e-mail, and even paper letters mailed via the postal service of your country. Often purports to be from a legitimate organization, such as a bank, credit card company, retailer, etc. Phishing is a form of social engineering. (2)

pinning A feature introduced in Windows 7 that allows you to place icons for applications and destinations on the taskbar and Start menu. Once pinned, an item's icon remains on the toolbar regardless of whether the program is open or closed. Simply click it to open the application or destination. (6)

plug and play The ability of a computer to automatically detect and configure a hardware device. To work, the computer, the device, and the OS must all comply with the same plug and play standard. (7)

pop-up An ad that runs in a separate browser window that you must close before you can continue with your present task. (2)

pop-up blocker A program that works against pop-ups. (2)

pop-up download A program that is downloaded to a user's computer through the use of a pop-up page that appears while surfing the Web. (2)

primary partition A partition type that can only have one logical drive, which is assigned to the entire space defined by the partition. MS-DOS and Windows 9x can only have a single primary partition, while Windows NT/2000/XP can have up to four primary partitions. (4)

private IP address An address from one of three ranges of IP addresses designated for use only on private networks and not to be used on the Internet. The private IP address ranges are 10.0.0.0 through 10.255.255.255, 172.16.0.0 through 172.31.255.255, and 192.168.0.0 through 192.168.255.255. (10)

processor See *microprocessor*.

Program Compatibility wizard A Windows wizard that enables you to set compatibility options for an older application that will "trick" the older program into thinking that the OS is actually the earlier version of Windows required by the application (such as Windows 95). You can also set these options manually from the properties of the application's shortcut or program file. (5)

protected mode A mode of modern processors that allows the processor and the OSs to access vast amounts of memory addresses. This mode also supports multitasking, a basic feature of today's Windows, OS X, and Linux OSs. (4)

public IP addresses IP addresses assigned to hosts on the Internet. (10)

raw write A utility that once came with most distributions of Linux and is used to create a bootable floppy disk. (8)

real mode The mode in which an Intel processor starts when the computer is first turned on. It is very limited, offers the operating system just a small amount of memory to work with, and does not allow for multitasking, protection of the hardware from other software, or support for virtual machines. (4)

real-time operating system (RTOS) A very fast and relatively small OS, often embedded into the circuitry of a device, it runs real-time applications. A real-time application responds to certain inputs extremely quickly—thousandths or millionths of a second—and runs medical diagnostics equipment, life-support systems, machinery, scientific instruments, and industrial systems, for example. (1)

Recovery Console A character-mode boot-up environment with a command-line interface, accessed either from the installation disk or from the hard drive if you installed it from the disk. You can enter advanced command-line commands to attempt to recover from a major OS failure. (5)

registry A database of all configuration settings in Windows. (7)

restore point A snapshot of Windows, its configuration, and all installed programs. If your computer has nonfatal problems after you have made a change, you can use System Restore to roll it back to a restore point. (5)

ROM BIOS (read only memory basic input output system) A set of program instructions for starting the computer, as well as for controlling communications between the processor and other components (input and output). (1)

root The most powerful account on a Linux (or UNIX) computer, and, like the Administrator account on a Windows computer, an account that is capable of doing anything. It can access any file or program on a computer and is required to shut down Linux from the command prompt. (8)

root directory In a FAT file system, a directory with special characteristics: It is at the top level of the directory hierarchy, and it is the only directory created automatically when a logical drive is formatted. (4)

root key In the Windows registry, the top five folders are root keys, often called subtrees in Microsoft documentation. Each of these subtrees is the top of a hierarchical structure containing folders called keys. (7)

rootkit Malware that hides itself from detection by anti-malware programs, by concealing itself within the OS code or any other program running on the computer. (2)

router A network device that sits between networks and directs (routes) traffic to destinations beyond the local network. (10)

Safe Mode A start-up mode in which Windows starts without using all of the drivers and components that would normally be loaded. Use Safe Mode when your Windows computer will not start normally. (5)

secret key A special code that can be used to decrypt encrypted data. (2)

Secure HTTP (HTTPS) A form of the HTTP protocol that supports encryption of the communications. HTTPS uses the Secure Sockets Layer (SSL) security protocol. (2)

Secure Sockets Layer (SSL) A security protocol for encrypting network data. (2)

Secure Virtual Memory A Mac OS X feature that encrypts the swap file. (9)

security An operating system function that provides password-protected authentication of the user before allowing access to the local computer. Security features may restrict what a user can do on a computer. (1)

security account In a security accounts database, a security account is a listing of information about a user, group, or computer. A user or computer account used for authentication; both user and group accounts are used for authorization with assigned permissions. (2)

security ID (SID) A unique string of numbers preceded by *S-1-5* that identifies a security principal in a Windows security accounts database. (7)

server A computer that plays one or more of several important roles on a network. In all of these roles, the server provides services to other computers (clients). (1)

Server Message Block (SMB) A file and print sharing protocol used on Microsoft networks that is being replaced by a newer protocol, Common Internet File System (CIFS). (10)

server virtualization A single machine hosting multiple servers, each of which performs tasks independently from the others as separate physical machines would. (3)

share A connecting point to which network clients with the correct permissions may connect. It is visible as a folder over the network, but it is a separate entity from the disk folder to which it points.

shell The operating system component that provides the character-mode user interface—processing commands and issuing error messages and other limited feedback. (8)

shell commands Commands used in the shell. (8)

shortcut An icon that represents a link to an object, such as a file or program. Activating a shortcut (by clicking on it) is a quick way to access an object or to start a program from any location without having to find the actual location of the object on your computer. (5)

Snow Leopard The eighth major release of Mac OS X that improved on the previous release, Leopard, with a speed increase and size decrease in memory usage and required disk space. (9)

social engineering The use of persuasion techniques to gain the confidence of individuals—for both good and bad purposes. People with malicious intent use social engineering to persuade someone to reveal confidential information or to obtain something else of value. (2)

spam Unsolicited e-mail. This includes e-mail from a legitimate source selling a real service or product, but if you did not give permission to send such information to you, it is spam. (2)

spim An acronym for "Spam over Instant Messaging"; the perpetrators are called spimmers. (2)

Spotlight A Mac OS X search utility that, much like Search in Windows, is a live search, so it starts presenting results as soon as you start typing. (9)

spyware A category of software that runs surreptitiously on a user's computer, gathers information without permission from the user, and then sends that information to the people or organizations that requested the information. (2)

standard user account An account for an "ordinary" user without administrator status. (2)

Startup Repair A Windows recovery tool that will scan for problems with missing or damaged system files and attempt to replace the problem files. (6)

static IP address An IP address that is manually configured for a host and can, therefore, be considered semipermanent—that is, it stays with the device until someone takes action to change it. (10)

storage virtualization Utilizing many hard drives as though they are one. (3)

subdirectory A directory contained within another directory. It is sometimes called a child directory. (4)

subkey In the Windows registry, a key that exists within another key. (7)

subnet mask An important IP configuration parameter as critical as the address itself, because it takes what looks like a single address and divides it into two addresses by masking off part of the address. (10)

superuser Another name for the root account in Linux, although the login name is "root." (8)

syntax A set of rules for correctly entering a specific command at the command line. The rules include the placement of the command name and the parameters that you can use to modify the behavior of the command. (4)

System Image Recovery A Windows recovery tool that will let you restore a complete PC Image backup, providing you created one. This is a replacement for the Automated System Recovery (ASR) tool previously found in Windows XP. (6)

System Preferences The Mac OS X application for applying and changing system-wide settings. (9)

System Restore A recovery tool that creates restore points, which are snapshots of Windows, its configuration, and all installed programs. If your computer has nonfatal problems after you have made a change, you can use System Restore to roll it back to a restore point. (5)

task management An operating system function in multitasking OSs that controls the focus. The user can switch between tasks by bringing an application to the foreground, which gives the focus to that application. (1)

Task Manager A program for removing errant programs. This Windows utility allows you to see the state of the individual processes and programs running on the computer and to stop one of them, if necessary. (5)

TCP/IP A suite of protocols that work together to allow both similar and dissimilar computers to communicate. This protocol suite is needed to access the Internet and is the most common protocol suite used on private intranets. It gets its name from two of its many protocols: Transmission Control Protocol (TCP) and Internet Protocol (IP)—the core protocols of TCP/IP. (10)

terminal client Software on a computer that establishes a connection to a terminal server. (3)

terminal services Software running on servers to which users connect from their desktop PCs using terminal client software. (3)

terminal window A window in a Linux GUI that provides a command line for entering Linux shell commands. (8)

terminate and stay resident (TSR) The characteristic of some small DOS programs that stay loaded in memory when inactive but can be quickly activated when needed. (4)

thin client A minimally configured network computer. (3)

third-party cookie A cookie that originates with a domain name beyond the one shown in your URL. (2)

token A physical device that can be used in authentication, either alone or together with a user name and password. (2)

Transmission Control Protocol (TCP) The protocol responsible for the accurate delivery of messages, verifying and resending pieces that fail to make the trip from source to destination. Several other protocols act as sub-protocols, helping TCP accomplish this. (10)

Trojan horse A program that is installed and activated on a computer by appearing to be something harmless, which the user innocently installs. This is a common way that a virus or a worm can infect a computer. (2)

Type I hypervisor A hypervisor that can run directly on a computer without an underlying host operating system—sometimes called a bare-metal hypervisor. (3)

Type II hypervisor A Type II hypervisor requires a host operating system. (3)

upgrade An installation of an OS that installs directly into the folders in which a previous version was installed, preserving all your preferences and data. (6)

Upgrade Advisor A compatibility checker that you can run from the Windows XP CD by selecting Check System Compatibility on the Welcome To Microsoft Windows XP screen that runs automatically (autorun) or after invoking the Setup program. (5)

user account A record in an accounts database that represents a single person and that is used for authentication. (2)

User Account Control (UAC) A security feature that prevents unauthorized changes to Windows. A user logged on with a privileged account with administrative rights only has the privileges of a standard account until the user (or a malicious program) attempts to do something that requires higher privileges. (2)

user interface The software layer, sometimes called the shell, through which the user communicates with the OS, which, in turn, controls the computer. (1)

user right In Windows, the privilege to perform a system-wide function, such as access the computer from the network, log on locally, log on to a computer from the network, back up files, change the system time, or load and unload device drivers. (2)

utility A program that allows you to perform handy tasks, usually computer management functions or diagnostics such as upgrading the program in your computer's ROM-BIOS or looking for errors on your disk. (4)

value entry The settings within a Windows registry key. (7)

vector A mode of malware infection, such as e-mail, code on Web sites, Trojan horses, searching out unprotected computers, sneakernet, back doors, rootkits, pop-up downloads, drive-by downloads, war driving, and Bluesnarfing. (2)

version Each Microsoft Windows version is a new level of the Windows operating system, with major changes to the core components of the operating system as well as a distinctive and unifying look to the GUI. (1)

virtual desktop infrastructure (VDI) The term used for hosting and managing multiple virtual desktops on network servers. (3)

virtual machine A software simulation of a computer. In Windows, when a DOS application is launched, the OS creates a DOS virtual machine that simulates both the hardware of a PC and the DOS operating system. When a 16-bit (Windows 3.*x*) Windows application is launched, Windows creates a virtual machine that includes the Windows 3.*x* OS. (3)

virtual machine monitor (VMM) Another name for hypervisor. A software layer that emulates the necessary hardware for an operating system to run in. (3)

virtual memory A system of memory management in which the OS moves programs and data in and out of memory as needed. (1)

virtual private network (VPN) A virtual tunnel created between two end points over a real network or internetwork. This is done by encapsulating the packets. Other security methods are also usually applied, such as encryption of the data and encrypted authentication. When set up in combination with properly configured firewalls, a VPN is the safest way to connect two private networks over the Internet. (10)

virtual world An online simulated communal environment within which users, often using an animated computer-generated human (avatar), can interact with one another and create and use various objects. (3)

virtualization The creation of an environment that seems real, but isn't. (3)

virus In the broadest sense, a virus is the term used for all malware, as it is a program that is installed and activated on a computer without the knowledge or permission of the user. At the least the intent is mischief, but most often it is genuinely damaging in one way or another. (2)

war driving The act of moving through a neighborhood in a vehicle or on foot, using either a laptop equipped with Wi-Fi wireless network capability or a simple Wi-Fi sensor available for a few dollars from many sources. War drivers seek to exploit open hotspots, areas where a Wi-Fi network connects to the Internet without the use of security to keep out intruders. (2)

warm boot Restarting a computer without a power-down and power-up cycle, by using a key combination (for example, CTRL-ALT-DELETE) or a hardware reset button. (4)

Web browser A special type of client software used to navigate the Web. Examples include Netscape, Chrome, and Internet Explorer. (10)

Web mail A generic term for Web-based e-mail services such as Hotmail, Gmail, and Yahoo that keep your messages stored on the Internet, allowing you to access them via a Web browser from any computer. (10)

Windows 7 Upgrade Advisor A utility you can run on a Windows computer to discover any hardware or software incompatibilities. (6)

Windows Aero Microsoft's name for a group of GUI desktop features and visual themes introduced in Windows Vista. (6)

Windows Defender A free built-in anti-spyware product now integrated into the Windows 7 Action Center where you can configure spyware scanning and updates. (6)

Windows Easy Transfer (WET) A utility that will transfer your data, e-mail, and settings for the Windows desktop and your applications from an old installation of Windows to Windows 7. (6)

Windows Explorer The primary tool for copying, moving, renaming, and deleting files in Windows. (6)

Windows Memory Diagnostic Tool A Windows recovery tool that tests the system's RAM because RAM problems can prevent Windows from starting. (6)

Windows Preinstallation Environment (PE) A scaled-down Windows operating system. Much like the old Windows Setup program, it has limited drivers for basic hardware and support for the NTFS file system, TCP/IP, certain chipsets, mass storage devices, and 32-bit and 64-bit programs. Windows PE supports the Windows Setup GUI, collecting configuration information. (6)

Windows Update A Windows program that allows you to interactively connect to the Windows Update Web page. (5)

Windows XP Mode Introduced in Windows 7; Windows Virtual PC with a free and legal Windows XP VM preinstalled. (6)

wireless LAN (WLAN) A local area network using one of the standards referred to as Wi-Fi (for wireless fidelity). The Wi-Fi standards of the Institute of Electrical and Electronics Engineers (IEEE) include 802.11a, 802.11b, 802.11g, and 802.11n. The distance covered by a WLAN is usually measured in feet (or meters) rather than miles. (10)

wireless wide area network (WWAN) A digital wireless network that extends over a large geographical area. A WWAN receives and transmits data using radio signals over cellular sites and satellites, which makes the network accessible to mobile computer systems. At the switching center, the WWAN splits off into segments and then connects to either a specialized public or private network via telephone or other high-speed communication links. The data then links to an organization's existing LAN/WAN infrastructure. (10)

worm A self-replicating computer virus. (2)

X Window System The program code used as the basis for many GUIs for Linux or UNIX. (8)

zombie An individual computer in a botnet. (2)

zone In Internet Explorer, an area that contains one or more Web sites to which you can assign restrictions that control how Internet Explorer handles cookies. A zone may be an area such as the Internet or local intranet or a list of sites grouped together, as in trusted sites and restricted sites. (10)

Index